Historic Documents
of 2010

Historic Documents
of 2010

Heather Kerrigan, Editor

INCLUDES CUMULATIVE INDEX, 2006–2010

Los Angeles | London | New Delhi
Singapore | Washington DC

CQ Press
2300 N Street, NW, Suite 800
Washington, DC 20037

Phone: 202-729-1900; toll-free, 1-866-4CQ-PRESS (1-866-427-7737)

Web: www.cqpress.com

Sponsoring and Development Editor: Andrew Boney
Volume Editor: Heather Kerrigan
Contributors: Hilary Ewing, Linda Fecteau, Melissa Feinberg, Heather Kerrigan, Anastazia Skolnitsky, Roger K. Smith
Copy Editor: Lawrence W. Baker
Production Editor: Sarah Fell
Cover Designer: Malcolm McGaughy, McGaughy Design
Cover Photos: Left: Associated Press; Center (top): Reuters/Daniel Aguilar; Center (bottom): Reuters/Sean Gardner; Right: Reuters/Eddie Keogh.
Composition: C&M Digitals (P) Ltd.
Indexer: Indexing Partners, LLC

♾ The paper used in this publication exceeds the requirements of the American National Standard for Information Sciences—Permanence of Paper for Printed Library Materials, ANSI Z39.48–1992.

Printed and bound in the United States of America

15   14   13   12   11   1   2   3   4   5

The Library of Congress cataloged the first issue of this title as follows:
Historic documents. 1972–
Washington. Congressional Quarterly Inc.

1. United States—Politics and government—1945—Yearbooks.
2. World politics—1945—Yearbooks. I. Congressional Quarterly Inc.
E839.5H57   917.3´03´9205   72-97888

ISSN 0892-080X
ISBN 978-1-60871-724-8

Contents

JANUARY

FEBRUARY

MARCH

APRIL

statement by Sen. Dick Durbin, D-Ill., also on April 22, 2010, in support of the Dodd-Frank legislation; and a statement by President Barack Obama on July 21, 2010, upon signing the Wall Street reform legislation into law.

MAY

AUGUST

SEPTEMBER

OCTOBER

NOVEMBER

DECEMBER

Thematic Table of Contents

HEALTH AND SOCIAL SERVICES

INTERNATIONAL AFFAIRS
Africa

INTERNATIONAL AFFAIRS
Asia

INTERNATIONAL AFFAIRS
Europe

INTERNATIONAL AFFAIRS
Latin America and the Caribbean

INTERNATIONAL AFFAIRS
Middle East

INTERNATIONAL AFFAIRS
Russia and Former Soviet Republics

INTERNATIONAL AFFAIRS
Global Issues

NATIONAL SECURITY AND TERRORISM

RIGHTS, RESPONSIBILITIES, AND JUSTICE

U.S. GOVERNMENT AND POLITICS

List of Document Sources

CONGRESS

EXECUTIVE DEPARTMENTS,
AGENCIES, AND OTHER FEDERAL OFFICES

INTERNATIONAL GOVERNMENTAL AND NONGOVERNMENTAL ORGANIZATIONS

JUDICIARY

NON-U.S. GOVERNMENTS

U.S. NONGOVERNMENTAL ORGANIZATIONS

U.S. STATE AND LOCAL GOVERNMENTS AND ORGANIZATIONS

WHITE HOUSE AND THE PRESIDENT

Preface

Republican victories in the midterm election, a devastating oil spill in the Gulf of Mexico, the passage of landmark health care legislation, the repeal of the military's "Don't Ask, Don't Tell" policy, a major shift in political power in the United Kingdom, and a landmark Supreme Court decision on campaign finance are just a few of the topics of national and international significance chosen for discussion in *Historic Documents of 2010*. This edition marks the thirty-ninth volume of a CQ Press project that began with *Historic Documents of 1972*. This series allows students, librarians, journalists, scholars, and others to research and understand the most important domestic and foreign issues and events of the year through primary source documents. To aid research, many of the lengthy documents written for specialized audiences have been excerpted to highlight the most important sections. The official statements, news conferences, speeches, special studies, and court decisions presented here should be of lasting public and academic interest.

Historic Documents of 2010 opens with an "Overview of 2010," a sweeping narrative of the key events and issues of the year that provides context for the documents that follow. The balance of the book is organized chronologically, with each article comprising an introduction entitled "Document in Context" and one or more related documents on a specific event, issue, or topic. The introductions provide context and an account of further developments during the year. A thematic table of contents (page xvii) and a list of documents organized by source (page xxi) follow the standard table of contents and assist readers in locating events and documents.

As events, issues, and consequences become more complex and far-reaching, these introductions and documents yield important information and deepen understanding about the world's increasing interconnectedness. As memories of current events fade, these selections will continue to further understanding of the events and issues that have shaped the lives of people around the world.

How to Use This Book

Each of the 70 entries in this edition consists of two parts: a comprehensive introduction followed by one or more primary source documents. The articles are arranged in chronological order by month. Articles with multiple documents are placed according to the date of the first document. There are several ways to find events and documents of interest:

By date: If the approximate date of an event or document is known, browse through the titles for that month in the table of contents. Alternatively, browse the monthly tables of contents that appear at the beginning of each month's articles.

By theme: To find a particular topic or subject area, browse the thematic table of contents.

By document type or source: To find a particular type of document or document source, such as the White House or Congress, review the list of document sources.

By index: The five-year index allows researchers to locate references to specific events or documents as well as entries on the same or related subjects. The index in this volume covers the years 2006–2010. A separate volume, *Historic Documents Index, 1972–2005,* may also be useful.

Each article begins with a section entitled "Document in Context." This feature provides historical and intellectual contexts for the documents that follow. Documents are reproduced with the spelling, capitalization, and punctuation of the original or official copy. Ellipsis points indicate textual omissions (unless they were present in the documents themselves, as indicators of pauses in speech), and brackets are used for editorial insertions within documents for text clarification. The excerpting of Supreme Court opinions has been done somewhat differently than other documents. Other excerpting exceptions are presented in brackets preceding the document text. In-text references to laws and other cases have been removed to improve the readability of opinions. In those documents, readers will only find ellipses used when sections of narrative text have been removed. Full citations appear at the end of each document. If a document is not available on the Internet, this too is noted. For further reading on a particular topic, consult the "Other Historic Documents of Interest" section at the end of each article. This section provides cross-references for related articles in this edition of *Historic Documents* as well as in previous editions. References to articles from past volumes include the year and page number for easy retrieval.

Overview of 2010

The year 2010 was characterized by domestic policy struggles and international civil unrest. In January, President Barack Obama laid out his plans for the coming months during his State of the Union address, hopeful that his primary legislative efforts, including passage of health care reform and the repeal of "Don't Ask, Don't Tell," would be signed prior to the November midterm congressional elections. The impending November vote colored the decisions made by those in Congress who wanted to ensure a successful reelection bid. When the votes were tallied, Republicans, driven by the popularity of their more conservative Tea Party members, gained control of the U.S. House of Representatives, picking up sixty-three seats from Democrats who were in the majority in 2009 and 2010. The Senate remained in Democratic control, but Republicans saw a gain of six seats.

Around the world, 2010 brought new leaders, natural disasters, continued financial distress, and sometimes violent struggles for land and political dominance. In Europe, protests erupted over austerity measures that would cut government spending and, in turn, government services. Chile and Haiti experienced damaging earthquakes from which they are still recovering. Chile was hit with a second near-disaster in August when a mine collapsed, trapping thirty-three miners who were all found alive and rescued in October. Three African nations—Côte d'Ivoire, Guinea, and Somalia—experienced significant spikes in violence. In Côte d'Ivoire and Guinea, presidential election results were rejected by the losing parties, leading to recounts, allegations of fraud, and renewed ethnic violence. In Somalia, the weak central government worked to instill order, but without much authority, antigovernment forces gained ground and attacked government officials and civilians.

GLOBAL ECONOMICS

The global economic downturn showed signs of slowing in 2010, but events made clear that it was not yet over. In the United States, the U.S. Census Bureau reported that the nation's poverty rate reached its highest level in fifteen years in 2009. Americans in nearly all sectors were affected, but commentary and the bureau's report indicated that investments made in expanding the unemployment insurance, food stamp, and other welfare benefits programs had a significant impact on a number of Americans.

In 2010, the U.S. housing market was still taking a hit from the effects of the recession that began in 2007. After reaching a peak in April, bolstered by an $8,000 homebuyer's tax credit, existing-home sales fell 27 percent in July. With housing sales closely linked to the nation's overall economy, immediate speculation began that one of the major drivers behind the current recession could cause another economic tumble. But by the end of the year, optimism in the real estate market was growing cautiously as existing-home sales began climbing again.

In Europe, hard-hit public coffers and ailing economies resulted in the euro losing value and public anger over austerity measures, bank bailouts, and a new European Union (EU) monetary policy. In May, Greece accepted a $146 billion bailout from the EU and International Monetary Fund (IMF) to shore up its credit market, and in November, Ireland accepted a similar $118 billion bailout to help stabilize its banking system. In an effort to rein in spending by member nations, the EU approved new economic governance policies for member states. These policies would put a limit on public debt and presented the possibility of extensive fines for noncompliance. A number of European governments had already begun passing austerity measures to reduce government spending to stave off their own debt crises. These measures prompted protests across the continent, led by public employee unions facing layoffs and pension reductions.

In Asia, economic statistics from the first half of 2010 officially marked China's ascent to become the world's second largest economy, surpassing Japan. The shift was driven by powerful export growth in China, while Japan's economy lagged with nearly zero growth during much of the first decade of the twenty-first century. Japanese analysts said long-term trends in Chinese growth indicate that the nation could overtake the United States to become the world's largest economy by 2025.

China's global dominance was not felt across the country, nor was it without global critics. Nearly 10 percent of the Chinese population lives below the World Bank's poverty line, set at $2 per day. And the communist government's crackdown on democratic movements and alleged human rights violations showed little sign of slowing. In October 2010, the Nobel committee announced that it would be awarding the year's Nobel Peace Prize to Liu Xiaobo, an imprisoned Chinese dissident. The Chinese government encouraged invited nations to boycott the Nobel ceremony, calling the award an encroachment on internal Chinese affairs. In turn, the Nobel committee, and many Western nations, called for Liu's release and asked China to recognize that its new position in the world would mean increased vigilance and criticism of its state affairs.

Domestic Affairs

At the start of his second year in office, President Barack Obama faced a number of pressing domestic problems—the economy, which remained weak even after a $787 billion infusion of federal funds; climbing unemployment; and the wars in Iraq and Afghanistan. High on the president's list of priorities was passage of his health care reform legislation, and on March 23, 2010, one year of debate and partisan squabbling came to an end when Obama signed a landmark health care reform bill into law. The new law would guarantee access to medical insurance for tens of millions of uninsured Americans and gave additional coverage guarantees to those already insured. The bill had been passed without Republican support, and the party made health care reform a cornerstone of the 2010 midterm congressional elections, promising to challenge the law through any means necessary and available.

As the American combat mission in Iraq drew to a close and the war in Afghanistan raged on, the president was also faced with following through on his promise to repeal the military's "Don't Ask, Don't Tell" policy. The policy that disallowed gay and lesbian soldiers from openly serving in the military was supported by key Republicans in the Senate and some senior military officials, while gay rights organizations, Democrats, and other military officials—including the chairman of the Joint Chiefs of Staff—supported repeal of the policy. A November report from the Pentagon stated that repeal of the policy presented a low risk to U.S. military operations and turned the tide in favor of repeal. By December, Congress passed and the president signed legislation to end the ban.

Continued economic recovery in the United States also took center stage in Congress and the White House in 2010. In February, in an effort to help bring the federal budget under control, President Obama created the National Commission on Fiscal Responsibility and Reform, a body tasked with developing a financial plan that would reduce the U.S. deficit to no more than 3 percent of the U.S. economy by 2015. The commission released its final report on December 1, proposing cuts to discretionary and defense spending and the elimination of some tax breaks. The commission needed fourteen of its eighteen members to vote to approve the report's recommendations before they could be presented to Congress. Only eleven votes in favor of the report were tallied, leaving open the question of how the recommendations might play into the budget plans of the White House and 112th Congress.

Financial reform was also in play in July, when the president signed the Dodd-Frank Wall Street Reform and Consumer Protection Act. The bank bailouts of 2009 were met with distaste from many Americans questioning why the government would protect big businesses and left Washington to find a way to avoid future financial collapse. Dodd-Frank was a step toward greater security for the U.S. financial system. It reorganized the Federal Deposit Insurance Corporation (FDIC) that oversees the financial industry and gave the government increased power to prevent future bailouts.

With nearly 10 percent of the nation unemployed, job creation was key to helping improve the economy. On March 18, 2010, President Obama signed the Hiring Incentives to Restore Employment (HIRE) Act of 2010. The act provided incentives for employers to begin hiring more unemployed individuals, including payroll tax credits and tax breaks for retaining the employee for at least one year. The HIRE Act was expected to create as many as 250,000 new jobs, but it would only make a small dent in the 8.4 million jobs lost since late 2007.

The economy's slow growth and sustained unemployment put Republicans in Congress in a position of power following the 2010 midterm elections held on November 4. The GOP took control of the House of Representatives, gaining a net sixty-three seats. In the Senate, Republicans won six seats, but Democrats remained in power. In state legislative and gubernatorial elections, Republicans gained control of nineteen legislative chambers and six governorships, winning key elections in swing states including Ohio, Pennsylvania, and Wisconsin. Republican dominance in the election was driven by a portion of the most conservative wing of the GOP, the Tea Party. Tea Party candidates experienced a number of primary and general election victories, campaigning on a platform of smaller government, reduced spending, and lower taxes.

The uptick in support for Republican candidates was called into question in December when the U.S. Census Bureau released preliminary numbers from its 2010 decennial count. The population of the United States had grown to more than three hundred million people, and this population was continuing its shift toward heavy concentration in western states where Republicans often have more support. The 2010 census data would be used to redraw congressional district lines and reapportion seats in the House of Representatives for the Congress that will meet beginning in 2013. Although Republicans will likely enjoy additional power in the short term, the growth in the

U.S. population between 2000 and 2010 was driven largely by immigrants, both legal and illegal. Two-thirds of the twenty-seven million new residents were immigrants, and these residents, while concentrated in many western states, typically support Democratic candidates in elections. But how that impact will be felt is unknown as illegal immigrants, while counted in the census for representation purposes, are unable to vote.

Immigration has been a controversial topic for a number of years as the United States works to determine the best way to control the influx of immigrants, specifically those who enter the United States illegally from Mexico. In April 2010, Arizona's Republican governor, Jan Brewer, brought the discussion back into the headlines when she signed the nation's toughest and most controversial immigration law. The law required police to question those they suspect to be in the country illegally and required legal immigrants to carry proof of their residency with them at all times. Opponents said the law would lead to racial profiling. The Obama administration led the fight against Arizona's new law, filing suit in federal court, while some cities and counties around the country refused to do business with the state of Arizona until the law was repealed.

Energy resources presented another key topic of debate in 2010. President Obama, in an outreach to Republicans, proposed opening additional portions of the coastal United States to offshore drilling, a move aimed at ensuring less dependence on often volatile foreign oil. In March, the president said he would open parts of the Gulf of Mexico and Atlantic Ocean to oil exploration. One month later, the offshore oil drilling platform Deepwater Horizon exploded, releasing millions of gallons of oil into the Gulf of Mexico and putting a hold on offshore drilling plans. The Deepwater Horizon accident was considered the biggest environmental disaster in U.S. history and damage stretched along the Gulf Coast, affecting habitats of coastal-dwelling animals, slowing tourism, and shuttering fishing operations, the lifeblood of the Gulf region. Under pressure from the Obama administration, British Petroleum (BP), which was leasing the well at the time of the explosion, set up a $20 billion fund to compensate those affected by the spill and assist with cleanup costs. Although the full extent of the damage will not be known for years, Obama placed a new ban on offshore drilling and declared areas of the Gulf of Mexico and Atlantic and Pacific Oceans closed to drilling for at least the next seven years.

The Gulf oil spill increased national attention on renewable energy sources, including offshore wind generation, that have less potential environmental impact. After nine years of working through government red tape and fighting opposition, in April 2010 the U.S. Department of the Interior approved the nation's first offshore wind farm, set to be built five miles off the Massachusetts coast. Cape Wind was expected to begin generating power in 2012 and would produce enough to power two hundred thousand homes. Eleven other offshore wind farm projects were in development at the time awaiting Interior Department approval, but by the end of 2010, none of these projects had received necessary clearance for building, and Cape Wind remained at a standstill.

SUPREME COURT DECISIONS

The U.S. Supreme Court welcomed a new justice, Elena Kagan, and handed down significant rulings on *Miranda* rights, spending on political campaigns, material support of terrorism, gun rights, and juvenile prison terms. To replace retiring justice John Paul Stevens, who had served on the court for nearly thirty-five years, President Obama chose U.S. solicitor general Kagan. Upon confirmation, Kagan became the first justice since William Rehnquist to ascend to the Court without having previously served as a judge, marking Obama's desire to choose a unique candidate who would be above the political fray. Kagan's lack of judicial experience was a key tenet of debate in Senate confirmation hearings, where Republicans said her inexperience would not allow her to properly follow the rule of law. Democrats glazed over the issue, and Kagan was confirmed by the Senate 63 to 37. Because of her time as solicitor general, Kagan made it clear that she planned to recuse herself from a number of cases on the Court's 2010–2011 docket.

One issue on the Court's 2010 docket involved spending by corporations and labor unions on political campaigns. On January 21, 2010, the Court ruled 5–4 in the landmark *Citizens United v. Federal Election Commission* that spending on political campaigns as a form of free speech extended beyond private citizens, and that the federal government cannot stop corporations and labor unions from spending to support or oppose a political candidate. The Court stopped short, however, of allowing these organizations to give money directly to candidates. The decision overturned a two-decade-old ruling that had prohibited unions and corporations from paying for campaign advertisements. The ruling also partially overturned *McConnell v. Federal Election Commission,* a case that upheld the constitutionality of the Bipartisan Campaign Reform Act of 2002, which forbids corporations or labor unions from paying for political advertisements during the final days of the campaign. Democrats, led by the Obama administration, expressed discontent with the ruling, noting that it would give undue influence to large corporations—and even foreign corporations—during elections. The ruling had its first impact on the 2010 midterm congressional elections held in November, when a record was set for the amount of money spent on campaigning. Much of the spending used for television advertisements was funneled to candidates by corporations and labor unions.

The Court took up the issue of *Miranda* rights in *Berghuis v. Thompkins,* ruling that criminal suspects who do not want to talk to the police, but rather want to exercise their right to remain silent, must speak up unambiguously to assert that right. Prior to the Court's 5–4 ruling, suspects could invoke their *Miranda* rights simply by remaining silent to avoid self-incrimination.

The only terrorism-related case to be heard in 2010 did not involve the rights of detainees at Guantánamo Bay, but rather the USA PATRIOT Act, a sweeping law passed shortly after the terrorist attacks of September 11, 2001. On June 21, 2010, the Court ruled 6–3 in *Holder v. Humanitarian Law Project,* upholding a key section of the Patriot Act that prohibits the provision of "material support" to foreign organizations deemed terrorists by the U.S. secretary of state. By ruling for the government, the Court decided that even the actions of humanitarian organizations, which wanted to provide training and advocacy for peaceful, lawful activity, could be prosecuted under the act.

For the second time in as many years, the 2010 Court docket included the issue of Second Amendment rights. In 2008, a groundbreaking decision by the Court in *District of Columbia v. Heller* overturned the District of Columbia's ban on handgun ownership. Because of D.C.'s status as a federal district, the ruling applied only to federal laws, which cover a fraction of handgun owners in the United States. In 2010, a narrowly divided Court ruled in *McDonald v. Chicago* that individuals in all states and municipalities have the right to bear arms, thus overturning a number of state and local gun bans.

The Court also took up the issue of sentencing of juvenile offenders who have not committed homicide. A movement that began during a rise in violent crime in the 1990s led state legislatures to crack down on juvenile crime, thus enacting harsher penalties. The result was thousands of children being tried as adults and sentenced to life in prison without the possibility of parole. In *Graham v. Florida* the Court ruled 6–3 to ban the sentence of life in prison without the chance of parole for juvenile offenders who commit a crime that does not involve a killing.

FOREIGN AFFAIRS

Around the world, 2010 was a year wrought with devastation brought on by natural disasters, political strife, and ethnic unrest. In early 2010, Haiti and Chile were struck by earthquakes of historic magnitude. Thousands of Haitians were killed, infrastructure in both nations was destroyed, and the two nations continue to struggle with recovery and rebuilding. The Haitian earthquake, which occurred on January 12, measured a magnitude of 7.0 on the Richter scale, and the impact was devastating. Entire cities were completely destroyed, and despite billions of dollars in pledges, by the end of 2010, 98 percent of debris had yet to be removed and more than one million Haitians remained displaced. Adding to Haiti's difficulty in rebuilding was an outbreak of cholera that killed more than two thousand of those living in temporary tent camps in the capital city of Port-au-Prince in mid-December. Chile's 8.8 magnitude earthquake was the strongest to hit the nation in fifty years. More than seven hundred were killed in the February 27 quake. The low death toll in Chile was directly related to its advanced building standards that far exceeded requirements in Haiti and kept modern buildings secure during the earthquake.

Chile, however, faced a second disaster on August 5, 2010, when the roof of the San José copper and gold mine collapsed, trapping thirty-three miners inside. More than two weeks later, as rescue workers drilled in an attempt to make contact with the miners, a note came to the surface letting Chileans know that all the miners were alive inside a mine shelter. An international team of experts worked around the clock to drill rescue tunnels and build a capsule that could safely bring the miners to the surface. On October 12, extraction began and slowly each miner was brought to the surface alive to the cheers of families and the nation's president.

In Europe and the Middle East, weather patterns caused drought and heavy rains and brought air traffic to a standstill. In mid-April, an Icelandic volcano erupted, sending a plume of ash into the atmosphere that grounded flights, stranding travelers across the European continent for more than one week. The airspace closures and flight delays renewed European focus on centralizing air traffic control within one European Union organization.

The summer of 2010 brought extreme weather patterns to Pakistan and Russia. In Pakistan, provinces were devastated by the worst flooding seen in the nation in eighty years. As the flood waters rose, roads, bridges, homes, schools, and government buildings were destroyed. The devastation was blamed on the nation's "timber mafia," a key driver behind deforestation. The price tag on Pakistan's disaster called into question how quickly the government could recover and whether it could maintain security to root out Taliban safe havens. In Russia, the worst drought in more than one hundred years was brought on by the hottest summer on record and sparked devastating wildfires across the country that destroyed homes and croplands. The destruction of Russia's grain crop led to a ban on grain exports into 2011 that drove up global food prices.

Elections in 2010 brought new leaders with new governing plans in some nations and sparked violence in others. In May 2010, the United Kingdom's Labour Party lost its grip on power for the first time in more than a decade. A new governing coalition, formed by the Conservatives and Liberal Democrats and led by David Cameron, took control and was charged with the responsibility of reviving the economically recessed European nation. Brazilians also went to the polls in 2010 and elected the nation's first female president. Dilma Rousseff won a runoff election by a double-digit margin despite being relatively unknown before her campaign began.

Guinea, one of Africa's poorest nations, held its first democratic elections in June 2010. The first vote, featuring former prime minister Cellou Dalein Diallo and opposition leader Alpha Condé, triggered a runoff election that was twice postponed because of violent clashes between the two ethnic groups supporting the presidential candidates. Condé was declared the victor of the November runoff election, but Diallo refused to accept the results, accusing Condé of suppressing votes from Diallo's ethnic Peuhl supporters. The United Nations reported a number of human rights violations following the election outcome, including hundreds of injuries and deaths. It was not until December 22 that Condé's government was able to officially take over Guinea's government.

A similar situation unfolded in Côte d'Ivoire, where a long-awaited presidential election and subsequent runoff took place in October and November. Both candidates, then-president Laurent Gbagbo and former prime minister and opposition leader Alassane Ouattara, claimed victory after the runoff election. Gbagbo, who controlled the nation's security forces, cracked down on the opposition movement, killing, wounding, and kidnapping Ouattara supporters. The UN peacekeeping force in the nation attempted to uphold Ouattara's government, being run from a heavily guarded luxury hotel. Ouattara promised to take complete control of the government by January 2011, but it was not until April that Gbagbo was captured, signaling the end of his reign.

Elections were not the only cause of worldwide violence in 2010. Violence between Armenia and Azerbaijan was reignited after a ceasefire violation over the autonomous Nagorno-Karabakh region. Mediation efforts led by Russia produced few breakthroughs by late 2010 and left governments on both sides of the conflict unconvinced that peace would soon return to the region. In Somalia, where the nation has existed in a state of near anarchy since the collapse of its central government in 1991, violence peaked in the summer and fall of 2010, displacing residents and causing a number of deaths. International security forces were unable to maintain order as they tried to install a new, weak central government, leaving open the question of whether the nation would follow through on holding its first official election in 2011.

In Kyrgyzstan, one of the former Soviet bloc's poorest nations, unrest that began in April over a government decision to raise utility prices by 200 percent stretched into the summer. The persistent high prices and government corruption reached a breaking point, and hundreds were killed in the fighting that pitted ethnic Kyrgyz against Uzbeks. The violence resulted in the collapse of Kyrgyzstan's government and the installation of a new parliamentary republic. Thailand experienced similar political unrest in March and April 2010, when rallies erupted into clashes between the military and antigovernment forces. Unlike the situation in Kyrgyzstan, however, the Thai government stood its ground and refused the protestors' calls for new elections, further underscoring the nation's tenuous political situation.

Violence broke out in Ecuador in September 2010 after the government stalled in its implementation of the president's controversial reform plans that would increase government involvement in the nation's economy. Although the measures were met with significant resistance in parliament, President Rafael Correa used a number of tactics, including veto power, to ensure passage of some key pieces of his reform plan and rewrite others he did not support. Alienation of opposition leaders and a number of austerity

measures that hit members of the military and police led to a protest that quickly escalated into violence.

Long-standing tension on the Korean peninsula was heightened in March 2010 when
a torpedo sank a South Korean naval vessel in the nation's territorial waters, killing forty-
six sailors. Media outlets were quick to point a finger at North Korea as the responsible
party, but South Korea's government called for calm until an official investigation could
be completed. When results of the investigation were announced in May, it was made
clear that the torpedo that sank the vessel was of North Korean origin. North Korea
refused to accept the results and promised "unpredictable strikes" against South Korea.
The South Korean government, in cooperation with allies, including the United States,
chose to impose financial sanctions on the North rather than retaliate with military
action.

During the summer and fall of 2010, the relationship between the North and South
looked as though it was beginning to improve. North Korea reached out to the South,
asking to resume allowing families split by the border to reunite, and also calling for a new
round of humanitarian and military discussions. The goodwill fell apart on November 23
when North Korea launched an artillery attack at Yeonpyeong Island, just off South
Korea's coast, where the South Korean military was preparing for its annual offensive drill
training. The North condemned the drills as an act of aggression, and South Korea
returned fire. While reason for the attack was unclear, North Korea, which was preparing
for the handover of power from Kim Jong-il to his son Kim Jong-un, said the continent
was on the "brink of war."

Security in the United States and Abroad

American military action abroad came under fire in 2010 when a website called WikiLeaks
began publishing confidential government documents, some containing key elements of
U.S. foreign policy. The website had previously published reports on U.S. military operations, but the flow of secret information rose to new levels in 2010. In April, WikiLeaks
founder Julian Assange released a military video at a Washington, D.C., press conference
that featured American troops shooting Iraqi civilians from an Apache helicopter. The
U.S. military claimed the helicopter had been flown in to assist coalition forces engaged
in combat, but the video featured soldiers congratulating each other on shooting skills
and mocking the dead civilians. Three months later, the website released 92,000 U.S.
documents on military operations in Afghanistan. An October release followed with
390,000 reports on U.S. military action in Iraq. Details of combat operations, civilian
casualties, meeting records, and even information that suggested that the Pakistan Inter-
Services Intelligence Agency might be working with the Taliban were contained in the
documents. In November, 250,000 diplomatic cables from U.S. embassies around the
world were released. The U.S. government met each release with outrage, while governments in nations including Russia criticized the American government's actions and
called its outrage an attempt at a cover-up.

Following up on a promise made by President Obama during his first months in
office, on August 19, 2010, the last U.S. combat brigade left Iraq, signaling the end of the
seven-and-a-half-year Operation Iraqi Freedom. The withdrawal of American combat
troops was uncertain in March when Iraqis went to the polls to vote for their new members of parliament. The newly elected government would be in charge of working with
the United States on combat troop withdrawal. Iraqis voted in large numbers, and little

violence was reported, but the vote totals, placing the secular Iraqiya Party ahead of Prime Minister Nuri Kamal al-Maliki's State of Law coalition, ushered in a period of political uncertainty for the nation. Maliki refused to accept the results and called for a recount, which he did not receive. Ayad Allawi, head of the Iraqiya Party, could not form a governing coalition, which opened the door for the State of Law coalition to remain in power. The United States stuck to its withdrawal plan and by September 1 had entered into its new role in Iraq—that of security force trainer and adviser. It was not until November that a tentative agreement for a coalition government, to be led by Maliki, was reached.

As the United States drew down its troops in Iraq, it maintained its combat forces in Afghanistan. These forces were instrumental in helping keep peace during Afghanistan's September parliamentary elections. Amid threats of violence from the Taliban, Afghanis went to the polls on September 18, 2010, but initial vote counts led to widespread allegations of fraud, and a number of recounts took place. It was not until December 1, 2010, that the election results were certified, and ethnic Pashtuns claimed a majority of parliamentary seats. The 2010 election was another indication of the need for election reform in Afghanistan that was most recently highlighted by Afghan president Hamid Karzai's 2009 election, which was wrought with fraud and brought legitimacy of his government under fire.

Maintaining security in the Middle East remains a top priority of Western governments. More specifically, these nations, led by the United States, have worked to eliminate safe havens for Taliban and al-Qaeda terrorists. The global effort in increased security came to a head in late October 2010 when two package bombs, bound for the United States on United Parcel Service (UPS) and FedEx cargo planes, were seized in the United Kingdom and Dubai. Neither of the packages made it to U.S. soil, and both were defused before they could cause damage. Cooperation between Saudi Arabia, the United States, and the United Kingdom helped avoid disaster. This cooperation was also instrumental in helping investigators quickly pinpoint the responsible party—al-Qaeda in the Arabian Peninsula. The knowledge that the bombs had come from Yemen increased U.S. military aid to the nation's central government, which was losing control of much of its territory to extremist organizations. Yemen refused U.S. encroachment on its internal affairs.

Not all terrorist acts in 2010 came from abroad. On May 1, 2010, in New York City's crowded Times Square, police were alerted to a smoking car, where they found a bomb hidden inside. The attempted bombing was linked to a Pakistani immigrant who had trained with the militant extremist group Tehrik-e-Taliban Pakistan. The organization had never before tried to carry out an attack on American soil, but federal counterterrorism officials said the attempt may indicate the strengthening of the organization and a move away from its usual targets in Pakistan. A similar plot unfolded in Oregon in November when a naturalized citizen from Somalia attempted to detonate a remote bomb at a Christmas tree–lighting ceremony. Federal Bureau of Investigation (FBI) agents had been tracking the responsible party and had even provided him with the materials to build a fake bomb. Both the New York and the Oregon incidents renewed fears of homegrown terrorism in the United States.

—Heather Kerrigan

January

Asian Carp Invade the Great Lakes

JANUARY 5, FEBRUARY 8, AND DECEMBER 16, 2010

Asian carp, a fish species introduced into the United States in the 1960s, have been slowly making their way up the Mississippi River toward the Great Lakes, leaving environmental degradation in their wake. Fearful of the potential impact on both fisheries and the ecosystems of the Great Lakes, states in the region have taken steps to keep the invasive species out. The fish are considered extremely dangerous to the Great Lakes ecosystem because of their large size, appetites, reproduction rate, and lack of natural predators. Because of the Asian carp's migration toward the Great Lakes region, neighboring states and the federal government have been working to find new methods to combat their spread, although not without controversy.

The controversy came to a head in December 2009 when Michigan filed suit against Illinois to close the canals in the Chicago River in order to stop the movement of Asian carp into Lake Michigan. Minnesota, Indiana, Ohio, and Wisconsin later joined Michigan's lawsuit. The suits threatened to open a nearly ninety-year-old Supreme Court case on Chicago's diversion of water from Lake Michigan.

The Supreme Court refused to hear Michigan's case, but the federal government did intervene, calling on a group of federal departments to investigate the best methods for stopping the spread of Asian carp in the Great Lakes region. The departments released their initial solutions on February 8, 2010. The final 2011 Asian Carp control framework was released on December 16, 2010.

ASIAN CARP

Asian carp, as the name implies, are native to Asia. However, because of the similar climate, the Great Lakes region is well suited to support them. Asian carp first came to the United States in 1963. The U.S. Fish and Wildlife Service brought the fish to Arkansas as a means to control weeds in the state's waterways. As the benefit of the fish became clear, fish farms began buying additional Asian carp to keep their own ponds clean. By 1966, the fish had begun spreading into the Mississippi River. When the river flooded in the 1990s, the fish spread even further.

Because of their ability to reproduce quickly, the Asian carp have taken over parts of the Mississippi and many rivers that flow into it. The fish have quickly traveled upstream where the climate is more suitable and food more plentiful for their needs. The worry for wildlife experts is the threat to other fish that support the ecosystems of U.S. waterways. Asian carp can consume 40 percent of their body weight in food per day, and they have no natural predator or known disease to ensure population control.

Four species are currently found in U.S. waterways—bighead, black, grass, and silver. Bighead carp and silver carp are of the greatest concern. Bighead carp eat constantly because they lack a stomach. The fish can become a danger to humans in the water as they can grow up to four feet in length and eighty-five pounds. Silver carp have been known to leap out of the water when a boat or other water sport vehicle disturbs them. The large, flying fish can hurt anyone in their path. Because of the dangerous nature of the Asian carp, water sports in the Illinois River have become less common. "You don't see people water-skiing or flying down the Illinois River in boats anymore," said Chris McCloud of the Illinois Department of Natural Resources. A lack of water sports means a decrease in tourism and recreation dollars for the state.

If the carp make it into the Great Lakes, they could cause considerable damage. As the world's largest freshwater ecosystem, the Great Lakes support a fishing and recreation industry that brings in $7 billion annually.

THE CHICAGO CANAL SYSTEM

Currently of greatest concern in the Great Lakes region is a two-hundred-foot-wide canal that links the Mississippi River to the Great Lakes. This canal is part of the larger Chicago Sanitary and Ship Canal, which was built more than a century ago to reverse the flow of the Chicago River and carry sewage out of Chicago and away from Lake Michigan. Once the canal was built, three locks were also put in place to allow for commercial and recreational ship traffic. The Controlling Works lock, which sits at the end of the Chicago River and controls flow from Lake Michigan, sees more than fifty thousand vessels pass through each year. Combined, 19.3 million tons of goods were moved through the locks in 2008, the most recent year for which data are available.

Due to Clean Water Act regulations and new technology, Chicago no longer dumps raw sewage into the river. However, the entire canal system is still vital to the region for clean drinking water, transportation, commercial shipping, and recreation.

Since its reversal, the Chicago River and its canal system have drawn concern from states surrounding Lake Michigan. When the canal was originally built, it diverted water away from Lake Michigan to provide additional clean water to flush sewage safely into the Mississippi River and eventually out into the Gulf of Mexico. That water is crucial to the ecosystem of the Chicago River.

In 1967, Great Lakes states brought a case to the U.S. Supreme Court, seeking to restrict the amount of water Illinois was able to take from Lake Michigan. The Court ruled that Illinois could take water from the Great Lakes but would have to limit its diversion to 2.1 billion gallons per day. However, the Court decided, if other states in the region could prove that Illinois's diversion was causing them harm, they could file another lawsuit. The 1967 decision formed the basis of Michigan's 2009 lawsuit.

CONTROL EFFORTS

To help stop Asian carp from moving from Chicago waterways to Lake Michigan, the Army Corps of Engineers built a series of underwater electric barriers. The first barrier was built in 2002, and a second, more powerful barrier was added in 2006. In 2010, the Corps used funds from the American Recovery and Reinvestment Act to install a third electric barrier. The electric barriers, the world's largest fish barriers, cost the Corps tens of thousands of dollars per month to operate. The barriers are electrified to a level that is not harmful to humans; they do not kill the fish, but rather repel them.

In the spring of 2009, the Corps worked with the University of Notre Dame to take environmental DNA samples (eDNA) from the Chicago waterways to check for the presence of Asian carp. These samples tested positive for the fish, and the Corps subsequently increased the voltage on the first two electric barriers. A second sample was taken in November of the same year, and again Asian carp were present, this time past the electric barrier. Fortunately they were still miles from the lock that separates the Chicago River from Lake Michigan.

In response, Illinois worked with commercial fishermen who were skilled in capturing Asian carp. In December 2009, one thousand fish were caught in the canal system during this exercise, and none were Asian carp. As an added precaution, the Illinois Department of Natural Resources (IDNR) dumped fish poison into the canal, south of the electric barrier. Tens of thousands of fish were killed, and only one bighead carp was found. Given the evidence the Corps and IDNR collected, both asserted that the electric barriers are working as intended and are keeping Asian carp out of the Great Lakes.

Even if new regulations are imposed or new technologies created to stop the spread of Asian carp, ensuring that the fish never make it into the Great Lakes could be an impossible task. Since they were first brought to the United States, Asian carp have become common in many U.S. rivers. As a result, it is likely that the best engineers will be able to do is control the spread of the invasive fish, but never fully stop it.

Michigan Files Suit

Although the Chicago canal still serves as an important passageway for treated water and shipping vessels, in December 2009, Michigan filed suit to permanently close the waterway locks to stop movement of the fish. Attorney General Mike Cox of Michigan filed the suit in federal court to protect the revenue Lake Michigan provides for the state and its citizens. According to Cox, thousands of jobs are dependent on Lake Michigan. The suit called for immediate closure of the locks, but it indicated that the state would eventually like to see the Mississippi River and Great Lakes separated permanently.

Illinois attorney general Lisa Madigan responded to Michigan's lawsuit in a statement sent to the U.S. Supreme Court, refuting Michigan's argument. "Even a temporary closure of the locks will devastate the local economy and Illinois's role in the regional, national, and global economies, endanger public safety, and cause serious environmental harm," said Madigan. She claimed that closure of the locks would hinder the Chicago police and fire departments' efforts to effectively respond to large incidents or possible terror attacks in the area; curb commercial ship traffic, causing harm to businesses that use the waterway; increase energy prices; upset grain pricing; reduce state revenue from recreation; and degrade the quality of the water in the Chicago River, thereby harming its ecosystem.

Suzanne Malec-McKenna, commissioner of Chicago's Department of Environment, also responded to the lawsuit, saying, "While we recognize that Asian carp pose a significant threat to the Great Lakes, shutting down the waterway system in Northeastern Illinois before fully understanding the impact it would have on the movement of people, goods and storm water is a shortsighted answer to a complex problem." The president of the Metropolitan Water Reclamation District of Greater Chicago, Terrence O'Brien, added that closing the locks would be "a disservice to public health and safety."

Michigan's suit threatened to impact the Great Lakes Compact. In 2008, the Great Lakes states agreed to a compromise that stops the diversion of water from any of the lakes unless all of the states and nearby Canadian provinces agree. The compact's original intention was to stop drought-ridden regions from tapping into and using the lakes' water.

However, on January 19, 2010, the U.S. Supreme Court refused to order Illinois to close the locks immediately. The Court offered no comment on its decision, and on February 4, 2010, Cox filed another motion with the Court, asking it to reconsider its decision. The new motion, Cox said, should be considered because of new evidence that Asian carp are present in Lake Michigan. The second motion was also denied by the U.S. Supreme Court on March 22, 2010. The Court further rejected Michigan's request to file another lawsuit on the same issue.

A NEW ACTION PLAN

With a lack of agreement among the Great Lakes states, on February 8, 2010, the White House convened the Summit for Great Lakes Governors on the Threat of Asian Carp to the Great Lakes. The Barack Obama administration wanted states to use this time to discuss and explore options available to prevent the spread of the fish. Here the administration also unveiled its Asian Carp Control Strategy Framework, which outlines possible future funding sources and prevention techniques.

The framework included both short- and long-term recommendations. The short-term recommendations, implemented on May 15, 2010, ensured that state and federal departments had the resources to quickly respond to any Asian carp; ramped up monitoring efforts; and encouraged research on potential biological controls. Before 2020, the White House called for additional feasibility studies on additional electric barriers or other spread prevention structures; biological controls; development of an Asian carp market; and controlled lock operations.

On December 16, the White House announced that the 2011 Asian Carp Control Strategy Framework had been released. Building off of the White House summit and earlier frameworks, the 2011 strategy added thirteen new goals to help combat Asian carp. These new strategies included evaluating the impact some commercial traffic has on the reliability of the electronic barriers; limiting the wastewater treatment chemicals used in Chicago to reduce food sources available to Asian carp; developing new methods to trap the fish; and expanding the use and reliability of eDNA.

"The Obama Administration has taken an aggressive, unprecedented approach to protect our Great Lakes and the communities and economies that depend on them from the threat of Asian carp," said John Goss, Asian carp director for the White House Council on Environmental Quality. "This Framework builds on the successes we accomplished in 2010 by leveraging our cross-government, regional coordination on immediate preventative actions and multi-tiered strategies for the longer term."

—Heather Kerrigan

Following is a response from Illinois attorney general Lisa Madigan, on January 5, 2010, to Michigan's request for a preliminary injunction; a press release from February 8, 2010, announcing the strategy devised by the U.S. Army Corps of Engineers, the Environmental Protection Agency, the Department of the Interior, and the U.S. Coast Guard to combat the onslaught of Asian carp in the Great Lakes; and a White House press release from December 16, 2010, announcing the final 2011 Asian Carp strategy framework.

DOCUMENT

Illinois Responds to Michigan's Request for Preliminary Injunction

January 5, 2010

[The table of contents and footnotes have been omitted.]

Introduction

The motion for preliminary injunction should be denied. As an initial matter, this case does not fall within the scope of the decades' old Consent Decree on which Michigan and the joining States (hereinafter "Michigan") chiefly rely as a source for this Court's jurisdiction. The Decree reconciles States' competing claims to water from Lake Michigan, and it would stretch the Decree's scope well past the breaking point to argue that it resolves any dispute related in any way to Illinois canals, particularly where, as here, Michigan disclaims any interest in reducing the amount of Lake Michigan water that Illinois may divert. But without the Decree, Michigan has little on which to proceed, especially against the State of Illinois, which operates neither the locks nor the sluice gates that Michigan wants closed or regulated. In fact, Michigan does not—and cannot—specify a single action within Illinois' legal authority that it has not undertaken already to ensure that the Asian carp do not reach the Great Lakes.

Illinois is intensely concerned about, and invested in, the ecology and health of the Great Lakes. Its own environmental and commercial stake in the Lakes' well-being is unsurpassed, and Illinois is as much a victim of the release of Asian carp into the Mississippi years ago by fish farmers in the South as any of the complainants. Indeed, the State is doing everything within its legal authority over a federal, navigable waterway to combat the carps' progress. The Illinois Department of Natural Resources ("IDNR") spent millions of dollars in 2009 alone in a massive effort to kill all aquatic life over a six-mile stretch of water—hand in hand with officials from Michigan and other Great Lakes States, who have participated in the effort—notwithstanding this measure's devastating effect on water life. And this is only a small fraction of the work the State has done, within its limited authority in this area, to stop the progress of Asian carp. Alongside officials from each of the Great Lakes States and Canada, Illinois has been an active participant for years in efforts to keep the carp and other invasive species from entering the Lakes, contributed $1.8 million toward the construction by the Army Corps of Engineers ("Corps") of an electric barrier to prevent Asian carp from passing into Lake Michigan, and sponsored commercial and "electrofishing" efforts to detect the presence of Asian carp. Having participated in these efforts, Michigan makes no specific demand of Illinois, and accordingly this case does not fall within this Court's exclusive, original jurisdiction. At best, it is a thinly veiled end-run around the Administrative Procedure Act, under which Michigan would need to sue the Corps in federal district court to close the locks.

But Michigan has another problem, beyond the fact that it has sued in the wrong court and demands nothing specific from Illinois. The harm that it identifies is speculative. Illinois has deployed a battery of tests to detect the presence of Asian carp above the protective barrier that the Corps built to keep the fish from Lake Michigan, without finding a single fish. The "fish kill" that devastated all aquatic life over a six-mile stretch revealed one Asian carp, and even that was *south* of the barrier. In the end, plaintiffs rely on "eDNA" evidence suggesting that some fish matter north of the barrier tested positive for the presence of Asian carp DNA. But putting aside the fact that eDNA testing is a nascent, unpublished practice, every effort to find even a single actual Asian carp above the barrier has come up empty. And against this speculation, Michigan understates the massive health, safety, and economic effects of even a temporary shut-down of the lock system.

Finally, there is yet another, independently fatal defect in Michigan's extraordinary request for preliminary injunctive relief from this Court: it cannot show any likelihood of success on the underlying merits of its claim. Without the argument that the 1967 decree somehow resolves this dispute, Michigan must contend that Illinois has violated the common law of nuisance. But this is absurd on its face. That Asian carp would be introduced into the Mississippi by third parties and make their way toward the Great Lakes was wholly unforeseeable at the time the Chicago waterway system was constructed, and Illinois lacks control over the locks and sluice gates on which Michigan premises its claim for relief. And where Illinois does have control, it has worked cooperatively with other States in ensuring that the carp do not enter the Great Lakes, and has used what legal authority it has, and substantial resources, to fulfill this mission.

For each of these several, independent reasons, Michigan's motion for preliminary injunction should be denied. . . .

[The Statement of Facts, Argument, and Conclusion sections have been omitted.]

SOURCE: State of Illinois. Office of the Attorney General. "Attorney General Madigan Files Response to Asian Carp Lawsuit." January 5, 2010. http://www.illinoisattorneygeneral.gov/pressroom/2010_01/ILLINOIS_RESPONSE_01-05-2010_15-04-18.pdf.

Federal Officials Unveil Strategy to Combat Asian Carp in the Great Lakes

February 8, 2010

Federal officials from the U.S. Army Corps of Engineers, the Environmental Protection Agency, the Department of the Interior, and the U.S. Coast Guard today unveiled a strategy that outlines over 25 short and long-term actions and $78.5 million in investments to combat the spread of Asian carp. The draft Asian Carp Control Strategy Framework (Framework) is an unparalleled effort to control the invasive species, unifying Federal, state, and local action, and introducing a multi-tiered defense of the Great Lakes to prevent Asian carp from developing self-sustaining populations while longer term biological controls are being developed.

"As with many great eco-systems across the country, invasive species have harmed the Great Lakes, and an invasion of Asian carp threatens to be particularly ecologically and economically damaging," said Nancy Sutley, Chair of the White House Council on Environmental Quality. "Today, we have an opportunity to work together to prevent environmental and economic damage before it happens. This Framework utilizes the best available science and its multi-tiered strategy will ensure coordination and the most effective response."

"EPA has helped to develop this coordinated strategy on such an urgent issue and assisted in building a coalition to act to keep Asian carp from becoming established in the Great Lakes," said EPA Administrator Lisa P. Jackson. "The combined resources and expertise of the interagency partnership are our best tools for protecting the Great Lakes ecosystem and economy."

"The Army Corps of Engineers remains committed to aggressively using all available authorities to protect the Great Lakes from this invasive species," said Jo-Ellen Darcy, Assistant Secretary of the Army for Civil Works. "We cannot do this alone. All parties must bring the full force of their resources to this challenge. We are working intensively with its Federal, State, provincial, bi-national, and municipal agency partners to achieve this goal."

"Interior and its bureaus are committed to working in partnership with the States of Illinois, Michigan and Wisconsin, the affected communities and other Federal agencies to tackle the complex threat posed by Asian carp to the ecological and economic health of the Great Lakes," said Tom Strickland, Assistant Secretary for Fish and Wildlife and Parks. "We are providing immediate financial, technical and research assistance for Asian carp control efforts in South Chicago waterways, and will continue to do everything we can to keep carp out of Lake Michigan."

In the near term, the Framework focuses on keeping carp from establishing populations in the Great Lakes. It calls for reduced openings of Chicago's navigational locks to prevent carp movement. In addition, Federal agencies will deploy enlarged field crews for physical and sonar observation, electro-shocking and netting operations within the waterway. Turnaround times on eDNA verification will be expedited and testing capacity will be doubled to 120 samples per week.

In March, 2010, a $13.2M contract will be awarded for construction of barriers between the Chicago Sanitary and Ship Canal and Des Plaines River, which will prevent fish passage around the electric barrier in the event of flooding where the two water bodies mix. A $10.5M contract will also be awarded for construction and operation of a third electric barrier (IIB). The Framework expedites a U.S. Army Corps of Engineers' study of the feasibility and impacts of permanent lock closure, the effectiveness of lock closings to block carp movement, the risks and costs associated with closure, and a discussion of alternatives.

The Framework identifies a variety of longer term Asian carp management techniques for the duration of 2010 and beyond. This includes $3M in funds for commercial market enhancements and $5M for additional chemical treatments in the case of barrier failure. It also puts forth over $1.5M in new research funding. Several research efforts will receive significant funding in the coming months to help inform decision makers of additional tools that might be available for Asian carp management, including development of biological controls like Asian carp-specific poisons, methods to disrupt spawning and egg viability, sonic barriers, and assessment of food sources and potential habitats.

The Framework also identifies educational and enforcement tools to prevent Asian carp from being sold or purposefully transferred, and an investigation of Asian carp transfer in ballast and bilge water. The Framework will be updated as new partners and new action options are identified to help stop the spread of Asian carp. Federal agencies will continue to work together and in collaboration with state and local agencies to fight the spread of Asian carp into the Great Lakes. The entire Framework is available at www.asiancarp.org.

SOURCE: U.S. Executive Office of the President. "Federal Officials Unveil Aggressive Strategy to Reduce Threat of Asian Carp in the Great Lakes." February 8, 2010. http://www.whitehouse.gov/administration/eop/ceq/Press_Releases/February_8_2010.

2011 Asian Carp Framework Released

December 16, 2010

The Obama Administration today announced a series of new measures to protect the Great Lakes from Asian carp, building on the unprecedented proactive plan to prevent this invasive species from developing self-sustaining populations in the Great Lakes that the Administration established in February 2010.

The 2011 Asian Carp Control Strategy Framework adds 13 new initiatives to the comprehensive effort to combat Asian carp, including expanding eDNA testing capacity and developing cutting-edge biological controls and monitoring technology, among other measures.

The original Framework, created in February 2010 and updated in May, established the Asian Carp Regional Coordinating Committee (ACRCC), consisting of state and municipal agencies, the U.S. Army Corps of Engineers, the U.S. Fish and Wildlife Service, the U.S. Geological Survey, the U.S. Environmental Protection Agency, and the U.S. Coast Guard to synchronize the response to Asian carp.

"The Obama Administration has taken an aggressive, unprecedented approach to protect our Great Lakes and the communities and economies that depend on them from the threat of Asian carp," said John Goss, Asian Carp Director for the White House Council on Environmental Quality. "This Framework builds on the successes we accomplished in 2010 by leveraging our cross-government, regional coordination on immediate preventative actions and multi-tiered strategies for the longer term."

"Thanks to the Great Lakes Restoration Initiative established by President Obama and strongly supported by Congress, we can take important steps to protect these vital waters," said Cameron Davis, Senior Advisor to the Administrator (Great Lakes), U.S. Environmental Protection Agency. "We are working to maintain this ecosystem, which represents the nation's largest source of fresh surface water and is the cornerstone of local jobs and the regional economy."

"The Army Corps of Engineers continues its commitment to protect the Great Lakes from Asian carp. Our achievements in 2010 demonstrate the success of this integrated framework, of working together to keep the carp out of this treasured ecosystem. Our success further motivates us to accomplish new initiatives in 2011," said Jo-Ellen Darcy, Assistant Secretary of the Army for Civil Works.

"From a biological standpoint we face a great challenge protecting the Great Lakes ecosystems and fisheries from invasion by the Asian carp," said Tom Strickland, Assistant Secretary for Fish and Wildlife and Parks at the Department of the Interior. "The U.S. Fish and Wildlife Service and the U.S. Geological Survey are working on the ground as part of an Administration-wide intensive comprehensive strategy to stop the spread of Asian carp. This effort is unprecedented and is a major priority for the Department of the Interior."

The original Asian Carp Control Strategy Framework included 32 Federally-funded initiatives, all of which have been completed or are underway. The 2011 Asian Carp Control Strategy Framework now includes 45 short- and long-term initiatives in an aggressive, multi-tiered strategy to combat Asian carp.

Key accomplishments in 2010 in response to the Asian Carp threat include:

- Enhanced the fish barrier system to include strengthened electric barriers, physical barricades to stop carp migration during floods, and closed off smaller waterway connections to the Great Lakes.
- Constructed a third electric fish barrier in the Chicago Waterway for extra protection in the primary path of concern for carp migration into Lake Michigan.
- Established Asiancarp.org to provide up-to-date information about Asian Carp efforts.
- Utilized emergency authority provided through Section 126 of Energy and Water Development Act of 2010 to block flood waters from the Des Plaines River with a 13-mile fish barrier and a permanent block in the Illinois and Michigan Canal to keep Asian carp from crossing into the Chicago Waterway.
- Installed a 1,500 foot fish barrier fence at Eagle Marsh, near Fort Wayne, IN, once considered an alternate pathway of greatest concern, to block advancement of Asian carp from the Wabash to the Maumee and Lake Erie.
- Identified 18 other potential pathways at risk across all the Great Lakes states for the potential transfer of aquatic invasive species between the Great Lakes and Mississippi River Basins.
- Began implementing the Asian Carp Prevention and Control Act following the President's signing of the bill on December 14, 2010. This legislation prohibits live bighead carp from being shipped or imported into the United States.
- Coordinated Federal agencies to deploy larger field crews to conduct electro shock and netting operations, and increased eDNA testing capacity to 220 samples a week.
- Increased collaboration across all levels of government by integrating the Great Lakes states into the Asian Carp Regional Coordinating Committee and our Asian Carp Control Strategy Framework actions.

New projects in the 2011 Framework include:

- Validation of eDNA as an effective tool for monitoring and tracking Asian Carp through analysis and refinement of the eDNA processes to determine the number and distribution of positive detections of Asian carp.
- Development of eDNA genetic markers to more accurately and efficiently detect Asian carp concentrations.
- Expansion of the USFWS lab in LaCrosse, WI to increase capacity of eDNA testing in all of the Great Lakes.
- Development of alternate trap and net designs for Asian carp.
- Development of rapid genetic-based methods to detect Asian carp to allow for faster results than eDNA.
- Evaluation of the affect of removing Asian carp food sources by reducing phosphorus and nitrogen from waste water treatment plant discharges into the CAWS/ Upper Illinois Watershed.
- Assessment of the impact of steel hulled barges on the electric barriers.
- Evaluation of a permanent separation between the Wabash-Maumee watersheds.

Key ongoing projects include:

- Continuation of the Great Lakes and Mississippi River Interbasin Study (GLM-RIS), including study of aquatic nuisance species controls and hydrologic separation of the basins.
- Development of permanent blockages for aquatic invasive species pathways throughout the Great Lakes states.
- Evaluation of electric barrier effectiveness through fish tagging and by utilizing Didson cameras.
- Deployment of an enhanced, more efficient system to monitor, sample and capture Asian carp.
- Enforcement of carp inspections at bait shops, fish processors, fish markets and retail food establishments.
- Enabling American commercial fishermen to develop markets for Asian carp, reducing Asian carp population in the Illinois River and creating jobs.
- Public engagement through outreach and enforcement.
- Collaboration with stakeholders groups, commercial fishermen, industry and recreational boaters to mitigate the damage Asian carp inflict upon waterway users.
- Investment of Great Lakes Restoration Initiative funds in research and development of long term fish management strategies for Asian carp, eDNA sampling, and habitability assessments.
- Improvement of hydro gun techniques to herd or eradicate and test as a barrier when locks are opened.
- Development of biological interference to reduce Asian carp breeding.
- Establishment and continual updating of www.asiancarp.org as a comprehensive source for information about Asian carp activities. . . .

SOURCE: U.S. Executive Office of the President. "Obama Administration Releases 2011 Asian Carp Control Strategy Framework." December 16, 2010. http://www.whitehouse.gov/administration/eop/ceq/Press_Releases/December_16_2010.

OTHER HISTORIC DOCUMENTS OF INTEREST

FROM PREVIOUS *HISTORIC DOCUMENTS*

Earthquakes Devastate Haiti and Chile

JANUARY 15 AND 17, FEBRUARY 27, AND JUNE 2010

Early in 2010, two earthquakes of historic magnitude struck the countries of Haiti and Chile, causing widespread destruction. Hundreds of thousands of Haitians lost their lives, while Chileans living in coastal regions contended with treacherous tsunami waves. Despite an outpouring of international support and millions of dollars in contributions received, both countries continue to struggle with their recovery efforts.

DEVASTATION IN HAITI

On January 12, 2010, an earthquake struck Haiti approximately ten miles southwest of the capital city of Port-au-Prince. Measuring a magnitude of 7.0 on the Richter scale, it was the strongest earthquake to hit the country in more than two hundred years. The quake was caused by the release of seismic tension along a fault line between the Caribbean and North American tectonic plates, a fault line running directly underneath the island of Hispaniola. A series of aftershocks followed the initial quake, fifteen of which were a magnitude 5.0 or higher. The Pacific Tsunami Warning Center issued a tsunami warning immediately following the quake, but quickly withdrew it when a tsunami did not materialize.

The impact of the quake was immediate and devastating. The southern towns of Jacmel and Léogâne reported significant damage, but Port-au-Prince suffered the greatest destruction. The buildings of the presidential palace, Palace of Justice, National Assembly, and Supreme Court were destroyed, as were the Haitian tax office and ministries of foreign affairs and commerce. The headquarters of the United Nations (UN) peacekeeping mission collapsed and killed sixteen members of the peacekeeping force, making it one of the deadliest single days for UN employees. The quake also destroyed the Prison Civile de Port-au-Prince, enabling four thousand inmates to escape into the streets. According to Minister of Education Joel Jean-Pierre, half of the nation's schools and the three main universities in the capital were damaged, and approximately fifty health care facilities were destroyed. Thousands of Haitians became trapped in the rubble of their homes and other buildings, with the American Red Cross estimating that as many as three million people had been affected by the disaster. Electricity, running water, and phone service were cut, leaving survivors in the dark and unable to access food and clean water.

Immediately following the quake, thousands of Haitians took to the streets, sleeping on sidewalks, in parks, or in hastily built shanty towns. Thousands more fled to the countryside where there was less damage. Those who remained began the rescue effort, searching collapsed homes for signs of survivors. "You have thousands of people sitting in the streets with nowhere to go. There are people running, crying, screaming. People are trying to dig victims out with flashlights," said Rachmani Domersant, an operations manager with Food for the Poor. The United Nations later estimated that 105,000 homes had been destroyed with another 208,000 damaged, while the Inter-American Development Bank placed the death toll between 200,000 and 250,000. Many pointed to Haiti's lack of strong building standards as a key factor contributing to the widespread devastation; in addition, some neighborhoods had barely recovered from damage sustained during the 2008 hurricane season.

RELIEF EFFORTS

Expressions of sympathy and pledges of humanitarian aid poured in from around the world, including a promise of $4.4 million from the European Union and a United Nations (UN) commitment to release $10 million from the Central Emergency Response Fund. "There is no doubt that we are facing a major humanitarian emergency and that a major relief effort will be required. . . . I urge all members of the international community to come to Haiti's aid in this hour of need," said UN secretary general Ban Ki-moon.

In the United States, the American Red Cross played a central role in mobilizing aid. On January 15, 2010, the organization announced the release of $10 million to support aid efforts; the following day, it announced that a truck convoy carrying fifty-bed field hospitals and water purification systems had arrived in the capital. The group also organized an innovative mobile fundraising campaign, in which those wishing to donate to the relief effort could use their cellular phones to make a $10 contribution. Within two days of its launch, the campaign raised more than $3 million.

The global relief effort was quickly hampered by Haiti's lack of sufficient infrastructure. The country's system of roads and bridges was already weakened by a brutal 2008 hurricane season, but it was further damaged by the quake. Combined with a shortage of fuel, this made the transportation of aid and rescue workers extremely difficult. The traffic control tower at Haiti's Toussaint Louverture International Airport had also been damaged, further restricting the airport's already limited capacity to handle the overwhelming number of military and civilian planes attempting to deliver supplies and forcing some groups to transport supplies by boat or over land to Port-au-Prince from the Dominican Republic. Approximately 375 aid organizations had registered with the UN in Haiti, but officials believed many more had made their way into the country, including a number of inexperienced groups that became known as "humanitarian tourists." This further complicated an inefficient system of communications among the various groups.

Hoping to expedite the receipt of international aid, the Haitian government signed control of the airport over to the United States on January 15. Two days later, the two countries issued a joint communiqué in which the United States reaffirmed its commitment to providing aid and Haiti welcomed U.S. assistance. Yet the United States quickly drew criticism from the United Nations and aid groups who claimed important food deliveries were being delayed and that U.S. military planes were receiving preferential treatment. On January 22, the United States and United Nations signed a memorandum of understanding to formalize their roles in the aid process and put the United Nations in charge of coordinating relief work and peacekeeping efforts. Tensions were also relieved when the United States began flying military planes into the airport during off-peak hours to better accommodate international aid flights.

Haitians soon became frustrated by the lack of a government response to the disaster. A leadership crisis began to develop as it became increasingly clear that the government could not control the relief effort and was slow to clear debris and identify safe relocation sites for those who had lost their homes. Many expressed particular disappointment in President René Préval's seeming inaction. Security was also a major concern as looters raided damaged shops in search of anything they could sell, aid distribution stations erupted in chaos when supplies ran out, and children went unaccounted for.

On February 4, Haitian prosecutors charged a group of ten Americans with kidnapping and criminal association, after alleging it may have been part of a child-trafficking scheme. The group, New Life Children's Refuge, mostly affiliated with Baptist churches in Idaho, had tried to take thirty-three Haitian children over the border into the Dominican Republic after claiming the children had been orphaned during the quake. Several of the children were identified as still having parents. The group claimed it was not planning to offer the children for adoption but rather intended to build a new orphanage for them in the Dominican Republic. On February 19, a judge ordered eight of the Americans be released after parents of some of the children testified that they had voluntarily given their children to the group, but said the group leader, Laura Silsby, would need to remain in Haiti for further questioning.

DISASTER STRIKES IN CHILE

As Haiti struggled to recover, Chile faced its own disaster. On February 27, an earthquake measuring a magnitude of 8.8 struck at 3:34 a.m. local time. It was the strongest quake to hit Chile in fifty years, and, according to the U.S. Geological Survey, it was tied for the fifth strongest quake recorded since 1900. The epicenter was located approximately seventy miles northeast of the coastal city of Concepción and two hundred miles south of the capital city of Santiago, but its force could be felt as far away as Brazil. Geologists later reported that the force of the quake had been strong enough to move Concepción ten feet to the west.

The quake quickly triggered a tsunami warning of possible "widespread damage" from the Pacific Tsunami Warning Center for fifty-three countries and island chains throughout the Pacific region, though only a few experienced wave surges. Tsunami waves hit Chile's own islands and coastal regions, which caused the majority of casualties, including approximately 350 deaths in hardest-hit Concepción.

Initial reports from the Ministry of the Interior claimed that the quake had killed at least 214 Chileans, but President Michele Bachelet later announced that there were 708 known deaths. Casualties were reported throughout the regions of Maule, Santiago, O'Higgins, Biobio, Araucania, and Valparaiso. Though stronger than the Haiti earthquake, the low death toll was attributed to Chile's advanced building standards, which prevented many newer structures from collapsing. As in Haiti, Chileans were without electricity and running water, and Internet and cell phone services were sporadic. Highways were destroyed, bridges collapsed, and a fire broke out at a chemical plant on the outskirts of Santiago. The city's airport was damaged and was closed for three days, and rescue teams had difficulty travelling to Concepción because of infrastructure damage. Insurance companies estimated the total damage at about $30 billion.

Governments around the world offered their condolences and pledged to provide any aid needed. U.S. secretary of state Hillary Clinton issued a statement saying, "Our hemisphere comes together in times of crisis, and we will stand side by side with the people of

Chile in this emergency." Though Bachelet described the earthquake as "a catastrophe of such unthinkable magnitude that it will require a giant effort," she did not request assistance from the international community until March 1. That same day, Secretary Clinton arrived in Chile as part of a previously scheduled five-nation tour of Latin America, bringing satellite phones with her as a first installment of U.S. aid. The United States would provide extensive aid to Chile through June, including temporary shelters, water purification systems, and electrical generators. A six-member team from the U.S. Agency for International Development was also dispatched to assist in the relief effort.

Some looting broke out immediately following the earthquake, but Bachelet quickly mobilized thousands of Chileans to assist law enforcement officials in Santiago and Concepción in maintaining security. She also announced that any essentials on the shelves of major supermarkets would be given away for free, while law enforcement officials would also be distributing food and water. In addition, Bachelet imposed a curfew from 9:00 p.m. to 6:00 a.m., during which time only emergency personnel and security forces would be allowed outside. While these efforts restored relative calm to Santiago within a matter of days, looting would continue in Concepción and other coastal towns.

PAINSTAKING RECOVERY

Since shortly after the earthquakes, the recovery effort in both countries has been ongoing. In mid-April, the Haitian Parliament approved the creation of the Interim Haiti Reconstruction Commission, to be led by former U.S. president Bill Clinton and Haitian prime minister Jean-Max Bellerive. The commission was charged with overseeing $5.3 billion that had been pledged by private donors for the first eighteen months of Haiti's recovery, yet only ten percent of those funds had been delivered as of the beginning of 2011. As of July 2010, only 28,000 of the 1.5 million displaced Haitians had moved into new homes, and as much as 98 percent of the debris had not been cleared. Meanwhile, global criticism of the aid effort continues to grow. The Disaster Accountability Project released a report in early July 2010 pointing to the lack of transparency among aid groups on the ground in Haiti, while the U.S. Senate Foreign Relations Committee released a report criticizing the groups for poor coordination. Adding to the devastation, a cholera outbreak swept through rural Haiti and into the tent camps of Port-au-Prince in October 2010, killing more than two thousand people by mid-December 2010.

Frustration also lingers among the residents of Chile's coastal towns, where the recovery has been far slower than in Santiago. Much of the debris remains, and the government has yet to provide reconstruction assistance. Six months after the earthquake, many were still living in temporary camps without running water. "Six months later and there's no solution," said Dichato resident Eglantina Chavez. "The government can't just leave us here, tossed aside."

—Linda Fecteau

Following are two press releases from the American Red Cross regarding American recovery assistance after the earthquake in Haiti on January 15 and January 17, 2010; a joint statement by the United States and Haiti on January 17, 2010, regarding the aftermath of the earthquake; a statement by U.S. secretary of state Hillary Clinton on February 27, 2010, regarding the earthquake in Chile; and a press release from the U.S. Embassy in Chile on American earthquake recovery assistance from June 2010.

American Red Cross Announces Donation to Haiti

January 15, 2010

With estimates that as many as three million people may be affected by the catastrophic earthquake which hit Haiti Tuesday, the American Red Cross is releasing an additional $9 million for earthquake relief, bringing its total commitment so far to $10 million to support relief efforts in Haiti.

Priority needs in Haiti are food, water, temporary shelter, medical services and emotional support. Thousands of local Red Cross volunteers are aiding their fellow Haitians. American Red Cross Disaster management specialists are scheduled to arrive today from the United States, Peru and Mexico to join local Red Cross staff already on the ground in the disaster zone. As soon as airports begin accepting relief shipments, tarps, hygiene items and cooking sets for approximately 5,000 families will come from the Red Cross warehouse in Panama.

The American Red Cross is also helping the injured who may need blood. Blood and blood products were shipped to the U.S. Naval Air Station in Jacksonville, Florida, and then on to Guantanamo Bay in support of medical evacuees from Haiti.

The International Committee of the Red Cross (ICRC) has a plane full of mostly medical items on the way to Haiti from Geneva. ICRC staff, including engineers, a surgeon and family linking specialists are expected to arrive in Port-au-Prince this morning. Other Red Cross partners have deployed a mobile hospital, medical teams, and 40 staff to help with sheltering, providing water, sanitation, and telecommunications.

ICRC is helping reconnect separated families in Haiti through a special web site which enables people in Haiti and outside the country to search for and register the names of relatives missing since the earthquake. In the first twenty-four hours, more than 6,000 people have been registered. . . .

SOURCE: American Red Cross. "American Red Cross Releases $10 Million to Help Haiti." January 15, 2010. http://www.redcross.org/portal/site/en/menuitem.94aae335470e233f6cf911df43181aa0/?vgnextoi d=99b36d585ce26210VgnVCM10000089f0870aRCRD.

American Red Cross Statement on Resources Sent to Haiti

January 17, 2010

Truckloads of Red Cross supplies arrived in Port-au-Prince today and thousands of responders are traveling the streets providing water and first aid as well as finding lost loved ones and transporting people with serious injuries to nearby health facilities.

"America's support—donations made in the United States to the American Red Cross—is reaching the hands of survivors in Haiti," said Steve McAndrew, disaster relief specialist with the American Red Cross in Port-au-Prince.

Within the convoy that arrived today are 50-bed field hospitals and purification equipment capable of producing 10,000 gallons of drinking water per day. The mobile hospitals have a dedicated section to help people cope with emotional trauma. Toys and specially-trained volunteers will be available to comfort children, who are particularly vulnerable.

An additional seven truckloads of equipment and materials including medical supplies, that were on Red Cross planes re-routed to Dominican Republic Friday, are traveling overland and are expected to arrive in Port-au-Prince by Sunday. Two flights will arrive in the capital city, carrying enough relief supplies for more than 32,000 families, on Monday as well.

The American Red Cross team and responders from more than 30 countries, totaling more than 100, have now arrived and are providing a wide-range of support, including food, water, field hospitals, emotional support and sanitation services.

"We are working with the Haitian Red Cross volunteers, who have intimate knowledge of the community," said McAndrew. "Survivors are receiving aid from their neighbors, who they know and trust, with support from the international community."

On Tuesday, American Red Cross President & CEO Gail McGovern will travel to Port-au-Prince to join other Red Cross leaders in assessing the relief efforts and planning for long-term recovery.

"Our focus now is on the immediate relief for the people of Haiti, but make no mistake, this is going to be a massive long-term recovery operation," McGovern said.

Since the earthquake struck, more than 19,300 people have registered with the International Committee of the Red Cross-sponsored Web site (www.icrc.org/familylinks) helping to reconnect families separated during the earthquake. Almost all of the registrations were from people searching for news about their relatives, although around 1,400 people have so far used the site to say they are safe and well.

Source: American Red Cross. "Red Cross Aid Reaches Haitian Earthquake Survivors." January 17, 2010. http://www.redcross.org/portal/site/en/menuitem.94aae335470e233f6cf911df43181aa0/?vgnextoid= 6bbee033e1636210VgnVCM10000089f0870aRCRD.

United States and Haiti Release Joint Statement Regarding Haitian Earthquake

January 17, 2010

President René Préval of Haiti and Secretary of State Hillary Rodham Clinton of the United States of America met in Port-au-Prince in the wake of the catastrophic earthquake of January 12, 2010 and its tragic aftermath, and issued the following joint communiqué:

Recognizing:

the long history of friendship between the people of Haiti and the people of the United States and their mutual respect for each other's sovereignty;

the grievous suffering of the people of Haiti, including the massive loss of life, widespread injuries, and extensive damage to public infrastructure and private property;

the urgent need for an immediate response to the requests by the Government of Haiti and the paramount importance of safe, swift and effective implementation of rescue, relief, recovery, and reconstruction efforts;

the current, unprecedented challenges facing the Haitian Government; and

the January 15, 2010 conversation between President Obama and President Préval underscoring the urgency of the needs of Haiti and its people, President Obama's pledge of the full support of the American people for the Government and people of Haiti in relation to both the immediate recovery effort and the long-term rebuilding effort, and the two Presidents' commitment to coordinate assistance among the various parties, including the Haitian Government, the United Nations, the United States and the many international partners and organizations on the ground;

President Préval, on behalf of the Government and people of Haiti, welcomes as essential the efforts in Haiti by the Government and people of the United States to support the immediate recovery, stability and long-term rebuilding of Haiti and requests the United States to assist as needed in augmenting security in support of the Government and people of Haiti and the United Nations, international partners and organizations on the ground;

Secretary Clinton, on behalf of the Government and people of the United States, reaffirms the intention of the United States, through its assistance, to stand by the Haitian people in this time of great tragedy; and

President Préval and Secretary Clinton jointly reaffirm that the Governments of Haiti and the United States will continue to cooperate under this shared understanding to promote the most safe and effective rescue, relief, recovery and reconstruction efforts possible.

SOURCE: Embassy of Haiti in Washington, D.C. "17 Jan—Joint Communique of the Governments of the United States and Haiti." January 17, 2010. http://www.haiti.org/index.php?option=com_content&view=article&id=166.

U.S. Secretary of State Clinton on the Situation in Chile

February 27, 2010

We are closely monitoring reports from Chile and across the Pacific rim, and our thoughts and prayers are with all those who have loved ones affected by this tragedy.

The United States stands ready to provide necessary assistance to Chile in the days and weeks ahead and is coordinating closely with senior Chilean officials on the content and timing of such support. Our Embassy in Santiago has established a command center and is working to ensure the safety of any affected American citizens.

I leave for the region tomorrow and will be in close contact with President Bachelet and other leaders. Our Hemisphere comes together in times of crisis, and we will stand side by side with the people of Chile in this emergency.

SOURCE: U.S. Department of State. Office of the Secretary of State. "Earthquake in Chile." February 27, 2010. http://www.state.gov/secretary/rm/2010/02/137382.htm.

U.S. Government Announces Aid Work in Chile Following Earthquake

June 2010

(Prepared by the Office of Public Affairs at the U.S. Embassy in Santiago)

The United States Government is working as quickly and effectively as possible to provide many of the items identified by the Government of Chile as necessary to assist the victims of the February 27 earthquake. As of June 8, the United States Government has provided the following assistance:

HUMANITARIAN ASSISTANCE

33 U.S. Humanitarian Projects Reach Communities in Four Regions of Chile.

USAID Disaster Assistance Response Team (DART): A Disaster Assistance Response Team has been operating in Chile since March 5 to assess, identify, and respond to humanitarian needs in disaster-affected areas. At its peak, the team comprised 17 members, including field teams working in the affected areas.

Water Purification Units: The U.S. Agency for International Development's Office of U.S. Foreign Disaster Assistance (USAID/OFDA) provided eight mobile water treatment units. Each unit is capable of producing approximately 100,000 liters of safe drinking water daily for an estimated 10,000 individuals.

Satellite Phones: The U.S. government has donated over 50 satellite telephones phones and made several dozen more available to facilitate communications until telephone networks in affected areas are repaired.

C-130 Aircraft: The U.S. Department of Defense (DoD) provided two C-130 Hercules cargo aircraft and a team of airmen and maintenance and logistics personnel to support U.S. and international relief efforts from March 7–14. The two aircraft participated in the air bridge between Santiago and Concepcion, transporting over 300,000 pounds of cargo and 300 passengers (including more than 200 evacuees) on 17 humanitarian flights.

Humanitarian Assistance/Disaster Response (HA/DR) Command and Control Center: The U.S. military established a Command and Control center at U.S. Embassy Santiago to coordinate DoD support for the HA/DR effort.

Expeditionary Medical Support (EMEDS) Unit: USAID provided funding for the deployment of a U.S. Air Force Expeditionary Medical Support (EMEDS) unit to meet medical needs in Angol. The unit includes a 57-person medical team, 26 support staff, tents, and medical equipment and supplies to treat up to 3,000 patients. USG personnel began treating patients on March 13. The USG formally transferred the entire facility (tents, equipment, and beds) to Chilean Ministry of Health and Defense authorities on March 24.

Heavy Duty Tents/Tools: DoD donated 84 heavy-duty tents to meet humanitarian needs in earthquake-affected areas. Seven of the tents will be provided to the EMEDS unit in Angol to increase its capacity; in addition, USAID/OFDA is providing four heavy-duty Alaska tents to augment the EMEDS unit. The remaining tents will be consigned to ONEMI and may be used for medium-term replacement of health clinics, schools or other public facilities in affected areas. The tents arrived in Santiago via DoD airlift on March 22. In addition, DoD and USAID are providing tools and hardware to be used in reconstructing homes or buildings.

Temporary Shelter and Sanitation Assistance: USAID/OFDA has funded the Adventist Development and Relief Agency (ADRA) to provide emergency shelter and sanitation assistance for 5,000 people in the Maule and Bio Bio regions. USAID/OFDA plans to airlift an additional 140 rolls of plastic sheeting (300 rolls of 24x100 foot plastic sheeting were delivered on March 3 for use in emergency shelters) to Chile for ADRA to use in constructing transitional shelters funded under this project.

Electrical generators: 20 dual voltage generators (19 of them 25 kilowatt units and one 45 kilowatt unit) arrived in Santiago on March 12 and have been consigned to ONEMI.

Cash: USAID/OFDA donated $1 million to the International Federation of Red Cross and Red Crescent Societies (IFRC) to support the organization's emergency appeal.

U.S. Scientific Support

Satellite Images: A U.S. interagency group (including the Departments of Interior, Agriculture, NASA, the U.S. Geological Service, and USAID/OFDA) is providing pre- and post-earthquake satellite images to the Government of Chile.

Seismometers/Earthquake Experts:

Experts from the U.S. Geological Survey (USGS) have been visiting Chile to consult with Chilean agencies and provide technical support, including seismology equipment.

Two USGS seismologists installed 6 seismometers to measure aftershocks, conducted public outreach, and will prepare after action report.

The Incorporated Research Institutions for Seismology (IRIS), composed of over 100 universities, is working with the University of Chile to install 50–100 sensors along the Chilean coast.

SOUTHCOM facilitated the transport of 60 seismological stations belonging to the Incorporated Research Institutions for Seismology (IRIS); the equipment arrived on March 21.

Earthquake Engineering Research Institute (EERI) and Geo-engineering Extreme Events Reconnaissance (GEER) are assessing structural damage.

Scripps Institute of Oceanography will survey the seafloor.

Other USG Assistance

Mobile Command Center: The FBI made available a Virtual Command Center (VCC) to Chilean law enforcement agencies and provided VCC training to law enforcement personnel. The VCC is an internet-based, "real-time" crisis and incident management system that gives law enforcement personnel the ability to securely track and manage incidents, forces, and operations from any location with internet access.

Biometric Records Assistance: The FBI's Criminal Justice Information Service Global Initiatives Unit is supporting Chilean law enforcement personnel in the identification of victims through searches of biometric records.

Navy Technical Assessment Team: Per a Chilean Navy request, a 12-member U.S. Navy technical team assisted in the assessment of damage to the Talcahuano port and Chilean Navy base March 8–14.

Chile and California sign joint statement on cooperation for natural disasters: Chile's Foreign Affairs Minister, Alfredo Moreno, and the director of the California Emergency Management Agency, Matthew Bettenhausen, signed on April 5 a joint statement on emergency and disaster cooperation. The joint statement expresses the desire of the State of California and the Government of Chile to carry out research and training projects in risk assessment and natural disasters to develop procedures to prevent, mitigate, and improve the response and recovery after catastrophes. The cooperation will be carried out in accordance to the agreements already in place between the government of Chile and the State of California.

Emergency Management Experts Share Experiences in Santiago: International consultant on disaster management Richard Andrews, and California Emergency Management Agency (CalEMA) Secretary Matthew R. Bettenhausen shared their experiences in the field at the seminar "2010 Issues: Chile Reconstruction," held in Santiago on April 6. . . .

SOURCE: Embassy of the United States in Santiago, Chile. "The United States Assists Chile Earthquake Relief." June 2010. http://chile.usembassy.gov/2010press0304-relief.html.

OTHER HISTORIC DOCUMENTS OF INTEREST

FROM THIS VOLUME

Supreme Court on Campaign Contributions

JANUARY 21, 2010

On January 21, 2010, the U.S. Supreme Court ruled 5–4 in *Citizens United v. the Federal Election Commission* that spending on political campaigns is a form of free speech extended beyond private citizens, and that the federal government cannot stop corporations and labor unions from spending to support or oppose a political candidate. These corporations or unions will still be unable to give money directly to candidates; however, these groups may use political advertisements to persuade the public to vote in a certain way. The decision overturned a two-decade-old ruling, *Austin v. Michigan Chamber of Commerce*, that prohibited unions and corporations from paying for campaign advertisements. In addition, the ruling partially overturned *McConnell v. Federal Election Commission* (2003), which upheld the constitutionality of the Bipartisan Campaign Reform Act of 2002 (BCRA), commonly referred to as the McCain-Feingold campaign finance law, which disallows corporations or labor unions from paying for campaign ads during the final days of a campaign.

The Barack Obama administration expressed discontent with the *Citizens United* ruling. One of Obama's platforms during the 2008 presidential campaign had been to stop corporations and unions from pushing candidates into office with their often unlimited funding sources. It was widely speculated that both the Obama administration and the Democratic Party saw the ruling as another blow to the Democrats' chances of retaining the House and Senate during the 2010 congressional midterm elections and the White House in 2012.

THE RULING

The case of *Citizens United v. the Federal Election Commission* was referred to the U.S. Supreme Court by the U.S. District Court for the District of Columbia. The case revolved around a documentary titled *Hillary: The Movie*. The film, produced by Citizens United, a conservative nonprofit corporation, was released during the 2008 presidential primaries. The movie was filled with political commentary in opposition to Democratic presidential candidate Hillary Clinton, at the time a U.S. senator from New York. In 2008, the Federal Election Commission (FEC) banned its showing, on the basis that it violated McCain-Feingold. Citizens United sued, alleging that its movie was nonpartisan and therefore conformed to the 2002 BCRA law. Citizens United lost its case, and it appealed to the U.S. Supreme Court.

In its decision, the U.S. Supreme Court's majority concluded that a corporation's right to run political ads could not be taken away because of protections afforded by the First Amendment. In writing for the majority, Justice Anthony M. Kennedy wrote, "If the First Amendment has any force, it prohibits Congress from fining or jailing citizens, or associations of citizens, for simply engaging in political speech." Justice Kennedy was joined by the Court's four other conservative members in his opinion: Chief Justice John G. Roberts and Justices Antonin Scalia, Samuel Alito, and Clarence Thomas.

In its decision, the Court overturned two rulings. The first, *Austin v. Michigan Chamber of Commerce*, decided in 1990, upheld a ban on a corporation's ability to spend money to support or oppose a candidate. The second, earlier ruling, which was partially overturned, was the Court's 2003 decision in *McConnell v. Federal Election Commission*, which upheld McCain-Feingold.

The Court also overturned part of the McCain-Feingold campaign finance law, passed in 2002, which in part put a stop to ads broadcast by corporations and labor unions in the days before an election. The law bans the transmission of "electioneering communications" on broadcast, cable, or satellite television that is paid for by corporations or labor unions out of their general funds thirty days before a presidential primary or sixty days before a general election.

The majority opinion upheld bans on direct contributions to candidates, which was a major point of contention in the divided Court. Those in the opposition said there was little difference between "selling a vote and selling access." Justice John Paul Stevens wrote for the minority.

The complete opinion, which included five written statements, ran more than 180 pages, with Justice Stevens contributing half with his dissent. Stevens called the decision by the majority a grave error. In his sharply worded critique of the majority opinion, Stevens wrote, "The court's ruling threatens to undermine the integrity of elected institutions across the nation." Furthermore, "In a democratic society, the longstanding consensus on the need to limit corporate campaign spending should outweigh the wooden application of judge-made rules. . . . At bottom, the Court's opinion is thus a rejection of the common sense of the American people, who have recognized a need to prevent corporations from undermining self government since the founding, and who have fought against the distinctive corrupting potential of corporate electioneering since the days of Theodore Roosevelt. It is a strange time to repudiate that common sense. While American democracy is imperfect, few outside the majority of this Court would have thought its flaws included a dearth of corporate money in politics."

Though the Court was divided, eight of the nine justices agreed that Congress has the right to ask corporations about their spending on campaigns, and require them to answer honestly, and can also require disclaimers on any and all political ads run by a corporation or labor union. "Disclosure permits citizens and shareholders to react to the speech of corporate entities in a proper way," said Justice Kennedy. Justice Clarence Thomas was the only justice who did not agree with this argument, stating that "the Court's constitutional analysis does not go far enough."

The ruling had its first impact on the 2010 midterm congressional elections, which took place on November 4. During the election cycle, a record was set for the amount of money spent on campaigning, much of which was used for television advertisements and was funneled to candidates by corporations and labor unions. *New York Times* writer Michael Luo said donations were driven more by the psychological impact of the *Citizens United* ruling than the legal changes. Ex-FEC chairman Trevor Porter told Luo,

"The difference between the law pre– and post–*Citizens United* is subtle to the expert observer. . . . To the casual observer, what they have heard is the court has gone from a world that prohibited corporate political speech and activity, even though that isn't actually the case, to suddenly for the first time that it's allowed. It's that change in psychology that has made a difference in terms of the amount of money now being spent."

Further out, political analysts said the Court's shift in thinking could change the way campaigns and elections are carried out.

REACTION

President Obama issued the sharpest critique of the Court's ruling, saying, "The Supreme Court has given a green light to a new stampede of special interest money in our politics. It is a major victory for big oil, Wall Street banks, health insurance companies and the other powerful interests that marshal their power every day in Washington to drown out the voices of everyday Americans." He also expressed concern that America was opening itself up to influence by foreign entities.

Other Democrats expressed their sentiment that the law would give unions and corporations too large a position in elections. "The bottom line is," said Sen. Charles Schumer, D-N.Y., "the Supreme Court has just predetermined the winners of next November's election. It won't be the Republicans or the Democrats and it won't be the American people; it will be corporate America."

The Republican Party, with many members who are long-time opponents of McCain-Feingold, celebrated the ruling. "For too long, some in this country have been deprived of full participation in the political process," said Senate minority leader Mitch McConnell, R-Ky.

Because of the Court's ruling, state laws would be affected. Two dozen states have laws that stop or restrict labor unions and corporations from encouraging the public to vote for or against a particular candidate through the use of campaign advertisements. These states will now be required to change their campaign finance laws.

In Congress, Democrats introduced bills to try to limit the effectiveness of the Court's decision. In the House of Representatives, the DISCLOSE Act, which would require corporations to report additional information on their campaign expenditures and stop campaign spending by U.S. companies with 20 percent or more foreign ownership, was introduced. It faced heavy criticism because of stipulations that would allow some special interest organizations, such as AARP and the National Rifle Association (NRA), to be exempt. Representatives equated this to allowing some companies to buy themselves out of the laws. "They are auctioning off pieces of the First Amendment in this bill," said Rep. Dan Lungren, R-Calif. However, House supporters of the bill said the exemption was necessary to ensure that the powerful lobbies of these associations would not derail passage. Even given the resistance, the act passed in the House, but failed twice in the Senate.

QUESTIONS REMAIN

The long Court opinion left some questions open for future debate. One question left unanswered was whether unions will be as free as corporations to indirectly spend on local and nationwide campaigns. The ruling implies that unions and corporations will be treated equally, but the ruling never directly addressed the issue. In Kennedy's opinion, he uses the two types of organizations interchangeably. In addition, the portion of the campaign finance law that was struck down applies to both groups equally.

The Court also left open the idea of whether foreign corporations that operate in the United States will be able to indirectly spend money on political campaigns. The Court stated that it did not plan to rule on this issue.

Another issue left open by the Court is known as the flat ban. This ban has been in effect for more than a century for corporations and more than sixty years for labor unions; the ban stops both groups from giving money directly to a candidate. Both supporters and opponents had hoped to see a ruling on this issue, stating that there is little difference between directly financing a candidate and running an ad encouraging the public to vote for the candidate.

Finally, the Court did reject the ban that forbid corporate funds from being used on ads that ask voters to vote for or against a particular candidate, calling it a free-speech issue. This raises a question of how much power Congress will maintain in determining what types of political advertisements will be permitted. The Court has stated that Congress has more power to stop ads that ask voters to choose one candidate over the other, rather than issue advocacy ads. With its ruling, however, the Court appears to have taken that power away from Congress.

—Heather Kerrigan

Following is the text of the U.S. Supreme Court's 5–4 decision of January 21, 2010, in Citizens United v. Federal Elections Commission, *in which the Court overruled the ban on independent campaign expenditures by corporations.*

Citizens United v. Federal Election Commission

January 21, 2010

No. 08–205

Citizens United, Appellant	On appeal from the
v.	United States District Court
Federal Election Commission	for the District of Columbia

[January 21, 2010]

[Footnotes and case citations have been omitted.]

JUSTICE KENNEDY delivered the opinion of the Court.

Federal law prohibits corporations and unions from using their general treasury funds to make independent expenditures for speech defined as an "electioneering communication" or for speech expressly advocating the election or defeat of a candidate. Limits on electioneering communications were upheld in *McConnell v. Federal Election Comm'n*. The holding of *McConnell* rested to a large extent on an earlier case, *Austin v. Michigan*

Chamber of Commerce. Austin had held that political speech may be banned based on the speaker's corporate identity.

In this case we are asked to reconsider *Austin* and, in effect, *McConnell*. It has been noted that "*Austin* was a significant departure from ancient First Amendment principles," *Federal Election Comm'n v. Wisconsin Right to Life, Inc.* . . . We agree with that conclusion and hold that stare decisis does not compel the continued acceptance of *Austin*. The Government may regulate corporate political speech through disclaimer and disclosure requirements, but it may not suppress that speech altogether. We turn to the case now before us. . . .

[Background on the case, contained in sections I and II, which includes the argument presented by Citizens United, has been omitted.]

III

The First Amendment provides that "Congress shall make no law . . . abridging the freedom of speech." Laws enacted to control or suppress speech may operate at different points in the speech process. . . . The law before us is an outright ban, backed by criminal sanctions. Section 441b makes it a felony for all corporations—including nonprofit advocacy corporations—either to expressly advocate the election or defeat of candidates or to broadcast electioneering communications within 30 days of a primary election and 60 days of a general election. Thus, the following acts would all be felonies under §441b: The Sierra Club runs an ad, within the crucial phase of 60 days before the general election, that exhorts the public to disapprove of a Congressman who favors logging in national forests; the National Rifle Association publishes a book urging the public to vote for the challenger because the incumbent U. S. Senator supports a handgun ban; and the American Civil Liberties Union creates a Web site telling the public to vote for a Presidential candidate in light of that candidate's defense of free speech. These prohibitions are classic examples of censorship.

Section 441b is a ban on corporate speech notwithstanding the fact that a PAC created by a corporation can still speak. . . .

Section 441b's prohibition on corporate independent expenditures is thus a ban on speech. As a "restriction on the amount of money a person or group can spend on political communication during a campaign," that statute "necessarily reduces the quantity of expression by restricting the number of issues discussed, the depth of their exploration, and the size of the audience reached." Were the Court to uphold these restrictions, the Government could repress speech by silencing certain voices at any of the various points in the speech process. . . . If §441b applied to individuals, no one would believe that it is merely a time, place, or manner restriction on speech. Its purpose and effect are to silence entities whose voices the Government deems to be suspect.

Speech is an essential mechanism of democracy, for it is the means to hold officials accountable to the people. . . . The right of citizens to inquire, to hear, to speak, and to use information to reach consensus is a precondition to enlightened self-government and a necessary means to protect it. The First Amendment "'has its fullest and most urgent application' to speech uttered during a campaign for political office." . . .

For these reasons, political speech must prevail against laws that would suppress it, whether by design or inadvertence. Laws that burden political speech are "subject to strict scrutiny," which requires the Government to prove that the restriction "furthers a compelling interest and is narrowly tailored to achieve that interest." . . .

Premised on mistrust of governmental power, the First Amendment stands against attempts to disfavor certain subjects or viewpoints. . . . As instruments to censor, these categories are interrelated: Speech restrictions based on the identity of the speaker are all too often simply a means to control content.

Quite apart from the purpose or effect of regulating content, moreover, the Government may commit a constitutional wrong when by law it identifies certain preferred speakers. By taking the right to speak from some and giving it to others, the Government deprives the disadvantaged person or class of the right to use speech to strive to establish worth, standing, and respect for the speaker's voice. The Government may not by these means deprive the public of the right and privilege to determine for itself what speech and speakers are worthy of consideration. The First Amendment protects speech and speaker, and the ideas that flow from each.

The Court has upheld a narrow class of speech restrictions that operate to the disadvantage of certain persons, but these rulings were based on an interest in allowing governmental entities to perform their functions. . . . The corporate independent expenditures at issue in this case, however, would not interfere with governmental functions, so these cases are inapposite. These precedents stand only for the proposition that there are certain governmental functions that cannot operate without some restrictions on particular kinds of speech. By contrast, it is inherent in the nature of the political process that voters must be free to obtain information from diverse sources in order to determine how to cast their votes. At least before *Austin*, the Court had not allowed the exclusion of a class of speakers from the general public dialogue.

We find no basis for the proposition that, in the context of political speech, the Government may impose restrictions on certain disfavored speakers. Both history and logic lead us to this conclusion.

A

1

The Court has recognized that First Amendment protection extends to corporations. . . .

This protection has been extended by explicit holdings to the context of political speech. . . . Under the rationale of these precedents, political speech does not lose First Amendment protection "simply because its source is a corporation." . . . The Court has thus rejected the argument that political speech of corporations or other associations should be treated differently under the First Amendment simply because such associations are not "natural persons." . . .

[The history of the Court's rulings on First Amendment protections for corporations has been omitted.]

B

The Court is thus confronted with conflicting lines of precedent: a pre-*Austin* line that forbids restrictions on political speech based on the speaker's corporate identity and a post-*Austin* line that permits them. No case before *Austin* had held that Congress could prohibit independent expenditures for political speech based on the speaker's corporate identity. Before *Austin* Congress had enacted legislation for this purpose, and the Government urged the same proposition before this Court. . . .

1

As for *Austin*'s antidistortion rationale, the Government does little to defend it. . . . And with good reason, for the rationale cannot support §441b.

If the First Amendment has any force, it prohibits Congress from fining or jailing citizens, or associations of citizens, for simply engaging in political speech. If the antidistortion rationale were to be accepted, however, it would permit Government to ban political speech simply because the speaker is an association that has taken on the corporate form. The Government contends that *Austin* permits it to ban corporate expenditures for almost all forms of communication stemming from a corporation. . . . If *Austin* were correct, the Government could prohibit a corporation from expressing political views in media beyond those presented here, such as by printing books. The Government responds "that the FEC has never applied this statute to a book," and if it did, "there would be quite [a] good as applied challenge." . . . This troubling assertion of brooding governmental power cannot be reconciled with the confidence and stability in civic discourse that the First Amendment must secure.

Political speech is "indispensable to decision making in a democracy, and this is no less true because the speech comes from a corporation rather than an individual." . . . This protection for speech is inconsistent with *Austin*'s antidistortion rationale. . . . It is irrelevant for purposes of the First Amendment that corporate funds may "have little or no correlation to the public's support for the corporation's political ideas." . . . All speakers, including individuals and the media, use money amassed from the economic marketplace to fund their speech. The First Amendment protects the resulting speech, even if it was enabled by economic transactions with persons or entities who disagree with the speaker's ideas. . . .

[Discussion on an exemption for media corporations has been omitted.]

[The Court's refute of the Government's argument has been omitted, which includes brief discussion on direct contributions to candidates by corporations.]

C

Our precedent is to be respected unless the most convincing of reasons demonstrates that adherence to it puts us on a course that is sure error. "Beyond workability, the relevant factors in deciding whether to adhere to the principle of stare decisis include the antiquity of the precedent, the reliance interests at stake, and of course whether the decision was well reasoned." . . . We have also examined whether "experience has pointed up the precedent's shortcomings." . . .

These considerations counsel in favor of rejecting *Austin*, which itself contravened this Court's earlier precedents in *Buckley* and *Bellotti*. "This Court has not hesitated to overrule decisions offensive to the First Amendment." . . .

For the reasons above, it must be concluded that *Austin* was not well reasoned. . . .

Due consideration leads to this conclusion: *Austin*, 494 U. S. 652, should be and now is overruled. . . .

D . . .

Given our conclusion we are further required to overrule the part of *McConnell* that upheld BCRA §203's extension of §441b's restrictions on corporate independent expenditures. . . .

[Citizens United challenge of BCRA's disclaimer and disclosure provisions has been omitted.]

The judgment of the District Court is reversed with respect to the constitutionality of 2 U. S. C. §441b's restrictions on corporate independent expenditures. The judgment is affirmed with respect to BCRA's disclaimer and disclosure requirements. The case is remanded for further proceedings consistent with this opinion.

It is so ordered.

[The concurring opinion of Justice Roberts and Justice Alito has been omitted.]

[The concurring opinion of Justices Scalia and Alito, which Justice Thomas joined in part, has been omitted.]

JUSTICE STEVENS, with whom JUSTICE GINSBURG, JUSTICE BREYER, and JUSTICE SOTOMAYOR join, concurring in part and dissenting in part.

The real issue in this case concerns how, not if, the appellant may finance its electioneering. Citizens United is a wealthy nonprofit corporation that runs a political action committee (PAC) with millions of dollars in assets. Under the Bipartisan Campaign Reform Act of 2002 (BCRA), it could have used those assets to televise and promote *Hillary: The Movie* wherever and whenever it wanted to. It also could have spent unrestricted sums to broadcast *Hillary* at any time other than the 30 days before the last primary election. Neither Citizens United's nor any other corporation's speech has been "banned," *ante,* at 1. All that the parties dispute is whether Citizens United had a right to use the funds in its general treasury to pay for broadcasts during the 30-day period. The notion that the First Amendment dictates an affirmative answer to that question is, in my judgment, profoundly misguided. Even more misguided is the notion that the Court must rewrite the law relating to campaign expenditures by for-profit corporations and unions to decide this case.

The basic premise underlying the Court's ruling is its iteration, and constant reiteration, of the proposition that the First Amendment bars regulatory distinctions based on a speaker's identity, including its "identity" as a corporation. While that glittering generality has rhetorical appeal, it is not a correct statement of the law. Nor does it tell us when a corporation may engage in electioneering that some of its shareholders oppose. It does not even resolve the specific question whether Citizens United may be required to finance some of its messages with the money in its PAC. The conceit that corporations must be treated identically to natural persons in the political sphere is not only inaccurate but also inadequate to justify the Court's disposition of this case. . . .

[Earlier Court decisions and the scope of the case have been omitted.]

The majority suggests that a facial ruling is necessary because anything less would chill too much protected speech. . . . In addition to begging the question what types of corporate spending are constitutionally protected and to what extent, this claim rests on the assertion that some significant number of corporations have been cowed into quiescence by FEC "'censor[ship].'" . . . That assertion is unsubstantiated, and it is hard to square with practical experience. It is particularly hard to square with the legal landscape following WRTL, which held that a corporate communication could be regulated under §203 only if it was "susceptible of no reasonable interpretation other than as an appeal to vote for or against a specific candidate." . . . The whole point of this test was to make §203 as simple and speech-protective as possible. The Court does not explain how, in the span of a single election cycle, it has determined THE CHIEF JUSTICE's project to be a failure. In this respect, too, the majority's critique of line-drawing collapses into a critique of the as-applied review method generally.

The majority suggests that, even though it expressly dismissed its facial challenge, Citizens United nevertheless preserved it—not as a freestanding "claim," but as a potential argument in support of "a claim that the FEC has violated its First Amendment right to free speech." . . . By this novel logic, virtually any submission could be reconceptualized as "a claim that the Government has violated my rights," and it would then be available to the Court to entertain any conceivable issue that might be relevant to that claim's disposition. Not only the as-applied/facial distinction, but the basic relationship between litigants and courts, would be upended if the latter had free rein to construe the former's claims at such high levels of generality. There would be no need for plaintiffs to argue their case; they could just cite the constitutional provisions they think relevant, and leave the rest to us.

Finally, the majority suggests that though the scope of Citizens United's claim may be narrow, a facial ruling is necessary as a matter of remedy. Relying on a law review article, it asserts that Citizens United's dismissal of the facial challenge does not prevent us "'from making broader pronouncements of invalidity in properly "as applied" cases.'" . . . The majority is on firmer conceptual ground here. Yet even if one accepts this part of Professor Fallon's thesis, one must proceed to ask which as-applied challenges, if successful, will "properly" invite or entail invalidation of the underlying statute. The paradigmatic case is a judicial determination that the legislature acted with an impermissible purpose in enacting a provision, as this carries the necessary implication that all future as-applied challenges to the provision must prevail. . . .

Citizens United's as-applied challenge was not of this sort. . . .

II . . .

In the end, the Court's rejection of *Austin* and *McConnell* comes down to nothing more than its disagreement with their results. Virtually every one of its arguments was made and rejected in those cases, and the majority opinion is essentially an amalgamation of resuscitated dissents. The only relevant thing that has changed since *Austin* and *McConnell* is the composition of this Court. Today's ruling thus strikes at the vitals of stare decisis, "the means by which we ensure that the law will not merely change erratically, but will develop in a principled and intelligible fashion" that "permits society to presume that bedrock principles are founded in the law rather than in the proclivities of individuals." . . .

[Further dissent regarding BCRA has been omitted.]

IV

Having explained why this is not an appropriate case in which to revisit *Austin* and *McConnell* and why these decisions sit perfectly well with "First Amendment principles," I come at last to the interests that are at stake. The majority recognizes that *Austin* and *McConnell* may be defended on anticorruption, antidistortion, and shareholder protection rationales. . . . It badly errs both in explaining the nature of these rationales, which overlap and complement each other, and in applying them to the case at hand. . . .

V

Today's decision is backwards in many senses. It elevates the majority's agenda over the litigants' submissions, facial attacks over as-applied claims, broad constitutional theories over narrow statutory grounds, individual dissenting opinions over precedential holdings, assertion over tradition, absolutism over empiricism, rhetoric over reality. Our colleagues have arrived at the conclusion that *Austin* must be overruled and that §203 is facially unconstitutional only after mischaracterizing both the reach and rationale of those authorities, and after bypassing or ignoring rules of judicial restraint used to cabin the Court's lawmaking power. Their conclusion that the societal interest in avoiding corruption and the appearance of corruption does not provide an adequate justification for regulating corporate expenditures on candidate elections relies on an incorrect description of that interest, along with a failure to acknowledge the relevance of established facts and the considered judgments of state and federal legislatures over many decades.

In a democratic society, the longstanding consensus on the need to limit corporate campaign spending should outweigh the wooden application of judge-made rules. The majority's rejection of this principle "elevate[s] corporations to a level of deference which has not been seen at least since the days when substantive due process was regularly used to invalidate regulatory legislation thought to unfairly impinge upon established economic interests." . . . At bottom, the Court's opinion is thus a rejection of the common sense of the American people, who have recognized a need to prevent corporations from undermining self government since the founding, and who have fought against the distinctive corrupting potential of corporate electioneering since the days of Theodore Roosevelt. It is a strange time to repudiate that common sense. While American democracy is imperfect, few outside the majority of this Court would have thought its flaws included a dearth of corporate money in politics.

I would affirm the judgment of the District Court.

[The opinion of Justice Thomas, concurring in part and dissenting in part, has been omitted.]

SOURCE: U.S. Supreme Court. Citizens United v. Federal Election Commission, 558 U.S. ____ (2010). http://www.supremecourt.gov/opinions/09pdf/08-205.pdf.

OTHER HISTORIC DOCUMENTS OF INTEREST

FROM THIS VOLUME

FROM PREVIOUS *HISTORIC DOCUMENTS*

State of the Union Address and Republican Response

JANUARY 27, 2010

On January 27, 2010, President Barack Obama laid out his plan for the second year of his presidency in his first official State of the Union address. Obama addressed a number of issues during his speech: the economy, which remained weak even with a $787 billion infusion of funds; climbing unemployment; the wars in Iraq and Afghanistan; and his own battle of ensuring the passage of his health care reform plans.

Speaking to a joint session of the Democratic-controlled U.S. House and Senate, the president expressed a desire to face these challenges head on. "We do not give up. We do not quit. We do not allow fear or division to break our spirit," he said. Though his speech contained a list of what his administration sought to accomplish during the next twelve months, Obama broke from the mold to criticize and scold both Democrats and Republicans. His accusatory manner, analysts said, was intended to help him overcome what many describe as a remote, detached, and clinical manner. Prior to his speech, analysts said the president would have to connect with Americans and let them know that he is working for them and is above the fray of politics as usual in Washington. In an effort to do so, the president explained why Americans feel cynical about their government and why Republicans and Democrats need to put aside their differences to "start anew."

In addition to his focus on jobs, the economy, and health care reform, Obama also touched on a need for clean energy and the benefits of offshore drilling, his olive branch to Republicans. As is typical with a Democratic president's State of the Union address, Obama spent little time discussing foreign affairs, even though he was facing wars in both Iraq and Afghanistan. However, the attempted airplane bombing on a flight bound for Detroit, Michigan, on Christmas Day 2009 made it imperative that he address national security and the country's work to stop terrorists abroad before they enter the United States. At home, the president said, "we are filling unacceptable gaps revealed by the failed Christmas attack, with better airline security and swifter action on our intelligence."

Looking abroad, Obama said the Iraq war would be swiftly coming to an end, a promise of his campaign, and that all of the troops would be brought home. He also restated his position on gay rights in the military, calling again for a repeal of "Don't Ask, Don't Tell," which he said "denies gay Americans the right to serve the country they love because of who they are."

The president called for international cooperation on an end to nuclear weapons, which he considered to be the "greatest danger to the American people." He set a goal of securing all nuclear materials around the world within the next four years to ensure that terrorists are unable to use them in the United States and abroad.

Jobs and the Economy

Before Obama's speech, the Congressional Budget Office (CBO) released a report on the federal deficit. In its evaluation, the CBO concluded that the nation was on track for a $1.3 trillion deficit in 2010. Obama had previously reacted to the federal deficit, calling for a freeze on all federal discretionary spending, which, he said during his State of the Union address, would begin in 2011. The CBO had also reported on Obama's plan for the freeze and said it would only save $250 billion over the next decade.

The nation's economic outlook was central to Obama's first State of the Union address—led by his focus on job creation. "Jobs must be our number one focus in 2010," the president said. To begin spurring job creation in the private sector, he called on Congress to pass a new jobs bill. "People are out of work. They are hurting. They need our help. And I want a jobs bill on my desk without delay," Obama said. The president proposed that the jobs bill provide tax breaks for small businesses, as well as tax credits for new hiring and equipment purchase. He further asked the federal government to work to double American exports over the next two years, which he said would support two million jobs.

The president also addressed both the bank bailout of 2009 and the stimulus program, both of which he indicated were vital to the nation's economic recovery. On the bailout, Obama admitted that it was largely unpopular, even saying that he "hated" it. But, he said, without the bailout, "more businesses would certainly have closed. More homes would have surely been lost."

The president celebrated the American Recovery and Reinvestment Act (ARRA) for getting the country through the worst of the recession, but he reminded listeners that many Americans were still struggling. "The worst of the storm has passed, but the devastation remains," he said. He further stated that his economic plan had cut taxes for 95 percent of working families, a claim that earned no response from Republicans. "I thought I'd get some applause on that one," Obama quipped.

Health Care Reform

Prior to his address, Obama's press secretary, Robert Gibbs, told the *Today* show that the president's focus on health care would cover "why we can't walk away from making sure the high cost of health care doesn't choke off an economic recovery." Health care reform was a top priority for Obama when he came into office, but after both the House and Senate passed their own versions of a reform bill in late 2009, compromise or a reconciliation bill was stalled by January. Though reform of the health insurance industry was a major issue on the president's agenda for 2010, he spent only five minutes of his seventy-minute speech on the issue. The president used his address to call on lawmakers to go back to the table and work together to pass legislation that would benefit the American people. "By the time I'm finished speaking tonight, more Americans will have lost their health insurance. Millions will lose it this year. Our deficit will grow. Premiums will go up. Patients will be denied the care they need. Small-business owners will continue to drop coverage altogether. I will not walk away from these Americans, and neither should the people in this chamber," the president said.

Placing Blame

The president took a scolding tone when he addressed both parties in Congress and even the U.S. Supreme Court. He told legislators to "put aside the schoolyard taunts" on terrorism and international security issues. In a surprise move, Obama even took aim at his own party. Even though Democrats had a larger majority in Congress than they had in decades, "the people expect us to solve problems, not run for the hills," the president said. But he reminded Republicans that even though they did not hold a majority, "the responsibility to govern is now yours as well." He continued, "Just saying no to everything may be good short-term politics, but it's not leadership."

Criticism of the U.S. Supreme Court came after its recent 5–4 decision to allow corporations and labor unions to fund political campaign ads, in *Citizens United v. Federal Election Commission*. Changing corporate spending limits, the president said, "reversed a century of laws that would open the floodgates for special interests—including foreign corporations—to spend without limit in our elections." He called on Congress to pass a set of regulations that would correct the Court's decision and ensure that the largest American and foreign corporations are not able to control the elections in the United States.

The president also blamed himself for some of the failures during the first year of his presidency. Specifically, he spoke of the inability to pass effective health care reform legislation that both parties could agree to and that could win support from the American public. "I take my share of blame for not explaining it more clearly to the American people," Obama said.

In closing, the president focused on his campaign promise of change. "Right now," he said, "I know there are many Americans who aren't sure if they still believe we can change—or that I can deliver it. But remember this—I never suggested that change would be easy or that I can do it alone. Democracy in a nation of three hundred million people can be noisy and messy and complicated. And when you try to do big things and make big changes, it stirs passions and controversy. That's just how it is." But, he concluded, "We don't quit. I don't quit. Let's seize this moment—to start anew, to carry the dream forward, and to strengthen our union once more."

REPUBLICAN RESPONSE

Gov. Bob McDonnell of Virginia was chosen by his party to deliver the Republican response to the president's address. The theme of McDonnell's speech, delivered from the Virginia statehouse, was excess. "Today, the federal government is simply trying to do too much," McDonnell opened. "Good government policy should spur economic growth, and strengthen the private sector's ability to create new jobs. We must enact policies that promote entrepreneurship and innovation, so America can better compete with the world. What government should not do," McDonnell continued, "is pile on more taxation, regulation, and litigation that kills jobs and hurt the middle class."

McDonnell went on to criticize the Democrats, led by Obama, for not creating jobs quickly enough. He pointed to promises made by the party in 2009 that said federal spending programs, mainly the ARRA, would create more jobs "immediately" and keep unemployment below 8 percent. However, McDonnell explained, current statistics showed that three million Americans had lost their jobs in the past year, while Democratic spending continued to increase without any indication that it would create jobs in the near future.

In addition to his criticism of Obama's work on jobs, McDonnell also took aim at Congress's proposed health care reform plan. Specifically, he addressed the idea of the public option in which the government would provide health insurance to rival the private sector. "Most Americans do not want to turn over the best medical care system in the world to the federal government," McDonnell said. He encouraged congressional leaders to take a look at plans offered by Republicans in Congress that, he said, would not increase taxes or place additional burden on states to pay for Medicaid. However, while Republicans in Congress spoke out about health care reform, they did not introduce a formal plan or legislation to rival the Democrats' proposals. McDonnell was also critical of the length of the bill, at over one thousand pages, which he said catered to special interests and did not give lawmakers enough time to fully review before a vote.

The governor and president did agree on one point—bipartisan cooperation. While Obama scolded both parties in Congress for failing to work together on various pieces of legislation, McDonnell used the example of the election of Sen. Scott Brown, R-Mass., to fill the late Sen. Ted Kennedy's vacant Senate seat. "The American people have made clear that they want government leaders to listen and act on the issues most important to them. We want results, not rhetoric. We want cooperation, not partisanship," McDonnell said.

—Heather Kerrigan

Following is the full text of President Barack Obama's State of the Union address and the Republican response given by Virginia governor Bob McDonnell, both on January 27, 2010.

DOCUMENT *The State of the Union Address*

January 27, 2010

Madam Speaker, Vice President Biden, members of Congress, distinguished guests, and fellow Americans:

Our Constitution declares that from time to time, the President shall give to Congress information about the state of our union. For 220 years, our leaders have fulfilled this duty. They've done so during periods of prosperity and tranquility. And they've done so in the midst of war and depression; at moments of great strife and great struggle.

It's tempting to look back on these moments and assume that our progress was inevitable—that America was always destined to succeed. But when the Union was turned back at Bull Run, and the Allies first landed at Omaha Beach, victory was very much in doubt. When the market crashed on Black Tuesday, and civil rights marchers were beaten on Bloody Sunday, the future was anything but certain. These were the times that tested the courage of our convictions, and the strength of our union. And despite all our divisions and disagreements, our hesitations and our fears, America prevailed because we chose to move forward as one nation, as one people.

Again, we are tested. And again, we must answer history's call.

One year ago, I took office amid two wars, an economy rocked by a severe recession, a financial system on the verge of collapse, and a government deeply in debt. Experts from across the political spectrum warned that if we did not act, we might face a second depression. So we acted—immediately and aggressively. And one year later, the worst of the storm has passed.

But the devastation remains. One in 10 Americans still cannot find work. Many businesses have shuttered. Home values have declined. Small towns and rural communities have been hit especially hard. And for those who'd already known poverty, life has become that much harder.

This recession has also compounded the burdens that America's families have been dealing with for decades—the burden of working harder and longer for less; of being unable to save enough to retire or help kids with college.

So I know the anxieties that are out there right now. They're not new. These struggles are the reason I ran for President. These struggles are what I've witnessed for years in places like Elkhart, Indiana; Galesburg, Illinois. I hear about them in the letters that I read each night. The toughest to read are those written by children—asking why they have to move from their home, asking when their mom or dad will be able to go back to work.

For these Americans and so many others, change has not come fast enough. Some are frustrated; some are angry. They don't understand why it seems like bad behavior on Wall Street is rewarded, but hard work on Main Street isn't; or why Washington has been unable or unwilling to solve any of our problems. They're tired of the partisanship and the shouting and the pettiness. They know we can't afford it. Not now.

So we face big and difficult challenges. And what the American people hope—what they deserve—is for all of us, Democrats and Republicans, to work through our differences; to overcome the numbing weight of our politics. For while the people who sent us here have different backgrounds, different stories, different beliefs, the anxieties they face are the same. The aspirations they hold are shared: a job that pays the bills; a chance to get ahead; most of all, the ability to give their children a better life.

You know what else they share? They share a stubborn resilience in the face of adversity. After one of the most difficult years in our history, they remain busy building cars and teaching kids, starting businesses and going back to school. They're coaching Little League and helping their neighbors. One woman wrote to me and said, "We are strained but hopeful, struggling but encouraged."

It's because of this spirit—this great decency and great strength—that I have never been more hopeful about America's future than I am tonight. Despite our hardships, our union is strong. We do not give up. We do not quit. We do not allow fear or division to break our spirit. In this new decade, it's time the American people get a government that matches their decency; that embodies their strength.

And tonight, tonight I'd like to talk about how together we can deliver on that promise.

It begins with our economy.

Our most urgent task upon taking office was to shore up the same banks that helped cause this crisis. It was not easy to do. And if there's one thing that has unified Democrats and Republicans, and everybody in between, it's that we all hated the bank bailout. I hated it—I hated it. You hated it. It was about as popular as a root canal.

But when I ran for President, I promised I wouldn't just do what was popular—I would do what was necessary. And if we had allowed the meltdown of the financial system, unemployment might be double what it is today. More businesses would certainly have closed. More homes would have surely been lost.

So I supported the last administration's efforts to create the financial rescue program. And when we took that program over, we made it more transparent and more accountable. And as a result, the markets are now stabilized, and we've recovered most of the money we spent on the banks. Most but not all.

To recover the rest, I've proposed a fee on the biggest banks. Now, I know Wall Street isn't keen on this idea. But if these firms can afford to hand out big bonuses again, they can afford a modest fee to pay back the taxpayers who rescued them in their time of need.

Now, as we stabilized the financial system, we also took steps to get our economy growing again, save as many jobs as possible, and help Americans who had become unemployed.

That's why we extended or increased unemployment benefits for more than 18 million Americans; made health insurance 65 percent cheaper for families who get their coverage through COBRA; and passed 25 different tax cuts.

Now, let me repeat: We cut taxes. We cut taxes for 95 percent of working families. We cut taxes for small businesses. We cut taxes for first-time homebuyers. We cut taxes for parents trying to care for their children. We cut taxes for 8 million Americans paying for college.

I thought I'd get some applause on that one.

As a result, millions of Americans had more to spend on gas and food and other necessities, all of which helped businesses keep more workers. And we haven't raised income taxes by a single dime on a single person. Not a single dime.

Because of the steps we took, there are about two million Americans working right now who would otherwise be unemployed. Two hundred thousand work in construction and clean energy; 300,000 are teachers and other education workers. Tens of thousands are cops, firefighters, correctional officers, first responders. And we're on track to add another one and a half million jobs to this total by the end of the year.

The plan that has made all of this possible, from the tax cuts to the jobs, is the Recovery Act. That's right—the Recovery Act, also known as the stimulus bill. Economists on the left and the right say this bill has helped save jobs and avert disaster. But you don't have to take their word for it. Talk to the small business in Phoenix that will triple its workforce because of the Recovery Act. Talk to the window manufacturer in Philadelphia who said he used to be skeptical about the Recovery Act, until he had to add two more work shifts just because of the business it created. Talk to the single teacher raising two kids who was told by her principal in the last week of school that because of the Recovery Act, she wouldn't be laid off after all.

There are stories like this all across America. And after two years of recession, the economy is growing again. Retirement funds have started to gain back some of their value. Businesses are beginning to invest again, and slowly some are starting to hire again.

But I realize that for every success story, there are other stories, of men and women who wake up with the anguish of not knowing where their next paycheck will come from; who send out resumes week after week and hear nothing in response. That is why jobs must be our number-one focus in 2010, and that's why I'm calling for a new jobs bill tonight.

Now, the true engine of job creation in this country will always be America's businesses. But government can create the conditions necessary for businesses to expand and hire more workers.

We should start where most new jobs do—in small businesses, companies that begin when—companies that begin when an entrepreneur—when an entrepreneur takes a chance on a dream, or a worker decides it's time she became her own boss. Through sheer grit and determination, these companies have weathered the recession and they're ready to grow. But when you talk to small businessowners in places like Allentown, Pennsylvania, or Elyria, Ohio, you find out that even though banks on Wall Street are lending again, they're mostly lending to bigger companies. Financing remains difficult for small business owners across the country, even those that are making a profit.

So tonight, I'm proposing that we take $30 billion of the money Wall Street banks have repaid and use it to help community banks give small businesses the credit they need to stay afloat. I'm also proposing a new small business tax credit—one that will go to over one million small businesses who hire new workers or raise wages. While we're at it, let's also eliminate all capital gains taxes on small business investment, and provide a tax incentive for all large businesses and all small businesses to invest in new plants and equipment.

Next, we can put Americans to work today building the infrastructure of tomorrow. From the first railroads to the Interstate Highway System, our nation has always been built to compete. There's no reason Europe or China should have the fastest trains, or the new factories that manufacture clean energy products.

Tomorrow, I'll visit Tampa, Florida, where workers will soon break ground on a new high-speed railroad funded by the Recovery Act. There are projects like that all across this country that will create jobs and help move our nation's goods, services, and information.

We should put more Americans to work building clean energy facilities—and give rebates to Americans who make their homes more energy-efficient, which supports clean energy jobs. And to encourage these and other businesses to stay within our borders, it is time to finally slash the tax breaks for companies that ship our jobs overseas, and give those tax breaks to companies that create jobs right here in the United States of America.

Now, the House has passed a jobs bill that includes some of these steps. As the first order of business this year, I urge the Senate to do the same, and I know they will. They will. People are out of work. They're hurting. They need our help. And I want a jobs bill on my desk without delay.

But the truth is, these steps won't make up for the seven million jobs that we've lost over the last two years. The only way to move to full employment is to lay a new foundation for long-term economic growth, and finally address the problems that America's families have confronted for years.

We can't afford another so-called economic "expansion" like the one from the last decade—what some call the "lost decade"—where jobs grew more slowly than during any prior expansion; where the income of the average American household declined while the cost of health care and tuition reached record highs; where prosperity was built on a housing bubble and financial speculation.

From the day I took office, I've been told that addressing our larger challenges is too ambitious; such an effort would be too contentious. I've been told that our political system is too gridlocked, and that we should just put things on hold for a while.

For those who make these claims, I have one simple question: How long should we wait? How long should America put its future on hold?

You see, Washington has been telling us to wait for decades, even as the problems have grown worse. Meanwhile, China is not waiting to revamp its economy. Germany is not waiting. India is not waiting. These nations—they're not standing still. These nations aren't playing for second place. They're putting more emphasis on math and science. They're rebuilding their infrastructure. They're making serious investments in clean energy because they want those jobs. Well, I do not accept second place for the United States of America.

As hard as it may be, as uncomfortable and contentious as the debates may become, it's time to get serious about fixing the problems that are hampering our growth.

Now, one place to start is serious financial reform. Look, I am not interested in punishing banks. I'm interested in protecting our economy. A strong, healthy financial market makes it possible for businesses to access credit and create new jobs. It channels the savings of families into investments that raise incomes. But that can only happen if we guard against the same recklessness that nearly brought down our entire economy.

We need to make sure consumers and middle-class families have the information they need to make financial decisions. We can't allow financial institutions, including those that take your deposits, to take risks that threaten the whole economy.

Now, the House has already passed financial reform with many of these changes. And the lobbyists are trying to kill it. But we cannot let them win this fight. And if the bill that ends up on my desk does not meet the test of real reform, I will send it back until we get it right. We've got to get it right.

Next, we need to encourage American innovation. Last year, we made the largest investment in basic research funding in history—an investment that could lead to the world's cheapest solar cells or treatment that kills cancer cells but leaves healthy ones untouched. And no area is more ripe for such innovation than energy. You can see the results of last year's investments in clean energy—in the North Carolina company that will create 1,200 jobs nationwide helping to make advanced batteries; or in the California business that will put a thousand people to work making solar panels.

But to create more of these clean energy jobs, we need more production, more efficiency, more incentives. And that means building a new generation of safe, clean nuclear power plants in this country. It means making tough decisions about opening new offshore areas for oil and gas development. It means continued investment in advanced biofuels and clean coal technologies. And, yes, it means passing a comprehensive energy and climate bill with incentives that will finally make clean energy the profitable kind of energy in America.

I am grateful to the House for passing such a bill last year. And this year I'm eager to help advance the bipartisan effort in the Senate.

I know there have been questions about whether we can afford such changes in a tough economy. I know that there are those who disagree with the overwhelming scientific evidence on climate change. But here's the thing—even if you doubt the evidence, providing incentives for energy-efficiency and clean energy are the right thing to do for our future—because the nation that leads the clean energy economy will be the nation that leads the global economy. And America must be that nation.

Third, we need to export more of our goods. Because the more products we make and sell to other countries, the more jobs we support right here in America. So tonight, we set a new goal: We will double our exports over the next five years, an increase that will support two million jobs in America. To help meet this goal, we're launching a National Export Initiative that will help farmers and small businesses increase their exports, and reform export controls consistent with national security.

We have to seek new markets aggressively, just as our competitors are. If America sits on the sidelines while other nations sign trade deals, we will lose the chance to create jobs on our shores. But realizing those benefits also means enforcing those agreements so our trading partners play by the rules. And that's why we'll continue to shape a Doha trade agreement that opens global markets, and why we will strengthen our trade relations in Asia and with key partners like South Korea and Panama and Colombia.

Fourth, we need to invest in the skills and education of our people.

Now, this year, we've broken through the stalemate between left and right by launching a national competition to improve our schools. And the idea here is simple: Instead of rewarding failure, we only reward success. Instead of funding the status quo, we only invest in reform—reform that raises student achievement; inspires students to excel in math and science; and turns around failing schools that steal the future of too many young Americans, from rural communities to the inner city. In the 21st century, the best anti-poverty program around is a world-class education. And in this country, the success of our children cannot depend more on where they live than on their potential.

When we renew the Elementary and Secondary Education Act, we will work with Congress to expand these reforms to all 50 states. Still, in this economy, a high school diploma no longer guarantees a good job. That's why I urge the Senate to follow the House and pass a bill that will revitalize our community colleges, which are a career pathway to the children of so many working families.

To make college more affordable, this bill will finally end the unwarranted taxpayer subsidies that go to banks for student loans. Instead, let's take that money and give families a $10,000 tax credit for four years of college and increase Pell Grants. And let's tell another one million students that when they graduate, they will be required to pay only 10 percent of their income on student loans, and all of their debt will be forgiven after 20 years—and forgiven after 10 years if they choose a career in public service, because in the United States of America, no one should go broke because they chose to go to college.

And by the way, it's time for colleges and universities to get serious about cutting their own costs—because they, too, have a responsibility to help solve this problem.

Now, the price of college tuition is just one of the burdens facing the middle class. That's why last year I asked Vice President Biden to chair a task force on middle-class families. That's why we're nearly doubling the child care tax credit, and making it easier to save for retirement by giving access to every worker a retirement account and expanding the tax credit for those who start a nest egg. That's why we're working to lift the value of a family's single largest investment—their home. The steps we took last year to shore up the housing market have allowed millions of Americans to take out new loans and save an average of $1,500 on mortgage payments.

This year, we will step up refinancing so that homeowners can move into more affordable mortgages. And it is precisely to relieve the burden on middle-class families that we still need health insurance reform. Yes, we do.

Now, let's clear a few things up. I didn't choose to tackle this issue to get some legislative victory under my belt. And by now it should be fairly obvious that I didn't take on health care because it was good politics. I took on health care because of the stories I've heard from Americans with preexisting conditions whose lives depend on getting coverage; patients who've been denied coverage; families—even those with insurance—who are just one illness away from financial ruin.

After nearly a century of trying—Democratic administrations, Republican administrations—we are closer than ever to bringing more security to the lives of so many Americans. The approach we've taken would protect every American from the worst practices of the insurance industry. It would give small businesses and uninsured Americans a chance to choose an affordable health care plan in a competitive market. It would require every insurance plan to cover preventive care.

And by the way, I want to acknowledge our First Lady, Michelle Obama, who this year is creating a national movement to tackle the epidemic of childhood obesity and make kids healthier. Thank you. She gets embarrassed.

Our approach would preserve the right of Americans who have insurance to keep their doctor and their plan. It would reduce costs and premiums for millions of families and businesses. And according to the Congressional Budget Office—the independent organization that both parties have cited as the official scorekeeper for Congress—our approach would bring down the deficit by as much as $1 trillion over the next two decades.

Still, this is a complex issue, and the longer it was debated, the more skeptical people became. I take my share of the blame for not explaining it more clearly to the American people. And I know that with all the lobbying and horse-trading, the process left most Americans wondering, "What's in it for me?"

But I also know this problem is not going away. By the time I'm finished speaking tonight, more Americans will have lost their health insurance. Millions will lose it this year. Our deficit will grow. Premiums will go up. Patients will be denied the care they need. Small business owners will continue to drop coverage altogether. I will not walk away from these Americans, and neither should the people in this chamber.

So, as temperatures cool, I want everyone to take another look at the plan we've proposed. There's a reason why many doctors, nurses, and health care experts who know our system best consider this approach a vast improvement over the status quo. But if anyone from either party has a better approach that will bring down premiums, bring down the deficit, cover the uninsured, strengthen Medicare for seniors, and stop insurance company abuses, let me know. Let me know. Let me know. I'm eager to see it.

Here's what I ask Congress, though: Don't walk away from reform. Not now. Not when we are so close. Let us find a way to come together and finish the job for the American people. Let's get it done. Let's get it done.

Now, even as health care reform would reduce our deficit, it's not enough to dig us out of a massive fiscal hole in which we find ourselves. It's a challenge that makes all others that much harder to solve, and one that's been subject to a lot of political posturing. So let me start the discussion of government spending by setting the record straight.

At the beginning of the last decade, the year 2000, America had a budget surplus of over $200 billion. By the time I took office, we had a one-year deficit of over $1 trillion and projected deficits of $8 trillion over the next decade. Most of this was the result of not paying for two wars, two tax cuts, and an expensive prescription drug program. On top of that, the effects of the recession put a $3 trillion hole in our budget. All this was before I walked in the door.

Now—just stating the facts. Now, if we had taken office in ordinary times, I would have liked nothing more than to start bringing down the deficit. But we took office amid a crisis. And our efforts to prevent a second depression have added another $1 trillion to our national debt. That, too, is a fact.

I'm absolutely convinced that was the right thing to do. But families across the country are tightening their belts and making tough decisions. The federal government should do the same. So tonight, I'm proposing specific steps to pay for the trillion dollars that it took to rescue the economy last year.

Starting in 2011, we are prepared to freeze government spending for three years. Spending related to our national security, Medicare, Medicaid, and Social Security will not be affected. But all other discretionary government programs will. Like any cash-strapped family, we will work within a budget to invest in what we need and sacrifice what we don't. And if I have to enforce this discipline by veto, I will.

We will continue to go through the budget, line by line, page by page, to eliminate programs that we can't afford and don't work. We've already identified $20 billion in savings for next year. To help working families, we'll extend our middle-class tax cuts. But at a time of record deficits, we will not continue tax cuts for oil companies, for investment fund managers, and for those making over $250,000 a year. We just can't afford it.

Now, even after paying for what we spent on my watch, we'll still face the massive deficit we had when I took office. More importantly, the cost of Medicare, Medicaid, and Social

Security will continue to skyrocket. That's why I've called for a bipartisan fiscal commission, modeled on a proposal by Republican Judd Gregg and Democrat Kent Conrad. This can't be one of those Washington gimmicks that lets us pretend we solved a problem. The commission will have to provide a specific set of solutions by a certain deadline.

Now, yesterday, the Senate blocked a bill that would have created this commission. So I'll issue an executive order that will allow us to go forward, because I refuse to pass this problem on to another generation of Americans. And when the vote comes tomorrow, the Senate should restore the pay-as-you-go law that was a big reason for why we had record surpluses in the 1990s.

Now, I know that some in my own party will argue that we can't address the deficit or freeze government spending when so many are still hurting. And I agree—which is why this freeze won't take effect until next year—when the economy is stronger. That's how budgeting works. But understand—understand if we don't take meaningful steps to rein in our debt, it could damage our markets, increase the cost of borrowing, and jeopardize our recovery—all of which would have an even worse effect on our job growth and family incomes.

From some on the right, I expect we'll hear a different argument—that if we just make fewer investments in our people, extend tax cuts including those for the wealthier Americans, eliminate more regulations, maintain the status quo on health care, our deficits will go away. The problem is that's what we did for eight years. That's what helped us into this crisis. It's what helped lead to these deficits. We can't do it again.

Rather than fight the same tired battles that have dominated Washington for decades, it's time to try something new. Let's invest in our people without leaving them a mountain of debt. Let's meet our responsibility to the citizens who sent us here. Let's try common sense. A novel concept.

To do that, we have to recognize that we face more than a deficit of dollars right now. We face a deficit of trust—deep and corrosive doubts about how Washington works that have been growing for years. To close that credibility gap we have to take action on both ends of Pennsylvania Avenue—to end the outsized influence of lobbyists; to do our work openly; to give our people the government they deserve.

That's what I came to Washington to do. That's why—for the first time in history—my administration posts on our White House visitors online. That's why we've excluded lobbyists from policymaking jobs, or seats on federal boards and commissions.

But we can't stop there. It's time to require lobbyists to disclose each contact they make on behalf of a client with my administration or with Congress. It's time to put strict limits on the contributions that lobbyists give to candidates for federal office.

With all due deference to separation of powers, last week the Supreme Court reversed a century of law that I believe will open the floodgates for special interests—including foreign corporations—to spend without limit in our elections. I don't think American elections should be bankrolled by America's most powerful interests, or worse, by foreign entities. They should be decided by the American people. And I'd urge Democrats and Republicans to pass a bill that helps to correct some of these problems.

I'm also calling on Congress to continue down the path of earmark reform. Democrats and Republicans. Democrats and Republicans. You've trimmed some of this spending, you've embraced some meaningful change. But restoring the public trust demands more. For example, some members of Congress post some earmark requests online. Tonight, I'm calling on Congress to publish all earmark requests on a single Web site before there's a vote, so that the American people can see how their money is being spent.

Of course, none of these reforms will even happen if we don't also reform how we work with one another. Now, I'm not naïve. I never thought that the mere fact of my election would usher in peace and harmony—and some post-partisan era. I knew that both parties have fed divisions that are deeply entrenched. And on some issues, there are simply philosophical differences that will always cause us to part ways. These disagreements, about the role of government in our lives, about our national priorities and our national security, they've been taking place for over 200 years. They're the very essence of our democracy.

But what frustrates the American people is a Washington where every day is Election Day. We can't wage a perpetual campaign where the only goal is to see who can get the most embarrassing headlines about the other side—a belief that if you lose, I win. Neither party should delay or obstruct every single bill just because they can. The confirmation of—I'm speaking to both parties now. The confirmation of well-qualified public servants shouldn't be held hostage to the pet projects or grudges of a few individual senators.

Washington may think that saying anything about the other side, no matter how false, no matter how malicious, is just part of the game. But it's precisely such politics that has stopped either party from helping the American people. Worse yet, it's sowing further division among our citizens, further distrust in our government.

So, no, I will not give up on trying to change the tone of our politics. I know it's an election year. And after last week, it's clear that campaign fever has come even earlier than usual. But we still need to govern.

To Democrats, I would remind you that we still have the largest majority in decades, and the people expect us to solve problems, not run for the hills. And if the Republican leadership is going to insist that 60 votes in the Senate are required to do any business at all in this town—a supermajority—then the responsibility to govern is now yours as well. Just saying no to everything may be good short-term politics, but it's not leadership. We were sent here to serve our citizens, not our ambitions. So let's show the American people that we can do it together.

This week, I'll be addressing a meeting of the House Republicans. I'd like to begin monthly meetings with both Democratic and Republican leadership. I know you can't wait.

Throughout our history, no issue has united this country more than our security. Sadly, some of the unity we felt after 9/11 has dissipated. We can argue all we want about who's to blame for this, but I'm not interested in re-litigating the past. I know that all of us love this country. All of us are committed to its defense. So let's put aside the schoolyard taunts about who's tough. Let's reject the false choice between protecting our people and upholding our values. Let's leave behind the fear and division, and do what it takes to defend our nation and forge a more hopeful future—for America and for the world.

That's the work we began last year. Since the day I took office, we've renewed our focus on the terrorists who threaten our nation. We've made substantial investments in our homeland security and disrupted plots that threatened to take American lives. We are filling unacceptable gaps revealed by the failed Christmas attack, with better airline security and swifter action on our intelligence. We've prohibited torture and strengthened partnerships from the Pacific to South Asia to the Arabian Peninsula. And in the last year, hundreds of al Qaeda's fighters and affiliates, including many senior leaders, have been captured or killed—far more than in 2008.

And in Afghanistan, we're increasing our troops and training Afghan security forces so they can begin to take the lead in July of 2011, and our troops can begin to come home.

We will reward good governance, work to reduce corruption, and support the rights of all Afghans—men and women alike. We're joined by allies and partners who have increased their own commitments, and who will come together tomorrow in London to reaffirm our common purpose. There will be difficult days ahead. But I am absolutely confident we will succeed.

As we take the fight to al Qaeda, we are responsibly leaving Iraq to its people. As a candidate, I promised that I would end this war, and that is what I am doing as President. We will have all of our combat troops out of Iraq by the end of this August. We will support the Iraqi government—we will support the Iraqi government as they hold elections, and we will continue to partner with the Iraqi people to promote regional peace and prosperity. But make no mistake: This war is ending, and all of our troops are coming home.

Tonight, all of our men and women in uniform—in Iraq, in Afghanistan, and around the world—they have to know that we—that they have our respect, our gratitude, our full support. And just as they must have the resources they need in war, we all have a responsibility to support them when they come home. That's why we made the largest increase in investments for veterans in decades—last year. That's why we're building a 21st century VA. And that's why Michelle has joined with Jill Biden to forge a national commitment to support military families.

Now, even as we prosecute two wars, we're also confronting perhaps the greatest danger to the American people—the threat of nuclear weapons. I've embraced the vision of John F. Kennedy and Ronald Reagan through a strategy that reverses the spread of these weapons and seeks a world without them. To reduce our stockpiles and launchers, while ensuring our deterrent, the United States and Russia are completing negotiations on the farthest-reaching arms control treaty in nearly two decades. And at April's Nuclear Security Summit, we will bring 44 nations together here in Washington, D.C. behind a clear goal: securing all vulnerable nuclear materials around the world in four years, so that they never fall into the hands of terrorists.

Now, these diplomatic efforts have also strengthened our hand in dealing with those nations that insist on violating international agreements in pursuit of nuclear weapons. That's why North Korea now faces increased isolation, and stronger sanctions—sanctions that are being vigorously enforced. That's why the international community is more united, and the Islamic Republic of Iran is more isolated. And as Iran's leaders continue to ignore their obligations, there should be no doubt: They, too, will face growing consequences. That is a promise.

That's the leadership that we are providing—engagement that advances the common security and prosperity of all people. We're working through the G20 to sustain a lasting global recovery. We're working with Muslim communities around the world to promote science and education and innovation. We have gone from a bystander to a leader in the fight against climate change.

We're helping developing countries to feed themselves, and continuing the fight against HIV/AIDS. And we are launching a new initiative that will give us the capacity to respond faster and more effectively to bioterrorism or an infectious disease—a plan that will counter threats at home and strengthen public health abroad.

As we have for over 60 years, America takes these actions because our destiny is connected to those beyond our shores. But we also do it because it is right. That's why, as we meet here tonight, over 10,000 Americans are working with many nations to help the people of Haiti recover and rebuild. That's why we stand with the girl who yearns to go to school in Afghanistan; why we support the human rights of the women marching through the streets of Iran; why we advocate for the young man denied a job by corruption in Guinea. For America must always stand on the side of freedom and human dignity. Always.

Abroad, America's greatest source of strength has always been our ideals. The same is true at home. We find unity in our incredible diversity, drawing on the promise enshrined in our Constitution: the notion that we're all created equal; that no matter who you are or what you look like, if you abide by the law you should be protected by it; if you adhere to our common values you should be treated no different than anyone else.

We must continually renew this promise. My administration has a Civil Rights Division that is once again prosecuting civil rights violations and employment discrimination. We finally strengthened our laws to protect against crimes driven by hate. This year, I will work with Congress and our military to finally repeal the law that denies gay Americans the right to serve the country they love because of who they are. It's the right thing to do.

We're going to crack down on violations of equal pay laws—so that women get equal pay for an equal day's work. And we should continue the work of fixing our broken immigration system—to secure our borders and enforce our laws, and ensure that everyone who plays by the rules can contribute to our economy and enrich our nation.

In the end, it's our ideals, our values that built America—values that allowed us to forge a nation made up of immigrants from every corner of the globe; values that drive our citizens still. Every day, Americans meet their responsibilities to their families and their employers. Time and again, they lend a hand to their neighbors and give back to their country. They take pride in their labor, and are generous in spirit. These aren't Republican values or Democratic values that they're living by; business values or labor values. They're American values.

Unfortunately, too many of our citizens have lost faith that our biggest institutions—our corporations, our media, and, yes, our government—still reflect these same values. Each of these institutions are full of honorable men and women doing important work that helps our country prosper. But each time a CEO rewards himself for failure, or a banker puts the rest of us at risk for his own selfish gain, people's doubts grow. Each time lobbyists game the system or politicians tear each other down instead of lifting this country up, we lose faith. The more that TV pundits reduce serious debates to silly arguments, big issues into sound bites, our citizens turn away.

No wonder there's so much cynicism out there. No wonder there's so much disappointment.

I campaigned on the promise of change—change we can believe in, the slogan went. And right now, I know there are many Americans who aren't sure if they still believe we can change—or that I can deliver it.

But remember this—I never suggested that change would be easy, or that I could do it alone. Democracy in a nation of 300 million people can be noisy and messy and complicated. And when you try to do big things and make big changes, it stirs passions and controversy. That's just how it is.

Those of us in public office can respond to this reality by playing it safe and avoid telling hard truths and pointing fingers. We can do what's necessary to keep our poll numbers high, and get through the next election instead of doing what's best for the next generation.

But I also know this: If people had made that decision 50 years ago, or 100 years ago, or 200 years ago, we wouldn't be here tonight. The only reason we are here is because generations of Americans were unafraid to do what was hard; to do what was needed even when success was uncertain; to do what it took to keep the dream of this nation alive for their children and their grandchildren.

Our administration has had some political setbacks this year, and some of them were deserved. But I wake up every day knowing that they are nothing compared to the setbacks that families all across this country have faced this year. And what keeps me going—what keeps me fighting—is that despite all these setbacks, that spirit of determination and optimism, that fundamental decency that has always been at the core of the American people, that lives on.

It lives on in the struggling small business owner who wrote to me of his company, "None of us," he said, " . . . are willing to consider, even slightly, that we might fail."

It lives on in the woman who said that even though she and her neighbors have felt the pain of recession, "We are strong. We are resilient. We are American."

It lives on in the 8-year-old boy in Louisiana, who just sent me his allowance and asked if I would give it to the people of Haiti.

And it lives on in all the Americans who've dropped everything to go someplace they've never been and pull people they've never known from the rubble, prompting chants of "U.S.A.! U.S.A.! U.S.A.!" when another life was saved.

The spirit that has sustained this nation for more than two centuries lives on in you, its people. We have finished a difficult year. We have come through a difficult decade. But a new year has come. A new decade stretches before us. We don't quit. I don't quit. Let's seize this moment—to start anew, to carry the dream forward, and to strengthen our union once more.

Thank you. God bless you. And God bless the United States of America.

Source: The White House. Office of the Press Secretary. "Remarks by the President in State of the Union Address." January 27, 2010. http://www.whitehouse.gov/the-press-office/remarks-president-state-union-address.

Virginia Governor McDonnell
Response to the President's Address

January 27, 2010

Good evening. I'm Bob McDonnell. Eleven days ago I was honored to be sworn in as the 71st governor of Virginia.

I'm standing in the historic House Chamber of Virginia's Capitol, a building designed by Virginia's second governor, Thomas Jefferson.

It's not easy to follow the President of the United States. And my twin 18-year old boys have added to the pressure, by giving me exactly ten minutes to finish before they leave to go watch SportsCenter.

I'm joined by fellow Virginians to share a Republican perspective on how to best address the challenges facing our nation today.

We were encouraged to hear President Obama speak this evening about the need to create jobs.

All Americans should have the opportunity to find and keep meaningful work, and the dignity that comes with it.

Many of us here, and many of you watching, have family or friends who have lost their jobs.

1 in 10 American workers is unemployed. That is unacceptable.

Here in Virginia we have faced our highest unemployment rate in more than 25 years, and bringing new jobs and more opportunities to our citizens is the top priority of my administration.

Good government policy should spur economic growth, and strengthen the private sector's ability to create new jobs.

We must enact policies that promote entrepreneurship and innovation, so America can better compete with the world.

What government should not do is pile on more taxation, regulation, and litigation that kill jobs and hurt the middle class.

It was Thomas Jefferson who called for "A wise and frugal Government which shall leave men free to regulate their own pursuits of industry. . . . and shall not take from the mouth of labor the bread it has earned . . ." He was right.

Today, the federal government is simply trying to do too much.

Last year, we were told that massive new federal spending would create more jobs 'immediately' and hold unemployment below 8%.

In the past year, over three million Americans have lost their jobs, yet the Democratic Congress continues deficit spending, adding to the bureaucracy, and increasing the national debt on our children and grandchildren.

The amount of this debt is on pace to double in five years, and triple in ten. The federal debt is already over $100,000 per household.

This is simply unsustainable. The President's partial freeze on discretionary spending is a laudable step, but a small one.

The circumstances of our time demand that we reconsider and restore the proper, limited role of government at every level.

Without reform, the excessive growth of government threatens our very liberty and prosperity.

In recent months, the American people have made clear that they want government leaders to listen and act on the issues most important to them.

We want results, not rhetoric. We want cooperation, not partisanship.

There is much common ground.

All Americans agree, we need a health care system that is affordable, accessible, and high quality.

But most Americans do not want to turn over the best medical care system in the world to the federal government.

Republicans in Congress have offered legislation to reform healthcare, without shifting Medicaid costs to the states, without cutting Medicare, and without raising your taxes.

We will do that by implementing common sense reforms, like letting families and businesses buy health insurance policies across state lines, and ending frivolous lawsuits against doctors and hospitals that drive up the cost of your healthcare.

And our solutions aren't thousand-page bills that no one has fully read, after being crafted behind closed doors with special interests.

In fact, many of our proposals are available online at solutions.gop.gov, and we welcome your ideas on Facebook and Twitter.

All Americans agree, this nation must become more energy independent and secure.

We are blessed here in America with vast natural resources, and we must use them all.

Advances in technology can unleash more natural gas, nuclear, wind, coal, and alternative energy to lower your utility bills.

Here in Virginia, we have the opportunity to be the first state on the East Coast to explore for and produce oil and natural gas offshore.

But this Administration's policies are delaying offshore production, hindering nuclear energy expansion, and seeking to impose job-killing cap and trade energy taxes.

Now is the time to adopt innovative energy policies that create jobs and lower energy prices.

All Americans agree, that a young person needs a world-class education to compete in the global economy. As a kid my dad told me, "Son, to get a good job, you need a good education." That's even more true today.

The President and I agree on expanding the number of high-quality charter schools, and rewarding teachers for excellent performance. More school choices for parents and students mean more accountability and greater achievement.

A child's educational opportunity should be determined by her intellect and work ethic, not by her zip code.

All Americans agree, we must maintain a strong national defense. The courage and success of our Armed Forces is allowing us to draw down troop levels in Iraq as that government is increasingly able to step up. My oldest daughter, Jeanine, was an Army platoon leader in Iraq, so I'm personally grateful for the service and the sacrifice of all of our men and women in uniform, and a grateful nation thanks them.

We applaud President Obama's decision to deploy 30,000 more troops to Afghanistan. We agree that victory there is a national security imperative. But we have serious concerns over recent steps the Administration has taken regarding suspected terrorists.

Americans were shocked on Christmas Day to learn of the attempted bombing of a flight to Detroit. This foreign terror suspect was given the same legal rights as a U.S. citizen, and immediately stopped providing critical intelligence.

As Senator-elect Scott Brown says, we should be spending taxpayer dollars to defeat terrorists, not to protect them.

Here at home government must help foster a society in which all our people can use their God-given talents in liberty to pursue the American Dream. Republicans know that government cannot guarantee individual outcomes, but we strongly believe that it must guarantee equality of opportunity for all.

That opportunity exists best in a democracy which promotes free enterprise, economic growth, strong families, and individual achievement.

Many Americans are concerned about this Administration's efforts to exert greater control over car companies, banks, energy and health care.

Over-regulating employers won't create more employment; overtaxing investors won't foster more investment.

Top-down one-size fits all decision making should not replace the personal choices of free people in a free market, nor undermine the proper role of state and local governments in our system of federalism. As our Founders clearly stated, and we Governors understand, government closest to the people governs best.

And no government program can replace the actions of caring Americans freely choosing to help one another. The Scriptures say "To whom much is given, much will be required." As the most generous and prosperous nation on Earth, it is heartwarming to see Americans giving much time and money to the people of Haiti. Thank you for your ongoing compassion.

Some people are afraid that America is no longer the great land of promise that she has always been. They should not be.

America will always blaze the trail of opportunity and prosperity.

America must always be a land where liberty and property are valued and respected, and innocent human life is protected.

Government should have this clear goal: Where opportunity is absent, we must create it. Where opportunity is limited, we must expand it. Where opportunity is unequal, we must make it open to everyone.

Our Founders pledged their lives, their fortunes and their sacred honor to create this nation.

Now, we should pledge as Democrats, Republicans and Independents—Americans all—to work together to leave this nation a better place than we found it.

God Bless you, and God Bless our great nation.

SOURCE: Office of the Governor of Virginia. "Republican Address to the Nation." January 27, 2010. http://www.governor.virginia.gov/News/viewRelease.cfm?id=27.

OTHER HISTORIC DOCUMENTS OF INTEREST

FROM THIS VOLUME

FROM PREVIOUS *HISTORIC DOCUMENTS*

February

President Obama Establishes the National Commission on Fiscal Responsibility and Reform

---

FEBRUARY 18 AND DECEMBER 1, 2010

In January 2010, the United States continued to face a bleak fiscal environment. The country's economy remained in recession, while high unemployment and foreclosure rates provided proof of the lingering effects of the 2008 financial crisis. At the same time, government spending continued to expand as federal officials scrambled to cover the growing costs of entitlement programs, the wars in Iraq and Afghanistan, a series of tax cuts approved by former president George W. Bush, and a $787 billion economic stimulus package signed by President Barack Obama. The national debt had reached $12.3 trillion, and the White House was projecting a record budget deficit of $1.56 trillion for fiscal year 2010. As part of his effort to bring the federal budget under control, President Obama established the National Commission on Fiscal Responsibility and Reform through an executive order on February 18 after a failed attempt by Congress to create a similar body.

FISCAL CHALLENGES AND A FAILED PROPOSAL

On January 20, a group of Democratic senators proposed a bill to raise the U.S. government's legal limit on borrowing by $1.9 trillion, for a total of $14.3 trillion, to ensure the government could secure enough funds to continue daily operations. The measure was immediately unpopular with Republicans and moderate Democrats, particularly as it followed closely on the heels of a short-term debt increase of $290 billion, approved by Congress in December 2009. In exchange for their votes in favor of the measure, moderate Democrats in the Senate demanded a vote on a proposal to establish a national commission that would study and recommend ways to reduce the deficit.

Such a proposal had been introduced in December 2009 by Sens. Kent Conrad, D-N.D., and Judd Gregg, R-N.H., the chair and ranking member of the Senate Budget Committee, respectively. The Bipartisan Task Force for Responsible Fiscal Action Act of 2009 called for the creation of an eighteen-member bipartisan commission that would produce a multiyear plan to reduce annual deficits. The commission would provide its recommendations after the midterm elections in November, with Congress voting on the proposed plan in December.

To help appease moderate Democrats, Sens. Gregg and Conrad added their proposal as an amendment to the debt ceiling bill. Yet several powerful Democrats remained opposed to the measure, such as Senate Finance Committee chair Max Baucus, D-Mont., and Sen. Robert Byrd, D-W.Va., who expressed concern that the amendment required Congress to use "expedited procedures" to consider the commission's recommendations. Republicans also objected to the measure, claiming such a commission would only lead to tax increases, and called for the panel's focus to be limited to recommending spending cuts.

On January 23, three days before the debt limit bill was scheduled for a vote, President Obama issued a statement offering his formal endorsement of the fiscal commission proposed by Sens. Gregg and Conrad. "These deficits did not happen overnight, and they won't be solved overnight. We not only need to change how we pay for policies, but we also need to change how Washington works. The only way to solve our long-term fiscal challenge is to solve it together—Democrats and Republicans," Obama said.

Despite Obama's endorsement, opposition to the commission remained strong. Several Republicans who signed on as co-sponsors to the initial bill to create the commission dropped their support shortly before the vote, and the amendment ultimately failed.

EXECUTIVE ORDER 13531

The failed Gregg-Conrad amendment did not spell the end of the fiscal commission. President Obama had made it clear that if Congress did not vote for such a body, he would create the panel by executive order.

On February 18, President Obama signed Executive Order 13531, officially establishing the National Commission on Fiscal Responsibility and Reform. Similar to the Gregg-Conrad proposal, the commission would have eighteen members. Democrats would hold ten seats on the commission; the Republicans would hold eight. Congressional Democrats and Republicans would each select six sitting members of Congress to serve on the commission while Obama would appoint the remaining six, including two co-chairs.

The goal of the commission was to produce a fiscal reform plan that would reduce the deficit to 3 percent of the U.S. economy by 2015, which would put the country's budget in balance with the exception of payments on old debt. Commission members were charged with considering any and all ideas that would achieve this goal, including tax increases, spending cuts, and changes to entitlement programs such as Social Security. The commission's final report would be due to Congress by December 1.

The key difference between the president's commission and that proposed by Sens. Gregg and Conrad was that it would not have the authority to force Congress to vote on the commission's ultimate recommendations. Some, including Gregg, saw this as a major weakness. "Unless you have fast-track approval, unless you have an up-and-down vote, unless you have no amendments . . . you don't get bipartisanship, you don't get fairness, and you don't get action," Gregg said.

Upon signing the executive order, Obama named Erskine Bowles and Alan Simpson as the co-chairs of the commission. Bowles previously served in the Bill Clinton administration, first as the head of the Small Business Administration, then as White House chief of staff. As chief of staff, Bowles worked with the Republican leadership in Congress to craft the Balanced Budget Act of 1997, which helped to generate the first balanced budget in nearly thirty years. Simpson previously served three terms as a U.S. senator from Wyoming. During his senate career, Simpson served as the Republican whip, chaired the Senate Finance Committee's Subcommittee on Social Security, and voted in favor of bipartisan deficit-reduction measures. Both men "know how to disagree without being disagreeable, and there's a sense of civility and a sense that there are moments where you set politics aside to do what's right. That's the kind of spirit we need," Obama said.

Immediately following the signing of the executive order, the Republican congressional leadership would not confirm whether Republican members would participate in the commission, citing lingering concerns that the commission would lead to tax increases. "After trillions in new and proposed spending, Americans know our problem is not that we tax too little, but that Washington spends too much—that should be the focus of this commission," said Senate minority leader Mitch McConnell, R-Ky.

The commission also met resistance from labor unions and AARP. These groups questioned the necessity of a deficit commission and argued that a small group led by unelected officials should not have the power to propose major changes to programs such as Social Security and Medicare. "We come in as a skeptic," said David Sloane, senior vice president for government relations and advocacy for AARP. "We believe this is a situation where in essence Congress has abdicated its responsibility."

The Work Begins

Despite the concerns identified by some, officials began the process of staffing the commission and holding public hearings on possible deficit reduction measures. By the end of March, the remaining commission members had been announced. President Obama appointed David Cote, chairman and CEO of Honeywell International; Ann Fudge, former CEO of Young & Rubicam Brands; Alice Rivlin, senior fellow at the Brookings Institution; and Andrew Stern, president of Service Employees International Union (SEIU). The Democratic congressional leadership named Sen. Max Baucus, D-Mont.; Rep. Xavier Becerra, D-Calif.; Sen. Kent Conrad, D-N.D.; Sen. Richard Durbin, D-Ill.; Rep. Jan Schakowsky, D-Ill.; and Rep. John Spratt, D-S.C. The Republican congressional leadership selected Rep. Dave Camp, R-Mich.; Sen. Tom Coburn, R-Okla.; Sen. Mike Crapo, R-Idaho; Sen. Judd Gregg, R-N.H.; Rep. Jeb Hensarling, R-Texas; and Rep. Paul Ryan, R-Wis.

On March 25, commission chairs Bowles and Simpson announced that Democratic Leadership Council CEO Bruce Reed would serve as the commission's executive director. On June 7, Josh Odintz was detailed from the Department of the Treasury's Office of Tax Policy to serve as the commission's chief tax counsel.

Throughout the spring and summer, the commission held a series of five public meetings where it heard testimony from a variety of academic scholars and current and former government officials from the Federal Reserve, Congressional Budget Office (CBO), the Government Accountability Office (GAO), and the Office of Management and Budget (OMB). The commission also hosted a public forum on June 30 and invited seventy-five organizations, think tanks, policy experts, and individual citizens to share their ideas for balancing the federal budget. Attendees included representatives of the AFL-CIO, Business Roundtable, Economic Policy Institute, Institute for America's Future, and the Pew Charitable Trusts.

News surrounding the commission's proceedings remained quiet until late August, when co-chair Simpson's use of colorful language called his ability to lead the commission into question. Upon reading a column about Social Security penned by National Older Women's League (OWL) executive director Ashley Carson, Simpson wrote Carson a strongly worded e-mail comparing Social Security to "a milk cow with 310 million tits," and urged her to find "honest work." Simpson quickly apologized for the incident, but not before Carson, Sen. Bernard Sanders, I-Vt., and Reps. Peter DeFazio, D-Ore., and Raúl Grijalva, D-Ariz., called for his resignation. Simpson retained his co-chairmanship, and the commission continued its work into the fall.

INITIAL RECOMMENDATIONS

On November 10, chairs Bowles and Simpson released a draft report outlining the commission's initial recommendations. The report included proposed cuts to discretionary spending that would total $1.4 trillion over ten years, as well as cuts to defense spending and farm subsidies. The report also called for the elimination of a number of tax breaks, including the deductibility of mortgage interest payments, and a simplification of the tax code. In addition, the chairs recommended reducing Social Security benefits to most future retirees and raising the retirement age to sixty-eight by 2050. Further recommendations included freezing the salaries of federal employees for three years and cutting the federal workforce by 10 percent. None of the proposals would take effect until 2012 to ensure that they would not impede the country's economic recovery. "We have harpooned every whale in the ocean and some of the minnows," said Simpson.

Reaction to the draft report was swift and mostly critical. House Speaker Nancy Pelosi, D-Calif., called the plan "simply unacceptable," while commission member Schakowsky said, "This is not the way to do it." AFL-CIO president Richard Trumka claimed the commission chairs had told "working Americans to drop dead," citing the report's proposed changes to Social Security and Medicare. Some criticism was more subdued. In a joint statement, Republican commission members Ryan, Hensarling, and Camp said, "This is a provocative proposal, and while we have concerns with some of their specifics, we commend the co-chairs for advancing the debate." Others defended the recommendations. "This is one of the rare, tangible and comprehensive approaches that have come through the political process to deal with an issue that everyone should be concerned about. I, for one, will resist efforts to reject the co-chairs' proposals out of hand," said Rep. Earl Blumenauer, D-Ore.

The commission co-chairs released their final report, "The Moment of Truth: Report of the National Commission on Fiscal Responsibility and Reform," on December 1 with minor changes and scheduled a vote on their recommendations for December 3. Fourteen of the commission's eighteen members were required to approve the report before it could be finalized and presented to Congress for possible legislative action. However, only eleven commission members ultimately voted in favor of the co-chairs' recommendations. This was a higher vote tally than many political observers expected and reflected bipartisan support for the co-chairs' recommendations, leading some to speculate the 112th Congress may try to adopt certain proposals during the annual budget process or otherwise use the report as a framework for future fiscal debates.

—Linda Fecteau

Following are President Barack Obama's remarks on creating the National Commission on Fiscal Responsibility and Reform and the Executive Order establishing the commission, both released on February 18, 2010, and excerpts from the "Moment of Truth: Report of the National Commission on Fiscal Responsibility and Reform," released on December 1, 2010.

President Obama's Remarks on Establishing the National Commission on Fiscal Responsibility and Reform

February 18, 2010

Hello, everybody. All right. Good morning, everybody. When I took office, America faced three closely linked challenges. One was a financial crisis brought on by reckless speculation that threatened to choke off all lending. And this helped to spark the deepest recession since the Great Depression, from which we're still recovering. That recession, in turn, helped to aggravate an already severe fiscal crisis brought on by years of bad habits in Washington.

Now, the economic crisis required the Government to make immediate emergency investments that added to our accumulated debt, critical investments that have helped to break the back of the recession and lay the groundwork for growth and job creation. But now, with so many Americans still out of work, the task of recovery is far from complete. So in the short term, we're going to be taking steps to encourage business to create jobs. That will continue to be my top priority. Still there's no doubt that we're going to have to also address the long-term quandary of a Government that routinely and extravagantly spends more than it takes in. When I walked into the door of the White House, our Government was spending about 25 percent of GDP, but taking in only about 16 percent of GDP. Without action, the accumulated weight of that structural deficit, of ever-increasing debt, will hobble our economy, it will cloud our future, and it will saddle every child in America with an intolerable burden.

Now, this isn't news. Since the budget surpluses at the end of the 1990s, Federal debt has exploded. The trajectory is clear, and it is disturbing. But the politics of dealing with chronic deficits is fraught with hard choices, and therefore, it's treacherous to officeholders here in Washington. As a consequence, nobody's been too eager to deal with it.

That's where these two gentlemen come in. Alan Simpson and Erskine Bowles are taking on the impossible: They're going to try to restore reason to the fiscal debate and come up with answers as Cochairs of the new National Commission on Fiscal Responsibility and Reform. I'm asking them to produce clear recommendations on how to cover the costs of all Federal programs by 2015 and to meaningfully improve our long-term fiscal picture. I've every confidence that they'll do that because nobody's better qualified than these two.

Now, Alan Simpson is a flinty, Wyoming truthteller. [*Laughter*] If you look in the dictionary, it says "flinty," and then it's got Simpson's picture. [*Laughter*] Through nearly two decades in the United States Senate, he earned a reputation for putting common sense and the people's welfare ahead of petty politics. As the number-two Republican in the Senate, he made the tough choices necessary to close deficits and he played an important role in bipartisan deficit reduction agreements.

Erskine Bowles understands the importance of managing money responsibly in the public sector, where he ran the Small Business Administration and served as President Clinton's Chief of Staff. In that capacity, he brokered the 1997 budget agreement with Republicans that helped produce the first balanced budget in nearly 30 years.

One's a good Republican, the other a good Democrat, but above all, both are patriotic Americans who are answering their country's call to free our future from the stranglehold of debt.

The Commission they'll lead was structured in such a way as to rise above partisanship. There's going to be 18 members. In addition to the two Cochairs, four others will be appointed by me; six will be appointed by Republican leaders, six by Democratic leaders. Their recommendations will require the approval of 14 of the Commission's 18 members, and that ensures that any recommendation coming out of this effort and sent forward to Congress has to be bipartisan in nature.

This Commission is patterned on a bill that I supported for a binding commission that was proposed by Democratic Senator Kent Conrad and Republican Senator Judd Gregg. Their proposal failed recently in the Senate. But I hope congressional leaders in both parties can step away from the partisan bickering and join this effort to serve the national interest.

Now, as important as this Commission is, our fiscal challenge is too great to be solved with any one step alone, and we can't wait to act. And that's why last week, I signed into law the PAYGO bill—says very simply that the United States of America should pay as we go and live within our means again, just like responsible families and businesses do. This law is what helped get deficits under control in the 1990s and produced surpluses by the end of the decade. It was suspended in the last decade, and during that period, we saw deficits explode again. By reinstituting it, we're taking an important step towards addressing the deficit problem in this decade and in decades to come.

That's also why, after taking steps to cut taxes and increase access to credit for small businesses to jump-start job creation this year, I've called for a 3-year freeze on discretionary spending starting next year. This freeze won't affect Medicare, Medicaid, or Social Security spending, and it won't affect national security spending, including veterans' benefits, but all other discretionary spending will be subject to this freeze.

These are tough times, and we can't keep spending like they're not. And that's why we're seeking to reform our health insurance system, because if we don't, soaring health care costs will eventually become the single largest driver of our Federal deficits. Reform legislation in the House and the Senate would bring down deficits, and I'm looking forward to meeting with members of both parties and both Chambers next week to try to get this done.

And that's also why this year, we're proposing a responsible budget that cuts what we don't need to pay for what we do. We've proposed budget reductions and terminations that would yield about $20 billion in savings. We're ending loopholes and tax giveaways for oil and gas companies and for the wealthiest 2 percent of Americans. So taken together, these and other steps would provide more than $1 trillion in deficit reduction over the coming decade. That's more savings than any administration's budget in the past 10 years.

I know the issue of deficits has stirred debate. And there's some on the left who believe that this issue can be deferred. There are some on the right who won't enter into serious discussions about deficits without preconditions. But those who preach fiscal discipline have to be willing to take the hard steps necessary to achieve it. And those who believe Government has a responsibility to meet these urgent challenges have a great stake in bringing our deficits under control, because if we don't, we won't be able to meet our most basic obligations to one another.

So America's fiscal problems won't be solved overnight. They've been growing for years. They're going to take time to wind down. But with the Commission that I'm establishing today and the other steps we're pursuing, I believe we are finally putting America on the path towards fiscal reform and fiscal responsibility.

And I want to again thank Alan and Erskine for taking on what is a difficult and, perhaps, thankless task. I'm grateful to them for their willingness to sacrifice their time and their energy in this cause. I know that they're going to take up their work with a sense of integrity and a sense of commitment that America's people deserve and America's future demands.

And I think part of the reason they're going to be effective is, although one's a strong Democrat and one's a strong Republican, these are examples of people who put country first. And they know how to disagree without being disagreeable, and there's a sense of civility and a sense that there are moments where you set politics aside to do what's right.

That's the kind of spirit that we need. And I am confident that the product that they put forward is going to be honest, it's going to be clear, it's going to give a path to both parties in terms of how we have to address these challenges.

All right. Thank you very much. Come on, let's sign this thing. . . .

SOURCE: U.S. Executive Office of the President. "Remarks on Signing an Executive Order Establishing the National Commission on Fiscal Responsibility and Reform and an Exchange With Reporters." February 18, 2010. *Daily Compilation of Presidential Documents* 2010, no. 00103 (February 18, 2010). http://www.gpo.gov/fdsys/pkg/DCPD-201000103/pdf/DCPD-201000103.pdf.

Executive Order Establishing the National Commission on Fiscal Responsibility and Reform

DOCUMENT

February 18, 2010

By the authority vested in me as President by the Constitution and the laws of the United States of America, it is hereby ordered as follows:

Section 1. Establishment. There is established within the Executive Office of the President the National Commission on Fiscal Responsibility and Reform (Commission).

Sec. 2. Membership. The Commission shall be composed of 18 members who shall be selected as follows:

(a) six members appointed by the President, not more than four of whom shall be from the same political party;

(b) three members selected by the Majority Leader of the Senate, all of whom shall be current Members of the Senate;

(c) three members selected by the Speaker of the House of Representatives, all of whom shall be current Members of the House of Representatives;

(d) three members selected by the Minority Leader of the Senate, all of whom shall be current Members of the Senate; and

(e) three members selected by the Minority Leader of the House of Representatives, all of whom shall be current Members of the House of Representatives.

Sec. 3. Co-Chairs. From among his appointees, the President shall designate two members, who shall not be of the same political party, to serve as Co-Chairs of the Commission.

Sec. 4. Mission. The Commission is charged with identifying policies to improve the fiscal situation in the medium term and to achieve fiscal sustainability over the long run. Specifically, the Commission shall propose recommendations designed to balance the budget, excluding interest payments on the debt, by 2015. This result is projected to stabilize the debt-to-GDP ratio at an acceptable level once the economy recovers. The magnitude and timing of the policy measures necessary to achieve this goal are subject to considerable uncertainty and will depend on the evolution of the economy. In addition, the Commission shall propose recommendations that meaningfully improve the long-run fiscal outlook, including changes to address the growth of entitlement spending and the gap between the projected revenues and expenditures of the Federal Government.

Sec. 5. Reports.

(a) No later than December 1, 2010, the Commission shall vote on the approval of a final report containing a set of recommendations to achieve the mission set forth in section 4 of this order.

(b) The issuance of a final report of the Commission shall require the approval of not less than 14 of the 18 members of the Commission.

Sec. 6. Administration.

(a) Members of the Commission shall serve without any additional compensation, but shall be allowed travel expenses, including per diem in lieu of subsistence, as authorized by law for persons serving intermittently in Government service (5 U.S.C. 5701–5707), consistent with the availability of funds.

(b) The Commission shall have a staff headed by an Executive Director.

Sec. 7. General.

(a) The Commission shall terminate 30 days after submitting its final report.

(b) Nothing in this order shall be construed to impair or otherwise affect:

(i) authority granted by law to an executive department, agency, or the head thereof; or

(ii) functions of the Director of the Office of Management and Budget relating to budgetary, administrative, or legislative proposals.

(c) This order is not intended to, and does not, create any right or benefit, substantive or procedural, enforceable at law or in equity by any party against the United States, its departments, agencies, or entities, its officers, employees, or agents, or any other person.

BARACK OBAMA
The White House,
February 18, 2010.

SOURCE: U.S. Executive Office of the President. "Executive Order 13531—National Commission on Fiscal Responsibility and Reform." February 18, 2010. *Daily Compilation of Presidential Documents* 2010, no. 00 104 (February 18, 2010). http://www.gpo.gov/fdsys/pkg/DCPD-201000104/pdf/DCPD-201000104.pdf.

Report of the National Commission on Fiscal Responsibility and Reform

December 1, 2010

[The table of contents, tables and figures, and footnotes have been omitted.]

PREAMBLE

Throughout our nation's history, Americans have found the courage to do right by our children's future. Deep down, every American knows we face a moment of truth once again. We cannot play games or put off hard choices any longer. Without regard to party, we have a patriotic duty to keep the promise of America to give our children and grandchildren a better life.

Our challenge is clear and inescapable: America cannot be great if we go broke. Our businesses will not be able to grow and create jobs, and our workers will not be able to compete successfully for the jobs of the future without a plan to get this crushing debt burden off our backs.

Ever since the economic downturn, families across the country have huddled around kitchen tables, making tough choices about what they hold most dear and what they can learn to live without. They expect and deserve their leaders to do the same. The American people are counting on us to put politics aside, pull together not pull apart, and agree on a plan to live within our means and make America strong for the long haul.

As members of the National Commission on Fiscal Responsibility and Reform, we spent the past eight months studying the same cold, hard facts. Together, we have reached these unavoidable conclusions: The problem is real. The solution will be painful. There is no easy way out. Everything must be on the table. And Washington <u>must</u> lead. . . .

The President and the leaders of both parties in both chambers of Congress asked us to address the nation's fiscal challenges in this decade and beyond. We have worked to offer an aggressive, fair, balanced, and bipartisan proposal – a proposal as serious as the problems we face. None of us likes every element of our plan, and each of us had to tolerate provisions we previously or presently oppose in order to reach a principled compromise. We were willing to put our differences aside to forge a plan because our nation will certainly be lost without one.

We do not pretend to have all the answers. We offer our plan as the starting point for a serious national conversation in which every citizen has an interest and all should have a say. Our leaders have a responsibility to level with Americans about the choices we face, and to enlist the ingenuity and determination of the American people in rising to the challenge.

We believe neither party can fix this problem on its own, and both parties have a responsibility to do their part. The American people are a long way ahead of the political system in recognizing that now is the time to act. We believe that far from penalizing their leaders for making the tough choices, Americans will punish politicians for backing down – and well they should. . . .

After all the talk about debt and deficits, it is long past time for America's leaders to put up or shut up. The era of debt denial is over, and there can be no turning back. We sign our names to this plan because we love our children, our grandchildren, and our country too much not to act while we still have the chance to secure a better future for all our fellow citizens.

[Discussion on the mission of the commission has been omitted.]

OVERVIEW

We propose a six-part plan to put our nation back on a path to fiscal health, promote economic growth, and protect the most vulnerable among us. Taken as a whole, the plan will:

- Achieve nearly $4 trillion in deficit reduction through 2020, more than any effort in the nation's history.
- Reduce the deficit to 2.3% of GDP by 2015 (2.4% excluding Social Security reform), exceeding President's goal of primary balance (about 3% of GDP).[2]
- Sharply reduce tax rates, abolish the AMT, and cut backdoor spending in the tax code.
- Cap revenue at 21% of GDP and get spending below 22% and eventually to 21%.
- Ensure lasting Social Security solvency, prevent the projected 22% cuts to come in 2037, reduce elderly poverty, and distribute the burden fairly.
- Stabilize debt by 2014 and reduce debt to 60% of GDP by 2023 and 40% by 2035.

The plan has six major components:

1) Discretionary Spending Cuts: Enact tough discretionary spending caps to force budget discipline in Congress. Include enforcement mechanisms to give the limits real teeth. Make significant cuts in both security and non-security spending by cutting low-priority programs and streamlining government operations. Offer over $50 billion in immediate cuts to lead by example, and provide $200 billion in illustrative 2015 savings.

2) Comprehensive Tax Reform: Sharply reduce rates, broaden the base, simplify the tax code, and reduce the deficit by reducing the many "tax expenditures"—another name for spending through the tax code. Reform corporate taxes to make America more competitive, and cap revenue to avoid excessive taxation.

3) Health Care Cost Containment: Replace the phantom savings from scheduled Medicare reimbursement cuts that will never materialize and from a new long-term care program that is unsustainable with real, common-sense reforms to physician payments, cost-sharing, malpractice law, prescription drug costs, government-subsidized medical education, and other sources. Institute additional long-term measures to bring down spending growth.

4) Mandatory Savings: Cut agriculture subsidies and modernize military and civil service retirement systems, while reforming student loan programs and putting the Pension Benefit Guarantee Corporation on a sustainable path.

5) Social Security Reforms to Ensure Long-Term Solvency and Reduce Poverty: Ensure sustainable solvency for the next 75 years while reducing poverty among seniors. Reform Social Security for its own sake, and not for deficit reduction.

6) Process Changes: Reform the budget process to ensure the debt remains on a stable path, spending stays under control, inflation is measured accurately, and taxpayer dollars go where they belong. . . .

[The recommendations on how to achieve these goals have been omitted.]

SOURCE: National Commission on Fiscal Responsibility and Reform. "The Moment of Truth: Report of the National Commission on Fiscal Responsibility and Reform." December 1, 2010. http://www.fiscal commission.gov/sites/fiscalcommission.gov/files/documents/TheMomentofTruth12_1_2010.pdf.

OTHER HISTORIC DOCUMENTS OF INTEREST

FROM THIS VOLUME

- State of the Union Address and Republican Response, p. 33

Federal Hiring Incentives Bill Signed

FEBRUARY 22 AND 24, AND MARCH 18, 2010

In an effort to spark continued economic recovery, on March 18, 2010, President Barack Obama signed the Hiring Incentives to Restore Employment (HIRE) Act of 2010, commonly referred to as the "jobs bill." At the time of the bill's signing, the United States was facing a nearly 10 percent unemployment rate with approximately fourteen million Americans looking for, but unable to find, stable employment. The HIRE Act would provide incentives for employers to begin hiring more unemployed individuals and would also provide a tax break for businesses investing in new equipment. Also in the bill was $20 billion for mass transit and other transportation projects and an extension of the Build America Bonds program. Both the Obama administration and congressional leaders were quick to remind Americans that this was just one of many steps being taken to spur economic recovery.

In February, the president signed a debt-limit bill into law that focused on the idea of pay-as-you-go (paygo) principles. Paygo was used in the early 1990s as a way for the federal government to create balanced budgets and surpluses. By signing a new paygo bill into law, the president said that Congress would have to pay for anything it funded without increasing the deficit. Because of the large spending increase called for in the HIRE Act, Republicans were highly critical of the bill, saying it was a violation of new paygo regulations.

OBAMA'S PUSH FOR A LEGISLATIVE VICTORY

President Obama's proposal for a bill to spur more hiring in the private sector put Democrats in the hot seat. The president's party had suffered a series of embarrassing congressional losses in the midterm elections, and Democratic leaders were determined to show that they could pass this piece of legislation. In January, the president visited Ohio, a state with an unemployment rate higher than the national average that had seen its fair share of job loss from the closure of car manufacturing plants. He reminded Ohioans that even though his administration had worked to bail out Wall Street and car companies, everything he does is for the American public. "This is not about me," Obama told the crowd. "This is about you. . . . I think that I win when you win."

During his speech, the president called on Congress to include tax breaks for small businesses that increase hiring and for those who are working to make their own homes more energy efficient. It had been the president's goal to fit these two points into the House's $174 billion stimulus package passed in December 2009, but he failed to win approval from Congress to ensure their inclusion and passage.

In January, President Obama made an official call for a jobs bill. "People are out of work," he said during his State of the Union address. "They are hurting. They need our help. And I want a jobs bill on my desk without delay." He proposed that the jobs bill include tax breaks for small businesses and tax credits for new hiring and equipment purchases.

HOUSE AND SENATE DEBATE

The Senate's version of the bill contained two main provisions. First, businesses that hired previously unemployed Americans would be able to forgo paying the 6.2 percent Social Security tax through December 2010 for eligible employees. If the employer retained the new employee for one year, the employer would receive a $1,000 tax credit. The second provision of the bill added $20 billion to highway and mass transit projects to encourage hiring and additional labor at a time when revenue from the gas tax, which typically funds infrastructure projects, was lower than expected.

Much of the debate in the Senate was focused on the funding for infrastructure projects. In her floor statement, Sen. Barbara Boxer, D-Calif., read and discussed letters she had received from major transportation associations and some states that were afraid of being able to maintain safe roads, bridges, and public transportation without additional funding to make up for lost gas tax revenue. "Clearly, the two infrastructure pieces in the Reid bill are essential in both saving jobs and creating new jobs. Investments in infrastructure are a crucial component of job creation in our Nation. As we work our way out of this recession, the last thing we want to do is create uncertainty about our transportation funding. Too many people are counting on it," Boxer said.

Republicans criticized the Democrats for proposing a bill that, while it could spur job creation, made a mockery of the recent paygo legislation. In his floor statement, Sen. Judd Gregg, R-N.H., said "I don't think we get people back to work in this nation by loading more and more debt onto the next generation," he said. Gregg claimed the jobs bill would add billions in debt to the federal books.

Before the measure was brought to a final vote, senators had to vote to end debate on the bill and bring it to the floor. In this first vote, five Republicans broke with their party and voted in its favor. By supporting the closure of debate, Sens. George Voinovich, R-Ohio, Olympia Snowe, R-Maine, Susan Collins, R-Maine, Kit Bond, R-Mo., and Scott Brown, R-Mass., helped avoid a filibuster of the bill. Sen. Brown, the newest member of the Senate after winning a surprise victory in a special election to fill the late senator Ted Kennedy's vacant seat, said he knew the bill was not perfect but hoped that it would be a stepping stone in getting America back on the right track. "I hope my vote today is a strong step toward restoring bipartisanship in Washington," he said. The Senate's version of the bill was expected to cost $35 billion and passed in February, 70 to 28. The final vote in the Senate was 68-29. Thirteen Republicans voted in favor of passage of the bill. Sen. Ben Nelson, D-Neb., was the only Democrat to vote against the bill.

In December 2009, the House had passed a version of the bill that was far more expensive than what the Senate passed in February 2010. When the Senate passed its version and sent it back to the House, House leaders criticized it as not going far enough to ensure additional economic recovery because it focused more on tax cuts than on investment and spending.

During final passage, the House voted 217 to 201, with six Republicans voting in favor of the bill. The House version included a stipulation regarding paygo. The additional measure meant that the bill had to go back to the Senate for another approval before being sent to the president. When the bill went back to the Senate, it passed 68 to 29 on March 17. President Obama signed the bill on March 18, 2010. Upon signing the bill, the president congratulated members of Congress for working together. "I want to commend all the Members of Congress, and their leadership is what made this bill possible. Many of them are here today. I'm also gratified that over a dozen Republicans agreed that the need for this jobs bill was urgent, and that they were willing to break out of the partisan morass to help us take this forward step for the American people. I hope this is a prelude to further cooperation in the days and months to come, as we continue to work on digging our way out of the recession and rebuilding our economy in a way that works for all Americans and not just some Americans."

Provisions and Benefits of the New Law

The major provisions in the law are aimed at lowering the unemployment rate by spurring hiring in the private sector. First, employers who hired new employees between February 3, 2010, and January 1, 2011, may be eligible for a payroll tax credit. To be eligible for the credit, the new hire must have been unemployed during the sixty days prior to being hired or working fewer than forty hours per week under another employer. The payroll tax credit means that employers did not have to pay the 6.2 percent Social Security payroll tax for the new hires through the end of 2010. Should the employer choose to keep the employee for a minimum of one year, after that year, the employer can receive a $1,000 tax break. Not all employees meeting the above two criteria are credit eligible, however. Ineligible hires include those earning more than $106,000 per year or a new hire who took a job away from a current employee, unless the current employee was fired or left on his or her own accord.

The HIRE Act was expected to create as many as 250,000 new jobs. While this makes only a small dent in the 8.4 million jobs lost since the recession began in late 2007, according to Treasury Secretary Tim Geithner, it is vital to ensuring economic recovery. "This is one of a series of critical measures to get more Americans back to work and strengthen economic growth," he said after the Senate passed its version of the bill in February.

It will still take time, however, to see whether the new law will have an impact. It is possible that some businesses opted to hire new employees sooner than they would have without an incentive, but others might have chosen to hold back and wait for a stronger economic plan or a bigger indication of recovery. "This is just the first, certainly not the last, piece of legislation that we will put forward in relation to jobs," said HIRE Act sponsor Sen. Charles Schumer, D-N.Y., a sentiment President Obama echoed when signing the bill. As promised, Democrats introduced additional pieces of legislation in 2010 to continue job growth and creation, though few came to a floor vote or were passed.

—Heather Kerrigan

Following is a statement delivered on the Senate floor by Sen. Barbara Boxer, D-Calif., on February 22, 2010, in support of the HIRE Act; a statement delivered on the Senate floor by Sen. Judd Gregg, R-N.H., on February 24, 2010, in opposition to the HIRE Act; and a statement delivered by President Barack Obama upon signing the HIRE Act on March 18, 2010.

Sen. Boxer, D-Calif., in Support of the HIRE Act

February 22, 2010

Mr. President, we all went home over this recess—most of us did—and we heard very clear messages. At least I can tell you I did. The messages are: Address the problems that face us and reach out a hand across the aisle and do it together. Pretty simple.

Today we have a chance to do that. Today we have a very clear chance to do that and to lift the spirits of the American people. The bill we will be voting on—actually we are voting to take it up, in essence; we need 60 votes to do that, unfortunately, because there is a filibuster again on this—is a very simple, straightforward jobs bill. . . .

[Among other comments, the text of a letter from the American Association of State Highway and Transportation Officials, the American Road and Transportation Builders Association, the Associated General Contractors of America, the U.S. Chamber of Commerce, the Laborers International Union, and the International Union of Operating Engineers has been omitted.]

Today, we have a chance to have a fresh start by voting for cloture—in other words, ending a filibuster—on this package of four bills, two tax breaks for businesses and two very important investments in our infrastructure. . . .

If we fail to pass an extension, period, we would lose 1 million jobs in this great Nation.

So there are two scenarios. One is if we fail to extend the program, this is what will happen. The States will lose jobs immediately. If we don't authorize this program, we will lose 1 million jobs. Without the transfer, this highway trust fund will not have any funds by the summer. Some people say June. Some people say August. I ask my colleagues who may be watching this debate: Please consider what it will be like when you have your contractors come and tell you they have had to stop a project in midstream—a highway, a bike path, a freeway, fixing a bridge that is perhaps in danger of collapsing.

So I will tell my colleagues I don't think we have a choice. . . .

[An estimate of job loss without an extension of the highway trust fund has been omitted.]

Mr. President, this is a pretty straightforward vote for us today. In essence, everything in this jobs bill is bipartisan. Everything in it is bipartisan. I can tell my colleagues right now that my Republican colleagues tell me they want to reauthorize this highway trust fund through the end of the year. They want to make sure the trust fund has the dollars it needs. Well, then, what is the reason why one might not vote to end the filibuster? . . .

Frankly, I don't know how anyone could face their constituents in a time of unemployment that we are seeing now. Even though we have certainly gone from bleeding—600,000 jobs a month, 700,000 jobs a month—to very few in comparison, we have a long way to go. Building the infrastructure of this Nation is done by the private sector. We hear the Republicans on the other side say: Well, we want this to be built by the private sector. That is how this program works. . . .

[Letters from the Missouri Department of Transportation, the American Highway Users Association, and a group of cement, asphalt, rock, and concrete associations have been omitted]

So we have an opportunity today to send the clearest of messages that we are ready to come together around a simple premise; that is, the transportation infrastructure of this Nation is not a political whipping boy. There is no time to play politics here—no time. We have one State already saying: Beware. We are putting off our contracting. What more do we need to see than that? This is just the beginning of what is going to happen. We know the Build America Bonds program, which will allow State and local governments to borrow at lower costs, is going to put people to work. Our treasurer, California treasurer Bill Lockyer, said Build America Bonds have enabled the State—our State—to sell more than $19 billion in general obligation funds to meet voter-approved mandates for more than 7,000 vital infrastructure projects, in turn creating or sustaining more than 100,000 solid, middle-class, private sector jobs and businesses, large and small, in California.

The Build America Bonds program is something our local people want, whether they are in California or anywhere else in the Nation. This program can cover bonds for school construction, clean energy, and all the rest. It will allow us to put people to work, and the decisions will not be made here but in our cities, our counties, and our States.

Clearly, the two infrastructure pieces in the Reid bill are essential in both saving jobs and creating new jobs. Investments in infrastructure are a crucial component of job creation in our Nation. As we work our way out of this recession, the last thing we want to do is create uncertainty about our transportation funding. Too many people are counting on it. . . .

SOURCE: Sen. Barbara Boxer. "Health Care and the Jobs Bill." *Congressional Record* 2010, 156 pt. S604-S607. http://www.gpo.gov/fdsys/pkg/CREC-2010-02-22/pdf/CREC-2010-02-22-pt1-PgS604.pdf.

Sen. Gregg, R-N.H., in Opposition to the HIRE Act

DOCUMENT

February 24, 2010

Mr. President, I believe the first obligation of a government—or one of the obligations, especially of Congress—is to live by its own words and live by its own rules. With great fanfare a couple weeks ago, the Democratic leadership and its membership passed a pay-go piece of legislation which says that when you bring spending legislation to the floor, it should be paid for. There was great breast-beating on the other side of the aisle about how this would discipline the government and make us fiscally responsible.

Now we see, as the first piece of legislation to come forward since the pay-go resolution passed, a bill which violates that pay-go resolution. This bill spends $12 billion that is not paid for under the pay-go rules over the next 5 years. It is in violation of the concepts and the rules which were put forward by the other side as the way we would discipline spending.

I understand—and I think most of us understand—the issue of the economy is critical, getting people back to work is critical, but I don't think we get people back to work by loading more and more debt onto the next generation. Probably we create an atmosphere where folks who are willing to go out and invest and create jobs are a little reticent to do so because they don't know how all that debt the Federal Government is putting on the books will be paid for. I presume that is one of the reasons the pay-go legislation was brought forward a couple of weeks ago, to try to give some certainty to the markets and to the American people who were upset with all the deficit and debt, that we would discipline ourselves.

Now the first bill that comes forward violates the rules of the Senate by adding $12 billion of spending which is not paid for, which will be deficit spending, and which will be added to the debt. I am not sure how you vote for this bill when it violates that rule which you just voted for 2 weeks ago. It seems a bit of inconsistency that is hard even for a political institution to justify.

On top of that, this bill has massive gamesmanship in the outyears. It is a bill of $15 to $18 billion in spending, but actually, because of the games played in the highway accounts, it adds $140 billion of spending that is not paid for which will be added to the debt if this bill is passed. That is a hard number. That is a big number. That is a real number.

The simple fact is, this bill, in the classic gamesmanship we see from the highway committee, spends money we don't have and then claims we have the money. In the end, all that money has to be borrowed because there are no revenues to cover it.

If this bill is passed, there will be $140 billion in new debt put on our kids' backs as a result of this alleged small number. . .

What they are claiming is that the highway fund, on which they have committed to spend much more money than is coming in, and they knew they would spend more money than was coming in because they wanted to spend more money than was coming in, what they are claiming is that highway fund lent the general fund money 10 years ago and that money should have had interest paid on it. Of course, at the time, they actually waived the interest, assuming interest should have been paid on that. That interest has been recouped a couple of times now, allegedly, even if it were owed. But what they claim is that because the money is coming out of the general fund to fund the highway fund, they are calling that an offset so it won't score. . . .

Our children already have a fair amount of debt coming at them as a result of this Congress's profligacy. Under the President's budget, the deficit will double in the next 5 years and triple in the next 10 years. We will add $11 trillion of new debt to the backs of our children over the next 10 years under the President's initiatives, every year for the next 10 years. We will average deficits of $1 trillion.

The American people intuitively understand that cannot continue; it can't keep up. We are on an unsustainable course. We are running this Nation into a ditch on the fiscal side of the ledger. We are putting this Nation into financial bankruptcy because of the fact that we are running up deficits and debt far beyond our capacity to repay. In fact, if you look at these deficits and debt just in the context of what other industrialized nations do—for example, the European Union—they don't allow their states to exceed deficits of 3 percent or a public debt to GDP ratio of 60 percent. The way this works out, we are going to run deficits of about 5 percent every year for the next 10 years, we will have a public debt situation of well over 60 percent next year, and we will get to 80 percent before the next 10 years are up. Those are numbers which lead to one conclusion—that we are in deep trouble. We are in deep, deep trouble. Yet we come here today with a bill which aggravates that situation relative to the pay-go rules by $12 billion and relative to the highway fund by $140 billion. . . .

What we have before us today is a bill which, first, violates the pay-go rules which we just passed a couple of weeks ago to the tune of $12 billion and, second, puts in place a glidepath, which should be called a nosedive, toward $140 billion of new debt being put on the backs of our children, with the alleged justification that it is offset when, in fact, the offset is superficial, Pyrrhic, and nonexistent. . . .

We can not keep doing this. We cannot keep doing this to our children. We cannot keep coming out here and claiming we are being fiscally disciplined when we are doing just the opposite: spending money we don't have and passing the bill on to our kids.

SOURCE: Sen. Judd Gregg. "Commerce, Justice, Science, and Related Agencies Appropriations Act, 2010." *Congressional Record* 2010, 156, p. S719. http://www.gpo.gov/fdsys/pkg/CREC-2010-02-24/pdf/CREC-2010-02-24-pt1-PgS718-2.pdf.

DOCUMENT

President Obama's Remarks on Signing the HIRE Act

March 18, 2010

. . . In a few moments, I'll sign what's called the HIRE Act, a jobs bill that will encourage businesses to hire and help put Americans back to work. And I'd like to say a few words about what this jobs bill will mean for workers, for businesses, and for America's economic recovery.

There are a number of ways to look at an economic recovery. Through the eyes of an economist, you look at the different stages of recovery. You look at whether an economy has begun to grow, at whether businesses have begun to hire temporary workers or increase the hours of existing workers. You look at whether businesses, small and large, have begun to hire full-time employees again.

That's how economists measure a recovery, and by those measures, we are beginning to move in the right direction. But through the eyes of most Americans, recovery is about something more fundamental: Do I have a decent job? Can I provide for my family? Do I feel a sense of financial security?

The great recession that we've just gone through took a terrible toll on the middle class and on our economy as a whole. For every 1 of the over 8 million people who lost their jobs in recent years, there's a story of struggle, of a family that's forced to choose between paying their electricity bill or the car insurance or the daughter's college tuition, of weddings and vacations and retirements that have been postponed.

So here's the good news: A consensus is forming that partly because of the necessary, and often unpopular, measures we took over the past year, our economy is now growing again, and we may soon be adding jobs instead of losing them. The jobs bill I'm signing today is intended to help accelerate that process.

I'm signing it mindful that, as I've said before, the solution to our economic problems will not come from Government alone. Government can't create all the jobs we need nor can it repair all the damage that's been done by this recession.

But what we can do is promote a strong, dynamic private sector, the true engine of job creation in our economy. We can help to provide an impetus for America's businesses to start hiring again. We can nurture the conditions that allow companies to succeed and to grow.

And that's exactly what this jobs bill will help us do. Now, make no mistake, while this jobs bill is absolutely necessary, it's by no means enough. There's a lot more that we're going to need to do to spur hiring in the private sector and bring about full economic recovery, from helping creditworthy small businesses to get loans that they need to expand, to offering incentives to make homes and businesses more energy efficient, to investing in infrastructure so we can put Americans to work doing the work that America needs done.

Nevertheless, this jobs bill will make a difference in several important ways. First, we will forgive payroll taxes for businesses that hire someone who's been out of work at least 2 months. That's a tax benefit that will apply to unemployed workers hired between last month and the end of this year. So this tax cut says to employers, if you hire a worker who's unemployed, you won't have to pay payroll taxes on that worker for the rest of the year. And businesses that move quickly to hire today will get a bigger tax credit than businesses that wait until later this year.

This tax cut will be particularly helpful to small-business owners. Many of them are on the fence right now about whether to bring in that extra worker or two, or whether they should hire anyone at all. And this jobs bill should help make their decision that much easier. And by the way, I'd like to note that part of what health insurance reform would do is to provide tax credits for over 4 million small businesses so they don't have to choose between hiring workers and offering coverage.

The second thing this bill does is to encourage small businesses to grow and to hire by permitting them to write off investments they make in equipment this year. These kinds of expenses typically take years to depreciate, but under this law, businesses will be able to invest up to $250,000, let's say, in a piece of factory equipment, and write it off right away. Put simply, we'll give businesses an incentive to invest in their own future, and to do it today.

Third, we'll reform municipal bonds to encourage job creation by expanding investment in schools and clean energy projects. Say a town wants to put people to work rebuilding a crumbling elementary school or putting up wind turbines. With this law, we'll make it easier for them to raise the money they need to do what they want to do by using a model that we've called Build America Bonds, one of the most successful programs in the Recovery Act. We'll give Americans a better chance to invest in the future of their communities and of the country.

And finally, this jobs bill will maintain crucial investments in our roads and our bridges as we head into the spring and summer months, when construction jobs are picking up.

I want to commend all the Members of Congress, and their leadership is what made this bill possible. Many of them are here today. I'm also gratified that over a dozen Republicans agreed that the need for this jobs bill was urgent, and that they were willing to break out of the partisan morass to help us take this forward step for the American people. I hope this is a prelude to further cooperation in the days and months to come, as we continue to work on digging our way out of the recession and rebuilding our economy in a way that works for all Americans and not just some Americans. . . .

SOURCE: U.S. Executive Office of the President. "Remarks on Signing the Hiring Incentives to Restore Employment Act." March 18, 2010. *Daily Compilation of Presidential Documents* 2010, no. 00185 (March 18, 2010). http://www.gpo.gov/fdsys/pkg/DCPD-201000185/pdf/DCPD-201000185.pdf.

OTHER HISTORIC DOCUMENTS OF INTEREST

FROM THIS VOLUME

FROM PREVIOUS *HISTORIC DOCUMENTS*

March

Iraq Parliamentary Elections

MARCH 7 AND 8, 2010

On March 7, 2010, Iraqis went to the polls to vote for their new members of parliament. The nation last held parliamentary elections in December 2005, and the 2010 election was considered to be another step toward stable democracy. Whichever bloc won the largest number of seats would be given the chance to choose the prime minister and form a new government. This new government would be in charge of working with the United States as it removed the remaining combat troops from Iraq.

Iraqis voted in large numbers. Although some violence was reported and Islamic extremists attempted to keep Sunnis away from the polls, voters were not deterred. When the votes were counted, Prime Minister Nuri Kamal al-Maliki's State of Law coalition lost by a small margin to the secular Iraqiya Party, which was led by former interim prime minister Ayad Allawi. Maliki immediately challenged the outcome, ushering in a period of political uncertainty in the nation that could have bred violence and change plans for American troop withdrawal. The United States, however, maintained its withdrawal plan. In November, the parties reached a tentative agreement for a coalition government, to be led by Maliki, leading to Allawi walking out of parliament.

ELECTION RESULTS

As was the case in the 2005 elections, the only one held since the U.S. invasion in 2003, the 2010 parliamentary vote was split along regional and ethnic lines, reflecting the divide between Iraq's religious sects. The continued divide indicates that political stability remains elusive. Maliki was most popular in Baghdad and six Shiite provinces. Provinces with a Sunni-dominated population supported Allawi, though his popularity was attributed to voters tired of the nation being controlled by religious parties.

On election day, Western nations watched Kirkuk closely, where Allawi and the Kurdish Alliance gained seats. This region of Iraq contains billions of barrels of oil and is a hotbed of unrest as anyone who controls the region has a lot to gain from oil and political struggles. The Kurds want the region to be incorporated into Kurdistan, while the Arabs want it to remain a part of Iraq. Accusations of fraud were strong in this area. Western observers warned that whichever party ultimately won control of Iraq's government must proceed cautiously in this area to avoid further conflict.

In the end, Allawi's party proved more popular than Maliki's for various reasons, one being its secular nature. Iraq has long been split by religious factions, and many voters wanted a coalition focused on governing that was based on the needs and wants of

Iraqi people rather than on religious decree. Allawi was also seen as a stronger leader than Maliki, one who would not be as sympathetic to American interests in the region.

Though victorious, Allawi's win was not enough to allow his party to form the new government. The Iraqiya Party won ninety-one seats, while Maliki's party won eighty-nine seats. In order to form a new government in Iraq, the winning party must control at least 163 of the 325 parliamentary seats. This left Allawi in a position in which he would need to form a coalition government. In his former position as interim prime minister, Allawi had been considered a leader who would bend to American interests, which would make forming a governing coalition difficult and would most likely require Maliki's support. After the election, Allawi began softening his stance toward Maliki's government, stating, "We will not exclude anyone. Our coalition is open to all." Allawi would also need to win the favor of the Kurds and the Iraqi National Alliance, a largely Shiite party.

Because of his party's victory, even though it was by a small margin, Allawi was given thirty days to form a governing coalition. Failure to do so would mean that Maliki would be given the chance to form a coalition and would most likely remain prime minister.

CALL FOR A RECOUNT

When the votes were counted, Maliki accused the winning party of voter fraud. Those in his coalition, State of Law, and others in the nation also joined in the call for a recount. "No way we will accept the results," Maliki stated after the election. "These are preliminary results." Maliki demanded that the Independent High Electoral Commission begin a recount. He further asserted that he remained commander in chief during a recount. Without a recount and without a clear party in charge, Maliki claimed, Iraq could "return to violence." Though Maliki indicated he might use force to ensure a recount, he later said he would pursue peaceful, legal means to ensure a proper vote recount.

The Electoral Commission refused Maliki's calls for a recount. It said that there was no indication of widespread fraud and that it had investigated numerous fraud claims. What cases of fraud the commission did find were deemed to not have any major impact on the election results.

The United Nations (UN) and other election observers said they saw no reason to suspect widespread fraud in the election and, therefore, no reason for a recount. "We have not found evidence of systematic failure or fraud of widespread nature," said Ad Melkert, the UN's top representative in Iraq. Melkert asked the Iraqi public to accept the results of the election to ensure the peaceful development of a new government. "The UN calls on all candidates and parties to unite in accepting the results. This will set an example for a culture of democracy that requires commitment beyond elections. The UN also calls on all those newly elected to move resolutely to seat parliament and form the new government so that political, economic and social progress is not delayed."

REACTION IN IRAQ AND THE UNITED STATES

The United States had a strong stake in the election outcome, as President Barack Obama had made it a campaign promise to withdraw all troops from Iraq by mid-2011, with all of the combat troops leaving in 2010. The drawdown plan that the president agreed to and the generals in Iraq helped implement was dependent on stability in the Middle Eastern nation. The parliamentary election had the greatest possibility to change the timetable for troop withdrawal.

The U.S. ambassador to Iraq, Christopher Hill, released a joint statement on the election with General Ray Odierno, America's top military commander in Iraq. Together they called upon the people of Iraq and the newly elected members of parliament to "refrain from inflammatory rhetoric or action." President Obama called for patience on the part of Iraqis as the votes were counted and a new government was formed. "Today's voting makes it clear that the future of Iraq belongs to the people of Iraq," said the president, as he celebrated the seemingly peaceful elections.

In Iraq, the election was another reminder of the deep religious differences that still divide the country. Reaction in the streets ranged from citizens who cheered to citizens who stocked up on groceries because they feared a potential violent backlash against the new government.

The parliamentary campaigns, which began in mid-February, sparked excessive violence that targeted civilian areas and Iraqi government installations. When Election Day arrived, there was fear that another round of violence would break out. Al Qaeda's threat of election sabotage led the governments and independent organizations overseeing the elections to put two hundred thousand security forces on the streets in Baghdad, with thousands more spread around the country. In the end, thirty-eight Iraqis were killed on Election Day.

Forming a New Government

Allawi was given thirty days to form a governing coalition after his party was declared the winner of the largest number of seats in Iraq's parliament. Maliki, however, was not going to make this task easy for his opponent. Maliki undertook many methods to stall Allawi's work, including his call for a vote recount.

Because his party had not won the largest number of seats in parliament, Maliki was designated the prime minister caretaker, a position that is considered more of a ceremonial position than one for actual policy making. Maliki, however, did not see it this way. He signed trade agreements and continued to threaten those who did not accept his power with the reminder that he controlled Iraq's military forces.

Allawi's effort at forming a government was also curbed by the support Maliki received from the United States and Iran. Pressure from Iran convinced the Shiite parties to accept that Maliki would be prime minister of any coalition government that was formed. The Shiite parties had previously stated that they would accept an alliance with Maliki's State of Law coalition but would not accept him as leader. Seeking to curb any violence that might ensue, the United States pressured Allawi into accepting Maliki's leadership, which in turn brought the Iraqiya Party to the table to form a coalition government.

November Compromise

On November 11, all parties reached a compromise for a coalition government. The coalition formed by the compromise would be headed by Maliki. Allawi's failure to form a coalition government of his own, which could have led to his appointment as prime minister, had opened the door for Maliki to remain in power. The coalition government, agreed to by Maliki, Allawi and Kurdistan president Masoud Barzani, included representation of all major parties and ethnic groups.

The agreement was thought to set new standards for Iraq's government. For example, the nation's constitution gives an outline of general practices that the government should follow, but these were not legally binding and had no real way to be enforced. The agreement meant that the positions in the coalition government would be apportioned to the largest population groups to ensure fair, democratic leadership. Though no positions changed parties, the agreement laid out which group was entitled to hold which position in future elections—Shiites would control the prime minister's seat, Kurds would hold the presidency, and the Sunnis would receive the post of speaker of the Council of Representatives, Iraq's parliament. The seats were not equal in power. The president's position was mostly ceremonial, and the speaker can only be powerful if the council is able to work together to put pressure on the prime minister.

The agreement was not legally binding, meaning that Maliki and other party leaders would have to be fair about the positions. The loose agreement, however, was hard to maintain in a deeply divided nation with a strong prime minister.

Iraq's parliament met and elected the speaker and president after the agreement was signed. As planned, the president of the Council of Representatives called on Maliki to form the new government. Allawi's Iraqiya Party walked out of the session, stating that the November 11 agreement had been violated. While his party returned, Allawi did not rejoin the parliamentary session until late November. Maliki was given until late December 2010 to form his cabinet, a process that was expected to be difficult. On December 21, after weeks of negotiation and calls for Maliki to give up some of his military power, Iraq's parliament approved the new government. The new cabinet, which will be overseen by Maliki, consists of forty-two members, with each major party represented. Maliki and his new cabinet will be closely watched through the coming months as they attempt to stabilize their fledgling democracy while the United States continues to draw down troops.

—Heather Kerrigan

Following are two statements by the United Nations on the elections in Iraq, released on March 7 and 8, 2010; and a statement by President Barack Obama congratulating the Iraqi people on a successful parliamentary election on March 7, 2010.

DOCUMENT   *United Nations Supports Iraqi Elections*

March 7, 2010

On March 7, Iraqis will vote for 325 members of the Council of Representatives, the nation's parliament, from 18 governorate constituencies, the third election conducted since 2003.

In preparation for the elections, UNDP is providing support for the Out of Country Voting (OCV) programme of the Iraqi election commission Operation. The out-of-country voting will take place in 16 countries - Syria, Jordan, UK, Sweden, Germany, UAE, Australia, Lebanon, Iran, USA, Austria, Canada, Egypt, Netherlands, Denmark and Turkey. Iraqi High Electoral Commission (IHEC) Country Office Managers and UN technical advisors have been deployed to support the preparation and implementation of this operation. The OCV is to be treated the same as in-country, with votes counted against the governorate from which a voter originates.

Under the umbrella of the United Nations Assistance Mission in Iraq (UNAMI) Elections Assistance Team, UNDP has provided specialized technical assistance for the 2010 elections, including assistance to IHEC for drafting the standard operations for polling, which comprises measures to prevent, detect and address irregularities.

In addition, UNDP, together with UNOPS, has created a post-elections, long term programme to build the institutional capacity of IHEC developing the managerial skills, organisational know-how and strategic planning abilities. This will enable IHEC to become a leading independent institution with the appropriate institutional policies, personnel, and knowledge base, fulfilling the aspirations of the people of Iraq to live in a democratic society.

After decades of one-party rule, the first Council of Representatives was elected in the 2005 elections, marred by boycotts by some important political groups. This weakened the representation of all constituencies in the Council of Representatives; nevertheless the lawmaking body has emerged as a viable locus for national debate, in keeping with its constitutional mandate.

The January 2009 Provincial Council elections marked a turning point in Iraq's democratic process, notable for the broad participation of political groups, as well as the remarkable level of citizen security experienced immediately before, during and after the polling.

The 2005 and 2009 elections were conducted by the IHEC with substantial assistance from the international community. For these votes, UNDP, as part of the UNAMI–led Electoral Assistance Team, assisted Iraq's Independent High Electoral Commission through a range of projects, including the provision of technical assistance and support for fair, safe and professional media coverage.

The 2009 elections were noted for the innovative public outreach campaigns launched by IHEC using new media tools, such as the IHEC website, blogs, SMS, and YouTube, as well as traditional radio, TV and print media.

International assistance has been scaled back as the IHEC has continued to develop its own capacities, and the 2010 elections will be a milestone for IHEC, as it demonstrates its capacities as an independent, specialized elections institution.

The March 7, 2010, election represents the next major step in the political course of Iraq's nascent democracy. The electoral process has already registered some success in the operational readiness of IHEC. The final story will be defined by increased participation of all constituencies, the ability of IHEC to resolve disputes fairly and professionally, and the enhanced credibility that the Iraqi people will have developed in elections as a democratic tool for the citizens to elect their representatives for the next four years.

FACTS AND FIGURES ABOUT THE ELECTIONS

- Iraq is divided into 18 electoral constituencies based on governorates. Each governorate represents one electoral constituency.
- The Council of Representatives will be composed of 325 seats, up from the 275 seats in the 2005 Election. 6,529 candidates were nominated by 86 political entities. All candidates are under an obligatory vetting process with reference to their educational background, affiliation with the outlawed Ba'ath party, or criminal convictions.
- Approximately 18.9 million voters have registered to vote. The IHEC will establish around 10,000 polling centers throughout Iraq. Each center consists of one or more polling stations, totaling over 50,000. Each polling station is expected to serve up to 420 voters.

- To increase the participation of eligible voters, special polling centres have been identified to accommodate Internally Displaced People (IDPs) who have registered with the IHEC to vote for the governorate from which they have been displaced.
- In support of the Out of Country Voting programme that will take place in 16 countries, IHEC Country Office Managers have been deployed to these countries, to support the preparation and implementation of this operation.
- A Voter Registration Update was conducted in August and September 2009 to give voters the opportunity to check/correct details on the Voter List. More than 574,000 voters requested services and over 935,000 visited voter registration centers for these purposes.
- An estimated 300,000 political agents and national observers are expected to participate in the election.

SOURCE: United Nations. Assistance Mission for Iraq. "UNDP Supports Iraqis in Electing Their Future Government." March 7, 2010. http://www.uniraq.org/newsroom/getarticle.asp?ArticleID=1284.

President Obama Remarks on Iraq's Parliamentary Elections

March 7, 2010

Good afternoon, everybody. Today the people of Iraq went to the polls to choose their leaders in Iraq's second national election. By any measure, this was an important milestone in Iraqi history. Dozens of parties and coalitions fielded thousands of parliamentary candidates, men and women. Ballots were cast at some 50,000 voting booths. And in a strong turnout, millions of Iraqis exercised their right to vote with enthusiasm and optimism.

Today's voting makes it clear that the future of Iraq belongs to the people of Iraq. The election was organized and administered by Iraq's Independent High Electoral Commission, with critical support from the United Nations. Hundreds of thousands of Iraqis served as poll station workers and as observers.

As expected, there were some incidents of violence as Al Qaida in Iraq and other extremists tried to disrupt Iraq's progress by murdering innocent Iraqis who were exercising their democratic rights. But overall, the level of security and the prevention of destabilizing attacks speaks to the growing capability and professionalism of Iraqi security forces, which took the lead in providing protection at the polls.

I also want to express my admiration for the thousands of Americans on the ground in Iraq, for our civilians and our men and women in uniform who continue to support our Iraqi partners. This election's also a tribute to all who have served and sacrificed in Iraq over the last 7 years, including many who have given their lives.

We are mindful, however, that today's voting is the beginning and not the end of a long electoral and constitutional process. The ballots must be counted. Complaints must be heard, and Iraq, with the support of the United Nations, has a process in place to investigate and adjudicate any allegations of fraud. A parliament must be seated, leaders must be chosen, and a new Government must be formed. All of these important steps will take time—not weeks, but months.

In this process, the United States does not support particular candidates or coalitions. We support the right of the Iraqi people to choose their own leaders. And I commend the Iraqi Government for putting plans into place to ensure security and basic services for the Iraqi people during this time of transition.

We know that there will be very difficult days ahead in Iraq; there will probably be more violence. But like any sovereign, independent nation, Iraq must be free to chart its own course. No one should seek to influence, exploit, or disrupt this period of transition. Now's the time for every neighbor and nation to respect Iraq's sovereignty and territorial integrity.

A new Iraqi Government will face important decisions about Iraq's future. But as today's voting demonstrates, the Iraq people want disagreements to be debated and decided through a political process that provides security and prosperity for all Iraqis.

And as they go forward, the Iraqi people must know that the United States will fulfill its obligations. We will continue with the responsible removal of United States forces from Iraq. Indeed, for the first time in years, there are no—now fewer than 100,000 American troops serving in Iraq. By the end of August, our combat mission will end. As I said last year when I announced our new strategy in Iraq, we will continue to advise and assist Iraqi security forces, carry out targeted counterterrorism operations with our Iraqi partners, and protect our forces and civilians. And by the end of next year, all U.S. troops will be out of Iraq.

In the weeks and months ahead, the United States will continue to work closely with the Iraqi people as we expand our broad-based partnership based on mutual interest and mutual respect. And in that effort, I'm pleased that Vice President Biden will continue to play a leading role.

On behalf of the American people, I congratulate the Iraqi people on their courage throughout this historic election. Today, in the face of violence from those who would only destroy, Iraqis took a step forward in the hard work of building up their country. And the United States will continue to help them in that effort as we responsibly end this war and support the Iraqi people as they take control of their future.

Thanks very much.

SOURCE: U.S. Executive Office of the President. "Remarks on the Parliamentary Elections in Iraq." March 7, 2010. *Daily Compilation of Presidential Documents* 2010, no. 00153 (March 7, 2010). http://www.gpo.gov/fdsys/pkg/DCPD-201000153/pdf/DCPD-201000153.pdf.

UN Special Representative in Iraq
Remarks on Parliamentary Elections

March 8, 2010

I congratulate the more than 12 million Iraqis who went to the polls, some braving insecurity, to cast their ballots for a better future, marking the historic character of election day. This turnout was beyond the expectations of many. I commend the IHEC Board of Commissioners and the more than 300,000 Iraqis engaged by IHEC, for their efforts to conduct elections in a well organized and professional fashion. UNAMI is proud to have supported their work.

I congratulate the Iraqi Security forces, who were solely responsible for all security on election-day for safeguarding the electoral process, despite efforts by some to deter Iraqis from voting. There can be no doubt that the Iraqi people stand together in their wish that reason prevails over confrontation and violence.

UNAMI visited polling centers in Anbar, Ninewa, Kirkuk, Erbil, Najaf, Sulaimania, Salahadin, Diyala, Basra, Dohuk and Baghdad. We were pleased with the conduct of the vote and the evident enthusiasm for the elections among the different Iraqi communities. I join Iraqi and international leaders in the call for patience and restraint as the results are counted and tabulated. I also encourage political agents and observers to continue to monitor the process, and to direct any complaints to the IHEC in accordance with the law. Only IHEC can announce the official results of these elections, which will be certified by the Federal Supreme Court.

The most crucial moment will arrive when the results are announced. The UN calls on all candidates and parties to unite in accepting the results. This will set an example for a culture of democracy that requires commitment beyond elections. The UN also calls on all those newly elected to move resolutely to seat parliament and form the new government so that political, economic and social progress is not delayed.

SOURCE: United Nations. Assistance Mission for Iraq. "Statement from the Special Representative of the Secretary General for Iraq (SRSG), Ad Melkert, on the National Iraqi Elections." March 8, 2010. http://www.uniraq.org/newsroom/getarticle.asp?ArticleID=1286.

OTHER HISTORIC DOCUMENTS OF INTEREST

FROM THIS VOLUME

FROM PREVIOUS HISTORIC DOCUMENTS

Health Care Reform Signed into Law

MARCH 21 AND 23, 2010

In what was arguably the biggest legislative victory of his first two years in office, on March 23, 2010, President Barack Obama signed a landmark health care reform bill into law. By signing the bill, Obama guaranteed access to medical insurance for tens of millions of uninsured Americans and gave additional coverage guarantees to those already insured. As signed, the law is anticipated to cost $940 billion over the next decade and will be fully implemented by 2014.

Final passage of the health care reform bill, titled the Patient Protection and Affordable Care Act, came after nearly one year of debate and compromise between both congressional chambers and the White House. In the end, no Republicans voted in favor of the bill, sparking concern that implementation of the law would be a long and difficult process.

Republicans used health care reform as one of the cornerstones of the 2010 midterm congressional elections, promising to challenge the law through any means necessary and available. Some candidates even promised a complete repeal of the law. American conservatives rallied behind this idea in many states, led by the Tea Party, putting Republicans in control of the House and closing in on the Democratic majority in the Senate.

THE LONG FIGHT FOR HEALTH CARE REFORM

Obama was not the first president to call for health care reform, but he was the most successful. President Franklin D. Roosevelt attempted to include a national health insurance plan in the Social Security Act, but because of the Great Depression, another large financial undertaking by the government was not possible. Harry S. Truman proposed a similar program but failed to win support from Congress. His small victory, however, came through a presidential order stating that all Social Security recipients could receive sixty days of hospital care for free—a condition that is now a key component of Medicare and Medicaid.

Prior to 2009, the most recent, strong push for health reform came from President Bill Clinton. His ten months of work for reform ended with the Democratic Party's loss of both chambers of Congress in the 1994 midterm elections. Clinton's inability to successfully pass health care reform was largely caused by the insurance industry's unwillingness to sign onto the president's proposals.

The history of Democratic unsuccessful attempts at health care reform did not set an optimistic tone for Obama's push. However, as opposed to his predecessors, when the fight for reform began, the Democrats had a filibuster-proof majority in the Senate that would almost guarantee that even without Republican support a reform bill would pass. Any success, however, would be based on convincing the conservative wing of the Democratic Party of the importance of the bill.

In March 2009, Democratic leaders in the House and Senate agreed to major provisions they wanted to include in the bill. The measures at this stage included requiring all Americans to have health insurance, requiring employers to help pay for health insurance for their employees, and the offering of a public health insurance option that would compete with the private sector. The "public option" was the biggest point of contention between Democrats and Republicans, and even within the Democratic Party.

To ensure successful passage, and because of some disagreement within the party, the Democrats worked on different versions of legislation in 2009. In the House, Democrats completed a bill that included the public option, a tax on high-income earners, and penalties for companies that did not comply with the requirement to insure their employees. To get the more conservative members of the party on board, the House bill also included exemptions for some businesses that chose not to provide health care for their employees. In the Senate, Sen. Max Baucus, D-Mont., led the Health, Education, Labor, and Pensions (HELP) committee to a party-line agreement on a bill that did not include the public option. It was the opinion of Baucus that, because of its unpopularity with Republicans and some Democrats, any bill with a public option would never achieve passage.

When Congress returned to Washington after its summer recess, during which time Democratic legislators held townhall-style meetings on health care reform that in many cases turned into shouting matches, Baucus released his version of the health care reform bill in the Senate. The Baucus bill differed from other Democratic proposals in various ways. In addition to eliminating the public option, Baucus's bill included a provision that would tax insurance companies selling so-called "Cadillac plans." A Cadillac health insurance plan has an unusually high premium but often offers a low deductible and coverage for more expensive medical treatments. In addition, Baucus's bill did not require employers to provide coverage to their employees. Instead, any company employing more than fifty people that chose to not offer insurance would have to pay a fee to the government to help cover the cost of employees who bought their own health care plan.

The Baucus bill gained support from one Republican on the HELP committee—Sen. Olympia Snowe, R-Maine. With her support, the Baucus bill passed out of committee on October 13, 2009. In preparation to bring the legislation to the Senate floor, Senate majority leader Harry Reid, D-Nev., announced that he would add the public option back into the plan. Upon his announcement, Sen. Snowe declared that she would no longer support Baucus's bill.

HOUSE AND SENATE PASSAGE

The final bills that went to the floor in the House and Senate differed in a few critical ways. The Senate bill, unlike the House version, increased the Medicare payroll tax on those considered to be high-income earners. In addition, employers offering high-cost health care plans would be required to pay an excise tax. In the House bill, an amendment prohibited public option coverage of abortion, except in the case of rape, incest, or if the mother's life was in danger. The Senate version, in contrast to the House bill, did not impose strict penalties on employers who chose not to purchase health insurance plans for their employees.

In the House, Speaker Nancy Pelosi, D-Calif., made multiple concessions within her party to ensure swift passage. The final bill, House Democrats claimed, would provide health insurance coverage for thirty-six million Americans who were currently uninsured. The House bill retained the public option provision. In November 2009, the House passed its version of health care reform, 220 to 215.

As he had promised after the HELP committee passed its version of the bill, Sen. Reid inserted the public option back into the proposed Senate legislation before it went to the floor. Sen. Joe Lieberman, I-Conn., said he would not vote for the bill with the public option back in. The Democrats were reliant on both independent members of the Senate (Bernard Sanders of Vermont being the other) voting in favor of the bill. Reid conceded and dropped the provision. He had also added into the bill an opt-out clause, which would allow states to pass legislation banning the health care reform mandates from taking place in their states. This was a compromise for the Democrats in the Senate—the liberal members were able to maintain their desire for a national, rather than a state, health insurance plan, and conservative Democrats, and theoretically some Republicans, were happy because states maintained their Tenth Amendment rights.

The other hurdle to overcome before final passage was Sen. Ben Nelson, D-Neb. To get his vote, Senate Democrats dropped a provision from the bill thus allowing the insurance industry to keep its antitrust exemption, and added Medicaid funds specifically for Nebraska. In addition, the Senate version included a new abortion policy. Federal law currently prohibits federal funds from being used to pay for an abortion, meaning that women on Medicaid are unable to receive the procedure through the program. Some states offer women on Medicaid the ability to pay for an abortion out-of-pocket. The Senate's bill would allow women using the federal subsidy to purchase private health insurance through the exchange to choose plans that would cover abortion. However, anyone choosing this type of plan would have to pay for abortion coverage through a separate premium. In addition, states would be able to ban any plan on the exchange that covers abortion.

With Lieberman's and Nelson's votes, Democrats were ensured the filibuster-proof sixty votes needed to pass the bill. The Christmas Eve 2009 vote, which came after twenty-five days of debate on the bill, went along party lines 60 to 39.

RECONCILIATION AND A SUMMIT

In Washington, some lawmakers on Capitol Hill and those in the White House were skeptical that any significant health reform bill would reach the president's desk. With different bills passed in the two Houses of Congress, senators and representatives would need to agree to a compromise bill. Various proposals for ensuring passage were discussed, and after Scott Brown, a Republican from Massachusetts, won a special election to fill the late senator Ted Kennedy's seat, another successful vote in the Senate looked increasingly unlikely. House leaders said the easiest way to ensure passage would be for the House to approve the Senate's version of the bill, making a second Senate vote unnecessary. However, in January, the House announced that it was waiting for the Senate to take action before a decision was made.

With health care reform stalled in Congress, President Obama reminded legislators of the importance of the bill. During his first State of the Union address, the president called on legislators to work together to find a compromise. "Do not walk away from reform. Not now. Not when we are so close. Let's find a way to come together and finish the job for the American people," he said.

One month later, in a historic, seven-hour summit, Republican and Democratic congressional leaders met with President Obama to discuss the various health care reform proposals. Republicans criticized the Democrats, saying that they were trying to force through a bill that had not been fully vetted or debated, one that was not in line with what the American people wanted. By passing health care reform and increasing the number of insured Americans, they said, the United States would simply be putting itself in another entitlement hole that it could not afford. Democrats informed their counterparts that they planned to use a reconciliation bill to ensure passage. Though controversial, Democrats could pass health care with a simple majority vote in the Senate because rules do not allow for a filibuster of a reconciliation bill.

In the end, Democrats decided to pass the Senate version of the bill and an additional bill that would include some changes from the original House bill. Democrats felt they could pass the Senate's version of the bill in the House and now only needed to convince the Senate of the changes. However, it was not until the day of the vote for final passage that a majority in the House was ensured with a decision by Rep. Bart Stupak, D-Mich., to support the bill. His decision to vote in favor came from the president's promise to issue an executive order that would stop federal funds from being used for abortion. This time, the vote in the House came in at 219 to 212.

When the bill went back to the Senate, debate was heated. House minority leader John Boehner, R-Ohio, broke with floor procedure and was scolded by Rep. David Obey, D-Wis., the acting speaker, for his language. "Look at how this bill was written," said Boehner. "Can you say it was done openly, with transparency and accountability? Without backroom deals and struck behind closed doors hidden from the people? Hell, no, you can't."

House majority leader Steny Hoyer, D-Md., said in his floor statement, "American health care is on an unsustainable course. By the end of this debate, another family will have fallen into bankruptcy because someone had the bad fortune to become sick." But, he said, "We have before us a bill to change an unsustainable course."

After a long debate, the Senate passed the changes bill, 56 to 43. Changes in this bill included the removal of Sen. Nelson's Medicaid provision and an adjustment of the excise tax. The changes bill went back to the House for approval. The final House vote to approve health care reform was 220 to 207. President Obama signed the bill on March 23; he told the American people that "it was your work, your commitment, your unyielding hope that made this victory possible."

IMPLEMENTING THE NEW LAW

With unanimous disapproval from the Republicans, it was almost ensured that implementing the new law would be difficult. Immediately after the president signed the bill, twenty states banded together to file suit in federal court, seeking to block implementation of the law. The states filing suit, led by Florida, hope to not only stop implementation of the bill, but also to lessen the power of Congress to regulate interstate commerce.

The first of the health care reform provisions went into effect in September 2010 and included a ban on dropping sick or otherwise costly patients from coverage after finding technical mistakes on applications and also required health insurers to cover children on their parents' plan up to age twenty-six. Health insurers across the country were quick to fight the first rules, by threatening to find loopholes by moving out of some markets, refusing to sell various policies, or leaving the health insurance market.

The Obama administration, in an effort to keep the health insurance system afloat, had to make concessions to the health insurance companies. Nearly thirty insurers received one-year extensions on adhering to some of the new rules.

—Heather Kerrigan

Following is a statement delivered on the floor of the House of Representatives by Rep. Steny Hoyer, D-Md., in support of health care reform on March 21, 2010; a statement delivered on the floor of the House of Representatives by Rep. John Boehner, R-Ohio, in opposition to health care reform; and a statement by President Barack Obama, upon signing health care reform legislation into law on March 23, 2010.

Rep. Hoyer, D-Md., in Support of Health Care Reform

DOCUMENT

March 21, 2010

. . . Today, March 21, 2010, we will cross another bridge. It is not a physical bridge, but it is a bridge that too many Americans find that they cannot cross; a river that separates them from the security of having available the best health care that is available in the world available to them.

We are here to conclude a day of debate, which concludes months of debate, in a national conversation that began more than a century ago.

But this much is beyond debate. American health care is on an unsustainable course. By the end of this debate, another family will have fallen into bankruptcy because someone had the bad fortune simply to be sick. More families will have joined them in paying more and more for less and less health coverage. More businesses will have weighted bankruptcy against cutting their workers' care and their workers will have lost.

We have before us a bill to change an unsustainable course. That is our choice this evening. It is a historic choice. It's a choice that all of us volunteered to be put in the position to make. It is a choice that we will be honored to make this evening. We stood in this Chamber tonight with John Dingell, John Dingell, who stood at that rostrum with the gavel that the Speaker will use tonight to gavel through Medicare, that ensured that millions and millions and millions of seniors would not be crushed by poverty and put into bankruptcy by the cost of health care. . . .

But what a campaign of fear this bill has faced this last year. Its critics call it, without justification, and we will hear it tonight, a "government takeover." That's not true, but if you believe it's true, perhaps you think we ought to repeal veterans health care, which is clearly government-run health care. Perhaps we ought to repeal Medicare, government participated but private sector providers. Perhaps you believe Medicare should be repealed. I don't think you do; I hope you don't.

It is more control, however, for whom? For consumers, and less for insurance companies. It is the end of discrimination against Americans with preexisting conditions, and the end of medical bankruptcy and caps on benefits. It is coverage you can rely on whether you lose your job or become your own boss, coverage that reaches 95 percent of all Americans. Its critics call it tyranny. There is none.

It is a free, competitive, transparent marketplace where individuals and small businesses can pool together to buy private insurance at low rates. It is lower cost for the middle class and an end to the prescription drug doughnut hole that has faced too many struggling seniors. Its critics mock this as "out-of-control government."

In truth, it is the biggest definite-reduction bill any of us will have an opportunity to vote on in this Congress and, indeed, in other Congresses as well. Indeed, it's the deepest definite reduction since the Clinton budget of the 1990s that ushered in a budget surplus and historic prosperity. . . .

Yet there are some who hope for the bill's defeat. They would see that, I think, as the defeat of one party. One Senator made that observation and said this might be the President's Waterloo. If this bill fails, the Waterloo will be that of the people who are without health care insurance, the people who are struggling to make sure that their children are healthy and well and safe. But it would be a defeat for them and for our country, for a healthy America is a stronger America. . . .

. . . Ladies and gentlemen of this House, this bill, this bill will stand in the same company, for the misguided outrage of its opposition and for its lasting accomplishment of the American people. . .

SOURCE: Rep. Steny Hoyer. "Senate Amendments to H.R. 3590, Service Members Home Ownership Tax Act of 2009, and H.R. 4872, Health Care and Education Reconciliation Act of 2010." *Congressional Record* 2010, 156, pt. H1854-H1856. http://www.gpo.gov/fdsys/pkg/CREC-2010-03-21/pdf/CREC-2010-03-21-pt1-PgH1854-2.pdf.

Rep. Boehner, R-Ohio, in Opposition to Health Care Reform

March 21, 2010

Mr. Speaker and my colleagues, I rise tonight with a sad and heavy heart. Today we should be standing together reflecting on a year of bipartisanship and working to answer our country's call and their challenge to address the rising costs of health insurance in our country.

Today, this body, this institution, enshrined in the first article of the Constitution by our Founding Fathers as a sign of the importance they placed on this House, should be looking with pride on this legislation and our work.

But it is not so.

No, today we're standing here looking at a health care bill that no one in this body believes is satisfactory. Today we stand here amidst the wreckage of what was once the respect and honor that this House was held in by our fellow citizens. And we all know why it is so. We have failed to listen to America. And we have failed to reflect the will of our constituents. And when we fail to reflect that will, we fail ourselves, and we fail our country.

Look at this bill. Ask yourself, do you really believe that if you like the health plan that you have that you can keep it? No, you can't. You can't say that.

In this economy, with this unemployment, with our desperate need for jobs and economic growth, is this really the time to raise taxes, to create bureaucracies, and burden every job creator in our land? The answer is no.

Can you go home and tell your senior citizens that these cuts in Medicare will not limit their access to doctors or further weaken the program instead of strengthening it? No, you cannot.

Can you go home and tell your constituents with confidence that this bill respects the sanctity of all human life and that it won't allow for taxpayer funding of abortions for the first time in 30 years? No, you cannot.

And look at how this bill was written. Can you say it was done openly, with transparency and accountability? Without backroom deals and struck behind closed doors hidden from the people? Hell, no, you can't.

Have you read the bill? Have you read the reconciliation bill? Have you read the manager's amendment? Hell, no, you haven't. . .

Mr. Speaker, in a few minutes we will cast some of the most consequential votes that any of us will ever cast in this Chamber. The decision we make will affect every man, woman, and child in this Nation for generations to come. If we're going to vote to defy the will of the American people, then we ought to have the courage to stand before them and announce our votes, one at a time. . . .

When we came here, we each swore an oath to uphold and abide by the Constitution as representatives of the people. But the process here is broken. The institution is broken. And as a result, this bill is not what the American people need nor what our constituents want.

Americans are out there making sacrifices and struggling to make a better future for their kids, and over the last year as the damn-the-torpedoes outline of this legislation became more clear, millions of Americans lifted their voices and many, for the first time, asking us to slow down, not to try to cram through more than this system could handle, not to spend money that we didn't have. In this time of recession, they wanted us to focus on jobs, not more spending, not more government, and certainly not more taxes.

But what they see today frightens them. . . .

Shame on us. Shame on this body. Shame on each and every one of you who substitutes your will and your desires above those of your fellow countrymen.

Around this Chamber, looking upon us are the lawgivers from Moses, to Gaius, to Blackstone, to Thomas Jefferson. By our actions today, we disgrace their values. We break the ties of history in this Chamber. We break our trust with America. . . .

If we pass this bill, there will be no turning back. It will be the last straw for the American people. In a democracy, you can only ignore the will of the people for so long and get away with it. And if we defy the will of our fellow citizens and pass this bill, we're going to be held to account by those who have placed us in their trust. We will have shattered those bonds of trust.

I beg you, I beg each and every one of you on both sides of the aisle: Do not further strike at the heart of this country and this institution with arrogance, for surely you will not strike with impunity.

I ask each of you to vow to never let this happen again—this process, this defiance of our citizens. It's not too late to begin to restore the bonds of trust with our Nation and return comity to this institution.

And so join me. Join me in voting against this bill so that we can come together, together anew and addressing the challenge of health care in a manner that brings credit to this body and brings credit to the ideals of this Nation, and most importantly, that reflects the will of the American people.

SOURCE: Rep. John Boehner. "Senate Amendments to H.R. 3590, Service Members Home Ownership Tax Act of 2009, and H.R. 4872, Health Care and Education Reconciliation Act of 2010." *Congressional Record* 2010, 156, pt. H1895. http://www.gpo.gov/fdsys/pkg/CREC-2010-03-21/pdf/CREC-2010-03-21-PT2-PgH1891.pdf.

President Obama on Signing Health Care Reform into Law

March 23, 2010

. . . After a century of striving, after a year of debate, after a historic vote, health care reform is no longer an unmet promise, it is the law of the land. It is the law of the land.

And although it may be my signature that's affixed to the bottom of this bill, it was your work, your commitment, your unyielding hope that made this victory possible. When the special interests deployed an army of lobbyists, an onslaught of negative ads to preserve the status quo, you didn't give up. You hit the phones, and you took to the streets. You mobilized, and you organized. You turned up the pressure, and you kept up the fight.

When the pundits were obsessing over who was up and who was down, you never lost sight of what was right and what was wrong. You knew this wasn't about the fortunes of a party; this was about the future of our country. And when the opposition said this just wasn't the right time, you didn't want to wait another year or another decade or another generation for reform. You felt the fierce urgency of now.

You met the lies with truth. You met cynicism with conviction. Most of all, you met fear with a force that's a lot more powerful, and that is faith in America. You met it with hope.

Despite decades in which Washington failed to tackle our toughest challenges, despite the smallness of so much of what passes for politics these days, despite those who said that progress was impossible, you made people believe that people who love this country can still change it. So this victory is not mine; it is your victory. It's a victory for the United States of America.

For 2 years on the campaign trail, and for the past year as we've worked to reform our system of health insurance, it's been folks like you who have propelled this movement and kept us fixed on what was at stake in this fight. And rarely has a day gone by that I haven't heard from somebody personally—whether in a letter, or an e-mail, or at a town hall—who's reminded me of why it was so important that we not give up, who reminded me why we could not quit. . . .

Now, let me tell you what change looks like, because those fighting change are still out there, still making a lot of noise—[laughter]—about what this reform means. So I want the American people to understand it and look it up for yourself. Go on our web site, whitehouse.gov, or go to any credible news outlet's web site and look in terms of what reform will mean for you. [Laughter]

I said this once or twice, but it bears repeating: If you like your current insurance, you will keep your current insurance. No Government takeover; nobody is changing what you've got if you're happy with it. If you like your doctor, you will be able to keep your doctor. In fact, more people will keep their doctors because your coverage will be more secure and more stable than it was before I signed this legislation.

And now that this legislation is passed, you don't have to take my word for it. You'll be able to see it in your own lives. I heard one of the Republican leaders say this was going to be Armageddon. Well, 2 months from now, 6 months from now, you can check it out. We'll look around—[laugher]—and we'll see. You don't have to take my word for it. . . .

This year, insurance companies will no longer be able to drop people's coverage when they get sick, or place lifetime limits or restrictive annual limits on the amount of care they can receive. This year, all new insurance plans will be required to offer free preventive care. And this year, young adults will be able to stay on their parents' policies until they're 26 years old. That all happens this year.

This year, seniors who fall in the coverage gap known as the doughnut hole will get some help to help pay for prescription drugs. And I want seniors to know, despite what some have said, these reforms will not cut your guaranteed benefits. Let me repeat that: They will not cut your guaranteed benefits, period. I'd be wary of anybody who claimed otherwise.

So these are the reforms that take effect right away. These reforms won't give the Government more control over your health care. They certainly won't give the insurance companies more control over your health care. These reforms give you more control over your health care. And that's only the beginning.

That's only the beginning. After more than a decade, we finally renewed the Indian Health Care Improvement Act. And the other changes I'm signing into law will take several years to implement fully, but that's because this is a difficult, complex issue and we want to get it right. . . .

Now, for those of us who fought so hard for these reforms and believe in them so deeply, I have to remind you our job is not finished. We're going to have to see to it that these reforms are administered fairly and responsibly. And this includes rooting out waste and fraud and abuse in the system. That's how we'll extend the life of Medicare and bring down health care costs for families and businesses and governments. And in fact, it is through these reforms that we achieve the biggest reduction in our long-term deficits since the Balanced Budget Act of the 1990s.

So for all those folks out there who are talking about being fiscal hawks and didn't do much when they were in power, let's just remind them that according to the Congressional Budget Office, this represents over a trillion dollars of deficit reduction, but it's being done in a smart way.

And for those who've been suspicious of reform—and there are a lot of wonderful folks out there who, with all the noise, got concerned because of the misinformation that has marred this debate—I just repeat: Don't take my word for it. Go to our web site, whitehouse.gov; go to the web sites of major news outlets out there; find out how reform will affect you. And I'm confident that you will like what you see: a commonsense approach that maintains the private insurance system, but makes it work for everybody; makes it work not just for the insurance companies, but makes it work for you.

So that's what health reform is all about. Now, as long as a road that this has been, we all know our journey is far from over. There's still the work to do to rebuild this economy.

There's still work to do to spur on hiring. There's work to do to improve our schools and make sure every child has a decent education. There's still work to do to reduce our dependence on foreign oil. There's more work to do to provide greater economic security to a middle class that has been struggling for a decade.

So this victory does not erase the many serious challenges we face as a nation. Those challenges have been allowed to linger for years, even decades, and we're not going to solve them all overnight.

But as we tackle all these other challenges that we face, as we continue on this journey, we can take our next steps with new confidence, with a new wind at our backs. Because we know it's still possible to do big things in America. Because we know it's still possible to rise above the skepticism, to rise above the cynicism, to rise above the fear. Because we know it's still possible to fulfill our duty to one another and to future generations.

So, yes, this has been a difficult 2 years. There will be difficult days ahead. But let us always remember the lesson of this day and the lesson of history: That we, as a people, do not shrink from a challenge; we overcome it. We don't shrink from our responsibilities; we embrace it. We don't fear the future; we shape the future. That's what we do. That's who we are. That makes us the United States of America. . . .

SOURCE: U.S. Executive Office of the President. "Remarks on the Patient Protection and Affordable Care Act." March 23, 2010. *Daily Compilation of Presidential Documents* 2010, no. 00197 (March 23, 2010). http://www.gpo.gov/fdsys/pkg/DCPD-201000197/pdf/DCPD-201000197.pdf.

OTHER HISTORIC DOCUMENTS OF INTEREST

FROM THIS VOLUME

FROM PREVIOUS *HISTORIC DOCUMENTS*

South Korean Naval Vessel Sunk by Torpedo

MARCH 27 AND MAY 20, 2010

On March 26, 2010, tensions on the Korean peninsula were heightened when a torpedo sank the *Cheonan*, a South Korean naval vessel, in South Korea's territorial waters. Forty-six of the 104 sailors onboard were killed in the attack that took place near waters disputed by North and South Korea. Given the long-running tension between the two countries, Western media outlets quickly placed blame with North Korea's leader, Kim Jong Il. South Korea, however, was slower to place blame. It was not until May when South Korea's foreign minister, Yu Myung-kwan, called it "obvious" that the North Koreans were behind the attack. Officials in North Korea's capital city of Pyongyang, however, continued to deny involvement, even after stating before the attacks that the country was prepared to make "unpredictable strikes" against South Korea and the United States over a belief that the two nations were planning for possible political instability when power transferred from Kim to one of his children.

NORTH KOREAN INVOLVEMENT

South Korean president Lee Myung-bak called for patience while local and international investigators reviewed the case to decide who was at fault for the torpedo attack. "We should wait patiently, although it will be painful, as a joint investigation team from the government, military, and civilians is already looking into the case," he said. Lee asked that those involved in the investigation not make a "hasty conjecture or obscure prediction" in determining who was at fault for the attack.

In May, South Korea said it had evidence of North Korea's involvement. The smoking gun, it claimed, was a propeller that powered a torpedo that was found at the bottom of the ocean. According to a team of international investigators, the serial number font and technique was in a North Korean style. Yoon Duk-yong, who co-chaired the committee investigating the attack, said the "torpedoes that were exported from North Korea and the letters and the fonts on the torpedo are the same that are used by North Korea. This torpedo was manufactured in North Korea." Yoon said that a North Korean submarine "fired the torpedo that sunk the *Cheonan* vessel and retreated back to [its] border."

In response to the attacks and blame placed by the South, Kim called for a joint investigation by North and South Korea. He said this investigation would help "to verify objectively the truth of the incident." The North Korean National Defense Commission responded, "We had already warned the South Korean group of traitors not to make reckless remarks concerning the sinking of warship *Cheonan* of the puppet navy. Nevertheless, the group of traitors had far-fetchedly tried to link the case with us without offering any material evidence."

SOUTH KOREA'S LIMITED OPTIONS

The sinking of the *Cheonan* was not the first military engagement between the two nations. Twice during the past ten years, North and South Korea have engaged in naval battle. The last of these battles occurred in 2002 when six South Korean sailors were killed. These attacks were largely overlooked by the South Korean government in adherence to its "sunshine policy" toward North Korea. The sunshine policy, which ended after Lee's election in 2008, was built on cooperation between the North and South. The policy outlined an agreement in which the South stated that it did not want to incorporate the North and the North agreed that it would not take up arms to provoke the South in any way. The goal of the policy was not to unify the two governments, but rather to create a peaceful coexistence on the peninsula.

Lee's government, however, looked differently upon North Korean advances. Much of the South's confidence and new way of dealing with the North derived from its now stronger economy and military and its powerful allies.

Regardless of whether the North was at fault for the attack, South Korea's government was faced with limited options. Any sanctions or retaliation would have to be carefully weighed against a number of factors. One of the major issues impacting any response by the South is its close economic ties with its Northern neighbor. Kaesong, the special economic zone located in North Korea, contains more than one hundred South Korean companies that employ forty thousand North Koreans. These companies, many of which are textile-producing factories, use the inexpensive North Korean labor to compete with Chinese imports.

South Korea's response would also need to take regional issues into consideration, including the possible involvement of China. Although China is viewed as an ally of North Korea, if the Chinese government cut ties with the North under pressure from the United States or Japan, it would cripple North Korea, which is dependent upon external trade to and oil shipments from China.

While the world waited for South Korea's response, Lee told Australian prime minister Kevin Rudd that he was interested in ensuring that pressure was put on the North by a variety of international partners. "We will take resolute countermeasures against North Korea and make it admit its wrongdoings through strong international cooperation and return to the international community as a responsible member," Lee said. In the end, South Korea chose to suspend trade with North Korea and began anew its propaganda broadcasts into North Korea that spoke against Kim's government.

UNITED NATIONS RESPONSE

In addition to ending its trade ties with North Korea, the South also asked the United Nations to review the situation and enforce new sanctions against North Korea. After reviewing the *Cheonan* sinking and the response by North Korea, the United Nations elected not to issue additional sanctions. Instead, the international body did not directly blame North Korea, but rather expressed "deep concern" about the situation. In a unanimous vote, the UN Security Council called for "appropriate and peaceful measures to be taken against those responsible." The council's statement also took note of North Korea's claim that it was not responsible.

The United Nations further called on North and South Korea to adhere to the Korean Armistice Agreement. Though still technically at war to this day, in 1953 the two countries agreed to a ceasefire. The ceasefire agreement did not end the war; it simply split the country along the thirty-eighth parallel, now known as the demilitarized zone (DMZ). The DMZ is still patrolled by North and South Korean troops, and occasionally the two sides trade fire.

Representatives from Western nations said that Chinese opposition caused the decision not to issue new sanctions. The Western representatives said China, a permanent member of the Security Council, feared retaliation by its often unstable North Korean ally.

Whether sanctions would have had an impact on North Korea is unknown. Earlier financial and trade sanctions had been placed on the country by the United Nations because of its nuclear tests in 2006 and 2009. Without regard to the stiff sanctions, the North continued to build and test nuclear weapons.

DAMAGE TO THE SIX-PARTY TALKS

In its response, the United States was forced to choose whether it wanted to condemn North Korea and risk the end of the six-party nuclear talks involving North and South Korea, China, Japan, and Russia, or work to uphold the negotiations. Possible sanctions the United States considered included cutting off North Korea's access to U.S. financial institutions or putting the nation back on the U.S. list of state sponsors of terrorism after it was removed in 2008. Analysts said that financial sanctions would send the strongest message to Pyongyang, but they could risk another North Korean nuclear test.

U.S. president Barack Obama spoke with South Korean president Lee shortly before the announcement about the torpedo propeller and pledged to support South Korea in imposing stronger sanctions against the North. "This act of aggression is one more instance of North Korea's unacceptable behavior and defiance of international law," said Obama's press secretary, Robert Gibbs. "This attack constitutes a challenge to international peace and security and is a violation of the Armistice Agreement." Obama made it clear to Lee that the United States would support South Korea in its defense against the North. "North Korea must understand that belligerence towards its neighbors and defiance of the international community are signs of weakness, not strength. Such unacceptable behavior only deepens North Korea's isolation. It reinforces the resolve of its neighbors to intensify their cooperation to safeguard peace and stability in the region against all provocations," said Gibbs.

The United States would need to wait for an ultimate decision on military action from South Korea as it is bound to assist South Korea through a mutual defense treaty, of which Japan is also a party. The treaty says the nations will defend "against any aggression" if a military situation were to arise in one of the nations.

ADDITIONAL TENSIONS

During the summer and fall of 2010, the relationship between North and South Korea looked as though it was beginning to improve. The North Korean government said it would resume allowing families split by the border to reunite and also called for new military talks. In a gesture of goodwill, the South responded by sending rice to areas of North

Korea that were hit by heavy flooding. Prior to the Yeonpyeong incident, North Korea's government requested permission to come to South Korea to talk about military issues on the peninsula.

The goodwill fell apart, however, on November 23, with a North Korean artillery attack at Yeonpyeong Island, just off South Korea's coast. The South Korean military had been on the island preparing for its annual offensive drill training. North Korea called the drills an act of aggression and attacked the island. South Korea returned fire. Two South Korean soldiers and two civilians were killed in the attacks on Yeonpyeong, and there is no information available on injuries or casualties on the North Korean side.

There is no clear indication of why the North fired on the South. Some international analysts suggested that the island's proximity to the Yellow Sea border, which is disputed by the two nations, prompted the action. Others said that Kim was using the military exercise to strengthen the power of both the nation and his son, Kim Jong-un, who had recently been named as Kim's successor.

The attack fueled renewed tensions between the two Koreas. North Korea claimed that the attack and continuing drills, which included the U.S. Navy, had brought the continent to the "brink of war."

—Heather Kerrigan

Following is a press release from South Korea regarding the sinking of the naval ship Cheonan, *issued on March 27, 2010; a statement by South Korea's defense commission on May 20, 2010, announcing the results of the investigation into the* Cheonan's *sinking; and a statement by North Korea's government on May 20, 2010, responding to South Korea's investigation.*

South Korean Statement on the Sinking of the Cheonan

DOCUMENT

March 27, 2010

President Lee Myung-bak is presiding over a national security-related ministers meeting that began at 7:30 a.m.

The President instructed the Armed Forces authorities to do all they can to rescue as many survivors as possible. At the same time, he said that the authorities concerned should find out what exactly transpired in the incident in a speedy and thorough manner, considering all possibilities.

There were no reports made at the meeting indicating that North Korea is behaving abnormally in connection with the incident.

The President also said, "The Government should notify families of the victims in detail and faithfully about the incident. It also has to explain the situation to the member countries of the Six-Party Talks in Beijing. The Government should accurately inform the ruling and opposition parties about the development of the incident as well."

The President told the participating cabinet members to "take every measure so that the citizens will not be overly worried about the incident."

Throughout the meeting, President Lee expressed sorrow and anguish over the missing of the 46 crew members and the agony of their families. The meeting is still continuing at the moment. I will try to brief the media organizations often even while the meeting is going on so that they will be fully informed about the situation.

SOURCE: Korean Culture and Information Service. Government News. "Briefing by Cheong Wa Dae Regarding Sinking of South Korean Navy Ship." March 27, 2010. http://www.korea.net/news.do?mode= detail&thiscode=eng030001&guid=45180.

Results of the South Korean Investigation into the Cheonan *Sinking*

May 20, 2010

The Joint Civilian-Military Investigation Group (JIG) conducted its investigation with 25 experts from 10 top Korean expert agencies, 22 military experts, 3 experts recommended by the National Assembly, and 24 foreign experts constituting 4 support teams from the United States, Australia, the United Kingdom and the Kingdom of Sweden. The JIG is composed of four teams—Scientific Investigation Team, Explosive Analysis Team, Ship Structure Management Team, and Intelligence Analysis Team.

In our statement today, we will provide the results attained by Korean and foreign experts through an investigation and validation process undertaken with a scientific and objective approach.

The results obtained through an investigation and analysis of the deformation of the hull recovered from the seabed and evidence collected from the site of the incident are as follows:

The JIG assesses that a strong underwater explosion generated by the detonation of a homing torpedo below and to the left of the gas turbine room caused Republic of Korea Ship(ROKS) "Cheonan" to split apart and sink.

The basis of our assessment that the sinking was caused by a torpedo attack is as follows:

Precise measurement and analysis of the damaged part of the hull indicates that a shockwave and bubble effect caused significant upward bending of the CVK (Center Vertical Keel), compared to its original state, and shell plate was steeply bent, with some parts of the ship fragmented.

On the main deck, fracture occurred around the large openings used for maintenance of equipment in the gas turbine room and significant upward deformation is present on the port side. Also, the bulkhead of the gas turbine room was significantly damaged and deformed.

The bottoms of the stern and bow sections at the failure point were bent upward. This also proves that an underwater explosion took place.

Through a thorough investigation of the inside and outside of the ship, we have found evidence of extreme pressure on the fin stabilizer, a mechanism to reduce significant rolling of the ship; water pressure and bubble effects on the bottom of the hull; and wires cut with no traces of heat. All these point to a strong shockwave and bubble effect causing the splitting and the sinking of the ship.

We have analyzed statements by survivors from the incident and a sentry on Baekryong-do.

The survivors made a statement that they heard a near-simultaneous explosion once or twice, and that water splashed on the face of a port-side lookout who fell from the impact; furthermore, sentry on the shore of Baekryong-do stated that he witnessed an approximately 100-meter-high "pillar of white flash" for 2~3 seconds. The aforementioned phenomenon is consistent with damage resulting from a shockwave and bubble effect.

Regarding the medical examination on the deceased service members, no trace of fragmentation or burn injury were found, but fractures and lacerations were observed. All of these are consistent with damage resulting from a shockwave and bubble effect.

The seismic and infrasound wave analysis result conducted by the Korea Institute of Geoscience and Mineral Resources (KIGAM) is as follows:

Seismic wave intensity of 1.5 degrees was detected by 4 stations.

2 infrasound waves with a 1.1-second interval were detected by 11 stations.

The seismic and infrasound waves originated from an identical site of explosion.

This phenomenon corresponds to a shock wave and bubble effect generated by an underwater explosion.

Numerous simulations of an underwater explosion show that a detonation with a net explosive weight of 200~300kg occurred at a depth of about 6~9m, approximately 3m left of the center of the gas turbine room.

Based on the analysis of tidal currents off Baekryong-do, the JIG determined that the currents would not prohibit a torpedo attack.

As for conclusive evidence that can corroborate the use of a torpedo, we have collected propulsion parts, including propulsion motor with propellers and a steering section from the site of the sinking.

The evidence matched in size and shape with the specifications on the drawing presented in introductory materials provided to foreign countries by North Korea for export purposes. The marking in Hangeul, which reads "1번 (or No. 1 in English)", found inside the end of the propulsion section, is consistent with the marking of a previously obtained North Korean torpedo. The above evidence allowed the JIG to confirm that the recovered parts were made in North Korea.

Also, the aforementioned result confirmed that other possible causes for sinking raised, including grounding, fatigue failure, mines, collision and internal explosion, played no part in the incident.

In conclusion,

The following sums up the opinions of Korean and foreign experts on the conclusive evidence collected from the incident site; hull deformation; statements of relevant personnel; medical examination of the deceased service members; analysis on seismic and infrasound waves; simulation of underwater explosion; and analysis on currents off Baekryong-do and collected torpedo parts.

ROKS "Cheonan" was split apart and sunk due to a shockwave and bubble effect produced by an underwater torpedo explosion.

The explosion occurred approximately 3m left of the center of the gas turbine room, at a depth of about 6~9m.

The weapon system used is confirmed to be a high explosive torpedo with a net explosive weight of about 250kg, manufactured by North Korea.

In addition, the findings of the Multinational Combined Intelligence Task Force, comprised of 5 states including the US, Australia, Canada and the UK and operating since May 4th, are as follows:

The North Korean military is in possession of a fleet of about 70 submarines, comprised of approximately 20 Romeo class submarines (1,800 tons), 40 Sango class submarines (300 tons) and 10 midget submarines including the Yeono class (130 tons).

It also possesses torpedoes of various capabilities including straight running, acoustic and wake homing torpedoes with a net explosive weight of about 200 to 300kg, which can deliver the same level of damage that was delivered to the ROKS "Cheonan."

Given the aforementioned findings combined with the operational environment in the vicinity of the site of the incident, we assess that a small submarine is an underwater weapon system that operates in these operational environment conditions. We confirmed that a few small submarines and a mother ship supporting them left a North Korean naval base in the West Sea 2-3 days prior to the attack and returned to port 2-3 days after the attack.

Furthermore, we confirmed that all submarines from neighboring countries were either in or near their respective home bases at the time of the incident.

The torpedo parts recovered at the site of the explosion by a dredging ship on May 15th, which include the 5x5 bladed contra-rotating propellers, propulsion motor and a steering section, perfectly match the schematics of the CHT-02D torpedo included in introductory brochures provided to foreign countries by North Korea for export purposes. The markings in Hangeul, which reads "1 번 (or No. 1 in English)", found inside the end of the propulsion section, is consistent with the marking of a previously obtained North Korean torpedo. Russian and Chinese torpedoes are marked in their respective languages.

The CHT-02D torpedo manufactured by North Korea utilizes acoustic/wake homing and passive acoustic tracking methods. It is a heavyweight torpedo with a diameter of 21 inches, a weight of 1.7 tons and a net explosive weight of up to 250kg.

Based on all such relevant facts and classified analysis, we have reached the clear conclusion that ROKS "Cheonan" was sunk as the result of an external underwater explosion caused by a torpedo made in North Korea. The evidence points overwhelmingly to the conclusion that the torpedo was fired by a North Korean submarine. There is no other plausible explanation.

THU. 20 MAY, 2010
The Joint Civilian-Military
Investigation Group

SOURCE: South Korean Ministry of National Defense. "Investigation result on the sinking of ROKS 'Cheonan.'" May 20, 2010. http://www.korea.net/news.do?mode=detail&thiscode=eng030001&guid=46843.

North Korea Disputes South Korea's Cheonan *Investigation Findings*

May 20, 2010

The south Korean conservative group at the NPT review conference now under way in the U.S. behaved so recklessly as imploring for "more tightened international sanctions" against the DPRK, while making groundless accusations against it with a hue and cry over "a blatant challenge to nuclear non-proliferation." At the 25th south Korea-U.S. "meeting on security policy initiative" the group was so foolish as to beg its master for "military cooperation" in the moves against the DPRK while vociferating about what it called "provocation" and "threat".

Rodong Sinmun Thursday observes in a signed commentary carried in this regard:

The puppet group's above-said behavior is nothing but a treacherous criminal act to do harm to the DPRK in collusion with foreign forces under the pretext of "nuclear non-proliferation".

This betrays the despicable ambition of the group of traitors to stand in the way of the process for building a peace-keeping regime on the Korean Peninsula as servants for the aggressors, push the inter-Korean relations to a catastrophe and, furthermore, ignite a nuclear war of aggression against the DPRK at any cost.

The puppet ruling forces are the nuclear criminals gravely threatening the destiny of the country and the nation by shipping nuclear weapons of foreign aggressor forces into south Korea and frantically stepping up the moves to ignite a war.

All the fellow countrymen will never pardon the clique of traitors, which finds fault with fellow countrymen, though it has committed so hideous acts of treachery, and gets frantic with the scheme to bring the dark clouds of a nuclear war, but mete out a stern punishment to it on behalf of the nation.

SOURCE: Korea Central News Agency. "S. Korea's Groundless Accusations against DPRK Refuted." May 20, 2010. http://www.kcna.co.jp/item/2010/201005/news20/20100520-15ee.html.

OTHER HISTORIC DOCUMENTS OF INTEREST

FROM PREVIOUS *HISTORIC DOCUMENTS*

- Joint Statement on Six-Party Talks on North Korean Nuclear Program, *2005*, p. 604
- Joint Statement by Leaders of North and South Korea, *2000*, p. 359

Race to the Top Education Funds Awarded

MARCH 29 AND AUGUST 24, 2010

When the American Recovery and Reinvestment Act (ARRA) was passed in 2009, the package included $4.35 billion in education funds that would be given to states to improve their K-12 education systems and to support the development of a twenty-first-century workforce that can help America compete in the global economy. To decide how to apportion the funds, the U.S. Department of Education created Race to the Top, a contest for states to improve their education systems and the methods through which they evaluate student and teacher performance. On March 29, 2010, the department announced the first two states to win the funds—Delaware and Tennessee. In August, it announced the remaining ten winners.

The funding proved controversial, as some states that did not win in the first round complained that they would be unable to compete with smaller states because teachers' unions would not agree to some of the changes required to obtain the funding. Other states that never submitted an application, such as Texas, criticized the program's requirements and the federal government's interference in state policy. "Texas is on the right path toward improved education, and we would be foolish and irresponsible to place our children's future in the hands of unelected bureaucrats and special interest groups thousands of miles away in Washington, virtually eliminating parents' participation in their children's education," Texas governor Rick Perry said. "If Washington were truly concerned about funding education with solutions that match local challenges, they would make the money available to states with no strings attached," he said.

NEW EDUCATION PERFORMANCE STANDARDS

When it was first created, Race to the Top sought to achieve four major education goals of the Barack Obama administration. First, the program called on states to reform their education standards for students to better prepare them for postsecondary education or future careers. Without a highly educated population, the United States would find it increasingly difficult to compete with countries around the world that have stricter education standards. In addition to the money allocated to states, the Department of Education was prepared to work toward this improvement goal on a national level by keeping $350 million of the ARRA education funds to spend on improving its own data systems.

Second, the administration wanted school districts and states to maintain or build data systems that could track students during their time in the education system. This would help state and local education officials determine if the educational reforms put in place were working to improve student achievement. It would also help schools quickly identify students who were falling behind.

A third goal of the competition was to change the way American public school teachers are compensated. The department recommended that teachers serving in low-performing schools, or those who excelled at teaching priority areas such as math and science, be paid based on skill level and expertise.

Finally, the Department of Education wanted to use Race to the Top funding as a way for states to identify and turn around low-performing schools. This goal was linked to data systems, but it required that states formulate a plan for helping low-performing schools raise their standards to the level other schools have achieved or, in many cases, risk closure or other discipline.

Phase One

To apply for Race to the Top funds, the Department of Education asked states to send information detailing successes of their past education reform. In addition, states were required to submit a plan that would reform or improve on their current K-12 education system. This plan would need to include college- and career-ready standards for classes; a way to choose and train teachers that would be more effective than their current system of selection and training; the creation or improvement of educational data systems that can track student progress; and a strategy for turning around low-performing schools. The Obama administration also sought states that were prepared to lift caps on the number of charter schools allowed to operate within their borders and that were willing to pay teachers based on performance. States wishing to compete must also sign on to the National Governors Association's new education standards—something that only two states had failed to do when the competition was announced.

Forty states applied for funding during the first phase. To choose the finalists, panels of peer reviewers met and discussed each application. The Department of Education then reviewed the scores and ranked the applications from highest to lowest to determine which applicants would be invited to complete their application for phase one funding. The chosen finalists were Colorado, Delaware, Florida, Georgia, Illinois, Kentucky, Louisiana, Massachusetts, New York, North Carolina, Ohio, Pennsylvania, Rhode Island, South Carolina, Tennessee, and Washington, D.C. According to Secretary of Education Arne Duncan, "These states are an example for the country of what is possible when adults come together to do the right thing for children."

Each finalist was invited to Washington, D.C., to present its proposals for education reform. This presentation gave the Department of Education a chance to ask questions about each project to fully vet its merits. In selecting winners from the presentation process, the department sought states that had a well-devised plan that included both an understanding of the work needed to follow through on the plan and a capacity and ability to deliver results.

From the beginning, the Department of Education indicated that it did not plan to have many winners in the first phase, but it did encourage anyone not chosen as a winner to reapply for the second phase. The number of winners was determined solely on the merit of each application. "We are setting a high bar and we anticipate very few winners in phase 1," Duncan said.

Secretary Duncan held a conference call with reporters to announce that Delaware and Tennessee were the winners of phase one and would be awarded $100 million and $500 million, respectively. He mentioned that both states had existing data systems in place that could be used for teacher evaluation. Delaware stood out in part because of its adherence to Obama's wish that teachers be judged on student performance. In its application, Delaware noted that it would begin giving tenure only to those teachers who could demonstrate student growth. Tennessee's application focused on dealing with its failing schools by creating an Achievement School District where low performers would be grouped together. Both states were able to convince teachers' unions of the benefit of implementing new performance measures, a point of contention for larger states that applied but were not awarded phase one funds.

"The biggest distinguishing thing for me is that the two state winners were touching 100 percent of their students," Duncan said after announcing the winners. "This is about systemic change." Duncan took aim at criticism the Department of Education had received regarding teachers' unions, saying, "Buy-in was a piece of the application, but by no means the determining factor."

PHASE TWO

Heading into phase two, finalists from phase one had to make a difficult decision about whether they wanted to spend additional time and money to reapply with a new education reform plan. Duncan had encouraged Washington, D.C., and the forty-eight remaining states to apply during his phase one winner announcement, saying "I want to challenge every state to put their best foot forward. Just by participating in the process, states are bringing people together to collaborate and create the policies that will accelerate student achievement."

After losing in phase one, Virginia governor Bob McDonnell decided the commonwealth should reapply in phase two. However, in May he removed Virginia from the competition, saying that it would not win if it adopted stricter measures than what the Department of Education had called for. "To create criteria that they've created, to mandate us putting national standards in when we've got great, verifiable working standards that have been in for 15 years, that people know and appreciate, we just can't do it, even for a couple hundred million dollars," McDonnell said.

Thirty-six states applied for phase two, with nineteen being chosen as finalists. After the rounds of applications, nine states and Washington, D.C., were awarded a total of $3.4 billion, which was split between the states in a method determined by the Department of Education. The winners of phase two were Florida, Georgia, Hawaii, Maryland, Massachusetts, New York, North Carolina, Ohio, Rhode Island, and Washington, D.C. In announcing the winners, Duncan said, "Every state that applied showed a tremendous amount of leadership and bold commitment to education reform. The creativity and innovation in each of these applications is breathtaking. We set a high bar and these states met the challenge."

The Obama administration has asked for an additional $1.35 billion in its fiscal year 2011 budget to support a third phase of Race to the Top. "We're very hopeful there will be a Phase 3 of Race to the Top and have requested $1.35 billion in next year's budget. In the meantime, we will partner with each and every state that applied to help them find ways to carry out the bold reforms they've proposed in their applications," Secretary Duncan said. This partnership included bringing states together with Department of Education officials to learn from each other's successes and failures.

RESISTANCE FROM EDUCATORS

Educators showed the strongest resistance to Race to the Top funding. Although teachers' unions were included in statewide and nationwide negotiations, they resisted change that would affect tenure and pay decisions. Secretary Duncan told teachers that he wanted change to happen "with teachers, not to teachers." The argument against the Department of Education's methods came to a head when Duncan and Obama commended Central Falls High School in Rhode Island for its decision to fire all of its teachers for not being supportive of reform ideas. "President Obama's comments . . . condoning the mass firing of the Central Falls High School teachers do not reflect the reality on the ground and completely ignore the teachers' significant commitment to working with others to transform this school," said Randi Weingarten, president of the American Federation of Teachers. The Obama administration, however, has stood by its call for more accountability on the part of teachers for student growth and performance.

The National Conference of State Legislatures (NCSL) has also taken issue with Race to the Top requirements. The organization, which represents legislators in all fifty states, opposes the federal government's new role in education created by this program. NCSL said that the Obama administration is stepping over its normal role in education. "The administration has made a decision that they're going to try to use limited federal resources to leverage change in the entire system," said David Shreve, an NCSL education policy expert.

—Heather Kerrigan

Following is a statement by U.S. Department of Education secretary Arne Duncan announcing the winners of phase one Race to the Top funds on March 29, 2010; and a press release from the department announcing the phase 2 winners on August 24, 2010.

Secretary Duncan Announces Race to the Top Winners

March 29, 2010

Thank you for joining me today for this historic announcement.

Today, I'm proud to announce that Delaware and Tennessee have won grants in the first phase of Race to the Top.

We received many strong proposals from states all across America, but two applications stood out above all others: Delaware and Tennessee. These states received the two highest scores in the competition. Both of them have statewide buy-in for comprehensive plans to reform their schools. They have written new laws to support their policies. And they have demonstrated the courage, capacity, and commitment to turn their ideas into practices that can improve outcomes for students.

All along, we said we would set a very high bar for success because we know that real and meaningful change in public education will only come from doing hard work and setting the highest expectations.

Both Delaware and Tennessee cleared that bar. They made commitments to raise their standards. They have strong plans to create meaningful teacher evaluation systems. Their schools rest on foundations rich with data, and they will be using this data to help teachers and principals accelerate student achievement. Both states have made deep commitments to turning around their struggling schools and their innovative plans reflect that commitment.

Tennessee's application includes examples of excellence from its cities, suburban towns, and rural areas. Tennessee's plan truly is a statewide effort. In particular, it will reach rural areas with a STEM initiative to increase high school rigor and has a specific plan to recruit teachers into rural areas.

Delaware also has a strong application that will reach every corner of the state and has the full support of its teacher's union.

Perhaps most importantly, every one of the districts in Delaware and Tennessee is committed to implementing the reforms in Race to the Top, and they have the support of the state leaders as well as their unions. We're confident that all students in both states will benefit from this program. We will be working with them to finalize their budgets and will closely monitor whether they're reaching their benchmarks over the course of the four years of their grants.

Although we have two winners for Phase 1, every state that applied is a winner. Everyone who applied is helping to chart the path forward for education reform in America. And the biggest winners of all are the students.

And the Race to the Top doesn't end today.

The good news is that about $3.4 billion remains to be awarded. Every other state in the country will have the opportunity to apply in the second phase. I want to challenge every state to put their best foot forward. Just by participating in the process, states are bringing people together to collaborate and create the policies that will accelerate student achievement.

We want to help states improve their proposals and share great ideas. On our Web site, we're posting the scores for every application and all of the reviewers' comments. By the end of next week, we'll post the video of every finalist's presentation to the peer reviewers. We also have asked teams from Tennessee and Delaware to participate in our April 21 workshop for Phase 2 applicants to share their ideas and approaches to statewide collaboration and reform.

We're providing all of these resources to help states succeed in creating comprehensive reform plans that will result in better results for children. I urge all states to set high expectations for themselves and take advantage of the opportunity to create strong plans to move reform forward. Applications for Phase 2 are due on June 1. That leaves time for states to do the hard work necessary to write the comprehensive plans necessary to succeed in school reform.

Finally, I want to announce that we are making one change to the Phase 2 application. In order to fund as many states with strong applications as possible, we are capping budgets. For Phase 2, states' budget requests have to be within the ranges that were suggested in our notice inviting applications. We will not accept budgets that exceed the top of a state's range. You can read about the proposed change on the Department's website today or in the Federal Register later this week.

So far, the Race to the Top has been an extraordinary success. It's been little more than a year since Race to the Top was created in the American Recovery and Reinvestment Act. Since then, this historic program has been a catalyst for education reform across this country, prompting states to think deeply about how to improve the way we prepare our students for success in a competitive, 21st century economy and workplace.

We now have two states that will blaze the path for the future of school education reform. I fully expect all 48 states to be refining and improving their ideas, vying to join them as leaders for reform in decades to come. We look forward to supporting that hard work in Phase 2 and beyond. President Obama has proposed an additional $1.35 billion for Race to the Top in fiscal 2011 so we can continue to support more states in moving reform forward.

Let me close, then, by thanking Delaware and Tennessee for their leadership, and by urging everyone else to continue to use this opportunity to drive meaningful educational reform across your states.

Thank you for your time. I'm joined here by Joanne Weiss, who's leading this effort on behalf of the Department. Joanne and I are ready to take your questions.

SOURCE: U.S. Department of Education. "U.S. Secretary of Education Arne Duncan's Statement on Race to the Top Phase 1 Winners." March 29, 2010. http://www.ed.gov/news/speeches/us-secretary-education-arne-duncans-statement-race-to-top-phase-1-winners.

Secretary Duncan Announces Phase II Race to the Top Winners

August 24, 2010

U.S. Secretary of Education Arne Duncan announced today that 10 applicants have won grants in the second phase of the Race to the Top competition. Along with Phase 1 winners Delaware and Tennessee, 11 states and the District of Columbia have now been awarded money in the Obama Administration's groundbreaking education reform program that will directly impact 13.6 million students, and 980,000 teachers in 25,000 schools.

The 10 winning Phase 2 applications in alphabetical order are: the District of Columbia, Florida, Georgia, Hawaii, Maryland, Massachusetts, New York, North Carolina, Ohio, and Rhode Island.

"These states show what is possible when adults come together to do the right thing for children," said Secretary Arne Duncan. "Every state that applied showed a tremendous amount of leadership and a bold commitment to education reform. The creativity and innovation in each of these applications is breathtaking," Duncan continued. "We set a high bar and these states met the challenge."

While peer reviewers rated these 10 as having the highest scoring plans, very few points separated them from the remaining applications. The deciding factor on the number of winners selected hinged on both the quality of the applications and the funds available.

"We had many more competitive applications than money to fund them in this round," Duncan said. "We're very hopeful there will be a Phase 3 of Race to the Top and have requested $1.35 billion dollars in next year's budget. In the meantime, we will partner with each and every state that applied to help them find ways to carry out the bold reforms they've proposed in their applications."

A total of 46 states and the District of Columbia put together comprehensive education reform plans to apply for Race to the Top in Phases 1 and 2. Over the course of the Race to the Top competition, 35 states and the District of Columbia have adopted rigorous common, college- and career-ready standards in reading and math, and 34 states have changed laws or policies to improve education.

Every state that applied has already done the hard work of collaboratively creating a comprehensive education reform agenda. In the coming months, the Department plans to bring all States together to help ensure the success of their work implementing reforms around college- and career-ready standards, data systems, great teachers and leaders, and school turnarounds.

In addition to the reforms supported by Race to the Top, the Department has made unprecedented resources available through reform programs like the Investing in Innovation Fund, the Teacher Incentive Fund, and the School Improvement Grants under Title I.

Through all of these programs, the Department of Education will be distributing almost $10 billion to support reform in states and local communities.

"As we look at the last 18 months, it is absolutely stunning to see how much change has happened at the state and local levels, unleashed in part by these incentive programs," Duncan said.

As with any federal grant program, budgets will be finalized after discussions between the grantees and the Department, and the money will be distributed over time as the grantees meet established benchmarks.

The $4.35 billion Race to the Top Fund is an unprecedented federal investment in reform. The program includes $4 billion for statewide reform grants and $350 million to support states working together to improve the quality of their assessments, which the Department plans to award in September. The Race to the Top state competition is designed to reward states that are leading the way in comprehensive, coherent, statewide education reform across four key areas:

- Adopting standards and assessments that prepare students to succeed in college and the workplace;
- Building data systems that measure student growth and success, and inform teachers and principals how to improve instruction;
- Recruiting, developing, rewarding, and retaining effective teachers and principals, especially where they are needed most; and
- Turning around their lowest-performing schools.

The 10 winning applicants have adopted rigorous common, college- and career-ready standards in reading and math, created pipelines and incentives to put the most effective teachers in high-need schools, and all have alternative pathways to teacher and principal certification.

In the first round of competition supporting state-based reforms, Delaware and Tennessee won grants based on their comprehensive plans to reform their schools and the statewide support for those plans.

The Department of Education has posted all Phase 2 applications online. Phase 2 peer reviewers' comments, and scores will be available on the website by August 25th; videos of states' presentations will be posted by September 10th. Phase 1 materials are available online.

	Phase 2 Grantee	Budget Not to Exceed	Phase 2 Score	Phase 1 Score	Score Change
1	Massachusetts	$250,000,000	471.0	411.4	59.6
2	New York	$700,000,000	464.8	408.6	56.2
3	Hawaii	$75,000,000	462.4	364.6	97.8
4	Florida	$700,000,000	452.4	431.4	21
5	Rhode Island	$75,000,000	451.2	419.0	32.2
6	District of Columbia	$75,000,000	450.0	402.4	47.6
7	Maryland	$250,000,000	450.0	N/A	N/A
8	Georgia	$400,000,000	446.4	433.6	12.8
9	North Carolina	$400,000,000	441.6	414.0	27.6
10	Ohio	$400,000,000	440.8	418.6	22.2

SOURCE: U.S. Department of Education. "Nine States and the District of Columbia Win Second Round Race to the Top Grants." August 24, 2010. http://www.ed.gov/news/press-releases/nine-states-and-district-columbia-win-second-round-race-top-grants.

OTHER HISTORIC DOCUMENTS OF INTEREST

FROM THIS VOLUME

- State of the Union Address and Republican Response, p. 33

FROM PREVIOUS *HISTORIC DOCUMENTS*

- Bush and Governors' Statements on Education Goals, *1990*, p. 153
- Statements at the Education Summit, *1989*, p. 561
- Education Report: 'A Nation at Risk,' *1983*, p. 413

Moscow Subway Attacked by Suicide Bombers

MARCH 29 AND 31, 2010

On March 29, 2010, two females entered crowded Moscow, Russia, subway trains and detonated bombs attached to them, killing thirty-nine and wounding dozens more during the city's morning rush hour. The suicide bombing sparked renewed fears that Islamic extremists operating in the region's North Caucasus would commit further terrorist acts throughout the city. Chechen rebels operating in the North Caucasus have over time been blamed for multiple terrorist attacks on Russian cities, in what they call a fight for their independence from Russia. The subway attack was the worst to hit the nation's capital city in six years. In February 2004, forty-one people were killed on a Moscow subway train, an attack that was blamed on Chechen rebels.

Russian president Dmitry Medvedev and prime minister Vladimir Putin together called on security forces to find those responsible for the attacks and bring them to justice. "I am confident that law enforcement bodies will spare no effort to track down and punish the criminals," Putin said. "I have no doubt that we will find and destroy them all," Medvedev echoed.

Immediately after the attacks, Medvedev faced criticism that his government reorganizations were not working to thwart terrorist attacks. As a result, he ordered his government to propose and implement a new transportation security plan that would focus not only on either Moscow or the subway system, but on transportation systems throughout the country.

Foreign leaders from around the world offered condolences to the families of those killed and wounded during the subway bombing. The Group of 8 was beginning security talks in Huntsville, Ontario, Canada, when the attack occurred, and members promised to "continue to collaborate to thwart and constrain terrorists." Leaders in Europe and the United States condemned the bombings and promised to work with Russian leaders to bring those responsible to justice.

SUBWAY ATTACKS

Moscow's subway system is one of the world's busiest, carrying some 5.5 million riders each day. On March 29, during Moscow's morning rush hour, two bombs were set off less than one hour apart at two separate stations.

The first suicide bombing occurred before 8 a.m. and killed twenty-four people. The station was close to the Federal Security Service (FSB) headquarters; analysts said that the proximity of the blast was intended as a warning to leaders in Moscow. The second blast, at a nearby subway station, killed fifteen more people.

The attacks occurred just weeks after Russian security forces announced the killing of leaders of the Chechen rebels. Putin officials presented this victory to the Russian people as a clear example that the government's reorganization in the name of security had been working as planned. "We have been able to break the spine of terrorism," said Ramzan Kadyrov, Moscow's appointed governor in Chechnya. The March 29 attacks seemed to be a clear retaliation for the killing of the Chechen leaders.

No group immediately stepped forward to claim responsibility for the attacks; however, according to the FSB, early reports indicated that the body parts found belonging to the two female bombers indicated that the women were from the North Caucasus. On March 30, a Chechen rebel leader, Doku Umarov, claimed that he ordered the attacks on the Moscow subway.

On the day of the attacks, officials opened two criminal cases under the charge of terrorism. Russia's prosecutor general, Yury Chaika, set up a thirty-member group to investigate the crime and to ensure that those responsible were quickly brought to justice.

CHECHEN REBELS IN RUSSIA

Suicide bombings have been carried out over the years in and around Russia's capital city. Many of these attacks have been blamed on Chechen rebels who are fighting for independence from Russia.

Recent suicide bombings in or near subway stations include forty-one killed in February 2004 and an additional ten killed in August of the same year. In August 2000, thirteen were killed in an attack on a subway tunnel.

The Chechen rebellion against Russia began in the 1990s. The rebellion was formed by Chechnya's ethnic groups, many of which felt that their relocation to Central Asia in the 1940s under Josef Stalin's rule had been unjust. Two wars have been fought in Chechnya during the rebellion between Russian military units and Chechen rebels. The first took place from 1994 through 1996, and the second from 1999 through 2005.

The rebellion has intensified as Islamic militants from outside of Russia, some operating on the Afghanistan-Pakistan border, have joined the fight, helping the rebels organize their attacks. Thousands have been killed during the two decades of fighting, and five hundred thousand Chechens have been displaced. However, Russian security says the rebellion is not just coming out of Chechnya. The neighboring republics of Ingushetia and Dagestan have also joined in the fight.

Following the Kadyrov announcement, Umarov released an Internet video warning Russian officials that the violence was not over. "Blood will no longer be limited to our cities and towns. The war is coming to their cities," the video warned. "If Russians think the war only happens on television, somewhere far away in the Caucasus where it can't reach them, then God willing, we plan to show them that the war will return to their homes." The video came as a warning that the Kremlin's claim of victory over the Chechen rebels was not yet ensured.

FALLOUT FROM THE BOMBING

Tension between Moscow and the North Caucasus region are long-standing. However, the recent attacks prompted a more pressing response from the Kremlin. Further complicating Moscow's reaction is the power structure between Medvedev and Putin.

When Putin was president, he responded to terrorist attacks by completely overhauling his government. In doing so, he took much of the power away from local government and centralized it in Moscow. Security services were strengthened, and to ensure that his policies would win approval, Putin made regional governors political appointees, thus eliminating direct election of these positions.

Since becoming president, Medvedev has worked to address the cause of insurgency, rather than simply reacting to terrorist acts. Putin stood by while Medvedev attempted to implement his new policies. The suicide bombing on March 29, critics said, was evidence that Medvedev's strategy is not working, even though many of his policies had yet to take effect.

BLACK WIDOWS

In Russia, female suicide bombers are referred to as "black widows." This is derived from the black mourning clothes the women wear when completing an attack. Chechen rebels began the technique of using women as suicide bombers more than a decade ago. A rebel leader at the time, Shamil Basayev, determined that women could more easily get explosives past Russian security checkpoints. The women in the brigade consider themselves martyrs and are generally the wives or mothers of Chechens killed by Russian military.

After Basayev's death, the use of female suicide bombers grew less routine, and it was thought that the brigade of women formed for this purpose had disbanded. The March bombing indicates, however, that the group has reformed.

The metro bombing was not the first attack in recent memory when females were used as suicide bombers. In 2002, women helped take control of a Moscow theater and were killed by security forces along with their hostages. Another Moscow attack resulted in fourteen deaths at a concert. In 2004, women attacked two Russian airliners and a school.

Experts in Russia say that as the violence between Chechnya and Russia continues, and conditions worsen in the region, more women may turn to black widow brigades in an effort to fight for their lost loved ones.

NEW SECURITY PLANS

"Preventing these kinds of terrorist attacks and ensuring security in the transport system are very difficult tasks, as recent experience shows," Medvedev told government leaders on the day of the attacks. "We need to intensify substantially our efforts in this area and address this problem in comprehensive fashion on the national scale. It is not enough to focus on just one type of transport or just one specific location. We need to address this problem at the national level. The measures taken to date are clearly insufficient," he said.

On March 31, Medvedev announced that the comprehensive transportation security program would soon be approved. This program gave the government one year to install technical systems and devices that could help stop future attacks. These systems would first be placed in locations around the country that are most vulnerable to attack. By 2014, the entire country would be equipped with the system.

—Heather Kerrigan

Following is a transcript of a special meeting called by Russian president Dmitry Medvedev following the Moscow metro bombings on March 29, 2010; and a press release detailing Medvedev's call for enhanced security on public transportation systems on March 31, 2010.

Russian President Medvedev Holds
Special Meeting After Subway Attacks

March 29, 2010

The President instructed the heads of Russia's law enforcement agencies to keep the investigation into the attacks under their constant supervision and report on developments.

The Government has been told to provide any necessary aid to all of the victims.

Mr Medvedev also gave an instruction to tighten security measures throughout Russia's transport system.

Earlier, the heads of the Federal Security Service, Prosecutor General's Office, Emergency Situations Ministry and Healthcare and Social Development Ministry briefed the President on what is being done to help those injured in the attacks, and on the investigation now underway.

* * *

PRESIDENT OF RUSSIA DMITRY MEDVEDEV: Two terrorist attacks were committed in the Moscow metro this morning. Let us first of all honour the victims' memory with a minute of silence.

Turning now to the actual details of the events, let's hear first from *Mr [Alexander] Bortnikov*. Please, brief us on the chronology of events and the main conclusions so far on what took place.

DIRECTOR OF THE FEDERAL SECURITY SERVICE ALEXANDER BORT-NIKOV: The first blast took place at 7.57 this morning at Lubyanka metro station, and the second occurred at 8.37 at Park Kultury metro station. The death toll currently stands at 36 people.

Preliminary forensic tests show that the explosive used was hexogen, up to four kilograms in the first blast, and 1.5-2 kilograms in the second. The explosive devices were filled with cut steel chips and bolts to act as shrapnel.

Our preliminary conclusion is that these terrorist attacks were committed by a terrorist group with links to the North Caucasus region. We consider this the most likely version of events because preliminary analysis of the fragments of the terrorists' bodies found at the sites suggests that the blasts were carried out by two female suicide bombers with links to the North Caucasus.

A federal operations headquarters has begun work, the necessary investigation work and operations are underway, and a criminal case has been opened under the charge of terrorism. The Federal Security Service and Interior Ministry operations officers are working in intensive regime. We are doing everything necessary to identify as rapidly as possible the people connected to this terrorist attack and are taking all necessary measures to exclude any possible further attacks.

DMITRY MEDVEDEV: *Mr Shoigu*, what have the rescuers been doing, what is the situation now? Have the wounded been evacuated, and where have they been sent?

EMERGENCY SITUATIONS MINISTER SERGEI SHOIGU: The rescue services all reacted quite fast. All of the injured have been evacuated to 12 hospitals and treatment facilities around Moscow. We currently have 54 people in hospital. Most of the casualties were at Lubyanka station. Of course, it is hard to say where things are worse, but I am talking simply of the numbers – we had 41 casualties there.

We engaged all the necessary services and agencies, including 342 people and 100 vehicles from the Emergency Situations Ministry, as well as two helicopters that we also used to transport the injured to hospitals. They are currently being examined by medical personnel. Of course, the Moscow City Government and the Healthcare Ministry are also taking all necessary steps to provide needed medicines and blood supplies. We have opened hotlines, of course, to inform peoples' families.

We also used the Aksion public address system that has been developed together with the Interior Ministry and FSB to inform people using the metro system or travelling by road. Moscow transport services were quick to organise buses, around 130 buses [replacing the closed metro line].

All the services responded quite fast. As for additional conclusions, they will follow over the next 24 hours.

DMITRY MEDVEDEV: Mr Luzhkov, you visited the scene of these attacks. What is the situation there now in your view, and what are the Moscow city authorities doing to support people?

MOSCOW MAYOR YURY LUZHKOV: We went to the scene and together with the Emergency Situations Ministry and law enforcement agencies organised immediate evacuation and took measures to prevent the panic and crushes that, unfortunately, always follow this kind of tragic event. People were evacuated from the metro, public transport was restored, the needed numbers of extra buses were organised, and the way was cleared for ambulances, fire engines and special transport.

We organised everything quite fast so as not to disrupt traffic on the Garden Ring and main roads. Together with the Emergency Situations Ministry we organised urgent transportation of the injured to our hospitals. All of the hospitals are fully provided with the necessary medicines and everything they need for their work.

DMITRY MEDVEDEV: Where have the injured been taken?

YURY LUZHKOV: They are in nine different hospitals. This work has been organised by our ambulance system, which has the latest information technology at its disposal.

We opened several telephone hotlines. We are also taking all the necessary organisational steps regarding the sad consequences of this tragedy – cemeteries and so on.

But our first task is to help the victims and fully restore traffic. To restore traffic on the metro we need the services (the prosecutor's office and investigators) to finish their work as quickly as possible, because until then, we cannot remove the damaged carriages. Once the investigators have finished their work we will need no more than an hour to restore traffic on the Sokolnicheskaya metro line.

Everything has been organised, including a draft order on providing aid for the victims, including financial help for the families of those killed.

DMITRY MEDVEDEV: Mr Nurgaliyev, what is being done to return the transport system to normal and ensure that the law enforcement agencies have it under their control? After all, this is the responsibility of the police and the Interior Ministry in general. What is the situation now?

INTERIOR MINISTER RASHID NURGALIYEV: A rapid response group was dispatched immediately to Lubyanka metro station. More than 300 Interior Ministry officers are now keeping order there. As for Park Kultury metro station, we now have around 150 officers there. All the necessary measures have been taken and the operational and investigation groups are at work.

At the same time, we have sent specific instructions to all of our regional offices to heighten vigilance and ensure our citizens' safety throughout the entire transport infrastructure, and especially in cities that have metro systems.

The situation is under control. We are working with the Moscow investigators to carry out immediate investigation of these crimes.

DMITRY MEDVEDEV: *Mr Chaika*, a criminal case has been opened?

PROSECUTOR GENERAL YURY CHAIKA: Two criminal cases have been opened under the charge of terrorism. An operational and investigation group of 30 people has been set up. I have already given the instruction to add more people to the group so as to complete examination of the crime sites faster. The investigators from the Investigative Committee are receiving help from the Federal Security Service's investigations service. They are working actively with us collecting all the evidence.

My deputy, the heads of the Investigative Committee, investigators from the Investigative Committee and from the central office have all been to the crime sites. Given the importance of this case I decided that the Prosecutor General's Office Investigative Committee will handle it. I think we have the grounds for consolidating these two cases into one, seeing as the two attacks were carried out in such identical fashion, and this will allow us to concentrate more attention on the investigation work.

At 10.30 this morning I already held a meeting and heard a report on the investigation so far. My deputies reported on the developments. The Moscow City prosecutor and my deputy, who visited the scene, have already reported on the investigation. We will make every possible effort to solve this crime. I am keeping this case under my supervision.

DMITRY MEDVEDEV: Yes, keep it under your control.

Now, one final issue regarding transport, Mr Levitin, we have transport that comes under the federal authorities' responsibility, and transport that comes under local authorities' responsibility. But we nevertheless have an overall national transport policy. What proposals are there on how to organise security in the transport system in general, and in city transport systems, including the metro?

TRANSPORT MINISTER IGOR LEVITIN: In accordance with the law on transport security, we drew up regulations together with the Interior Ministry and Federal Security Service on establishing a transport counterterrorism system, including for the metro.

We have metro system in seven Russian cities. These cities have put in place public address systems that can be used in the event of terrorist attacks such as that in Moscow today. The legal framework issues are coordinated with owners of the infrastructure – with the Moscow city authorities here, and with the local authorities in the other cities. Although these metro systems are municipal and regional property, we are developing the legal framework at federal level, working in coordination with the regions.

DMITRY MEDVEDEV: Preventing these kinds of terrorist attacks and ensuring security in the transport system are very difficult tasks, as recent experience shows. We need to intensify substantially our efforts in this area and address this problem in comprehensive fashion on the national scale. It is not enough to focus on just one type of transport or just one specific location. We need to address this problem at the national level. The measures taken to date are clearly insufficient.

As for the concrete steps to take right now, we need, of course, to help the people affected, first of all, provide help and support to the families of those killed and help all the victims, help those now in hospitals. They must get all necessary aid from the Moscow authorities and from the federal government.

I have instructed the Government to hold a meeting today to discuss all of these issues in detail. I ask the Government to carry this out.

Regarding the situation in general, we need to remain vigilant. The sad truth is that these kinds of attacks are clearly always well-planned, calculated to cause as many victims as possible, and aimed at destabilising our country and society. The Interior Ministry and the security services must therefore work to raise public awareness and keep tight control on the situation. Of course, they must respect citizens' rights, but keep things under tight control, intervening and responding as necessary if circumstances call for it.

Such practice exists throughout the world and in Russia too. Sadly, this is not the first time we find ourselves facing this sort of event. We therefore need to have precise and prepared responses in this kind of situation.

The Prosecutor General's Office and the Investigative Committee must continue collecting evidence and conducting a thorough investigation, though without hampering traffic in the metro system, of course. Traffic must resume as soon as the investigations work has been completed, so as not to cause problems for the city.

All versions advanced so far need to be investigated as thoroughly as possible. This is very clearly a continuation of the terrorist activity we have already encountered, and the investigation will no doubt be based primarily on this version. Keep the investigation under your control and report to me on developments.

One final point I want to make is that we will continue our efforts to stamp out and combat terrorism in our country. We will continue our counterterrorist operations with unflinching resolve until we have defeated this scourge. I want all of you, the heads of our law enforcement and security agencies, to remember this and make it your guiding principle – we will act unflinchingly and not stop until terrorism is defeated.

We will hold another meeting soon on specific consequences of these attacks. Now we need to get on with our immediate duties, and so I propose that we all get back to our respective work.

SOURCE: Office of the President of Russia. "Dmitry Medvedev Gave a Series of Instructions at a Special Meeting Following the Terrorist Attacks in the Moscow Metro." March 29, 2010. http://eng.kremlin.ru/news/139.

Russian President Medvedev Calls for Enhanced Transportation Security

DOCUMENT

March 31, 2010

The Government has been set a deadline of four months for approving a comprehensive programme to guarantee public safety in the transport systems, above all in the metro and other types of public transport. The programme will unite the efforts and resources of executive authorities responsible for transport safety at every level.

The Government has been given until March 31, 2011 to equip the most vulnerable means of transport and parts of the transport infrastructure with specialised technical systems and devices to protect them from unlawful interference. A comprehensive system to ensure public safety, prevent emergency situations and terrorist attacks and protect users is to be in place throughout the transport system by January 1, 2014.

The Government has been instructed to select the organisations to be charged with developing the new technical systems, and to ensure the necessary funding from the federal budget for the comprehensive transport safety system's operation.

The Transport Ministry will oversee the comprehensive system's establishment.

SOURCE: Office of the President of Russia. "Dmitry Medvedev Signed an Executive Order on Creating a Comprehensive Transport Safety System." March 31, 2010. http://eng.kremlin.ru/news/129.

OTHER HISTORIC DOCUMENTS OF INTEREST

FROM THIS VOLUME

- Attempted Bombing in Times Square, p. 207

FROM PREVIOUS *HISTORIC DOCUMENTS*

- Medvedev on His Inauguration as President of Russia, *2008*, p. 169
- Russian President Putin on Hostage-Taking Tragedy, *2004*, p. 564
- UN Human Rights Officials on the War in Chechnya, *1999*, p. 909

April

Federal Court Rules in Net Neutrality Case

APRIL 6, 2010

In a decision that came as a significant blow to the Barack Obama administration, a federal appeals court ruled on April 6, 2010, that the Federal Communications Commission (FCC) cannot regulate the way in which Internet service providers (ISPs) manage their user traffic. The decision overturned a 2008 ruling by the FCC against Comcast, which had been managing user traffic by blocking some content that used large amounts of bandwidth, such as file sharing programs. Congress and the White House saw the decision as a defeat after previously trying to pass legislation on net neutrality, a policy of unrestricted Internet service offered by ISPs, under the assumption that the FCC would have such power.

RULING AGAINST THE FCC

In *Comcast v. Federal Communications Commission*, the FCC argued that with no overarching federal law dictating who was in charge of regulating ISPs, it was the job of the FCC to do so and ensure that the practices of these companies were in line with a net neutrality–focused policy.

At trial, the FCC argued that it had ancillary authority to order Comcast to stop regulating traffic from BitTorrent, an online file sharing site, by its customers. This authority, it said, came from earlier U.S. Supreme Court decisions. However, the FCC did not argue that it had the express authority to regulate Internet service provided by cable companies. It instead called its regulation powers "reasonably ancillary to the . . . effective performance of its statutorily mandated responsibilities," which it claimed it received from the Communications Act first passed in 1934. The act states that the United States will continue to promote the development of the Internet to maximize each user's control over what he or she can see or do. The D.C. Court found that if the FCC was given leeway to regulate over all policies found in the Communications Act in this fashion, its reach would be limitless and U.S. courts would be unable to regulate its power.

In recent cases, the D.C. Circuit Court ruled that the FCC could only use the Communications Act argument if the data being regulated were covered by Title I of the Communications Act, thus giving the FCC power to make decisions about that data, or if the regulations could reasonably be considered necessary to the FCC effectively carrying out its federally mandated responsibilities. In the instance of *Comcast v. FCC*, the court ruled that while the commission could not argue that cable Internet fell within Title I of the Communications Act, it could argue that the regulations were necessary to carry out FCC duties.

The U.S. Court of Appeals for the D.C. Circuit disagreed with the FCC's arguments. In an overwhelming 3–0 vote, the court wrote, "The Commission may exercise this 'ancillary' authority only if it demonstrates that its action—here barring Comcast from interfering with its customers' use of peer-to-peer networking applications—is 'reasonably ancillary to the . . . effective performance of its statutorily mandated responsibilities.'" The FCC, the court ruled, had failed to prove this. According to the ruling, the FCC's argument "relies principally on several Congressional statements of policy, but under Supreme Court and D.C. Circuit case law statements of policy, by themselves, do not create 'statutorily mandated responsibilities.'"

Republicans on Capitol Hill cheered the ruling. Sen. Kay Bailey Hutchison, R-Texas, who had previously threatened to block the FCC from enacting net neutrality policies from her position on the Senate Commerce Committee, said, "It would be wrong to double down on excessive and burdensome regulations, and I hope the FCC Chairman will now reconsider his decision to pursue expanded commission authority over broadband services in current proceedings before the agency."

WINNERS AND LOSERS

The FCC was the biggest loser in the decision, and the ruling would deal a strong blow to the National Broadband Plan, which was released in early 2010 with the assumption that the FCC would be able to regulate ISPs in an effort to make broadband more universally accessible—even in the country's most rural areas. Now, in order to implement its plan, the FCC must find a way to classify broadband under Title II of the Communications Act, which would make it a telecommunication service and give the commission power to enact net neutrality. In its current Title I state, the FCC does not have authority to regulate ISPs. After the ruling, the FCC maintained its commitment to providing broadband for all Americans, saying "the Court in no way disagreed with the importance of preserving a free and open Internet; nor did it close the door to other methods for achieving this important end."

The net neutrality ruling, while dealing a significant blow to legislation in Washington, would be a significant win for Internet and wireless providers. Both groups had been fighting the FCC's 2008 ruling in which Comcast was ordered to stop blocking content that was bogging down its servers. The biggest Internet providers, including Comcast and AT&T, would benefit the most in this case because they would be able to immediately restrict traffic to certain sites to ensure that everyone maintains an equal level of bandwidth usage. This opened the door for such providers to begin charging file download sites extra to use a larger amount of bandwidth. The wireless providers, many of which were already dealing with bandwidth demands from smartphones, say the ruling is a necessity in controlling these problems.

The caveat of the benefit for Internet and wireless providers was that there is no telling when or if Congress would become involved in an attempt to give the FCC power to regulate net neutrality. However, because of the National Broadband Plan, there was a clear indication that Congress would eventually step in.

Large Internet companies, like Google, will likely be impacted by the ruling. These groups are often supporters of net neutrality legislation and also supported the 2008 ruling against Comcast. Collectively, large Internet companies disagree with an ISP's ability to decide how to devote bandwidth to each web site. Google posted a statement on its public policy blog after the federal court's decision stating, "Carriers should not be allowed to degrade access to competitors' web sites." With the court's decision, companies like Google could see a decrease in bandwidth provided to their web sites by ISPs, thus slowing a user's experience on the site.

FCC NET NEUTRALITY COMPROMISE

In December, the FCC again took up the issue of net neutrality, and, in a 3–2 party-line vote, FCC commissioners agreed to methods through which ISPs would be able to control user access. The new regulations were defined by whether a person is accessing the Internet wirelessly or through a landline. The split between Republicans and Democrats on the commission was mainly caused by a difference of opinion over whether the FCC has the right to enact net neutrality regulations and whether they were necessary. One FCC commissioner, Republican Robert McDowell, gave four main reasons why he chose not to vote for the new rules, starting with "nothing is broken with the current system."

Before the vote, FCC chairman Julius Genachowski stressed the importance of continuing work on the regulations that had been debated for more than a year. "On one end of the spectrum, there are those who say government should do nothing at all," he said. "On the other end are those who would adopt extensive detailed and rigid regulations. . . . I reject both extremes in favor of a strong and sensible non-ideological framework—one that protects Internet freedom and openness and promotes robust innovation and investment."

Under the FCC's December net neutrality regulations, anyone providing broadband service would not be able to block access to web sites that are legal. This means that the FCC decided that ISPs would not be able to slow traffic to sites that take up a large amount of bandwidth or any sites that compete with the ISPs' own offerings. However, ISPs will be able to charge sites that want a larger amount of bandwidth, but they will have to disclose the amounts they charge and the regulations they are placing on these sites. Because of the federal court's decision in April, the FCC's December net neutrality decision was seen as a compromise put forth to avoid further court action, but it set up the possibility of additional future net neutrality regulations.

Any Internet site that is reached wirelessly, even through a smartphone, will have fewer restrictions. The ISP will still not be allowed to block traffic to certain web sites, but it will be allowed to block specific applications, unless they provide voice or video service.

Although Democrats on the Hill have advocated for net neutrality rules, they saw the FCC's December decision as an insignificant version of what they had hoped for. Sen. Al Franken, D-Minn., said, "If the FCC passes this weak rule, Verizon will be able to cut off access to the Google Maps app on your phone and force you to use their own mapping program, Verizon Navigator, even if it is not as good. And even if they charge money, when Google Maps is free." Republicans argued against the FCC's December decision as well, seeing it as an encroachment of big government into business and the lives of Americans. House minority leader John Boehner, R-Ohio, called the FCC decision "job killing." He continued: "Today's action by the FCC will hurt our economy, stifle private-sector job creation, and undermine the entrepreneurship and innovation of Internet-related American employers."

Obama celebrated the FCC's decision. "Today's decision will help preserve the free and open nature of the Internet while encouraging innovation, protecting consumer choice, and defending free speech. Throughout this process, parties on all sides of this issue—from consumer groups to technology companies to broadband providers—came together to make their voices heard. This decision is an important component of our overall strategy to advance American innovation, economic growth, and job creation," he said.

—Heather Kerrigan

The following are excerpts from Comcast v. Federal Communications Commission, *in which the D.C. Circuit Court ruled 3–0 against the Federal Communications Commission, stating that the FCC does not have the authority to regulate the way in which Internet service providers (ISPs) regulate traffic on their networks.*

Comcast v. Federal Communications Commission

April 6, 2010

Argued January 8, 2010   Decided April 6, 2010

No. 08–1291

Comcast Corporation, Petitioner

v.

Federal Communications Commission and United States of America, Respondents

NBC Universal, et al., Intervenors

   On Petition for Review of an Order of the Federal Communications Commission

[The names and titles of those involved in the case have been omitted.]

TATEL, *Circuit Judge:* In this case we must decide whether the Federal Communications Commission has authority to regulate an Internet service provider's network management practices. Acknowledging that it has no express statutory authority over such practices, the Commission relies on section 4(i) of the Communications Act of 1934, which authorizes the Commission to "perform any and all acts, make such rules and regulations, and issue such orders, not inconsistent with this chapter, as may be necessary in the execution of its functions." The Commission may exercise this "ancillary" authority only if it demonstrates that its action—here barring Comcast from interfering with its customers' use of peer-to-peer networking applications—is "reasonably ancillary to the . . . effective performance of its statutorily mandated responsibilities." The Commission has failed to make that showing. It relies principally on several Congressional statements of policy, but under Supreme Court and D.C. Circuit case law statements of policy, by themselves, do not create "statutorily mandated responsibilities." The Commission also relies on various provisions of the Communications Act that do create such responsibilities, but for a variety of substantive and procedural reasons those provisions cannot support its exercise of ancillary authority over Comcast's network management practices. We therefore grant Comcast's petition for review and vacate the challenged order.

I.

In 2007 several subscribers to Comcast's high-speed Internet service discovered that the company was interfering with their use of peer-to-peer networking applications. Peer-to-peer programs allow users to share large files directly with one another without going through a central server. Such programs also consume significant amounts of bandwidth. . . .

[The background of the Comcast case have been omitted.]

Following a period of public comment, the Commission issued the order challenged here. The Commission began by concluding not only that it had jurisdiction over Comcast's network management practices, but also that it could resolve the dispute through adjudication rather than through rulemaking. On the merits, the Commission ruled that Comcast had "significantly impeded consumers' ability to access the content and use the applications of their choice," id. at 13,054, ¶ 44, and that because Comcast "ha[d] several available options it could use to manage network traffic without discriminating" against peer-to-peer communications, id. at 13,057, ¶ 49, its method of bandwidth management "contravene[d] . . . federal policy," id. at 13,052, ¶ 43. Because by then Comcast had agreed to adopt a new system for managing bandwidth demand, the Commission simply ordered it to make a set of disclosures describing the details of its new approach and the company's progress toward implementing it. The Commission added that an injunction would automatically issue should Comcast either fail to make the required disclosures or renege on its commitment.

Although Comcast complied with the *Order*, it now petitions for review, presenting three objections. First, it contends that the Commission has failed to justify exercising jurisdiction over its network management practices. Second, it argues that the Commission's adjudicatory action was procedurally flawed because it circumvented the rulemaking requirements of the Administrative Procedure Act and violated the notice requirements of the Due Process Clause.

Finally, it asserts that parts of the *Order* are so poorly reasoned as to be arbitrary and capricious. We begin—and end—with Comcast's jurisdictional challenge.

II.

Through the Communications Act of 1934, ch. 652, 48 Stat. 1064, as amended over the decades, 47 U.S.C. § 151 et seq., Congress has given the Commission express and expansive authority to regulate common carrier services, including landline telephony, id. § 201 et seq. In this case, the Commission does not claim that Congress has given it express authority to regulate Comcast's Internet service. . . .

Courts have come to call the Commission's section 4(i) power its "ancillary" authority, a label that derives from three foundational Supreme Court decisions: *United States v. Southwestern Cable Co.*, 392 U.S. 157 (1968), *United States v. Midwest Video Corp.*, 406 U.S. 649 (1972) (*Midwest Video I*), and *FCC v. Midwest Video Corp.*, 440 U.S. 689 (1979) (*Midwest Video II*).

All three cases dealt with Commission jurisdiction over early cable systems at a time when, as with the Internet today, the Communications Act gave the Commission no express authority to regulate such systems. (Title VI, which gives the Commission jurisdiction over "cable services," was not added to the statute until 1984.) . . .

We recently distilled the holdings of these three cases into a two-part test. In *American Library Ass'n v. FCC*, we wrote: "The Commission . . . may exercise ancillary jurisdiction only when two conditions are satisfied: (1) the Commission's general jurisdictional grant under Title I [of the Communications Act] covers the regulated subject and (2) the regulations are reasonably ancillary to the Commission's effective performance of its statutorily mandated responsibilities." Comcast concedes that the Commission's action here satisfies the first requirement because the company's Internet service qualifies as "interstate and foreign communication by wire" within the meaning of Title I of the Communications Act. 47 U.S.C. § 152(a). Whether the Commission's action satisfies *American Library's* second requirement is the central issue in this case.

III.

Before addressing that issue, however, we must consider two threshold arguments the Commission raises. First, it asserts that given a contrary position Comcast took in a California lawsuit, the company should be judicially stopped from challenging the Commission's jurisdiction over the company's network management practices. Second, the Commission argues that even if Comcast's challenge can proceed, we need not go through our usual ancillary authority analysis because a recent Supreme Court decision, *National Cable & Telecommunications Ass'n v. Brand X Internet Services*, 545 U.S. 967, makes clear that the Commission had authority to issue the *Order.* . . .

[Discussion of the FCC's threshold arguments have been omitted.]

IV.

The Commission argues that the *Order* satisfies *American Library's* second requirement because it is "reasonably ancillary to the Commission's effective performance" of its responsibilities under several provisions of the Communications Act. These provisions fall into two categories: those that the parties agree set forth only congressional policy and those that at least arguably delegate regulatory authority to the Commission. We consider each in turn.

A.

The Commission relies principally on section 230(b), part of a provision entitled "Protection for private blocking and screening of offensive material," 47 U.S.C. § 230, that grants civil immunity for such blocking to providers of interactive computer services, id. § 230(c)(2). Setting forth the policies underlying this protection, section 230(b) states, in relevant part, that "[i]t is the policy of the United States . . . to promote the continued development of the Internet and other interactive computer services" and "to encourage the development of technologies which maximize user control over what information is received by individuals, families, and schools who use the Internet." In this case the Commission found that Comcast's network management practices frustrated both objectives.

In addition to section 230(b), the Commission relies on section 1, in which Congress set forth its reasons for creating the Commission in 1934: "For the purpose of regulating interstate and foreign commerce in communication by wire and radio so as to make available, so far as possible, to all the people of the United States . . . a rapid, efficient, Nation-wide, and world-wide wire and radio communication service . . . at reasonable charges, . . . there is created a commission to be known as the 'Federal Communications Commission.' . . ." The Commission found that "prohibiting unreasonable network discrimination directly furthers the goal of making broadband Internet access service both 'rapid' and 'efficient.'"

Comcast argues that neither section 230(b) nor section 1 can support the Commission's exercise of ancillary authority because the two provisions amount to nothing more than congressional "statements of policy." Pet'r's Br. 46. Such statements, Comcast contends, "are not an operative part of the statute, and do not enlarge or confer powers on administrative agencies. As such, they necessarily fail to set forth 'statutorily mandated responsibilities'" within the meaning of *American Library*.

The Commission acknowledges that section 230(b) and section 1 are statements of policy that themselves delegate no regulatory authority. Still, the Commission maintains that the two provisions, like all provisions of the Communications Act, set forth "statutorily mandated responsibilities" that can anchor the exercise of ancillary authority. "The operative provisions of statutes are those which *declare the legislative will*," the Commission asserts. "Here, the legislative will has been declared by Congress in the form of a policy, along with an express grant of authority to the FCC to perform all actions necessary to execute and enforce all the provisions of the Communications Act."

In support of its reliance on congressional statements of policy, the Commission points out that in both *Southwestern Cable* and *Midwest Video I* the Supreme Court linked the challenged Commission actions to the furtherance of various congressional "goals," "objectives," and "policies." In particular, the Commission notes that in *Midwest Video I*, the plurality accepted its argument that the Commission's "concern with CATV carriage of broadcast signals . . . extends . . . to requiring CATV affirmatively to further statutory *policies*." According to the Commission, since congressional statements of policy were sufficient to support ancillary authority over cable television, it may likewise rely on such statements—section 230(b) and section 1—to exercise ancillary authority over the network management practices of Internet providers.

We read *Southwestern Cable* and *Midwest Video I* quite differently. . . .

The Commission exceeded those "outer limits" in both *NARUC II* and *Midwest Video II*. In *NARUC II*, the Commission defended its exercise of ancillary authority over non-video cable communications (as it does here with respect to Comcast's network management practices) on the basis of section 1's "overall statutory mandate to make available, so far as possible, to all the people of the United States a rapid, efficient, [N]ation-wide, and world-wide wire and radio communications service." The Commission "reasoned that this language called for the development of a nationwide broadband communications grid in which cable systems should play an important part." We rejected that argument. Relying on *Southwestern Cable* and *Midwest Video I*, we began by explaining that the Commission's ancillary authority "is really incidental to, and contingent upon, specifically delegated powers under the Act."

Applying that standard, we found it "difficult to see how any action which the Commission might take concerning two-way cable communications could have as its primary impact the furtherance of any broadcast purpose." Because the regulations had not been "justified as reasonably ancillary to the Commission's power over broadcasting," id. at 612, we vacated them.

In *Midwest Video II*, the Supreme Court rejected the Commission's assertion of ancillary authority to impose a public access requirement on certain cable channels because doing so would "relegate[] cable systems . . . to common-carrier status." Pointing out that the Communications Act expressly prohibits common carrier regulation of *broadcasters*, *id.* at 702, the Court held that given the derivative nature of ancillary jurisdiction the same prohibition applied to the Commission's regulation of *cable providers*. The Commission had opposed this logic, arguing that it could regulate "so long as the rules promote statutory objectives." Id. The Court rejected that broad claim and, revealing the flaw in the argument the Commission makes here, emphasized that "without reference to the provisions of the Act *directly governing broadcasting*, the Commission's [ancillary] jurisdiction . . . would be unbounded." Id. at 706 (emphasis added). "Though afforded wide latitude in its supervision over communication by wire," the Court added, "the Commission was not delegated unrestrained authority." . . .

Attempting to avoid this conclusion, the Commission argues that in several more recent cases we upheld its use of ancillary authority on the basis of policy statements alone. In each of those cases, however, we sustained the exercise of ancillary authority because, unlike here, the Commission had linked the cited policies to express delegations of regulatory authority. . . .

[Additional cases addressed by the FCC have been omitted.]

B.

This brings us to the second category of statutory provisions the Commission relies on to support its exercise of ancillary authority. Unlike section 230(b) and section 1, each of these provisions could at least arguably be read to delegate regulatory authority to the Commission.

We begin with section 706 of the Telecommunications Act of 1996, which provides that "[t]he Commission . . . shall encourage the deployment on a reasonable and timely basis of advanced telecommunications capability to all Americans . . . by utilizing . . . price cap regulation, regulatory forbearance, measures that promote competition in the local telecommunications market, or other regulating methods that remove barriers to infrastructure investment." As the Commission points out, section 706 does contain a direct mandate—the Commission "shall encourage . . . ." In an earlier, still-binding order, however, the Commission ruled that section 706 "does not constitute an independent grant of authority." . . .

The Commission now insists that this language refers only "to whether section 706(a) supported *forbearance* authority," Resp't's Br. 41, i.e., the Commission's authority to free regulated entities from their statutory obligations in certain circumstances, see 47 U.S.C. § 160. According to the Commission, it "was not opining more generally on the effect of section 706 on ancillary authority." But the order itself says otherwise: "[S]ection 706(a) does not constitute an independent grant of forbearance authority *or of authority to employ other regulating methods*." Because the Commission has never questioned, let alone overruled, that understanding of section 706, and because agencies "may not . . . depart from a prior policy sub silentio," *FCC v. Fox Television Stations, Inc.,* 129 S. Ct. 1800, 1811 (2009), the Commission remains bound by its earlier conclusion that section 706 grants no regulatory authority. . . .

The Commission's attempt to tether its assertion of ancillary authority to section 256 of the Communications Act suffers from the same flaw. Section 256 directs the Commission to "establish procedures for . . . oversight of coordinated network planning . . . for the effective and efficient interconnection of public telecommunications networks." In language unmentioned by the Commission, however, section 256 goes on to state that "[n]othing in this section shall be construed as expanding . . . any authority that the Commission" otherwise has under law, id. § 256(c)—precisely what the Commission seeks to do here. . . .

[Additional argument presented by the FCC and refuted by the Court has been omitted.]

V.

It is true that "Congress gave the [Commission] broad and adaptable jurisdiction so that it can keep pace with rapidly evolving communications technologies." It is also true that "[t]he Internet is such a technology," id., indeed, "arguably the most important innovation in communications in a generation," id. at 30. Yet notwithstanding the "difficult regulatory problem of rapid technological change" posed by the communications industry, "the allowance of wide latitude in the exercise of delegated powers is not the equivalent of untrammeled freedom to regulate activities over which the statute fails to confer . . . Commission authority." Because the Commission has failed to tie its assertion of ancillary authority over Comcast's Internet service to any "statutorily mandated responsibility," *Am. Library*, 406 F.3d at 692, we grant the petition for review and vacate the *Order.*
   So ordered.

SOURCE: United States Court of Appeals for the District of Columbia Circuit. *Comcast Corporation v. FCC.* April 6, 2010. http://www.cadc.uscourts.gov/internet/opinions.nsf/EA10373FA9C20DEA85257807 005BD63F/$file/08-1291-1238302.pdf.

The United States and Russia Agree to New Arms Treaty

APRIL 8, 2010

After months of negotiation, on April 8, 2010, U.S. president Barack Obama and Russian Federation president Dmitry Medvedev signed a landmark agreement to further limit each nation's stock of nuclear weapons. The agreement replaced the 1991 Strategic Arms Reduction Treaty (START), which expired in December 2009. "Today is an important milestone for nuclear security and nonproliferation, and for U.S.-Russia relations," Obama said upon signing the treaty. Although the agreement faced relatively little resistance in the Russian parliament, where approval was required, the U.S. Senate put up a battle in the waning days of the 111th Congress.

NUCLEAR WEAPONS IN RUSSIA AND THE UNITED STATES

Since the start of the nuclear age, the United States and Russia have maintained a stockpile of nuclear weapons. The two countries combined hold nearly 95 percent of all nuclear weapons in the world. Near the end of the Soviet Union, in an effort to forge new agreements toward nonproliferation, the two superpowers came to the table to put together an arms reduction strategy on which both nations could agree.

START I had been in the works for more than ten years before it was signed in 1991, originally proposed by U.S. president Ronald Reagan under the guise of a third round of Strategic Arms Limitation Talks, or SALT III. The first round of SALT negotiations had begun in 1969 and resulted in the Anti-Ballistic Missile Treaty. SALT II culminated in arms reduction agreements in 1979, but the United States chose not to ratify the proposed treaty and withdrew entirely from SALT II discussions in 1986.

The 1991 START I agreement barred Russia and the United States from deploying any more than six thousand nuclear warheads and also limited the nuclear weapon carrying devices to sixteen hundred. When it was signed, the treaty was the most far-reaching of its kind in history. It went into effect in 1994, a delay that was largely caused by the fall of the Soviet Union and the security concerns it raised, which took priority over START. The two nations worked to create the START II treaty in 1993, but it was never ratified by the Russian Federation because of its protest of American involvement in Iraq and Kosovo.

A New Arms-Reduction Treaty

Negotiators in Russia and the United States, including both nations' presidents, debated for months before finally agreeing on language for the new treaty. Although both sides admitted that they had made concessions and were still in disagreement on a few points, they felt that the overall spirit of the treaty was necessary, especially to show a united front against nations like Iran and North Korea, who have defied international requests to end their nuclear weapon programs.

In the new treaty, the number of warheads allowed in each country was reduced to 1,550. In addition, limits on the number of deployed delivery vehicles, including heavy bombers and ballistic missiles, were set at no more than seven hundred. Each vehicle, however, was allowed to carry more than one nuclear warhead and still only count toward one of the delivery vehicles. The treaty includes terms that allow each nation to verify the other's compliance with weapons limits. On-site inspections, exhibitions, exchange of data, and other technical monitoring were agreed to by both parties.

The overall intent of the treaty was not to limit either nation, but to begin a conversation toward creating safer conditions around the world with regard to nuclear weapons. Medvedev called the final plan a win-win for both countries. "The result we have obtained is good," Medvedev said. "We have got a document that fully maintains the balance of interests between Russia and the U.S. The main thing is that there are no victors or losers here." The treaty was also a key effort toward restoring the relationship between the two nations, which had deteriorated significantly during the administration of President George W. Bush.

The biggest point of contention in treaty negotiations was the United States' plan to build a missile defense shield in Europe. In 2009, President Obama announced plans to put missile interceptors in Poland and the Czech Republic. He withdrew these plans in late 2009 but did announce his intent to seek a similar shield and interceptors in Romania. However, regardless of U.S. plans, Russia admitted the treaty was within its best interest because it would no longer be financially burdened to replace aging Soviet-era missiles.

Russian officials have made it clear to the United States that even though they agreed to ratify the treaty, they would withdraw support if the missile defense system became a perceived threat to Russia. Russia had made a similar threat during negotiations over START I, but it never followed through.

Both countries admitted that this treaty was only the start of a partnership they hoped would ensure further arms reduction around the world. "While the New START treaty is an important first step forward, it is just one step on a longer journey. The treaty will set the stage for further cuts, and going forward, we hope to pursue discussions with Russia on reducing both our strategic and tactical weapons, including non-deployed weapons," Obama said at the signing event in April.

Senate Debate and Approval

To win final approval, the treaty would need to be ratified in both the Russian parliament and the U.S. Senate. Approval in Russia was never a question, as members of parliament rarely vote against something that comes with overwhelming approval from the Kremlin.

In the U.S. Senate, however, sixty-seven votes were needed for approval, meaning that Democrats would need to convince a number of Republicans to vote for the treaty.

Republican leaders warned that they would not approve any treaty that got rid of any potential future missile-defense system. Senate Republicans expressed further concern about rules on weapons monitoring. While the new treaty allowed inspectors from either nation to count the number of warheads and delivery vehicles, similar language had been included in START I, but the Russians never conceded to full inspections by American observers.

During debate, some Republicans stressed the importance of approving the treaty in order to keep a watchful eye on Russia. Sen. Richard Lugar, R-Ind., the ranking member on the Senate Foreign Relations Committee, said in a floor statement, "It would be an incredible strategic blunder to sever our START relationship with Russia when that country still possesses thousands of nuclear weapons. We would be distancing ourselves from a historic rival in the area where our national security is most affected and where cooperation already has delivered successes. When it comes to our nuclear arsenals we want to keep Russia close."

Sen. John Kerry, D-Mass., chair of the Foreign Relations Committee, called on all members to support the measure to ensure safety worldwide. "This is one of those rare times in the United States Senate . . . when we have it in our power to safeguard or endanger human life on this planet," he said. "More than any other, this issue should transcend politics. . . . More than at almost any other time, the people of the world are watching us because they rely on our leadership," Kerry continued.

Final approval by the Senate was based on the Democrats' agreement to two amendments introduced by Republicans and accepted on a voice vote with little resistance. The amendments reemphasized the desire for a missile-defense program and sought continued funding to modernize the U.S. nuclear weapons complex. The amendments are nonbinding and do not affect the language of the treaty in a direct fashion. Republican attempts at changing the treaty language were thwarted by Democrats who warned that slight changes could create Russian resistance. The final vote on December 22, 2010, resulted in a 71–26 victory for the Obama administration's treaty, with thirteen Republicans joining all of the Senate Democrats in approval.

NON-PROLIFERATION IN THE OBAMA ADMINISTRATION

Ratification and approval of the new arms-reduction treaty was seen as a large victory for the Obama administration's policies on non-proliferation. The initial approval came shortly before crucial meetings were set to take place between Nuclear Non-Proliferation Treaty signatory nations.

Just before the April 8 signing, Obama had released his Nuclear Posture Review, which laid out the limited instances in which the United States would use nuclear weapons, making it clear that such weapons could be used in response to threats by North Korea and Iran. "The United States will not use or threaten to use nuclear weapons against non-nuclear weapons states that are party to the Nuclear Non-Proliferation Treaty and in compliance with their nuclear non-proliferation obligations," Obama's plan read. Iran is considered in non-compliance, and North Korea withdrew itself from the treaty in 2003. The Review also promised not to develop new nuclear weapons, which faced significant resistance from the Pentagon.

On the missile defense shield, Obama pledged to hold more conversations with Russian leaders to reach an agreement that would be amendable to both nations. Medvedev said that he felt a compromise on missile defense would eventually be reached, and he admitted that Russia agreed with the idea of the missile defense shield but shied away from the idea of interceptors that would be placed close to Russian borders.

During the signing ceremony in April, President Obama remarked that working together through the treaty and the missile defense issue was essential. "When the United States and Russia are not able to work together on big issues, it's not good for either of our nations, nor is it good for the world. Together we've stopped that drift and proven the benefits of cooperation."

—Heather Kerrigan

The following is the text of the new arms reduction treaty agreed to on April 8, 2010, by the United States and the Russian Federation.

Arms Treaty Between the United States and Russia

April 8, 2010

The United States of America and the Russian Federation, hereinafter referred to as the Parties,

Believing that global challenges and threats require new approaches to interaction across the whole range of their strategic relations,

Working therefore to forge a new strategic relationship based on mutual trust, openness, predictability, and cooperation,

Desiring to bring their respective nuclear postures into alignment with this new relationship, and endeavoring to reduce further the role and importance of nuclear weapons,

Committed to the fulfillment of their obligations under Article VI of the Treaty on the Non-Proliferation of Nuclear Weapons of July 1, 1968, and to the achievement of the historic goal of freeing humanity from the nuclear threat,

Expressing strong support for on-going global efforts in non-proliferation,

Seeking to preserve continuity in, and provide new impetus to, the step-by-step process of reducing and limiting nuclear arms while maintaining the safety and security of their nuclear arsenals, and with a view to expanding this process in the future, including to a multilateral approach,

Guided by the principle of indivisible security and convinced that measures for the reduction and limitation of strategic offensive arms and the other obligations set forth in this Treaty will enhance predictability and stability, and thus the security of both Parties,

Recognizing the existence of the interrelationship between strategic offensive arms and strategic defensive arms, that this interrelationship will become more important as strategic nuclear arms are reduced, and that current strategic defensive arms do not undermine the viability and effectiveness of the strategic offensive arms of the Parties,

Mindful of the impact of conventionally armed ICBMs and SLBMs on strategic stability,

Taking into account the positive effect on the world situation of the significant, verifiable reduction in nuclear arsenals at the turn of the 21st century,

Desiring to create a mechanism for verifying compliance with the obligations under this Treaty, adapted, simplified, and made less costly in comparison to the Treaty Between the United States of America and the Union of Soviet Socialist Republics on the Reduction and Limitation of Strategic Offensive Arms of July 31, 1991, hereinafter referred to as the START Treaty,

Recognizing that the START Treaty has been implemented by the Republic of Belarus, the Republic of Kazakhstan, the Russian Federation, Ukraine, and the United States of America, and that the reduction levels envisaged by the START Treaty were achieved,

Deeply appreciating the contribution of the Republic of Belarus, the Republic of Kazakhstan, and Ukraine to nuclear disarmament and to strengthening international peace and security as non-nuclear-weapon states under the Treaty on the Non-Proliferation of Nuclear Weapons of July 1, 1968,

Welcoming the implementation of the Treaty Between the United States of America and the Russian Federation on Strategic Offensive Reductions of May 24, 2002,

Have agreed as follows:

ARTICLE I

1. Each Party shall reduce and limit its strategic offensive arms in accordance with the provisions of this Treaty and shall carry out the other obligations set forth in this Treaty and its Protocol.

2. Definitions of terms used in this Treaty and its Protocol are provided in Part One of the Protocol.

ARTICLE II

1. Each Party shall reduce and limit its ICBMs and ICBM launchers, SLBMs and SLBM launchers, heavy bombers, ICBM warheads, SLBM warheads, and heavy bomber nuclear armaments, so that seven years after entry into force of this Treaty and thereafter, the aggregate numbers, as counted in accordance with Article III of this Treaty, do not exceed:

(a) 700, for deployed ICBMs, deployed SLBMs, and deployed heavy bombers;

(b) 1550, for warheads on deployed ICBMs, warheads on deployed SLBMs, and nuclear warheads counted for deployed heavy bombers;

(c) 800, for deployed and non-deployed ICBM launchers, deployed and non-deployed SLBM launchers, and deployed and non-deployed heavy bombers.

2. Each Party shall have the right to determine for itself the composition and structure of its strategic offensive arms.

ARTICLE III

1. For the purposes of counting toward the aggregate limit provided for in subparagraph l(a) of Article I1 of this Treaty:

(a) Each deployed ICBM shall be counted as one.

(b) Each deployed SLBM shall be counted as one.

(c) Each deployed heavy bomber shall be counted as one.

2. For the purposes of counting toward the aggregate limit provided for in subparagraph l(b) of Article II of this Treaty:

(a) For ICBMs and SLBMs, the number of warheads shall be the number of reentry vehicles emplaced on deployed ICBMs and on deployed SLBMs.

(b) One nuclear warhead shall be counted for each deployed heavy bomber.

3. For the purposes of counting toward the aggregate limit provided for in subparagraph l(c) of Article II of this Treaty:

(a) Each deployed launcher of ICBMs shall be counted as one.

(b) Each non-deployed launcher of ICBMs shall be counted as one.

(c) Each deployed launcher of SLBMs shall be counted as one.

(d) Each non-deployed launcher of SLBMs shall be counted as one.

(e) Each deployed heavy bomber shall be counted as one.

(f) Each non-deployed heavy bomber shall be counted as one.

4. For the purposes of this Treaty, including counting ICBMs and SLBMs:

(a) For ICBMs or SLBMs that are maintained, stored, and transported as assembled missiles in launch canisters, an assembled missile of a particular type, in its launch canister, shall be considered to be an ICBM or SLBM of that type.

(b) For ICBMs or SLBMs that are maintained, stored, and transported as assembled missiles without launch canisters, an assembled missile of a particular type shall be considered to be an ICBM or SLBM of that type.

(c) For ICBMs or SLBMs that are maintained, stored, and transported in stages, the first stage of an ICBM or SLBM of a particular type shall be considered to be an ICBM or SLBM of that type.

(d) Each launch canister shall be considered to contain an ICBM or SLBM from the time it first leaves a facility at which an ICBM or SLBM is installed in it, until an ICBM or SLBM has been launched from it, or until an ICBM or SLBM has been removed from it for elimination. A launch canister shall not be considered to contain an ICBM or SLBM if it contains a training model of a missile or has been placed on static display. Launch canisters for ICBMs or SLBMs of a particular type shall be distinguishable from launch canisters for ICBMs or SLBMs of a different type.

5. Newly constructed strategic offensive arms shall begin to be subject to this Treaty as follows:

(a) an ICBM, when it first leaves a production facility;

(b) a mobile launcher of ICBMs, when it first leaves a production facility;

(c) a silo launcher of ICBMs, when the silo door is first installed and closed;

(d) an SLBM, when it first leaves a production facility;

(e) an SLBM launcher, when the submarine on which that launcher is installed is first launched;

(f) a heavy bomber equipped for nuclear armaments, when its airframe is first brought out of the shop, plant, or building in which components of such a heavy bomber are assembled to produce complete airframes; or when its airframe is first brought out of the shop, plant, or building in which existing bomber airframes are converted to such heavy bomber airframes.

6. ICBMs, SLBMs, ICBM launchers, SLBM launchers, and heavy bombers shall cease to be subject to this Treaty in accordance with Parts Three and Four of the Protocol to this Treaty. ICBMs or SLBMs of an existing type shall cease to be subject to this Treaty if all

ICBM or SLBM launchers of a type intended for such ICBMs or SLBMs have been eliminated or converted in accordance with Part Three of the Protocol to this Treaty.

7. For the purposes of this Treaty:

(a) A missile of a type developed and tested solely to intercept and counter objects not located on the surface of the Earth shall not be considered to be a ballistic missile to which the provisions of this Treaty apply.

(b) Within the same type, a heavy bomber equipped for nuclear armaments shall be distinguishable from a heavy bomber equipped for non-nuclear armaments.

(c) Heavy bombers of the same type shall cease to be subject to this Treaty or to the limitations thereof when the last heavy bomber equipped for nuclear armaments of that type is eliminated or converted, as appropriate, to a heavy bomber equipped for non-nuclear armaments in accordance with Part Three of the Protocol to this Treaty. . . .

[Part 8, which describes types of intercontinental ballistic missiles (ICBMs), has been excerpted.]

ARTICLE IV

1. Each Party shall base:
(a) deployed launchers of ICBMs only at ICBM bases;
(b) deployed heavy bombers only at air bases.

2. Each Party shall install deployed launchers of SLBMs only on ballistic missile submarines.

3. Each Party shall locate:
(a) non-deployed launchers of ICBMs only at ICBM bases, production facilities, ICBM loading facilities, repair facilities, storage facilities, conversion or elimination facilities, training facilities, test ranges, and space launch facilities. Mobile launchers of prototype ICBMs shall not be located at maintenance facilities of ICBM bases;
(b) non-deployed ICBMs and non-deployed SLBMs only at, as appropriate, submarine bases, ICBM or SLBM loading facilities, maintenance facilities, repair facilities for ICBMs or SLBMs, storage facilities for ICBMs or SLBMs, conversion or elimination facilities for ICBMs or SLBMs, test ranges, space launch facilities, and production facilities. Prototype ICBMs and prototype SLBMs, however, shall not be located at maintenance facilities of ICBM bases or at submarine bases.

4. Non-deployed ICBMs and non-deployed SLBMs as well as nondeployed mobile launchers of ICBMs may be in transit. Each Party shall limit the duration of each transit between facilities to no more than 30 days.

5. Test launchers of ICBMs or SLBMs may be located only at test ranges.

6. Training launchers may be located only at ICBM bases, training facilities, and test ranges. The number of silo training launchers located at each ICBM base for silo launchers of ICBMs shall not exceed one for each type of ICBM specified for that ICBM base.

7. Each Party shall limit the number of test heavy bombers to no more than ten.

8. Each Party shall base test heavy bombers only at heavy bomber flight test centers. Non-deployed heavy bombers other than test heavy bombers shall be located only at repair facilities or production facilities for heavy bombers.

9. Each Party shall not carry out at an air base joint basing of heavy bombers equipped for nuclear armaments and heavy bombers equipped for non-nuclear armaments, unless otherwise agreed by the Parties.

10. Strategic offensive arms shall not be located at eliminated facilities except during their movement through such facilities and during visits of heavy bombers at such facilities.

11. Strategic offensive arms subject to this Treaty shall not be based outside the national territory of each Party. The obligations provided for in this paragraph shall not affect the Parties' rights in accordance with generally recognized principles and rules of international law relating to the passage of submarines or flights of aircraft, or relating to visits of submarines to ports of third States. Heavy bombers may be temporarily located outside the national territory, notification of which shall be provided in accordance with Part Four of the Protocol to this Treaty.

ARTICLE V

1. Subject to the provisions of this Treaty, modernization and replacement of strategic offensive arms may be carried out.

2. When a Party believes that a new kind of strategic offensive arm is emerging, that Party shall have the right to raise the question of such a strategic offensive arm for consideration in the Bilateral Consultative Commission.

3. Each Party shall not convert and shall not use ICBM launchers and SLBM launchers for placement of missile defense interceptors therein. Each Party further shall not convert and shall not use launchers of missile defense interceptors for placement of ICBMs and SLBMs therein. This provision shall not apply to ICBM launchers that were converted prior to signature of this Treaty for placement of missile defense interceptors therein.

ARTICLE VI

1. Conversion, elimination, or other means for removal from accountability of strategic offensive arms and facilities shall be carried out in accordance with Part Three of the Protocol to this Treaty.

2. Notifications related to conversion, elimination, or other means for removal from accountability shall be provided in accordance with Parts Three and Four of the Protocol to this Treaty.

3. Verification of conversion or elimination in accordance with this Treaty shall be carried out by:
    (a) national technical means of verification in accordance with Article X of this Treaty; and
    (b) inspection activities as provided for in Article XI of this Treaty.

ARTICLE VII

1. A database pertaining to the obligations under this Treaty shall be created in accordance with Parts Two and Four of the Protocol to this Treaty. Categories of data for this database are set forth in Part Two of the Protocol to this Treaty.

2. Each Party shall notify the other Party about changes in data and shall provide other notifications in a manner provided for in Part Four of the Protocol to this Treaty.

3. Each Party shall use the Nuclear Risk Reduction Centers in order to provide and receive notifications, unless otherwise provided for in this Treaty.

4. Each Party may provide additional notifications on a voluntary basis, in addition to the notifications specified in paragraph 2 of this Article, if it deems this necessary to ensure confidence in the fulfillment of obligations assumed under this Treaty.

5. The Parties shall hold consultations within the framework of the Bilateral Consultative Commission on releasing to the public data and information obtained during the implementation of this Treaty. The Parties shall have the right to release to the public such data and information following agreement thereon within the framework of the Bilateral Consultative Commission. Each Party shall have the right to release to the public data related to its respective strategic offensive arms.

6. Geographic coordinates relating to data provided for in Part Two of the Protocol to this Treaty, unique identifiers, site diagrams of facilities provided by the Parties pursuant to this Treaty, as well as coastlines and waters diagrams provided by the Parties pursuant to this Treaty shall not be released to the public unless otherwise agreed by the Parties within the framework of the Bilateral Consultative Commission.

7. Notwithstanding paragraph 5 of this Article, the aggregate numbers of deployed ICBMs, deployed SLBMs, and deployed heavy bombers; the aggregate numbers of warheads on deployed ICBMs, deployed SLBMs, and nuclear warheads counted for deployed heavy bombers; and the aggregate numbers of deployed and nondeployed ICBM launchers, deployed and non-deployed SLBM launchers, and deployed and non-deployed heavy bombers, may be released to the public by the Parties. . . .

[Article VIII has been omitted.]

ARTICLE IX

By mutual agreement of the Parties, telemetric information on launches of ICBMs and SLBMs shall be exchanged on a parity basis. The Parties shall agree on the amount of exchange of such telemetric information.

ARTICLE X

1. For the purpose of ensuring verification of compliance with the provisions of this Treaty, each Party undertakes:

    (a) to use national technical means of verification at its disposal in a manner consistent with generally recognized principles of international law;

    (b) not to interfere with the national technical means of verification of the other Party operating in accordance with this Article; and

    (c) not to use concealment measures that impede verification, by national technical means of verification, of compliance with the provisions of this Treaty.

2. The obligation not to use concealment measures includes the obligation not to use them at test ranges, including measures that result in the concealment of ICBMs, SLBMs, ICBM launchers, or the association between ICBMs or SLBMs and their launchers

during testing. The obligation not to use concealment measures shall not apply to cover or concealment practices at ICBM bases or to the use of environmental shelters for strategic offensive arms.

ARTICLE XI

1. For the purpose of confirming the accuracy of declared data on strategic offensive arms subject to this Treaty and ensuring verification of compliance with the provisions of this Treaty, each Party shall have the right to conduct inspection activities in accordance with this Article and Part Five of the Protocol to this Treaty.

2. Each Party shall have the right to conduct inspections at ICBM bases, submarine bases, and air bases. The purpose of such inspections shall be to confirm the accuracy of declared data on the numbers and types of deployed and non-deployed strategic offensive arms subject to this Treaty; the number of warheads located on deployed ICBMs and deployed SLBMs; and the number of nuclear armaments located on deployed heavy bombers. Such inspections shall hereinafter be referred to as Type One inspections.

3. Each Party shall have the right to conduct inspections at facilities listed in Section VII of Part Five of the Protocol to this Treaty. The purpose of such inspections shall be to confirm the accuracy of declared data on the numbers, types, and technical characteristics of non-deployed strategic offensive arms subject to this Treaty and to confirm that strategic offensive arms have been converted or eliminated.

In addition, each Party shall have the right to conduct inspections at formerly declared facilities, which are provided for in Part Two of the Protocol to this Treaty, to confirm that such facilities are not being used for purposes inconsistent with this Treaty.

The inspections provided for in this paragraph shall hereinafter be referred to as Type Two inspections.

4. Each Party shall conduct exhibitions and have the right to participate in exhibitions conducted by the other Party. The purpose of such exhibitions shall be to demonstrate distinguishing features and to confirm technical characteristics of new types, and to demonstrate the results of conversion of the first item of each type of strategic offensive arms subject to this Treaty.

ARTICLE XII

To promote the objectives and implementation of the provisions of this Treaty, the Parties hereby establish the Bilateral Consultative Commission, the authority and procedures for the operation of which are set forth in Part Six of the Protocol to this Treaty.

ARTICLE XIII

To ensure the viability and effectiveness of this Treaty, each Party shall not assume any international obligations or undertakings that would conflict with its provisions. . . .

ARTICLE XIV

1. This Treaty, including its Protocol, which is an integral part thereof, shall be subject to ratification in accordance with the constitutional procedures of each Party. This Treaty shall enter into force on the date of the exchange of instruments of ratification.

2. This Treaty shall remain in force for 10 years unless it is superseded earlier by a subsequent agreement on the reduction and limitation of strategic offensive arms. If either Party raises the issue of extension of this Treaty, the Parties shall jointly consider the matter. If the Parties decide to extend this Treaty, it will be extended for a period of no more than five years unless it is superseded earlier by a subsequent agreement on the reduction and limitation of strategic offensive arms.

3. Each Party shall, in exercising its national sovereignty, have the right to withdraw from this Treaty if it decides that extraordinary events related to the subject matter of this Treaty have jeopardized its supreme interests. It shall give notice of its decision to the other Party. Such notice shall contain a statement of the extraordinary events the notifying Party regards as having jeopardized its supreme interests. This Treaty shall terminate three months from the date of receipt by the other Party of the aforementioned notice, unless the notice specifies a later date.

4. As of the date of its entry into force, this Treaty shall supersede the Treaty Between the United States of America and the Russian Federation on Strategic Offensive Reductions of May 24, 2002, which shall terminate as of that date. . . .

[Articles XV, XVI, and the signatures have been omitted.]

Source: U.S. Department of State. "Treaty Between the United States of America and the Russian Federation on Measures for the Further Reduction and Limitation of Strategic Offensive Arms." April 8, 2010. http://www.state.gov/documents/organization/140035.pdf.

Other Historic Documents of Interest

From Previous *Historic Documents*

Unrest in Kyrgyzstan

Kyrgyzstan, one of the former Soviet bloc's poorest nations, erupted in days of unrest in April, which stretched into the summer of 2010. Protests broke out after the government announced it would raise utility prices 200 percent. The persistent high prices and government corruption had finally reached a breaking point for Kyrgyzstan's citizens. Hundreds were killed in the violence, and many fled into Uzbekistan. In the end, the government was toppled, and the new president ushered in a new era of reform, quickly rewriting the nation's constitution to form a parliamentary republic.

CAUSES OF UNREST

Kyrgyzstan, a poor, but progressive Central Asian state, has often found itself on the brink of unrest. Its economy collapsed in the 1990s and has never recovered. Many citizens feel that the government does not fully provide for them and that they have no way of bringing themselves out of poverty with the consistently rising prices of essential goods and services. Kyrgyzstan provides little for itself by way of food, oil, and other raw materials. Forty percent of the nation's gross domestic product (GDP) is made up of remittances sent from family members working in the more lucrative job market in Russia. The global economic crisis, however, caused jobs in Russia to dry up, thereby causing additional economic strain in Kyrgyzstan.

Tensions between ethnic groups in the country further destabilized the nation. The country is predominantly ethnically Kyrgyz, and minority groups are made up of Uzbeks, Russians, and a number of other ethnicities. In some areas, the Uzbeks, which comprise 15 percent of the nation's population, hold a majority. The two groups have a long history of conflict, ever since Josef Stalin divided the Fergana Valley into three sections—one for Uzbekistan, one for Kyrgyzstan, and a third for Tajikistan.

In April 2010, economic tension in the nation reached a breaking point, and citizens took to the streets to protest utility price hikes imposed by President Kurmanbek Bakiyev's government. Although Bakiyev had maintained some popularity after agreeing to reduce his presidential powers in 2006—a surprising move that was intended to fulfill a promise to end political corruption—the nation had recently turned against him. Opponents claimed that he had failed to take actual steps to implement any of the programs he had promised to create during the Tulip Revolution of March-April 2005 that had brought him to power. Although Bakiyev claimed to be working toward reducing corruption, his appointment of family and friends to top political posts reflected poorly on this goal.

Another of Bakiyev's promises during the Tulip Revolution was to keep utility costs low. Bakiyev said the 2010 price hikes were unavoidable because the government could no longer afford to subsidize utilities as a result of the global economic crisis. Many citizens, however, were unwilling to accept that they would need to put a large portion of their monthly salaries toward utilities.

Riots in the capital city of Bishkek turned violent, and early accounts reported that seventy-five people were killed. During the fighting, Bakiyev fled to southern Kyrgyzstan and Foreign Minister Roza Otunbayeva worked to rally support to rebuild the government under her leadership. Bakiyev agreed to resign if he was granted permission to safely leave the country. Otunbayeva announced that she had received an official resignation notice from Bakiyev and that she would become the leader of the government until official elections could be held.

The 2010 violence pitted the ethnic Kyrgyz and Uzbeks against one another. Reports from those in the country said that Kyrgyz groups were burning down the homes of Uzbeks and attempting to kill any they could find.

The crisis in the spring and summer of 2010 was not the first power struggle Kyrgyzstan has witnessed. During the last days of the Soviet Union, fighting broke out in Osh, the nation's second largest city, which quickly turned deadly. A state of emergency was declared to keep the peace. After the violence subsided, Askar Akayev was declared the nation's first president. Akayev was a brutal ruler, but he managed to keep violence between the ethnic sects to a minimum. In 2005, shortly after Akayev announced his intention to rewrite the nation's constitution to indefinitely retain his position as head of state, Bakiyev, then the leader of the People's Movement of Kyrgyzstan, led the Tulip Revolution, forcing Akayev from power. When he assumed the presidency, Bakiyev promised to fight the corruption that had been rampant in Akayev's administration, and he also promised to champion the people and bring them out of poverty.

At that time, international observers thought Bakiyev's governing style would be a positive influence in Central Asia, one that would turn Kyrgyzstan into a truly democratic state. The Tulip Revolution only led to one night of violent protests, and by the time Bakiyev had assumed power, he held a large amount of support from the people of Kyrgyzstan, even those in the southern regions, who were often caught up in the violent ethnic struggle.

New Power

After the ouster, Otunbayeva was named the interim president and leader of the "people's government." Although Otunbayeva had been an early supporter of Bakiyev, she called the revolt "our answer to the repression and tyranny by the Bakiyev regime." She promised the people of Kyrgyzstan that she would hold elections in the fall to allow them to choose their own leader. After resigning and fleeing the country following his ouster from power, Bakiyev was found in Belarus in mid-April, where he claimed that he still maintained power in Kyrgyzstan and would remain the legitimate leader until his death. Bakiyev later sent another official letter of resignation to Otunbayeva.

Otunbayeva's government got off to a strong start, but quickly began facing problems in trying to keep the police and military under its control. Crime levels rose, and unrest again broke out around the country. In June, renewed violence was sparked when Kyrgyz soldiers stormed a village near Osh. There are varying accounts of the incident, with

Kyrgyzstan saying that the soldiers entered the village and were fired upon, while witnesses said the Kyrgyz soldiers beat Uzbeks in the village without provocation.

The violence spread, leading to twenty-two hundred deaths in an outbreak of mass riots and looting. The Kyrgyz fighters saw the violence as a struggle for their ethnic survival. Otunbayeva was sympathetic to the Uzbeks, a position not shared by her predecessor, and in retaliation to her government's power, Bakiyev supporters took control of provincial government buildings, holding then until Otunbayeva's military was able to regain control.

Otunbayeva blamed the violence on her predecessor and admitted that she did not yet have full control of the government, especially security forces. "There are a number of people in key positions loyal to Bakiyev, and in the local governments, too," she said. "They're working hard and certainly, absolutely [engaging in] sabotage." After the June violence, Otunbayeva came under significant scrutiny for failure to put measures in place to quell future violence and seek a resolution to the long-standing ethnic tensions.

Because of the increase in violence, officials decided to delay the presidential election until December 2011, but would still hold parliamentary elections as scheduled in October 2010. This gave Otunbayeva the opportunity to rewrite the nation's constitution, turning it into a parliamentary republic. "We hope to rebuild the democratic system . . . and in particular freedom of speech and human rights," Otunbayeva said. In June, the nation overwhelmingly supported the referendum to remake the government, which Otunbayeva described as a "caretaker government."

Otunbayeva's government will face significant challenges before the 2011 election. To find a way to bring the people of Kyrgyzstan out of poverty, the government will need to reduce the nation's reliance on its neighbors to provide food and fuel. Otunbayeva will be forced to respond to the ethnic clashes, but bringing both the Kyrgyz and Uzbeks to the table to find an amendable agreement will not be easy.

WORLDWIDE IMPACT

Both Russia and the United States maintain a heavy stake in the politics of Kyrgyzstan, and both maintain air bases within the country. The United States uses its air base as a staging ground for NATO missions to Afghanistan. In 2009, the U.S. base was nearly closed when the Russian government promised to send extensive aid to Kyrgyzstan if it refused to allow the Americans to stay. The Obama administration, in turn, agreed to pay a significant amount more to maintain the base, and Otunbayeva agreed to extend the lease on the base until 2011.

When violence broke out, the United States renewed its call for a partnership to aid Kyrgyzstan on its continuing path toward democracy. "We urge that calm be restored to Bishkek and other affected areas in a manner consistent with democratic principles and with respect for human rights," said White House press secretary Robert Gibbs. "The United States looks forward to continuing our productive relationship with the people of Kyrgyzstan and the renewal of Kyrgyzstan's democratic path."

In Russia, the Kremlin believes that it still has some influence over Kyrgyzstan as one of its former republics. As such, after the unrest broke out, the Russian government agreed to send $50 million in aid to Otunbayeva's government. In addition, after rejecting early calls from the Kyrgyz government, Russia agreed to send peacekeeping paratroopers who would protect Russia's military outposts. Russia sent materials to the Kyrgyz government—including helicopters and trucks—to help stop the violence. "This is extremely dangerous for this region and it is necessary to do everything possible to put an end to such acts," said Russian Federation president Dmitry Medvedev. The assistance from Russia would go no further than material support, Medvedev said, renewing his stance that Russia would not become directly involved in the violence.

Uzbekistan was significantly impacted during the fighting, as one hundred thousand Uzbek refugees from Kyrgyzstan fled over the border between April and June to escape the fighting. Uzbekistan's government set up temporary refugee camps on its side of the border to provide space and assistance for the Uzbeks. In late June, however, Uzbekistan's government determined that without support from international organizations, it could no longer accept additional Uzbek refugees. "Today we will stop accepting refugees from the Kyrgyz side because we have no place to accommodate them and no capacity to cope with them," said Uzbekistan's deputy prime minister, Abdullah Aripov. The United Nations pleaded with the country to keep its borders open, but Uzbekistan refused until additional resources could be found. "If we have the ability to help them and to treat them of course we will open the border," said Aripov.

—Heather Kerrigan

Following is a press release issued by the U.S. Department of State on April 8, 2010, in response to unrest in Kyrgyzstan; a statement by White House press secretary Robert Gibbs on April 8, 2010, in response to the situation in Kyrgyzstan; a statement by the U.S. Embassy in Kyrgyzstan on April 11, 2010, regarding unrest in the nation; and a press release from the United Nations on June 15, 2010, on renewed violence in Kyrgyzstan.

U.S. Expresses Concern over Violence in Kyrgyzstan

April 8, 2010

Washington—The United States expressed deep concern about the loss of life in Kyrgyzstan following two days of bloody protests and unrest that started in northwestern Kyrgyzstan on April 6 and spread throughout the capital, Bishkek, on April 7.

"We have reached out to government and civil society leaders to urge calm, nonviolence and respect for the rights of citizens, especially under emergency situations," U.S. Ambassador Ian Kelly said April 8 in Vienna at a meeting of the Permanent Council of the Organization for Security and Co-operation in Europe (OSCE).

White House press secretary Robert Gibbs told reporters April 8 that President Obama has been kept informed about the crisis in Kyrgyzstan. Gibbs is traveling with the president, who was in Prague for the signing of a new arms-reduction treaty with Russian President Dmitry Medvedev.

"The president has been closely following the events in Kyrgyzstan, and continues to monitor the situation with his national security team," Gibbs said. "We urge that calm be restored to Bishkek and other affected areas in a manner consistent with democratic principles and with respect for human rights."

Gibbs added that the United States deplores the use of deadly force by some of the Kyrgyz security services against the demonstrators and by some of the demonstrators against the security forces, and continues to be concerned about looting and disorder.

"The United States looks forward to continuing our productive relationship with the people of Kyrgyzstan and the renewal of Kyrgyzstan's democratic path," Gibbs said.

Thousands of protesters, furious over corruption and rising energy costs, seized government buildings in Talas on April 6 and in Bishkek April 7 and clashed with police and security forces. Police and security forces opened fire in Bishkek, killing dozens and wounding hundreds more, according to news reports. In the aftermath of the clashes, Kyrgyzstan President Kurmanbek Bakiyev fled the capital after declaring a state of emergency, and an opposition group has formed a transitional government. News reports on April 8 said Bakiyev was in a southern Kyrgyzstan city.

At the OSCE, Kelly said the United States has endorsed an April 6 statement from U.N. Secretary-General Ban Ki-moon that calls for restraint and immediate talks aimed at lowering tensions. Ban dispatched Ján Kubiš, the executive secretary of the U.N. Economic Commission for Europe, as his special envoy to the Central Asian nation. Ban was in Bishkek April 2–3, and had urged leaders there to uphold human rights and guarantee freedom of speech.

OSCE Chairperson-in-Office Kanat Saudabayev, who is Kazakhstan's secretary of state and foreign minister, announced April 8 that he was sending special envoy Zhanybek Karibzhanov to Kyrgyzstan. Karibzhanov is deputy speaker of the Majilis (the lower house of parliament) of Kazakhstan, chairman of the Kazakh-Kyrgyz inter-parliamentary group and a former Kazakh ambassador. Saudabayev also announced that Ambassador Herbert Salber, director of the OSCE Conflict Prevention Centre in Vienna, will travel to Bishkek to support Karibzhanov.

The United States maintains a military transit center at the Manas airport, near Bishkek, which it uses to support operations in Afghanistan. Russia also maintains an air base in the country. U.S. officials said the transit center at Manas was operating, but personnel were confined to the facility.

SOURCE: U.S. Department of State. "U.S. Concerned by Unrest in Kyrgyzstan." April 8, 2010. http://www.america.gov/st/peacesec-english/2010/April/20100408154911dmslahrellek0.4479792.html#.

White House Statement on Unrest in *Kyrgyzstan*

DOCUMENT

April 8, 2010

"The President has been closely following the events in Kyrgyzstan, and continues to monitor the situation with his National Security Team. We urge that calm be restored to Bishkek and other affected areas in a manner consistent with democratic principles and with respect for human rights. We deplore the use of deadly force by some of the security services against the demonstrators and by some demonstrators and continue to be concerned by ongoing looting and disorder. The United States looks forward to continuing our productive relationship with the people of Kyrgyzstan and the renewal of Kyrgyzstan's democratic path."

SOURCE: U.S. Department of State. "Statement on Unrest in Kyrgyzstan." April 8, 2010. http://www.america.gov/st/texttrans-english/2010/April/20100408171939xjsnommis0.5371973.html&distid=ucs#.

U.S. Embassy in Kyrgyzstan Statement on Unrest

April 11, 2010

I have just returned to Kyrgyzstan from the United States this morning. Along with the President and the Secretary of State, I have been closely following the recent events in the Kyrgyz Republic. I would like to express my sincere condolences to all of those who have lost loved ones or experienced injuries during the events of the last few days.

I am deeply committed to our continued partnership with Kyrgyzstan for the benefit of the Kyrgyz people. I look forward to continuing to support the economic and democratic development of Kyrgyzstan.

We are working with the provisional government and I plan to meet with its members in the near future. As you are aware, Secretary Clinton spoke with Ms. Otunbayeva yesterday evening. She encouraged peaceful resolution to the political problems Kyrgyzstan is currently experiencing and expressed hope for the renewal of Kyrgyzstan's path to democracy.

We are providing humanitarian assistance and plan to contribute more in the coming weeks. We have been providing medical supplies and assistance through the Transit Center at Manas. We are still assessing needs and considering what more we can do to help the Kyrgyz people in the recovery and development of their country.

We continue to encourage all parties to refrain from violence, so Kyrgyzstan can move forward on a productive and democratic path. I intend to put forth my full effort to support a bright and democratic future in this beautiful country, which has been and will continue to be a vital partner of the United States.

Source: Embassy of the United States in Bishkek, Kyrgyzstan. "Statement in Response to Recent Events in Kyrgyzstan." April 11, 2010. http://bishkek.usembassy.gov/2010_0411_ambassador_statement.html.

United Nations Statement on Violence in Kyrgyzstan

June 15, 2010

Two Special Advisers of United Nations Secretary-General Ban Ki-moon, Francis Deng on the Prevention of Genocide and Edward Luck on the responsibility to protect, expressed grave concern on Tuesday over the recent eruption of violence in Kyrgyzstan. "I am extremely concerned about the violence in South Kyrgyzstan, which has broken out along ethnic lines. I encourage the Interim Government and international actors to do all in their power to stop the violence and ensure the protection of vulnerable minority communities," stated Mr. Deng.

The Special Advisers have been monitoring the situation in Kyrgyzstan closely since April 2010, when the ouster of President Kurmanbek Bakiyev brought ethnic tensions to the surface, particularly between the Kyrgyz and Uzbek communities in the south. The Special Advisers noted that the violence that started on 10 June appears to have targeted ethnic Uzbeks in particular. "The pattern and scale of the violence, which has resulted in the mass displacement of Uzbeks from South Kyrgyzstan, could amount to ethnic cleansing," warned Special Adviser Luck. He reminded all parties that the 2005 World Summit banned either the commission or the incitement of ethnic cleansing, genocide, war crimes, or crimes against humanity.

Given the requests by the Interim Government for international assistance to the people of Kyrgysztan, the Special Advisers called on the international community to operationalise its "responsibility to protect" by providing coordinated and timely assistance to stop the violence and its incitement. They underscored the urgency of ensuring that the violence does not spread to other regions of Kyrgyzstan or to neigbouring countries.

The Special Advisers called on the Interim Government, neighboring states, and the larger international community to take all possible steps to reduce the risk of violence along ethnic lines in the future. "The current crisis in Kyrgyzstan has revealed a clear ethnic fault-line that has developed over decades. Once they have curbed the violence, the Kyrgyzstan authorities should acknowledge and address its underlying causes in order to prevent any recurrence, put in place a process of reconciliation in collaboration with civil society, and work to preserve the country's ethnic diversity and heritage. The United Nations and the international community stand ready to assist in these efforts."

SOURCE: United Nations. "UN Special Advisers of the Secretary-General on the Prevention of Genocide and on the Responsibility to Protect on the Situation in Kyrgyzstan." June 15, 2010. http://www.un.org/en/preventgenocide/adviser/pdf/Statement%20of%20Special%20Advisers%20Deng%20and%20Luck%20on%20the%20situation%20in%20Kyrgyzstan%2015%20June%202010.pdf.

OTHER HISTORIC DOCUMENTS OF INTEREST

FROM PREVIOUS *HISTORIC DOCUMENTS*

Polish President and Top Politicians Killed in Plane Crash

APRIL 18 AND AUGUST 6, 2010

On April 10, a plane carrying Polish president Lech Kaczyński, his wife, and many top Polish politicians crashed in western Russia, killing everyone aboard. The outpouring of grief from around the world was immediate, but the country quickly worked to find a new leader. The ensuing election pitted the president's brother, Jarosław Kaczyński, a former prime minister, against the leader of Poland's lower house of parliament, Bronisław Komorowski. Jarosław Kaczyński's unpopularity during his tenure as prime minister gave the win to Komorowski. In August, Komorowski took office, promising to end corruption in Polish politics and carve out a space for the nation as a leader within the European Union, breaking a pro-U.S. trend set by his predecessor.

President Kaczyński

Lech Kaczyński was born in 1949 and had his first claim to fame starring with his twin brother in a movie called *The Two Who Stole the Moon*. It was with his brother, Jarosław, that Kaczyński would climb through the ranks of Polish politics. Throughout the 1970s and 1980s, the two were active members of anticommunist groups, and they served as advisers in the Solidarity movement, the first noncommunist trade union to sprout up in Poland. Because of the labor union's popularity, the Polish government tried to shut it down during a period of political repression in the 1980s. Kaczyński's involvement with the movement at this time led to his one-year internment. Solidarity maintained its popularity and was invited to negotiate with future governments.

His ascension to the Polish presidency began when Kaczyński was elected as a senator shortly before being appointed to the position of chief security adviser under Lech Wałęsa, who was elected president in 1990. After a falling out with Wałęsa, Kaczyński was fired from his position. Kaczyński went on to serve as the justice minister from 2000 to 2001 and gained notoriety and popularity for his anticrime projects. In 2001, Kaczyński was elected mayor of Warsaw, where he enjoyed popularity because of his anticorruption and no-nonsense form of governing.

Kaczyński's background in the anticommunist movement, however, cost him some supporters who felt that he was trying to drive all former communists from Poland. His record on human rights issues was also brought into question when he attempted to stop a gay rights parade from taking place in Warsaw, stating that he feared the parade would promote a "homosexual lifestyle." Poland was taken to the European Court of Human

Rights over this and other issues pertaining to the free speech afforded to gay and lesbian citizens of the country. Kaczyński represented the nation and lost. The court ruled that Poland was in direct violation of freedom of assembly.

In September 2005, the Law and Justice political party, which was founded and headed by Jarosław Kaczyński, won the parliamentary election. One month later, Lech Kaczyński was elected president of Poland, riding a platform of combating corruption and creating a stronger Poland. The following year, the Law and Justice party chose Jarosław Kaczyński as prime minister, and the twin brothers held both positions at the top of Polish government. Lech Kaczyński continued to enjoy support from the people of Poland, while Jarosław Kaczyński's popularity waned. Jarosław Kaczyński was often unwilling to compromise with other members of Poland's parliament, and his strong views against communism left many fearing that he intended to rid the nation, by any means, of anyone who had previously supported the Communist Party.

Upon being elected to the presidency, Lech Kaczyński made it clear that his loyalties were more tied to the United States than the European Union (EU), often putting him at odds with the organization. He tried to maintain a distance from the EU in an attempt to ensure that the nation could retain its conservative values, especially when it came to the Lisbon Treaty, an EU document that disallowed discrimination against European citizens on the basis of sexual orientation. President Kaczyński called on the United States to place its missile defense shield inside Poland, which he called mutually beneficial. He garnered support for this plan from former U.S. president George W. Bush, but his successor, Barack Obama, was forced to draw down plans in an effort to appease Russia. One of Lech Kaczyński's greatest aspirations was to expand membership in the North Atlantic Treaty Organization (NATO) by encouraging the body to admit the Ukraine and Georgia. Western nations, and the EU as a whole, believed that this idea could only lead to increased tensions between the East and West and that Russia would feel threatened.

In domestic affairs, Lech Kaczyński called for a radical transformation of Poland from its former communist self to what he called a new Fourth Republic, which would be based on justice for all in society, no matter each person's political beliefs.

The reign of the brothers lasted until 2007, when Jarosław Kaczyński lost his position as prime minister after his governing coalition could not garner enough support in the parliamentary election. Lech Kaczyński, however, remained immensely popular, especially with the Polish Jewish community. He was the first president of Poland to attend a service at a synagogue in a gesture of goodwill toward the community.

On April 10, 2010, Lech Kaczyński was with his wife, army chief, deputy foreign minister, central bank governor, and many legislators traveling to Russia to commemorate the seventieth anniversary of the World War II killing of twenty-two thousand Polish officers by Soviet security forces. Their plane crashed in western Russia, approximately one-half mile from the Smolensk airport. Witnesses said the plane hit a grove of trees before breaking apart and catching fire. There were no survivors.

Investigations into the cause of the plane crash were launched in both Russia and Poland. In January 2011, Russia released its report, which faulted pilot error as the reason behind the crash. According to the report, the pilot ignored warnings of bad weather, fearing that landing at another airport would upset the president. Poland's government rejected the Russian report, calling it incomplete. Jarosław Kaczyński and some conspiracy theorists questioned the idea that the plane had simply suffered mechanical troubles while trying to land, and they instead placed blame on the Russian government. Lech Kaczyński had previously expressed concern about his presidential plane after it experienced mechanical problems during a 2008 trip to Asia. "Any flight brings with it a certain risk, but a very serious risk attaches to the responsibilities of a president, because it is necessary to fly constantly," Lech Kaczyński said.

Following the plane crash, the speaker of Poland's lower house of parliament, Bronisław Komorowski, took control of the government. He immediately consoled the nation, saying, "There is no right or left today. There is no separation, no difference. We are together in our condolences to the families of those who have died."

PRESIDENTIAL ELECTION

Komorowski, though appointed the interim president, could not hold that seat without a proper election. There was already a presidential election scheduled for the fall, but it was moved into the early summer in order to find a replacement for President Kaczyński. Two candidates rose to the top—Komorowski and Kaczyński's brother, Jarosław. Both candidates first became politically active in earlier anticommunist movements and shared similar views on the role government should play in the lives of Poles. Kaczyński gained popularity from older voters in rural areas because of his strong ties to the Catholic Church. Komorowski, on the other hand, was from a rich family with a Catholic background and preferred a government that was more separate from the church.

After his fall from the prime minister post in 2007, Kaczyński became relatively unpopular in Poland because of his governing style—he was often combative in debate and unwilling to take different viewpoints into consideration while legislation was being crafted. However, after his brother's death, public opinion toward Kaczyński softened and Poles began to look past what they had earlier called a "witch hunt" to root out former communists.

Polling before the election showed Kaczyński faring poorly, but as the election drew near, he gained ground but could never quite close the gap with Komorowski. As the votes were counted, Komorowski retained his seat with approximately 53 percent of the vote.

In his concession speech, Kaczyński did not express discontent over his loss, but reminded Poland's residents of his brother's legacy. "I would like to mention here the man, the people who are the reason for our being here: my brother and all those killed in the Smolensk catastrophe. Let us remember them because this result grew out of their martyr-like deaths. A new quality grew out of my brother's work and service, a return to values, a return to patriotism."

NEW PRESIDENT TAKES OFFICE

Before the final election results had been announced, Poland's prime minister, Donald Tusk, said, "If this result is confirmed, this will be one of the happiest days of my life." Having Komorowski in the position of president presumably creates a stronger coalition between the posts of president and prime minister. Both Komorowski and Tusk are members of the Civic Platform party, which was created by Tusk. As such, any legislation proposed by the party in parliament would not likely be vetoed by the new president. Tusk supports closer ties to the EU, a position shared by Komorowski, which is especially important, as Poland assumed the presidency of the EU in 2011. In outlining his party's platform, Komorowski invited all Poles to join in his government. "I am willing to cooperate with you and consider the most important issues for Poland," he said. "I invite representatives of different parties, various philosophies of life and social groups. The seat of

Poland's president will be an open place in which roads of all Poles can meet. . . . Our state's development and modernization—and as a result, the possibility to fully benefit from our change of civilization—depends on our mutual confidence, willingness and ability to cooperate and the size of social capital."

Komorowski supports not only closer ties to the EU but also stronger ties with Germany and Russia, two countries that have had a volatile relationship with Poland since the end of World War II. Economics will also play a central role in Komorowski's presidency. Although the nation is often less financially sound than its neighbors, it was the only European nation in 2009 to escape recession. In 2010, however, the budget deficit had begun to creep up and tax revenues had fallen in the months before the election.

—Heather Kerrigan

Following is a press release from the Office of the President of the Republic of Poland on April 18, 2010, announcing the burial of Polish president Lech Kaczyński; and the speech by new Polish president Bronisław Komorowski, on August 6, 2010, outlining his government's plans for the coming years.

DOCUMENT   *Poland's President Buried*

April 18, 2010

On Sunday, President Lech Kaczyński and his wife Maria were laid to rest in the Wawel. The family and friends of the deceased, as well as the representatives of the highest authorities and 18 foreign delegations, took part in the funeral ceremony. About 150,000 people gathered in the Market Square of Cracow, in the adjacent streets, in the Błonia Park and near the Sanctuary in Łagiewniki.

The invited foreign guests that attended the ceremony included: the presidents of Russia Dmitry Medvedev, Germany, Horst Koehler, Ukraine, Viktor Yanukovych, the Czech Republic, Vaclav Klaus, Latvia, Valdis Zatlers, and Lithuania, Dalia Grybauskaite as well as the prime Minister of Estonia Andrus Ansip. According to the Ministry of Foreign Affairs, delegations of 18 countries took part in the funeral ceremonies. The head of the European Parliament, Jerzy Buzek, also arrived at the Basilica.

In St. Mary's Basilica, the coffins were placed on catafalques in front of the main altar by Veit Stoss, with a guard of honour beside them. The church was decorated with national flags and flowers. At 2 p.m. the mass began, in which the official delegations took part. The emissary of Pope Benedict XVI, the Dean of the College of Cardinals, Cardinal Angelo Sodano, had been expected to celebrate the mass. However, due to the closed airspace, he was unable to arrive in Cracow on Sunday. He was replaced by the papal nuncio in Poland, Archbishop Józef Kowalczyk, who read out the homily prepared by Cardinal Sodano.

"70 years ago Katyń made two nations grow apart and attempts at concealing the truth of the innocent blood spilt there prevented painful wounds from healing. The tragedy that happened eight days ago has brought out the good in people and nations. The compassion and support that we were offered in those days from our Russian brothers revives our hopes for rapprochement and reconciliation between our two Slavonic nations," said Cardinal Stanisław Dziwisz while beginning the ceremonial service.

"I direct these words to the President of Russia," said the metropolitan bishop of Cracow, turning to Dmitry Medvedev, present at the mass. He added that the reconciliation was a task for our generation. "Let us accept it with magnanimity," he appealed. He reminded those gathered that this was also the wish of the deceased president and the speech that he never managed to give in Katyń included the following words: "we ought to walk the road that brings our nations closer together, without stopping and without moving backwards."

In his homily, Cardinal Sodano wrote that Poles have always been able to "properly respond to times of trial" and to "find a way to better social coexistence and to great national unity." "Nations do not perish, as successive popes have repeated on various occasions," wrote Sodano. He appealed for the "bonds of friendship and collaboration between nations" in Europe and all over the world to be strengthened.

"The sacrifice of those who died tragically in the Smoleńsk disaster cannot be in vain and it ought to encourage reconciliation within the Polish people and between Poles and Russians," said the speaker of the Polish Sejm, Bronisław Komorowski, in his speech at the end of the Sunday mass. He emphasised that the sound of the Royal Sigismund Bell in Cracow asked everyone not to let the deaths of the 96 Poles to be a "futile sacrifice" and it urged that "the sense of community, the community that is mourning the pilgrims of the Polish cause who died tragically, bear good fruit."

He added that the Sigismund Bell appeals to "the mourners to stay together by the side of freedom, solidarity and truth." "It calls for our good will and kindness to outlast the time of mourning. It appeals for reconciliation within the Poles," said Komorowski. According to him, this should also lead to reconciliation with the Russian nation "in the name of overcoming the tragedy of Katyń."

The speaker of the Sejm stated that Lech Kaczyński had intended to say important words in Katyń, words reminding us of the tragedy of 1940: "Katyń has been a painful wound in Polish history and for long decades it has been poisoning relations between Poles and Russians." He added that the president had not managed to express his wish for the "wound of Katyń to finally be able to heal." "This last will (. . .) ought to be carried out through rapprochement and reconciliation," he said.

"No one has remained as faithful to the values of Solidarity as Lech Kaczyński. We will be proud to call him 'the man of Solidarity,'" said the leader of the Independent Self-Governing Trade Union 'Solidarity,' Janusz Śniadek. He added that the president has reminded us what it means to be Polish and the example of his life and his tragic death yet again revived the spirit of solidarity in Polish hearts. "Mocked for out-of-date patriotism, faithful to God and our country, we raised our heads. Let us do our best not to let the flame lit in our hearts and minds burn out," said Śniadek.

The presidential couple were accompanied in their journey from St. Mary's Basilica to the Wawel by a funeral procession of several hundred people. As the procession was passing the Katyń Cross located at the foot of the Wawel, the Sigismund Bell reverberated.

Only the closest family and friends were present while the coffins were laid into the sarcophagus. The funeral ceremonies ended with a national salute—21 gun salvos to honour the presidential couple. The national salute was given by 6 saluting guns of the Ceremonial Guard Battalion of the Polish Army based on a 1939 howitzer design.

After the funeral ceremony, members of the official delegations conveyed their condolences to the family of the presidential couple and to the representatives of the Polish authorities. The closest family of Lech and Maria Kaczyński, their daughter, Marta and the president's brother, Jarosław, received condolences. Polish authorities were represented by the speakers of the Sejm and the Senate—Bronisław Komorowski and Bogdan Borusewicz, the Prime Minister, Donald Tusk and the Minister for Foreign Affairs, Radosław Sikorski.

Having paid their condolences, each person signed the book of condolence. In the evening, access to the crypt with the bodies of Lech and Maria Kaczyński was provided to all the participants of the funeral ceremony, who were able to pay their last respects to the couple.

Source: President of the Republic of Poland. "President Lech Kaczyński and his wife Maria laid to rest in the Wawel." April 18, 2010. http://www.prezydent.pl/en/archive/news-archive/news-2010/art,12,124, president-lech-kaczynski-and-his-wife-maria-laid-to-rest-in-the-wawel,1.html.

DOCUMENT

New President of Poland Addresses the Nation

August 6, 2010

Respected Speakers, Honourable National Assembly,
  Distinguished Guests,
  Dear Compatriots,
  It is difficult for me to hide my emotions when I stand at such moment in the place where one can feel the heart of Polish democracy beating. I have heard this pulse of Polish democracy; I have felt it for 19 years while working in Parliament. I would like to thank both Chambers for these 19 years of working together with many people that sit in this room today as well.
  Ladies and Gentlemen,
  Today it is a great honour for me to accept this strong commitment. Thus, I would like to thank those of you who share this significant moment with me and my family, both here in the Polish Sejm and at home. The swearing-in ceremony of the President is always a celebration of Polish statehood and Polish democracy. A celebration in which each and every Pole participates and should participate.
  Therefore, I would like to thank the nearly nine million Poles who brought me to the President's office. I would like to assure you that I will do my best not to disappoint your expectations and hopes. I also remember that almost eight million Polish citizens voted for my rival. I will try to perform my duties as president in such a manner to win their understanding and appreciation. I would also like to address those of my compatriots who did not participate in the elections, who did not vote. I wish to encourage those discouraged or indifferent to be more active citizens, because public affairs considerably affect the lives of all of us.
  I am taking the highest office in the Republic of Poland after elections held in special circumstances, when Poland had to face a great national tragedy—the death of President Lech Kaczyński and his wife in the Smoleńsk plane crash together with many of Poland's elite and distinguished representatives of Polish public and social life. This was our

common tragedy, our common mourning which brought sorrow and severe pain to us. But it also showed all of us that our society, state, democracy, and constitution can rise to such a situation. We all did it. The democratic institutional order which we have built over the last 20 years of change in Poland managed to maintain continuity of power in this difficult time. We were able to pay due tribute to the victims of the crash. Now I would like to evoke our memories from 13th April when the Polish Sejm was the first Polish institution to honour the memory of all victims of the Smoleńsk crash in an exceptional manner, in particular Members of Parliament representing all political parties. The memory of those events, the memory of those who were killed in the plane crash near Smoleńsk is not only our duty, but also my duty as President of the Republic of Poland.

Honourable National Assembly, Ladies and Gentlemen,

As of today I will hold the duty of many different tasks and challenges. I am aware of the emotions accompanying these events, but I am also willing and determined to rise to those challenges. . . .

Today our nation can confidently look to the future. We are free and live in a free world, in a free state. There is no one threatening our Polish freedom, no one threatening us.

We live in an independent and secure state that is respected worldwide. Even now, despite the global crisis and difficulties we face, we have the opportunity to develop our economy. We are experiencing actual growth in education. Our skills and qualifications are improving. Working better and more effectively, Poles are changing their state for the better. . . .

Ladies and Gentlemen, . . .

We need more peace and understanding, less fighting, dislike, contempt, and sometimes hatred. I am convinced that this is what most of us want, regardless of our political opinions, philosophy of life and background. We should not accept a situation where in experiencing a collective feeling of community—so beautiful and required—we are only joined by great and dramatic moments but separated by daily life. Yet cooperation and mutual respect do not mean we should avoid discussions and disputes or eliminate differences. Democracy should not be confused with unanimity. I have always been a man of Solidarity, a great national movement against dictatorship, whose 30th anniversary will be celebrated later this month. Solidarity allowed us to regain freedom and sovereignty, but also the right to be different. It brought us the normality we wanted so much for our Homeland. And it only depends on us whether we will create a gap between each other by taking part in inevitable disputes, or will show respect and care for the most important issues by holding a democratic debate. This is what a great Pole—John Paul II—expected from us when he gave a speech here, in this place.

The public domain is more than disputes and political struggles. It needs to be filled with citizens' activities to a much larger degree.

Twenty years ago two great values were reborn in Poland: our own independent and democratic state together with a free and active society. They both have to be harmonized and complement each other. Local authority, whose restoration was one of the biggest achievements of the last 20 years, has already changed the face of our state. It has contributed to the improvement of the living conditions of residents of Polish villages, towns and cities. However, the process of its development is not yet complete. The process of creating a civil society and development of various forms of social self-organisation is also still under way. At present the potential, energy and creativity of Poles need to be discussed, thoroughly discussed, and provided with good initiatives to realise an ambitious task—strengthening a civil model for our democracy. I want to support this debate and these initiatives. I want to take patronage over them.

I am willing to cooperate with you and consider the most important issues for Poland. I invite representatives of different parties, various philosophies of life and social groups. The seat of Poland's president will be an open place in which roads of all Poles can meet. I believe in dialogue which enriches and prevents the sense of national community from collapsing amid disputes and quarrelling. This is also extremely significant because our state's development and modernization—and as a result, the possibility to fully benefit from our chance of civilization—depends on our mutual confidence, willingness and ability to cooperate and the size of social capital. We need to seize the opportunity for Poland owing to our strong roots in the developing world, in the West.

Ladies and Gentlemen,

The Constitution indicates foreign affairs and security of state to be areas of particular involvement and shared responsibility of the President.

Six years ago Poland joined the European Union. Then, it was Europe telling us and the countries from our region, "Come with us." And as a result, now we can not only look after Polish interests efficiently, but also inspire joint actions in the spirit of openness and solidarity. Poland has initiated the Eastern Partnership and suggested more extensive talks on a Common Security Defence Policy. We are joining the group of European leaders; we want to strengthen, inspire and dynamize the old continent, to which Poland's EU presidency in the second half of 2011 will also contribute. I will support the government in dealing with this important task. However, at the same time, I would like the President's office to become a centre for reflection over the future of a common Europe. As discussion on this topic is already going on in Europe and Poland's voice cannot be unheard. This should be a far-reaching voice of all Poles. . . .

One of the pillars of Poland's foreign policy is close relations with the United States and the transatlantic bond. As a NATO member Poland is conscious of its allied obligations. We understand that for the sake of our own and collective security we should commit our forces to allied actions. Poland has acted in this way many times. It is, however, important that objectives, resources and responsibility for such ventures be defined in a joint debate. . . .

There will be no stable development of this part of Europe without co-operation with Russia. I will support the process of Polish-Russian reconciliation and the process of forming closer Polish-Russian relations. This is an important challenge facing both Poland and Russia.

Looking for partners among states on different continents we cannot forget our great Polish community, a family that is always close to our hearts and can constantly rely on Polish assistance.

Honourable Assembly,

Poland has changed a lot over the last two decades. But we still face big challenges. In the next few years we have to strengthen the foundations for the permanent social and economic development—invest in infrastructure, improve the quality of public services, keep state finances in tight rein. We have to improve the quality of education and ensure access to it for all; we have to invest in scientific research, and provide better financing to cultural institutions. Poland needs people that are creative and able to think independently. Poland needs non-governmental organisations. Education, the internet and civic activities will define our place in the future and not only in today's world.

We have to eliminate obstacles making a start in life difficult for young people. Jobs, housing, kindergartens, nurseries must not be scarce goods and services. The health service and pension systems are among those areas that require radical improvement so that Poles can work longer, if they wish, and retire living to a certain standard through an adequate pension. . . .

Work is a key to the future and quality of life for all citizens. Good work determines Polish patriotism of the 21st century. . . . The President's task is, and will be, to ensure that no one is deprived of their chance to be part of the community and to receive aid in a difficult situation due to their origin, capacities, age, education or place of residence. . . .

Compatriots, fellow citizens,

Today I address this message to each and all of you; to all Poles, wherever you are, and whatever your political opinions and beliefs.

I will strengthen and support relationships between us in cooperation for the development and success of Poland, the cooperation of all of us.

I am aware that you will judge me by acts, not by words. The declarations I have made today about cooperation, dialogue and openness will be an unwavering direction for me and my activities. I believe in the path of Poland. I believe that we may follow it with courage and move bravely forward. I believe in Poland, I believe in the patriotism of everyday effort, everyday work. I believe in our Polish abilities and capabilities because, quite simply, I believe in us, Poles.

Thank you very much.

Source: President of the Republic of Poland. "Address of the New President of the Republic of Poland." August 6, 2010. http://www.prezydent.pl/en/news/news/art,133,address-of-the-new-president-of-the-republic-of-poland,1.html.

Volcanic Ash Spreads across Europe

In mid-April, an Icelandic volcano erupted for the second time in one month, spreading a plume of ash into the atmosphere that grounded flights and stranded travelers across the European continent for more than a week. Air traffic came to a halt in what some considered the worst travel chaos since the September 11, 2001, terrorist attacks on the United States. The travel nightmare caused by the growing ash cloud, which was rarely visible from the ground, spread around the world as flights were rerouted or unable to reach their intended destinations. "I would think Europe was probably experiencing its greatest disruption to air travel since 9/11," said a spokesperson for the Civil Aviation Authority, which regulates the United Kingdom's aviation programs. "In terms of closure of airspace, this is worse than after 9/11. The disruption is probably larger than anything we've probably seen."

VOLCANIC ASH IMPACT

The impact of the volcanic ash, which originated in Iceland below the Eyjafjallajökull glacier, was felt across Europe. The ash spewed four to seven miles into the atmosphere, a height that wreaks havoc on plane engines and bodies because the ash, made up of silicate, a material much like glass fiber, can cause engines to catch fire and stall. The situation was unprecedented, and as the ash moved across the continent, airspace that had been open was quickly closed, causing airlines and flight controllers to think on their feet in an effort to keep passengers safe. "This demonstrates the dynamic and rapidly changing conditions in which we are working," the National Air Traffic Services, the main provider of air traffic service in the United Kingdom, said in a statement.

There was little question as to whether flights would be able to continue in the ash plume. A similar incident occurred in Indonesia in 1982 when a volcano's ash caused a British Airways plane to lose power in all four of its engines. The plane coasted toward the ground but luckily all of the engines restarted, allowing the plane to land safely. Because of this earlier incident, European air traffic controllers decided it was best to take little to no risk.

Airports in Great Britain, France, Germany, Hungary, and Romania were completely shut down, stranding passengers inside the airports and forcing them to either wait out the ash or to find alternate routes home. Many passengers attempted to book travel on the Eurail train lines, only to find that tickets had quickly sold out after the crisis began. Others found cabs back to their destinations, in some cases paying thousands of dollars to get home.

When flights are grounded, the airlines feel a significant impact to their bottom line. Some estimates put the total loss to airlines across Europe at nearly $200 million per day. The question quickly became whether, if the chaos continued for much longer, the economic impact felt by the airlines would spread into other sectors of the economy, essentially halting the slow economic recovery around the continent. "Given that the recovery of the euro-area economy is anyway so weak, it might have an impact," said Daniel Gros, director of the Centre for European Policy Studies in Brussels, Belgium. The ultimate economic impact would be determined by how long the ash cloud impacted travel. After a majority of the airspace was reopened by April 23, however, it seemed that Europe would remain on track for its recovery, despite the setback.

There was also some concern that other nations might feel the economic impact if flights remained on the ground for days or weeks. Those countries, for example, that rely on goods, services, or raw materials from Europe delivered by plane were on standby until the atmosphere cleared. The problem was most significant for perishable items. The same was true for nations relying on Europe as a main point of exports. Israel and North Africa, for example, ship large amounts of fruits and vegetables into Europe via plane, which is their largest market for perishable food. If the crisis continued, their revenue from Europe would quickly decrease.

Energy prices were also impacted. Demand for oil quickly fell as flights were grounded, and, according to JBC Energy oil analyst David Wech, some of the demand in Europe would never be regained because some flights would never take place, while others would simply take place later than expected. The impact on oil was estimated at 1.87 million barrels of unused oil for every forty-eight hours the crisis continued.

EUROPEAN UNION TAKES ACTION

With no way of knowing how long the ash cloud would last or whether the volcano would continue to erupt, the European Union (EU) took immediate action. It worked with individual airspace agencies in its member nations to shut down large swaths of air to non-emergency travel. This meant a reduction in air travel from twenty-eight thousand flights a day that travel through European airspace to less than half of that volume in the days following the volcano's eruption. Working in cooperation with Spain's air traffic agency, the EU determined that with the rate of movement and the placement of the ash cloud, it could predict how it would act over the coming days, causing some flights to be able to leave as planned as early as April 20. Throughout the crisis, Spain's airspace, along with that in Italy and a handful of other southern European nations, remained open to some flights and did not experience the blanket air traffic ban experienced in northern Europe.

The World Health Organization, located in Geneva, Switzerland, began a public information campaign, urging Europeans to remain indoors if the ash began to fall. A number of health risks are associated with breathing in large amounts of volcanic ash because of the silicates and other particles of rock, glass, and sand found within it. In the end, however, the crisis posed few health risks as it did not affect the air quality and the ash never fell in large enough amounts to call for Europeans to remain in their homes.

REACTION TO THE EUROPEAN RESPONSE

European air carriers responded with outrage at the EU's response to the ash cloud. Many said that the organization had blown the threat out of proportion. Others complained about the slow response and lack of coordination across member nations. Giovanni

Bisignani, CEO of the International Air Transport Association, which represents major airline companies, said, "It's embarrassing, and a European mess. . . . It took five days to organize a conference call with the ministers of transport and we are losing $200 million per day [and] 750,000 passengers are stranded all over. Does it make sense?" Airlines complained that test flights should have been run earlier than they were after data showed that there was little reason for a complete shutdown of European airspace. The problem, EU transportation commissioners said, was a lack of data on and knowledge of how damaging volcanic ash could be. The Civil Aviation Authority stood by its response, saying it had made decisions based on the best knowledge available at the time and in line with the body's air control policies.

In Europe, calls for faster and more coordinated responses to future disasters came immediately from EU member nations. According to Jo Leinen, chair of the European Parliament's environment committee, the crisis showed that Europe is "ill-prepared for natural disasters. . . . We see that the crisis management has many shortcomings." In its defense, the EU placed blame on member nations, reminding them that ultimately, each country is in charge of its own air traffic control.

EU transportation commissioner Siim Kallas did admit, however, that more needs to be done to ensure that countries at least know how other member states are planning to respond. "Fragmentation caused by a patchwork of different national decisions is limiting available airspace." His office indicated that letting each country make its own decisions had dangerous consequences, especially given the varying levels of expertise with the damage volcanic ash can cause and how it moves in the atmosphere. The Civil Aviation Authority stated that it was planning to work with nations across Europe to create a more coordinated effort in preparation for future problems. Airlines have also conducted research on the damage caused by ash clouds.

In May, another ash cloud spread over Iceland and toward the United Kingdom, sparking renewed concern that airspace would be shut down. However, British aviation controllers said that they had learned from the previous month's shutdown how to determine what is an actual threat and what is simply an inconvenience. After the April disaster, EU member states immediately formed a crisis group that would be on call to handle future air traffic emergencies. In addition, plans for the Single European Sky initiative, which would create a single European airspace and had been in the works for years, were accelerated. EU members also agreed to study the dangers and possible movement of volcanic ash to prepare for future problems. They said this study could redefine how airplane engines should be built to withstand volcanic ash, which could make flights safer for travelers around the globe.

After the ash cloud moved out of European airspace and allowed flights to begin again, transportation agencies around the world began looking at their own travel networks and studying the effect of volcanic ash on air travel to be sure that the crisis, which canceled one hundred thousand flights, would not be repeated in their countries.

In the United States, the House of Representatives Committee on Science and Technology heard testimony on May 5 from the National Aeronautics and Space Administration (NASA), the Air Line Pilots Association, the Federal Aviation Administration (FAA), and a number of other private and public sector groups involved in air travel to discuss the impact of volcanic ash on air travel in an effort to better understand how to prepare the FAA for possible future disruptions.

NASA spoke about its experience flying through a similar ash cloud in 2000. In this instance, those piloting the aircraft, which was headed for Sweden, did not notice that they were flying through volcanic ash. It was up to scientists aboard the flight, who could detect the particles in the air, to alert them of possible danger. After their safe landing and subsequent flight back to the United States, NASA sent the engines for inspection to see if any internal damage had been done. Those inspecting the engines found that though no external damage was detected on the plane or its engines, the inside showed significant wear. What this meant for future flights, the inspectors said, was that while the engine would not show immediate problems, after less than 100 hours of flight, it had the potential to lose some or all of its functionality.

—Heather Kerrigan

The following is a memo released by the European Union on April 20, 2010, regarding the impact of the volcanic ash on Europe and the response by the European Union.

European Union Releases Memo on Volcanic Ash

April 20, 2010

The purpose of this memo is to respond to the most frequently asked questions concerning the current volcanic ash crisis, notably in relation to the Commission's role in opening up Europe's airspace, while fully respecting safety requirements, to passenger rights and to the economic response for sectors hit by the crisis.

While decisions on airspace management are a national competence, faced with a situation which had become unsustainable the Commission intervened to help facilitate European solutions—to maximise available airspace, within strict safety controls. The Commission has worked tirelessly since Friday, 16th April to work with all key actors to open up corridors of European airspace. Progressively opening up airspace holds the key to providing the most immediate relief to stranded passengers and hard hit economic sectors, while ensuring that safety concerns remain paramount.

SECTION 1: THE EUROPEAN COMMISSION'S ROLE IN FACILITATING A PROGRESSIVE RE-OPENING OF EUROPEAN AIRSPACE

The context:

This is an <u>unprecedented crisis</u> facing Europe. A unique combination of 3 factors coming together have resulted in an almost complete lock-down of European airspace:
   We have seen:

1. Severe and prolonged volcanic disruption;

2. Weather conditions that mean the ash cloud has remained over Europe; and

3. A risk management model based on a strict precautionary principle

Treated separately, or even with two of these factors coinciding the crisis would have been much less severe.

Faced with this crisis, who is responsible for managing Europe's airspace?

1. The decision to open or shut airspace is <u>entirely national</u>. Only a Member State Authority can decide to open or close its national airspace.

2. Those national decisions on airspace are implemented by EuroControl (an independent agency in Brussels with 38 Member countries). EuroControl co-ordinates all the information and then approves flight plans for air companies across the different Member States, depending on the available airspace.

3. There is <u>NO EU competence for air traffic management</u> or in relation to decisions taken to open and close airspace i.e. the European Commission and European Parliament have NO role—it is for individual Member State Governments to decide.

So what happened when the volcano erupted? What procedures were followed?

Safety is the first priority of aviation policy. When the volcano erupted last Thursday, Member States (Civil Aviation Authorities with National Air Traffic Controllers) started to close airspace—based on the scientific advice from the Volcanic Ash Centre in London (linked to the London Met office) and applying the risk assessment models agreed by Member States under ICAO Guidelines for Europe (International Civil Aviation Organisation).

   Member states were absolutely right to react as they did in applying the model and procedures agreed for the European area in line with International Civil Aviation organisation guidelines. Safety is the first priority of aviation policy and must remain so.

What was the Commission's intervention as the situation evolved?

From Thursday onwards large parts of the European Airspace were shut down by national authorities. From an average of 28,000 flights a day in Europe, by Friday less than half of Europe's airspace was in use. Thousands of air passengers were stranded, air companies and other economic sectors were very hard hit.

   The cloud was not moving. And Europe was facing into another week of major traffic disruption. As the situation evolved, the model and risk management procedures were tested. It became clear to Member States, national safety authorities, national air traffic controllers, the industry and EuroControl that a more differentiated approach was needed. But no member state acting independently could take the first step to introduce change.

   At the end of last week, the European Commission, working with the Spanish Presidency and Eurocontrol proposed a European Framework which could move the situation forwards.

What did the European Commission do?

The Commission worked intensively with Eurocontrol, with the Volcanic Ash Centre, with Scientists, with the National Authorities across the Member States as well as with the airlines and airport sectors.

The result was the following:

- 11.00 Monday 19 April: Extraordinary Meeting co-chaired by Euro-Control and the European Commission in Brussels (Euro-control building) to look at possible ways to increase European co-operation on air traffic management. The meeting brought together national civil aviation authorities, air navigation providers, representatives of the airline and airport industry as well as the Spanish Presidency.

The participants had been asked by European Commission Vice President Siim Kallas, responsible for Transport, to provide a technical recommendation or a series of recommendations to Ministers later that that day on how to move forwards.

The meeting agreed <u>unanimously</u> on one recommendation to put to Transport Ministers:

That option allowed for a more <u>differentiated assessment</u> of risk from the ash cloud, while still respecting safety concerns. As well as more <u>harmonised/uniform implementation</u> of the risk assessment. The new procedures are fully in line with the ICAO Guidelines for the European Area.

- At 16.00 Monday 19th, Vice President Kallas, presented the technical recommendation to an Extra-ordinary meeting of Transport Ministers, chaired by Spanish Minister José Blanco, and the recommendations were endorsed.
- The new measures came into force at 8.00 CET time Tuesday 20 April. The more differentiated risk assessment and more harmonized implantation of decisions across the Member States, has allowed for a progressive, opening of more airspace.

If it were NOT for European Commission intervention since the end of last week, large parts of Europe's skies would still be unnecessarily closed.

What has been the result?

We are pleased to see that today (Tuesday, 20 April) there are more flights taking place today.

Overall the forecasts for flights for today are 14,500 as compared with 9,000 yesterday, for example, limited operations out of Paris, Amsterdam, as well as in Frankfurt Airport and for Italian domestic travel.

This is substantially due to the new more **pragmatic approach** agreed by Transport ministers on the initiative taken by the Commission.

The Commission will continue to monitor the situation closely.

What happens next?

National Safety Authorities, national air traffic authorities, and Euro-Control will now continue to operate the revised procedures. The scientific assessments will be updated every six hours—with no-fly zones, a large buffer area, and an intermediary zone where Member States can allow flights but with additional restrictions and safety controls, and an area where there is no contamination.

Can you ensure the same safety levels are guaranteed as with today's model?

Yes, because before any piece of airspace is opened up, a thorough safety assessment is carried out. We are not taking any additional risks, merely determining more precisely where the risk that we want to avoid is located.

Why do we not go directly to the US model (Option 2) as they seem to have no problems even though airspace is kept open?

Firstly we want our model to be safer, by ensuring that the assessment is done by those with best information and least vested interest. Otherwise the aircraft operators might be putting intolerable pressure on pilots to fly even when it is not safe.

Secondly the European Union law requires that the decision to open airspace is done by the air navigation service providers through a pre-determined methodology approved by the National Supervisory Authorities.

Where is the Volcanic Ash Advisory Centre in all this? They are the real professionals of assessing volcanic ash risk.

The VAAC is indeed the body responsible for assessing where ash might be encountered. However the decision to open or close airspace is not theirs alone. That is why we called upon all the central players to develop this methodology and that involves obviously also the VAAC itself.

What about thirds countries? Opening European airspace alone is not enough.

They are brought on board by the Eurocontrol machinery as the ones closest to EU are also Eurocontrol members. That is why Eurocontrols role in this is so central. . . .

[Section 2, detailing passengers rights, has been omitted.]

SECTION 3: WHAT ABOUT THE ECONOMIC IMPACT ON THE INDUSTRY

The aviation sector as well as other economic sectors have been hit very hard by this crisis.

European Commission President Barroso decided to set up an ad-hoc group to assess the impact of the situation created by the volcanic ash cloud on the air travel industry and the economy in general.

The aim is to ensure that the EU has the right analysis to be able to respond appropriately, if needed, and that any measures taken across the EU to respond to economic consequences of this situation are properly coordinated.

President Barroso asked Vice-President Kallas, responsible for Transport, to lead this work, assisted by Vice President Almunia (Competition and State Aids) and Commissioner Rehn (Economic and Monetary Affairs).

That work is moving ahead quickly.

- The process of gathering the economic data on the effects of the crisis has begun this weekend.
- Vice President Kallas met with representatives of European airlines and airports on Monday this week to discuss the economic impact.
- Working and expert meetings within the European Commission have taken place to define how the process will move forwards.

Assessing the economic impact of this crisis will take time.

Representatives of the airline industry, when they spoke with Vice President Kallas on Monday said they simple cannot at this stage accurately estimate the impact on their sector. It will take time for the full impact to become clear.

Equally, the ad hoc group will look carefully at the broader economic impact on other sectors of industry which have also been hard hit.

Is it possible for Member States to grant state aid to compensate airlines for the consequences of the ash cloud according to EU rules?

The Treaty allows Member States to grant State aid to "make good the damage caused by "natural disasters and exceptional occurrences" (Art 107 2b).

No Member State has notified any state aid plans as of yet.

The Commission clarified in the aftermath of the September 11 terrorist attacks, how those rules applied to the airline sector with regard to that particular event. Similar compatibility criteria, as the ones fixed in 2001, could apply:

- compensation in a non-discriminatory way to all airline companies of a Member State;
- amount of the compensation limited to the real costs of the traffic interruption;
- no hidden aid for restructuration of companies.

VP Almunia, who is part of the ad-hoc group examining the economic impact of the problem, has said his services could rapidly update the guidance for Member States.

In the event Member States were to notify any aid, the Commission could rapidly assess such requests.

Section 4: Other Aspects of the Crisis What about the Health Risks?

Is there a health risk in the current situation?

According to the preliminary assessments made by the Member States, risks in relation to public health are generally limited. The cloud of ash moves at a high altitude and is spread over large areas, resulting in a decrease in the concentration of particles which could nevertheless lead to low exposure. The public health impact of such low exposure is difficult to estimate at present especially in the absence of the detailed composition of the cloud. The current situation is estimated to be similar to peaks of air pollution experienced in the Member States.

Any health effects are likely to be short term. Furthermore, as long as the ash remains in the upper statosphere, there will not be an increased risk to health.

Nevertheless, there are some specific health issues which may demand attention, e.g. air rescue and continuation of healthcare of people stranded abroad because of the interruption of air traffic.

What's the Commission doing on this issue?

In order to discuss public health related impact of the interruption of air traffic and the volcanic ash clouds drifting across Europe, the European Commission's health services are in contact with several key health organisations, including the World Health Organization and the European Centre for Disease Prevention and Control, as well with Member States and Iceland. The potential impact on human health, as well as animal health, will be monitored in the coming weeks.

WHAT ABOUT VISA PROBLEMS?

Is the European Commission aware of the situation of third country nationals obliged to stay in the EU due to recent disruptions of the air travel and what action does it consider necessary?

The closure of the European airspace since 15 April 2010 has meant that travel of a number of third country nationals subject to the visa requirement for staying in or transiting through the territory of the Schengen States has been disrupted and urgent measures must be taken to overcome the different situations of distress occurring. The European Commission is recommending Member States to apply special derogations to certain categories of travellers and in particular to people holding a short stay visa that has expired on or after 15 April 2010 and to people who did not intend to enter into the territory of the Member States but are forced to do so.

How will the European Union deal with people holding a short stay visa that has expired on or after 15 April 2010?

Many people have not been able to leave the territory of the Member States before the expiry of their short stay Schengen visa. Given the extraordinary situation and the high numbers of persons concerned, the European Commission recommends a derogation from the general rules for persons whose visas have expired or will expire in the period from 15 April 2010 until the reopening of the European airspace. These people will be allowed to remain within the territory of the Schengen States until the normalisation of air traffic without having to apply for the extension of their visas. The passport of these persons should be stamped upon exit without considering these persons as having stayed beyond the authorised period.

What about those who did not intend to enter into the area of the Member States but are forced to do so?

Two categories of persons are considered: firstly, persons who cannot return to their country of residence by air and who wish to transit by land (e.g. a person holding a return ticket from London to Tirana, but who wishes to return by ferry and train). Secondly, persons who intended to transit via the international transit area of a Schengen airport but are forced to leave the airport to find accommodation until the onward journey can take place. The Commission recommends that these persons should be issued visas at the external borders in accordance with Article 35 of the Visa Code and the Handbook for the processing of visa applications and the modification of issued visas. Since the third country nationals concerned had no intention of entering into the territory of the Member States but are compelled to do so for reasons of "force majeure," the Commission recommends derogating from certain provisions and in particular to waive the visa fee and not to insist on the applicant being in possession of travel medical insurance.

What is the role of the EU's Civil Protection Mechanism in this crisis?

The Monitoring and Information Centre (MIC) is the central operational hub of the EU Civil Protection Mechanism, through which the European Commission can facilitate and support the deployment and coordination of civil protection assistance in the event of major emergencies. The current transport situation across Europe has not yet led to any calls for assistance but the MIC continues to coordinate and monitor the situation closely. This is important as the EU needs to be prepared for all possible scenarios, identify all possible effects and anticipate possible needs for support or cooperation.

What has the MIC done so far?

The MIC has been in close contact with Iceland's civil protection authorities since Thursday and has regularly briefed Member States on the situation both in Iceland and across Europe. It convened an urgent coordination meeting with the civil protection representatives of Member States and Iceland to take stock of the effects of the volcanic ash cloud to be in a position to anticipate possible needs for support and coordination at EU level. The MIC has created a platform to ensure exchange of information between Member States which aims at enabling a coordinated EU action. In practical terms this means that Member States will feed information into the system to create an overview of the situation in their countries. The MIC is also in the process of centralising key data from the Member States on the numbers of stranded passengers, both inside the EU and in third countries, in order to assess the scope of the problems. This means that the EU has the possibility -if the need arises- to facilitate repatriation by coordinating the efforts of the 27 Member States.

The MIC also works closely with DG SANCO, which is monitoring the possible health effects of the ash cloud moving over Europe.

SOURCE: European Union. Press Room. "Volcanic Ash Crisis: Frequently Asked Questions." April 20, 2010. http://europa.eu/rapid/pressReleasesAction.do?reference=MEMO/10/143&format=HTML&aged =0&language=EN&guiLanguage=en%20.

OTHER HISTORIC DOCUMENTS OF INTEREST

FROM PREVIOUS *HISTORIC DOCUMENTS*

Senate Debates Dodd-Frank Wall Street Reform Legislation

APRIL 22 AND JULY 21, 2010

President Barack Obama signed into law one of his administration's signal achievements, the Dodd-Frank Wall Street Reform and Consumer Protection Act, on July 21, 2010. The financial reform legislation is named for its two main congressional sponsors, Sen. Christopher Dodd, D-Conn., chair of the Senate Banking Committee, and Rep. Barney Frank, D-Mass., chair of the House Financial Services Committee. Among the act's many provisions are the creation of several new government bodies, including the Consumer Financial Protection Bureau (CFPB), an independent agency housed within the Federal Reserve, and the Financial Services Oversight Council, consisting of senior officials. In the wake of a severe recession exacerbated by a near-collapse of the financial system, Dodd-Frank reorganizes the regulatory regime that polices the financial industry with the aim of arming government with tools to protect the economy and prevent future bank bailouts. At the signature ceremony at the Ronald Reagan Building and International Trade Center in Washington, D.C., President Obama said, "Our financial system only works, our market is only free when there are clear rules and basic safeguards that prevent abuse, that check excess, that ensure that it is more profitable to play by the rules than to game the system. And that's what these reforms are designed to achieve, no more, no less."

Dealing with the Financial Crisis

A central factor sparking the nation's economic woes, beginning in 2006, was declining home values, which had risen for decades to reach a historic peak. When the housing bubble burst, the number of home foreclosures jumped, especially among those under adjustable-rate, "sub-prime" mortgages. The trouble in the mortgage market had especially broad ramifications for the economy due to the role of investment banks. Major Wall Street firms had developed a huge, highly lucrative, and largely deregulated trade in mortgage debt. Trillions of dollars were changing hands annually in investment vehicles called derivatives, including credit default swaps, collateralized debt obligations, and mortgage-backed securities. By 2008, with the housing market still dropping, financial firms began to find themselves short of capital.

The government stepped in to prevent the collapse of Wall Street's Bear Stearns and mortgage giants Fannie Mae and Freddie Mac after Federal Reserve chairman Ben Bernanke pronounced them "too big to fail." The government's intervention in Bear Stearns failed and ultimately led to the sale of the company to JPMorgan Chase in March 2008 at the behest of the Treasury Department and Federal Reserve. The crisis peaked in September when another Wall Street firm, Lehman Brothers, and insurance giant AIG (American International Group) announced nearly simultaneously that they were approaching bankruptcy. The stock market plummeted and credit slowed to a crawl as the nation hurtled into the steepest recession since the 1930s. Three major legislative initiatives arose in response to the emergency. First, the final months of the George W. Bush administration saw the $700 billion bank bailout and the creation of the Troubled Asset Relief Program (TARP). In February 2009, a month after Obama's inauguration, Congress approved the $787 billion stimulus package. The third piece, financial regulatory reform, was declared one of the president's top legislative priorities, along with health care reform and a bill to revamp energy policy in light of the climate crisis. Obama introduced his proposals for financial reform on June 17, 2009. Most of these proposals—including the creation of a consumer watchdog agency and a council of senior regulators, tighter regulation of derivatives trading, the transfer of bank regulation authority from the Office of Thrift Supervision to other governmental bodies, and empowerment of the Federal Deposit Insurance Corporation (FDIC) to dispose of failing financial firms—made it into the final bill. The president's program stopped short of restructuring the industry itself, by mandating the breakup of companies deemed "too big to fail" or reimposing the separation of investment banks and securities firms from depository and commercial banks. The latter was a key plank of the Glass-Steagall Act of 1933, the New Deal financial reform that the Gramm-Leach-Bliley Act repealed in 1999.

HOUSE, SENATE, AND CONFERENCE

Obama's speech and the start of congressional work on the issue was the cue for a round of intense lobbying and advocacy. Liberal groups supportive of the president's agenda lined up behind the reform effort, although the proposal struck some Democrats as overly cumbersome. Most Republicans opposed the initiative, and business groups such as the U.S. Chamber of Commerce swiftly began lobbying and sponsoring advertisements against the legislation.

In the House Financial Services Committee, Rep. Frank divided the bill into seven components: derivatives trading, bank regulation, the "too big to fail" problem, monitoring of the private sector companies that provide credit ratings, consumer protection, investor protection, and executive compensation. Despite the bill's complexity, the comfortable Democratic majority in the House made its eventual passage somewhat assured. One flashpoint in the debate was the proposed CFPB. Industry groups pushed hard for an amendment brought by Rep. Walt Minnick, a conservative Blue Dog Democrat from Idaho, to strip the new agency from the bill. The amendment was defeated by a vote of 223–208, despite the support of thirty-three Democrats. The House legislation called for the major banks to contribute $150 billion to a government fund to cover the costs of liquidating failing firms. Jokingly referring to an unrelated political controversy, Frank quipped, "If a company fails, it will be put to death. Yes, we have death panels, but they got the death panels in the wrong bill. The death panels are in this bill." On December 12, 2009 the full House approved the bill 223–202, with no Republicans voting yes.

Movement in the Senate was slower. Sen. Dodd introduced a draft to the Banking Committee on November 10, 2009 and committee work continued through the winter. The Senate draft was closely aligned with its House counterpart in most respects, although it called for a wider reorganization of the regulatory regime. The Senate offered a stronger likelihood of bipartisan cooperation, and Dodd allowed time for discussions with Republicans such as Sen. Richard Shelby of Alabama. In late April, Dodd and his fellow Democrats moved to start floor debate on the bill. On May 20, 2010, the full Senate approved the legislation on a 59–39 vote, with four Republicans in favor and two Democrats opposed.

Most of the work of reconciling the two versions of the bill was accomplished in one twenty-hour conference session on June 24–25. Two notable compromises marked the evening. The proposal by Sen. Blanche Lincoln, D-Ark., to ban most derivatives trading by commercial banks, which was included in the Senate bill, was softened in conference. The Senate bill also contained the so-called Volcker Rule, named for former Fed chairman Paul Volcker, banning proprietary trading, or banks using their own money to invest in the market, such as through hedge funds or private equity funds. Sen. Scott Brown, R-Mass., one of the few Republicans to support the legislation, won a compromise allowing banks to retain up to 3 percent of their capital in hedge or private equity funds. President Obama said the final bill kept 90 percent of what he wanted. The House passed the conference report 237–192 on June 30, and the Senate followed on July 15 with a 60–39 tally.

Provisions of Dodd-Frank

The bill Obama signed on July 21 represents the most dramatic reform of the rules governing American finance since the New Deal era. The 848-page document affects virtually every aspect of the relationship between financial institutions and the government. Among its major provisions are the following:

– Establishment of the Financial Stability Oversight Council, a group of senior officials (including the secretary of the treasury and the Fed chairman) tasked with identifying and responding to threats to the overall financial system.

– Authorization for the seizure and orderly liquidation of troubled firms on the verge of bankruptcy, under the direction of the FDIC. The law stipulates that no taxpayer funds shall be used for bailouts of troubled corporations. Public funds may be used to cover resolution costs, but regulators would recoup these costs by collecting up to $50 billion from the firms with the largest capitalization.

– Streamlining bank regulation by transferring powers from the Office of Thrift Supervision to the Office of the Comptroller of the Currency, the Federal Reserve, and the FDIC. The law increases federal insurance on bank deposits from $100,000 to $250,000.

– Improvements to the regulation of derivatives trading, hedge funds, and other securities. Over-the-counter derivatives must now be sold on regulated exchanges or clearinghouses to increase transparency and accountability. Regulators will have the authority to require investment banks to maintain higher capital reserves. Banks may continue to trade in certain derivatives in order to hedge risk or for purposes directly related to core banking operations. Other derivatives must be spun off to a subsidiary with its own capital reserves. Banks will have two years to close out their proprietary trading in accordance with the Volcker Rule.

– Investor protections. The law institutes investor advocacy and whistleblower incentives within the Securities and Exchange Commission (SEC) in an effort to prevent regulatory failures such as the Bernard Madoff scandal. Companies that sell asset-backed securities will be required to maintain a percentage of the credit risk of those securities, keeping a "skin in the game" (in the words of billionaire investor Warren Buffett). Company shareholders will be permitted to have input and a non-binding vote on executive compensation, or a "say on pay."

– Enhanced regulation of credit ratings agencies, to ensure that risk is competently and independently assessed and to prevent conflicts of interest at companies that provide credit ratings. The failure of these agencies to flag risky investments contributed to the current financial crisis.

– Creation of the Consumer Financial Protection Bureau, to serve as a watchdog and public advocate in the financial sector. This bureau will be able to create and enforce rules for banking, credit cards, mortgages, and other financial services, consolidating in one office a set of responsibilities previously spread across the federal bureaucracy. The CFPB will be an independent agency within the Federal Reserve, with a director appointed by the president and confirmed by the Senate.

– Clarified standards for mortgage underwriting, in order to curtail predatory lending and ensure that lenders establish prospective borrowers' ability to pay.

– A little-noted provision proposed by Sen. Dick Durbin, D-Ill., authorizes the Federal Reserve to regulate and limit the per-transaction "swipe fees" (interchange fees) imposed on merchants by credit and debit card companies. Such fees amount to nearly $20 billion annually.

The Warren Debate

Despite the magnitude of the achievement, passage of Dodd-Frank did little to boost President Obama's popularity or improve prospects for Democrats in the 2010 congressional elections. Republicans blasted the bill as a bureaucratic monster that would impose burdens on business and drag down credit and economic growth. Some progressives faulted the legislation as too weak, to address the power of the giant firms and leaving too much authority in the hands of the same regulators who failed to prevent the crisis. Since the law gave regulators wide leeway to institute new market rules, the rule-making process inevitably became the focus of intense lobbying and potential conflict of interest, given that regulators often go to work for the industry after leaving government.

Following the law's passage, speculation turned to who the president would nominate to direct the CFPB. The front-runner was Harvard law professor Elizabeth Warren, head of congressional oversight for the TARP. Warren was credited with originating the idea of the consumer protection agency, but her reputation as a zealous consumer advocate had earned her the enmity of some industry figures and Republicans. For many on the left, Warren's appointment became an important litmus test of President Obama's commitment to an agenda of progressive change. Few Democrats denied her suitability for the position, but Senator Dodd and others publicly questioned whether she could survive the confirmation process. On September 17, Obama named Warren as a special assistant to the president and the treasury secretary. The appointment allowed Warren to lead in the establishment of the consumer protection bureau without requiring her confirmation. A nominee for the director's post, who may or may not be Warren, is likely to be named in 2011.

—Roger K. Smith

Following is a floor statement by Sen. Mitch McConnell, R-Ky., on April 22, 2010, in opposition to the Dodd-Frank Wall Street reform legislation; a floor statement by Sen. Dick Durbin, D-Ill., also on April 22, 2010, in support of the Dodd-Frank legislation; and a statement by President Barack Obama on July 21, 2010, upon signing the Wall Street reform legislation into law.

Sen. McConnell in Opposition to
Wall Street Reform

April 22, 2010

Mr. McCONNELL. Reserving the right to object, and I will object, here we go again. The majority leader is once again moving to a bill, even while bipartisan discussions on the content of the bill are still underway.

Just about an hour ago, the majority leader said:

> I'm not going to waste any more time of the American people while they come up with some agreement.

Well, I do not think bipartisanship is a waste of time. I do not think a bill with the legitimacy of a bipartisan agreement is a waste of time.

Is it a waste of time to ensure that the taxpayers never again bail out Wall Street firms? Is it a waste of time to ensure that the bill before us does not drive jobs overseas or dry up lending to small businesses? Is it too much to ask, should an agreement be reached, that we take the time to make sure every Member of the Senate and our constituents can actually read the bill and understand the details?

This bill potentially affects every small bank and lending institution in our country. It has serious implications for jobs and the availability of credit to spur economic growth. It has important consequences for the taxpayers, if done incorrectly.

I think Americans expect more of us. I think they expect us to take the time to do it right. I would add, my impression was that serious discussions were going on. I think they should continue. Therefore, Mr. President, I object.

SOURCE: Sen. Mitch McConnell. "Restoring American Financial Stability Act of 2010—Motion to Proceed." *Congressional Record* 2010, pt. 156, S2553. http://www.gpo.gov/fdsys/pkg/CREC-2010-04-22/pdf/CREC-2010-04-22-pt1-PgS2553.pdf.

Sen. Durbin in Support of
Wall Street Reform

April 22, 2010

Mr. DURBIN. . . .

Mr. President, I hope that soon we will be moving to financial regulatory reform. It is a Washington term known as Wall Street reform, or basically trying to clean up the mess that was created by this last recession. This is a bill that is controversial. It has been worked on by many committees in the Senate. Senator Blanche Lincoln in the Agricultural Committee took on a big part of it. Most people are surprised to think of Wall Street and the Ag Committee at the same time, but those of us from Chicago are not. We have a futures market which has been in place for almost a century, starting with the Chicago Board of Trade, and it deals in futures—derivatives, if you will—that are based on agricultural commodities and currency and interest rates and a certain index. That operation in Chicago is governed and regulated by the Commodity Futures Trading Commission. The jurisdiction of that, as it started with agricultural products, has been relegated to the Agriculture Committee.

Senator Lincoln met this week and did an outstanding job of reporting a bill on that section of the bill related to derivatives and futures regulated by the Commodity Futures Trading Commission. She was successful in reporting the bill from her committee, with the support of Senator Grassley of Iowa making it a bipartisan effort. Another Republican Senator expressed an interest in helping as well. So I give her high praise in this charged political atmosphere in which we work in this body. It says a lot for her that she can put together this type of bipartisan coalition.

At the same time, Senator Dodd, in the Banking Committee, has been working on a bill as well, trying to bring the two together on the Senate floor and have a joint effort to deal with this issue.

Now, why are we doing this? Well, we are doing this for very obvious reasons. We know that leading into this recession, Wall Street and the big banks in America got away with murder. At the end of the day, the taxpayers of this country were called on to rescue these financial institutions from their own perfidy.

When we look at the things they did in the name of profit, it turned out to be senseless greed. At the end of the day, many people suffered. As a result of this recession, $17 trillion was extracted from the American economy—$17 trillion in losses. Mr. President, $17 trillion is more than the annual gross national product of the United States. So if we took the sum total value of all the goods and services produced in our country in 1 year, we lost that much value in this recession. It was the hardest hit the American economy has taken since the Great Depression in 1929.

Of course, a lot of it had to do with bad decisions. Some individual families and businesses made bad decisions. They borrowed money when they shouldn't have. They got in too deeply, bought homes that were too expensive. They might have been lured into it, but they made bad decisions. The government made some bad decisions. We thought, as a general principle, encouraging home ownership was great for our country; that the more people who own a home, the more likely they will make that home a good investment for themselves, and the more likely they will be engaged in their neighborhood and their churches and in their communities, and the stronger we will be as a nation. That was the starting point. So we opened up opportunities for home ownership, reaching down to levels that had not been tried before, and, unfortunately, that went too far.

The private sector was to blame. When we look at so many people who were lured into mortgages and borrowing far beyond their means, we see there was also a lot of deception going on. People were told they could get a mortgage and make an easy monthly payment and weren't told their mortgage would explode right in front of them, as the subprime mortgage, in a matter of months or years, would have a monthly payment far beyond their means. They weren't told there was a provision in that mortgage which had a pre-payment penalty that stopped them from refinancing, and that they were stuck with high interest rates from which they couldn't escape. They weren't told that just making an oral representation about their income was not nearly enough; that they needed to produce documentation about their real net worth.

These so-called no-doc closings, which became rampant in some areas, led to terrible decisions, encouraged by greedy speculators in the financial industries. So the net result was that the bottom fell out of the real estate market and $17 trillion in value was lost in the American economy. Most of us felt it in our 401(k)s, in our savings accounts, and in our retirement plans. We saw it with businesses that lost their leases and lost their businesses and had to lay off their employees. . . .

At the same time, though, as we go through this painful process of coming out of this recession, we have to make changes in Wall Street and the financial institutions to guarantee that we would not face this again. That means taking an honest look at some of the practices that are taking place today, and that are legal today. We got into this thinking—and I was part of it; most of us were—that if we had an expanding financial sector in the United States, it would expand jobs and opportunities and business growth and global competition.

Unfortunately, it went overboard. Many financial institutions, which are now being called on the carpet, took the authority given them by the Federal Government to an extreme. That is what we are trying to change. We want to make sure there is some accountability on Wall Street and with the big banks, so that we understand what they are doing and that their investments don't end up being a gamble where people can lose their life savings or investments.

We want to make sure as well that we empower consumers in the United States. This bill that is going to come before us has the strongest consumer financial protection ever enacted into law in the United States. We are going to create an agency which is going to protect and empower consumers—protect them from the tricks and traps and shadowy agreements and fine print stuck in mortgages and credit card statements, in student loans, in retirement plans, and all of the things that people engage in daily in their lives where one sentence stuck in a legal document can end up being someone's downfall.

We want to protect consumers from that and empower consumers to make the right decisions, so that there will be clarity in these legal documents that can bring a person's financial empire to ruin. That kind of clarity and plain English is going to be guaranteed by a Federal group that is going to keep an eye on the financial industries.

Some of these large banks are fighting us. They don't want to see this happen. They do not believe there should be this kind of consumer financial protection. But we are going to fight to make that happen so consumers across America have a fighting chance when they enter into agreements, so that they will have a legal document they can understand and one that they can work with, and then they will have an agency to back them up.

Currently, we have only had one Republican Senator vote for this kind of reform—Senator Grassley of Iowa voted for it in the Agriculture Committee version that came out of Senator Lincoln's committee. But on the Banking Committee, not a single Republican would vote for it. I hope they will have a change of heart.

I understand there are negotiations underway, but I hope the negotiations don't water down the basic agreement in this bill. We need a strong bill. We need a bill that meets the test of what we have been through as a nation. After all of the suffering that has taken place—the businesses lost, the savings lost, the jobs lost—for goodness' sake, let's not come up with some halfhearted effort. Let's stand up to the Wall Street lobbyists who are going to try to water down this bill and tell them no. We are going to call for a vote on a bill that has some teeth in it, something worth voting for, something that will guarantee that we will never go through this kind of recession ever again in our economy.

I think we owe that to the American people, and I hope that next week, come Monday afternoon at 5 o'clock, when this Senate convenes for a vote, I hope we have a strong bipartisan vote to move forward on this whole idea of Wall Street reform. . . .

SOURCE: Sen. Dick Durbin. "Restoring American Financial Stability Act of 2010—Motion to Proceed." *Congressional Record* 2010, pt. 156, S2557–S2559. http://www.gpo.gov/fdsys/pkg/CREC-2010-04-22/pdf/ CREC-2010-04-22-pt1-PgS2553.pdf.

President Obama Signs Wall Street Reform Legislation

July 21, 2010

We are gathered in the heart of our Nation's Capital, surrounded by memorials to leaders and citizens who served our Nation in its earliest days and in its days of greatest trial. Now, today is such a time for America.

Over the past 2 years, we have faced the worst recession since the Great Depression. Eight million people lost their jobs. Tens of millions saw the value of their homes and retirement savings plummet. Countless businesses have been unable to get the loans they need, and many have been forced to shut their doors. And although the economy is growing again, too many people are still feeling the pain of the downturn.

Now, while a number of factors led to such a severe recession, the primary cause was a breakdown in our financial system. It was a crisis born of a failure of responsibility, from certain corners of Wall Street to the halls of power in Washington. For years, our financial sector was governed by antiquated and poorly enforced rules that allowed some to game the system and take risks that endangered the entire economy.

Unscrupulous lenders locked consumers into complex loans with hidden costs. Firms like AIG placed massive, risky bets with borrowed money. And while the rules left abuse and excess unchecked, they also left taxpayers on the hook if a big bank or financial institution ever failed.

Now, even before the crisis hit, I went to Wall Street and I called for commonsense reforms to protect consumers and our economy as a whole. And soon after taking office, I proposed a set of reforms to empower consumers and investors, to bring the shadowy deals that caused this crisis into the light of day, and to put a stop to taxpayer bailouts once and for all. . . .

Passing this bill was no easy task. To get there, we had to overcome the furious lobbying of an array of powerful interest groups and a partisan minority determined to block change. So the Members who are here today, both on the stage and in the audience, they have done a great service in devoting so much time and expertise to this effort, to looking out for the public interests and not the special interests. And I also want to thank the three Republican Senators who put partisanship aside, judged this bill on the merits, and voted for reform. We're grateful to them and the Republican House Members. Good to see you, Joe.

Now, let's put this in perspective. The fact is, the financial industry is central to our Nation's ability to grow, to prosper, to compete, and to innovate. There are a lot of banks that understand and fulfill this vital role, and there are a whole lot of bankers out there who want to do right—and do right—by their customers. This reform will help foster innovation, not hamper it. It is designed to make sure that everybody follows the same set of rules so that firms compete on price and quality, not on tricks and not on traps. It demands accountability and responsibility from everyone. It provides certainty to everybody, from bankers to farmers to business owners to consumers. And unless your business model depends on cutting corners or bilking your customers, you've got nothing to fear from reform.

Now, for all those Americans who are wondering what Wall Street reform means for you, here's what you can expect. If you've ever applied for a credit card, a student loan, or a mortgage, you know the feeling of signing your name to pages of barely understandable fine print. What often happens as a result is that many Americans are caught by hidden fees and penalties or saddled with loans they can't afford. That's what happened to Robin Fox, hit with a massive rate increase on her credit card balance, even though she paid her bills on time. That's what happened to Andrew Giordano, who discovered hundreds of dollars in overdraft fees on his bank statement, fees he had no idea he might face. And both are here today. Well, with this law, unfair rate hikes, like the one that hit Robin, will end for good, and will ensure that people like Andrew aren't unwittingly caught by over-draft fees when they sign up for a checking account.

With this law, we'll crack down on abusive practices in the mortgage industry. We'll make sure that contracts are simpler, putting an end to many hidden penalties and fees in complex mortgages, so folks know what they're signing. With this law, students who take out college loans will be provided clear and concise information about their obligations. And with this law, ordinary investors, like seniors and folks saving for retirement, will be able to receive more information about the costs and risks of mutual funds and other investment products so that they can make better financial decisions as to what will work for them.

So all told, these reforms represent the strongest consumer financial protections in history—in history. And these protections will be enforced by a new consumer watchdog with just one job: looking out for people—not big banks, not lenders, not investment houses—looking out for people as they interact with the financial system.

And that's not just good for consumers; that's good for the economy. Because reform will put a stop to a lot of the bad loans that fueled a debt-based bubble. And it will mean all companies will have to seek customers by offering better products instead of more deceptive ones.

Now, beyond the consumer protections I've outlined, reform will also rein in the abuse and excess that nearly brought down our financial system. It will finally bring trans-parency to the kinds of complex and risky transactions that helped trigger the financial crisis. Shareholders will also have a greater say on the pay of CEOs and other executives, so they can reward success instead of failure.

And finally, because of this law, the American people will never again be asked to foot the bill for Wall Street's mistakes. There will be no more tax-funded bailouts, period. If a large financial institution should ever fail, this reform gives us the ability to wind it down without endangering the broader economy. And there will be new rules to make clear that no firm is somehow protected because it is too big to fail, so we don't have another AIG.

That's what this reform will mean. Now, it doesn't mean our work is over. For these new rules to be effective, regulators will have to be vigilant. We may need to make adjust-ments along the way as our financial system adapts to these new changes and changes around the globe. No law can force anybody to be responsible; it's still incumbent on those on Wall Street to heed the lessons of this crisis in terms of how they conduct their businesses. . . .

In the end, our financial system only works, our market is only free when there are clear rules and basic safeguards that prevent abuse, that check excess, that ensure that it is more profitable to play by the rules than to game the system. And that's what these reforms are designed to achieve, no more, no less. Because that's how we will ensure that our economy works for consumers, that it works for investors, that it works for financial institutions, that it works for all of us. This is the central lesson not only of this crisis but of our history.

Ultimately, there's no dividing line between Main Street and Wall Street. We rise or fall together as one nation. So these reforms will help lift our economy and lead all of us to a stronger, more prosperous future.

And that's why I'm so honored to sign these reforms into law, and I'm so grateful to everybody who worked so hard to make this day possible. Thank you very much, everybody.

SOURCE: U.S. Executive Office of the President. "Remarks on Signing the Dodd-Frank Wall Street Reform and Consumer Protection Act." July 21, 2010. *Daily Compilation of Presidential Documents* 2010, no. 000617 http://origin.www.gpo.gov/fdsys/pkg/DCPD-201000617/pdf/DCPD-201000617.pdf.

OTHER HISTORIC DOCUMENTS OF INTEREST

FROM PREVIOUS *HISTORIC DOCUMENTS*

Arizona Passes Nation's Toughest Immigration Law

APRIL 23 AND JULY 6, 2010

In April 2010, Arizona's Republican governor, Jan Brewer, signed the nation's toughest, and most controversial, immigration law, ushering in a flood of lawsuits and accusations of racial profiling. The Arizona legislature approved the new law during a period of heightened anxiety over illegal immigrants and their impact on the U.S. economy, coupled with a rise in criminal activity along the U.S.-Mexican border. Arizona, which shares a nearly four-hundred-mile border with Mexico, receives a large influx of illegal immigrants each year. To escalate deportation efforts, Gov. Brewer's law required police to question those they suspect to be in the country illegally and required legal immigrants to carry proof of their residency with them at all times. The Barack Obama administration, which had advocated for nationwide immigration reform since taking control of the executive branch in 2009, was the first to attempt to put a stop to Arizona's law through the federal courts.

ILLEGAL IMMIGRATION IN AMERICA

While the exact number is not known, the Pew Hispanic Center estimates that there were approximately 11.1 million illegal immigrants living in the United States in 2009. As violence continues to increase along the Mexican border and spill over into the United States, and without a strong, unified federal policy on immigration, states have attempted to deal with illegal immigrants themselves. Each year, a growing number of state laws are introduced with regard to illegal immigration, dealing with everything from health care and education to driver's licenses. In 2005, three hundred such bills were introduced in state legislatures. This number grew to more than fifteen hundred in 2007 with relatively the same number introduced in 2009. Approximately 15 percent have been enacted. These laws often face tough resistance in the state legislatures and from police forces already facing depleted resources.

The federal government argues that it has the greatest authority to regulate illegal immigration and has left limited power to state governments. The last push for immigration reform occurred in 2005, when Sens. Ted Kennedy, D-Mass., and John McCain, R-Ariz., introduced the McCain-Kennedy Act, which would have created a guest-worker program to allow employers to temporarily hire foreign laborers for positions they are unable to fill with Americans. The legislation was held up in the Senate and never came to the floor for a vote.

On the campaign trail in 2008 and during his first years in office, President Obama called for nationwide immigration reform. "As other states and localities go their own ways, we face the prospect that different rules for immigration will apply in different parts of the country," Obama said in a speech shortly after Arizona's law was passed. "A patchwork of local immigration rules where we all know one clear national standard is needed."

Toward this goal, in 2010 the U.S. House of Representatives and Senate introduced the Development, Relief, and Education for Alien Minors (DREAM) Act, which would have allowed illegal immigrants who were brought to the country at a young age to remain in the United States if they finished two years of college or military service and met a number of other requirements. The House passed the DREAM Act, but the motion failed to garner support in the Senate. Sen. Jeff Sessions, R-Ala., said that during the economic downturn, it was not the place of the federal government to focus on overhauling immigration policy. Instead, he suggested that Congress and the White House "take targeted steps to deal with the crisis at the border, increase the usage of the E-Verify program, and enhance prosecutions of employers who knowingly hire illegal workers." A vote required to advance the legislation to the Senate floor failed 55–41 on December 18, 2010.

ARIZONA'S LAW

The Support Our Law Enforcement and Safe Neighborhoods Act, passed in the Arizona legislature and signed by Gov. Brewer, is the toughest regulation of immigration ever seen in the United States. While the law encompasses a number of rules, there are two main provisions that have sparked controversy. These include: a requirement for police to verify that anyone they suspect of being an illegal immigrant prove otherwise; and a requirement that legal immigrants carry proper documentation of their status at all times. Upon signing the law, Gov. Brewer said, "The bill I'm about to sign into law—Senate Bill 1070—represents another tool for our state to use as we work to solve a crisis we did not create and the federal government has refused to fix." She continued, "Let me be clear, though: My signature today represents my steadfast support for enforcing the law—both against illegal immigration and against racial profiling." The requirement that police question anyone they suspect of being illegally in the country has been the biggest point of contention. Critics, including the American Civil Liberties Union (ACLU), said the law does in fact foster the type of profiling Gov. Brewer spoke against.

To alleviate the fear of racial profiling by Arizona law enforcement officials, one week after signing the original bill, Gov. Brewer signed into law a bill that would make changes to the Support Our Law Enforcement and Safe Neighborhoods Act. The original version of the law stated that officers "may not solely consider race" when deciding whether to question someone about their immigration status. The revisions stated, "A law enforcement official or agency of this state or a county, city, town or other political subdivision of this state may not consider race, color or national origin in implementing the requirements of this subsection except to the extent permitted by the United States or Arizona Constitution."

Legal experts said this change did little to clarify the law or ensure that questioning would be less racially charged. For example, behavior or clothing would still be allowed to be considered when an officer decides whether to question someone on his or her immigration status. Many wanted Arizona to instead adopt the language of earlier court cases. In 1975, the U.S. Supreme Court ruled 9–0 in *United States v. Brignoni-Ponce* that race alone does not justify stopping and questioning someone about his or her residency. The majority wrote, "The likelihood that any given person of Mexican ancestry is an alien is high enough to make Mexican appearance a relevant factor"; however, "standing alone it does not justify stopping all Mexican-Americans to ask if they are aliens." The U.S. Court of Appeals for the Ninth Circuit, which covers Arizona and some surrounding areas, went further, saying that it is not permissible to stop someone simply on the basis of his or her appearance as a person of Hispanic descent.

After passage, civil rights groups and some cities and counties, including Los Angeles, San Francisco, Boston, and Cook County, Illinois, boycotted and criticized Arizona. In some instances, cities refused to do business with the state or any vendors located in Arizona and would not allow government business–related travel to the state. Convention centers, hotels, and other recreational establishments were hardest hit. By November, it was reported that the state had lost a total of $141 million in meeting and convention services.

LEGAL CHALLENGES

Arizona has faced past legal challenges on its immigration laws. The 2007 Legal Arizona Workers Act required prosecutors in the state to investigate any complaint that illegal immigrants were working in a particular business and file suit to suspend the business license of that employer unless the allegations were "false and frivolous." The case was heard by the U.S. Supreme Court in December 2010. Those opposing the law, including the U.S. Chamber of Commerce and Obama administration, said that it violated the 1986 Federal Immigration Reform and Control Act, which states that federal regulations supersede "state or local law imposing civil or criminal sanctions." There was concern of a 4–4 split on the decision as the newest justice, Elena Kagan, would recuse herself from the case because she had been involved in its early stages as the U.S. solicitor general. If the Court is split, the Legal Arizona Workers Act will remain intact.

Almost as soon as the governor signed the 2010 immigration bill into law, the Obama administration filed suit in federal court to block its implementation. The brief filed with the U.S. District Court of Arizona stated that "the Constitution and federal law do not permit the development of a patchwork of state and local immigration policies throughout the country."

Sen. McCain, a supporter of immigration reform, issued a statement with the state's Republican junior senator, Jon Kyl, against the administration's decision to file suit. "Instead of wasting taxpayer resources filing a lawsuit against Arizona and complaining that the law would be burdensome, the Obama administration should have focused its efforts on working with Congress to provide the necessary resources to support the state in its efforts to act where the federal government has failed to take responsibility."

U.S. secretary of homeland security Janet Napolitano, Brewer's predecessor as Arizona governor, supported the Obama administration's decision. "I vetoed several similar pieces of legislation as Governor of Arizona because they would have diverted critical law enforcement resources from the most serious threats to public safety and undermined the vital trust between local jurisdictions and the communities they serve," she said.

After hearing the case, Judge Susan Bolton issued a preliminary injunction against Arizona's law. The injunction does not rule out the law being implemented at a later date; it only indicates that the Justice Department would likely uphold her ruling. "Preserving the status quo through a preliminary injunction is less harmful than allowing state laws that are likely pre-empted by federal law to be enforced," Bolton said during her ruling.

Bolton only blocked the most controversial portions of the law, including police questioning and the requiring of documents to always be carried. In her decision, Bolton wrote, "There is substantial likelihood that officers will wrongfully arrest legal resident aliens. By enforcing this statute, Arizona would impose a 'distinct, unusual and extraordinary' burden on legal resident aliens that only the federal government has the authority to impose." Bolton wrote that it was her opinion that the law would lead to the unlawful arrest of legal aliens and would also restrict the liberty of those legally in the country.

Bolton also blocked a provision that would have allowed police to hold anyone until immigration status was determined and one that would have banned illegal immigrants from soliciting work in public places at day laborer centers or outside of other businesses.

After Bolton's ruling, Gov. Brewer called for an appeal. "This fight is far from over," Brewer said. "In fact, it is just the beginning, and at the end of what is certain to be a long legal struggle, Arizona will prevail in its right to protect our citizens."

—Heather Kerrigan

Following is a statement issued by Gov. Jan Brewer on April 23, 2010, upon signing Arizona's Support Our Law Enforcement and Safe Neighborhoods Act; and a press release issued by the U.S. Department of Justice on July 6, 2010, announcing the department's intent to file suit to block implementation of Arizona's immigration law.

Gov. Brewer on Passage of Arizona's Immigration Law

April 23, 2010

[Ellipses and emphases in original document]

Thank you for being here today, to join me as we take another step forward in protecting the state of Arizona.

The bill I'm about to sign into law—Senate Bill 1070—represents another tool for our state to use as we work to solve a crisis we did not create and the federal government has refused to fix . . .

. . . The crisis caused by illegal immigration and Arizona's porous border.

This bill, the Support Our Law Enforcement and Safe Neighborhoods Act, strengthens the laws of our state.

It protects all of us, every Arizona citizen and everyone here in our state lawfully.

And, it does so while ensuring that the constitutional rights of ALL in Arizona remain solid—stable and steadfast.

I will now sign Senate Bill 1070.

For weeks, this legislation has been the subject of vigorous debate and intense criticism. My decision to sign it was by no means made lightly.

I have listened patiently to both sides. I have considered the significance of this new law long into the night. I have prayed for strength and prayed for our state.

I've decided to sign Senate Bill 1070 into law because, though many people disagree, I firmly believe it represents what's best for Arizona. Border-related violence and crime due to illegal immigration are critically important issues to the people of our state, to my Administration and to me, as your Governor and as a citizen.

There is no higher priority than protecting the citizens of Arizona. We cannot sacrifice our safety to the murderous greed of drug cartels. We cannot stand idly by as drop houses, kidnappings and violence compromise our quality of life.

We cannot delay while the destruction happening south of our international border creeps its way north.

We in Arizona have been more than patient waiting for Washington to act.

But decades of federal inaction and misguided policy have created a dangerous and unacceptable situation.

Yesterday, I announced the steps I was taking to enhance security along our border.

Today—with my unwavering signature on this legislation—Arizona strengthens its security WITHIN our borders.

Let me be clear, though: My signature today represents my steadfast support for enforcing the law—both AGAINST illegal immigration AND against racial profiling.

This legislation mirrors federal laws regarding immigration enforcement.

Despite erroneous and misleading statements suggesting otherwise, the new state misdemeanor crime of willful failure to complete or carry an alien registration document is adopted, verbatim, from the same offense found in federal statute.

I will NOT tolerate racial discrimination or racial profiling in Arizona.

Because I feel so strongly on this subject, I worked for weeks with legislators to amend SB 1070, to strengthen its civil rights protections.

That effort led to new language in the bill, language prohibiting law enforcement officers from "solely considering race, color, or national origin in implementing the requirements of this section . . ."

The bill already required that it "shall be implemented in a manner consistent with federal laws regulating immigration, protecting the civil rights of all persons and respecting the privileges and immunities of United States citizens."

While the general protection was already included, I believe the issue is so important, we needed to make it CRYSTAL clear.

And I believe that we need to more than simply inscribe it in statute.

Words in a law book are of no use if our police officers are not properly trained on the provisions of SB 1070, including its civil rights provisions.

Today I am issuing an executive order directing the Arizona Peace Officer Standards and Training Board—AZPOST—to develop training to appropriately implement SB 1070.

Importantly, this training will include what DOES—and DOES NOT—constitute "reasonable suspicion" that a person is not legally present in the United States.

Currently, AZPOST serves approximately 170 law enforcement agencies encompassing over 16,000 sworn peace officers, 9,000 correctional service officers, and 16 training academies.

The AZPOST Board of Directors includes the Arizona Attorney General, the Directors of the Arizona Department of Public Safety, the Arizona Department of Corrections, several county sheriffs, and local police departments.

I am also asking the Board to make recommendations on possible improvements to SB 1070 before the end of the year.

For 28 years in public service, I have worked without fail to solve problems diligently and practically. I have done so always with an eye toward civility, and always with the greatest respect for the rule of law.

This new law is no different: As committed as I am to protecting our state from crime associated with illegal immigration I am EQUALLY committed to holding law enforcement accountable should this statute ever be misused to violate an individual's rights.

Respect for the rule of law means respect for every law. I have led that way every day in every office I have ever held. That will not change.

I have also spent my career in service to Arizona working to bring people together, no matter the color of their skin and no matter the depth of our disagreements.

This bill—and this issue—will be no exception.

While protecting our citizens is paramount, it cannot come at the expense of the diversity that has made Arizona so great. Nor can safety mean a compromise of freedom for some, while we, the many, turn a blind eye.

We must acknowledge the truth—people across America are watching Arizona, seeing how we implement this law, ready to jump on even the slightest misstep.

Some of those people from outside our state have an interest in seeing us fail.

They will wait for a single slip-up, one mistake, and then they will work day and night to create headlines and get the face time they so desperately covet.

We cannot give them that chance.

We must use this new tool wisely, and fight for our safety with the honor Arizona deserves.

We must react calmly.

We must enforce the law evenly, and without regard to skin color, accent, or social status.

We must prove the alarmists and the cynics wrong.

I know in my heart that this great state, my home for more than 40 years, is up to the task.

I believe every one of us wants to be safe, and none of us wants to compromise on the subject of civil rights.

I believe we must love and honor those who fight beside us—just as we must love and honor those who look and believe nothing like we do.

I believe Arizona, like America, is governed by laws.

Good laws . . . well-intentioned laws . . . laws that confer respect and that demand respect in return.

In his third State of the Union address, President Theodore Roosevelt said, "No man is above the law and no man is below it; nor do we ask any man's permission when we require him to obey it.

Obedience to the law is demanded as a right; not asked as a favor."

So, let us move forward—ever mindful of our rights . . .

—ever faithful to the law . . . and ever conscious of our bond as Arizonans, and the blessing we share together.

Thank you."

Source: State of Arizona. Office of Governor Jan Brewer. "Statement by Governor Jan Brewer." April 23, 2010. http://azgovernor.gov/dms/upload/PR_042310_StatementByGovernorOnSB1070.pdf.

U.S. Justice Department Files Suit Against Arizona Immigration Law

July 6, 2010

The Department of Justice challenged the state of Arizona's recently passed immigration law, S.B. 1070, in federal court today.

In a brief filed in the District of Arizona, the Department said S.B. 1070 unconstitutionally interferes with the federal government's authority to set and enforce immigration policy, explaining that "the Constitution and federal law do not permit the development of a patchwork of state and local immigration policies throughout the country." A patchwork of state and local policies would seriously disrupt federal immigration enforcement. Having enacted its own immigration policy that conflicts with federal immigration law, Arizona "crossed a constitutional line."

The Department's brief said that S.B. 1070 will place significant burdens on federal agencies, diverting their resources away from high-priority targets, such as aliens implicated in terrorism, drug smuggling, and gang activity, and those with criminal records. The law's mandates on Arizona law enforcement will also result in the harassment and detention of foreign visitors and legal immigrants, as well as U.S. citizens, who cannot readily prove their lawful status.

In declarations filed with the brief, Arizona law enforcement officials, including the Chiefs of Police of Phoenix and Tucson, said that S.B. 1070 will hamper their ability to effectively police their communities. The chiefs said that victims of or witnesses to crimes would be less likely to contact or cooperate with law enforcement officials and that implementation of the law would require them to reassign officers from critical areas such as violent crimes, property crimes, and home invasions.

The Department filed the suit after extensive consultation with Arizona officials, law enforcement officers and groups, and civil rights advocates. The suit was filed on behalf of the Department of Justice, the Department of Homeland Security, and the Department of State, which share responsibilities in administering federal immigration law.

"Arizonans are understandably frustrated with illegal immigration, and the federal government has a responsibility to comprehensively address those concerns," Attorney General Holder said. "But diverting federal resources away from dangerous aliens such as terrorism suspects and aliens with criminal records will impact the entire country's safety. Setting immigration policy and enforcing immigration laws is a national responsibility. Seeking to address the issue through a patchwork of state laws will only create more problems than it solves."

"With the strong support of state and local law enforcement, I vetoed several similar pieces of legislation as Governor of Arizona because they would have diverted critical law enforcement resources from the most serious threats to public safety and undermined the vital trust between local jurisdictions and the communities they serve," Department of Homeland Security Secretary Janet Napolitano said. "We are actively working with members of Congress from both parties to comprehensively reform our immigration system at the federal level because this challenge cannot be solved by a patchwork of inconsistent state laws, of which this is one. While this bipartisan effort to reform our immigration system progresses, the Department of Homeland Security will continue to enforce the laws on the books by enhancing border security and removing criminal aliens from this country."

The Department has requested a preliminary injunction to enjoin enforcement of the law, arguing that the law's operation will cause irreparable harm.

"Arizona impermissibly seeks to regulate immigration by creating an Arizona-specific immigration policy that is expressly designed to rival or supplant that of the federal government. As such, Arizona's immigration policy exceeds a state's role with respect to aliens, interferes with the federal government's balanced administration of the immigration laws, and critically undermines U.S. foreign policy objectives. S.B. 1070 does not simply seek to provide legitimate support to the federal government's immigration policy, but instead creates an unprecedented independent immigration scheme that exceeds constitutional boundaries," the Department said in its brief. . . .

[The supporting documents have been omitted.]

SOURCE: United States Department of Justice. Office of Public Affairs. "Citing Conflict with Federal Law, Department of Justice Challenges Arizona Immigration Law." July 6, 2010. http://www.justice.gov/opa/pr/2010/July/10-opa-776.html.

OTHER HISTORIC DOCUMENTS OF INTEREST

FROM PREVIOUS *HISTORIC DOCUMENTS*

Deepwater Horizon Explosion and Oil Spill

On April 20, 2010, the offshore oil drilling platform Deepwater Horizon, which was working in the Macondo oil and gas prospect in the Gulf of Mexico, exploded after a methane gas bubble traveled up the drilling line. The explosion killed eleven and wounded many of the rig's employees. Just over one day later the rig sank, and oil flowed freely into the Gulf of Mexico. Millions of gallons of oil from the well flowed into the Gulf for more than eighty days before it could be stopped, causing extensive damage to animals and wildlife habitats and raising questions about the dangerous nature of deep-water drilling needed to keep up with the U.S. and global demand for oil.

DEEPWATER HORIZON EXPLOSION

Deepwater Horizon, a drilling rig owned by Houston-based Transocean and leased by British Petroleum (BP) at the cost of approximately $450,000 per day, was located fifty miles off the Louisiana coast. The rig was considered one of the most advanced engineering projects in the world. The year before the explosion, it had reached a drill depth of thirty-two thousand feet into the earth's crust, something never before achieved. Rig workers later complained that these feats were achieved at the same time that BP had encouraged them to cut corners to save money.

On the evening of April 20, methane gas in the well moved quickly through the drill column, landing on the deck of the nine-year-old rig. The rig was equipped with a blowout preventer, a $15 million piece of equipment that is intended to stop oil from flowing too quickly up the drill column. The protector, however, failed because it had been poorly maintained. Before employees could stop the flow, the gas ignited, overtaking the entire platform. Most of those on the rig escaped via lifeboat, but eleven were killed in the blast. The rig burned for thirty-six hours before sinking into the Gulf.

One day after the spill, Coast Guard rear admiral Mary Landry said there was potential for eight thousand barrels of crude oil to be released into the Gulf of Mexico each day. This estimate was later revised to anywhere between twenty thousand and one hundred thousand barrels per day. Significant environmental impact was expected because there was no clear sense of how long the oil would continue to flow.

The first efforts to contain the spill took place on the surface. Miles of containment booms were deployed along the Louisiana coast to prevent it from entering coastal wetlands and beaches. The booms also attempted to corral the oil for burning or collection by skimmer ships. By April 27, however, many of the containment methods being used on the ocean's surface were failing as the oil slick grew to one hundred miles wide and situated itself only twenty miles from the Louisiana coast. The U.S. Environmental Protection Agency (EPA) encouraged BP to deploy a chemical dispersant that would break up the oil underwater, thereby mitigating the damage, but quickly retracted its plan after learning of the total amount to be used, which it considered far more dangerous to the environment than necessary. After receiving a directive in May from the EPA encouraging BP to stop using dispersant on the water's surface except in rare circumstances, BP continued to use the dispersant well into June.

In its first underwater attempt at stopping the flow of oil, BP developed a containment dome, which it expected to stop the oil until another well could be drilled to relieve the pressure and safely deliver the oil to the surface. The containment dome was an immediate failure.

BP next attempted to apply a device called a "top hat," a second version of a containment dome, while simultaneously injecting the oil pipe with packed debris to try and clog it. This clogging method, known as "top kill," combined with the top hat, was also declared a failure.

The final plan, which was ultimately successful, was deployed on July 15. BP cut the oil pipe and fit it with a cap to stop the flow. While Coast Guard commandant Thad Allen warned that it would only be a temporary fix, there was relief that for at least a moment no additional oil was spilling into the Gulf. After fitting the gushing pipe with a cap, BP deployed its "static kill" method in August, using mud to force the oil back and permanently plug the pipe with cement.

The Oil Spill's Impact

Drilling rig explosions are rare around the world. In 1988, an offshore oil rig in the North Sea exploded and killed 167 people, and in 2001, a rig operating off the coast of Brazil exploded, killing eleven. The Deepwater Horizon disaster, however, was not BP's first run-in with oil rig problems. In 2005, a rig also operating in the Gulf of Mexico nearly capsized because of a faulty isolation valve in the ballast system. On land, in 2005, a refinery in Texas City, Texas, exploded and killed fifteen, and the next year, a BP-owned pipeline in Alaska began leaking. All of these incidents, and more specifically the recent rig explosion, reminded Americans of the danger of oil exploration, said Robert Bryce, an energy expert at the Manhattan Institute. "Deep water drilling is already a high-stakes casino and as geological risk, capital risk, market risk and engineering risk all come together, they are becoming extraordinarily difficult to quantify," he said.

The first oil from the Deepwater well washed ashore on April 30 in Venice, Louisiana, one of the state's barrier islands. By May 19, the oil reached Louisiana's mainland shore. And by the beginning of June, tar balls, a word that would enter the nation's common parlance, washed up on Florida's coast, fueling great concern about the tourism industry on the Gulf Coast.

More than a month after the explosion, federal officials were calling the damage to the environment some of the worst seen in U.S. history. "This is probably the biggest environmental disaster we have ever faced in this country," said Carol Browner, director of the White House Office of Energy and Climate Change Policy. The damage stretched along the Gulf Coast and affected not only the habitats of water-dwelling and coastal animals; it slowed tourism and shuttered seafood companies, the lifeblood of the region.

In Alabama, Louisiana, and Mississippi, seafood production is one of the largest forms of employment and sources of revenue. Because of the pollutants in the water, the National Oceanic and Atmospheric Administration (NOAA) closed 25 percent of the Gulf to fishing. Louisiana was hardest hit. It supplies 40 percent of all U.S. seafood, bringing in $2.4 billion annually. To offset the impact, the federal government declared the area a "fishery disaster," which opened up federal funds to local fishermen.

The three states also reported an impact on tourism and recreation. But Florida was the hardest hit: it depends on its $60-billion-per-year tourism industry. As tar balls washed up on shore, hotels and resorts reported cancellations. To alleviate the fears of potential tourists, Alabama, Florida, and Mississippi put out ads—paid for by BP—early in the spill's timeline that said the beaches were free of oil. A report released in December 2010 by the Louisiana Office of Tourism found that although tourism in the state will be significantly impacted through 2013, it has been offset somewhat by the media, government officials, scientists, and others who came to the region immediately after the spill.

Environmental scientists say it will take years to determine the complete environmental damage caused by the oil spill. Because of the wildlife habitats ruined by the oil slick, many water-dwelling and coast-dwelling animals may not return to the Gulf for many years, harming the fragile ecosystem off Louisiana's coast. However, initial reports after the spill indicated that the damage was not as significant as originally feared.

Under pressure from the Barack Obama administration, BP agreed to set up a $20 billion fund to compensate those affected by the oil spill and help state and local governments cover cleanup costs. "We will continue to hold BP and all other responsible parties accountable," the president said after completing the agreement. "And I'm absolutely confident BP will be able to meet its obligations to the Gulf Coast and to the American people." The $20 billion will be paid out over four years and will come on top of a $100 million payout BP agreed to make to those who were put out of work by President Obama's moratorium on deep-sea drilling. Claims for portions of the $20 billion quickly came in and BP faced criticism for slow and small payments.

Cause of the Spill

The federal government and BP launched independent investigations into the cause of the explosion and oil spill. In announcing his investigation, U.S. secretary of the Interior Ken Salazar said that while it was important to continue work to contain the spill and clean up any damage done, it was also important to look ahead in an effort to stop future catastrophes. "We must take aggressive action to verify the safety of other offshore oil and gas operations, further tighten our oversight of industry's practices, and take a careful look at all the questions that this disaster is raising," Salazar said. The federal investigation would review whether human or mechanical error, or a combination of the two, led to the explosion on April 20. The results of the investigation were released in January 2011. The 138-page report pointed to a number of mistakes made by the well's owners that led to the disaster. It also called for additional government control over the energy industry.

In a separate investigation concluded in 2010, BP placed blame for the explosion on a number of factors, including human error, mechanical failure, the design of the rig, and its operations leading up to the spill. Not only that, BP said, but blame could be placed on itself as well as Halliburton, which had been in charge of the initial cementing of the rig, and Transocean, which owned the rig. "No single factor caused the Macondo well tragedy. Rather, a sequence of failures involving a number of different parties led to the explosion and fire which killed 11 people and caused widespread pollution in the Gulf of Mexico earlier this year," the BP report stated.

BP CEO Tony Hayward, who had taken significant heat after calling the spill "relatively tiny" when compared to the size of the ocean, responded to the report saying, "The investigation report provides critical new information on the causes of this terrible accident. It is evident that a series of complex events, rather than a single mistake or failure, led to the tragedy.... To put it simply, there was a bad cement job and a failure of the shoe track barrier at the bottom of the well, which let hydrocarbons from the reservoir into the production casing. The negative pressure test was accepted when it should not have been, there were failures in well control procedures and in the blow-out preventer; and the rig's fire and gas system did not prevent ignition."

Robert Dudley, who soon replaced Hayward, stated that his leadership team had accepted all of the report's findings and recommendations and would give it careful further review to determine how best to proceed on other drilling platforms. "We are determined to learn the lessons for the future and we will be undertaking a broad-scale review to further improve the safety of our operations. We will invest whatever it takes to achieve that. It will be incumbent on everyone at BP to embrace and implement the changes necessary to ensure that a tragedy like this can never happen again," Dudley said.

Obama's Drilling Ban

When he first came into office, President Obama announced that he planned to open up more areas of the coastal United States to offshore drilling exploration, a plan that was cheered by many Republicans and rebuked by Democrats and environmentalists. Obama's plan was aimed at ensuring that the United States reduced its dependence on foreign oil, a volatile commodity that could easily be taken away if any foreign power wanted to harm the United States.

In March, one month before the oil rig explosion, Obama announced his intention to open parts of the eastern Gulf of Mexico and other parts of the Atlantic Ocean to oil and gas exploration. The eastern portion of the Gulf of Mexico was at that point closed to exploration by a congressional moratorium, but the Obama administration said that it would fight to lift that ban in the interest of national security.

After the oil spill, Obama reversed this policy and said that there would be no new drilling in the eastern Gulf of Mexico or off the Atlantic and Pacific coasts. The president renewed this ban in December, saying that these areas would be closed for the next five to seven years. In a press statement, Secretary of the Interior Salazar said, "We are adjusting our strategy in areas where there are no active leases. [The Obama administration decided] not to expand to new areas at this time," he explained. Instead, the administration would focus on areas where drilling is currently active to ensure that adequate safety measures are put in place. "We see clear evidence every day, as oil spills from BP's well, of the need for a pause on deepwater drilling. Based on this ever-growing evidence, I will issue a new order in the coming days that eliminates any doubt that a moratorium is needed, appropriate, and within our authorities," Salazar said.

—Heather Kerrigan

Following are two press releases issued by the U.S. Department of the Interior. The first, released on April 27, 2010, announces the start of the investigation into the Deepwater Horizon spill; the second, released on April 30, 2010, announces Secretary of the Interior Ken Salazar's intent to investigate offshore drilling safety issues.

Secretaries Salazar and Napolitano Launch Deepwater Horizon Investigation

April 27, 2010

As they emphasized the importance of continued vigilance and interagency coordination in the joint response to the Deepwater Horizon incident in the Gulf of Mexico, Secretary of Homeland Security Janet Napolitano and Secretary of the Interior Ken Salazar today laid out the next steps for the investigation that is underway into the causes of the April 20 explosion that left 11 workers missing, three critically injured, and an ongoing oil spill that the responsible party and federal agencies are working to contain and clean up.

"As we continue to work with our federal, state, local and private sector partners to respond to this ongoing incident, we must also effectively determine and address its causes," said Secretary Napolitano. "Secretary Salazar and I share President Obama's commitment to devoting every available resource to a comprehensive and thorough investigation."

"We will remain focused on providing every resource we can to support the massive response effort underway at the Deepwater Horizon, but we are also aggressively and quickly investigating what happened and what can be done to prevent this type of incident in the future," said Secretary of the Interior Ken Salazar.

Secretary Salazar and Secretary Napolitano made the announcement as they signed an order establishing the next steps for a joint investigation that is underway into the causes of the explosion of the drilling rig Deepwater Horizon in the Gulf of Mexico. The U.S. Coast Guard (USCG) and the Minerals Management Service (MMS) share jurisdiction for the investigation. The MMS is responsible for investigating incidents related to systems associated with exploration, drilling, completion, work over, production, pipeline, and decommissioning operations for hydrocarbons and other minerals on the Outer Continental Shelf. The USCG investigates maritime industry deaths, injuries, property loss, and environmental damage to determine the causes of accidents. The Coast Guard also investigates merchant mariner negligence or misconduct and possible criminal and civil offenses; and analyzes trends and risks in the maritime industries.

The joint investigation, which began on April 21, will proceed under a Joint Statement of Principles and Convening Order, and a Memorandum of Agreement, which lays out roles and responsibilities that relate to each agency's area of expertise. The joint investigation will have the power to issue subpoenas, hold public hearings, call witnesses, and take other steps that may be needed to determine the cause of the incident.

Later today, Assistant to the President for Energy and Climate Change Carol Browner and White House Senior Advisor Valerie Jarrett, Secretary Napolitano, U.S. Coast Guard Commandant Admiral Thad Allen, and Secretary Salazar and DOI Deputy Secretary David Hayes are holding meetings with BP senior leadership—including the CEO of BP Group, the President and Chairman of BP America, and Executive Vice President of BP America—to discuss the response effort and to ensure all is being done to respond to this incident.

A unified, coordinated response continues among federal, state, local and private sector partners to stop the flow of oil and minimize its environmental impact. 1,000 total personnel are currently deployed and have used nearly 15,000 gallons of oil dispersant so far. Nearly 50,000 gallons of oily water have been collected. 11 offshore response vessels, eight skimming boats and multiple aircraft are conducting containment and cleanup operations in the area. . . .

SOURCE: U.S. Department of the Interior. "Salazar and Napolitano Launch Full Investigation of Deepwater Horizon Incident in the Gulf of Mexico." April 27, 2010. http://www.doi.gov/news/pressre leases/SECRETARY-NAPOLITANO-AND-SECRETARY-SALAZAR-LAUNCH-FULL-INVES TIGATION-OF-DEEPWATER-HORIZON-INCIDENT-IN-THE-GULF-OF-MEXICO.cfm.

Secretary of the Interior Salazar Launches First Full Review of Offshore Drilling Safety

DOCUMENT

April 30, 2010

As part of the federal government's coordinated oversight and support of BP's response to its spill in the Gulf of Mexico, the Department of the Interior will establish a new Outer Continental Shelf Safety Board, conduct a full review of offshore drilling safety and technology issues, and further tighten oversight of industry equipment testing, Secretary of the Interior Ken Salazar announced today.

"In this eleventh day of the massive, coordinated response to the Deepwater Horizon incident, we must continue to do everything we can to oversee and support BP's efforts to stop and clean up the oil that is spilling from the well head," said Salazar, during a visit to command centers in Houma and Robert, Louisiana, with Secretary of Homeland Security Janet Napolitano. "At the same time, we must take aggressive action to verify the safety of other offshore oil and gas operations, further tighten our oversight of industry's practices, and take a careful look at all the questions that this disaster is raising."

The Department of the Interior's Outer Continental Shelf Safety Oversight Board, established today by Secretarial Order, will provide recommendations regarding interim measures that may enhance OCS safety and recommendations for improving and strengthening the Department's overall management, regulation and oversight of OCS operations. The Oversight Board, on which Assistant Secretary for Land and Minerals Management Wilma Lewis, DOI Inspector General Mary Kendall, and Assistant Secretary for Policy, Management and Budget Rhea Suh will serve, will also provide oversight of the MMS regarding the Joint Investigation that MMS and the United States Coast Guard have undertaken into the Deepwater Horizon incident. Secretary Salazar will provide a report to President Obama within 30 days on what, if any, immediate additional precautions and technologies should be required.

Salazar also said that MMS will continue rigorous oversight of industry operations to ensure compliance with all drilling laws and regulations. . . . At Secretary Salazar's direction, MMS is conducting immediate inspections of all 30 deepwater drilling rigs and 47 deepwater production platforms in the Gulf of Mexico. This operation is underway and consists of targeted inspections ensuring that tests of BOP (blowout preventer) stacks have been completed, related records are available for inspection, and that emergency well control exercises are taking place. MMS inspectors should complete inspections of deepwater drilling rigs within seven days, whereupon they will immediately start inspecting all deepwater production platforms.

Salazar urged oil and gas leaders and technical experts yesterday evening to do everything possible to assist BP with its response to its spill and to take every available precaution as they conduct their own operations. At Salazar's direction, MMS today issued a special safety alert to operators emphasizing that all safety procedures and testing must be conducted fully and that operators should verify that BOP stacks are properly tested and configured.

The findings of the Joint Investigation and the recommendations of the Oversight Board will help inform the implementation of the Obama Administration's comprehensive energy strategy for the Outer Continental Shelf, said Salazar. "As we evaluate new areas for potential exploration and development in the OCS, we will conduct thorough environmental analysis and scientific study, gather public input and comment, and carefully examine the potential safety and spill risk considerations, including the findings of the Joint Investigation and the recommendations of the new oversight board."

Interior agencies with responsibility for public lands and natural resources are working with federal and state officials to place boom barriers around sensitive areas of the Gulf Coast.

This effort has already deployed about 100,000 feet of boom along sensitive Louisiana sites, including 23,000 feet of boom to protect pelican nesting colonies at North and New Harbor Islands (behind Chandeleur Islands) and 23,000 feet deployed around the Breton National Wildlife Refuge, where additional boom is being deployed.

Booms are being placed to protect coastal marshes in southeast Louisiana and ecologically sensitive areas in Florida. In Alabama and Mississippi, the placement of booms to protect priority areas has been initiated and will continue through the next few days. Priority areas include ecologically sensitive areas identified by U.S. Fish and Wildlife Service and National Park Service as part of the Area Contingency Plan and Environmental Sensitivity Index Map planning processes. . . .

The Mobile Offshore Drilling Unit Deepwater Horizon, located in the Gulf of Mexico about 51 miles southeast of Venice, Louisiana exploded and caught fire on April 20 and sank on April 22. The National Response Team was immediately activated and Unified and Area Commands were established near New Orleans to coordinate search and rescue operations and oil spill response efforts. Interior Deputy Secretary David J. Hayes was on scene to assist with coordination and response. Interior's Minerals Management Service, which oversees the leasing and operation of oil and gas exploration rigs and production platforms on the Outer Continental Shelf, activated its Emergency Operations Center in New Orleans and deployed additional personnel to the Houston, Texas—Incident Command Center for British Petroleum. The Interior Department, Minerals Management Service, and other Interior agencies continue to provide their full support to the U.S. Coast Guard's oil spill response and coastal protection efforts and the Department's land and wildlife management agencies in the Gulf are protecting sensitive areas with boom barriers and taking other measures to protect natural resources.

Estimated production from the federal waters Gulf of Mexico as of October 2009 is 1.7 million barrels of oil per day and 6.6 billion cubic feet of gas per day. This represents about 30 percent of domestic oil production and about 11 percent of domestic natural gas production. About 35,000 workers are engaged in offshore Gulf of Mexico activities at any one time. Ninety rigs are currently drilling or working-over in federal waters Gulf of Mexico, including 68 Mobile Offshore Drilling Units and 22 platform rigs. There are about 3,500 production platforms in federal waters in the Gulf of Mexico; 978 of those are manned.

SOURCE: U.S. Department of the Interior. "Salazar Launches Full Review of Offshore Drilling Safety Issues during Visit to Oil Spill Command Centers on Gulf Coast." April 30, 2010. http://www.doi.gov/news/pressreleases/Salazar-Launches-Full-Review-of-Offshore-Drilling-Safety-Issues-during-Visit-to-Oil-Spill-Command-Centers-on-Gulf-Coast.cfm.

OTHER HISTORIC DOCUMENTS OF INTEREST

FROM THIS VOLUME

FROM PREVIOUS *HISTORIC DOCUMENTS*

First U.S. Offshore Wind Farm Approved

APRIL 28 AND OCTOBER 6, 2010

After nine years of working through government red tape and fighting opposition from environmentalists and citizen groups, in April 2010, the United States' first offshore wind farm project was approved. Cape Wind, which is slated to be built five miles off the Massachusetts coast, could begin generating power in 2012 if the U.S. Department of the Interior, Cape Wind's owners, and Massachusetts residents and politicians are able to agree on placement, color, and number of turbines of the wind farm. "America needs offshore wind power," said Massachusetts governor Deval Patrick upon U.S. Interior secretary Ken Salazar's approval of the wind farm. "With this project, Massachusetts will lead the nation. . . . Cape Wind is good for our environment and good for our energy needs." As renewable energy advocates around the United States rejoiced at Salazar's decision, by the end of 2010, Cape Wind had yet to break ground as the political battle raged on.

CAPE WIND

In 2001, Energy Management Inc., a New England–based energy company, announced its intention to build the United States' first offshore wind farm, which would supply energy to the Cape Cod, Martha's Vineyard, and Nantucket Sound areas of Massachusetts. Not only would the wind farm be able to generate 75 percent of the power in this area, Energy Management claimed, it would also create jobs and put America on track to develop additional renewable energy sources.

The company's chief executive officer, Jim Gordon, knew the fight would not be easy. By situating the wind turbines in Nantucket Sound, he was interfering with, among other things, the view from the Kennedy family compound in Martha's Vineyard. The late senator Ted Kennedy, D-Mass., had been a strong opponent of the project. Kennedy's nephew, Robert Kennedy Jr., wrote an op-ed article in the *New York Times* in 2005 supporting wind power, but opposing the Cape Wind project. "Cape Wind's proposal involves construction of 130 giant turbines whose windmill arms will reach 417 feet above the water and be visible for up to 26 miles. These turbines are less than six miles from shore and would be seen from Cape Cod, Martha's Vineyard and Nantucket. Hundreds of flashing lights to warn airplanes away from the turbines will steal the stars and nighttime views. The noise of the turbines will be audible onshore. A transformer substation rising 100 feet above the sound would house giant helicopter pads and 40,000 gallons of potentially hazardous oil," he wrote.

In April 2010, Salazar announced that he would approve the project. "I am approving the Cape Wind project," said Salazar. "This will be the first of many projects up and down the Atlantic coast." Although the federal government was throwing its backing to the project, Salazar's approval did include restrictions. For example, Salazar requested that the 170 turbines originally asked for be reduced to 130 and that some be repositioned to accommodate the concerns of residents and environmentalists. Finally, Salazar requested that the turbines be painted off-white to make them less visible on the horizon.

In his approval remarks, Salazar noted that not only would the wind farm move the United States forward in renewable energy production, it would also significantly cut carbon dioxide emissions. According to the interior secretary, the reduction in carbon dioxide would be equivalent to removing 175,000 cars from the road.

With initial federal approval secured, Cape Wind's developers turned to obtaining the proper state and local permits to break ground. In the summer of 2010, the Massachusetts Supreme Judicial Court ruled on a case brought by community groups who opposed the Cape Wind project. The court ruled in favor of the state, saying it had the power to overrule any concern brought forth by community groups and activists in order to ensure that Cape Wind received the proper state and local permits to begin building.

In October, Salazar officially signed a twenty-eight-year lease for the $1 billion project on Nantucket Sound. "Responsibly developing this clean, renewable, domestic resource will stimulate investment in cutting-edge technology, create good, solid jobs for American workers, and promote our nation's competiveness, security, and prosperity," Salazar said. The Federal Aviation Administration also signed off on the project, declaring that it would not present a hazard for incoming planes.

In November, Massachusetts finalized a deal between Cape Wind and one of the state's largest electric companies, National Grid, to purchase half of the power generated by Cape Wind at a cost of 18.7 cents per kilowatt hour. Massachusetts helped to finalize the deal to work toward reaching Gov. Patrick's goal of generating 20 percent of the state's electricity with renewable sources by 2020. To cover the cost of its purchase, National Grid's customers in Massachusetts will likely pay higher prices for their electricity, but the increase in price is expected to be minimal. The project's approval process was completed in early January 2011 when the U.S. Environmental Protection Agency (EPA) and the U.S. Army Corps of Engineers issued their permits.

WIND FARMS AROUND THE COUNTRY AND WORLD

Europe and China have led the United States in development of offshore wind farms. In China, a little more than 100 megawatts are currently generated by its first offshore wind farm located off the coast of Shanghai. A second approved offshore wind farm near the city will produce another 100 megawatts. In total, Chinese officials expect that their collection of offshore wind farms will be able to produce nearly 1,000 megawatts of power by 2020. Cape Wind officials hope that its farm will generate 468 megawatts, enough to power 200,000 homes.

In Europe, where onshore wind farms are largely unfeasible because of the lack of available space, offshore wind generation has been met with little resistance. Denmark was responsible for building the world's first offshore wind farm more than twenty years before Cape Wind received U.S. approval. While European nations have faced obstacles in the most economical and efficient ways to deliver power from offshore sources to land, turbines have been built in large numbers.

Eleven other offshore wind farm projects are currently in development in the United States and are awaiting approval from the Interior Department, as of the end of 2010. These projects are slated to be built in Delaware, Massachusetts, New Jersey, North Carolina, Ohio, Rhode Island, and Texas. States on the Atlantic Coast and in the Great Lakes region are best suited for wind farms because of the shallow water along the coast. In the west and south, the coast quickly drops off into deep water, presenting significant challenges for placing turbines.

WIND FARM OPPONENTS

Opposition to Cape Wind has come from a number of sources, including members of the government, environmental groups, and Massachusetts residents who would be able to see the turbines from shore.

Environmental groups, though pleased with the development of renewable energy, which is gathered in a method less destructive to the environment, are still worried that the turbines could damage the habitats of some water-dwelling birds and animals in the region. According to Michael Fry, the conservation advocacy director for the American Bird Conservancy, Cape Wind could "reduce prime offshore sea-duck foraging habitat." He also indicated that there is reason to believe that loons would leave the area and that endangered roseate terns could be impacted. Two major environmental groups, Greenpeace and the Sierra Club, however, have supported the project. In 2009, the Department of the Interior's Minerals Management Service released a study stating that no major environmental damage would be caused by the wind farm.

Residents of Massachusetts worry about the visual impact brought on by the turbines. Some have claimed that Nantucket Sound, a tourist destination, will lose its allure if the turbines appear off the coast and reduce opportunities for boating and recreational income for the region. "We will not stand by and allow our treasured public lands to be marred forever by a corporate giveaway to private industrial energy developers," said Audra Parker, president of the Alliance to Protect Nantucket Sound.

Residents have further expressed financial concerns. Although Massachusetts has a plan to purchase the power, it will still be more costly to consumers than traditional sources of energy. According to state and local research, however, the additional cost would only be $1.50 per month per home. Updating the power grid and power lines to ensure efficient delivery of wind energy to homes and businesses presents another potential cost for residents. The expectation is that the upgrade will cost $10 billion, a sum that is likely to be passed down to taxpayers.

Nantucket Sound holds historical significance for two local Native American tribes that have fought to get the sound added to the National Register of Historic Places. "No amount of mitigation will change the fact that this is a site of great historical and cultural significance for our tribe, and is inappropriate for this project," said Cedric Cromwell, chair of the Mashpee Wampanoag Tribe. By building Cape Wind, the tribes claim the developer would be ruining important Native American rituals and desecrating sacred burial grounds located under the sound.

Some concern was mitigated after the Deepwater Horizon oil rig explosion, which brought to the forefront the dangers of America's most heavily used resources. According to Energy Management's Gordon, the disaster underscores the problems with traditional energy. "It gives the nation pause to reflect on, really, what are our energy choices, and how are we going to live with them?" Gordon said. "We are on our way, and if we get clean energy right, the whole world will be our customers," said Gov. Patrick.

Gordon has pressed on despite the pushback his project has received. "We've been developing this project for 10 years," he said. "This project has the potential to catalyze the industry. There's tremendous potential. There's over 900,000 megawatts of offshore wind identified off our coast." The potentially available megawatts surrounding the United States could have the ability to power the entire country.

—Heather Kerrigan

Following are two press releases from the U.S. Department of the Interior—the first, on April 28, 2010, announcing the approval of the first U.S. offshore wind farm at Cape Wind; and the second, on October 6, 2010, announcing Secretary Ken Salazar's signing of the lease for the space for Cape Wind.

DOCUMENT

Interior Secretary Salazar Announces Approval of First U.S. Offshore Wind Farm

April 28, 2010

Secretary of the Interior Ken Salazar today approved the Cape Wind renewable energy project on federal submerged lands in Nantucket Sound, but will require the developer of the $1 billion wind farm to agree to additional binding measures to minimize the potential adverse impacts of construction and operation of the facility.

"After careful consideration of all the concerns expressed during the lengthy review and consultation process and thorough analyses of the many factors involved, I find that the public benefits weigh in favor of approving the Cape Wind project at the Horseshoe Shoal location," Salazar said in an announcement at the State House in Boston. "With this decision we are beginning a new direction in our Nation's energy future, ushering in America's first offshore wind energy facility and opening a new chapter in the history of this region."

The Cape Wind project would be the first wind farm on the U.S. Outer Continental Shelf, generating enough power to meet 75 percent of the electricity demand for Cape Cod, Martha's Vineyard and Nantucket Island combined. The project would create several hundred construction jobs and be one of the largest greenhouse gas reduction initiatives in the nation, cutting carbon dioxide emissions from conventional power plants by 700,000 tons annually. That is equivalent to removing 175,000 cars from the road for a year.

A number of similar projects have been proposed for other northeast coastal states, positioning the region to tap 1 million megawatts of offshore Atlantic wind energy potential, which could create thousands of manufacturing, construction and operations jobs and displace older, inefficient fossil-fueled generating plants, helping significantly to combat climate change.

Salazar emphasized that the Department has taken extraordinary steps to fully evaluate Cape Wind's potential impacts on traditional cultural resources and historic properties, including government-to-government consultations with the Wampanoag Tribe of Gay Head (Aquinnah) and the Mashpee Wampanoag Tribe and that he was "mindful of our unique relationship with the Tribes and carefully considered their views and concerns."

Because of concerns expressed during the consultations, Interior has required the developer to change the design and configuration of the wind turbine farm to diminish the visual effects of the project and to conduct additional seabed surveys to ensure that any submerged archaeological resources are protected prior to bottom disturbing activities.

Under these revisions, the number of turbines has been reduced from 170 to 130, eliminating turbines to reduce the visual impacts from the Kennedy Compound National Historic Landmark; reconfiguring the array to move it farther away from Nantucket Island; and reducing its breadth to mitigate visibility from the Nantucket Historic District. Regarding possible seabed cultural and historic resources, a Chance Finds Clause in the lease requires the developer to halt operations and notify Interior of any unanticipated archaeological find.

Salazar said he understood and respected the views of the Tribes and the Advisory Council on Historic Preservation, but noted that as Secretary of the Interior, he must balance broad, national public interest priorities in his decisions. "The need to preserve the environmental resources and rich cultural heritage of Nantucket Sound must be weighed in the balance with the importance of developing new renewable energy sources and strengthening our Nation's energy security while battling climate change and creating jobs," Salazar said.

"After almost a decade of exhaustive study and analyses, I believe that this undertaking can be developed responsibly and with consideration to the historic and cultural resources in the project area," Salazar said. "Impacts to the historic properties can and will be minimized and mitigated and we will ensure that cultural resources will not be harmed or destroyed during the construction, maintenance, and decommissioning of the project."

He pointed out that Nantucket Sound and its environs are a working landscape with many historical and modern uses and changing technologies. These include significant commercial, recreational and other resource-intensive activities, such as fishing, aviation, marine transport and boating, which have daily visual and physical impacts, and have long coexisted with the cultural and historic attributes of the area and its people.

A number of tall structures, including broadcast towers, cellular base station towers, local public safety communications towers and towers for industrial and business uses are located around the area. Three submarine transmission cable systems already traverse the seabed to connect mainland energy sources to Martha's Vineyard and Nantucket Island. Visual and physical impacts associated with Nantucket Sound and its associated shorelines abound; it is not an untouched landscape.

Salazar disagreed with the Advisory Council's conclusion that visual impacts from the proposed wind farm, which will be situated between and at substantial distance from Cape Cod, Nantucket Island and Martha's Vineyard, provide a rationale for rejecting the siting of the project. The viewshed effects are not direct or destructive to onshore traditional cultural properties. In no case does the turbine array dominate the viewshed. The project site is about 5.2 miles from the mainland shoreline, 13.8 miles from Nantucket Island and 9 miles from Martha's Vineyard.

Nevertheless, Interior has required the developer to reduce the number of turbines and reconfigure the array to diminish its visual effects. Moreover, the developer will be required to paint the turbines off-white to reduce contrast with the sea and sky yet remain visible to birds.

No daytime Federal Aviation Administration lighting will be on the turbines, unless the U.S. Coast Guard requires some "day beacons" to ensure navigation safety. FAA nighttime lighting requirements have been reduced, lessening potential nighttime visual impacts. The upland cable transmission route was located entirely below ground within paved roads and existing utility rights of way to avoid visual impacts and potential impacts to unidentified archeological or historic resources.

These mitigation measures, coupled with the overall distance from which the turbine array will be viewed at any location, will reduce the visual impacts of the project. Lease terms also require the developer to decommission the facility when the project has completed its useful service life, deconstructing the turbines and towers and removing them from the site.

The Secretary also disagreed that it is not possible to mitigate the impacts associated with installation of piers for wind turbines in the seabed, noting that piers for bridges, transmission lines and other purposes are routinely built in relatively shallow waters consistent with those found in Horseshoe Shoals. A number of marine archaeological studies have indicated that there is low probability that the project area contains submerged archaeological resources. Most of the area has been extensively reworked and disturbed by marine activities and geological processes.

Nonetheless, Interior will require additional and detailed marine archaeological surveys and other protective measures in the project area. A full suite of remote sensing tools will be used to ensure seafloor coverage out to 1000 feet beyond the Area of Potential Effect. More predictive modeling and settlement pattern analyses also will be conducted as well as geotechnical coring and analyses to aid in the identification of intact landforms that could contain archaeological materials. Moreover, the Chance Finds Clause in the lease will not only halt operations if cultural resources or indicators suggesting the possibility of cultural habitation are found but also allow the Tribes to participate in reviewing and analyzing such potential finds.

The Advisory Council's regulations provide that the Interior Department must take into account the Council's comments on particular projects. The Department, as the decision-making authority, is required to consider the Council's comments but is not legally bound to follow its recommendations or conclusions.

The Cape Wind Associates, LLC facility would occupy a 25-square-mile section of Nantucket Sound and generate a maximum electric output of 468 megawatts with an average anticipated output of 182 megawatts. At average expected production, Cape Wind could produce enough energy to power more than 200,000 homes in Massachusetts. Horseshoe Shoals lies outside shipping channels, ferry routes and flight paths but is adjacent to power-consuming coastal communities. One-fifth of the offshore wind energy potential of the East Coast is located off the New England coast and Nantucket Sound receives strong, steady Atlantic winds year round. The project includes a 66.5-mile buried submarine transmission cable system, an electric service platform and two 115-kilovolt lines connecting to the mainland power grid.

SOURCE: U.S. Department of the Interior. "Secretary Salazar Announces Approval of Cape Wind Energy Project on Outer Continental Shelf off Massachusetts." April 28, 2010. http://www.doi.gov/news/press releases/Secretary-Salazar-Announces-Approval-of-Cape-Wind-Energy-Project-on-Outer-Continental-Shelf-off-Massachusetts.cfm.

Interior Secretary Salazar Signs Lease for Cape Wind

October 6, 2010

Secretary of the Interior Ken Salazar and Cape Wind Associates, LLC today signed the nation's first lease for commercial wind energy development on the Outer Continental Shelf (OCS).

"This is the beginning of a new era for our Nation in offshore energy production," Secretary Salazar said in a speech to the American Wind Energy Association in Atlantic City, New Jersey, where he signed the lease. "Responsibly developing this clean, renewable, domestic resource will stimulate investment in cutting-edge technology, create good, solid jobs for American workers, and promote our nation's competitiveness, security, and prosperity."

"This is an important milestone in the development of offshore wind energy," said Bureau of Ocean Energy Management, Regulation and Enforcement (BOEM) Director Michael R. Bromwich, whose agency is responsible for reviewing proposed renewable energy projects on the OCS. "This is the first chapter of what we hope will be a continuing story of offshore renewable energy development that will allow us to expand the nation's energy resource portfolio. As we move forward, we hope to expedite the process of reviewing and approving such applications."

The area offered in the lease is comprised of 25 square miles on the OCS in Nantucket Sound offshore Massachusetts. The 130 planned wind turbines could generate a maximum electric output of 468 megawatts with an average anticipated output of 182 megawatts. At average expected production, Cape Wind could produce enough energy to power more than 200,000 homes in Massachusetts. The site of the project on Horseshoe Shoals lies outside shipping channels, ferry routes and flight paths but is adjacent to power-consuming coastal communities.

The Cape Wind energy project would be the first wind farm on the OCS, potentially generating enough power to meet 75 percent of the electricity demand for Cape Cod, Martha's Vineyard and Nantucket Island combined.

The 28-year lease for the area off the coast of Cape Cod, Mass. will cost the company $88,278 in annual rent prior to production, and a 2 to 7 percent operating fee during production. The fee is based on revenues from selling the offshore wind energy in regional markets.

On April 28, 2010, Secretary Salazar signed the Record of Decision for the Cape Wind project, which paved the way for BOEM's decision to issue a commercial wind lease to Cape Wind Associates, LLC, a subsidiary of Energy Management Inc. The Record of Decision reflects the commitments that the company must satisfy to ensure that the company's lease activities are conducted in a manner that prevents or minimizes impacts on environmental or cultural resources.

The project site is about 5 miles from the mainland shoreline, 13 miles from Nantucket Island, and 9 miles from Martha's Vineyard. One-fifth of the offshore wind energy potential of the East Coast is located off the New England coast, and Nantucket Sound receives strong, steady Atlantic winds year round. The project includes a 66.5-mile buried submarine transmission cable system, an electric service platform and two 115-kilovolt lines connecting to the mainland power grid.

Source: U.S. Department of the Interior. "Salazar Signs First U.S. Offshore Commercial Wind Energy Lease with Cape Wind Associates, LLC." October 6, 2010. http://www.doi.gov/news/pressreleases/Salazar-Signs-First-US-Offshore-Commercial-Wind-Energy-Lease-with-Cape-Wind-Associates-LLC.cfm.

Other Historic Documents of Interest

From this volume

- Deepwater Horizon Explosion and Oil Spill, p. 183

From Previous *Historic Documents*

- Bush Task Force Plans for a National Energy Policy, *2001*, p. 331

May

Greek Financial Crisis

Members of the European Union (EU) began circulating its common currency, the euro, in 2002. While heralded at the time as a means of fostering ever closer integration, monetary union was achieved without coordination of fiscal policy, resulting in a division that could crudely be categorized along cultural lines. Northern European states, with some exceptions, generally responded to the easy credit and myriad opportunities offered during the boom times of the last decade with more caution than their southern neighbors, whose consumption and public debt rose broadly in line with gross domestic product (GDP) output, regardless of whether that growth was based on sustainable trends.

Fiscal discipline proved more politically difficult to implement than the currency itself, with the EU softening criteria for euro adoption and subsequent aid disbursements in order to advance the power and collective identity of Europe. This implicit pact between prudent budgeters such as Germany, who provided a disproportionate share of funds, and liberal Mediterranean spenders continued without obvious consequences prior to the global economic crisis that accelerated from 2008.

However, as governments drained national accounts to stimulate their ailing economies, the consequences of admitting weaker members to the euro became clear. Bereft of control over a national currency, they could not devalue to effectively reduce the sum of their debt. Previously undisclosed liabilities affected not only their citizens, who faced grim domestic austerity measures as a necessary corrective to structural deficits, but also other EU states, whose taxpayers would be called upon to fund emergency bailout packages. Ironically, despite the resentment of voters in donor countries towards their hapless counterparts, poor economic performance in the south of the continent weighed down the value of the euro, improving the competitiveness of export businesses in stronger economies.

Although other member states, including Ireland, Portugal, Spain, and Italy, would later face either the threat or the reality of insolvency, Greece stood alone as a byword for profligacy as its financial woes multiplied in early 2010. By May, the Greek government had acknowledged that it would need to access the rescue funds conditionally offered by the EU and the International Monetary Fund (IMF).

GREECE'S ECONOMY

Greece has had five major defaults since gaining its independence in 1829 and has habitually run a budget deficit, due to a combination of ever-rising public sector benefits and widespread tax evasion. The country hoped to join the inaugural members of the

European Monetary Union in 1999 but failed the EU's Maastricht criteria, which called for states adopting the euro to have budget deficits equal to no more than 3 percent of their annual GDP and total public debt equaling no more than 60 percent of GDP. After implementing an unpopular package of cuts, Greece was approved to join the euro currency in 2001, putting the currency in circulation in 2002. However, critics questioned whether the EU had been excessively lenient in allowing Greece to adopt the currency, noting the country's enduring structural problems.

In 2004, it was revealed that despite cutbacks, Greece had actually exceeded the EU budget deficit limit required for euro entry, which it achieved on the basis of its 1999 data. While adoption of the currency had afforded it more favorable interest rates than it would have merited under the Greek currency, the drachma, the government leveraged this windfall to fund wage increases and large projects such as the 2004 Athens Olympics on credit, instead of addressing long-term imbalances in the public finances. Underlying weaknesses were partially disguised with the assistance of external financial advisers, who arranged cross-currency swaps at artificial exchange rates. In one example, this method could allow the government to receive the equivalent of $11 billion in euros for a $10 billion bond and underreport its value in the public accounts. The Greek government would later suggest the possibility of suing these advisers, notably those employed by Goldman Sachs, for their role in enabling Greece to acquire so much debt. By 2010, public wages had risen by almost 100 percent in ten years, and the government's pension obligations, which could equal over 90 percent of workers' salaries, were expanding in response to an aging population.

LEAD UP TO THE CRISIS

Following snap elections in 2009, the Panhellenic Socialist Movement (PASOK) ousted the conservative New Democracy government, which had been seeking a mandate for economic reforms. The winning party pledged a new era of development and revival but later learned that the public finances were more precarious than acknowledged under the previous government, with new prime minister George Papandreou describing the economy as being in "intensive care." By the end of the year, the budget deficit totaled 13.6 percent of GDP. These revelations alarmed investors. Accordingly, ratings agencies Fitch and Standard and Poor's downgraded Greek bonds in December 2009.

Stripped of its investment grade rating, Greece saw its bond yields rise through early 2010, even as Prime Minister Papandreou presented an aggressive deficit-reduction plan. On March 3, the government announced that public sector wages would be cut, affecting the traditional bonuses equivalent to two extra months' salary, in addition to the extra payment usually awarded at Easter. Pensions were also frozen and bonuses were stopped for public sector servants, and the public was informed that the only alternative was national bankruptcy.

Although a bond sale held the next day was successful, observers remained wary of Greece's long-term prospects, as France continued its efforts to convince Germany of the necessity of establishing a European bailout fund. Germany remained resistant to the notion due to its unpopularity with German voters: Chancellor Angela Merkel had in February categorically dismissed the idea, arguing that Greece was responsible for its own debt. Jaded observers surmised that French president Nicolas Sarkozy was seeking to use the crisis to enhance member states' dependence on the EU, in which France and Germany hold the greatest influence.

International opinion continued to denigrate the credibility of the Greek market, rendering its access to credit progressively more prohibitive and depressing the value of the euro. An emergency EU summit was called for March 25. Ahead of the summit Chancellor Merkel insisted that the IMF be a party to any EU rescue, which would only be granted as a last resort. This position contrasted with the French preference for a unilateral EU agreement. Additionally, Merkel called for stricter consequences for liberal spenders within the EU, advocating stronger deficit procedures and targeted sanctions against erring members. Germans, meanwhile, questioned the desirability of additional integration in the EU as German courts considered the constitutionality of EU aid. The European finance ministers agreed on an initial aid sum of $39 billion in April, easing market pressure on the euro.

Accessing Aid and Facing the Public

Greece, however, continued to pay a premium for its credit, and the government announced that it would access the EU-IMF emergency fund on April 23. With IMF and EU funding confirmed at $145 billion in May, Greek finance minister Giorgos Papaconstantinou announced that public debt was expected to rise from 120 percent of GDP in 2010 to 150 percent of GDP by 2014 despite the additional funding. He also said that additional cuts would be required to avoid insolvency, including an increase in value-added tax to 21 percent and taxes on luxury goods.

The IMF and EU affirmed their support for the country's plan for economic recovery, noting that Greece would receive 3,200 percent of its aid quota. The Greek ruling party would pay a high price for the bailout later that month, forfeiting its control of the upper house in local elections. Nevertheless, Greek voters saw some of their concerns addressed in the conditions attached to this remarkable aid package. The Greek government agreed to work towards reducing the deficit to 8.7 percent of GDP in 2010, and further to 8 percent of GDP in 2011. Additional spending cuts equal to 11 percent of GDP would reduce the total debt-to-GDP ratio beginning in 2013, bringing the deficit within EU limits by 2014. Civil servants would be particularly affected, as public sector pay and benefits accounted for 75 percent of non-interest spending by the government. Essential social services for the poor, however, would be retained.

While lauding its commitment to reforms that protected the most vulnerable groups, IMF managing director Dominique Strauss-Kahn suggested that the success of the policy program would depend on collective commitment to its goals from all political parties and social groups outside the parliament.

The Greek public has been neither supportive nor stoic in its reaction to the policy package, which has provoked occasionally violent protests led by the public sector unions. Equally challenging is the silent rebellion of millions of tax evaders in the private sector, who will face redoubled collection efforts and stricter consequences for illegally withholding revenue from the government. Both groups feel entitled to their benefits and income, respectively, without acknowledging the tenuous position of relying on an unfunded government. While Greeks generally accept the inevitability of the cuts, many do not recognize their rationale or their justice but believe that international speculators, this time in the form of the IMF, are forcing them to pay for the mistakes that those very speculators made in the first place.

Some observers, meanwhile, are not completely convinced that existing funds will be sufficient to enable economic recovery. Euroskeptics have also suggested that Greece will have to restructure its debts entirely, either by forcing investors to take an outright loss or by exiting the euro in order to achieve devaluation of its external debts. The latter option would entail unpredictable consequences that could further damage the county's fragile economy. EU and IMF support will prove indispensible to the viability of its consolidation over the longer term. Greece sought to extend its aid repayment period in December 2010.

—Anastazia Skolnitsky

Following is a statement by the International Monetary Fund (IMF) on May 2, 2010, announcing its intent to provide Greece with monetary aid during its economic crisis; and a joint statement by the European Union and IMF on May 2, 2010, discussing the Greek financial crisis.

DOCUMENT

IMF Announces Monetary Plan to Aid Greek Economic Crisis

May 2, 2010

Mr. Dominique Strauss-Kahn, Managing Director of the International Monetary Fund (IMF) issued the following statement today on Greece:

"The Greek government has designed an ambitious policy package to address the economic crisis facing the nation. It is a multi-year program which begins with substantial up-front efforts to correct Greece's grave fiscal imbalances, make the economy more competitive and—over time—restore growth and jobs. We believe these efforts, along with the government's firm commitment to implement them, will get the economy back on track and restore market confidence.

"Fiscal policy and pro-growth measures are the two main pillars of the government's program. A combination of spending cuts and revenue increases amounting to 11 percent of GDP—on top of the measures already taken earlier this year—are designed to achieve a turnaround in the public debt-to-GDP ratio beginning in 2013 and will reduce the fiscal deficit to below 3 percent of GDP by 2014. Measures for 2010 involve a reduction of public sector wages and pension outlays—which are unavoidable given that those two elements alone constitute some 75 percent of total (non-interest) public spending in Greece.

"Pro-growth measures will be aimed at modernizing the economy and boosting its competitiveness so that it can emerge from the crisis as quickly as possible. Steps include strengthening income and labor markets policies; better managing and investing in state enterprises and improving the business environment. Reforms to fight waste and corruption—eliminating non-transparent procurement practices, for example–are also being undertaken.

"In addition, the government is taking decisive steps to strengthen and safeguard the financial system. A Financial Stability Fund—fully financed under the program—will ensure a sound level of bank equity.

"The authorities' program is designed with fairness in mind. There will be a more progressive tax scale for all sources of income; a clampdown on tax evasion and a step up in prosecution of the worst offenders; and stronger enforcement and audit of high-wealth individuals.

"In addition, there will be protection for the most vulnerable groups. The reductions in wages and pensions are designed largely to exempt those living on the minimum. Social expenditures also will be revised to strengthen the safety net for the most vulnerable people.

"Finally, there will be a significant reduction in military expenditures during the program period.

"To support Greece's effort to get its economy back on track the Euro Area members have pledged a total of €80 billion (about US$105 billion) in bilateral loans. An IMF staff mission, in consultation with representatives from the European Commission and the European Central Bank, also reached agreement today with the Greek authorities to support this program with a three-year SDR 26 billion (about €30 billion; or US$40 billion) Stand-By Arrangement. Our joint commitment will bring total financing to €110 billion (about US$145 billion). We have also activated the Fund's fast-track procedures for consideration of Greece's Stand-By Arrangement, and I expect the arrangement will go to the Executive Board for approval within the week.

"We believe these strong measures by the Greek government, along with the significant risks of spillover to other countries, merit an exceptional level of access to IMF resources—equivalent to 3200 percent of Greece's quota in the Fund. This represents the largest access granted to a member country and it indicates the Fund's high level of support for the program and for Greece.

"The success of Greece's recovery program will depend, first and foremost, on the commitment of its government and people. While the initial implementation period will be difficult, we are confident that the economy will emerge more dynamic and robust from this crisis—and able to deliver the growth, jobs and prosperity that the country needs for the future.

"Our collective effort will contribute to the stability of the euro, will benefit all of Europe and will help to promote global financial stability and a secure recovery in the global economy."

Greece, which became a member of the IMF on December 27, 1945, currently has an IMF quota amounting to SDR 823 million.

Source: International Monetary Fund. "IMF Reaches Staff-level Agreement with Greece on €30 Billion Stand-By Arrangement." May 2, 2010. http://www.imf.org/external/np/sec/pr/2010/pr10176.htm.

EU and IMF Issue Statement on Greek Financial Crisis

May 2, 2010

The European Commissioner for Economic and Monetary Affairs, Olli REHN, and the Managing Director of the International Monetary Fund (IMF), Dominique Strauss-Kahn, issued the following joint statement on Greece today:

"We strongly support the economic program announced today by the Government of Greece. The steps being taken, while difficult, are necessary to restore confidence in the

Greek economy and to secure a better future for the Greek people. The program is unprecedented in the scope of the national effort required, as well as in the scale of the financial support—€110 billion–being provided by euro area countries and IMF. We are confident that Greece will rise to the challenge and succeed.

"We recognize that the program demands great sacrifice from the Greek people and, given the serious situation facing their country, it cannot be expected to turn the economy around overnight. A sustained, multi-year effort will be needed to bring down Greece's debt and spur competitiveness. If implemented effectively–and we believe it will be–the program will lead to a more dynamic economy that will deliver the growth, jobs, and prosperity that Greece needs in the future.

"We believe that the program is the right thing to do to put the economy back on track. Importantly, the authorities have also designed their program with fairness in mind so as to protect the poorest and most vulnerable, and ask for a fair sharing of the burden across Greek society. That is the right thing to do as well.

"To be successful, the program will require a national commitment that goes beyond political party lines. The support from European countries, the European Commission and the European Central Bank, and the IMF demonstrates a very high level of external commitment–and attests to the goodwill for Greece from the international community. Our collective effort will also contribute to the stability of the euro and will benefit all of Europe."

SOURCE: European Union. "Joint Statement on Greece by EU Commissioner Olli Rehn and IMF Managing Director Dominique Strauss-Kahn." May 2, 2010. http://europa.eu/rapid/pressReleasesAction .do?reference=IP/10/484&format=HTML&aged=0&language=EN&guiLanguage=en.

OTHER HISTORIC DOCUMENTS OF INTEREST

FROM PREVIOUS *HISTORIC DOCUMENTS*

Attempted Bombing in Times Square

MAY 4, 2010

On May 1, 2010, amid New York City's crowded and bustling Times Square, a food cart vendor noticed a Pathfinder parked on a busy street with its hazard lights on. While the car would have been a normal sight on most days, the vendor noticed that this car was smoking, and quickly alerted police who secured the area and dismantled the bomb that was found inside. The attempted bombing in Times Square immediately put the United States on high alert as the hunt for those responsible began. In the end, the failed plot stretched all the way to a terrorist organization in Pakistan and renewed fears of homegrown terrorism in the United States.

TIMES SQUARE PLOT

When police arrived on the scene of the smoking Pathfinder, they found a bomb made from fertilizer, fireworks, gasoline, and propane tanks. Immediately, the area around Times Square was cordoned off and shut down for eleven hours while police dismantled the bomb and searched the area, ensuring that no additional devices had been placed nearby. Local law enforcement, cooperating with the Federal Bureau of Investigation (FBI) because of the possible link to terrorism, also began collecting surveillance footage from the multiple cameras mounted outside of buildings in Times Square. Police hoped these tapes would help them identify and locate those responsible.

After dismantling and inspecting the bomb and its components, police determined that it could have created a fireball leading to shrapnel damage, but that the effect would not have been as extensive as the attempted bomber had intended. Secretary of Homeland Security Janet Napolitano called the bombing attempt "amateurish."

Speaking after the attack, New York City mayor Michael Bloomberg said, "This was an act that was designed to kill innocent civilians and strike fear into the hearts of Americans. And I'm happy to say that it failed on both counts. We will not be intimidated by those who hate the freedoms that make this city and this country so great."

Using the evidence gathered from the scene—namely the vehicle identification number (VIN) removed from the Pathfinder's engine—police were able to track down the vehicle's registered owner who said he had sold the car weeks earlier in a cash transaction on Craigslist. With this knowledge and the available video footage, federal investigators could identify those potentially responsible.

Faisal Shahzad, one of the men who could be seen in the surveillance video, had immigrated to the United States in early 2009 from Pakistan. Because of new border security measures enacted after September 11, 2001, police had access to Shahzad's photo and personal information, which the Pathfinder's previous owner used to identify Shahzad as the buyer.

Police tracked Shahzad, a thirty-year-old Pakistani, to his home in Connecticut. Unable to locate his current whereabouts from neighbors, police got a lucky break when a ticket agent at the Emirates Airline ticket counter alerted police over suspicion about a man who had purchased a one-way ticket to Dubai with cash. Before the Emirates plane took off from John F. Kennedy International Airport in New York, law enforcement boarded the plane and took Shahzad into custody.

Trial and Sentencing

Immediately after his arrest, Shahzad began cooperating with police and answering their questions without the presence of a lawyer. He signed documents repeatedly indicating that he willingly waived his *Miranda* rights and would cooperate with the questioning. Shortly after being taken into custody, Shahzad told police that he had been planning another attack within weeks of the Times Square failed bombing.

As questioning and research into Shahzad continued, officials learned that he had received explosives training in Pakistan in 2009 with the intent to cause massive damage in the United States. After five months of training, Shahzad, a naturalized U.S. citizen, returned to the United States on a one-way ticket, telling U.S. Customs and Border Protection that he had been visiting family in Pakistan.

Investigators announced that in addition to his training in Pakistan, Shahzad could be clearly linked to the militant extremist group Tehrik-e-Taliban Pakistan (TTP). He was reportedly receiving phone calls originating in Pakistan, which stopped three days before the attempted bombing.

Ten charges were filed against Shahzad, five of which were federal counts. The charges included: intent to use a weapon of mass destruction; terrorism transcending national boundaries; use of a destructive device in connection with criminal activity; transporting and receiving explosives; and damage and destruction of property by means of a fire.

Shahzad pled guilty on all counts in June and was sentenced to life in prison in October. During his trial and sentencing hearing, Shahzad repeatedly spoke of his hatred of the United States and intent to continue to harm American citizens. "Brace yourselves," he said during his sentencing, "the war with Muslims has just begun. Consider me the first droplet of the flood that will follow." The defeat of the United States, he said, is "imminent and will happen in the near future."

With Shahzad's guilty plea and his manner in court, he gave little resistance to the final sentence. As she read the sentence, U.S. district judge Miriam Goldman Cedarbaum said, "The defendant has repeatedly expressed his total lack of remorse and his desire, if given the opportunity, to repeat the crime." She noted that Shahzad "has now announced and, by his conduct, has evidenced his desire is not to defend the United States or Americans, but to kill them."

Pakistan Claims Responsibility

In videos posted on YouTube, members of the Pakistani Taliban claimed responsibility for the attempted bombing, saying, "The time is very near when our fedayeen will attack the American states in their major cities . . . in some days or a month's time." The videos further offered "congratulations to the Muslim ummah on the jaw-breaking blow to Satan's USA." The Taliban operating in Pakistan had previously claimed responsibility for terrorist and attempted terrorist acts that it was never party to, prompting federal officials to call for pause on immediate blame of the group.

The Pakistani Taliban had never before attempted to carry out an attack on American soil. The failed bombing in Times Square, federal counterterrorism officials said, may signal that that group is gaining strength and moving away from its usual targets in Pakistan. However, John Brennan, the top counterterrorism adviser at the White House, said that the attack's crude nature and its failure to cause extensive damage were indications that the current counterterrorism strategy being employed by the United States was working. "Because of our success in degrading the capabilities of these terrorist groups overseas, preventing them from carrying out these attacks, they are now relegated to trying to do these unsophisticated attacks, showing that they have inept capabilities in training," Brennan said.

Because of previous terrorist attempts by other radical Islamic groups in Pakistan and Shahzad's claim that he was planning another attack, hundreds of federal agents were sent out to investigate a number of leads regarding potential terrorist threats after the Times Square incident. "Federal law enforcement agents are vigorously and expeditiously pursuing leads relating to this and other information provided by the defendant, a process which has required the participation of hundreds of agents in different cities working around the clock since the defendant's arrest," reads a letter from prosecutors in the Shahzad case sent to the chief judge of the U.S. district court in Manhattan and the magistrate judge assigned to the case. It further detailed the continued questioning of Shahzad in order to gather as much intelligence as possible on future attacks or those who are facilitating such attacks.

After the incident, President Barack Obama called on Pakistan to continue to fight the Taliban on its own soil in an effort to protect not only its own citizens but also those around the world. Secretary of State Hillary Clinton reminded Pakistan that if "an attack like this that we can trace back to Pakistan were to have been successful, there would be very severe consequences." Attorney General Eric Holder placed blame squarely on the Pakistani Taliban, after earlier announcing that evidence indicated that Shahzad had acted alone without training.

As commander in chief, Obama spoke to the nation and the world, making it clear that the United States would not back down to terrorists. "We know that the aim of those who try to carry out those attacks is to force us to live in fear," Obama said. "But as Americans and as a nation, we will not be terrorized. We will not cower in fear. We will not be intimidated."

OREGON BOMB PLOT

In a similar incident in November, a nineteen-year-old naturalized citizen from Somalia tried twice to detonate a remote bomb that was located near a Christmas tree lighting ceremony in downtown Portland, Oregon. Fortunately, the bomb was never successfully detonated, and it was later learned that the man responsible, Mohamed Osman Mohamud, had received the bomb materials from undercover FBI agents.

The plot had unfolded in 2009 when the FBI intercepted messages from Mohamud that indicated he was consulting with terrorist organizations in Pakistan in an attempt to learn how to create a bomb to detonate in a crowded venue inside the United States.

Undercover agents responded to Mohamud, providing him with fake bomb materials and instructions, and even meeting him in a remote location to discuss the plan. At the meeting, Mohamud admitted that he had wanted to detonate a bomb to harm Americans since age fifteen. When agents asked Mohamud whether he thought he was doing the right thing and whether he would be able to look at the bodies after the bomb exploded, he indicated that he would forge ahead with his plan. "Our investigation shows that Mohamud was absolutely committed to carrying out an attack on a very grand scale," said Oregon FBI agent Arthur Balizan.

After the failed attempt, the U.S. Attorney's Office made it clear that no one was ever in danger. A statement read, "The device was in fact inert." Mohamud was arrested and charged with attempting to use a weapon of mass destruction. He faces life in prison and a fine of up to $250,000 if convicted.

The case in Oregon was similar to other recent events, including one in which a naturalized immigrant from Pakistan was planning to bomb the Metro subway system in Washington, D.C., and a slew of incidents involving agents giving fake bomb materials and cell phone detonators to suspects in Illinois, Texas, and New York.

—Heather Kerrigan

The following is a statement by New York City mayor Michael Bloomberg on May 4, 2010, in response to the attempted bombing in Times Square.

Mayor Bloomberg Responds to Attempted Times Square Bombing

DOCUMENT

May 4, 2010

"Welcome. We are joined here by Speaker Christine Quinn, Lance who I'm going to introduce in a minute, Sal Cassano the Commissioner of the Fire Department, and Chief Kilduff who is the highest ranking uniformed officer in the Fire Department. When the engines show up he's the one that sends them, so be nice to him. We also have Steve Cassidy and Al Hagen from the UFA and UFOA. So welcome guys, see you back there.

"Let me start with an update on last night's arrest. First, let me express my gratitude to the NYPD, the FBI, the U.S. Customs and Border Protection agents, and all of the other local, state, city, and federal authorities who played a role in identifying and apprehending Faisal Shahzad. They have been on the job around-the-clock since Saturday night, and the fact that they cracked the case so quickly I think is a testament to their professionalism and their patriotism, and the fact that they work so well together.

"But let me stress that this is an ongoing investigation. There is still plenty of work to do. But I have every confidence that the NYPD and FBI will fully unravel this case—and bring the guilty to justice.

"There will be a briefing in Washington at 1:00 PM, and Police Commissioner Kelly is on his way down there right now so it will be a chance for you to ask questions there or have one of your representatives ask questions.

"This was an act that was designed to kill innocent civilians and strike fear into the hearts of Americans. And I'm happy to say that it failed on both counts. We will not be intimidated by those who hate the freedoms that make this city and this country so great. The fact that so many people are out and about in Times Square today, where I just came from, really shows that.

"And I want to make clear that we will not tolerate any bias or backlash against Pakistani or Muslim New Yorkers. All of us live in this City and among any group there's always a few bad apples, but the people who live in this city are proud of the fact that this is the city that gives everybody from every place in the world an opportunity, no matter what religion they practice, no matter where they or their parents came from. It's the City where you can practice your religion and say what you want to say and be in charge of your own destiny, and we're going to keep it that way. People from every corner of the world come and live here in the same buildings and the same neighborhoods, and that's what makes this the greatest city on Earth.

"We will continue doing everything we possibly can to protect New Yorkers from terrorist attacks. We have, as you know, built the most comprehensive and sophisticated counter-terrorism operation of any local police force in the world. Every day, 1,000 of our best officers are performing counter-terrorism and intelligence duties and the Lower Manhattan Security Initiative is the most advanced and comprehensive security effort anyplace in the world, and we're working to bring those same tools to the protection of Midtown.

"And I did want to thank Senators Schumer and Gillibrand for pledging to seek federal funding for the midtown security project, and it's hard to imagine a better investment of Homeland Security dollars.

"We have to take every precaution, as you know, because we remain a prime target for terrorists. That's something that all New Yorkers understand—and it's something that we need Washington to understand, as well. We have a very strong partnership with the FBI through the Joint Terrorism Task Force, which for decades has been staffed jointly by the NYPD and the FBI. Dozens of our officers are working on that Task Force.

"Now so many agencies worked together to lead us to this day. The reason I came here was to personally thank the FDNY for the important role that they played. I came here today to meet the members of Engine Company 54, Ladder 4, and Battalion 9. And I would just like to point out near the front door, if you look on the walls, you will see a lot of brass plaques. This Fire Department has a custom that one year after somebody dies in the line of duty, they put up a brass plaque in memory of that person, but mainly I think to tell the young recruits that come into these fire houses that somebody has paid a terrible price but they are the role models for all of us. Those are people that put their lives in danger and unfortunately didn't come out. And there were 15 from this house who lost their lives on 9/11. And I wanted to thank all of them, and you see some of the young ones here, for their deft and professional response to the car bombing in Times Square.

"I was able to shake hands with a lot of them at about two in the morning on Sunday morning. Members of this fire house responded when Police Officer Rhatigan saw a fire in the car and immediately notified his superiors that something was awry. The vehicle was parked haphazardly, the engine was running and the smoke emanating from the rear was white which is unusual for a vehicle fire. The fire officers on the scene then used thermal imaging cameras to detect the heat source, and once they saw that that the only heat was coming from the engine itself and the smoke had a different source, they worked hand-in-hand with the NYPD to evacuate the area and keep the public at a safe distance so the bomb squad could arrive and do its work. And then they stayed throughout the night to help secure the area.

"Our Bravest did exactly what they have been trained to do in such situations. They knew not to apply water or any other extinguishing agent. Their quick thinking and restraint preserved important evidence—evidence that could be very significant in the ongoing investigation of this act.

"Of course, this is not the first time that members of this firehouse have put themselves in harm's way to protect us from a terrorist attack. I told you what they did on 9/11 and they stand ready no matter what the emergency is to go into danger when the rest of us react to our normal reactions and run away from danger.

"The losses this firehouse has suffered have only strengthened the resolve of its members to protect our city and its residents. Their bravery was on display again this past Saturday, and I think we all owe them a great debt of gratitude for demonstrating the extraordinary judgment that helped keep the public safe.

"In addition to the NYPD and the FDNY, I'd also like to express my thanks to the Office of Emergency Management and the Department of Environmental Protection for their work and cooperation in this matter.

"Two nights ago, as many of you reported, I had dinner with Officer Rhatigan and the NYPD Mounted Unit. He did not bring along his horse. And today I wanted to give a special thanks to Lance Orton, who is with us today. As you know, Lance is the person who first alerted us to a suspicious vehicle in Times Square. He was one of the vendors that sell merchandise there. Lance, you should know, served his country once before in the Vietnam War, and today he is looking out for his fellow Americans and fellow New Yorkers.

"He did exactly what I keep saying every New Yorker should do—he saw something and he said something. And his actions, along with the actions of our first responders, helped keep everyone safe. It is a good lesson for all of us. Nobody expects us to be professionals and fighting terrorism or fires or crime or anything else. We have professionals for that, but we all have eyes and ears and a brain, and we see something that just isn't quite right, say something to a professional. Pick up the phone to 911. There's always a firefighter or a fire truck stopped at the traffic light or a cop at the corner. There's plenty of opportunities for you to call in those who are trained to deal with any of these situations.

"Lance, on behalf of all New Yorkers: Thank you very much, and I just wanted to on behalf of everybody to say thank you."

SOURCE: Office of the Mayor of New York City. "Mayor Michael R. Bloomberg Updates New Yorkers on Arrest and Investigation of Incident in Times Square." May 4, 2010. http://www.nyc.gov/portal/site/nycgov/menuitem.c0935b9a57bb4ef3daf2f1c701c789a0/index.jsp?pageID=mayor_press_release&catID=1194&doc_name=http%3A%2F%2Fwww.nyc.gov%2Fhtml%2Fom%2Fhtml%2F2010a%2Fpr197-10.html&cc=unused1978&rc=1194&ndi=1.

OTHER HISTORIC DOCUMENTS OF INTEREST

FROM PREVIOUS *HISTORIC DOCUMENTS*

Political Crisis in Thailand

Thailand experienced another bout of severe political unrest in March and April 2010. What began as large-scale rallies evolved into violent clashes between antigovernment protestors and the military that left twenty-one dead and over one thousand injured. The government refused to bow to the protestors' demands for the dissolution of parliament and fresh elections. The events of early 2010 underscore Thailand's great political divide.

HIGHLY POLARIZED POLITICAL ATMOSPHERE

On one side of the political divide is the United Front for Democracy Against Dictatorship (UDD), a red-shirted antigovernment movement whose *de facto* leader is a controversial former prime minister, Thaksin Shinawatra. The UDD has continued to call for the resignation of Prime Minister Abhisit Vejjajiva, the dissolution of parliament, and fresh elections. The so-called "redshirts" are a mixture of Thaksin supporters and a larger movement that seeks to challenge the established royalist elite that is dominated by the military. Thaksin was ousted from power in a military coup in 2006 and subsequently convicted *in absentia* in 2008 for abuse of power and sentenced to two years in prison. He remains in self-imposed exile but has continued to exert significant political influence over his followers. The former prime minister has regularly addressed meetings of redshirts via a video link and recorded messages.

On the other side of the divide is Abhisit, prime minister since December 2008, who is backed by the monarchy, the military, the bureaucracy, and other elites, and who is considered to be a representative of the establishment that seeks to maintain its grip on power. Abhisit took office on the back of political maneuvering by the military and has not won a popular election. The prime minister has denied claims by the UDD that he came to power illegitimately, and he asserts that Thaksin is supporting the redshirt movement for his own personal gain.

Thailand's political scene was previously defined as a struggle between Thaksin's supporters and his opponents. The former are comprised primarily of the rural poor from the north and northeast of the country, while the latter are made up of the urban middle class. The struggle has shifted to one between those who support the political status quo, which features a powerful and unelected elite class, and those who support changes to the balance of power.

LARGE-SCALE REDSHIRT RALLIES IN BANGKOK RAISE TENSIONS

On March 12, 2010, large-scale rallies took place on the streets of the capital, Bangkok. Around 100,000 to 150,000 redshirts took to the streets, calling for the dissolution of parliament and fresh elections. This was the largest protest in recent years in Thailand. In anticipation of the protests, the government deployed around fifty thousand unarmed security personnel and authorized the Internal Security Act, which gave the Internal Security Operation Command, a military unit, additional powers, including the ability to impose curfews, restrict the movement of demonstrators, and set up checkpoints. On March 14, the UDD reiterated its demands, giving the government twenty-four hours to acquiesce. Prior to the deadline, Abhisit addressed the Thai public on national television, stating that political decisions must be "based on ultimate national interest and accommodating all opinions from every group in society" and refusing to give in to the redshirts' demands. The UDD responded by threatening to escalate the protests, with the aim of paralyzing the capital. On March 16, the UDD called on its supporters to give blood in a symbolic gesture of support for the protestors. The UDD subsequently threw the blood (the UDD claimed it collected six hundred liters) over Abhisit's home and the headquarters of his ruling Democratic Party (DP).

At the same time, the DP's relations with its coalition partners in government appeared solid, with the latter supporting the prime minister's decision to not dissolve parliament. The prime minister also had the explicit support of the military: Abhisit was holed up at a military base in Bangkok—from which he gave interviews to the international press—at the start of the protests in mid-March.

Tensions eased slightly after the prime minister agreed to meet with his redshirt counterparts on March 28. The face-to-face meeting was broadcast live on national television. Abhisit was joined by the secretary-general of the prime minister's office, Korbsak Sabhavasu, and the secretary-general of the DP, Chamni Sakdiset. The UDD was represented by three senior members of the redshirt movement, Jatuporn Prompan, Weng Tojirakarn, and Veera Musikapong. The UDD was able to air its political grievances and be seen to be accepted by the government as a legitimate movement. Despite the assertion by Abhisit that the government and the UDD were in agreement on some issues, there appeared to be little common middle ground. Indeed, the government and the UDD disagreed on the most important issues at hand—dissolving parliament and calling for fresh elections. Neither the first nor a subsequent meeting resulted in substantive progress.

THE GOVERNMENT DECLARES A STATE OF EMERGENCY

Just a week later, tensions between the redshirt protestors and the government escalated dramatically, forcing the government to declare a state of emergency in Bangkok and five neighboring provinces. The state of emergency was invoked after protestors temporarily blockaded parliament, which forced some lawmakers to be airlifted to safety. The protestors, which now included many Bangkok residents in addition to the UDD's traditional rural support base, also blockaded key commercial areas of the city, calling again for the dissolution of parliament and for elections to be called. Meanwhile, in spite of facing increased pressure from within his own party to restore order, Prime Minister Abhisit continued to refuse to acknowledge that the protestors had genuine political grievances regarding democracy and social justice. Despite the rising tensions in the capital, Abhisit resisted enlisting help from the security forces to suppress the protestors, as civilian fatalities would have undermined his legitimacy and could have resulted in his party being forced from office.

On April 9, the government moved to shut down the redshirts' satellite television station, People's Television (PTV). In justifying taking the channel off the air, the government claimed that broadcasts aired disinformation that could endanger national security. In response, skirmishes broke out between UDD protestors and the military outside a broadcasting station on the outskirts of Bangkok.

Violent Clashes Erupt

Political tensions escalated further the following day when a deputy prime minister, Suthep Thaugsuban, ordered the military to disperse protestors gathered near the Democracy Monument, a landmark that has long been the center for protests. Violence subsequently broke out, resulting in the deaths of twenty people, including five soldiers, while nearly nine hundred were injured. The military fired tear gas and rubber bullets at the protestors, who responded with improvised weapons, including bottles and sticks. Overnight, the level of violence increased, with each side attacking the other with grenades and assault rifles. Video footage of the skirmishes showed both sides using live rounds and grenades. The street battles discredited the redshirts' claim that their movement was wholly nonviolent.

In the aftermath of the violence, the military retreated to its bases while the redshirts continued to occupy key areas of the city. As an emergency decree issued by the government banned such encampments, the UDD viewed the military's failure to remove the redshirts as a *de facto* victory. In the days that followed, both the UDD and the government sought to win the ongoing propaganda war. Videos of the military's hard-line tactics during the skirmishes were aired on large video screens at the UDD rally point in Bangkok, while the protestors also paraded the coffins of the redshirts killed through the streets. The government's own public relations campaign claimed that there were "terrorist elements" within the UDD and that these individuals intended to topple the current political order.

By April 21, the UDD had moved its rally site to the main shopping and hotel district, Rajaprasong, where members barricaded themselves behind a periphery fence made primarily of sharpened bamboo sticks. Meanwhile, the military camped nearby and warned that it would respond to provocation with decisive force if necessary.

The violence resumed on the night of April 22, when two grenades exploded in Bangkok's business district, killing one person and injuring around seventy-five others. Both sides denied responsibility for the attack. Meanwhile, pro-government activists converged on the business district and confrontations between the two opposing sides ensued. In the aftermath of the grenade attack, Abhisit met with security officials and assigned additional military personnel to the area.

Other Political Forces Remain Active

A so-called "third hand" was suspected of contributing to the violence on April 10. In particular, a military general, Major General Khattiya Sawasdiphol, known as Seh Daeng, reportedly claimed that armed men loyal to him operated alongside UDD protestors and fired at soldiers on the government side. These agent provocateurs are also suspected of involvement in the April 22 grenade attacks. A month later, Seh Daeng was assassinated.

The royalist conservative yellow-shirted movement, the People's Alliance for Democracy (PAD), was notably absent from the streets of Bangkok during the protests and UDD clashes with the military. Nevertheless, the group, which is staunchly anti-Thaksin and contributed to the military's ousting of his government in late 2006, was vocal in its position. The PAD sought to prevent the UDD from succeeding in its calls for fresh elections, which the former feared would result in a pro-Thaksin government returning to power. A leader of the PAD, Chamlong Srimuang, stated that if the government did not deal with the redshirt "terrorists," the yellowshirts would step in to protect the royal family and the country. The group claims that Thaksin was not democratically elected, but instead bought his votes from the uneducated and rural electorate. The views of the PAD underline the political divide in Thailand.

—Hilary Ewing

The following is a press release issued by the Thailand Ministry of Foreign Affairs on May 4, 2010, regarding a briefing by the foreign minister to ambassadors on the political situation in Thailand; a press release also from the Thailand Ministry of Foreign Affairs on May 6, 2010, on the foreign minister's remarks addressing concerns about Thailand's political situation; and a statement by the Association of Southeast Asian Nations (ASEAN) on May 23, 2010, on the political situation in Thailand.

Foreign Minister Briefs Ambassadors on Thailand Political Situation

May 4, 2010

On 29 April 2010, Mr. Kasit Piromya, Minister of Foreign Affairs, held a cordial meeting with Permanent Representatives of ASEAN and Ambassadors to ASEAN from non-ASEAN Member States from 41 Embassies in Jakarta at the ASEAN Secretariat during his visit to Indonesia. The meeting was also attended by Mr. Manasvi Srisodapol, Permanent Representative of Thailand to ASEAN.

On this occasion, Foreign Minister Kasit briefed the participants on the background, circumstances and context of the current political situation in Thailand. He took this opportunity to reiterate the Royal Thai Government's determination to avoid using force against the protestors, while also safeguarding the rule of law.

Foreign Minister Kasit also spent time separately with the Permanent Representatives from the 10 ASEAN Member States to share his views on the role of the Committee of Permanent Representatives in the ASEAN Community building process and in coordinating ASEAN's external relations together with ASEAN Committees in Third Countries and ASEAN capitals.

During both meetings, Foreign Minister Kasit gave time to respond to questions from the participants on the Royal Thai Government's view and policies.

Source: Thailand Ministry of Foreign Affairs. "Foreign Minister Kasit Briefs Ambassadors in Jakarta on Current Political Situation in Thailand." May 4, 2010. http://www.mfa.go.th/web/35.php?id=24332.

Foreign Minister Addresses Concern Regarding Political Situation in Thailand

May 6, 2010

On 3 May 2010, Mr. Yap Swee Seng, Director of the Asian Forum for Human Rights and Development (Forum-Asia), on behalf of a group of 43 non-governmental organisations (NGOs) and civil society bodies in the Asia-Pacific region, including Thai NGOs, submitted a statement on the current political situation in Thailand to the Royal Thai Government through Foreign Minister Kasit Piromya at the Ministry of Foreign Affairs.

Expressing appreciation for their concerns, Foreign Minister Kasit noted at the outset the fact that they—as NGOs—could carry out their work freely, meeting him at the Foreign Ministry and visiting the protest site, which reflects the fact that Thailand is an open and democratic society and a country in the process of democratization towards becoming a full-fledged democracy. He also stated that the present Government does not interfere in the work of independent bodies and that it works closely with all stakeholders in society.

Affirming the Government's adherence of the Constitution, the Foreign Minister assured the NGO representatives that the Government has done its utmost to observe the rule of law, including with regard to the use of force. It had been trying, up to this point, to avoid the use of weapons. He pointed out that the protestors have clearly gone beyond their constitutional rights in exercising their freedom of expression; they are armed and aim to bring down a legitimate and democratic government, as the Prime Minister assumed office in accordance with the letter and spirit of the Constitution. The Foreign Minister added that currently, the Government has been asking innocent protesters who have real grievances to leave the protest area in order to separate them from the group of people who are engaged in armed insurrection—an action that cannot be tolerated by any government which values public safety, law and order.

Emphasising that the Government respect the people's constitutional right to freedom of expression, the Foreign Minister observed that there has been use of certain media to attack individuals and to incite hatred and divisions within the country to the point of attempting to instigate the use of violent means to suppress the expression of different opinions and to bring down the Government. This, he stated, went beyond the legitimate exercise of such freedoms. The Government, therefore, has to deal with such activities in accordance with the law.

Foreign Minister Kasit urged the NGO representatives to examine the evolution of Thai democracy on the whole so that they would have an objective and balanced view of the situation in the country. He also asked that they have confidence in the belief and spirit of the Thai society in moving democracy forward, affirming that the present Government has been working very hard to maintain and promote human rights and the rule of law, and accepts differences of opinions, as evident in its readiness to sit down and enter into dialogue with the protest leaders. Nevertheless, the Government could not accept ultimatum such as that on parliamentary dissolution put forward by the protesters as precondition before negotiations could begin. The matter, he noted, must proceed on the basis of the rule of law as it affects not only the Government but also every stakeholder in society.

Finally, Foreign Minister Kasit reaffirmed the commitment of both the present Government and the Prime Minister to the values of democracy and human rights, with the intention of contributing positively to the promotion of human rights in the ASEAN Community and also in the world at large, which is why Thailand has become a candidate for the United Nations' Human Rights Council. Additionally, he gave assurances that he would forward the NGOs' statement to the Government for its consideration and that an official written reply to the group's statement would be given in due course.

SOURCE: Thailand Ministry of Foreign Affairs. "FM Addresses NGOs' Concerns Regarding Current Political Situation in Thailand." May 6, 2010. http://www.mfa.go.th/web/35.php?id=24324.

ASEAN Statement on Thailand Political Situation

May 23, 2010

On 23 May 2010, Ms. Vimon Kidchob, Director-General of the Department of Information and Foreign Ministry Spokesperson, informed the press about the statement issued on 21 May 2010 by Vietnam, in its capacity as Chairman of ASEAN, regarding the situation in Thailand. According to the said statement, the ASEAN member countries, while expressing their concerns over developments in the Kingdom, emphasised their support and solidarity with the people and the Government of Thailand in finding a peaceful solution to the present challenge, as well as expressed their support for a swift restoration of law and order, national reconciliation, and a return to normalcy.

The Spokesperson stated that the Royal Thai Government appreciates the concern expressed by other ASEAN member countries, particularly their support and solidarity. This, she said, was in line with the Government's attempt to restore normalcy and move forward with the reconciliation process in accordance with the five point reconciliation plan previously announced by Prime Minister Abhisit Vejjajiva, which underscored the importance of a participatory process involving all sectors of society. The Royal Thai Government also wishes to reassure its fellow ASEAN members that it would do its utmost to bring back peace to its people as soon as possible.

SOURCE: Thailand Ministry of Foreign Affairs. "ASEAN Chairman's Statement on the Situation in Thailand." May 23, 2010. http://www.mfa.go.th/web/35.php?id=24417.

OTHER HISTORIC DOCUMENTS OF INTEREST

FROM PREVIOUS *HISTORIC DOCUMENTS*

Elena Kagan Nominated to U.S. Supreme Court

MAY 10 AND JUNE 28, 2010

In the second year of his presidency, Barack Obama was given another opportunity to nominate a justice to the U.S. Supreme Court. To replace ninety-year-old retiring justice John Paul Stevens, who served on the court for thirty-five years, the president chose Elena Kagan, the U.S. solicitor general. Kagan's confirmation would make her the only justice since William Rehnquist to ascend to the Court without having previously served as a judge. Obama's decision to nominate someone without a judicial record was anticipated, as some senators had called for him to nominate a unique candidate from outside the judicial establishment. Obama achieved his mission, choosing someone he considered more interested in the law than in political bickering. "Her open-mindedness may disappoint some who want a sure liberal vote in almost every issue. Her pragmatism may disappoint those who believe that mechanical logic can decide all cases. All her progressive personal values will not endear her to the hard right. But that is exactly the combination the president was seeking," said Walter Dellinger, a former acting solicitor general in President Bill Clinton's administration.

KAGAN'S RISE TO THE SUPREME COURT

Kagan was raised in Manhattan, where her father served as a lawyer for community groups, including those fighting apartment management organizations that were turning buildings into co-ops. Teachers and friends who knew Kagan while she was growing up said that she emulated her father and was smart and driven. At an early age, she indicated to friends that it was her intention to one day serve as a U.S. Supreme Court justice.

Kagan, like the eight other justices on the court, was an Ivy League graduate. She attended Princeton for her undergraduate work and received her law degree from Harvard. Her experience in the field of law was wide ranging. Kagan served as a clerk for then–Supreme Court justice Thurgood Marshall, a position she took in 1987 at the age of twenty-seven.

In 1991, Kagan joined the faculty of the University of Chicago to teach law. It was during this time that she met the man who would go on to be the forty-fourth president of the United States. In 1993, Kagan took a position working for then-senator Joe Biden, D-Del., while he was chair of the Senate Judiciary Committee. She went on to serve as President Clinton's domestic policy adviser through most of his second term. In 1999, Clinton nominated her to the D.C. Circuit Court. Senate Republicans, however, blocked a chance for her nomination to come up for debate and a vote. Instead, future chief justice John Roberts received the post. After her nomination failed, Kagan went on to become the dean of the Harvard Law School.

In 2009, Obama nominated Kagan to become the first female solicitor general of the United States, a position often referred to as the "tenth justice." During her confirmation process, Kagan received support from Republicans and Democrats alike. "I look forward to supporting you," said Sen. Lindsey Graham, R-S.C. "I have no doubt in hearing you that you're up to the task," stated Sen. Tom Coburn, R-Okla. during her confirmation process.

Senators did, however, raise questions about her lack of judicial experience. Kagan supported herself, saying, "One of the things I would hope to bring to the job is not just book learning, not just the study that I've made of constitutional and public law, but a kind of wisdom and judgment, a kind of understanding of how to separate the truly important from the spurious."

Kagan argued six cases in front of the U.S. Supreme Court as the federal government's lawyer during her stint as solicitor general.

Nomination and Confirmation

When Justice Stevens announced his retirement, Obama and his advisers created a short list of a dozen candidates for the position. When that list was whittled down, two candidates emerged at the top—Kagan and Seventh Circuit judge Diane Wood. Both Kagan and Wood had been considered for the Court by Obama in 2009 when he instead nominated Sonia Sotomayor, the first Hispanic woman to serve on the Court. Obama's 2010 nomination decision largely came down to Kagan's lack of judicial experience.

In his announcement nominating Kagan, Obama called her a "trailblazing leader." He continued, "Elena's respected and admired not just for her intellect and record of achievement, but also for her temperament, her openness to a broad array of viewpoints, her habit—to borrow a phrase from Justice Stevens—'of understanding before disagreeing,' her fair-mindedness and skill as a consensus builder. . . . I hope that the Senate will act in a bipartisan fashion, as they did in confirming Elena to be our Solicitor General last year."

Kagan echoed Obama's remarks of her fair-mindedness, reminding those listening that everyone in front of the Court is due the respect of honest consideration of any topic. "The court is an extraordinary institution in the work it does and in the work it can do for the American people by advancing the tenets of our Constitution, by upholding the rule of law and by enabling all Americans, regardless of their background or their beliefs, to get a fair hearing and an equal chance at justice," she said, accepting the president's nomination.

Throughout her time with the Clinton administration and during her confirmation hearings as solicitor general, Kagan received broad support from both Republicans and Democrats in Congress, indicating that her confirmation would be a fairly smooth process. Obama's description of her as a "consensus builder" was addressed many times in the Senate and in the media, especially by those on the left who thought she might be able to sway more moderate members of the court to her position on any case. "She has brought people together of every ideological stripe," said Senate majority leader Harry Reid, D-Nev.

Her lack of a judicial record put little on the table for debate. However, this point did raise concern for liberals, who feared she would not be as progressive as Stevens, but would instead maintain a moderate political position—something the left did not want to see as the Court was already weighted toward the right, 5 to 4.

In her opening remarks before the Senate Judiciary Committee, Kagan promised to be impartial to all those appearing before the Court. "I will listen hard, to every party before the Court and to each of my colleagues. I will work hard. And I will do my best to consider every case impartially, modestly, with commitment to principle, and in accordance with law." This, she said, is what she owes to her grandparents and all other immigrants who came to this country looking for a better way of life and a place to have a voice.

Prior experience became a key tenet of debate in the Senate. Republicans heavily criticized Kagan and questioned whether her lack of experience would allow her to properly follow the rule of law. Sen. Jeff Sessions, R-Ala., the ranking member of the Senate Judiciary Committee, criticized the president for nominating "someone who shares his progressive, elitist vision and is willing to advance it from the bench." Senate minority leader Mitch McConnell, R-Ky., called Kagan "someone who has worked tirelessly to advance a political agenda."

Democrats, however, largely looked past the issue. Sen. Dianne Feinstein, D-Calif., viewed Kagan's background as bringing a unique and new experience to the Court, and one that would focus on "the impact of the law on human beings."

After hearings on her confirmation, senators voted 63–37 to allow Kagan to become the 112th justice of the court. Five Republicans supported her confirmation—including Sens. Judd Gregg of New Hampshire; Lindsey Graham of South Carolina; Susan Collins and Olympia Snowe, both of Maine; and Richard Lugar, of Indiana. Sen. Ben Nelson, D-Neb., voted against her confirmation.

DEBATE OVER KAGAN'S RECORD

Without a judicial record to use as a basis for debate during her Supreme Court confirmation hearings, senators instead turned to briefs and memos she had written in her earlier positions. As a law clerk for Justice Marshall, Kagan wrote a memo questioning the constitutionality of allowing religious organizations to collect federal funding for the purpose of discouraging teen pregnancy and providing care for pregnant teens. Her concern, she wrote, was that religion would certainly be injected into any care the teens received. During her 2009 solicitor general hearing, however, Kagan regretted her position of two decades earlier, calling it the "dumbest thing I've ever heard."

Of greater interest was a 2003 *amicus* brief filed by Kagan, who was then dean of the Harvard Law School, in a case challenging the constitutionality of the Solomon Amendment, which allowed the federal government to withhold funding from institutions of higher education that refused to allow Reserve Officer Training Corps (ROTC) programs and military recruiters on campus. In 2004, after a victory in the Third Circuit Court, Kagan banned recruiters from the Harvard Law School campus because the military's ban on gay and lesbian citizens serving in the armed forces conflicted with school antidiscrimination policies. The case was taken to the Supreme Court on appeal. Before the case was decided, Kagan reversed her decision after the federal government threatened to withhold funding from the school. In explaining her reversal, Kagan wrote, "I have said before how much I regret making this exception to our antidiscrimination policy. I believe the military's discriminatory employment policy is deeply wrong—both unwise and unjust. . . . I look forward to the time when all our students can pursue any career path they desire, including the path of devoting their professional lives to the defense of their country." The Supreme Court later ruled on the case and upheld the Solomon Amendment.

Another of Kagan's controversial activities came in 2005 when she joined other U.S. law school deans in protest of an amendment introduced in Congress that would have removed power from the federal courts to review cases brought by some Guantánamo Bay detainees. In expressing their discontent, the deans wrote, "When dictatorships have passed laws stripping their courts of power to review executive detention or punishment of prisoners, our government has rightly challenged such acts as fundamentally lawless. The same standards should apply to our own government."

New Makeup of the Court

Following Kagan's confirmation, all nine justices on the Court hailed from one of three Ivy League schools—Harvard, Yale, or Columbia. Kagan was the fourth new judge in five years to join the Court, giving it a much younger makeup than it had in its recent history, with Kagan becoming the youngest justice to serve on the current Court. The addition of Kagan meant that the Court now had more sitting females than it had in its entire history, with a total of three—Kagan, Sotomayor, and Ruth Bader Ginsburg. Justice Stevens's departure also marked the first time in the Court's history when there would be no Protestant members. Three-quarters of all of those who have served as a Supreme Court justice have been Protestant, and the new Court was now comprised of six Catholics and three Jews.

Because of her time as solicitor general, Kagan made it clear that she planned to recuse herself from more than one dozen different cases, including the first case of the Court's 2010–2011 term. These cases, she wrote in a letter to Sen. Sessions, were ones that she had argued for or written briefs for. It was left unclear whether Kagan would recuse herself from any potential case brought to the Court arguing against the Obama health care plan. As solicitor general, she had participated in conversations at the White House regarding potential backlash to the health care plan.

—Heather Kerrigan

Following is a statement by President Barack Obama on May 10, 2010, in which he nominates Elena Kagan to serve on the U.S. Supreme Court; and opening remarks delivered by Elena Kagan on June 28, 2010, at the start of her confirmation hearings before the U.S. Senate Judiciary Committee.

 **DOCUMENT**

President Obama Nominates Elena Kagan for the U.S. Supreme Court

May 10, 2010

Thank you very much. Everybody, please have a seat. Good morning, everybody. Of the many responsibilities accorded to a President by our Constitution, few are more weighty or consequential than that of appointing a Supreme Court Justice, particularly one to succeed a giant in the law like Justice John Paul Stevens.

For nearly 35 years, Justice Stevens has stood as an impartial guardian of the law, faithfully applying the core values of our founding to the cases and controversies of our time. He's done so with restraint and respect for precedent—understanding that a judge's job is to interpret, not make law—but also with fidelity to the constitutional ideal of equal justice for all. He's brought to each case not just mastery of the letter of the law, but a keen understanding of its impact on people's lives. And he has emerged as a consistent voice of reason, helping his colleagues find common ground on some of the most controversial and contentious issues the Court has ever faced.

While we can't presume to replace Justice Stevens's wisdom or experience, I have selected a nominee who I believe embodies that same excellence, independence, integrity, and passion for the law, and who can ultimately provide that same kind of leadership on the Court, our Solicitor General and my friend, Elena Kagan.

Elena is widely regarded as one of the Nation's foremost legal minds. She's an acclaimed legal scholar with a rich understanding of constitutional law. She's a former White House aide with a lifelong commitment to public service and a firm grasp of the nexus and boundaries between our three branches of Government. She's a trailblazing leader, the first woman to serve as dean of Harvard Law School, and one of the most successful and beloved deans in its history. And she is a superb Solicitor General, our Nation's chief lawyer representing the American people's interests before the Supreme Court, the first woman in that position as well. And she has won accolades from observers across the ideological spectrum for her well-reasoned arguments and commanding presence.

But Elena's respected and admired not just for her intellect and record of achievement, but also for her temperament, her openness to a broad array of viewpoints, her habit—to borrow a phrase from Justice Stevens—"of understanding before disagreeing," her fair-mindedness, and skill as a consensus builder.

These traits were particularly evident during her tenure as dean. At a time when many believed that the Harvard faculty had gotten a little one-sided in its viewpoint, she sought to recruit prominent conservative scholars and spur a healthy debate on campus. And she encouraged students from all backgrounds to respectfully exchange ideas and seek common ground, because she believes, as I do, that exposure to a broad array of perspectives is the foundation not just for a sound legal education, but of a successful life in the law.

And this appreciation for diverse views may also come in handy as a diehard Mets fan serving alongside her new colleague-to-be, Yankees fan, Justice Sotomayor, who I believe has ordered a pinstriped robe for the occasion.

But while Elena had a brilliant career in academia, her passion for the law is anything but academic. She's often referred to Supreme Court Justice Thurgood Marshall, for whom she clerked, as her hero. I understand that he reciprocated by calling her "Shorty." Nonetheless, she credits him with reminding her that, as she put it, "Behind law there are stories, stories of people's lives as shaped by the law, stories of people's lives as might be changed by the law." That understanding of law, not as an intellectual exercise or words on a page, but as it affects the lives of ordinary people, has animated every step of Elena's career, including her service as Solicitor General today.

And during her time in this office, she's repeatedly defended the rights of shareholders and ordinary citizens against unscrupulous corporations. Last year, in the Citizens United case, she defended bipartisan campaign finance reform against special interests seeking to spend unlimited money to influence our elections. Despite long odds of success, with most legal analysts believing the Government was unlikely to prevail in this case, Elena still chose it as her very first case to argue before the Court.

I think that says a great deal not just about Elena's tenacity, but about her commitment to serving the American people. I think it says a great deal about her commitment to protect our fundamental rights, because in a democracy, powerful interests must not be allowed to drown out the voices of ordinary citizens.

And I think it says a great deal about the path that Elena has chosen. Someone as gifted as Elena could easily have settled into a comfortable life in a corporate law practice; instead, she chose a life of service, service to her students, service to her country, service to the law and to all those whose lives it shapes.

And given Elena's upbringing, it's a choice that probably came naturally. Elena's the granddaughter of immigrants, whose mother was for 20 years a beloved public school-teacher, as are her two brothers, who are here today. Her father was a housing lawyer, devoted to the rights of tenants. Both were the first in their families to attend college. And from an early age, they instilled in Elena not just the value of a good education, but the importance of using it to serve others.

As she recalled during her Solicitor General confirmation hearings, "Both my parents wanted me to succeed in my chosen profession. But more than that, both drilled into me the importance of service, character, and integrity." Elena's also spoken movingly about how her mother had grown up at a time when women had few opportunities to pursue their ambitions and took great joy in watching her daughter do so.

Neither she nor Elena's father lived to see this day. But I think her mother would relish this moment. I think she would relish, as I do, the prospect of three women taking their seat on the Nation's highest Court for the first time in history, a Court that would be more inclusive, more representative, more reflective of us as a people than ever before.

And I think they would be tremendously proud of their daughter, a great lawyer, a great teacher, and a devoted public servant who I am confident will make an outstanding Supreme Court Justice.

So I hope that the Senate will act in a bipartisan fashion, as they did in confirming Elena to be our Solicitor General last year, and that they will do so as swiftly as possible, so she can get busy and take her seat in time to fully participate in the work of the Court this fall.

With that, I would like to invite the person who I believe will be the next Supreme Court Justice of the United States, Elena Kagan, to say a few words.

SOURCE: U.S. Executive Office of the President. "Remarks on the Nomination of Solicitor General Elena Kagan to Be a Supreme Court Associate Justice." *Daily Compilation of Presidential Documents* 2010, no. 000360, May 10, 2010. http://origin.www.gpo.gov/fdsys/pkg/DCPD-201000360/pdf/DCPD-201000360.pdf.

 ## Elena Kagan Testifies Before the Senate Judiciary Committee

June 28, 2010

Thank you very much, Mr. Chairman, Senator Sessions, and members of the Committee.

I'd like to thank Senators Kerry and Brown for those generous introductions.

I also want to thank the President again for nominating me to this position. I'm honored and humbled by his confidence.

Let me also thank all the members of the Committee, as well as many other Senators, for meeting with me in these last several weeks. I've discovered that they call these "courtesy visits" for a reason; each of you has been unfailingly gracious and considerate.

I know that we gather here on a day of sorrow for all of you, for this body, and for our nation, with the passing of Senator Byrd. I did not know him personally, as all of you did, but I certainly knew of his great love for this institution, his faithful service to the people of his state, and his abiding reverence for our Constitution, a copy of which he carried with him every day—a moving reminder to each of us who serves in government of the ideals we must seek to fulfill.

All of you, and all of Senator Byrd's friends and family, are in my thoughts and prayers at this time.

I would like to begin by thanking my family, friends, and students who are here with me today. I thank them for all the support they've given me, during this process and throughout my life. It's really wonderful to have so many of them behind me.

I said when the President nominated me that the two people missing were my parents, and I feel that deeply again today. My father was as generous and public-spirited a person as I've ever known, and my mother set the standard for determination, courage, and commitment to learning.

My parents lived the American dream. They grew up in immigrant communities; my mother didn't speak a word of English until she went to school. But she became a legendary teacher and my father a valued lawyer. And they taught me and my two brothers, both high school teachers, that this is the greatest of all countries, because of the freedoms and opportunities it offers its people. I know that they would have felt that today, and I pray that they would have been proud of what they did in raising me and my brothers.

To be nominated to the Supreme Court is the honor of a lifetime. I'm only sorry that, if confirmed, I won't have the privilege of serving there with Justice John Paul Stevens. His integrity, humility, and independence, his deep devotion to the Court, and his profound commitment to the rule of law—all these qualities are models for everyone who wears, or hopes to wear, a judge's robe. If given this honor, I hope I will approach each case with his trademark care and consideration. That means listening to each party with a mind as open as his to learning and persuasion and striving as conscientiously as he has to render impartial justice.

I owe a debt of gratitude to two other living Justices. Sandra Day O'Connor and Ruth Bader Ginsburg paved the way for me and so many other women in my generation. Their pioneering lives have created boundless possibilities for women in the law. I thank them for their inspiration and also for the personal kindnesses they have shown me. And my heart goes out to Justice Ginsburg and her family today. Everyone who ever met Marty Ginsburg was enriched by his incredible warmth and generosity, and I'm deeply saddened by his passing.

Mr. Chairman, the law school I had the good fortune to lead has a kind of motto, spoken each year at graduation. We tell the new graduates that they are ready to enter a profession devoted to "those wise restraints that make us free." That phrase has always captured for me the way law, and the rule of law, matters. What the rule of law does is nothing less than to secure for each of us what our Constitution calls "the blessings of liberty"—those rights and freedoms, that promise of equality, that have defined this nation since its founding. And what the Supreme Court does is to safeguard the rule of law, through a commitment to even-handedness, principle, and restraint.

My first real exposure to the Court came almost a quarter century ago when I began my clerkship with Justice Thurgood Marshall. Justice Marshall revered the Court—and for a simple reason. In his life, in his great struggle for racial justice, the Supreme Court stood as the part of government that was most open to every American—and that most often fulfilled our Constitution's promise of treating all persons with equal respect, equal care, and equal attention.

The idea is engraved on the very face of the Supreme Court building: Equal Justice Under Law. It means that everyone who comes before the Court—regardless of wealth or power or station—receives the same process and the same protections. What this commands of judges is even-handedness and impartiality. What it promises is nothing less than a fair shake for every American.

I've seen that promise up close during my tenure as Solicitor General. In that job, I serve as our government's chief lawyer before the Supreme Court, arguing cases on issues ranging from campaign finance, to criminal law, to national security. And I do mean "argue." In no other place I know is the strength of a person's position so tested and the quality of a person's analysis so deeply probed. No matter who the lawyer or who the party, the Court relentlessly hones in on the merits of every claim and its support in law and precedent. And because this is so, I always come away from my arguments at the Court with a renewed appreciation of the commitment of each Justice to reason and principle— a commitment that defines what it means to live in a nation under law.

For these reasons, the Supreme Court is a wondrous institution. But the time I spent in the other branches of government remind me that it must also be a modest one—properly deferential to the decisions of the American people and their elected representatives.

What I most took away from those experiences was simple admiration for the democratic process. That process is often messy and frustrating, but the people of this country have great wisdom, and their representatives work hard to protect their interests. The Supreme Court, of course, has the responsibility of ensuring that our government never oversteps its proper bounds or violates the rights of individuals. But the Court must also recognize the limits on itself and respect the choices made by the American people.

I am grateful, beyond measure, for the time I spent in public service, but the joy of my life has been to teach thousands of students about the law, and to have had the sense to realize that they had much to teach me.

I've led a school whose faculty and students examine and discuss and debate every aspect of our law and legal system. And what I've learned most is that no one has a monopoly on truth or wisdom. I've learned that we make progress by listening to each other, across every apparent political or ideological divide. I've learned that we come closest to getting things right when we approach every person and every issue with an open mind. And I've learned the value of a habit that Justice Stevens wrote about more than fifty years ago—of "understanding before disagreeing."

I will make no pledges this week other than this one—that if confirmed, I will remember and abide by all these lessons. I will listen hard, to every party before the Court and to each of my colleagues. I will work hard. And I will do my best to consider every case impartially, modestly, with commitment to principle, and in accordance with law.

That is what I owe to the legacy I share with so many Americans. My grandparents came to this country in search of a freer and better life for themselves and their families. They wanted to escape bigotry and oppression—to worship as they pleased and work as hard as they were able.

They found in this country—and they passed on to their children and their children's children—the blessings of liberty. Those blessings are rooted in this country's Constitution and its historic commitment to the rule of law. I know that to sit on our nation's highest court is to be a trustee of that inheritance. And if I have the honor to be confirmed, I will do all I can to help preserve it for future generations.

Thank you, Mr. Chairman. And thank you, members of the Committee.

SOURCE: U.S. Senate Committee on the Judiciary. "Opening Statement of Solicitor General Elena Kagan, Nominee for Associate Justice of the United States Supreme Court." June 28, 2010. http://judiciary.sen ate.gov/pdf/06-28-10%20Kagan%20Testimony.pdf.

OTHER HISTORIC DOCUMENTS OF INTEREST

FROM PREVIOUS *HISTORIC DOCUMENTS*

■ Sonia Sotomayor Confirmed as First Hispanic Supreme Court Justice, *2009*, p. 320

Power Shift in the United Kingdom

In May 2010, for the first time in thirteen years, the United Kingdom's Labour Party lost its grip on power to a coalition formed by the Conservatives and Liberal Democrats. The election came after Prime Minister Gordon Brown announced that he wanted to seek a "clear and straightforward mandate" to continue his economic recovery plans in the country. Brown had slowly been losing popularity as unemployment continued to climb in the nation. The new coalition government put David Cameron, leader of the Conservative, or Tory Party, at the helm of the fledgling coalition and squarely in the realm of responsibility for reviving the economically recessed European nation.

Brown Calls for an Election

In the political system of the United Kingdom, it is up to the prime minister to decide when an election will be called, as long as he or she does so once every five years, the length of the prime minister's term. In each election, all of the seats in Parliament are voted on, and the party that comes out with a majority of seats is given the opportunity to appoint the prime minister. In the case of a hung Parliament, which until 2010 had not occurred in thirty-six years, it is up to the various parties to try and form a coalition government to reach a majority of the seats.

It was widely speculated that Brown would call for an election in mid-2010, and he did so on April 6, calling for Queen Elizabeth II to dissolve Parliament and announcing that voting would take place on May 6. Brown was only three years into his term as prime minister, but the Labour Party's recent unpopularity led him to seek a mandate to continue his term. Because of the short election cycle, candidates immediately hit the campaign trail, traveling throughout the United Kingdom and drumming up support for their parties.

Brown's Labour Party was seeking its fourth term in the majority and, therefore, in the prime minister's seat. During his campaign, Brown called for a more transparent and accountable government that would lead the United Kingdom forward and out of the economic crisis. In his bid for his seat, he reminded voters that while still struggling, the United Kingdom was on the road to recovery. "We will not allow thirteen years of investment and reform in our public services, to build up the future of these great services, to be put at risk," he said on the campaign trail. He added that it was the intent of the Labour Party to continue fighting for all citizens of the nation. "Our cause is your cause," he told voters.

The Conservatives, headed by Cameron, led in the polls for most of the campaign cycle. Cameron's campaign was focused on criticism of the Labour Party, which he called "big government" that did nothing to help society or the hard working people of the United Kingdom. Cameron attacked Brown's record on the economy, telling voters that Brown had presided over the longest recession in more than sixty years. "It's the most important general election for a generation," Cameron told voters. "It comes down to this: You don't have to put up with another five years of Gordon Brown."

A third party making a strong run for the majority was the Liberal Democratic Party, led by Nick Clegg. Clegg focused his campaign on offering the nation something different from what it had experienced over the past decade with Labour in power. Clegg promised progress during his campaign and a way forward different from that offered by both the Labour and Conservative parties. The election, he said, would be a choice "between more of the same from the old parties . . . or real change, something different from the Liberal Democrats."

The 2010 election was unique in that it would be the first to feature televised debates between the three leading candidates and representatives of smaller parties jostling for seats in Parliament. Clegg was the standout during the debate, taking advantage of the platform to differentiate himself from Brown, who appeared stuffy on camera, and Cameron, who, while he was younger and more natural on television, failed to seize the opportunity to prove to voters why Labour had failed. "I'm here to persuade you there is an alternative . . . a fantastic opportunity to do things differently for once," Clegg said. Polls conducted after the televised debate showed Clegg as the clear winner, and his party received a subsequent bump in the polls.

One of the biggest issues facing the three leading candidates in the election, other than the economy, was immigration, specifically that from European Union (EU) member states. Brown was criticized early in the campaign after a report found that 98 percent of the jobs that had been created during Labour's thirteen years in power had been filled by immigrants. Clegg's idea for immigration reform was to allow anyone who had been in Britain for more than ten years to remain, a suggestion that proved unpopular with a large part of the country. Cameron suggested that he would cap the number of immigrants allowed into the country each year, but he refused to put a number on this policy. His opponents criticized his plan because it would not stop citizens of the EU from coming to the nation to seek work or live; it would only cap the number of those from non-EU nations.

Immigration impacted Brown in an unexpected way, when he hit a major speed bump in his campaign after encountering a constituent at a campaign event who voiced concern about immigration from Eastern Europe. When Brown returned to his car, his microphone was still on and caught him calling the woman "bigoted." The remark came at a critical time in the campaign, just one week before the election as the Labour Party tried to gain ground on the Conservatives. Brown apologized publicly and also visited the woman personally in her home. This gaffe, coupled with other setbacks the party had faced while in power, led to its ultimate defeat at the polls.

HUNG PARLIAMENT AND A RESIGNATION

After the May 6 votes were tallied, residents of the United Kingdom woke to a hung Parliament. A party seeking the majority needed to win at least 326 out of the 650 seats up for grabs. Heading into the election, Labour held a 48-seat majority, meaning that a loss of only two dozen seats would result in the party's fall from power. Conservatives picked up the biggest number of seats and experienced their largest victory since 1931. Some complaints came from the Liberal Democrats, who lost a number of seats in the election, stating that voters had been turned away from polling stations when they closed even though lines remained, and that many locations had run out of ballots. "That should never, ever happen again in a democracy," Clegg said.

With no clear winner in Parliament, Brown continued work on May 7, with the intent to continue to fight for his party and his position as prime minister. The Tories were still twenty seats short of having a majority and would need to form a governing coalition. Brown's party had been in discussions with Cameron's to form a coalition government that would leave Brown in the prime minister's seat, but the Conservatives would not stand for this outcome.

Recognizing that the Conservatives would need a strong partner, Cameron began courting the Liberal Democrats in an effort to form a governing coalition. In the end, Clegg conceded and joined Cameron, ensuring their victory.

On May 10, Brown knew that the coalition had sealed his fate, and he announced his resignation to Queen Elizabeth, as is customary in the United Kingdom, and subsequently held a press conference outside of 10 Downing Street to make his formal announcement. "I loved the job for its potential to make this country I love fairer, more tolerant, more green, more democratic, more prosperous and more just—truly a greater Britain. In the face of many . . . challenges up to and including the global financial meltdown, I have always tried to serve, to do my best in the interests of Britain, its values and its people," Brown said during his speech. He continued by wishing the new prime minister and governing coalition luck in their endeavors, and closed by saying "Thank you and goodbye."

After announcing his resignation, Brown spoke with Labour staff, telling them that he rested the party's loss of seats solely on himself. Harriet Harman succeeded Brown as the Labour Party's new leader in Parliament. Brown retained his seat in Parliament, representing the Kirkcaldy and Cowdenbeath constituency.

Cameron quickly took the stage as the nation's newest prime minister on May 12, speaking outside of 10 Downing Street to let the British public know that the queen had asked him to form a governing coalition. Briefly, Cameron described the biggest challenges the new government would face. "One of the tasks that we clearly have is to rebuild trust in our political system," Cameron said. "Yes that's about cleaning up expenses, yes that is about reforming parliament, and yes it is about making sure people are in control—and that politicians are always their servant and never their masters. But I believe in something else. It is about being honest about what government can achieve. Real change is not what government can do on its own—real change is when everyone pulls together," he continued. The message of togetherness continued throughout Cameron's first months in office.

A New Coalition

In forming the new coalition, Cameron agreed to make concessions to the Liberal Democrats. Other than appointing Clegg to act as his deputy, Cameron also appointed four Liberal Democrats to his cabinet. Cameron, the youngest prime minister in the United Kingdom's history, promised to forge a new direction for the country and open government up to all people in the nation. The leading pair promised to put their differences behind them in the interest of the country. Cameron called the appointment of Clegg and the other Liberal Democrats an example of "the strength and depth of the coalition and our sincere determination to work together, constructively."

Standing with Clegg outside of 10 Downing Street on May 20, 2010, Cameron outlined the coalition's plans for the new government. Not only would they try to end government corruption and make the political system more transparent to the citizens of the country, they also planned to cut the deficit to help bring the United Kingdom out of its economic crisis and would give more support to the troops fighting abroad, specifically those in Afghanistan. "It will be an administration united behind one key purpose and that is to give our country the strong and stable and determined leadership that we need for the long-term," Cameron said.

The new governing coalition will face a difficult road ahead with growing unemployment, which Cameron placed blame for on the Labour Party. He called the crisis a sign "of the economic mistakes of the past decade."

Clegg, to quell rumors that the bitter words exchanged between the two parties during the campaign would cause a riff in the coalition, said, "If it means swallowing some humble pie, and it means eating some of your words, I can't think of a more excellent diet." Clegg further told reporters that he would not have agreed to join the coalition if he did not think his party would be given a voice in the decisions made to help the citizens of the United Kingdom.

Members of the prime minister's new cabinet presented their governing plan on May 20, continuing the promise that the two parties would work togetherand invite all political parties in the nation to join them in forging a new path for the nation. Of his government's five-year plan, Cameron said, "Given the massive challenges this country faces, particularly the deficit, the national interest was not served by a minority government limping along. It was served by strong, stable, decisive government that could really act in the long-term interests of our country. But the more I see of this coalition in action, the more I see its potential. Not just in solving the problems that lie before us, but solving them with a shared set of values. Not just in working together day to day as governments have to do, but in changing our country for years to come. Not just in providing the strong, stable government I spoke about, but in being a genuinely radical reforming government."

—Heather Kerrigan

Following is the speech given by David Cameron on May 12, 2010, upon being chosen prime minister of the United Kingdom; and a press conference given on May 20, 2010, by Cameron and leaders in his party outlining the plans for the new government.

David Cameron upon Being Elected Prime Minister

DOCUMENT

May 12, 2010

Her Majesty the Queen has asked me to form a new government and I have accepted. Before I talk about that new government, let me say something about the one that has just passed. Compared with a decade ago, this country is more open at home and more compassionate abroad and that is something we should all be grateful for and on behalf of the whole country I'd like to pay tribute to the outgoing prime minister for his long record of dedicated public service.

In terms of the future, our country has a hung parliament where no party has an over-all majority and we have some deep and pressing problems—a huge deficit, deep social problems, a political system in need of reform. For those reasons I aim to form a proper and full coalition between the Conservatives and the Liberal Democrats.

I believe that is the right way to provide this country with the strong, the stable, the good and decent government that I think we need so badly. Nick Clegg and I are both political leaders that want to put aside party differences and work hard for the common good and for the national interest. I believe that is the best way to get the strong govern-ment that we need, decisive government that we need today.

I came into politics because I love this country. I think its best days still lie ahead and I believe deeply in public service. And I think the service our country needs right now is to face up to our really big challenges, to confront our problems, to take difficult decisions, to lead people through those difficult decisions, so that together we can reach better times ahead.

One of the tasks that we clearly have is to rebuild trust in our political system. Yes that's about cleaning up expenses, yes that is about reforming parliament, and yes it is about making sure people are in control—and that the politicians are always their servant and never their masters. But I believe it is also something else. It is about being honest about what government can achieve. Real change is not what government can do on its own—real change is when everyone pulls together, comes together, works together, where we all exercise our responsibilities to ourselves, to our families, to our communities and to others.

And I want to help try and build a more responsible society here in Britain. One where we don't just ask what are my entitlements, but what are my responsibilities. One where we don't ask what am I just owed, but more what can I give. And a guide for that society—that those that can should, and those who can't we will always help.

I want to make sure that my government always looks after the elderly, the frail the poorest in our country. We must take everyone through with us on some of the difficult decisions we have ahead.

Above all it will be a government that is built on some clear values. Values of freedom, values of fairness, and values of responsibility.

I want us to build an economy that rewards work. I want us to build a society with stronger families and stronger communities. And I want a political system that people can trust and look up to once again.

This is going to be hard and difficult work. A coalition will throw up all sorts of chal-lenges. But I believe together we can provide that strong and stable government that our country needs based on those values—rebuilding family, rebuilding community, above all, rebuilding responsibility in our country.

Those are the things I care about. Those are the things that this government will now start work on doing.

Thank you very much.

SOURCE: Office of the Prime Minister of the United Kingdom. "David Cameron's Speech Outside 10 Downing Street as Prime Minister." May 12, 2010. http://www.number10.gov.uk/news/speeches-and-transcripts/2010/05/david-camerons-speech-outside-10-downing-street-as-prime-minister-49929.

Prime Minister Cameron's Government Outlines Its New Strategy

May 20, 2010

DEPUTY PRIME MINISTER:

This document that we are launching today is unique. It is a programme for five years of partnership government. Even if you have read a hundred party manifestos, you have never read a document like this one. A joint programme for government based on shared ambition and shared goals. Compromises have, of course, been made on both sides, but those compromises have strengthened, not weakened, the final result.

From different traditions we have come together to forge a single programme for a united government, drawing on the strengths and traditions of both of our parties.

Just flick through the pages. This is a programme for fundamental and comprehensive reform that will transform our country for the better. We want this coalition to be defined by three words: freedom, fairness and responsibility. . . .

But today, it isn't just about ideas. Today is about action. This document sets out page by page, line by line, detailed ideas for changes that will make your life better. From now on, we get down to work.

What does that mean for you? If you are running a business, it means the banks will start lending to you again on fair terms. Unnecessary red tape will be cut back and government will play its role to promote the new industries, the new economy of the future. If you are a teacher, it means that government will stop interfering in what you do in the classroom, and will start giving you the money and the freedom you need so that all the children in your school can thrive. If you live in a rural community, it means more affordable homes for local people in empty farm buildings and on community land. It makes a fair deal from the supermarkets for farmers so your community can thrive.

If you are a pensioner, struggling to make ends meet, it means your pension will rise in line with earnings again starting next April. If you are out of work, it means help to find a job, but penalties if you refuse. If you are a police officer, it means less time in the police station and more time catching criminals. If you are a soldier, it means getting all the support you deserve on the front line. If you are a mother or a father, it means you will be able to share your paternity and maternity leave, and share the joys and challenges of parenting more equally.

And you'll get more control over how new homes and developments are built in your area, the right to register with any GP you want, a freeze in your council tax if your council participates in our scheme, a comprehensive plan so you know we really will do all we can to tackle climate change. . . .

Of course, these are difficult economic times. The challenge of restoring the public finances to health is both enormous and vital. As a government, we are united in saying that tackling the deficit is our first priority. Not because we relish cuts—far from it—but because, without sound finances, none of our ambitious programme for change and renewal will be possible. All parts of government now have the challenge of a lifetime to find savings so we can stop mortgaging the future of our children with unsustainable debts.

So let's be clear. Those spending proposals, set out in our initial coalition agreement, are our first priority for any new money. Fairer taxes, real-terms increases for the NHS, restoring the earnings link in pensions, the pupil premium, meeting our commitments on international aid: any other new spending proposals in this programme will be delivered only as and when resources allow.

Money may be short, but that does not mean our ambition is small. We understand that there is so much more to government than simply spending money. There is so much we can change, so much we can achieve, if we think differently, challenge assumptions, and for once, think about the 'what' and the 'how' of government, not just the 'how much.' That is what this coalition government will do.

Five years of radical reforming government, a stronger society, a sound economy, an accountable state, and power and responsibility in the hands of every citizen. This joint programme is the first step on that road. It is a road we look forward to travelling together. Thank you. I would now like to introduce the Home Secretary.

HOME SECRETARY:

As the Deputy Prime Minister has said, our coalition is united behind three key principles. And the first of those is freedom. We believe that a strong country needs strong citizens, free to make their own choices, not limited and hemmed in by state control. Now this might sound like stating the obvious, or the irrelevant. In a modern, open, democratic society such as Britain, we can take our liberty for granted; but if there is a lesson from our history, it is that freedom is never won.

Each generation, those of us who believe in freedom, in human potential, in the idea that the strength of our society comes from the energy and industry and creativity of our people, must make the case for freedom and fight for it over and over again. And that is certainly true in our country today. Over the past decade, we have seen the balance of power tip dramatically away from the individual and towards the state. The argument for more state power is that it is necessary for our safety, but the irony is that much of this authoritarianism has been ineffective, failing to guarantee our security, even sometimes endangering it, while at the same time undermining our fundamental rights.

So this coalition will be different. We will be hard-nosed defenders of our security and our freedoms. So yes, we will never compromise the security of our citizens, and we will do all that we can to protect them from every threat to their safety, be it terrorism or crime on their streets. But we will also restore civil liberties where they have been lost, and protect them where they still exist. Abolishing ID cards, stopping the powers people have to enter your home, bringing in rigorous regulation of CCTV, outlawing the fingerprinting of children at school, removing the ludicrous offences that have been created in the past decade.

But rebalancing the relationship between the state and the individual means more than just limiting the powers of the state. It means giving more control to people. This is the most radical programme of decentralisation this country has ever seen; from Whitehall to the Town Hall, from the central to the local, from bureaucrats to patients, parents and pupils, this coalition will disperse power and restore freedom, because we believe liberty builds bigger people, able to do more, change more, and achieve more.

And it's now my pleasure to ask the Business Secretary, Vince Cable to speak.

BUSINESS SECRETARY:

The second principle of the coalition is fairness, and without agreement on that, on the concept of fairness, the coalition would never have happened. We defined fairness as being a society where we protect the weakest, the most vulnerable and where everybody has the opportunity to fulfil their potential.

The principle of fairness is even more important in difficult times than in good times. These are difficult times and we have this priority—to deal with the budget deficit. And I just want to make it absolutely clear that I fully support the efforts of the Chancellor of the Exchequer, George Osborne, to deal with this problem urgently, because the problem of the financial crisis in Europe over the last few weeks has underlined the absolute priority for establishing confidence in the country. But the success of the government won't simply be measured by whether we deal with the budget deficit, but how we deal with it. And the programme of government makes it clear what our approach will be. And the approach is that the burdens have got to be fairly shared—and in the difficult times ahead, we won't balance the books on the backs of the poorest.

The coalition is also about more than the short term rescue of the economy. It is about stability, it is about government for the long term, changes that will last, and so we will put the principle of fairness at the heart of the economy in the long term. It will drive tax policy, because our aim is fairer, not higher, taxes. And that's why we've said we will increase the personal allowance for income tax to help lower and middle earners, lifting low earners out of tax, giving people an incentive to work, and we will increase the personal allowance to £10,000, making real-term steps towards meeting this policy objective. We will prioritise this over other tax cuts.

We will also put fairness at the heart of our reforms of the banking system. The banks that have been rescued or underwritten by the taxpayer must be treated as the servants, not the masters, of the economy. . . .

This coalition is a genuine partnership based on progress and reform, and a new era of politics will be underpinned by fairness. Thank you. I'll hand over to the Chancellor.

CHANCELLOR OF THE EXCHEQUER:

Thank you very much, Vince. The third principle that unites the work of this coalition is responsibility. And responsibility is easy to understand but difficult to define. Put simply, it is doing the right thing even when that is difficult: understanding your obligations, not just to yourself, but to those around you, to those you have never met, even to those who have not yet been born. But this value has been steadily eroded from our national life over decades. Spool back to the source of so many of the great problems we face as a country today, and they come back to a lack of responsibility. Our enormous debts, our massive welfare rolls, our deteriorating environment: at the root of these problems may be one person, a collection of people, or even a whole culture, saying, 'Let's do what we want, instead of what is right.'

So this coalition will put everything it does through this simple test: if it encourages responsibility we should do it; if it encourages irresponsibility, we shouldn't. We must start with government. We will bring responsibility to our public finances, saving £6 billion this year. And on Monday, we will be making further announcements about that.

This might not always be the easy thing to do, but it is right. We need to show the world that Britain can tackle its debts and live within its means if we are to sustain the recovery. . . .

We will do the difficult thing; the hard thing, the thing that no government has managed to do, and break the culture of welfare dependency that is wasting so many lives and so much money by saying to those who can work, 'You should work,' and to those who can't work, 'We will always look after you.' Bringing the value of responsibility back to the heart of our national life will not be a simple or short-term task, but this coalition government will play its part, by getting behind those people who want to do the right thing, and always doing the right thing ourselves, however difficult that may be.

I'd now like to hand over to the Prime Minister.

PRIME MINISTER: . . .

Given the massive challenges this country faces, particularly the deficit, the national interest was not served by a minority government limping along. It was served by strong, stable, decisive government that could really act in the long-term interests of our country. But the more I see of this coalition in action, the more I see its potential. Not just in solving the problems that lie before us, but solving them with a shared set of values. Not just in working together day to day as governments have to do, but in changing our country for years to come. Not just in providing the strong, stable government I spoke about, but in being a genuinely radical reforming government.

And that is evidenced, I believe, by the document we are publishing today. It is a full programme of reform for a full Parliament by a partnership government. In its pages are plans for a new green economy, where we set enterprise free, for fairer taxes, for open and accountable government, for radical school reform and for building the Big Society. Next week, in our first Queen's Speech, these transformative ideas will start moving from the pages of the document onto the statute book, beginning the work of change.

I think this document is significant. This coalition government has produced, in a rather short period of time, an extensive and detailed reform agenda. There is a reason why this has been possible. Yes, it is because the urgency of the hour required compromise and negotiation. Yes, it is because we had politicians on both sides who were willing to put aside party interests in favour of the national interest, but also because the more we talked, the more we listened, the more we realised that our visions for this country and the values that inspired them are strengthened and enhanced by the act of the two parties coming together. . . .

For me, the most important value underpinning this programme is the value of responsibility. On the steps of Downing Street, I said I wanted to help build a more responsible society, a Big Society: one where we do not just ask what our entitlements are, but what our responsibilities are; one where we do not just ask what we are owed, but what more we can give. A guide for that society is that those who can, should, and those who cannot, we always help.

You can see how the value of responsibility is woven through this policy programme. It is there in our plans to reform welfare. We will say to those who can work that you should work. If you do not and refuse a good job offer, your benefits will be cut. It is there in our plans to strengthen families. As we make savings from our welfare reforms, we will start to phase out the couples' penalty in the tax credit system that pays couples to live apart, which for years has sent out a completely crazy signal about what is responsible and what is not. It is there in our plans to cut crime. We are going to score a thick line between right and wrong through every community with our plans of real reform of our criminal justice system. The value of responsibility is there in our plans to limit immigration, because controlling our borders is the right thing to do by the people of this country.

Creating a responsible society has always been my mission in politics and that has not changed. For the most part, there has not been disagreement or compromise. We have found many areas where there was complete agreement in both mission and method. . . .

Now, we want to open this process out to the whole of our country. We want you to be involved, reclaim your democracy, have your say. This document and the programme for government contained within it will now enter a period of public scrutiny, consultation and comment. You will be able to guide its mission, policies and priorities. Next week, in the Queen's Speech, we will be announcing plans for a new public reading stage of all bills, so that you can help shape and form them. As Nick explained in his speech yesterday, we also want people to play a full part in developing our Freedom Bill, suggesting regulations that can go, laws that should be discarded and incursions of state power that should be rolled back.

This coalition, I believe, has the potential to be a great reforming government, united behind the three principles of freedom, fairness and responsibility, but above all, united in the purpose of bringing strong, stable, decisive government to our country. Thank you for coming this morning. Thank you for listening. We are happy to take questions. . . .

[The question and answer section has been omitted.]

SOURCE: Office of the Prime Minister of the United Kingdom. "Press Cconference on the Coalition: Our Programme for Government." May 20, 2010. http://www.number10.gov.uk/news/speeches-and-tran scripts/2010/05/press-conference-on-the-coalition-our-programme-for-government-50401.

OTHER HISTORIC DOCUMENTS OF INTEREST

FROM PREVIOUS *HISTORIC DOCUMENTS*

Supreme Court Rules on Life in Prison without Parole for Underage Offenders

MAY 17, 2010

An explosion in violent crime in the 1990s led to a nationwide sentencing movement towards harsher penalties and the elimination of parole. State legislatures cracked down on juvenile crime by enacting more punitive sentencing laws. This led to hundreds of thousands of children each year being transferred from juvenile courts to adult criminal courts. Of these, thousands of children, some as young as thirteen, have been sentenced as adults to life with no chance of parole. Most of these are serving time for homicide-related offences, but on May 17, 2010, the U.S. Supreme Court addressed the small minority of those minors serving life without parole sentences who did not commit homicide.

In *Graham v. Florida*, the Supreme Court created a new protection for the subset of juveniles who committed a crime that did not involve a killing. These juvenile offenders may no longer be sentenced to life in prison without any possibility of parole. A majority of the Court, in an opinion crafted by Justice Anthony Kennedy, found that such a sentence violates the "cruel and unusual punishment" prohibition in the Eighth Amendment to the Constitution. Although the Supreme Court has decreed hard and fast rules regarding when the death penalty can be imposed, this is the first time it has created such a rule for a term-of-years sentence. The ruling invalidates the laws of thirty-seven states but, practically, affects only a group of 129 prisoners convicted as minors to life with no chance of release—seventy-seven in Florida and the rest scattered across ten states and a few federal penitentiaries. But the Court was clear that this does not necessarily mean eventual freedom for these prisoners; it means only that they be given a chance at some point to try and prove that they are not the same people they were as teenagers, that they have matured enough in prison to be ruled "fit to rejoin society."

LEGAL BACKGROUND

This is the latest in a series of cases that relies on the Eighth Amendment to limit the kinds of punishments that are constitutionally permissible. The Eighth Amendment states: "Excessive bail shall not be required, nor excessive fines imposed, nor cruel and unusual punishment inflicted."

Precedents under this amendment have struck down punishments deemed "inherently barbaric," such as torture, and those where the length of a sentence is disproportionate to the crime given the circumstances in the particular case. In the last decade, however, the Court has defined Eighth Amendment standards of "cruel and unusual punishments" with a series of categorical rules. Two such recent opinions, each written by Justice Kennedy, laid the groundwork for the *Graham v. Florida* case. In 2005, in *Roper v. Simmons*, the Court focused on the characteristics of a class of defendants to hold that the death penalty for those who commit crimes before the age of eighteen can never be constitutional. According to *Roper*, juveniles are less culpable than adults because they have a "lack of maturity and an underdeveloped sense of responsibility" that renders them less deserving of the most severe punishment—the death penalty. Then, in 2008, Justice Kennedy wrote the majority opinion in *Kennedy v. Louisiana*, a case that limited the death penalty to only the most serious offenses, abolishing it for all crimes that do not involve homicide. These cases left open the question: Can an offender under eighteen be sentenced to what the Court referred to as "the second most severe penalty permitted by law," life in prison with no parole for a crime in which the victim was not killed? *Graham v. Florida* answered that question.

Terrance Jamar Graham

Terrance Jamar Graham was born in 1987 to parents addicted to crack cocaine. He was diagnosed in elementary school with attention deficit hyperactivity disorder and began drinking alcohol at age nine and smoking marijuana at age thirteen. When Graham was sixteen, he and three friends tried to rob a restaurant in Jacksonville, Florida. One of his accomplices struck the restaurant manager in the head, but they all ran out when he started yelling. The manager required stitches and no money was taken.

Graham was arrested, and the prosecutor elected to charge him as an adult with armed burglary with assault or battery, a first-degree felony carrying a maximum penalty of life without possibility of parole. Under a plea agreement, he pled guilty. In a letter to the court, he wrote: "This is my first and last time getting in trouble," and "if I get a second chance, I'm going to do whatever it takes to get into the NFL." The trial court agreed to withhold trial on the charges and sentenced him to a three-year probation with some time in the county jail.

Within this probationary period, when he was thirty-four days short of his eighteenth birthday, he was arrested again, this time for a home invasion robbery in which he and two accomplices forcibly entered a home, holding the owner at gunpoint while they ransacked his house. Later that night, in another attempted robbery, one of his accomplices was shot and he drove him to the hospital. Leaving the hospital, a police officer signaled for him to stop. After a high-speed chase, he crashed the car and was apprehended with three handguns in his car. He maintained that he had no involvement in the home invasion robbery, but he admitted that fleeing the officer violated his probation conditions.

The probation violation reopened sentencing on his original charges from when he was sixteen. At his sentencing, the Florida Department of Corrections recommended that Graham receive at most four years imprisonment and the prosecutor's office recommended thirty years. The trial judge, however, sentenced him to the maximum sentence authorized by law, life without the possibility of parole. He explained his sentence by saying "We can't do anything to deter you. This is the way you are going to lead your life, and

I don't know why you are going to. You've made that decision. I have no idea. But evidently that is what you decided to do."

On appeal, Graham challenged his sentence under the Eighth Amendment, and the Florida Court of Appeal denied the motion, concluding further that he was incapable of rehabilitation. The Florida Supreme Court denied review, and the U.S. Supreme Court granted *certiorari* to hear the Eighth Amendment issue.

THE OPINION OF THE COURT

The majority opinion, written by Justice Kennedy and joined by Justices John Paul Stevens, Ruth Bader Ginsburg, Stephen Breyer, and Sonia Sotomayor, held that if a state imposes the sentence of life on a juvenile who commits a crime in which no one is killed, the state "must provide him or her with some realistic opportunity to obtain release before the end of that term." Although the overall vote of the Court was 6–3, this is misleading because while Chief Justice John Roberts agreed that Graham's particular life without parole sentence violated the Eighth Amendment's prohibition on "cruel and unusual punishments," he did not go along with the majority on the need for a new constitutional rule that would prohibit such penalties for all juveniles convicted of non-homicide offences. The case triggered a fervent dissent written by Justice Clarence Thomas and joined by Justices Antonin Scalia and, partially, Samuel A. Alito Jr.

For the past century, the Supreme Court has interpreted the prohibition against "cruel and unusual punishments" by looking to the "evolving standards of decency that mark the progress of a maturing society." In starting this analysis, Justice Kennedy looked to see if there was a "national consensus" against such sentences. Although, as the dissent points out, a super-majority of states and the federal government have passed laws allowing life without parole sentences for juveniles, the majority looked beyond those numbers to show actual sentencing practices. Looking at the statistics, only 129 prisoners nationwide received such sentences and 77 of these were in Florida. Given how rarely the sentence is imposed, Kennedy wrote that "it is fair to say that a national consensus has developed against it."

As he did when banning the death penalty for minor offenders, Justice Kennedy focused on juveniles' "lack of maturity and underdeveloped sense of responsibility," their greater susceptibility to outside pressures, and their as-yet unformed characters to argue that they are "less deserving of the most severe punishments." In fact, the Court referenced *amici* briefs from the American Medical Association and American Psychological Association to point out that developments in psychology and brain science since *Roper* "continue to show fundamental differences between juvenile and adult minds. For example, parts of the brain involved in behavior control continue to mature through late adolescence."

The Court has repeatedly quoted "death is different" as a reason for categorical rules limiting the application of the death penalty, but this is the first time it has applied the categorical approach to a noncapital sentence. But life without parole is, according to the majority, an "especially harsh punishment for a juvenile," who will on average serve a far greater number of years and percentage of his or her life in prison than an adult offender. Denying all hope to a juvenile assumes that he or she is incapable of ever maturing.

Differentiating "transient immaturity" from "irreparable corruption" would be difficult, the Court points out, even for expert psychologists.

The Court held that the Eighth Amendment requires states to grant a prisoner who has been convicted of a non-homicide crime while a child in the eyes of the law the chance to "later demonstrate that he is fit to rejoin society." This does not mean that the state must guarantee the offender an eventual release; only that it must provide the offender with "some realistic opportunity to obtain release."

Justice Thomas, in his dissent, rejected the Court's entire "evolving standards of decency" approach to the Eighth Amendment, arguing instead that the Court was simply imposing its own morality over that of the state's elected representatives. Under Thomas's view, the Court must look to the practices at the time the Bill of Rights was adopted. Because laws at that time permitted capital punishment on people as young as seven, it is, he writes, "exceedingly unlikely that the imposition of a life-without-parole sentence on a person of Graham's age would run afoul of those standards." Justice Stevens wrote a separate concurring opinion rejecting what he characterized as Justice Thomas's "static approach" to the law. In a testy exchange, Stevens argued: "Society changes. Knowledge accumulates. We learn, sometimes, from our mistakes." Thomas responded, "Perhaps one day the Court will learn from this one."

EFFECT OF THE RULING

The practical effects of this ruling are far from clear. The Court did not specify what exactly was required to provide juvenile offenders with "some realistic opportunity" to seek release, leaving it to the states to explore mechanisms for compliance with the opinion's mandate. One open question is when such a review must occur and whether an extremely long sentence, rather than a life sentence, would likewise run afoul of the Eighth Amendment. For example, currently Colorado has no life-without-parole sentences for juvenile non-homicide offenders, but it does permit such offenders to be sentenced to terms of up to forty years.

In addressing the Court ruling, Florida's Republican attorney general, Bill McCollum, stressed this very point, stating, "The Court's ruling does not prohibit stern sentences for juveniles who commit violent crimes, and I fully expect the offender in this case to be resentenced to a very long term in prison." Florida lawmakers were expected to take up the issue of changing the state's juvenile justice and corrections systems to comply with the Court's ruling in early 2011. In November 2010, the Florida Prosecuting Attorneys Association, which represents the twenty state attorneys in Florida, endorsed a bill by Rep. Mike Weinstein, R-Jacksonville, that will set up a system for handling future juveniles who commit non-murder crimes. Under the bill, the juveniles could still receive life sentences but they would be eligible for parole after serving at least twenty-five years if they meet a series of criteria, including not having discipline problems in prison, completing education programs, and showing other signs of rehabilitation.

—Melissa Feinberg

The following are excerpts from the U.S. Supreme Court's ruling in Graham v. Florida, *in which the Court ruled 6–3 to ban the sentence of life in prison without the chance of parole for juvenile offenders.*

Graham v. Florida

May 17, 2010

No. 08–7412

Terrance Jamar Graham, Petitioner
v.
Florida

On writ of certiorari to the
District Court of Appeal of Florida,
First District

May 17, 2010

JUSTICE KENNEDY delivered the opinion of the Court.

The issue before the Court is whether the Constitution permits a juvenile offender to be sentenced to life in prison without parole for a nonhomicide crime. The sentence was imposed by the State of Florida. Petitioner challenges the sentence under the Eighth Amendment's Cruel and Unusual Punishments Clause, made applicable to the States by the Due Process Clause of the Fourteenth Amendment. . . .

[Section I, which contains background on the case, has been omitted.]

II

The Eighth Amendment states: "Excessive bail shall not be required, nor excessive fines imposed, nor cruel and unusual punishments inflicted." To determine whether a punishment is cruel and unusual, courts must look beyond historical conceptions to "'the evolving standards of decency that mark the progress of a maturing society.'" "This is because '[t]he standard of extreme cruelty is not merely descriptive, but necessarily embodies a moral judgment. The standard itself remains the same, but its applicability must change as the basic mores of society change.'"

The Cruel and Unusual Punishments Clause prohibits the imposition of inherently barbaric punishments under all circumstances. "[P]unishments of torture," for example, "are forbidden." These cases underscore the essential principle that, under the Eighth Amendment, the State must respect the human attributes even of those who have committed serious crimes.

For the most part, however, the Court's precedents consider punishments challenged not as inherently barbaric but as disproportionate to the crime. The concept of proportionality is central to the Eighth Amendment. Embodied in the Constitution's ban on cruel and unusual punishments is the "precept of justice that punishment for crime should be graduated and proportioned to [the] offense."

The Court's cases addressing the proportionality of sentences fall within two general classifications. The first involves challenges to the length of term-of-years sentences given all the circumstances in a particular case. The second comprises cases in which the Court implements the proportionality standard by certain categorical restrictions on the death penalty. . . .

[Further discussion of these classifications omitted.]

III

A

The analysis begins with objective indicia of national consensus. "[T]he 'clearest and most reliable objective evidence of contemporary values is the legislation enacted by the country's legislatures.'" Six jurisdictions do not allow life without parole sentences for any juvenile offenders. Seven jurisdictions permit life without parole for juvenile offenders, but only for homicide crimes. Thirty-seven States as well as the District of Columbia permit sentences of life without parole for a juvenile nonhomicide offender in some circumstances. Federal law also allows for the possibility of life without parole for offenders as young as 13. Relying on this metric, the State and its *amici* argue that there is no national consensus against the sentencing practice at issue.

This argument is incomplete and unavailing. "There are measures of consensus other than legislation." Actual sentencing practices are an important part of the Court's inquiry into consensus. Here, an examination of actual sentencing practices in jurisdictions where the sentence in question is permitted by statute discloses a consensus against its use. Although these statutory schemes contain no explicit prohibition on sentences of life without parole for juvenile nonhomicide offenders, those sentences are most infrequent. . . .

[Discussion of counting offenders has been omitted.]

. . . Thus, adding the individuals counted by the study to those we have been able to locate independently, there are 129 juvenile nonhomicide offenders serving life without parole sentences. A significant majority of those, 77 in total, are serving sentences imposed in Florida. The other 52 are imprisoned in just 10 States—California, Delaware, Iowa, Louisiana, Mississippi, Nebraska, Nevada, Oklahoma, South Carolina, and Virginia—and in the federal system. Thus, only 12 jurisdictions nationwide in fact impose life without parole sentences on juvenile nonhomicide offenders—and most of those impose the sentence quite rarely—while 26 States as well as the District of Columbia do not impose them despite apparent statutory authorization. . . .

B

Community consensus, while "entitled to great weight," is not itself determinative of whether a punishment is cruel and unusual. In accordance with the constitutional design, "the task of interpreting the Eighth Amendment remains our responsibility." The judicial exercise of independent judgment requires consideration of the culpability of the offenders at issue in light of their crimes and characteristics, along with the severity of the punishment in question. In this inquiry the Court also considers whether the challenged sentencing practice serves legitimate penological goals.

Roper established that because juveniles have lessened culpability they are less deserving of the most severe punishments. As compared to adults, juveniles have a "'lack of maturity and an underdeveloped sense of responsibility'"; they "are more vulnerable or susceptible to negative influences and outside pressures, including peer pressure"; and their characters are "not as well formed." These salient characteristics mean that "[i]t is difficult even for expert psychologists to differentiate between the juvenile offender whose crime reflects unfortunate yet transient immaturity, and the rare juvenile offender whose crime reflects irreparable corruption." Accordingly, "juvenile offenders cannot with reliability be classified among the worst offenders." A juvenile is not absolved of responsibility for his actions, but his transgression "is not as morally reprehensible as that of an adult."

No recent data provide reason to reconsider the Court's observations in *Roper* about the nature of juveniles. As petitioner's *amici* point out, developments in psychology and brain science continue to show fundamental differences between juvenile and adult minds. For example, parts of the brain involved in behavior control continue to mature through late adolescence. Juveniles are more capable of change than are adults, and their actions are less likely to be evidence of "irretrievably depraved character" than are the actions of adults. It remains true that "[f]rom a moral standpoint it would be misguided to equate the failings of a minor with those of an adult, for a greater possibility exists that a minor's character deficiencies will be reformed." These matters relate to the status of the offenders in question; and it is relevant to consider next the nature of the offenses to which this harsh penalty might apply.

The Court has recognized that defendants who do not kill, intend to kill, or foresee that life will be taken are categorically less deserving of the most serious forms of punishment than are murderers. There is a line "between homicide and other serious violent offenses against the individual." Serious nonhomicide crimes "may be devastating in their harm . . . but 'in terms of moral depravity and of the injury to the person and to the public,' . . . they cannot be compared to murder in their 'severity and irrevocability.'" This is because "[l]ife is over for the victim of the murderer," but for the victim of even a very serious nonhomicide crime, "life . . . is not over and normally is not beyond repair." *Ibid.* (plurality opinion). Although an offense like robbery or rape is "a serious crime deserving serious punishment," *Enmund, supra,* at 797, those crimes differ from homicide crimes in a moral sense.

It follows that, when compared to an adult murderer, a juvenile offender who did not kill or intend to kill has a twice diminished moral culpability. The age of the offender and the nature of the crime each bear on the analysis.

As for the punishment, life without parole is "the second most severe penalty permitted by law." It is true that a death sentence is "unique in its severity and irrevocability," yet life without parole sentences share some characteristics with death sentences that are shared by no other sentences. The State does not execute the offender sentenced to life by a forfeiture that is irrevocable. It deprives the convict of the most basic liberties without giving hope of restoration, except perhaps by executive clemency—the remote possibility of which does not mitigate the harshness of the sentence. *Solem,* 463 U. S., at 300–301. As one court observed in overturning a life without parole sentence for a juvenile defendant, this sentence "means denial of hope; it means that good behavior and character improvement are immaterial; it means that whatever the future might hold in store for the mind and spirit of [the convict], he will remain in prison for the rest of his days." . . .

Life without parole is an especially harsh punishment for a juvenile. Under this sentence a juvenile offender will on average serve more years and a greater percentage of his life in prison than an adult offender. A 16-year-old and a 75-year-old each sentenced to life without parole receive the same punishment in name only. See *Roper, supra,* at 572; cf. *Harmelin, supra,* at 996 ("In some cases . . . there will be negligible difference between life without parole and other sentences of imprisonment—for example, . . . a lengthy term sentence without eligibility for parole, given to a 65-year-old man"). This reality cannot be ignored. . . .

[The section discussing penological theories has been omitted.]

In sum, penological theory is not adequate to justify life without parole for juvenile nonhomicide offenders. This determination; the limited culpability of juvenile nonhomicide offenders; and the severity of life without parole sentences all lead to the conclusion that the sentencing practice under consideration is cruel and unusual. This Court now holds that for a juvenile offender who did not commit homicide the Eighth Amendment forbids the sentence of life without parole. This clear line is necessary to prevent the possibility that life without parole sentences will be imposed on juvenile nonhomicide offenders who are not sufficiently culpable to merit that punishment. Because "[t]he age of 18 is the point where society draws the line for many purposes between childhood and adulthood," those who were below that age when the offense was committed may not be sentenced to life without parole for a nonhomicide crime.

A State is not required to guarantee eventual freedom to a juvenile offender convicted of a nonhomicide crime. What the State must do, however, is give defendants like Graham some meaningful opportunity to obtain release based on demonstrated maturity and rehabilitation. It is for the State, in the first instance, to explore the means and mechanisms for compliance. It bears emphasis, however, that while the Eighth Amendment forbids a State from imposing a life without parole sentence on a juvenile nonhomicide offender, it does not require the State to release that offender during his natural life. Those who commit truly horrifying crimes as juveniles may turn out to be irredeemable, and thus deserving of incarceration for the duration of their lives. The Eighth Amendment does not foreclose the possibility that persons convicted of nonhomicide crimes committed before adulthood will remain behind bars for life. It does forbid States from making the judgment at the outset that those offenders never will be fit to reenter society.

C...

Terrance Graham's sentence guarantees he will die in prison without any meaningful opportunity to obtain release, no matter what he might do to demonstrate that the bad acts he committed as a teenager are not representative of his true character, even if he spends the next half century attempting to atone for his crimes and learn from his mistakes. The State has denied him any chance to later demonstrate that he is fit to rejoin society based solely on a nonhomicide crime that he committed while he was a child in the eyes of the law. This the Eighth Amendment does not permit.

D

There is support for our conclusion in the fact that, in continuing to impose life without parole sentences on juveniles who did not commit homicide, the United States adheres to a sentencing practice rejected the world over. This observation does not control our decision. The judgments of other nations and the international community are not dispositive as to the meaning of the Eighth Amendment. But "'[t]he climate of international opinion concerning the acceptability of a particular punishment'" is also "'not irrelevant.'" The Court has looked beyond our Nation's borders for support for its independent conclusion that a particular punishment is cruel and unusual.

Today we continue that longstanding practice in noting the global consensus against the sentencing practice in question. A recent study concluded that only 11 nations authorize life without parole for juvenile offenders under any circumstances; and only 2 of them, the United States and Israel, ever impose the punishment in practice. An updated version of the study concluded that Israel's "laws allow for parole review of juvenile offenders serving life terms," but expressed reservations about how that parole review is implemented. But even if Israel is counted as allowing life without parole for juvenile offenders, that nation does not appear to impose that sentence for nonhomicide crimes; all of the seven Israeli prisoners whom commentators have identified as serving life sentences for juvenile crimes were convicted of homicide or attempted homicide.

Thus, as petitioner contends and respondent does not contest, the United States is the only Nation that imposes life without parole sentences on juvenile nonhomicide offenders. . . .

* * *

The Constitution prohibits the imposition of a life without parole sentence on a juvenile offender who did not commit homicide. A State need not guarantee the offender eventual release, but if it imposes a sentence of life it must provide him or her with some realistic opportunity to obtain release before the end of that term. The judgment of the First District Court of Appeal of Florida is reversed, and the case is remanded for further proceedings not inconsistent with this opinion.

It is so ordered.

JUSTICE THOMAS, with whom JUSTICE SCALIA joins, and with whom JUSTICE ALITO joins as to Parts I and III, dissenting.

The Court holds today that it is "grossly disproportionate" and hence unconstitutional for any judge or jury to impose a sentence of life without parole on an offender less than 18 years old, unless he has committed a homicide. Although the text of the Constitution is silent regarding he permissibility of this sentencing practice, and although it would not have offended the standards that prevailed at the founding, the Court insists that the standards of American society have evolved such that the Constitution now requires its prohibition.

The news of this evolution will, I think, come as a surprise to the American people. Congress, the District of Columbia, and 37 States allow judges and juries to consider this sentencing practice in juvenile nonhomicide cases, and those judges and juries have decided to use it in the very worst cases they have encountered.

The Court does not conclude that life without parole itself is a cruel and unusual punishment. It instead rejects the judgments of those legislatures, judges, and juries regarding what the Court describes as the "moral" question of whether this sentence can ever be "proportionat[e]" when applied to the category of offenders at issue here.

I am unwilling to assume that we, as members of this Court, are any more capable of making such moral judgments than our fellow citizens. Nothing in our training as judges qualifies us for that task, and nothing in Article III gives us that authority.

I respectfully dissent. . . .

SOURCE: U.S. Supreme Court. *Graham v. Florida*, 560 U.S. ___ (2010). http://www.supremecourt.gov/opinions/09pdf/08-7412.pdf.

OTHER HISTORIC DOCUMENTS OF INTEREST

FROM PREVIOUS *HISTORIC DOCUMENTS*

Midterm Primary Elections

MAY 19 AND SEPTEMBER 15, 2010

The 2010 midterm primary elections were a tenuous time for Republicans and Democrats alike, with well-known incumbents losing the opportunity to keep their seats in the general election in the House, Senate, and across state legislatures and governorships. The roiling political landscape set up in 2009 by Barack Obama's assent to the presidency and the ensuing political infighting gave conservatives the upper hand heading into the primary elections, which were kicked off in January 2010 by Sen. Scott Brown, a Republican, securing the late Democratic senator Ted Kennedy's seat in a special election in Massachusetts. The Republican edge reached a peak in August when the Gallup organization's latest poll showed Republicans in congressional races leading Democrats by ten percentage points among likely voters, the biggest lead the GOP had experienced in sixty-eight years.

Democrats faced an uphill battle heading into the midterm elections with the economy weighing heavily on the minds of voters. Obama's declining popularity through the summer of 2010 and into the fall hurt Democrats running for Congress. In October, a Bloomberg poll found that four of ten likely midterm voters who once considered themselves Obama supporters were less supportive, or no longer supportive, of his presidency. Six of ten of those polled said Obama was responsible for the continued decline of the economy. With this national mood, Republicans built the midterm elections as a referendum against the president, swaying a number of independent voters to support their cause.

In some cases, this surge proved positive for Republican candidates, but in other instances, it was an upset as candidates of the newly formed Tea Party (Tea standing for Taxed Enough Already) made a strong showing in some races. A number of surprises came out of the primaries, sparking belief that the November election could set up a unique balance in the U.S. House and Senate. Not only would the election determine who would control Congress for the next two years, but in some instances it would also decide which political party would be in control of redrawing congressional district boundaries following the 2010 census.

THE TEA PARTY'S BIG UPSETS

The Tea Party, a coalition of community activist groups around the country, is a relative newcomer to politics and focuses on issues like limited government, tighter spending regulations, and a free market economy. The party, whose members ran on the Republican ticket, formed in 2009 amid rising anger and concern over the bailout of Wall Street banks coupled with rising federal debt and Obama's call for a nationwide health plan. There is no strong central organization, but rather local and regional chapters. In the primaries, their investments ranked in the millions of dollars.

In the Senate, the Tea Party won eight primary battles in Alaska, Colorado, Delaware, Florida, Kentucky, Nevada, Utah, and Wisconsin. Rand Paul, son of Rep. Ron Paul, R-Texas, a presidential candidate in the 1988 and 2008 elections, defeated the Republican favorite in Kentucky in a surprising upset on May 18. Republicans and Democrats closely watched this race to see how strong of an impact the Tea Party might have in the general election. "I have a message," Paul declared in his victory speech, "a message from the Tea Party, a message that is loud and clear and does not mince words: We've come to take our government back."

Alaska's Tea Party candidate, Joe Miller, led a big surprise win over incumbent Republican senator Lisa Murkowski, who announced that she would continue to pursue her seat as a write-in candidate, after first considering running as a Libertarian. "As disappointed as I am in the outcome of the primary and my belief that the Alaska Republican Party was hijacked by the Tea Party Express, an outside extremist group, I am not going to quit my party. I will not wrap myself in the flag of another political party for the sake of election at any cost."

In the primary race for the U.S. House of Representatives, the Tea Party won five decisive primary battles, in Alabama, Arizona, Colorado, Florida, and Maryland. Few of the House races were considered to be large upsets as compared to the Senate primary races.

In state government, four Tea Party–backed candidates won gubernatorial primaries in Colorado, Maine, New York, and South Carolina. In New York, Carl Paladino defeated former U.S. representative Rick Lazio by garnering 62 percent of the Republican vote. It had been expected that the state's Democratic attorney general, Andrew Cuomo, was on his way to an easy victory, but Paladino's surprising challenge would prove somewhat difficult.

Reaction to Tea Party Victories

Democrats across the country seemed happy with the Tea Party victories in primary elections, explaining that it showed a clear rift in the Republican Party. Political analysts also noted the likelihood that the Democrats would be able to hold on to seats, or gain seats, for which a Tea Party candidate would be running during the November general election. "The bottom line is," House majority leader Steny Hoyer, D-Md., said, "they're a deeply divided party." This division "is going to hurt them," he continued.

Democratic strategists and party leaders saw the Tea Party as posing very little threat to mainstream political parties. Former president Bill Clinton said the Tea Party candidates could make George W. Bush "look like a liberal." Democratic strategist Tanya Acker said, "The country is going to be presented with one party that seems to be auditioning for a talk radio show host. You've got folks like Sharron Angle saying things like take up arms against the government and the Democrats want to talk about unemployment benefits and Wall Street."

In states where Democrats were nearly assured a loss in the general election against Republican candidates, Tea Party victories and candidates backed by the party turned the tables in the Democrats' favor. For example, in Senate majority leader Harry Reid's home state of Nevada, Reid's defeat seemed certain. However, against Angle, a Republican who is favored and backed by the Tea Party, he edged up in the polls. Angle's platform included phasing out Social Security for young workers, closing the U.S. Department of Education, and opposing abortion in all cases, even in instances of rape and incest.

What Democrats saw as a major victory was the upset that occurred in the Delaware Senate primary, where Tea Party–backed Christine O'Donnell defeated a long-serving GOP candidate, Rep. Mike Castle. Castle, a nine-term representative, had been considered almost a shoo-in for the Senate seat. Without a victory in Delaware, the Republicans' chances for regaining control of the Senate would be drastically decreased.

"What happened for Democrats last night was very positive," said House Speaker Nancy Pelosi, D-Calif., after the Delaware election. "We were very pleased with the candidates that we drew, and they offer a great contrast in the election as to the clarity of the choice." Hoyer echoed Pelosi's remarks. "Our members are up. Our members are confident. Our members are engaged in the issues."

Republicans had railed against O'Donnell, who until a few weeks before the primary election had little chance of winning the nomination. The party's state chairman in Delaware, Tom Ross, called O'Donnell someone who "could not be elected dogcatcher." At the last minute, the Tea Party Express, financially backed by a California political action committee, spent nearly a quarter of a million dollars for O'Donnell's campaign. An endorsement by former vice presidential nominee Sarah Palin quickly followed, and O'Donnell was carried to victory.

Shortly after O'Donnell's win, the Republicans announced that they would not provide O'Donnell funding in the general election. O'Donnell, however, seemed unconcerned. "Never underestimate the power of 'We the People,'" she said. "'We the People' will have our voice heard once again in Washington, D.C."

Others saw any potential November Tea Party victories as a win-win for the Republican side. "The intensity gap that we're seeing between the two parties this election cycle is mainly being fed by the Tea Party movement on the Republican side. So, net-net, it's still a gain," said Republican strategist Dan Bartlett.

Sarah Palin's Impact on the Primaries

Palin, the former vice presidential nominee in 2008, was a driving force behind the Tea Party movement. When she threw her support to the party's candidates around the nation, they almost instantly received bumps in polling and additional campaign funds. One Republican analyst put the cash infusion at anywhere from $10,000 to $25,000 once Palin's support was received.

Palin downplayed her influence over the primaries, saying, "I think any credit given to me is way overblown because no one individual can tip it one way or another for a candidate." However, there was no hiding the fact that O'Donnell, along with a number of other female Tea Party candidates, were dark horse candidates until gaining Palin's support.

Political strategists say Palin's star power was the best Tea Party candidates could ask for because it elevated each candidacy in the eyes of voters. Republicans tried to downplay her influence as Palin-backed candidates pulled votes away from non–Tea Party Republicans. "The campaigns that won ran better races than their opponents. It's that simple," said Kevin Madden, a former campaign aid to 2008 presidential candidate Mitt Romney, denying that Palin's influence had been a factor.

Democrats, on the other hand, painted Palin as a major player in the Tea Party's wins, and all but encouraged her continued support. Democratic Congressional Campaign Committee spokesperson Ryan Rudominer said, "We think her involvement is a great thing across the board."

CAN THE TEA PARTY WIN IN NOVEMBER?

The big question on everyone's mind coming out of the primaries was whether the Tea Party candidates would be able to beat Democrats in the November general election. These candidates offered a return to more conservative politics, with a focus on limited government. Democrats and Republicans, on the other hand, weren't offering anything different in this campaign than they had in previous years.

The question before voters was how far they would want to go to fix what they saw as a broken political system. The Tea Party spurred conservative activists around the country and multiple rallies sprung up, some in support of the Republicans and others in support of the Tea Party. Sensing the importance of which party held power in the U.S. House and Senate in 2011 and 2012, conservative voters made it clear that their voices would be heard. The question soon became whether Democrats would be able to hold their two-house control in Congress. If the primaries were any indication, where Republican turnout far exceeded that of Democratic supporters, the party would have a long struggle ahead.

—Heather Kerrigan

Following is a statement by Republican National Committee (RNC) chair Michael Steele on May 19, 2010, after Rand Paul's victory in the Kentucky Senate primary; and a statement by Sen. John Cornyn. R-Texas, chair of the National Republican Senatorial Committee, on September 15, 2010, after Tea Party candidate Christine O'Donnell's primary victory in Delaware.

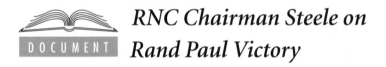

RNC Chairman Steele on Rand Paul Victory

May 19, 2010

Republican National Committee (RNC) Chairman Michael Steele released the following statement today:

"I would like to congratulate Rand Paul and all Republican nominees across the state of Kentucky who won their primaries today. Competitive and hard fought primaries give Republicans a chance to debate the ideas that move our party and our country forward. Trey Grayson should be congratulated for a hard fought campaign.

"Tonight, Republicans unite behind candidates that stand by our conservative principles of lower taxes, fiscal restraint and controlling the deficit. Voters are clearly frustrated with business-as-usual and Jack Conway, the Democrat nominee for Senate, will serve as nothing but a rubber stamp for the liberal policies of President Obama and Democrats in Washington. I am confident with Rand Paul leading the Republican ticket that Republicans will be successful this November."

SOURCE: Republican National Committee. "Statement from RNC Chairman Michael Steele on Kentucky Primaries." May 19, 2010. http://www.gop.com/index.php/news/comments/statement_from_rnc_chairman_michael_steele_on_kentucky_primaries#ixzz1CjjbGhy3.

Sen. Cornyn on Christine
O'Donnell's Primary Victory

September 15, 2010

"Let there be no mistake: The National Republican Senatorial Committee—and I personally as the committee's chairman—strongly stand by all of our Republican nominees, including Christine O'Donnell in Delaware.

"I reached out to Christine this morning, and as I have conveyed to all of our nominees, I offered her my personal congratulations and let her know that she has our support. This support includes a check for $42,000—the maximum allowable donation that we have provided to all of our nominees—which the NRSC will send to her campaign today.

"We remain committed to holding Democrat nominee New Castle County Executive Chris Coons accountable this November, as we inform voters about his record of driving his county to the brink of bankruptcy and supporting his party's reckless spending policies in Washington.

"In the weeks ahead, we will decide where to best allocate additional financial resources among the large number of competitive races at stake this November. While it's not in Republicans' interest to advertise our spending strategy to our opponents, it's worth noting that just yesterday, the NRSC's first independent expenditure ad aired in support of Dr. Rand Paul's campaign in Kentucky, where we firmly believe that he will win in November.

"It remains to be seen whether national Democrats will provide a similar level of support for many of their nominees, including in key battleground states like Indiana, Ohio, Florida, Arkansas, Illinois, and New Hampshire, among others. The Democrats' indecision reflects the fact that Republicans are on offense in at least 12 Democrat-held states and we are leading in the polls in seven of those 12 states.

"Finally, on the matter of the New Hampshire Senate race, while the results remain outstanding, we continue to monitor the Republican primary race, and we stand ready to fully support whichever candidate is chosen as the nominee."

SOURCE: National Republican Senatorial Committee. "NRSC Chairman Cornyn's Statement on Delaware Senate Race." September 15, 2010. http://www.nrsc.org/nrsc-chairman-cornyns-statement-on-delaware-senate-race.

OTHER HISTORIC DOCUMENTS OF INTEREST

FROM THIS VOLUME

- Responses to the 2010 Midterm Elections, p. 555

FROM PREVIOUS *HISTORIC DOCUMENTS*

- Congressional Debate on Health Care Reform, *2009*, p. 533

Violence in Jamaica

MAY 23 AND 25 AND JUNE 25, 2010

Violence spilled into the streets of Jamaica's capital Kingston in late May after the nation's prime minister, Bruce Golding, reversed an earlier decision and announced his intention to begin extradition proceedings against alleged drug lord Christopher "Dudus" Coke. Coke was wanted by U.S. authorities in connection with cocaine and arms trafficking in New York. The extradition decision had not come easily. Golding was largely dependent on Coke's influence over his neighborhood in West Kingston to not only ensure that peace was kept but also that the residents continued to support Golding. The impoverished citizens of West Kingston were, in turn, largely dependent on Coke to provide them with safety and basic necessities, which were rarely provided by the Jamaican government, and were willing to protect him from capture.

CRISIS IN JAMAICA

A popular tourist destination, Jamaica is often a nation on the brink of violent uprising as citizens languish in economic depression. Those who can provide basic necessities such as food, water, and clothing to impoverished citizens can gain an inordinate amount of power in a country where such services are largely not provided by the government. It is in this desperation that people like Coke can gain power and run illegal drug and arms trafficking rings, often using those who depend on them to sneak drugs into the United States.

Because of the tenuous political situation, political leaders rely on men known as "dons" to turn citizens out to vote for the dons' chosen candidates. These dons retain popularity in their communities by providing social support for poor communities. This can include buying food, sending children to school, and sponsoring parties for neighborhood children and families. Their supporters have made it clear that the failure of the Jamaican government is the reason for the high level of support the dons receive. The cycle of support is difficult to break. "This has been part of our history," said Victor Cummings, a former member of parliament. "It's been institutionalized. Every politician knows who the dons in their area are. If you want to be elected, you have to know them and you need their support." In the case of Coke, he supports the Jamaican Labor Party and its leader, Prime Minister Golding, which has helped Golding retain his hold on the nation's highest office.

Because of the support he receives from Coke, Golding refused to comply with an earlier extradition order for the alleged drug trafficker. The United States initially ordered an extradition in 2009 after allegations that Coke had shipped weapons from the United States to Jamaica. Golding refused, wanting to maintain support from Coke's neighborhood. Relations between the United States and Jamaica became strained. As support for his refusal to send Coke to the United States for trial, Golding claimed that the United States had used illegal wiretaps to gather evidence against Coke.

CHRISTOPHER "DUDUS" COKE

Coke, a resident of the West Kingston neighborhood in Jamaica, one of the country's most impoverished sections, grew up under the watch of his father, Lester, who controlled the Shower Posse gang, called by the Federal Bureau of Investigation (FBI) "the most violent and notorious criminal organization ever in America." The Shower Posse is said to have murdered more than one thousand people in the United States and Jamaica during the cocaine wars that broke out in the 1980s. Lester Coke was deported from the United States in 1987 after allegedly setting up American Shower Posse gangs. The United States demanded his extradition shortly after his return to Jamaica to face trial. While awaiting transport from Jamaica to the United States in 1992, Lester was killed in a mysterious fire that broke out in his jail cell.

Shortly after his father's extradition order, Coke, who owns a consulting company that receives millions of dollars in government contracts, took over as leader of the Shower Posse. From this position, Coke built a large drug trafficking and arms smuggling ring, which focuses its sales in New York. The money Coke makes from the sale of cocaine and weapons is used to buy additional weapons in Jamaica, which Coke uses to protect himself and his neighborhood. To get the cocaine into the United States, Coke uses those who rely most on him—the poor women of West Kingston. Coke has recruited women from his neighborhood, and around Jamaica, to smuggle drugs into the United States on commercial flights.

The United States' two extradition orders were not the first attempts at ending the reign of Coke and the Shower Posse; however, attempts by Jamaican authorities have been limited. In 2001, Jamaican police went to Tivoli Gardens to search for and round up Coke's weapons, only to be met by sniper fire that left twenty-six people dead after three days of fighting.

2010 EXTRADITION ORDER

The 2010 extradition order stemmed from conspiracy charges filed against Coke in the Southern District of New York. According to the U.S. Drug Enforcement Administration (DEA): "Since the early 1990s, Coke has led an international criminal organization known as the 'Shower Posse,' with members in Jamaica, the United States, and other countries. At Coke's direction and under his protection, members of his criminal organization sold marijuana and crack cocaine in the New York area and elsewhere, and sent the narcotics proceeds back to Coke and his co-conspirators. Coke and his co-conspirators also armed their organization with illegally trafficked firearms. Coke has been named by the U.S. Department of Justice to the list of Consolidated Priority Organization Targets. . . . The CPOT list includes the world's most dangerous narcotics kingpins." The DEA said Coke would be "charged with conspiracy to distribute cocaine and marijuana and conspiracy to illegally traffic in firearms." When Golding announced the reversal of his earlier standing on Coke's extradition, which he claimed rested on additional information received on U.S. claims made against Coke Jamaican residents responded in defiance and Coke barricaded himself inside his West Kingston neighborhood. In addition to agreeing to the extradition, Golding also admitted that he knew his Labour Party had hired a U.S. law firm to lobby, although unsuccessfully, the Barack Obama administration against extradition, a claim he had previously denied. This expression of knowledge led Jamaican political leaders to call for Golding's resignation, halfway through his five-year term in office.

When Coke barricaded himself, Jamaican police and soldiers stormed the area in West Kingston known as Tivoli Gardens. Citizens caught up in the fighting that went on for days were killed and wounded. Because of indications from residents that the police and soldiers sent to protect the area had abused citizens, a team including public defenders and the Jamaican Red Cross were sent to investigate. Golding promised to look into all deaths caused by police and soldiers, a claim many did not take seriously given the poor reputation of the Jamaican security forces and court system. "The government deeply regrets the loss of lives, especially those of members of the security services and innocent, law-abiding citizens caught in the crossfire," Golding told members of the nation's parliament. "The security forces were directed to take all practical steps to avoid casualties as much as possible."

The security forces had little success in trying to calm the violence, as gangs from across the Caribbean came to join the fight and protect Coke. In an indication of how dependent the citizens of Jamaica are on the dons, the barricaded section of West Kingston featured signs reading "Jesus died for us. We will die for Dudus," the gang leader's nickname.

In response to the fighting, the United States and many other nations issued travel warnings and informed tourists and expatriates in Jamaica that any nonemergency services would be suspended until further notice. Jamaica's government declared a state of emergency, closed businesses, and sent schoolchildren home. In his declaration, Golding said the state of emergency would "enable the security forces to exercise extraordinary powers necessary to deal with this extraordinary situation." The powers given to security forces under the state of emergency included the ability to restrict where citizens could travel to and freedom to search homes and detain anyone suspected to be involved with Coke without needing to secure a warrant first. Golding called these "necessary measures to restore order to a community that is now threatened."

Golding took a hard-line stance on the violence and vowed that the security forces would fight to the end to ensure that the gang stronghold on Jamaica might finally end. "This will be a turning point for us as a nation," said Golding in a public address, "to confront the powers of evil that have penalized the society and earned us the unenviable label as one of the murder capitals of the world." It was unclear, however, whether Golding sought to simply end the violence or if he also wanted to end the influence gangs hold over politicians. "My government is determined that Jamaica must be a land of peace, order and security; without this we will never achieve the happiness and prosperity that we seek," Golding said.

On June 22, 2010, Coke was arrested at a roadblock while attempting to surrender himself at the U.S. Embassy in Jamaica. Out of fear that Coke's followers would begin a second armed uprising upon his arrest and extradition, Jamaican police commissioner Owen Ellington called for calm. "I would like to appeal to the families, friends and sympathizers of Christopher Coke to remain calm." As a precaution, curfews were declared in Kingston. To calm fears of Coke's supporters that he would be mistreated by police, Ellington told the community that security forces were "taking every step possible to ensure his safety and wellbeing while he is in our custody." Seventy-six citizens and members of the security forces were killed in the violence leading up to Coke's capture.

Coke waived his right to an extradition trial and was instead flown within hours to the United States to await trial in New York. In a prepared statement, Coke said, "I take this decision for I now believe it to be in the best interest of my family, the community of western Kingston and in particular the people of Tivoli Gardens and above all Jamaica." He told the Jamaican court that he believed the United States would free him in little time and allow him to return to the Caribbean. Upon arrival in the United States, Coke pled not guilty to charges of arms and drug trafficking.

—Heather Kerrigan

The following are two statements issued by the Office of the President of Jamaica on May 23, 2010, declaring a state of emergency; a press release from the governor general of Jamaica on May 25, 2010, on the regulations to be followed during the state of emergency; and a statement by the U.S. Drug Enforcement Agency upon Christopher "Dudus" Coke's extradition to the United States on June 25, 2010.

Jamaican Government Declares a State of Emergency

May 23, 2010

A state of public emergency, limited to the parishes of Kingston and St. Andrew, has been declared and will come into effect at 6.00 P.M. today.

In a statement issued this afternoon, Prime Minister Bruce Golding said that based on an update and advice from the security forces, he summoned an emergency meeting of the Cabinet at 2.00 P.M today to consider the advice.

The Cabinet took the decision to advise the Governor-General to issue a Proclamation pursuant to Section 26 of the Constitution declaring that a state of public emergency exists in the parishes of Kingston and St. Andrew.

The Proclamation shall remain in force for a period of one month unless extended by the House of Representatives or revoked earlier.

SOURCE: Jamaican Information Service. Office of the Prime Minister. "State of Emergency Declared in Kingston and St. Andrew with Effect from 6:00 pm Today, May 23, 2010." May 23, 2010. http://www.jis .gov.jm/news/117/24049?mode=redirect.

Prime Minister's Statement on the Situation in Kingston

May 23, 2010

This afternoon, the Cabinet, in emergency session, took the decision to advise the Governor-General to issue a proclamation declaring a state of public emergency for the Corporate Area effective 6.00 PM today. This decision was based on information and advice provided by the security forces that actions were being taken which pose significant threats to law and order in the Corporate Area.

Since this morning, violent, orchestrated attacks have been launched on a number of police stations. Two members of the security forces have been shot and injured.

What is taking place is a calculated assault on the authority of the State that cannot be tolerated, and will not be allowed to continue.

The state of emergency will enable the security forces to exercise extraordinary powers necessary to deal with this extraordinary situation. These include the power to restrict the freedom of movement, search premises and detain persons suspected of involvement in unlawful activities without warrant. These are necessary measures to restore order to a community that is now threatened.

The security forces will be moving swiftly to bring the current situation under control. Criminal elements bent on violence and mayhem will be detained, and processed. The criminal element who have placed the society under siege will not be allowed to triumph.

The security forces have been instructed to observe and respect the rights of citizens to go about their lawful business. The city is not being shut down. People are assured that they are free to move about and go to work as usual. Schools will be in full session on Tuesday.

There will be some inconvenience as the security forces intensify their surveillance and efforts to ferret out the criminals and return the Corporate Area to a state of calm.

But let us make no mistake. The threats that have emerged to the safety and security of our people will be repelled with strong and decisive action.

The state of emergency will remain in effect for a period of one month unless the security forces advise that it should be revoked or unless it is extended by the House of Representatives.

This will be a turning point for us as a nation to confront the powers of evil that have penalized the society and earned us the unenviable label as one of the murder capitals of the world. We must confront this criminal element with determination and unqualified resolve.

Tonight, I appeal to all law-abiding citizens to remain calm and support these necessary measures. My government is determined that Jamaica must be a land of peace, order and security, without this we will never achieve the happiness and prosperity that we seek.

Good night and God bless you:

SOURCE: Jamaican Information Service. Office of the Prime Minister. "Address to the Nation on the State of Emergency by PM Golding, May 23, 2010." May 23, 2010. http://www.jis.gov.jm/news/opm-news/24052-officePM-address-to-the-nation-on-the-state-of-emergency-by-pm-golding-may-23.

State of Emergency Regulations Released

May 25, 2010

Governor General His Excellency the Most Honourable Sir Patrick Allen has signed off on the regulations that will govern the current period of public emergency that was declared Sunday May 23. The Jamaican Constitution requires that once a state of emergency is imposed, regulations be published detailing the powers of the authorities and the restrictions that apply to citizens.

The regulations speak of a Competent Authority and identify that authority as the Governor General, the Minister of National Security, the Chief of Staff of the Jamaica Defence Force, the Commissioner of Police, the Deputy Commissioner of Police, or the Senior Office of Police in the parish of Kingston and St. Andrew.

During the period of public emergency, which is scheduled to last for at least another 28 days and is limited to the corporate area, the regulations give the Competent Authority the power to do the following:

- Prevent persons from remaining in, preventing or blocking access to any structure or building.
- Prevent persons from blocking, obstructing or interfering with any road or path.
- Erect barriers, block access or divert any road or cordon any area, place or premises to prohibit or otherwise regulate access to such places. Where this power is exercised the Competent Authority should give notice to the public by the most effective methods. In certain instances the orders will have to be published in the gazette—the body of laws signed by the Governor General. In other cases, the Competent Authority may use its discretion to decide how to publish public notices, whether through posters, loudspeaker notification, flyers, banners etc.
- Establish cordons and curfews and require persons to stay indoors and not to leave without the required permit. Under the regulations persons who enter or leave an area where a curfew is in place without written or oral permission, are guilty of an offence and can be placed before the court for punishment.
- Direct persons in charge of vehicles to move them to some other point in a 10 mile radius.
- Search premises or vehicles where persons are suspected or are likely to endanger public safety.
- Stop and search vehicles if it's suspected that they are being used in a manner prejudicial to public safety.
- Have right of access to do work on land which is required for the perseveration of peace or regulating the supply and distribution of water, fuel, electricity transportation and other necessities (the statutory purpose).
- Take over on the order of the Governor General any premises or facility which provides essential services defined in the Regulations.
- Prevent trespass to public premises.
- Prevent trespass to premises of essential services.

- Protect public roads. This may include the setting up of road blocks and cordons which should be communicated to the public via notices in newspapers or though the electronic media. Once these road blocks or cordons are in place, persons will have to get permission to enter or leave the areas in question.
- Requisition essential services, by taking possession of premises apart from cash and securities after notice is given.
- Demand that persons furnish or produce to the Competent Authority articles or information in possession of persons who are deemed to have information or articles in their possession.
- Restrict publication of undesirable material which may be prejudicial to the public interest or which may incite persons to commit a breach of the peace.
- Prohibit assemblies of persons.
- Prohibit the carrying of a firearm or other lethal weapon.
- Prohibit the use of firearms and ammunition conditionally or unconditionally.
- Restrict access to certain areas for persons who are suspected of acting prejudicial to public safety.
- Prohibit the wearing of uniforms and emblems except for those engaged in lawful industrial action.
- Question persons and demand answers.
- Arrest and detain persons whose behavior gives reasonable grounds for suspecting that he/she is acting in a manner prejudicial to public safety, or has committed an offence against the Regulations. Such persons are to be detained up to a period not exceeding 24 hours. However, the Competent Authority has the power to extend that detention period by a further 5 days on the authority of a Resident Magistrate or a police officer not below the rank of Deputy Superintendent.
- Search persons and seize any article which is suspected or intended to be used in a manner prejudicial to public order and/or public safety.
- Confine persons to residences on the authority of the Minister to prevent such persons from acting in a manner prejudicial to public safety.
- Control places of public resort and entertainment which are specified in an order.
- Restrict the granting of bail for persons who contravene or fail to comply with provisions of the Regulations, and where it is believed that such persons would be likely to commit a similar offence against the Regulations.
- Deal with compensation for the use of property and equipment during the period of state of emergency.

Additionally, the Minister of National Security has the power to issue detention orders to exercise control over persons conditionally or unconditionally. Under the Constitution, a three-member Review Tribunal is to be established to examine cases of persons who have been detained by order of the Minister, or those who are the subject of restricted access. The Chief Justice is to appoint the Chairman of the Tribunal and the two other members appointed by the Governor General.

Source: Jamaican Information Service. Office of the Governor General. "Regulations Governing the Period of Public Emergency." May 25, 2010. http://www.jis.gov.jm/news/123/24063?mode=redirect.

DEA Announces Coke's Extradition to the United States on Drug and Arms Trafficking Charges

June 25, 2010

Special Agent in Charge of the U.S. Drug Enforcement Administration (DEA) John P. Gilbride, PREET BHARARA, the United States Attorney for the Southern District of New York, and Special Agent in Charge of DEA's Caribbean Division JAVIER F. PEÑA, announced that CHRISTOPHER MICHAEL COKE, a/k/a "Michael Christopher Coke," a/k/a "Paul Christopher Scott," a/k/a "Presi," a/k/a "General," a/k/a "President," a/k/a "Duddus," a/k/a "Shortman," arrived last night, June 24, 2010 in the Southern District of New York to face charges of conspiracy to distribute marijuana and cocaine and conspiracy to illegally traffic in firearms. COKE was arrested by Jamaican authorities on June 22, 2010, near Kingston, Jamaica, after a five-week pursuit by local authorities. COKE waived his right to judicial extradition proceedings in Jamaica and subsequently was transferred to the custody of the DEA and U.S. Marshals Service for transport to the United States. COKE is expected to be arraigned in Manhattan federal court today, June 25, 2010.

According to the Superseding Indictment filed in Manhattan federal court:

Since the early 1990s, COKE has led an international criminal organization known as the "Shower Posse," with members in Jamaica, the United States, and other countries. At COKE's direction and under his protection, members of his criminal organization sold marijuana and crack cocaine in the New York area and elsewhere, and sent the narcotics proceeds back to COKE and his co-conspirators. COKE and his co-conspirators also armed their organization with illegally trafficked firearms. COKE has been named by the U.S. Department of Justice to the list of Consolidated Priority Organization Targets ("CPOTs"). The CPOT list includes the world's most dangerous narcotics kingpins.

COKE, 40, is charged with conspiracy to distribute cocaine and marijuana and conspiracy to illegally traffic in firearms. If convicted on the narcotics charge, he faces a maximum sentence of life in prison and a mandatory minimum sentence of 10 years in prison, as well as a fine of up to $4 million or twice the pecuniary gain from the offense. He also faces a maximum sentence of five years in prison on the firearms trafficking charge, and a fine of up to $250,000 or twice the pecuniary gain. This case has been assigned to U.S. District Judge ROBERT P. PATTERSON.

Mr. BHARARA praised the investigative work of the DEA's New York Field Division and Caribbean Division's Jamaica Country Office. Mr. BHARARA also thanked the U.S. Department of Justice Office of International Affairs for their significant assistance in this case, as well as the U.S. Embassy in Kingston and the Office of the Legal Adviser at the Department of State.

DEA New York Special Agent-in-Charge JOHN P. GILBRIDE stated: "The arrest of Christopher Michael Coke takes one of the world's most dangerous narcotics kingpins off the streets. The case against Coke, built over the last three years, is a direct result of DEA New York Field Division's collaboration with its law enforcement partners, both domestically and internationally. This partnership is a testament to our unwavering dedication to clean up our communities and track down drug traffickers, wherever they hide. This arrest and extradition to face charges are the next steps in ensuring Coke and his 'Shower Posse' drug organization are brought to justice. I'd also like to commend the United States Attorney's Office for the Southern District of New York, the Jamaican authorities and DEA Caribbean Division's Kingston, Jamaica Country Office for their diligent work on this case."

U.S. Attorney PREET BHARARA stated: "As charged in the indictment pending against Coke in Manhattan federal court, drugs and guns were the bread and butter of Coke's 'Shower Posse.' We are relieved that Coke's arrest and transfer to New York was not marked by the violence that had gripped the streets of Jamaica for so many days. We look forward to presenting our case to a jury in a Manhattan courtroom and bringing Coke to justice."

Assistant United States Attorneys JOCELYN STRAUBER and JOHN ZACH are in charge of the prosecution, which is being handled by the Office's International Narcotics Trafficking Unit.

The charges contained in the Indictment are merely accusations and the defendant is presumed innocent unless and until proven guilty.

SOURCE: United States Drug Enforcement Administration. "Christopher Michael Coke Arrives in United States to Face Narcotics and Firearms Trafficking Charges in Manhattan Federal Court." June 25, 2010. http://www.justice.gov/dea/pubs/states/newsrel/2010/nyc062510.html.

U.S. Secretary of State Tours Asia

MAY 25, 2010

Hillary Rodham Clinton travelled to Asia in May 2010 for a week of diplomatic exchanges. It was her fifth visit to the continent since assuming the position of secretary of state in early 2009. Her itinerary took her to Tokyo, Shanghai, Beijing, and Seoul. The central event of this visit was the second U.S.-China Strategic and Economic Dialogue, a senior-level bilateral forum encompassing a range of issues concerning the two powers, from trade and monetary policy to climate change and cultural exchange. In her meetings with political leaders and the press, a good deal of attention was devoted to the March 26 sinking of a South Korean navy vessel in the Yellow Sea. An international investigation coordinated by the government of South Korea concluded that the ship was attacked by a torpedo fired from a North Korean submarine, killing forty-six sailors. This report was issued May 20, the day Secretary Clinton departed for Asia.

Japan: Problems with Regional Security

Clinton landed first in the Japanese capital for a brief but consequential stopover, meeting with Prime Minister Yukio Hatoyama and Foreign Minister Katsuya Okada. Both were members of the Democratic Party of Japan (DPJ), the center-left party that came to power after defeating Japan's dominant Liberal Democratic Party (LDP) in the August 2009 general election. Hatoyama's foreign policy centered on deemphasizing Japan's security alliance with the United States. He had terminated the agreement to allow American jets on their way to Afghanistan to refuel in Japan and asserted Japan's equality in relations with the United States. The sinking of the South Korean corvette *Cheonan*, however, served as a reminder of the value of the alliance with the Americans.

A pressing issue between the governments was the status of the American air base at Futenma on the island of Okinawa. More than half of the forty-seven thousand U.S. troops stationed in Japan were based on the island, located roughly halfway between Japan's southern tip and Taiwan. Their presence had long angered many Okinawans and sparked numerous protests over the years. In 2006, the LDP-led government had agreed to relocate the Futenma base to a less populated part of the island. In his 2009 campaign, however, Hatoyama promised to move the base off the island entirely. After his inauguration, the American and Japanese governments formed a high-level working group to decide on a new location for the base by the end of May 2010, but with the deadline approaching, the committee had yet to find a mutually suitable site off the island.

In their joint press conference on May 21, Clinton and Okada reaffirmed their intent to select a relocation site by the end of the month. "We both seek an arrangement that is operationally viable and politically sustainable," said Clinton. The two top diplomats also addressed the Korean situation. The expert report, which had been published the previous day, cited physical evidence of North Korean–made torpedo fragments found in the ocean near where the *Cheonan* was found. Clinton called the evidence "overwhelming and condemning" and added, "We cannot allow this attack on South Korea to go unanswered by the international community." Okada said, "We need to be aware this could happen to us," underlining the importance of the U.S. presence for security in the Northeast Asian region. North Korean spokespeople claimed the country had not carried out an attack and warned that any attempt at military retaliation would lead to war.

China: Tending to Issues and Relations

Secretary Clinton departed Tokyo for a four-day stop in China, to tend to one of the most complicated and integral diplomatic relationships in the geopolitical landscape. Two of the world's largest economies conducted more than $300 billion in bilateral trade annually, and the United States was the top destination for Chinese exports. The People's Republic was the largest foreign holder of U.S. government debt, a status that gave China considerable leverage in the financial dealings between the two nations. In addition, China and the United States led the globe in greenhouse gas emissions, accounting together for more than 40 percent of carbon dioxide released annually, according to the United Nations. The two states worked together in the United Nations (UN) Security Council and other diplomatic forums to address security challenges, such as the potential nuclear threats from North Korea and Iran.

U.S.-Chinese relations appeared to be in a downturn in early 2010. Beijing complained strongly when Washington announced a $6.4 billion weapons sale to the government of Taiwan in late January. Several weeks later, on February 18, President Barack Obama provoked another diplomatic flare-up by meeting with the Dalai Lama, the exiled Tibetan spiritual leader, in the White House. After both incidents, authorities in Beijing summoned the U.S. ambassador to China, Jon Huntsman, to express their displeasure. These episodes compounded more perennial sources of conflict between the two nations, such as trade barriers, digital piracy, human rights violations, and charges that China kept its currency undervalued through manipulation in order to benefit its export industries.

Part of Clinton's agenda in China, therefore, was to smooth over some of these rough patches in relations. Toward that end, her first stop was in Shanghai to visit the World Expo 2010. China was the first developing country ever to host a major World Expo, in the tradition of past world's fairs. More than 190 governments participated, and the organizers expected seventy million visitors over the course of six months. After visiting the U.S. and Chinese pavilions, Clinton spoke of the value of "people-to-people relations" as a source of international peace, a recurrent theme in her public diplomacy.

Clinton then headed for Beijing to take part in the two-day U.S.-China Strategic and Economic Dialogue. She and Treasury secretary Timothy Geithner headed a U.S. delegation consisting of over two hundred officials. Other prominent administration figures attending included Health and Human Services secretary Kathleen Sebelius, Federal Reserve chairman Ben Bernanke, Council of Economic Advisers chair Christina Romer, and Admiral Robert F. Willard, head of the U.S. Pacific Command. Vice Premier Wang Qishan and State Councilor Dai Bingguo headed the Chinese delegation. President Hu Jintao addressed the gathering at its opening session in the Great Hall of the People.

The dialogue, an annual event initiated in 2009 by Presidents Hu and Obama, is intended as a mechanism to overcome communication barriers and promote cooperation across the range of issues affecting the interests of the two powers. The strategic track included frank discussions of regional and global security issues, most prominently the international responses to North Korea's alleged provocation and Iran's nuclear ambitions. China, North Korea's sole diplomatic ally and major aid provider, had been all but mum on the subject of the *Cheonan* incident, calling it "unfortunate" but urging caution. The Americans stated that they would support South Korea's efforts to obtain a punitive UN Security Council resolution and tried to persuade the Chinese to join or at least not block this move. Earlier in May, China had agreed to support a fourth round of UN sanctions against Iran, on the condition that the measure not unduly hinder daily life in the Islamic Republic.

On the economic side, U.S. officials entered the dialogue seeking a more flexible, market-based exchange rate for the Chinese currency, the yuan. President Hu, in his opening speech, addressed his interlocutors' interest by referring to his commitment to reforming exchange rates, but the reforms he mentioned were not expected to make more than a modest impact. The Americans were also concerned about ensuring access to the Chinese market for their exports, in light of the Chinese industrial policy of "indigenous innovation," favoring companies whose intellectual property is created within China. The Chinese, for their part, displayed clear concerns about the rising U.S. national debt and deficit—in light of the sovereign debt crisis affecting European states such as Greece— and U.S. restrictions on exports of dual-use technologies (that is, civilian technologies deemed to have military applications). Both camps paid lip service to the idea of balanced economic growth, to be achieved by promoting Chinese domestic consumption while shoring up the economic recovery among U.S. households.

The two-day summit, Secretary Clinton said at its close, reflected the growing maturity in Sino-American relations. After the problems encountered earlier in the year, she said, "This dialogue mechanism, and the habits of cooperation it has helped create, along with the confidence it has built, helped put us rapidly back on a positive track."

SOUTH KOREA: DEEP CONCERN

Clinton spent a few hours in Seoul on May 26 before returning to the United States. She discussed the *Cheonan* incident with President Lee Myung-bak and held a press conference with Foreign Minister Yu Myung-hwan. She told reporters she greatly admired the calm and restraint with which the South Korean government had responded to the event and that "the international community has a responsibility and a duty to respond" forcefully. Having thoroughly discussed the *Cheonan* incident with Chinese leaders, Clinton expressed guarded optimism about the possibility that China could sign on to an international condemnation or censure of North Korea's behavior. She also used the occasion to suggest that "there's a different path for North Korea. And we believe it's in everyone's interest, including China, to make a persuasive case for North Korea to change direction."

On May 24, while Clinton was in China, Prime Minister Hatoyama of Japan admitted that he had been unable to persuade the United States to remove the Futenma airbase from Okinawa island and that he would abide by the agreement reached by his predecessors in 2006 to move the base across the island and transfer approximately eight thousand U.S. troops to Guam. Hatoyama apologized publicly "for the confusion

I have caused the people of Okinawa." Days later, the left-leaning Social Democratic Party withdrew from the ruling coalition, and on June 2, Hatoyama announced his resignation from the prime minister's post and the party leadership. Naoto Kan, also of the DPJ, was named the new prime minister on June 4 and formally appointed by Emperor Akihito on June 8.

On July 9 in New York, the UN Security Council unanimously approved a statement from its president deploring the attack on the *Cheonan*. The document, of lesser stature than a resolution, "calls for full adherence to the Korean Armistice Agreement and encourages the settlement of outstanding issues on the Korean peninsula by peaceful means." China, a veto-holding member of the Security Council, ensured that the statement neither censured the North Koreans nor directly attributed the attack to them. Thus, the council merely acknowledged with "deep concern" the international investigative report and its conclusion that North Korea perpetrated the attack, while concurrently taking note of North Korea's statement denying responsibility. Secretary Clinton welcomed the statement as an indication of "the unity of the international community."

—Roger K. Smith

Following is a statement by Secretary of State Hillary Rodham Clinton on May 25, 2010, on the economic relationship between the United States and China; and a joint statement by U.S. treasury secretary Timothy Geithner, Clinton, and Chinese vice premier Wang Qishan on May 25, 2010, at the close of discussions on the U.S.-China economic relationship.

Secretary of State Clinton Remarks on the U.S.-China Economic Dialogue

DOCUMENT

May 25, 2010

Thank you very much. On behalf of all of the American delegation, I want to thank our generous hosts, Vice-Premier Wang and State Councilor Dai, for their excellent preparation and the extraordinary time that has been given to this dialogue, along with the Chinese team and the American team. This dialogue is the premier forum for one of the most important and complex relationships in the world. And the breadth and depth of our delegation continues to grow, because it reflects the agenda that we are working on together.

Earlier this year, our relationship faced uncertainty, and many questioned the direction we were heading. Now, in an earlier era, we might have experienced a lasting setback. But this dialogue mechanism, and the habits of cooperation it has helped create, along with the confidence it has built, helped put us rapidly back on a positive track. This strategic and economic dialogue (inaudible), and it reflects the maturity, durability, and strength of our relationship. So, over the last days we discussed a wide range of the most complex bilateral, regional, and global challenges.

Now, as we have said many times, we do not agree on every issue. We don't agree even sometimes on the perception of the issue. But that is partly what this dialogue is about.

It is a place where we can discuss everything, as State Councilor Dai said, from Taiwan to universal human rights. And in the course of doing so, we are developing that positive, cooperative, and comprehensive understanding that leads to the relationship for the 21st century that both President Obama and President Hu Jintao put into motion when they agreed to do this dialogue.

The success of the U.S.-China relationship will ultimately be measured by the results we deliver to our people. Do our dialogues and our collaborations produce changes that people see in their daily lives, and that contribute to global progress or not? That is both our challenge and our responsibility.

So, this round of the dialogue did not solve all of our shared problems, but it did produce a number of concrete results, some of which you saw as Chinese and American officials came forward to sign memoranda of understanding.

One in particular is in our efforts to meet the challenges of climate change and clean energy. We signed an agreement that, for the first time, will allow American experts to work closely with Chinese colleagues to begin exploring China's vast natural gas potential. We believe that could well lead to new economic opportunities in both countries, and a lower carbon emission load for our planet. This is part of the broader drive for energy security and greater market transparency and efficiency, closer cooperation, and more focus on cleaner energy (inaudible).

Earlier today I was pleased to sign with State Councilor Liu (inaudible) U.S.-China consultation on people-to-people exchange. President Obama has announced a goal of sending 100,000 American students to China in the next 4 years to learn Mandarin, to experience Chinese culture, and to learn about the hospitality of the Chinese people, while they serve as ambassadors for the United States in China. And toward this end, I want to thank State Councilor Liu for her announcement of 10,000 scholarships for American students.

Our U.S.-China relationship must extend beyond the halls of government to our homes, our businesses, and our schools. And these exchanges really offer the opportunity for people to connect and collaborate, and they remind us of how much we have in common.

As part of this dialogue, we also had our most serious high-level discussion to date on development, which is a core pillar of our foreign policy, along with diplomacy and defense. And we had very frank and detailed conversations about international security challenges and regional hot spots, including Iran and North Korea. We stressed the importance of reaching a conclusion on resolution of the United Nations Security Council to send a message to Iran to, "Live up to your international responsibilities or face growing isolation and consequences."

Similarly, with respect to North Korea, the United States and China share the objective of peace and stability on the Korean Peninsula. Last year, we worked to pass and enforce a strong UN Security Council resolution in the wake of North Korea's nuclear test. Now we must work together again to address the serious challenge provoked by the sinking of the South Korean ship.

We are looking forward to working with our friends in South Korea. We appreciated the very statesmanlike approach that President Lee is following, and the prudent measures that he announced in his speech. No one is more concerned about the peace and stability in this region than the Chinese. We know this is a shared responsibility. And in the days ahead, we will work with the international community and our Chinese colleagues to fashion an effective and appropriate response. The consultations between China and the

United States have started here in Beijing. They continue very closely, and we expect to be working together to resolve this matter.

China and the United States are two great nations with a compelling interest in global stability and security. We have different histories, and are at different stages in our development. But we recognize that we share a responsibility for meeting the challenges of our time, from combating climate change to curbing nuclear proliferation and rebalancing the global economy. This dialogue is a mechanism to exercise that collective leadership and meet our collective responsibilities.

So, there is much that we have worked on and that we are accomplishing that can only happen when people come together and meet as we have. Yesterday, President Hu Jintao said in his opening remarks, "Not even the most sophisticated telecommunication technology can replace face-to-face exchanges." Well, he is absolutely right. So I am very pleased that we had face-to-face exchanges, and we developed greater understanding and deepened our relationship. And we look forward to hosting you, Vice Premier Wang and State Councilor Dai, next year in Washington for the third round of the strategic and economic dialogue.

SOURCE: U.S. Department of State. "Remarks at the Closing of the U.S.-China Strategic and Economic Dialogue." May 25, 2010. http://www.state.gov/secretary/rm/2010/05/142187.htm.

Secretary of State Clinton, Treasury Secretary Geithner, and Chinese Vice Premier Wang on Economic Relations

May 25, 2010

VICE-PREMIER WANG: (Via translator) Friends from the press, under the guidance of President Hu Jintao and President Obama, with the considered (inaudible) of both sides, the second round of China-U.S. S&ED have achieved complete success. This round fully illustrates the nature as being overriding, strategic, and long-term, and the principle of not replacing, not repeating, and not weakening exist dialogue mechanism between the related sectors of China and the United States. It has been candid, pragmatic, and successful.

China and the United States are respectively the largest developing country and developed country in the world. Our economic relationships (inaudible) and has had a global impact. Under the current extremely complicated circumstances, the two sides have had in-depth discussions, and expanded common ground on issues to each other's concerns, (inaudible) world economic situation, transform economic growth pattern, strengthen economic and financial cooperation, and reforming global economic governance (inaudible). Discussions, as such, are of a great importance to (inaudible) the upturn in our two economies and promoting strong, sustainable, and balanced growth of the world economy.

In fact, our two sides sitting together, having in-depth communications, candid exchanges, and rational discussions on our common interests and differences existing between us, this in itself is the most significant outcome of this round. As our economic relationship gets increasingly close, we are now able to take into full consideration our differences in history, culture, national conditions, development stage, economic structure, and market sophistication. We are now able to manage our differences and problems arising in the course of growing economic relationship with a more rational and mature manner. While upholding to our respective principles, we have better understood our positions, built a consensus (inaudible) cooperation, and achieved win-win.

Friends from press, I hope, through you, to make known to the world our firm confidence in working together to address challenges and promote the positive, cooperative, and comprehensive China-U.S. relationship (inaudible). Thank you. . . .

[State Councilor Dai's comments have been excerpted.]

SECRETARY CLINTON: . . . Earlier this year, our relationship faced uncertainty, and many questioned the direction we were heading. Now, in an earlier era, we might have experienced a lasting set-back. But this dialogue mechanism, and the habits of cooperation it has helped create, along with the confidence it has built, helped put us rapidly back on a positive track. This strategic and economic dialogue (inaudible), and it reflects the maturity, durability, and strength of our relationship. So, over the last days we discussed a wide range of the most complex bilateral, regional, and global challenges.

Now, as we have said many times, we do not agree on every issue. We don't agree even sometimes on the perception of the issue. But that is partly what this dialogue is about. It is a place where we can discuss everything, as State Councilor Dai said, from Taiwan to universal human rights. And in the course of doing so, we are developing that positive, cooperative, and comprehensive understanding that leads to the relationship for the 21st century that both President Obama and President Hu Jintao put into motion when they agreed to do this dialogue.

The success of the U.S.-China relationship will ultimately be measured by the results we deliver to our people. Do our dialogues and our collaborations produce changes that people see in their daily lives, and that contribute to global progress or not? That is both our challenge and our responsibility.

So, this round of the dialogue did not solve all of our shared problems, but it did produce a number of concrete results, some of which you saw as Chinese and American officials came forward to sign memoranda of understanding.

One in particular is in our efforts to meet the challenges of climate change and clean energy. We signed an agreement that, for the first time, will allow American experts to work closely with Chinese colleagues to begin exploring China's vast natural gas potential. We believe that could well lead to new economic opportunities in both countries, and a lower carbon emission load for our planet. This is part of the broader drive for energy security and greater market transparency and efficiency, closer cooperation, and more focus on cleaner energy (inaudible).

Earlier today I was pleased to sign with State Councilor Liu (inaudible) U.S.-China consultation on people-to-people exchange. President Obama has announced a goal of sending 100,000 American students to China in the next 4 years to learn Mandarin, to experience Chinese culture, and to learn about the hospitality of the Chinese people, while they serve as ambassadors for the United States in China. And toward this end, I want to thank State Councilor Liu for her announcement of 10,000 scholarships for American students.

Our U.S.-China relationship must extend beyond the halls of government to our homes, our businesses, and our schools. And these exchanges really offer the opportunity for people to connect and collaborate, and they remind us of how much we have in common.

As part of this dialogue, we also had our most serious high-level discussion to date on development, which is a core pillar of our foreign policy, along with diplomacy and defense. And we had very frank and detailed conversations about international security challenges and regional hot spots, including Iran and North Korea. We stressed the importance of reaching a conclusion on resolution of the United Nations Security Council to send a message to Iran to, "Live up to your international responsibilities or face growing isolation and consequences."

Similarly, with respect to North Korea, the United States and China share the objective of peace and stability on the Korean Peninsula. Last year, we worked to pass and enforce a strong UN Security Council resolution in the wake of North Korea's nuclear test. Now we must work together again to address the serious challenge provoked by the sinking of the South Korean ship.

We are looking forward to working with our friends in South Korea. We appreciated the very statesmanlike approach that President Lee is following, and the prudent measures that he announced in his speech. No one is more concerned about the peace and stability in this region than the Chinese. We know this is a shared responsibility. And in the days ahead, we will work with the international community and our Chinese colleagues to fashion an effective and appropriate response. The consultations between China and the United States have started here in Beijing. They continue very closely, and we expect to be working together to resolve this matter.

China and the United States are two great nations with a compelling interest in global stability and security. We have different histories, and are at different stages in our development. But we recognize that we share a responsibility for meeting the challenges of our time, from combating climate change to curbing nuclear proliferation and rebalancing the global economy. This dialogue is a mechanism to exercise that collective leadership and meet our collective responsibilities. . . .

SECRETARY GEITHNER: (Inaudible) offer my appreciation to Vice-Premier Wang and State Councilor Dai. (Inaudible.) I want to thank all of those who joined us from the administration here today, and to say what a pleasure (inaudible) together in China. (Inaudible.)

Our economic relationship is strong and will get stronger. It rests on recognition by Presidents Hu and Obama (inaudible) and shared responsibilities. Over the past year, we have acted together to help restore financial stability and economic growth to a (inaudible). And because we stood together, and because our presidents (inaudible) act quickly and decisively, (inaudible) in a much stronger condition (inaudible) to successfully overcome the challenges still ahead.

When people write the history of this economic crisis, they will point to the decisive role played by international cooperation, in stark contrast with much of the pattern in past crises, where division (inaudible) and nations turn (inaudible). And in writing that story, the story will point to the critical role played by the United States and China, and the remarkable story of two nations, with such different traditions and such different stages of development, coming together with common objectives (inaudible) action.

Last July, when we met in Washington, China and the United States (inaudible) economic growth. The G20 embraced that cause, and recognized it as a global (inaudible).

And since that time, China and the United States (inaudible). Americans are (inaudible) investing more, and borrowing less from the rest of the world, and China is consuming and importing more.

We work together, China the United States, (inaudible) substantial increase in financial resources for emerging markets and developing economies through the IMF and the multilateral development banks, and to restore trade (inaudible). And these commitments, these actions, were essential to arresting the freefall in global economic activity and averting much greater damage to the livelihoods of hundreds and millions of people around the world.

And, quietly but surely, we—China and the United States—are building a very strong network of cooperative arrangements on a range of goals, from boosting access to trade financial facilities for small and medium-sized enterprises, (inaudible), helping each (inaudible).

This second meeting of the strategic and economic dialogue takes place against the backdrop of a promising (inaudible) pave the road to China and the United States and across (inaudible), tempered by a recognition of the challenges faced by countries in Europe in (inaudible), sustainable, and promoting more balanced economic growth.

We agree here to do (inaudible) to strengthen and reinforce this global economic recovery, and we agree to support the strong programs of policy reforms and financial support now being undertaken by the nations of Europe. We welcome the strong commitment of President Hu to the process of economic reform to expand domestic demand and increase household consumption, to expand market access and keep with established international, economic, and trade goals, and to advance trade and investment liberalization.

We welcome the fact that China's leaders have recognized that reform of the exchange rate mechanism is an important part of their broader economic reform agenda. Allowing the exchange rate to reflect market forces is important, not just to give China the flexibility necessary to sustain more balanced economic growth with low inflation, but also to reinforce (inaudible) resources more productive, higher value-added activity (inaudible).

Now, this is, of course, China's choice. And we welcome the progress we have achieved to provide a more level playing field for American firms exporting to China and operating in China. China has taken a series of steps to adjust and modify its programs designed to promote (inaudible) and technological advancement. China has revised certain aspects of this (inaudible), such as the requirement that products be (inaudible) or trademarked in China, eligible for certain (inaudible). China has a firm commitment to abide by the principles of non-discrimination, market competition, open trade, intellectual property rights protection, and leaving the terms of technology transfer and production (inaudible) to agreements between enterprises.

And we have agreed to a process of dialogues in the coming weeks and months, led by my colleague, Ambassador Kirk, Secretary Locke, and Office of Science and Technologies Director, John Holdren to find ways to address our main concerns.

We also welcome (inaudible) procurement by July of 2010, as well as a commitment to reduce barriers (inaudible) high-technology goods, high-end (inaudible), and energy saving products (inaudible) facilitate more (inaudible). With this progress, it does not (inaudible) all our concern, but it gives us a set of (inaudible). And I want to thank Vice-Premier Wang, in particular, for his personal role in advancing the practical solutions to our concerns.

The relationship between our two countries is strong and beneficial to both sides. American exports to China are growing much more rapidly (inaudible). Compared to the first quarter of 2009, (inaudible) by the crisis. Our exports to China have risen by almost 50 percent, roughly double (inaudible). And these developments demonstrate (inaudible) the strength and dynamism of the American economy. It demonstrates the importance and the (inaudible) process (inaudible) in China, (inaudible). It demonstrates that our strengths are complementary. They demonstrate that American companies are leaders in innovation in the goods and services that the world needs to grow.

We are seeing a (inaudible) rise in private investments in the United States, dramatic ongoing (inaudible) supported by a stronger financial system, a carefully designed and very substantial commitment by the U.S. Government to promote investment, innovation, and basic research.

We bring to the dialogue respect for China's interests, and a commitment to close cooperation on all the major global challenges of our time. And we bring a recognition of the special responsibility of the United States to contribute to the stability of the global financial (inaudible).

I want to conclude, again, by expressing my sincere appreciation to President Hu, Premier Wen, Vice-Premier Wang (inaudible), for their commitment to work to strengthen this relationship, and we look forward to continuing progress in the forthcoming G20 meetings. (Inaudible.) Thank you.

SOURCE: U.S. Department of State. "Concluding Joint Statements at the U.S.-China Strategic and Economic Dialogue." May 25, 2010. http://www.state.gov/secretary/rm/2010/05/142207.htm.

OTHER HISTORIC DOCUMENTS OF INTEREST

FROM THIS VOLUME

FROM PREVIOUS *HISTORIC DOCUMENTS*

"Don't Ask, Don't Tell" Repealed

MAY 27, SEPTEMBER 21, AND NOVEMBER 30, 2010

As President Barack Obama began his second year in office, he faced continued pressure from gay rights organizations to fulfill his campaign promises aimed at providing gays and lesbians with more equal treatment, including the repeal of the military's "Don't Ask, Don't Tell" policy. While many members of Congress and key military leaders supported the push to repeal the long-standing policy, Obama faced considerable opposition from other senior military officials and among Republicans in the Senate, reigniting a divisive and highly emotional debate.

OPENING THE MILITARY

"Don't Ask, Don't Tell" first became law in 1993 when President Bill Clinton issued Defense Directive 1304.26. The directive was intended to loosen existing military policy, which, since 1982, had outright banned gays from serving. Under "Don't Ask, Don't Tell," military officials were prohibited from asking soldiers about their sexual orientation, but it also prevented openly gay, lesbian, or bisexual Americans from serving because their presence "would create an unacceptable risk to the high standards of morale, good order and discipline, and unit cohesion that are the essence of military capability." The law also held that any service members who revealed their homosexuality or engaged in homosexual acts could be dismissed.

The policy was instantly controversial and has since remained at the center of an emotionally charged debate as to whether it ought to be repealed and gay and lesbian citizens be allowed to serve openly. In the fifteen years between the law's implementation and the 2008 presidential campaign, lawmakers made several attempts to repeal "Don't Ask, Don't Tell," and interest groups such as the Log Cabin Republicans filed legal challenges in federal court. In 2008, Obama, then a U.S. senator from Illinois, revived the issue by promising during his presidential campaign that if elected he would repeal the ban and invite those discharged under the law, estimated at approximately fourteen thousand soldiers, to return to the military. He also pledged to provide antiharassment training for troops to help them deal with the policy change. When Obama won the presidency, advisers to his transition team stated that the president would delay pursuing repeal until he had an opportunity to confer with the Joint Chiefs of Staff and that a vote on the policy was not likely before 2010. Then on January 27, 2010, during his State of the Union address, Obama announced that he would work with Congress over the course of the year to repeal the ban, igniting a flurry of activity on Capitol Hill and at the Pentagon and prompting gay rights groups to mount a new national lobbying campaign.

MILITARY LEADERS BACK REPEAL

On February 2, 2010, U.S. defense secretary Robert Gates and Admiral Mike Mullen, chairman of the Joint Chiefs of Staff, appeared before the Senate Armed Services Committee at a hearing to discuss defense planning and budgeting for 2011, as well as "Don't Ask, Don't Tell." Admiral Mullen surprised many on the committee when he became the first sitting chairman of the Joint Chiefs of Staff to voice support for the policy's repeal, saying, "No matter how I look at this issue, I cannot escape being troubled by the fact that we have in place a policy which forces young men and women to lie about who they are in order to defend their fellow citizens." Gates also stated his support for repeal, noting that the real question was not if the ban would be lifted but how the Pentagon could best prepare for the change. Both officials said repeal would not occur anytime soon and that the Pentagon would launch a review of the policy and how lifting the ban might impact military readiness. Sen. John McCain, R-Ariz., led the Republican committee members in criticizing the officials, saying he was "deeply disappointed" in Admiral Mullen, and claiming Gates's testimony was biased.

Despite the negative reaction, Gates said that until "Don't Ask, Don't Tell" could be repealed, the military would explore ways in which the policy could be enforced in a "fairer manner." Gates ultimately approved new rules for discharging gay and lesbian soldiers under the law on March 25. The rules put higher-ranking officers in charge of discharge proceedings and imposed tougher requirements for evidence used against soldiers. This was intended to discourage the use of overheard statements, hearsay, or confidential statements made to individuals such as medical professionals and lawyers as evidence, or risk having a soldier's sexual orientation revealed by a "jilted lover."

CONGRESSIONAL ACTION AND INACTION

As the Pentagon began its review of "Don't Ask, Don't Tell," Congress also began taking steps toward the policy's repeal. In the House of Representatives, Rep. Patrick Murphy, D-Penn., introduced an amendment to the annual National Defense Authorization Act that would allow the Department of Defense and military commanders to repeal the ban. Murphy's amendment stipulated that the ban could only be lifted after the Pentagon had completed its review of the repeal's impact and military leaders such as Secretary Gates and Admiral Mullen had certified that it would not be disruptive or hamper military readiness. The repeal would take effect sixty days after this certification. On May 27, the House approved the amendment by a vote of 234–194, mostly along party lines. That same day, the Senate Armed Services Committee approved a similar amendment to the National Defense Authorization Act, sponsored by Sen. Joe Lieberman, I-Conn. In introducing the amendment, Lieberman said, "The 'don't ask, don't tell' policy doesn't serve the best interests of our military and doesn't reflect the best values of our country."

Despite seemingly having the support of many in Congress, the push to repeal "Don't Ask, Don't Tell" soon stalled in the Senate in the face of opposition led by Sen. McCain. McCain had encouraged the leaders of the Army, Navy, Air Force, and Marine Corps who had previously expressed their concern that lifting the ban may negatively impact their troops to write letters to other members of Congress, asking them to delay a vote on "Don't Ask, Don't Tell" until the Pentagon completed its review. "I think it's really going to be really harmful to the morale and battle effectiveness of our military," said McCain. He was joined by Rep. Mike Pence, R-Ind., who said the Democrats were trying to "advance a liberal social agenda." Others argued it was the wrong time to change the policy, as the military was already preoccupied with fighting two wars. "The issue isn't about individuals or liking gay people," said Elaine Donnelly, president of the Center for Military Readiness. "The issue is about what's best for the armed forces."

Democrats, on the other hand, compared lifting the ban to the desegregation of the military. They argued that the ban posed a fundamental challenge to the basic civil rights of those wishing to serve, and that it prevented thousands of able-bodied potential recruits from enlisting. They claimed Republicans were wrong to believe repealing the ban would harm the military, because under the measures proposed in the House and Senate, repeal would only occur once military leaders had certified it would not cause significant problems. Rep. Barney Frank, D-Mass., also argued in favor of repeal by pointing to other militaries, such as Israel's, that he said served as effective fighting forces even though they did not prevent gays and lesbians from serving openly.

Congressional debate on the ban came to a head on September 21, when Senate Republicans refused to begin debate on the National Defense Authorization Act while it included an amendment repealing "Don't Ask, Don't Tell" and Democrats could not secure the sixty votes needed to prevent a Republican filibuster. Republicans said they objected to majority leader Harry Reid, D-Nev., adding "politically motivated" proposals, such as the "Don't Ask, Don't Tell" repeal, to the broader bill, with McCain describing the provision as a "blatant political ploy" intended to help the Democrats garner more votes in the impending midterm elections. With the election only two weeks away, the defense bill would not be addressed again until the final days of the 111th Congress's lame duck session.

A LEGAL CHALLENGE

In the meantime, a lawsuit first filed in 2004 by the Log Cabin Republicans, the largest organization of gay Republicans, challenging "Don't Ask, Don't Tell" on behalf of several of its members, made its way to federal court. On September 9, U.S. district court judge Virginia Phillips ruled that the ban was unconstitutional, arguing that it violated the First and Fourteenth Amendment rights of gays and lesbians. Opponents of repeal immediately criticized the ruling. Tony Perkins, president of the Family Research Council, accused Phillips of "playing politics with our national defense." On October 12, Phillips took an additional step, issuing an injunction to prevent the government from enforcing "Don't Ask, Don't Tell" while it pursued an appeal of her ruling, which set off a cascade of legal maneuvering. The Department of Defense quickly appealed the injunction to the U.S. Court of Appeals for the Ninth Circuit to keep it from taking effect before the government could move to appeal the full case. The Ninth Circuit granted a stay of the injunction on November 1. Several days later, on November 6, the Log Cabin Republicans submitted a request to the U.S. Supreme Court to hear their case and lift the stay on Phillips's injunction, but the Court rejected their request, allowing the ban to stay in place during the appeals process.

THE PENTAGON REPORT

On November 30, the Pentagon released its report on the expected impact of repealing "Don't Ask, Don't Tell," concluding that allowing gays and lesbians to serve openly presents a low risk to the military's effectiveness, even at a time of war. The report also stated that out of 115,000 active-duty personnel surveyed, approximately 70 percent believed the impact of repeal on their units would be positive, mixed, or have no impact at all. Nearly 70 percent also believed they had already worked with a homosexual man or woman, and of those, 92 percent reported that it had been a good or neutral experience. Report authors Jeh C. Johnson, the Pentagon's chief counsel, and General Carter F. Ham said they believed any negative impacts of repeal could be overcome by effective leadership at senior levels and sufficient training. In announcing the report's findings, Secretary Gates described obtaining congressional approval of repeal as "a matter of urgency," lest it be decided by the courts instead. "We spend a lot of time in the military talking about integrity and honor and values," Gates said. "One of the things that is most important to me is personal integrity, and a policy or a law that in effect requires people to lie gives me a problem."

CONGRESS TRIES AGAIN

After a second unsuccessful attempt to move the National Defense Authorization Act forward with a provision to repeal "Don't Ask, Don't Tell," Sens. Lieberman and Susan Collins, R-Maine, introduced a separate, stand-alone bill to lift the ban on December 11 that contained the same language as the originally proposed amendment. Sen. Reid used his authority as majority leader to bring the bill directly to the Senate floor for a vote, where it passed with sixty-five votes in favor on December 18. The House had passed a similar stand-alone measure, sponsored by Rep. Murphy, on December 15. Several days later, on December 22, President Obama signed the bill into law, declaring, "No longer will tens of thousands of Americans in uniform be asked to live a lie or look over their shoulder in order to serve the country that they love."

Obama's signature did not mean the appeal would be effective immediately. The Pentagon must review its eighty-seven-page implementation plan for the repeal, and officials were expected to spend several weeks examining and rewriting a series of policies, regulations, and directives linked to "Don't Ask, Don't Tell." Once President Obama, Secretary Gates, and Admiral Mullen certified that repeal could move ahead, it would take effect sixty days later, permitting homosexual servicemen and -women to serve openly for the first time.

—Linda Fecteau

Following is a floor statement by Speaker of the House Nancy Pelosi, D-Calif., on May 27, 2010, in support of the repeal of "Don't Ask, Don't Tell"; a floor statement by Sen. John McCain, R-Ariz., on September 21, 2010, in opposition to the repeal of "Don't Ask, Don't Tell"; and excerpts from the Pentagon's report on "Don't Ask, Don't Tell," released on November 30, 2010.

Speaker Pelosi in Support of the Repeal of "Don't Ask, Don't Tell"

May 27, 2010

Ms. Pelosi: I thank the gentleman for yielding and for his leadership and service to our country.

Madam Chair, this weekend, on Memorial Day, America will come together to honor all those who have served our Nation in uniform, and those brave Americans have no better friend than the chairman of our Armed Services Committee, Mr. Skelton.

Today, by repealing the discriminatory Don't Ask, Don't Tell policy, we also honor the service and sacrifice of all who dedicated their lives to protecting the American people. We honor the values of our Nation, and we close the door on fundamental unfairness.

In 1993, I spoke on this same House floor, calling on the President "to act definitively to lift the ban that keeps patriotic Americans from serving in the U.S. Armed Forces because of their sexual orientation." Instead, despite everyone's good intentions, Don't Ask, Don't Tell was enacted—a policy which has been discriminatory to our brave men and women in uniform.

Under Don't Ask, Don't Tell, more than 13,000 men and women in uniform have been discharged from the military. Thousands more have decided not to reenlist. Fighter pilots, infantry officers, Arabic translators, and other specialists have been discharged at a time when our Nation is engaged in two wars.

That is why I support repealing Don't Ask, Don't Tell, and that support has come from all over the country. Nearly 8 out of 10 Americans want to end this era of discrimination.

Admiral Mullen, the current Chairman of the Joint Chiefs said, "It is my personal belief that allowing gays and lesbians to serve openly would be the right thing to do. We have in place a policy which forces young men and women to lie about who they are in order to defend their fellow citizens." He went on to say, "For me, personally, it comes down to integrity—theirs as individuals and ours as institutions."

General Colin Powell, who was Chairman of the Joint Chiefs when this policy was implemented, has said that he now thinks this restrictive policy should be repealed.

Then, in a letter to Congress, 51 retired generals, admirals, and a former Army Secretary called for the repeal of this policy, saying that they "have dedicated our lives to defending the rights of our citizens to believe whatever they wish."

Passing this amendment today respects the timeline of the Pentagon's Implementation Study Group. Repeal would take place only after the study group completes its work in December 2010 and after the President, the Joint Chiefs of Staff, and the Secretary of Defense all certify that repeal will not hurt military readiness or unit cohesion. No one in this body would jeopardize our national security.

America has always been the land of the free and the home of the brave. We are so because of our brave men and women in uniform who have been willing to fight for our country. Let us honor their service by recommitting to the values they fight for on the battlefield.

I urge my colleagues to vote for the repeal of this discriminatory policy of Don't Ask, Don't Tell and to make America more American.

SOURCE: Rep. Nancy Pelosi. "National Defense Authorization Act for Fiscal Year 2011—Continued." *Congressional Record* 2010, pt. 156, H4058. http://www.gpo.gov/fdsys/pkg/CREC-2010-5-27/pdf/CREC-2010-05-27-PT2-PgH4025.pdf.

Sen. McCain in Opposition to the Repeal of "Don't Ask, Don't Tell"

September 21, 2010

Mr. McCAIN. . . . Mr. President, I want to make it clear why I am opposed to moving to the National Defense Authorization Act of fiscal year 2011 at this time.

I am not opposed in principle to bringing up this Defense bill and debating it, amending it, and voting on it. I am not opposed to having a full and informed debate on whether to repeal the don't ask, don't tell law and then allowing the Senate to legislate.

What I am opposed to is bringing up the Defense bill now, before the Defense Department has concluded its survey of our men and women in uniform, which gives them a chance to tell us their views about don't ask, don't tell. Whether you agree or disagree with this policy, whether you want to keep it or repeal it, the Senate should not be forced to make this decision now, before we have heard from our troops. We have asked for their views, and we should wait to hear from them and then give their views the fullest consideration before taking any legislative action.

This isn't just my view. This is the view of all force service chiefs: GEN George Casey, Chief of Staff of the U.S. Army; ADM Gary Roughead, Chief of Naval Operations; GEN James Conway, Commandant of the Marine Corps; GEN Norton Schwartz, Chief of Staff of the Air Force. . . .

[The following five paragraphs have been omitted and include quotes from military leaders expressing their belief that Congress should wait to vote on repealing "Don't Ask, Don't Tell" until the Pentagon's review of the policy is completed.]

It could not be more clear what our uniformed service chiefs are saying: Complete this review before repealing the law.

Then the question is: Why would the chairman of the Senate Armed Services Committee and the majority leader ignore the very explicit recommendation of the four service chiefs? One can only draw one conclusion: November 2 is a few days away. The President of the United States, we all know, made a commitment to the gay and lesbian community that he would have as one of his priorities repeal of the don't ask, don't tell policy. Looking at a bleak electoral situation, they are now going to jam this legislation through—or try to—in direct contravention to the views of our service chiefs.

I spend a great deal of time with the men and women in the military. It is my job. It is my job to do so, both the Guard and Reserve in Arizona and traveling around the world to visit our men and women in places such as Kandahar, Baghdad, and other places around the world. Every place I go, the men and women are saying: Look, let's assess the impact of the repeal of this law. I get that from the senior enlisted men whose responsibilities are great. Why are we now trying to jam this through without the survey being completed and without a proper assessment of its impact?

I urge Members not to vote in favor of bringing the bill to the floor at this time so the troops can be heard. Let us hear from the men and women who are serving in the military.

I remind my colleagues that last year, they brought up the hate crimes bill and then put amendments on the hate crimes bill so there were no other amendments allowed until the hate crimes issue was resolved. That is the concern of the Senator from Maine, that the majority leader and/or the chairman will fill up the tree—in other words, make it so other amendments are not allowed until this issue is disposed of and then, of course, other issues.

In light of all the challenges that the Defense authorization bill entails—training, equipment, pay, benefits, all of the aspects of Defense authorizations that are so vital— why would the majority leader and the chairman want to bring up don't ask, don't tell, then the DREAM Act, then secret holds, and then reserve the rest of the issues for after we come back after the election?

Again, one can only draw the conclusion that this is all about elections, not about the welfare and well-being and the morale and the battle effectiveness of the men and women who are laying it on the line in Iraq and Afghanistan today.

The most fundamental thing we could do to honor the sacrifices of our troops is to take the time to listen respectfully and carefully to what they have to say about this major change before the Senate takes any legislative action.

If the Senate goes down this path, we would be ignoring the views of the troops and casting aside the professional military advice given by each of the four service chiefs, all four of whom oppose the Senate taking any action on don't ask, don't tell before we hear from the troops.

By the way, the way the legislation is framed, the service chiefs are not involved in the final decision; only the President, the Chairman of the Joint Chiefs of Staff, and the Secretary of Defense are. Why in the world before the certification is made would not the service chiefs be required to certify that as well?

This is not about filibustering. It is not about the reasons why we are not taking up this legislation or why I am opposing this legislation. It is all about the battle effectiveness, the morale of the men and women who are serving in the military today who have volunteered to put their lives on the line so the rest of us may live in a safe and secure environment. We owe them a right to have their voices heard before we act legislatively, motivated by the upcoming election.

SOURCE: Sen. John McCain. "National Defense Authorization Act for Fiscal Year 2011—Motion to Proceed." *Congressional Record* 2010, pt. 156, S7237–S7238. http://www.gpo.gov/fdsys/pkg/CREC-2010-09-21/pdf/CREC-2010-09-21-pt1-PgS7235-2.pdf.

Department of Defense Report on "Don't Ask, Don't Tell"

November 30, 2010

I. EXECUTIVE SUMMARY

On March 2, 2010, the Secretary of Defense appointed the two of us to co-chair a working group to undertake a comprehensive review of the impacts of repeal, should it occur, of Section 654 of Title 10 of the United States Code, commonly known as the "Don't Ask, Don't Tell" law. In this effort, we were aided by a highly dedicated team of 49 military and

19 civilian personnel from across the Department of Defense and the Military Services. Our assignment from the Secretary was two-fold: 1) assess the impact of repeal of Don't Ask, Don't Tell on military readiness, military effectiveness, unit cohesion, recruiting, retention, and family readiness; and 2) recommend appropriate changes, if necessary, to existing regulations, policies, and guidance in the event of repeal. The Secretary directed us to deliver our assessment and recommendations to him by December 1, 2010. This document constitutes our report of that assessment and our recommendations. The Secretary also directed us to develop a plan of action to support implementation of a repeal of Don't Ask, Don't Tell. That plan accompanies this report.

At the outset, it is important to note the environment in which we conducted our work: the Nation's military has been at war on several fronts for over 9 years. Much is being demanded from the force. The men and women in uniform who risk their lives to defend our Nation are, along with their families, stretched and stressed, and have faced years of multiple and lengthy deployments to Iraq, Afghanistan, and elsewhere. Some question the wisdom of taking on the emotional and difficult issue of Don't Ask, Don't Tell on top of all else. For these and other reasons, the Secretary directed that we "thoroughly, objectively and methodically examine all aspects of this question," and include, most importantly, the views of our men and women in uniform. Accordingly, over the last nine months we:

- solicited the views of nearly 400,000 active duty and reserve component Service members with an extensive and professionally-developed survey, which prompted 115,052 responses—one of the largest surveys in the history of the U.S. military;
- solicited the views of over 150,000 spouses of active duty and reserve component Service members, because of the influence and importance families play in the lives of Service members and their decisions to join, leave, or stay in the military, and received 44,266 responses;
- created an online inbox for Service members and their families to offer their views, through which we received a total of 72,384 entries;
- conducted 95 face-to-face "information exchange forums" at 51 bases and installations around the world, where we interacted with over 24,000 Service members—ranging from soldiers at Fort Hood, Fort Benning, and Fort Bragg, sailors at Norfolk, San Diego, and Pearl Harbor, airmen at Lackland, Langley, and Yokota in Japan, Marines at Camp Lejeune, Camp Pendleton, and Parris Island, cadets and midshipmen at our Service academies, and Coast Guardsmen on Staten Island, New York;
- conducted 140 smaller focus group sessions with Service members and their families;
- solicited the views of the Service academy superintendents and faculty, Service chiefs of chaplains, and Service surgeons general;
- solicited and received the views of various members of Congress;
- engaged RAND to update its 1993 study, *Sexual Orientation and U.S. Military Personnel Policy;*
- solicited and received the views of foreign allies, veterans groups, and groups both for and against repeal of the current law and policy; and
- during a two-week period prior to issuance, solicited and received the comments of the Secretaries of the Army, Navy and Air Force, and the Chiefs of each Service, on this report in draft form.

Finally, we heard the views and experiences of current and former Service members who are gay or lesbian. We knew that their viewpoints would be important, and we made affirmative efforts to reach them, though our ability to do so under the current Don't Ask, Don't Tell law was limited. The two of us personally interviewed former Service members who are gay or lesbian, including those who had been separated under Don't Ask, Don't Tell. To reach those currently in the military, we hired a private company to administer the survey of Service members and an interactive online confidential communications mechanism. This company was obligated to protect the identity of Service members and did not reveal identifying information to the Working Group. Through the confidential communications mechanism, the private company was able to engage a total of 2,691 Service members, 296 of whom self-identified as gay or lesbian, in interactive online conversations about their experiences.

Our Working Group also reviewed hundreds of relevant laws, regulations, and Department of Defense and Service policies and issuances (directives, instructions, and memoranda) and evaluated various policy options. As discussed in detail in section V, the breadth and depth of the Working Group's work was extensive. To our knowledge, our nine-month review and engagement of the force was the largest and most comprehensive in the history of the U.S. military, on any personnel-related matter.

Based on all we saw and heard, our assessment is that, when coupled with the prompt implementation of the recommendations we offer below, the risk of repeal of Don't Ask, Don't Tell to overall military effectiveness is low. We conclude that, while a repeal of Don't Ask, Don't Tell will likely, in the short term, bring about some limited and isolated disruption to unit cohesion and retention, we do not believe this disruption will be widespread or long-lasting, and can be adequately addressed by the recommendations we offer below. Longer term, with a continued and sustained commitment to core values of leadership, professionalism, and respect for all, we are convinced that the U.S. military can adjust and accommodate this change, just as it has others in history.

Significant to our assessment are the following:

The results of the Service member survey reveal a widespread attitude among a solid majority of Service members that repeal of Don't Ask, Don't Tell will not have a negative impact on their ability to conduct their military mission. The survey was conducted by Westat, a research firm with a long track record of conducting surveys for the U.S. military. The survey was one of the largest in the history of the military. We heard from over 115,000 Service members, or 28% of those solicited. Given the large number of respondents, the margin of error for the results was less than ±1%, and the response rate was average for the U.S. military.

The results of the survey are best represented by the answers to three questions:

- When asked about how having a Service member in their immediate unit who said he or she is gay would affect the unit's ability to "work together to get the job done," 70% of Service members predicted it would have a positive, mixed, or no effect.
- When asked "in your career, have you ever worked in a unit with a co-worker that you believed to be homosexual," 69% of Service members reported that they had.
- When asked about the actual experience of serving in a unit with a co-worker who they believed was gay or lesbian, 92% stated that the unit's "ability to work together" was "very good," "good," or "neither good nor poor."

Consistently, the survey results revealed a large group of around 50–55% of Service members who thought that repeal of Don't Ask, Don't Tell would have mixed or no effect;

another 15–20% who said repeal would have a positive effect; and about 30% who said it would have a negative effect. The results of the spouse survey are consistent. When spouses were asked about whether repeal of Don't Ask, Don't Tell would affect their preference for their Service member's future plans to stay in the military, 74% said repeal would have no effect, while only 12% said "I would want my spouse to leave earlier."

To be sure, these survey results reveal a significant minority—around 30% overall (and 40–60% in the Marine Corps and in various combat arms specialties)—who predicted in some form and to some degree negative views or concerns about the impact of a repeal of Don't Ask, Don't Tell. Any personnel policy change for which a group that size predicts negative consequences must be approached with caution. However, there are a number of other factors that still lead us to conclude that the risk of repeal to overall military effectiveness is low.

The reality is that there are gay men and lesbians already serving in today's U.S. military, and most Service members recognize this. . . .

Yet, a frequent response among Service members at information exchange forums, when asked about the widespread recognition that gay men and lesbians are already in the military, were words to the effect of: "yes, but I don't *know* they are gay." Put another way, the concern with repeal among many is with "open" service. . . .

In today's civilian society, where there is no law that requires gay men and lesbians to conceal their sexual orientation in order to keep their job, most gay men and lesbians still tend to be discrete about their personal lives, and guarded about the people with whom they share information about their sexual orientation. We believe that, in the military environment, this would be true even more so. . . .

In communications with gay and lesbian current and former Service members, we repeatedly heard a patriotic desire to serve and defend the Nation, subject to the same rules as everyone else. . . . Most said they did not desire special treatment, to use the military for social experimentation, or to advance a social agenda. Some of those separated under Don't Ask, Don't Tell would welcome the opportunity to rejoin the military if permitted. . . .

Given that we are in a time of war, the combat arms communities across all Services required special focus and analysis. Though the survey results demonstrate a solid majority of the overall U.S. military who predict mixed, positive or no effect in the event of repeal, these percentages are lower, and the percentage of those who predict negative effects are higher, in combat arms units. . . .

[Further discussion on the difference between combat arms units and the overall U.S. military has been omitted.]

It is also the case that the results of the survey indicate that, in this war-time environment, a solid majority of Service members believe that repeal will have positive, mixed, or no effect. Most of those surveyed joined our military after September 11, 2001, and have known nothing but a military at war. . . .

[A historical analysis of the situation has been omitted.]

Motivating many of our recommendations is the conclusion, based on our numerous engagements with the force, that repeal would work best if it is accompanied by a message and policies that promote fair and equal treatment of all Service members, minimize differences among Service members based on sexual orientation, and disabuse Service members of any notion that, with repeal, gay and lesbian Service members will be afforded some type of special treatment.

Included, also, should be a message to those who are opposed to "open" service on well-founded moral or religious grounds, that their views and beliefs are not rejected, and that leaders have not turned their backs on them. In the event of repeal, we cannot and should not expect individual Service members to change their personal religious or moral beliefs about homosexuality, but we do expect every Service member to treat all others with dignity and respect, consistent with the core values that already exist in each Service. These are not new concepts for the U.S. military, given the wide variety of views, races, and religions that already exist within the force. . . .

[Discussion of the final committee recommendations and closing remarks have been omitted.]

[The remainder of the report, section II through Appendix D, contains detailed information on the thoughts provided in the executive summary and has been omitted.]

Source: U.S. Department of Defense. "Report of the Comprehensive Review of the Issues Associated with a Repeal of 'Don't Ask, Don't Tell.'" November 30, 2010. http://www.defense.gov/home/features/2010/0610_gatesdadt/DADTReport_FINAL_20101130(secure-hires).pdf.

OTHER HISTORIC DOCUMENTS OF INTEREST

FROM PREVIOUS *HISTORIC DOCUMENTS*

Israel Raids Gaza Flotilla

MAY 31, 2010

Despite repeated attempts by U.S. president Barack Obama to restart peace talks, tensions between Israel and Palestine remained high in the early months of 2010. Israel's blockade of the Gaza Strip remained in place, despite claims from the international community that it had inflicted overwhelming poverty on Gazans and ought to be lifted. In May 2010, a flotilla organized to break the blockade became the center of a worldwide controversy after Israeli commandos attempted to stop the ships, killing nine of the activists on board in the process.

Containing a Threat, Cutting off the World

Israel and Egypt initially imposed a blockade on the Gaza Strip following an outbreak of violence in 2007 during which Hamas, a Palestinian Islamist militant movement, seized control of the region. The violence was the culmination of a lengthy power struggle that began when Hamas won a large majority of seats in the Palestinian Legislative Council in 2006 and defeated Fatah, the political party of President Mahmoud Abbas. Hamas and Fatah agreed to share governing power, with President Abbas maintaining control of Palestine's security forces. Yet Hamas began to suspect that a faction within Fatah was collaborating with Israel and the United States to isolate and weaken the movement. In June 2007, Hamas gunmen ousted security personnel loyal to Fatah and took Gaza by force.

Fearing what actions a more thoroughly empowered Hamas might take, Israeli officials quickly worked to blockade the Gaza Strip in an effort to prevent Hamas from obtaining any materials that could be used to make or deploy weapons. Nearly all imports and exports were banned, with only a limited amount of food and medical supplies allowed in. The Israeli navy also moved to close access to the Mediterranean Sea off of Gaza, up to twenty nautical miles out. Israel had allowed five seaborne shipments of international humanitarian aid into Gaza between August and December 2008, but it put an immediate end to these and other aid efforts following the three-week Gaza War of 2008–2009. Many in the international community spoke out against the tightening of the blockade despite Israel's reassurances that it allowed approximately fifteen thousand tons of aid into Gaza each week, an amount the United Nations (UN) said was less than a quarter of what was needed.

Breaking the Blockade

A number of international organizations believed Israel had placed a "stranglehold" on Gaza and began efforts to break the blockade and deliver aid. One such organization, the Free Gaza Movement, formed in direct response to the blockade. A coalition movement headquartered in Cyprus, the Free Gaza Movement had earned the endorsement of more than two hundred individuals and organizations worldwide, including many Europeans. Coalition members made nine attempts to deliver aid to Gaza between August 2008 and April 2010 but only succeeded three times. In May, the group began to organize a flotilla of passenger and cargo ships to deliver ten thousand tons of aid, including building materials, medical supplies, water filtration units, prefabricated homes, and school supplies. Israeli officials, who claimed the Free Gaza Movement was a threat to the Jewish state, warned the activists that their boats would not be allowed to reach Gaza, but that they could dock at the Israeli port of Ashdod. Their cargo would then be inspected, and any acceptable materials would then be transported by the Israelis over land to Gaza. The coalition declined the offer and continued with its plans. "What we're trying to do is open a sea lane between Gaza and the rest of the world," said Greta Berlin, spokesperson for the Free Gaza Movement. "We're not trying to be a humanitarian mission. We're trying to say to the world, 'You have no right to imprison a million and a half Palestinians.'"

Fearing a potential conflict between the activists and the Israeli military, UN secretary-general Ban Ki-moon issued a statement calling on all sides to act with care and responsibility and restating the UN's opposition to the blockade. Turkish prime minister Recep Tayyip Erdogan, whose country provided key support for the mission, also called on Israel to allow the boats through the blockade and warned that any effort to stop the flotilla could negatively impact relations between the two countries.

On May 30, a total of six ships from Turkey, Sweden, Ireland, and Greece, carrying approximately seven hundred activists and politicians from more than forty countries, met in international waters near Cyprus and began their journey to Gaza. Organizers had intended the flotilla to be larger, but three boats experienced sudden mechanical issues on their way to Cyprus, leading to accusations that Israeli officials may have somehow tampered with them. When the flotilla came within approximately eighty miles of the Gaza coast in the predawn hours of May 31, the Israeli navy contacted the captain of the lead ship, the *Mavi Marmara*, requesting that he identify himself and state where the ship was headed. Shortly thereafter, two naval vessels pulled alongside the ship. After issuing five warnings to the *Mavi Marmara* to turn back, all of which were ignored, the navy dispatched an elite commando unit by helicopter to begin a raid of the ship.

As the commandos rappelled down to the deck of the ship, they immediately clashed with the activists. Both sides later offered conflicting accounts of the incident. The activists claimed the Israelis initiated the violence and began firing weapons as they reached the ship. "They started off with some kind of paintball bullets with glass in them that left terrible soft tissue wounds. And then rubber bullets. And then live ammunition afterwards. And that's when things started to get really dangerous," said Espen Goffeng, a Norwegian activist onboard the ship. A reporter for Al-Jazeera who was sailing on the *Marvi Marmara* confirmed that the Israelis fired at the ship before boarding, while a Turkish television reporter said, "These savages are killing people here, please help." The Israeli soldiers claimed they were only carrying paintball guns and pistols and that they acted in self defense when the activists began attacking them with what one commando claimed were "knives, scissors, pepper spray and guns." Footage later provided by the military showed activists circling around the commandos as they reached the deck of the ship, beating them with sticks, while another commando said some of his colleagues jumped overboard to protect themselves. By the time the Israelis had taken control of the ship, nine activists had been killed and nearly thirty others wounded, including several Israeli soldiers. All six ships were towed to the port of Ashdod, and the remaining activists were arrested.

INTERNATIONAL CONDEMNATION

International reaction to the raid was swift and overwhelmingly critical of Israel's actions. The UN Security Council convened an emergency meeting and issued a statement condemning the attack. The council also called for an independent international investigation into the incident and the immediate release of all activists and their ships. President Abbas described the attack as a "massacre" and called for three days of mourning over the activists' deaths. Egypt, Spain, Sweden, Denmark, and Greece summoned the Israeli ambassadors in their countries for meetings to protest the violence. Protests broke out across Europe, with demonstrations in France, Italy, Sweden, Norway, Cyprus, and Greece. Reaction in the Arab world was equally intense. Jordanian protestors urged their government to cut ties with Israel, while citizens of Tehran and Baghdad gathered in the streets chanting "Death to Israel." Others questioned whether Israel had a legal right to confront the flotilla, as the ships were in international waters when the incident occurred, but the Israeli military dismissed this claim. "This happened in waters outside of Israeli territory, but we have the right to defend ourselves," said Israeli military spokesperson Avital Leibovich. Israeli prime minister Benjamin Netanyahu also defended the military's actions, claiming in a statement that the incident was "the result of an intentional provocation of forces which support Iran and its terrorist enclave, Hamas, in the Gaza Strip." Israel's deputy foreign minister, Danny Ayalon, described the convoy as an "armada of hate," and accused the activists of a "premeditated and outrageous provocation."

Perhaps the strongest condemnation came from Turkey, which had until then been a strong ally of Israel. All nine of the activists killed during the raid were Turkish. "Israel in no way can legitimize this murder, it cannot wash its hands of this blood," said Prime Minister Erdogan. Turkish officials announced that the country's ambassador to Israel would be withdrawn and issued three demands: that Israel apologize for the raid, organize an independent investigation into the incident, and lift the blockade of Gaza. Meanwhile, Turkish protestors attempted to storm the Israeli consulate in Istanbul, shouting, "Damn Israel." In the week following the raid, the Istanbul Prosecutor's Office launched a probe into Israel's attack on the flotilla, targeting officials such as Prime Minister Netanyahu, Defense Minister Ehud Barak, and Chief of the General Staff Gabi Ashkenazi, with hopes of compiling enough evidence to charge them with crimes such as murder and piracy. On June 4, a funeral was held for those killed during the raid, and 460 of the detained activists received a hero's welcome as they returned to Turkey. Some who gathered at the funeral described the incident as a "victory" because it succeeded in bringing attention to the blockade. The Foundation for Human Rights and Freedoms and Humanitarian Relief (IHH), an Islamic charity that was a primary organizer of the flotilla, described the deceased as martyrs and praised them for their willingness to fight.

SEARCHING FOR ANSWERS

In the weeks following the raid, Israel launched two separate investigations into the incident. On June 14, Israel's cabinet approved the formation of a panel led by former justice Jacob Turkel to examine whether the military's actions and the Gaza blockade conformed to international law. The Turkel Commission included two other Israelis and foreign observers: David Trimble, a Northern Ireland politician and Nobel Peace Prize winner, and Ken Watkin, a Canadian jurist. Turkish officials, as well as President Abbas and representatives of Hamas, claimed the panel would be biased, and UN officials continued to push for an independent, international investigation despite Israel's resistance.

On July 12, a second panel of eight Israeli military investigators, led by General Giora Eiland, concluded that the commandos were justified in their use of force, but that there had been "professional mistakes regarding intelligence and the decision-making process," such as a lack of coordination among different branches of military intelligence. The panel also claimed that it found "very clear evidence that in at least four cases the other side did use live fire" and that the activists came "to kill and be killed."

After months of negotiations with reluctant Israeli officials and the Turkish government, Secretary-General Ban announced on August 2 that the UN would launch its own inquiry. Ban said the panel would be led by former New Zealand prime minister Geoffrey Palmer, with outgoing Colombian president Alvaro Uribe serving as vice chair, and would review reports from Israeli and Turkish investigations into the raid, ultimately issuing recommendations on how to avoid similar incidents in the future. A separate UN fact-finding mission later released a report citing forensic and ballistic analyses to accuse the Israeli commandos of executing six of the flotilla passengers, including one activist who had dual U.S.-Turkish citizenship, and claimed their actions "betrayed an unacceptable level of brutality." The UN Human Rights Council voted to endorse the report on September 29, but all European countries abstained from the vote. The United States was the only country to vote against the endorsement, claiming the panel's findings were unbalanced, particularly because Israel had refused to allow the panel to interview Israeli witnesses.

The findings of Ban's panel and the Turkel Commission have yet to be released. While the Israeli cabinet voted on June 17, 2010, to ease the land blockade of Gaza and allow the import of items such as food, toys, kitchen utensils, and mattresses, the sea blockade remains in place, as does the ban on private imports of building materials.

—Linda Fecteau

Following is a condemnation by the United Nations Security Council, issued on May 31, 2010, in response to the Israeli operation against the Gaza flotilla; and a statement by Israeli prime minister Benjamin Netanyahu on May 31, 2010, in which he calls the attack an act of self defense.

UN Condemns Gaza Blockade

May 31, 2010

SECURITY COUNCIL CONDEMNS ACTS RESULTING IN CIVILIAN DEATHS DURING ISRAELI OPERATION AGAINST GAZA-BOUND AID CONVOY, CALLS FOR INVESTIGATION, IN PRESIDENTIAL STATEMENT

Also Briefed by United Nations Political Official, Who Says Bloodshed Would Have Been Avoided if Israel Had Lifted Unacceptable, Counterproductive Blockade

In the early morning hours of Tuesday, the Security Council expressed deep regret at the loss of life and injuries resulting from the use of force during the Israeli military operation early on Monday in international waters against the convoy sailing to Gaza, and condemned those acts which had killed at least 10 civilians and wounded many more.

Twelve hours after convening an emergency session on Monday in response to the Israeli "operation" on the Gaza-bound maritime convoy, the Council issued the statement, read out by Claude Heller of Mexico, whose delegation leads the Council in June (Lebanon was the Council President until midnight, 31 May), requesting the immediate release of the ships, as well as the civilians held by Israel.

The Council urged Israel to permit full consular access, to allow the countries concerned to retrieve their deceased and wounded immediately, and to ensure the delivery of humanitarian assistance from the convoy to its destination.

It took note of the statement of United Nations Secretary-General on the need to have a full investigation into the matter and it called for a prompt, impartial, credible and transparent investigation conforming to international standards.

Stressing that the situation in Gaza was not sustainable, the Council re-emphasized the importance of the full implementation of resolutions 1850 (2008) and 1860 (2009). In that context, it reiterated its grave concern at the humanitarian situation in Gaza and stressed the need for the sustained and regular flow of goods and people to Gaza, as well as unimpeded provision and distribution of humanitarian assistance throughout the enclave. The Council also expressed support for the proximity talks.

At an earlier meeting Monday afternoon, Oscar Fernandez-Taranco, Assistant Secretary-General for Political Affairs, briefed the Council on the incident, reporting that Israeli naval forces had boarded a six-ship convoy, which had been heading towards Gaza. The stated purpose of the convoy was to deliver humanitarian aid to Gaza and to break the Israeli blockade on Gaza, he said, making clear the United Nations has "no independent information on what transpired."

He said that in the lead-up to today's events, the Israeli authorities had conveyed their intention, both publicly and through diplomatic channels, not to allow the convoy to reach Gaza. The Israeli authorities had stated that if the convoy proceeded, contrary to those warnings, they would divert it to an Israeli port, inspect the cargo, facilitate the entry of only those goods that were allowed into Gaza in accordance with Israel's blockade, and deport those on-board.

The organizers of the convoy had indicated their intention to proceed with their convoy and to attempt to deliver their full consignment of cargo to Gaza and to break the blockade, he said. And a committee of persons organized by the de facto Hamas authorities in Gaza had been formed to receive the convoy.

According to the Israeli authorities, Israel naval forces had conveyed directly to the convoy in the early hours of Monday that they would not be allowed to reach port in Gaza, he said. However, the convoy had proceeded towards Gaza. At approximately 0400 hours local time, the Israeli navy had acted to intercept the convoy. That had reportedly taken place some 40 nautical miles off the coast, in international waters, and had reportedly involved Israeli military personnel boarding the vessels, supported by naval ships and helicopters.

Given the circumstances, he said, "it is not possible to state definitively the sequence or details of what happened." The Israeli Government had stated that the demonstrators on-board had used knives and clubs against Israel Defense Forces naval personnel, and possibly live fire, and that a weapon had been grabbed from one of its soldiers. Given that those who had been on-board were now in Israeli custody and had had their transmission equipment confiscated, further information from the convoy's organizers had been minimal since the incident.

He said that the Secretary-General had stated earlier on Monday in Kampala that he was "shocked" by the killings and injuries of people on the boats and had condemned the violence. He had called for a full investigation to determine exactly how the bloodshed had taken place and stressed that Israel must urgently provide a full explanation. In Mr. Fernandez Taranco's view, today's bloodshed would have been avoided if repeated calls on Israel to end the counterproductive and unacceptable blockade of Gaza had been heeded.

Turkey's Foreign Minister, Ahmet Davutoğlu, said he was distraught by the incident, which was a grave breach of international law and constituted banditry and piracy—it was "murder" conducted by a State, without justification. A nation that followed that path lost its legitimacy as a respectable member of the international community. The children of Gaza, meanwhile, did not know where their next meal was coming from; they had received no education and had no future. Today, many humanitarian workers returned home in body bags. Israel had "blood on its hands."

High-seas freedom, he said, freedom of navigation, was one of the oldest forms of international law; no vessel could be stopped or boarded without the consent of the captain or flag State. Any suspected violation of the law did not absolve the intervening State under international law. To treat humanitarian delivery as a hostile act and to treat aid workers as combatants could not be deemed legal or legitimate. Any attempt to legitimize the attack was futile.

This was an attack on the United Nations and its values, he said, adding that the international system had suffered a sharp blow, and now "it is our responsibility to rectify this and prove that common sense and respect to international law prevails." Israel must be prepared to face the consequences of its crimes. The processes in place had been suffocated by that one single act. Israel had become an advocate of aggression and the use of force. He called on the people of Israel to express dismay. Steps must be taken to reinstate Israel's status as a credible partner and responsible member of the international community.

The Security Council should react strongly and adopt a presidential statement today strongly condemning Israel and demanding an urgent inquiry and punishment for the perpetrators, he urged. He called on the body to step up and do what was expected of it.

The Palestinian Authority had declared a state of mourning for three days, said the Permanent Observer of Palestine to the United Nations, adding that everyone was a victim, to be mourned as martyrs of Palestine. It was high time for the Security Council to take decisive measures against Israel, which always acted beyond the law, he stressed.

The continuation of the Gaza blockade and the starvation of the people who lived there was what had led to today's crime and had allowed hundreds around the world "to be on our side."

He promised that the fleets would continue to come until the blockade was ended and the suffering ameliorated for the Palestinian people. The attack of those unarmed civilians aboard foreign ships in international waters was more proof that Israel acted as a country beyond the law. Hence, the international community must take "urgent and suitable" measures. It was time for the Council to put an end to the unjustifiable blockade imposed on 1.5 million Palestinians and to implement its resolution 1860 (2009).

Israel's representative told the Council that, although the flotilla was portrayed in the media as a humanitarian mission, it was anything but. If that were truly the case, the organizers of the mission would have accepted weeks ago Israel's offer to transfer the aid brought on the flotilla through the Israeli port of Ashdod and through the established Israeli procedures. Much material and merchandise was entering Gaza daily through those mechanisms. "I would like to stress there is no humanitarian crisis in Gaza," he said. The flotilla's organizers had not only rejected Israel's offer, but they had stated that their mission was not about delivering humanitarian supplies, but about breaking the Israeli siege on Gaza.

"What kind of humanitarian activists demand to bypass the United Nations, the Red Cross and other internationally recognized agencies?" he asked. "What kind of peace activists use knives, clubs and other weapons to attack soldiers who board a ship in accordance with international law?" he said. He asked what kind of activists embraced Hamas and terrorist organizations that openly shunned a two-State solution and called for Israel's destruction. "The answer is clear. They are not peace activists; they are not messengers of goodwill. They cynically use the guise of humanitarian aid to send a message of hate and to implement violence."

Council members around the table were generally united in strongly condemning the incident, deploring the loss of life and calling for a release by the Israeli authorities of the detainees. They agreed on the unambiguous need for an independent and in-depth investigation, with most suggesting that Israel bore the responsibility to provide a full account of what had occurred and to describe the efforts it had made to minimize the loss of life and injuries.

Context for today's tragedy, many said, were the Israeli restrictions on Gaza, which they insisted must be lifted, in line with resolution 1860 (2009). The current closure was deemed unacceptable and counterproductive, and ending it was among the highest priorities of many of their Governments and of the international community as a whole. There were calls for continued humanitarian reconstruction aid and economic development assistance for Gaza, with some speakers saying Monday morning's events had also highlighted the need, once again, for a comprehensive solution to the Arab-Israeli conflict.

Additional statements were made by the representatives of the United Kingdom, Mexico, Brazil, Austria, Japan, Nigeria, United States, Russian Federation, Uganda, China, France, Gabon, Bosnia and Herzegovina, and Lebanon.

The first meeting, on Monday, was called to order at 1:55 p.m. and adjourned at 3:19 p.m. The second meeting began at 1:43 a.m. on Tuesday and ended at 1:51 a.m.

Presidential Statement

The full text of the presidential statement, to be issued as document S/PRST/2010/9, reads as follows:

"The Security Council deeply regrets the loss of life and injuries resulting from the use of force during the Israeli military operation in international waters against the convoy sailing to Gaza. The Council, in this context, condemns those acts which resulted in the loss of at least 10 civilians and many wounded, and expresses its condolences to their families.

"The Security Council requests the immediate release of the ships as well as the civilians held by Israel. The Council urges Israel to permit full consular access, to allow the countries concerned to retrieve their deceased and wounded immediately, and to ensure the delivery of humanitarian assistance from the convoy to its destination.

"The Security Council takes note of the statement of the United Nations Secretary–General on the need to have a full investigation into the matter and it calls for a prompt, impartial, credible and transparent investigation conforming to international standards.

"The Security Council stresses that the situation in Gaza is not sustainable. The Council re-emphasizes the importance of the full implementation of resolutions 1850 (2008) and 1860 (2009). In that context, it reiterates its grave concern at the humanitarian situation in Gaza and stresses the need for sustained and regular flow of goods and people to Gaza as well as unimpeded provision and distribution of humanitarian assistance throughout Gaza.

"The Security Council underscores that the only viable solution to Israeli-Palestinian conflict is an agreement negotiated between the parties and re-emphasizes that only a two-State solution, with an independent and viable Palestinian State living side by side in peace and security with Israel and its other neighbours, could bring peace to the region.

"The Security Council expresses support for the proximity talks and voices concern that this incident took place while the proximity talks are under way and urges the parties to act with restraint, avoiding any unilateral and provocative actions, and all international partners to promote an atmosphere of cooperation between the parties and throughout the region." . . .

[The following nine pages include statements from Security Council member countries responding to the raid and have been omitted.]

SOURCE: United Nations Security Council. "Security Council Condemns Acts Resulting in Civilian Deaths During Israeli Operation Against Gaza-Bound Aid Convoy, Calls for Investigation, in Presidential Statement." May 31, 2010. http://unispal.un.org/UNISPAL.NSF/0/C37381B050B4D07B8 525773C0064CC48.

DOCUMENT

Israeli Prime Minister Netanyahu on the Gaza Flotilla

May 31, 2010

This regrettable incident was the result of an intentional provocation of forces which support Iran and its terrorist enclave, Hamas, in the Gaza Strip.

[Translated from Hebrew]

Last night a regrettable incident occurred, during which people were killed and others were injured. IDF soldiers who were compelled to defend their lives were also injured. This incident was the result of an intentional provocation of forces which support Iran and its terrorist enclave, Hamas, in the Gaza Strip. This enclave, Hamas, has fired thousands of missiles at the State of Israel, and it is amassing thousands more.

This is a clear case of self-defense. Israel cannot allow the free flow of weapons, rockets and missiles to the terrorist base of Hamas in Gaza. It's a terrorist base supported by Iran; it's already fired thousands of rockets at Israeli cities; it seeks to smuggle in thousands more, and this is why Israel must inspect the goods that come into Gaza. It's also a clear case of self-defense because as our soldiers were inspecting these ships, they were attacked—they were almost lynched. They were attacked with clubs, with knives, perhaps with live gunfire, and they had to defend themselves—they were going to be killed. Israel will not allow its soldiers to be lynched and neither would any other self-respecting country.

Our policy is simple. We say: any goods, any humanitarian aid to Gaza, can enter. What we want to prevent is their ability to bring in war materiel—missiles, rockets, the means for constructing casings for missiles and rockets. This has been our policy and yesterday we told the flotilla—which was not a simple, innocent flotilla—to bring their goods into Ashdod. We told them that we would examine their cargo and allow those goods that could not be used as weapons or shielding materials for Hamas into Gaza.

Five of the six ships accepted these terms without violence. Apparently, the sixth ship, the largest, which had on board hundreds of people, had a premeditated plan to harm IDF soldiers. When the first soldiers dropped down onto the deck of the ship, they were attacked by a violent mob and were compelled to defend their lives. That is when the unfortunate events took place.

We have a simple policy, which will continue. That policy is: we have no argument or fight with the population of Gaza. We are interested in allowing them to continue their regular routines. We want to prevent any humanitarian crisis in Gaza, but we are fighting the Hamas organization, which threatens the citizens of Israel and fires missiles at Israeli cities. It is our duty to defend the citizens of Israel, protect Israel's cities and ensure the security of the State of Israel—and we will continue to do so.

* * *

Statement following meeting with Canadian PM Stephen Harper (31 May 2010):

Gaza has become a base for Hamas terrorists backed by Iran, from which they fire thousands of rockets into Israel. They're amassing thousands more rockets to fire at our cities, at our towns, at our children. Our policy is this: we try to let in all humanitarian goods into Gaza, all peaceful commodities—food, medicine and the like. What we want to prevent coming into Gaza are rockets, missiles, explosives and war materiel that could be used to attack our civilians.

This is an ongoing policy and it was the one that guided our action yesterday. We told the flotilla of ships, we said: "You can take all your cargo. Put it in our port of Ashdod. We'll just ferret out if there are any war materiels and the rest will go through." We succeeded doing this peacefully with five of the six ships. The sixth ship, the largest, which had hundreds of people on it not only did not cooperate in this effort, they deliberately attacked the first soldiers that came on the ship. They were mobbed; they were clubbed; they were beaten; they were stabbed and there was even a report of gunfire.

Our soldiers had to defend themselves, defend their lives or they would have been killed, and regrettably, in this exchange at least ten people died. We regret this loss of life. We regret any of the violence that was there. I would like to wish speedy recovery to the wounded, including four of our own soldiers.

Our policy was and will continue to be that we will let humanitarian aid, any kinds of goods that are meant for peace to the civilian population in Gaza. We have no quarrel with the people of Gaza. We do have a conflict with the terrorist regime of Hamas, supported by Iran. We want to maintain a situation where we prevent weapons and raw materials from coming into Gaza. That is our main task.

SOURCE: Israeli Ministry of Foreign Affairs. "Gaza Flotilla: Statement by PM Netanyahu." May 31, 2010. http://www.mfa.gov.il/MFA/Government/Speeches+by+Israeli+leaders/2010/Gaza_flotilla-Statement_ PM_Netanyahu_31-May-2010.

OTHER HISTORIC DOCUMENTS OF INTEREST

FROM PREVIOUS HISTORIC DOCUMENTS

June

Supreme Court Rules on *Miranda* Rights

JUNE 1, 2010

Anyone who has ever watched a TV crime show has heard: "You have the right to remain silent and anything you say can be used against you in a court of law." Known as the *Miranda* warning, these words were crafted by the U.S. Supreme Court in the landmark 1966 case *Miranda v. Arizona* and were designed to protect suspects' constitutionally mandated rights against self-incrimination. After a suspect invokes the right to remain silent, all interrogation must cease and anything said to the police cannot be used at trial unless the suspect knowingly waives the right. In *Berghuis v. Thompkins*, the Court left in place *Miranda*'s requirement that suspects be told of their right to remain silent but reexamined how these rights can be invoked and waived. According to this ruling, criminal suspects who do not want to talk to the police, but rather want to exercise their right to remain silent, must speak up unambiguously to assert that right.

MIRANDA AND THE MURDER SUSPECT

The Court's *Miranda* decision in 1966 was extremely controversial. Before *Miranda*, police were unfettered in their ability to coerce confessions from suspects. Both police and prosecutors reacted with outrage to a decision they believed sided with criminals, warning that it would prevent them from solving crimes and sending criminals to prison. Conservatives continued to attack the decision, and it was widely thought that as soon as the Court had a five-member conservative majority *Miranda* would be overturned. But in 2000, Chief Justice William Rehnquist rejected the opportunity to do so, instead writing for a 7–2 majority in *Dickerson v. United States* and reaffirming the central holdings of *Miranda*. He argued that "*Miranda* has become embedded in routine police practice to the point where the warnings have become part of our national culture." But since that time, the Court has been incrementally, opinion by opinion, narrowing the scope of the *Miranda* ruling.

While statements obtained in violation of *Miranda* still cannot be used by prosecutors in their direct case, the Court has created an exception allowing those same statements to be used to impeach a defendant who testifies differently at trial. Just this year, the Court allowed police officers to vary the wording of the required warnings and to make further attempts to question suspects who have invoked their *Miranda* rights after they have been released from custody for two weeks. The Court also created a "public safety" exception that allows law enforcement officials to interrogate suspected terrorists for a limited time before advising them of their rights if the officers are "reasonably prompted by a concern for public safety." This exception was used to question terror suspects such as "underwear bomber" suspect Umar Farouk Abdulmutallab and Times Square bomber suspect Faisal Shahzad.

The events leading to *Berghuis v. Thompkins* began on January 10, 2000, with a shooting outside a mall in Southfield, Michigan, where one of the victims died from multiple gunshot wounds. Van Chester Thompkins fled the scene but was tracked down and arrested near Columbus, Ohio, a year later. The Michigan police traveled to Ohio to interrogate him. They read him his *Miranda* rights and, to determine that he understood English, asked him to read aloud the part that read: "You have the right to decide at any time before or during questioning to use your right to remain silent and your right to talk with a lawyer while you are being questioned." He complied, but then refused to sign a statement acknowledging that he understood his rights. In the face of an interrogation described by the officers as "very, very one-sided" and "nearly a monologue," Thompkins stayed almost completely silent and nonresponsive for almost three hours of this questioning, until the police asked three questions relating to his faith in God. They asked, "Do you believe in God?" Tears welled up in Thompkins's eyes as he said "yes." Then they asked, "Do you pray to God?" And, finally, "Do you pray to God to forgive you for shooting that boy down?" Thompkins reportedly answered "yes," and looked away. He refused to sign any written statements and interrogation ended. The answer to this third question was introduced as a confession at his murder trial where he was found guilty and sentenced to life in prison without parole.

Thompkins appealed this ruling to the Michigan Court of Appeals on the grounds that he invoked his right to remain silent by refusing to answer questions for such a long period of time and therefore his pretrial statement should have been suppressed. The appellate court rejected this *Miranda* claim, ruling that he had not invoked his right to remain silent and had waived it by speaking to the police. The Michigan Supreme Court declined to review the case. After losing on appeal in the state courts, Thompkins filed a challenge in the federal courts where the Sixth Circuit Court of Appeals ultimately ruled in his favor, holding that he had not waived his right to silence. Michigan filed a petition for *certiorari* to the U.S. Supreme Court, which was granted on September 30, 2009.

A Divided Court Sides with the Prosecution

Justice Anthony M. Kennedy wrote for the majority in *Berghuis v. Thompkins*, agreeing with the State of Michigan that Thompkins's confession was not obtained in violation of *Miranda* and was, therefore, properly introduced into his trial. The 5–4 decision was split along familiar ideological lines, with the Court's most conservative members, Chief Justice John G. Roberts and Justices Samuel A. Alito Jr., Antonin Scalia, and Clarence Thomas, joining the majority. Relatively new to the Court, Justice Sonia Sotomayor was a former Manhattan prosecutor, and many wondered if this would make her more likely to side with law enforcement than the other liberal members of the Court. Instead, she wrote a strongly worded dissent, characterizing the majority decision as turning *Miranda* "upside down."

The majority addressed two separate questions. First, whether Thompkins's silence during the interrogation invoked his right to remain silent. And second, whether Thompkins waived his right to remain silent when he made a statement to the police.

In addressing whether Thompkins's sustained silence in the face of hours of questioning invoked his right to remain silent, the Court cited a 1994 ruling, *Davis v. United States*, that addressed the other *Miranda* right—the right to counsel. *Davis* held that a suspect wanting to cut off interrogation until a lawyer can be present must invoke his right to counsel "unambiguously." Justice Kennedy found "no principled reason to adopt different standards for determining when an accused has invoked the *Miranda* right to remain silent and the *Miranda* right to counsel at issue in *Davis*. If Thompkins had wanted to cut off questioning, the Court reasoned, all he had to do was say that he wanted to remain silent or that he did not want to talk to the police. Either of these "simple unambiguous statements," the Court held, would have invoked his "right to cut off questioning," and Thompkins made neither. Requiring a clear assertion of the right to remain silent, the Court concluded, keeps the inquiry objective and prevents the suppression of voluntary confessions just because the police guessed wrong about a suspect's silence or ambiguous statement.

Next, the Court considered whether Thompkins had waived his right to remain silent when he answered "yes" to the question about praying for forgiveness for the shooting. Here the Court stepped back from the language of *Miranda*, which placed a "heavy burden on the government to demonstrate that a defendant knowingly and intelligently waived his privilege against self-incrimination" and clearly stated that "a valid waiver will not be presumed simply from the silence of the accused after warnings are given or simply from the fact that a confession was in fact eventually obtained." Instead, Justice Kennedy relied on the "course of decisions since *Miranda*," which he described as reaffirming *Miranda*'s main purpose of ensuring that the accused be told his or her rights and understands them, but reducing its impact on legitimate law enforcement. All the police need to do, the majority held, is show that a *Miranda* warning was given and that the accused understood it; then any subsequent uncoerced statement can be presumed to be a deliberate choice to waive the right to remain silent.

In her vigorous dissent, Justice Sotomayor described the majority opinion as a "substantial retreat from the protection against compelled self-incrimination." She criticized as counterintuitive the requirement that suspects must speak to invoke their rights not to speak. There is nothing in the warnings, she protested, that would hint to a suspect that his or her rights can only be acquired through certain "magic words," and it is unlikely that the police will provide guidance. The majority's opinion, she argued, undercuts the "heavy burden" the government should have to show that a defendant has given up the right against self-incrimination, reducing it to "the bare fact that a suspect made inculpatory statements after *Miranda* warnings were given and understood." This, she concludes, is "inconsistent with the fair-trial principles on which" *Miranda* and its subsequent interpretations are grounded. She was joined in dissent by Justices John Paul Stevens, Ruth Bader Ginsburg, and Stephen G. Breyer.

Reaction to the *Thompkins* Decision

Advocacy organizations on both sides of this case all agreed that the Court's opinion had scaled back the *Miranda* doctrine. Steven Shapiro, legal director of the American Civil Liberties Union (ACLU), which had filed an *amicus* brief in this case, said the decision provided police and prosecutors with a "roadmap" around *Miranda* and was not based on "the realities of custodial interrogation, the pressures confronting suspects who are being questioned by the police for a serious crime without a lawyer, and the risk of false confessions under those circumstances." Kent Scheidegger, legal director of the Sacramento-based Criminal Justice Legal Foundation, applauded the decision for recognizing "the practical realities that the police face in dealing with suspects." Suspects do not, he said, "always answer the waiver question clearly. When they do not, the bright-line rule of *Miranda* should not apply, and the statement should be admissible as long as it is not compelled."

Nationwide, the police procedure guides of many police departments now explicitly require more of officers questioning suspects than is required by the Supreme Court. Those departments will now have to decide if they still want to continue, for example, requiring explicit waivers from suspects before questioning, or if they want to take advantage of this new Court ruling.

—Melissa Feinberg

Following are excerpts from the U.S. Supreme Court ruling in Berghuis v. Thompkins, *in which the Court ruled 5–4 to make it easier for prosecutors to prove that suspects waived their* Miranda *rights.*

DOCUMENT ## Berghuis v. Thompkins

June 1, 2010

No. 08–1470

Mary Berghuis, Warden, Petitioner
v.
Van Chester Thompkins
[June 1, 2010]

On writ of certiorari to
the United States Court of
Appeals for the Sixth Circuit

JUSTICE KENNEDY delivered the opinion of the Court.

The United States Court of Appeals for the Sixth Circuit, in a habeas corpus proceeding challenging a Michigan conviction for first-degree murder and certain other offenses, ruled that there had been two separate constitutional errors in the trial that led to the jury's guilty verdict. First, the Court of Appeals determined that a statement by the accused, relied on at trial by the prosecution, had been elicited in violation of *Miranda* v. *Arizona*, 384 U. S. 436 (1966). Second, it found that failure to ask for an instruction relating to testimony from an accomplice was ineffective assistance by defense counsel. Both of these contentions had been rejected in Michigan courts and in the habeas corpus proceedings before the United States District Court. Certiorari was granted to review the decision by the Court of Appeals on both points. The warden of a Michigan correctional facility is the petitioner here, and Van Chester Thompkins, who was convicted, is the respondent....

[Sections I and II, containing background on the case, have been omitted.]

III

The *Miranda* Court formulated a warning that must be given to suspects before they can be subjected to custodial interrogation. The substance of the warning still must be given to suspects today. A suspect in custody must be advised as follows:

"He must be warned prior to any questioning that he has the right to remain silent, that anything he says can be used against him in a court of law, that he has the right to the presence of an attorney, and that if he cannot afford an attorney one will be appointed for him prior to any questioning if he so desires."

All concede that the warning given in this case was in full compliance with these requirements. The dispute centers on the response—or nonresponse—from the suspect.

A

Thompkins makes various arguments that his answers to questions from the detectives were inadmissible. He first contends that he "invoke[d] his privilege" to remain silent by not saying anything for a sufficient period of time, so the interrogation should have "cease[d]" before he made his inculpatory statements. *Id.*, at 474; see *Mosley*, 423 U. S., at 103 (police must "'scrupulously hono[r]'" this "critical safeguard" when the accused invokes his or her "'right to cut off questioning'" (quoting *Miranda, supra*, at 474, 479)).

This argument is unpersuasive. In the context of invoking the *Miranda* right to counsel, the Court in *Davis* v. *United States*, 512 U. S. 452, 459 (1994), held that a suspect must do so "unambiguously." If an accused makes a statement concerning the right to counsel "that is ambiguous or equivocal" or makes no statement, the police are not required to end the interrogation, *ibid.*, or ask questions to clarify whether the accused wants to invoke his or her *Miranda* rights, 512 U. S., at 461–462.

The Court has not yet stated whether an invocation of the right to remain silent can be ambiguous or equivocal, but there is no principled reason to adopt different standards for determining when an accused has invoked the *Miranda* right to remain silent and the *Miranda* right to counsel at issue in *Davis*. See, *e.g., Solem* v. *Stumes*, 465 U. S. 638, 648 (1984) ("[M]uch of the logic and language of *[Mosley]*," which discussed the *Miranda* right to remain silent, "could be applied to the invocation of the [*Miranda* right to counsel]"). Both protect the privilege against compulsory self-incrimination, *Miranda, supra*, at 467–473, by requiring an interrogation to cease when either right is invoked, *Mosley, supra*, at 103 (citing *Miranda, supra*, at 474); *Fare* v. *Michael C.*, 442 U. S. 707, 719 (1979).

There is good reason to require an accused who wants to invoke his or her right to remain silent to do so unambiguously. A requirement of an unambiguous invocation of *Miranda* rights results in an objective inquiry that "avoid[s] difficulties of proof and . . . provide[s] guidance to officers" on how to proceed in the face of ambiguity. If an ambiguous act, omission, or statement could require police to end the interrogation, police would be required to make difficult decisions about an accused's unclear intent and face the consequence of suppression "if they guess wrong." Suppression of a voluntary confession in these circumstances would place a significant burden on society's interest in prosecuting criminal activity. Treating an ambiguous or equivocal act, omission, or statement as an invocation of *Miranda* rights "might add marginally to *Miranda*'s goal of dispelling the compulsion inherent in custodial interrogation." But "as *Miranda* holds, full comprehension of the rights to remain silent and request an attorney are sufficient to dispel whatever coercion is inherent in the interrogation process."

Thompkins did not say that he wanted to remain silent or that he did not want to talk with the police. Had he made either of these simple, unambiguous statements, he would have invoked his "'right to cut off questioning.'" Here he did neither, so he did not invoke his right to remain silent.

B

We next consider whether Thompkins waived his right to remain silent. Even absent the accused's invocation of the right to remain silent, the accused's statement during a custodial interrogation is inadmissible at trial unless the prosecution can establish that the accused "in fact knowingly and voluntarily waived [Miranda] rights" when making the statement. The waiver inquiry "has two distinct dimensions": waiver must be "voluntary in the sense that it was the product of a free and deliberate choice rather than intimidation, coercion, or deception," and "made with a full awareness of both the nature of the right being abandoned and the consequences of the decision to abandon it."

Some language in Miranda could be read to indicate that waivers are difficult to establish absent an explicit written waiver or a formal, express oral statement. Miranda said "a valid waiver will not be presumed simply from the silence of the accused after warnings are given or simply from the fact that a confession was in fact eventually obtained." 384 U. S., at 475; see id., at 470 ("No effective waiver . . . can be recognized unless specifically made after the [Miranda] warnings . . . have been given"). In addition, the Miranda Court stated that "a heavy burden rests on the government to demonstrate that the defendant knowingly and intelligently waived his privilege against self-incrimination and his right to retained or appointed counsel."

The course of decisions since Miranda, informed by the application of Miranda warnings in the whole course of law enforcement, demonstrates that waivers can be established even absent formal or express statements of waiver that would be expected in, say, a judicial hearing to determine if a guilty plea has been properly entered. Cf. Fed. Rule Crim. Proc. 11. The main purpose of Miranda is to ensure that an accused is advised of and understands the right to remain silent and the right to counsel. Thus, "[i]f anything, our subsequent cases have reduced the impact of the Miranda rule on legitimate law enforcement while reaffirming the decision's core ruling that unwarned statements may not be used as evidence in the prosecution's case in chief."

One of the first cases to decide the meaning and import of Miranda with respect to the question of waiver was North Carolina v. Butler. The Butler Court, after discussing some of the problems created by the language in Miranda, established certain important propositions. Butler interpreted the Miranda language concerning the "heavy burden" to show waiver, 384 U. S., at 475, in accord with usual principles of determining waiver, which can include waiver implied from all the circumstances. And in a later case, the Court stated that this "heavy burden" is not more than the burden to establish waiver by a preponderance of the evidence.

The prosecution therefore does not need to show that a waiver of Miranda rights was express. An "implicit waiver" of the "right to remain silent" is sufficient to admit a suspect's statement into evidence. Butler made clear that a waiver of Miranda rights may be implied through "the defendant's silence, coupled with an understanding of his rights and a course of conduct indicating waiver." The Court in Butler therefore "retreated" from the "language and tenor of the Miranda opinion," which "suggested that the Court would require that a waiver . . . be 'specifically made.'"

If the State establishes that a Miranda warning was given and the accused made an uncoerced statement, this showing, standing alone, is insufficient to demonstrate "a valid waiver" of Miranda rights. The prosecution must make the additional showing that the accused understood these rights. See Colorado v. Spring, 479 U. S. 564, 573–575 (1987); Barrett, supra, at 530; Burbine, supra, at 421–422. Cf. Tague v. Louisiana, 444 U. S. 469, 469,

471 (1980) *(per curiam)* (no evidence that accused understood his *Miranda* rights); *Carnley* v. *Cochran*, 369 U. S. 506, 516 (1962) (government could not show that accused "understandingly" waived his right to counsel in light of "silent record"). Where the prosecution shows that a *Miranda* warning was given and that it was understood by the accused, an accused's uncoerced statement establishes an implied waiver of the right to remain silent.

Although *Miranda* imposes on the police a rule that is both formalistic and practical when it prevents them from interrogating suspects without first providing them with a *Miranda* warning, see *Burbine*, 475 U. S., at 427, it does not impose a formalistic waiver procedure that a suspect must follow to relinquish those rights. As a general proposition, the law can presume that an individual who, with a full understanding of his or her rights, acts in a manner inconsistent with their exercise has made a deliberate choice to relinquish the protection those rights afford. See, *e.g.*, *Butler*, *supra*, at 372–376; *Connelly*, *supra*, at 169–170 ("There is obviously no reason to require more in the way of a 'voluntariness' inquiry in the *Miranda* waiver context than in the [due process] confession context"). The Court's cases have recognized that a waiver of *Miranda* rights need only meet the standard of *Johnson* v. *Zerbst*, 304 U. S. 458, 464 (1938). See *Butler*, *supra*, at 374–375; *Miranda*, *supra*, at 475–476 (applying *Zerbst* standard of intentional relinquishment of a known right). As *Butler* recognized, 441 U. S., at 375–376, *Miranda* rights can therefore be waived through means less formal than a typical waiver on the record in a courtroom, cf. Fed.Rule Crim. Proc. 11, given the practical constraints and necessities of interrogation and the fact that *Miranda*'s main protection lies in advising defendants of their rights, see *Davis*, 512 U. S., at 460; *Burbine*, 475 U. S., at 427.

The record in this case shows that Thompkins waived his right to remain silent. There is no basis in this case to conclude that he did not understand his rights; and on these facts it follows that he chose not to invoke or rely on those rights when he did speak. First, there is no contention that Thompkins did not understand his rights; and from this it follows that he knew what he gave up when he spoke. . . .

Second, Thompkins's answer to Detective Helgert's question about whether Thompkins prayed to God for forgiveness for shooting the victim is a "course of conduct indicating waiver" of the right to remain silent. If Thompkins wanted to remain silent, he could have said nothing in response to Helgert's questions, or he could have unambiguously invoked his *Miranda* rights and ended the interrogation. The fact that Thompkins made a statement about three hours after receiving a *Miranda* warning does not overcome the fact that he engaged in a course of conduct indicating waiver. Police are not required to rewarn suspects from time to time. Thompkins's answer to Helgert's question about praying to God for forgiveness for shooting the victim was sufficient to show a course of conduct indicating waiver. This is confirmed by the fact that before then Thompkins had given sporadic answers to questions throughout the interrogation.

Third, there is no evidence that Thompkins's statement was coerced. Thompkins does not claim that police threatened or injured him during the interrogation or that he was in any way fearful. . . . In these circumstances, Thompkins knowingly and voluntarily made a statement to police, so he waived his right to remain silent.

C

Thompkins next argues that, even if his answer to Detective Helgert could constitute a waiver of his right to remain silent, the police were not allowed to question him until they obtained a waiver first. . . .

In order for an accused's statement to be admissible at trial, police must have given the accused a *Miranda* warning. If that condition is established, the court can proceed to consider whether there has been an express or implied waiver of *Miranda* rights. In making its ruling on the admissibility of a statement made during custodial questioning, the trial court, of course, considers whether there is evidence to support the conclusion that, from the whole course of questioning, an express or implied waiver has been established. Thus, after giving a *Miranda* warning, police may interrogate a suspect who has neither invoked nor waived his or her *Miranda* rights. On these premises, it follows the police were not required to obtain a waiver of Thompkins's *Miranda* rights before commencing the interrogation.

D

In sum, a suspect who has received and understood the *Miranda* warnings, and has not invoked his *Miranda* rights, waives the right to remain silent by making an uncoerced statement to the police. Thompkins did not invoke his right to remain silent and stop the questioning. Understanding his rights in full, he waived his right to remain silent by making a voluntary statement to the police. The police, moreover, were not required to obtain a waiver of Thompkins's right to remain silent before interrogating him. . . .

* * *

The judgment of the Court of Appeals is reversed, and the case is remanded with instructions to deny the petition.

It is so ordered.

JUSTICE SOTOMAYOR, with whom JUSTICE STEVENS, JUSTICE GINSBURG, and JUSTICE BREYER join, dissenting.

The Court concludes today that a criminal suspect waives his right to remain silent if, after sitting tacit and uncommunicative through nearly three hours of police interrogation, he utters a few one-word responses. The Court also concludes that a suspect who wishes to guard his right to remain silent against such a finding of "waiver" must, counterintuitively, speak—and must do so with sufficient precision to satisfy a clear-statement rule that construes ambiguity in favor of the police. Both propositions mark a substantial retreat from the protection against compelled self-incrimination that *Miranda* v. *Arizona*, 384 U. S. 436 (1966), has long provided during custodial interrogation. The broad rules the Court announces today are also troubling because they are unnecessary to decide this case, which is governed by the deferential standard of review set forth in the Antiterrorism and Effective Death Penalty Act of 1996 (AEDPA), 28U. S. C. §2254(d). Because I believe Thompkins is entitled to relief under AEDPA on the ground that his statements were admitted at trial without the prosecution having carried its burden to show that he waived his right to remain silent; because longstanding principles of judicial restraint counsel leaving for another day the questions of law the Court reaches out to decide; and because the Court's answers to those questions do not result from a faithful application of our prior decisions, I respectfully dissent. . . .

* * *

Today's decision turns *Miranda* upside down. Criminal suspects must now unambiguously invoke their right to remain silent—which, counterintuitively, requires them to speak. At the same time, suspects will be legally presumed to have waived their rights even if they have given no clear expression of their intent to do so. Those results, in my view, find no basis in *Miranda* or our subsequent cases and are inconsistent with the fair-trial principles on which those precedents are grounded. Today's broad new rules are all the more unfortunate because they are unnecessary to the disposition of the case before us.

I respectfully dissent.

Source: U.S. Supreme Court. *Berghuis v. Thompkins*, 560 U.S.___(2010). http://www.supremecourt.gov/opinions/09pdf/08-1470.pdf.

Other Historic Documents of Interest

From Previous *Historic Documents*

Supreme Court Rules on Material Support of Terrorist Organizations

JUNE 21, 2010

The only terrorism-related case to be heard in 2010 did not involve issues of detainee rights. Instead, the USA PATRIOT Act, the sweeping law passed just weeks after the September 11, 2001, attacks, went before the U.S. Supreme Court for the first time. In *Holder v. Humanitarian Law Project*, decided on June 21, 2010, the Supreme Court ruled on a free speech challenge to one of the government's most frequently used tools in the battle against terrorism. In this collision of free speech rights and security rights, the Court sided this time with the government. The 6–3 decision upheld a key section of the Patriot Act that prohibits the provision of "material support" to foreign organizations that have been designated as terrorists by the secretary of state. It held that this law could be applied to the actions of the humanitarian organization that challenged it, even though it wanted only to provide training and advocacy for peaceful, lawful activity.

THE LAW AND ITS CHALLENGERS

Six weeks after the September 11, 2001, attacks, Congress passed the USA PATRIOT Act to enhance federal antiterrorism investigations. Some of its provisions provided for roving wiretaps, intelligence-sharing, and secret searches of records, including library patrons' records. Signed into law with little debate, the sweeping act became more controversial over time for raising civil liberties and privacy concerns.

The provision at issue in this case was originally passed in the wake of the Oklahoma City bombing in 1996, expanded through the Patriot Act of 2001, and then amended again in 2004. With this law, Congress made it a federal crime to knowingly provide "material support or resources" to any foreign organizations designated by the secretary of state as a terrorist organization. Beyond assistance such as providing cash, weapons, or bomb-building expertise, the law defines the illegal "material support or resources" to include "service," "training," "expert advice or assistance," or "personnel." Anyone convicted under this statute could be imprisoned for up to fifteen years. Solicitor General Elena Kagan argued the government's case just before facing her confirmation hearings to be the newest member of the Supreme Court. She described the "material support" prohibition in the Patriot Act as vitally important to the government's antiterrorism legal campaign; it had been used to charge 150 defendants since 2001, resulting in seventy-five convictions.

The nonprofit Humanitarian Law Project and its president, Ralph Fertig, brought this lawsuit together with five nonprofit groups dedicated to the interests of persons of Tamil descent. Originally filed in 1998, the suit has had a long and complicated history, repeatedly starting over as the law was amended. None of the organizations were ever charged under the law; rather, they brought what is known as a "preenforcement action," arguing that their work on behalf of the peaceful goals of two organizations on the terrorist list brought a "credible threat of prosecution." Rather than waiting to be prosecuted, they sought a ruling that the law would be unconstitutional as applied to their work of helping these groups achieve peaceful goals.

Specifically, the Humanitarian Law Project and the other plaintiffs claimed that they wished to provide support for the humanitarian and political activities of two organizations on the terrorist list but could not do so for fear of prosecution. The first group on the terrorist list is the Kurdistan Workers' Party (PKK), an organization founded in 1974 with the goal of establishing an independent Kurdish state in southeastern Turkey. According to the State Department, the PKK insurrection has claimed more than twenty-two thousand lives. The second organization is the Liberation Tigers of Tamil Eelam (LTTE). Founded in 1976, this group has worked to pursue the creation of an independent Tamil state in Sri Lanka. The LTTE has an extensive history of suicide bombings and political assassinations. While both of these groups have committed numerous terrorist attacks, they both also engage in political as well as humanitarian activities.

The Humanitarian Law Project sought a ruling that it could safely continue its work training members of the PKK on how to use humanitarian and international law to peacefully resolve disputes, engage in political advocacy on behalf of the Kurds in Turkey, and teach PKK members how to petition the United Nations for relief. Many of the activities planned by the other plaintiffs on behalf of the LTTE were rendered moot by the group's recent defeat by the military of Sri Lanka.

According to the Court, both sides in this case took "extreme positions." The Court said that the plaintiffs made the extreme argument that their proposed advocacy of peaceful, lawful activities was "pure political speech" and as such cannot be a crime under the First Amendment to the Constitution. But the Court also characterized as extreme the government claims that the plaintiffs' interactions with the PKK and the LTTE are "pure" conduct and as such clearly outlawed by the statute. The majority rejected both parties' characterizations, holding that the First Amendment issues are "more refined than either the plaintiffs or the government would have it."

Ban on "Material Support" for Terror Groups May Ban Some Speech

Chief Justice John G. Roberts wrote the majority opinion and was joined by the Court's main conservatives, Justices Antonin Scalia, Anthony Kennedy, Clarence Thomas, and Samuel Alito, and also the Court's retiring liberal, Justice John Paul Stevens.

After relatively easily dismissing the concerns that the "material support" statute is unconstitutionally vague, the Court turned its attention to whether the statute violates the plaintiffs' freedom of speech. First, the Court rejected the government's arguments that the law regulated actions and not expression, characterizing what the plaintiffs want to do as "provide material support to the PKK and LTTE in the form of speech." When government regulation is related to expression, the Court will apply a more demanding standard.

Looking then to the government's interest in this law, the Court acknowledges that all parties agree that combating terrorism is an urgent objective of the highest order. However, it rejected the plaintiffs' argument that the government's interest is not served by banning the work of humanitarian organizations to advance the legitimate rather than violent activities of designated terrorist organizations. In analyzing whether it is possible to distinguish material support for violent activities from nonviolent activities, the Court cited congressional findings that "foreign organizations that engage in terrorist activity . . . are so tainted by their criminal conduct that any contribution to such an organization facilitates that conduct." Congress detailed multiple ways that material support meant only to further peaceful goals could result in increased terrorism. Such support could free up other resources that may be put to violent ends, lend legitimacy to the terrorist groups making recruiting members and raising funds easier, and strain U.S. relations with allies undermining cooperative efforts to prevent terrorist attacks. State Department findings further support the notion that "it is highly likely that any material support to these organizations will ultimately inure to the benefit of their criminal, terrorist functions—regardless of whether such support was ostensibly intended to support non-violent, non-terrorist activities."

These conclusions of the political branches of government are entitled to deference, according to the Court. While it is important, Chief Justice Roberts emphasized, that security interests do not automatically trump the Court's obligation to "secure the protection that the Constitution grants to individuals," he also noted that "neither the Members of this Court nor most federal judges begin the day with briefings that may describe new and serious threats to our Nation and its people." Further, "when it comes to collecting evidence and drawing factual inferences in this area, 'the lack of competence on the part of the courts is marked,' and respect for the Government's conclusions is appropriate." In this case, the Court found that, given the sensitive national security and foreign affairs interests, "the political branches have adequately substantiated their determination that, to serve the government's interest in preventing terrorism, it was necessary to prohibit providing material support in the form of training, expert advice, personnel, and services to foreign terrorist groups, even if the supporters meant to promote only the groups' nonviolent ends."

Although broadly deferring to the decisions of the executive and legislative branches about how to protect the United States from acts of terrorism, Chief Justice Roberts also emphasized the narrow scope of the decision. He made clear that the "material support" law does not prevent the plaintiffs from any "independent advocacy or expression of any kind," meaning the groups may say and write anything they want about the PKK and the LTTE, the governments of Turkey or Sri Lanka, human rights, or international law. They may advocate on issues before the United Nations, even become members of the groups. But, they must do so independently, on their own. Only speech "under the direction of, or in coordination with foreign groups that the speaker knows to be terrorist organizations" may be prohibited.

Justice Stephen Breyer not only wrote a dissenting opinion that was joined by Justices Ruth Bader Ginsburg and Sonia Sotomayor but also took the unusual step of reading a summary of his dissent aloud from the bench. In his view, the Court should have required the government to show with more specific evidence that its prohibition of peaceful speech-related activity is necessary to serve the compelling interest of combating terrorism. The majority's narrowing of its ruling to cover only material support provided in "coordination with" a terrorist group did not satisfy Breyer, who wrote, "There is no practical way to organize classes for a group (say, wishing to learn about human rights law) without 'coordination.'"

REACTION TO AND IMPACT OF THE OPINION

The decision triggered criticism from civil rights and humanitarian groups. The American Civil Liberties Union (ACLU), which had filed an *amicus* brief in the case, issued a statement projecting that the ruling will thwart "the efforts of human rights organizations to persuade violent actors to renounce violence or cease their human rights abuses and jeopardizes the provision of aid and disaster relief in conflict zones controlled by designated groups." Former president Jimmy Carter expressed his disappointment in the ruling as well, saying that the statute "inhibits the work of human rights and conflict resolution groups," leaving groups such as his Carter Center, which must work with groups that have engaged in violence, wondering if they "will be prosecuted for our work to promote peace and freedom."

Other groups, such as the Anti-Defamation League, described the ruling as "right on target." In a statement, the league said, "One cannot provide 'humanitarian' support . . . to a terrorist organization without helping [its] bottom line and facilitating violence, destruction and murder."

In September, several months after the Court decision, federal agents searched the homes of antiwar activists in both Minneapolis and Chicago, investigating possible links with terrorist organizations in the Middle East and South America. Steve Warfield, spokesperson for the Federal Bureau of Investigation in Minneapolis, described the searches as pursuant to warrants "seeking evidence in support of an ongoing Joint Terrorism Task Force investigation into activities concerning the material support of terrorism." According to foxnews.com, an attorney for a Chicago antiwar activist whose home was searched says that he believes the ruling in *Holder v. Humanitarian Law Project* has "opened the door for such raids."

—Melissa Feinberg

The following are excerpts from the U.S. Supreme Court ruling in Holder v. Humanitarian Law Project, *in which the Court ruled 6–3 to uphold the illegality of providing material support to terrorist organizations, even in the case of humanitarian aid.*

DOCUMENT # Holder v. Humanitarian Law Project

June 21, 2010

Nos. 08–1498 and 09–89

Eric H. Holder, Jr., Attorney General, et al., Petitioners v. Humanitarian Law Project et al. Humanitarian Law Project, et al., Petitioners v. Eric H. Holder, Jr., Attorney General, et al.	On writs of certiorari to the United States Court of Appeals for the Ninth Circuit

[June 21, 2010]

CHIEF JUSTICE ROBERTS delivered the opinion of the Court.

Congress has prohibited the provision of "material support or resources" to certain foreign organizations that engage in terrorist activity. That prohibition is based on a finding that the specified organizations "are so tainted by their criminal conduct that any contribution to such an organization facilitates that conduct." Antiterrorism and Effective Death Penalty Act of 1996 (AEDPA), §301(a)(7), 110 Stat. 1247, note following 18 U.S.C. §2339B (Findings and Purpose). The plaintiffs in this litigation seek to provide support to two such organizations. Plaintiffs claim that they seek to facilitate only the lawful, nonviolent purposes of those groups, and that applying the material-support law to prevent them from doing so violates the Constitution. In particular, they claim that the statute is too vague, in violation of the Fifth Amendment, and that it infringes their rights to freedom of speech and association, in violation of the First Amendment. We conclude that the material-support statute is constitutional as applied to the particular activities plaintiffs have told us they wish to pursue. We do not, however, address the resolution of more difficult cases that may arise under the statute in the future....

[Sections I, II, III, IV and V-A, containing case background, have been omitted.]

V

B

The First Amendment issue before us is more refined than either plaintiffs or the Government would have it. It is not whether the Government may prohibit pure political speech, or may prohibit material support in the form of conduct. It is instead whether the Government may prohibit what plaintiffs want to do—provide material support to the PKK and LTTE in the form of speech.

Everyone agrees that the Government's interest in combating terrorism is an urgent objective of the highest order. Plaintiffs' complaint is that the ban on material support, applied to what they wish to do, is not "necessary to further that interest." The objective of combating terrorism does not justify prohibiting their speech, plaintiffs argue, because their support will advance only the legitimate activities of the designated terrorist organizations, not their terrorism.

Whether foreign terrorist organizations meaningfully segregate support of their legitimate activities from support of terrorism is an empirical question. When it enacted §2339B in 1996, Congress made specific findings regarding the serious threat posed by international terrorism. One of those findings explicitly rejects plaintiffs' contention that their support would not further the terrorist activities of the PKK and LTTE: "[F]oreign organizations that engage in terrorist activity are so tainted by their criminal conduct that *any contribution to such an organization* facilitates that conduct."

Plaintiffs argue that the reference to "any contribution" in this finding meant only monetary support. There is no reason to read the finding to be so limited, particularly because Congress expressly prohibited so much more than monetary support in §2339B. Congress's use of the term "contribution" is best read to reflect a determination that any form of material support furnished "to" a foreign terrorist organization should be barred, which is precisely what the material-support statute does. Indeed, when Congress enacted §2339B, Congress simultaneously removed an exception that had existed in §2339A(a) (1994ed.) for the provision of material support in the form of "humanitarian assistance to persons not directly involved in" terrorist activity. That repeal demonstrates that Congress considered and rejected the view that ostensibly peaceful aid would have no harmful effects.

We are convinced that Congress was justified in rejecting that view. The PKK and the LTTE are deadly groups. "The PKK's insurgency has claimed more than 22,000 lives." The LTTE has engaged in extensive suicide bombings and political assassinations, including killings of the Sri Lankan President, Security Minister, and Deputy Defense Minister. *Id.*, at 130–132; Brief for Government 6–7. "On January 31, 1996, the LTTE exploded a truck bomb filled with an estimated 1,000 pounds of explosives at the Central Bank in Colombo, killing 100 people and injuring more than 1,400. This bombing was the most deadly terrorist incident in the world in 1996." It is not difficult to conclude as Congress did that the "tain[t]" of such violent activities is so great that working in coordination with or at the command of the PKK and LTTE serves to legitimize and further their terrorist means.

Material support meant to "promot[e] peaceable, lawful conduct," Brief for Plaintiffs 51, can further terrorism by foreign groups in multiple ways. "Material support" is a valuable resource by definition. Such support frees up other resources within the organization that may be put to violent ends. It also importantly helps lend legitimacy to foreign terrorist groups—legitimacy that makes it easier for those groups to persist, to recruit members, and to raise funds—all of which facilitate more terrorist attacks. "Terrorist organizations do not maintain *organizational* 'firewalls' that would prevent or deter . . . sharing and commingling of support and benefits." "[I]nvestigators have revealed how terrorist groups systematically conceal their activities behind charitable, social, and political fronts." M. Levitt, Hamas: Politics, Charity, and Terrorism in the Service of Jihad 2–3 (2006). "Indeed, some designated foreign terrorist organizations use social and political components to recruit personnel to carry out terrorist operations, and to provide support to criminal terrorists and their families in aid of such operations." McKune Affidavit, App. 135, ¶11; Levitt, *supra*, at 2 ("Muddying the waters between its political activism, good works, and terrorist attacks, Hamas is able to use its overt political and charitable organizations as a financial and logistical support network for its terrorist operations").

Money is fungible, and "[w]hen foreign terrorist organizations that have a dual structure raise funds, they highlight the civilian and humanitarian ends to which such moneys could be put." But "there is reason to believe that foreign terrorist organizations do not maintain legitimate *financial* firewalls between those funds raised for civil, nonviolent activities, and those ultimately used to support violent, terrorist operations." Thus, "[f]unds raised ostensibly for charitable purposes have in the past been redirected by some terrorist groups to fund the purchase of arms and explosives." *Id.*, at 134, ¶10. See also Brief for Anti-Defamation League as *Amicus Curiae* 19–29 (describing fundraising activities by the PKK, LTTE, and Hamas); *Regan v. Wald*, 468 U. S. 222, 243 (1984) (upholding President's decision to impose travel ban to Cuba "to curtail the flow of hard currency to Cuba—currency that could then be used in support of Cuban adventurism"). There is evidence that the PKK and the LTTE, in particular, have not "respected the line between humanitarian and violent activities."

The dissent argues that there is "no natural stopping place" for the proposition that aiding a foreign terrorist organization's lawful activity promotes the terrorist organization as a whole. But Congress has settled on just such a natural stopping place: The statute reaches only material support coordinated with or under the direction of a designated foreign terrorist organization. Independent advocacy that might be viewed as promoting the group's legitimacy is not covered.

Providing foreign terrorist groups with material support in any form also furthers terrorism by straining the United States' relationships with its allies and undermining cooperative efforts between nations to prevent terrorist attacks. We see no reason to question Congress's finding that "international cooperation is required for an effective response to terrorism, as demonstrated by the numerous multilateral conventions in force providing universal prosecutive jurisdiction over persons involved in a variety of terrorist acts, including hostage taking, murder of an internationally protected person, and aircraft piracy and sabotage." . . .

C

In analyzing whether it is possible in practice to distinguish material support for a foreign terrorist group's violent activities and its nonviolent activities, we do not rely exclusively on our own inferences drawn from the record evidence. We have before us an affidavit stating the Executive Branch's conclusion on that question. The State Department informs us that "[t]he experience and analysis of the U. S. government agencies charged with combating terrorism strongly suppor[t]" Congress's finding that all contributions to foreign terrorist organizations further their terrorism. See *Winter* v. *Natural Resources Defense Council, Inc.*, 555 U. S. ___, ___ (2008) (slip op., at 14–15) (looking to similar affidavits to support according weight to national security claims). In the Executive's view: "Given the purposes, organizational structure, and clandestine nature of foreign terrorist organizations, it is highly likely that any material support to these organizations will ultimately inure to the benefit of their criminal, terrorist functions—regardless of whether such support was ostensibly intended to support non-violent, non-terrorist activities."

That evaluation of the facts by the Executive, like Congress's assessment, is entitled to deference. This litigation implicates sensitive and weighty interests of national security and foreign affairs. The PKK and the LTTE have committed terrorist acts against American citizens abroad, and the material-support statute addresses acute foreign policy concerns involving relationships with our Nation's allies. We have noted that "neither the Members of this Court nor most federal judges begin the day with briefings that may describe new and serious threats to our Nation and its people." It is vital in this context "not to substitute . . . our own evaluation of evidence for a reasonable evaluation by the Legislative Branch."

Our precedents, old and new, make clear that concerns of national security and foreign relations do not warrant abdication of the judicial role. We do not defer to the Government's reading of the First Amendment, even when such interests are at stake. We are one with the dissent that the Government's "authority and expertise in these matters do not automatically trump the Court's own obligation to secure the protection that the Constitution grants to individuals." But when it comes to collecting evidence and drawing factual inferences in this area, "the lack of competence on the part of the courts is marked," *Rostker, supra*, at 65, and respect for the Government's conclusions is appropriate.

One reason for that respect is that national security and foreign policy concerns arise in connection with efforts to confront evolving threats in an area where information can be difficult to obtain and the impact of certain conduct difficult to assess. The dissent slights these real constraints in demanding hard proof—with "detail," "specific facts," and "specific evidence"—that plaintiffs' proposed activities will support terrorist attacks. That would be a dangerous requirement. In this context, conclusions must often be based on informed judgment rather than concrete evidence, and that reality affects what we may reasonably insist on from the Government. The material-support statute is, on its face, a preventive measure—it criminalizes not terrorist attacks themselves, but aid that makes the attacks more likely to occur. The Government, when seeking to prevent imminent harms in the context of international affairs and national security, is not required to conclusively link all the pieces in the puzzle before we grant weight to its empirical conclusions. See *Zemel* v. *Rusk*, 381 U. S., at 17 ("[B]ecause of the changeable and explosive nature of contemporary international relations, . . . Congress . . . must of necessity paint with a brush broader than that it customarily wields in domestic areas"). . . .

We also find it significant that Congress has been conscious of its own responsibility to consider how its actions may implicate constitutional concerns. First, §2339B only applies to designated foreign terrorist organizations. There is, and always has been, a limited number of those organizations designated by the Executive Branch, see, *e.g.*, 74 Fed. Reg. 29742 (2009); 62 Fed. Reg. 52650 (1997), and any groups so designated may seek judicial review of the designation. Second, in response to the lower courts' holdings in this litigation, Congress added clarity to the statute by providing narrowing definitions of the terms "training," "personnel," and "expert advice or assistance," as well as an explanation of the knowledge required to violate §2339B. Third, in effectuating its stated intent not to abridge First Amendment rights, see §2339B(i), Congress has also displayed a careful balancing of interests in creating limited exceptions to the ban on material support. The definition of material support, for example, excludes medicine and religious materials. In this area perhaps more than any other, the Legislature's superior capacity for weighing competing interests means that "we must be particularly careful not to substitute our judgment of what is desirable for that of Congress." Finally, and most importantly, Congress has avoided any restriction on independent advocacy, or indeed any activities not directed to, coordinated with, or controlled by foreign terrorist groups.

At bottom, plaintiffs simply disagree with the considered judgment of Congress and the Executive that providing material support to a designated foreign terrorist organization—even seemingly benign support—bolsters the terrorist activities of that organization. That judgment, however, is entitled to significant weight, and we have persuasive evidence before us to sustain it. Given the sensitive interests in national security and foreign affairs at stake, the political branches have adequately substantiated their determination that, to serve the Government's interest in preventing terrorism, it was necessary to prohibit providing material support in the form of training, expert advice, personnel, and services to foreign terrorist groups, even if the supporters meant to promote only the groups' nonviolent ends.

We turn to the particular speech plaintiffs propose to undertake. First, plaintiffs propose to "train members of [the] PKK on how to use humanitarian and international law to peacefully resolve disputes." Congress can, consistent with the First Amendment, prohibit this direct training. It is wholly foreseeable that the PKK could use the "specific skill[s]" that plaintiffs propose to impart, §2339A(b)(2), as part of a broader strategy to promote terrorism. The PKK could, for example, pursue peaceful negotiation as a means of buying time to recover from short-term setbacks, lulling opponents into complacency, and ultimately preparing for renewed attacks. See generally A. Marcus, Blood and Belief: The PKK and the Kurdish Fight for Independence 286–295(2007) (describing the PKK's suspension of armed struggle and subsequent return to violence). A foreign terrorist organization introduced to the structures of the international legal system might use the information to threaten, manipulate, and disrupt. This possibility is real, not remote.

Second, plaintiffs propose to "teach PKK members how to petition various representative bodies such as the United Nations for relief." The Government acts within First Amendment strictures in banning this proposed speech because it teaches the organization how to acquire "relief," which plaintiffs never define with any specificity, and which could readily include monetary aid. Indeed, earlier in this litigation, plaintiffs sought to teach the LTTE "to present claims for tsunami-related aid to mediators and international bodies," 552 F. 3d, at 921, n. 1, which naturally included monetary relief. Money is fungible, *supra*, at 26, and Congress logically concluded that money a terrorist group such as the PKK obtains using the techniques plaintiffs propose to teach could be redirected to funding the group's violent activities.

Finally, plaintiffs propose to "engage in political advocacy on behalf of Kurds who live in Turkey," and "engage in political advocacy on behalf of Tamils who live in Sri Lanka." As explained above, *supra*, at 19–20, plaintiffs do not specify their expected level of coordination with the PKK or LTTE or suggest what exactly their "advocacy" would consist of. Plaintiffs' proposals are phrased at such a high level of generality that they cannot prevail in this preenforcement challenge. . . .

All this is not to say that any future applications of the material-support statute to speech or advocacy will survive First Amendment scrutiny. It is also not to say that any other statute relating to speech and terrorism would satisfy the First Amendment. In particular, we in no way suggest that a regulation of independent speech would pass constitutional muster, even if the Government were to show that such speech benefits foreign terrorist organizations. We also do not suggest that Congress could extend the same prohibition on material support at issue here to domestic organizations. We simply hold that, in prohibiting the particular forms of support that plaintiffs seek to provide to foreign terrorist groups, §2339B does not violate the freedom of speech. . . .

[Section VI Freedom of Association discussion omitted.]

* * *

The Preamble to the Constitution proclaims that the people of the United States ordained and established that charter of government in part to "provide for the common defence." As Madison explained, "[s]ecurity against foreign danger is . . . an avowed and essential object of the American Union." We hold that, in regulating the particular forms of support that plaintiffs seek to provide to foreign terrorist organizations, Congress has pursued that objective consistent with the limitations of the First and Fifth Amendments.

The judgment of the United States Court of Appeals for the Ninth Circuit is affirmed in part and reversed in part, and the cases are remanded for further proceedings consistent with this opinion.

It is so ordered.

SOURCE: U.S. Supreme Court. *Holder v. Humanitarian Law Project*, 561 U.S.___(2010). http://www .supremecourt.gov/opinions/09pdf/08-1498.pdf.

Supreme Court Rules on Second Amendment Rights

JUNE 28, 2010

In 2008, in a groundbreaking decision, the U.S. Supreme Court ruled for the first time that the Second Amendment to the Constitution describes an individual right to own a gun and not, as had been widely assumed, a right of localities to form militias. That case, *D.C. v. Heller*, invalidated a broad District of Columbia ban on handguns but found in favor of one's right to have a gun in the home for self-defense. While this decision was historic, it was narrow. Because the nation's capital is a federal enclave and not a state, the ruling applied only to federal laws and so covered only a tiny fraction of the regulations governing the ninety million people in the United States who own as many as two hundred million guns, most of whom are governed by state and local laws.

Almost exactly two years after *Heller*, a narrowly divided Supreme Court ruled in *McDonald v. Chicago* that the Second Amendment to the Constitution provides an individual with a right to bear arms that applies to all states and municipalities.

The Challenger and the Chicago Gun Laws

In 1982, in response to rampant gang and firearm violence, Chicago and the suburb of Oak Park, Illinois, passed some of the strictest gun bans in the country. In defending the laws, the Chicago City Council cited that "the convenient availability of firearms and ammunition" leads to "increased firearm related deaths and injuries" and that handguns "play a major role in the commission of homicide, aggravated assaults and armed robbery." Under Chicago's city ordinance, long guns such as rifles and some shotguns are permitted in the home, but all handguns and automatic weapons are banned. According to the attorneys for the City of Chicago, the law focuses on handguns because they are at the root of 87 percent of violent crime in the city, they can be easily stolen and used by criminals, and they may be fired accidently or used in incidents of domestic violence. Oak Park's ban is similar to that of Chicago and extends to all guns small enough to be concealed on the person. In court papers defending the city's right to regulate handguns, Chicago Corporation counsel Mara S. Georges argued that cities are ultimately responsible for the safety of their citizens, because "the genius of our federal system ordinarily leaves this type of social problem to be worked out by state and local governments, without a nationally imposed solution excluding one choice or the other."

Otis McDonald is a seventy-six-year-old retired maintenance engineer who claimed to fear for his life after his home in a crime-ridden neighborhood of Chicago was broken into three times. He is an activist in his community trying to improve his neighborhood, and this has subjected him to violent threats from drug dealers. He was one of the people who sued to overturn his city's ban on handguns in the home. "We should have at least a deterrent," he said, "and I think that will give would-be robbers something to think about when they get ready to break into a house."

THE SUPREME COURT EXTENDS THE RIGHT TO OWN A GUN TO THE STATES

After already deciding in *Heller* that the Second Amendment guaranteed individuals the right to have a gun for private use and having struck down the D.C. law, which was very similar to the Chicago laws, the Supreme Court had only one issue before it in *McDonald*. Does the Second Amendment apply to states and localities? While it may seem strange that the Bill of Rights would not automatically apply to the states, its original intent was to restrict only the power of the federal government and not to provide a limit for what states could do. Constitutional amendments passed in the aftermath of the Civil War fundamentally changed the federal system. The Fourteenth Amendment was passed to protect individual rights and outlaw discrimination. It forbade states from passing laws that abridged "the privileges or immunities of citizens of the United States" and from depriving "any person of life, liberty, or property without due process of law."

In the late nineteenth century, the Supreme Court began to hold that the Due Process Clause of the Fourteenth Amendment prohibits states from infringing Bill of Rights protections if they are "fundamental to the Nation's scheme of ordered liberty." In this way, the Court selectively applied the provisions of the Bill of Rights, such as free speech and free press, to the states one at a time. Although there are a few rare exceptions, such as the requirement of unanimous jury verdicts, eventually the Court incorporated most of the provisions of the Bill of Rights, holding them to apply in full force to both the federal government and the states.

Justice Samuel Alito, writing for the majority in *McDonald v. Chicago*, addressed for the first time whether the Second Amendment right to keep and bear arms is similarly incorporated to the states through the concept of due process. The right would, as he articulated the framework, be incorporated if it were found to be "'fundamental to *our* scheme of ordered liberty'" or "'deeply rooted in this Nation's history and tradition.'" To reach his conclusion, Alito examined the United States' history with the Second and Fourteenth Amendments, starting with the recognition of the basic right to self-defense as recognized from ancient times to the present day. In the 1760s and 1770s, it was King George III's attempts to disarm the colonists that led to strong reactions by Americans invoking their rights to keep arms. These emotions were in evidence during the 1788 debates to ratify the Constitution, where the "fear that the federal government would disarm the people in order to impose rule through a standing army" were pervasive among those who insisted on the adoption of the Bill of Rights as a condition for ratification. The opinion addresses the period after the Civil War when throughout the South "armed parties, often consisting of ex-Confederate soldiers serving in the state militias, forcibly took firearms from newly freed slaves." The opinion cites evidence that the authors of the Fourteenth Amendment aimed, in part, to protect the rights of freed slaves to bear arms to defend themselves. "It is clear," Alito concluded, "that the Framers and ratifiers of the Fourteenth Amendment counted the right to keep and bear arms among those fundamental rights necessary to our system of ordered liberty." Therefore, the Court held that the "Due Process Clause of the Fourteenth Amendment incorporates the Second Amendment right recognized in *Heller*."

Justice Alito was joined in his majority opinion by Chief Justice John G. Roberts, Justices Antonin Scalia and Anthony Kennedy, and, in part, by Justice Clarence Thomas. Justice Thomas wrote a separate concurring opinion to reach the same conclusion but by adopting a new approach advocated by constitutional scholars. Under this approach, the decision to incorporate the Second Amendment would rest not on the Due Process Clause of the Fourteenth Amendment, but on its Privileges and Immunities Clause. This approach requires overturning precedent from over a hundred years ago, and the majority declined to reconsider old law when the case could be resolved with well-settled doctrine.

In the last dissent of his career, retiring justice John Paul Stevens disagreed with the majority's reading of the history. He counseled more caution, writing that "the reasons that motivated the framers to protect the ability of militiamen to keep muskets available for military use when our Nation was in its infancy, or that motivated the Reconstruction Congress to extend full citizenship to the freedmen in the wake of the Civil War, have only a limited bearing on the question that confronts the homeowner in a crime-infested metropolis today."

Impact of the Decision

While the *McDonald* case is a symbolic victory for supporters of gun rights, the Supreme Court sent the case back to the lower courts with very little guidance on how to analyze the inevitable flood of litigation that it will trigger. It seems clear that absolute bans on handgun ownership like those at issue in D.C. and Chicago will not pass constitutional muster, but the harder cases will involve gun regulation rather than prohibition. The Alito opinion, in a section that received only a plurality of the justices, explicitly rejected "doomsday proclamations" that incorporation would imperil all regulations regarding firearms, and it repeated language from *Heller* that the right to keep and bear arms is not "'a right to keep and carry any weapon whatsoever in any manner whatsoever and for whatever purpose.'" Further, the opinion reasserted that its Second Amendment holdings do not cast doubt on longstanding regulations such as those prohibiting "'the possession of firearms by felons and the mentally ill,'" or bans on firearms in sensitive places such as "'schools and government buildings.'" The Court, however, declined to articulate the standard under which gun regulations would be evaluated. Justice Stevens predicted the opinion would "mire the federal courts in fine-grained determinations about which state and local regulations comport with the *Heller* right," all "under a standard of review we have not even established." Justice Stephen Breyer also predicted havoc in the lower courts. "Consider," he wrote in dissent, "that countless gun regulations of many shapes and sizes are in place in every state and in many local communities."

This sense of uncertainty about the impact of *McDonald* was evident in the press release from Wayne LaPierre of the National Rifle Association. While acknowledging the victory as a "great moment in American history," he committed to "work to ensure this constitutional victory is not transformed into a practical defeat by activist judges, defiant city councils, or cynical politicians who seek to pervert, reverse, or nullify the Supreme Court's *McDonald* decision through Byzantine labyrinths of restrictions and regulations that render the Second Amendment inaccessible, unaffordable, or otherwise impossible to experience in a practical, reasonable way." Paul Helmke, president of the Brady Center to Prevent Gun Violence, said that he expects criminals convicted of gun charges will use the ruling to challenge their convictions, but, at the same time, he remains confident that most gun regulations will be "quickly upheld."

The predicted avalanche of firearm-related litigation has begun, with cases already filed challenging a ban on armor-piercing ammunition and large-capacity magazines. Other possible litigation may involve assault weapons bans; bans on certain kinds of handguns, such as so-called "junk guns"; laws requiring protections for children, such as trigger locks and storage requirements; and licensing requirements, including those for carrying concealed weapons. Other lawsuits may challenge the laws of eighteen states that either require or authorize removing handguns from the scene of a domestic violence incident. Because the Court did not specify a standard of review for the courts hearing these cases, it is likely they will reach contradictory results, keeping the courts busy for a long time.

—Melissa Feinberg

Following are excerpts from the U.S. Supreme Court's ruling in McDonald v. Chicago, *in which the Court ruled 5–4 that the Constitution affords individuals a right to bear arms in all states and localities.*

DOCUMENT McDonald v. Chicago

June 28, 2010

No. 08–1521

Otis McDonald, et al., Petitioners v. City of Chicago, Illinois, et al.	On writ of certiorari to the United States Court of Appeals for the Seventh Circuit

[June 28, 2010]

JUSTICE ALITO announced the judgment of the Court and delivered the opinion of the Court with respect to Parts I, II–A, II–B, II–D, III–A, and III–B, in which THE CHIEF JUSTICE, JUSTICE SCALIA, JUSTICE KENNEDY, and JUSTICE THOMAS join, and an opinion with respect to Parts II–C, IV, and V, in which THE CHIEF JUSTICE, JUSTICE SCALIA, and JUSTICE KENNEDY join.

Two years ago, in *District of Columbia* v. *Heller*, 554 U. S. ___ (2008), we held that the Second Amendment protects the right to keep and bear arms for the purpose of self-defense, and we struck down a District of Columbia law that banned the possession of handguns in the home. The city of Chicago (City) and the village of Oak Park, a Chicago suburb, have laws that are similar to the District of Columbia's, but Chicago and Oak Park argue that their laws are constitutional because the Second Amendment has no application to the States. We have previously held that most of the provisions of the Bill of Rights apply with full force to both the Federal Government and the States. Applying the standard that is well established in our case law, we hold that the Second Amendment right is fully applicable to the States. . . .

[Sections I, IIA, IIB, IIC, IID, containing background on the case, have been omitted.]

III

With this framework in mind, we now turn directly to the question whether the Second Amendment right to keep and bear arms is incorporated in the concept of due process. In answering that question, as just explained, we must decide whether the right to keep and bear arms is fundamental to *our* scheme of ordered liberty, *Duncan*, 391 U. S., at 149, or as we have said in a related context, whether this right is "deeply rooted in this Nation's history and tradition," *Washington* v. *Glucksberg*, 521 U. S. 702, 721 (1997) (internal quotation marks omitted).

A

Our decision in *Heller* points unmistakably to the answer. Self-defense is a basic right, recognized by many legal systems from ancient times to the present day, and in *Heller*, we held that individual self-defense is "the *central component*" of the Second Amendment right. 554 U. S., at ___ (slip op., at 26); see also *id.*, at ___ (slip op., at56) (stating that the "inherent right of self-defense has been central to the Second Amendment right"). Explaining that "the need for defense of self, family, and property is most acute" in the home, *ibid.*, we found that this right applies to handguns because they are "the most preferred firearm in the nation to 'keep' and use for protection of one's home and family," *id.*, at ___ (slip op., at 57) (some internal quotation marks omitted); see also *id.*, at ___ (slip op., at 56) (noting that handguns are "overwhelmingly chosen by American society for [the] lawful purpose" of self-defense); *id.*, at ___ (slip op., at 57) ("[T]he American people have considered the handgun to be the quintessential self-defense weapon"). Thus, we concluded, citizens must be permitted "to use [handguns] for the core lawful purpose of self-defense."

Heller makes it clear that this right is "deeply rooted in this Nation's history and tradition." *Heller* explored the right's origins, noting that the 1689 English Bill of Rights explicitly protected a right to keep arms for self defense, 554 U. S., at ___–___ (slip op., at 19–20), and that by 1765, Blackstone was able to assert that the right to keep and bear arms was "one of the fundamental rights of Englishmen," *id.*, at ___ (slip op., at 20).

Blackstone's assessment was shared by the American colonists. As we noted in *Heller*, King George III's attempt to disarm the colonists in the 1760's and 1770's "provoked polemical reactions by Americans invoking their rights as Englishmen to keep arms."

The right to keep and bear arms was considered no less fundamental by those who drafted and ratified the Bill of Rights. "During the 1788 ratification debates, the fear that the federal government would disarm the people in order to impose rule through a standing army or select militia was pervasive in Antifederalist rhetoric." Federalists responded, not by arguing that the right was insufficiently important to warrant protection but by contending that the right was adequately protected by the Constitution's assignment of only limited powers to the Federal Government. But those who were fearful that the new Federal Government would infringe traditional rights such as the right to keep and bear arms insisted on the adoption of the Bill of Rights as a condition for ratification of the Constitution. This is surely powerful evidence that the right was regarded as fundamental in the sense relevant here.

This understanding persisted in the years immediately following the ratification of the Bill of Rights. In addition to the four States that had adopted Second Amendment analogues before ratification, nine more States adopted state constitutional provisions protecting an individual right to keep and bear arms between 1789 and 1820. Founding-era legal commentators confirmed the importance of the right to early Americans. . . .

B

1

By the 1850's, the perceived threat that had prompted the inclusion of the Second Amendment in the Bill of Rights—the fear that the National Government would disarm the universal militia—had largely faded as a popular concern, but the right to keep and bear arms was highly valued for purposes of self-defense. And when attempts were made to disarm "Free-Soilers" in "Bloody Kansas," Senator Charles Sumner, who later played a leading role in the adoption of the Fourteenth Amendment, proclaimed that "[n]ever was [the rifle] more needed in just self-defense than now in Kansas." Indeed, the 1856 Republican Party Platform protested that in Kansas the constitutional rights of the people had been "fraudulently and violently taken from them" and the "right of the people to keep and bear arms" had been "infringed."

After the Civil War, many of the over 180,000 African Americans who served in the Union Army returned to the States of the old Confederacy, where systematic efforts were made to disarm them and other blacks. The laws of some States formally prohibited African Americans from possessing firearms. For example, a Mississippi law provided that "no freedman, free negro or mulatto, not in the military service of the United States government, and not licensed so to do by the board of police of his or her county, shall keep or carry fire-arms of any kind, or any ammunition, dirk or bowie knife."

Throughout the South, armed parties, often consisting of ex-Confederate soldiers serving in the state militias, forcibly took firearms from newly freed slaves. In the first session of the 39th Congress, Senator Wilson told his colleagues: "In Mississippi rebel State forces, men who were in the rebel armies, are traversing the State, visiting the freedmen, disarming them, perpetrating murders and outrages upon them; and the same things are done in other sections of the country." The Report of the Joint Committee on Reconstruction—which was widely reprinted in the press and distributed by Members of the 39th Congress to their constituents shortly after Congress approved the Fourteenth Amendment—contained numerous examples of such abuses. In one town, the "marshal [took] all arms from returned colored soldiers, and [was] very prompt in shooting the blacks whenever an opportunity occur[red]." As Senator Wilson put it during the debate on a failed proposal to disband Southern militias: "There is one unbroken chain of testimony from all people that are loyal to this country, that the greatest outrages are perpetrated by armed men who go up and down the country searching houses, disarming people, committing outrages of every kind and description."

Union Army commanders took steps to secure the right of all citizens to keep and bear arms, but the 39th Congress concluded that legislative action was necessary. Its efforts to safeguard the right to keep and bear arms demonstrate that the right was still recognized to be fundamental.

The most explicit evidence of Congress' aim appears in §14 of the Freedmen's Bureau Act of 1866, which provided that "the right . . . to have full and equal benefit of all laws and proceedings concerning personal liberty, personal security, and the acquisition, enjoyment, and disposition of estate, real and personal, *including the constitutional right to bear arms*, shall be secured to and enjoyed by all the citizens . . . without respect to race or color, or previous condition of slavery." Section 14 thus explicitly guaranteed that "all the citizens," black and white, would have "the constitutional right to bear arms."

The Civil Rights Act of 1866, 14 Stat. 27, which was considered at the same time as the Freedmen's Bureau Act, similarly sought to protect the right of all citizens to keep and bear arms. Section 1 of the Civil Rights Act guaranteed the "full and equal benefit of all laws and proceedings for the security of person and property, as is enjoyed by white citizens." This language was virtually identical to language in §14 of the Freedmen's Bureau Act, 14 Stat. 176–177 ("the right . . . to have full and equal benefit of all laws and proceedings concerning personal liberty, personal security, and the acquisition, enjoyment, and disposition of estate, real and personal"). And as noted, the latter provision went on to explain that one of the "laws and proceedings concerning personal liberty, personal security, and the acquisition, enjoyment, and disposition of estate, real and personal" was "the constitutional right to bear arms." Representative Bingham believed that the Civil Rights Act protected the same rights as enumerated in the Freedmen's Bureau bill, which of course explicitly mentioned the right to keep and bear arms. The unavoidable conclusion is that the Civil Rights Act, like the Freedmen's Bureau Act, aimed to protect "the constitutional right to bear arms" and not simply to prohibit discrimination. See also Amar, Bill of Rights 264–265 (noting that one of the "core purposes of the Civil Rights Act of 1866 and of the Fourteenth Amendment was to redress the grievances" of freedmen who had been stripped of their arms and to "affirm the full and equal right of every citizen to self defense").

Congress, however, ultimately deemed these legislative remedies insufficient. Southern resistance, Presidential vetoes, and this Court's pre-Civil-War precedent persuaded Congress that a constitutional amendment was necessary to provide full protection for the rights of blacks. Today, it is generally accepted that the Fourteenth Amendment was understood to provide a constitutional basis for protecting the rights set out in the Civil Rights Act of 1866.

In debating the Fourteenth Amendment, the 39th Congress referred to the right to keep and bear arms as a fundamental right deserving of protection. Senator Samuel Pomeroy described three "indispensable" "safeguards of liberty under our form of Government." One of these, he said, was the right to keep and bear arms:

> "Every man . . . should have the right to bear arms for the defense of himself and family and his homestead. And if the cabin door of the freedman is broken open and the intruder enters for purposes as vile as were known to slavery, then should a well-loaded musket be in the hand of the occupant to send the polluted wretch to another world, where his wretchedness will forever remain complete."

Even those who thought the Fourteenth Amendment unnecessary believed that blacks, as citizens, "have equal right to protection, and to keep and bear arms for self defense." . . .

In sum, it is clear that the Framers and ratifiers of the Fourteenth Amendment counted the right to keep and bear arms among those fundamental rights necessary to our system of ordered liberty. . . .

IV . . .

Municipal respondents assert that, although state constitutions protect firearms rights, state courts have held that these rights are subject to "interest-balancing" and have sustained a variety of restrictions. In *Heller*, however, we expressly rejected the argument that the scope of the Second Amendment right should be determined by judicial interest balancing, 554 U. S., at ___–___ (slip op., at 62–63), and this Court decades ago abandoned "the notion that the Fourteenth Amendment applies to the States only a watered-down, subjective version of the individual guarantees of the Bill of Rights," *Malloy, supra,* at 10–11 (internal quotation marks omitted).

As evidence that the Fourteenth Amendment has not historically been understood to restrict the authority of the States to regulate firearms, municipal respondents and supporting *amici* cite a variety of state and local firearms laws that courts have upheld. But what is most striking about their research is the paucity of precedent sustaining bans comparable to those at issue here and in *Heller*. Municipal respondents cite precisely one case (from the late 20th century) in which such a ban was sustained. See Brief for Municipal Respondents 26–27 (citing *Kalodimos v. Morton Grove*, 103 Ill. 2d 483, 470 N. E. 2d 266 (1984)); see also Reply Brief for Respondents NRA et al. 23, n. 7 (asserting that no other court has ever upheld a complete ban on the possession of handguns). It is important to keep in mind that *Heller*, while striking down a law that prohibited the possession of handguns in the home, recognized that the right to keep and bear arms is not "a right to keep and carry any weapon whatsoever in any manner whatsoever and for whatever purpose." We made it clear in *Heller* that our holding did not cast doubt on such longstanding regulatory measures as "prohibitions on the possession of firearms by felons and the mentally ill," "laws forbidding the carrying of firearms in sensitive places such as schools and government buildings, or laws imposing conditions and qualifications on the commercial sale of arms." We repeat those assurances here. Despite municipal respondents' doomsday proclamations, incorporation does not imperil every law regulating firearms. . . .

* * *

In *Heller*, we held that the Second Amendment protects the right to possess a handgun in the home for the purpose of self-defense. Unless considerations of *stare decisis* counsel otherwise, a provision of the Bill of Rights that protects a right that is fundamental from an American perspective applies equally to the Federal Government and the States. We therefore hold that the Due Process Clause of the Fourteenth Amendment incorporates the Second Amendment right recognized in *Heller*. The judgment of the Court of Appeals is reversed, and the case is remanded for further proceedings.

It is so ordered.

JUSTICE STEVENS, dissenting . . .

[Sections I, II, III, IV, V, VI, concerning case background, have been omitted.]

VII

The fact that the right to keep and bear arms appears in the Constitution should not obscure the novelty of the Court's decision to enforce that right against the States. By its terms, the Second Amendment does not apply to the States; read properly, it does not even apply to individuals outside of the militia context. The Second Amendment was adopted to protect the *States* from federal encroachment. And the Fourteenth Amendment has never been understood by the Court to have "incorporated" the entire Bill of Rights. There was nothing foreordained about today's outcome.

Although the Court's decision in this case might be seen as a mere adjunct to its decision in *Heller*, the consequences could prove far more destructive—quite literally—to our Nation's communities and to our constitutional structure. Thankfully, the Second Amendment right identified in *Heller* and its newly minted Fourteenth Amendment analogue are limited, at least for now, to the home. But neither the "assurances" provided by the plurality, *ante*, at 40, nor the many historical sources cited in its opinion should obscure the reality that today's ruling marks a dramatic change in our law—or that the Justices who have joined it have brought to bear an awesome amount of discretion in resolving the legal question presented by this case.

I would proceed more cautiously. For the reasons set out at length above, I cannot accept either the methodology the Court employs or the conclusions it draws. Although impressively argued, the majority's decision to overturn more than a century of Supreme Court precedent and to unsettle a much longer tradition of state practice is not, in my judgment, built "upon respect for the teachings of history, solid recognition of the basic values that underlie our society, and wise appreciation of the great roles that the doctrines of federalism and separation of powers have played in establishing and preserving American freedoms."

Accordingly, I respectfully dissent.

SOURCE: U.S. Supreme Court. *McDonald v. Chicago*, 561 U.S. ___ (2010). http://www.supremecourt.gov/opinions/09pdf/08-1521.pdf.

OTHER HISTORIC DOCUMENTS OF INTEREST

FROM PREVIOUS *HISTORIC DOCUMENTS*

July

The United States and Russia Exchange Spies

JULY 8, 2010

The fictional world of espionage and intrigue that plays out across movie screens around the world came to life in July when the governments of the United States and Russia reached an agreement to exchange a total of fourteen accused spies. Ten sleeper agents had been operating inside the United States on behalf of the Russian government for more than a decade, according to the Federal Bureau of Investigation (FBI) and the U.S. Department of Justice. Unbeknownst to the spies, they were being watched by the federal government, but because they had collected no sensitive material, the government never acted on charging and deporting the agents. But on July 9, 2010, two planes touched down within minutes of each other at Vienna International Airport, and ten spies departed to Russia while four boarded an American airplane, signaling the end of the largest spy swap since the Cold War.

THE SPY RING UNFOLDS

The ten Russian spies had been watched for more than a decade by officials from the FBI and the Department of Justice. They had infiltrated suburban American towns and had set up families on quiet streets, even raising children. The Russian government had instructed the sleeper agents to blend in with high-powered intellectuals and financiers, such as those at the Kennedy School of Government at Harvard University and along Wall Street. As they infiltrated these organizations, the Russian agents would send information to Moscow Center, a part of Russia's intelligence organization. Like in a spy movie, they sent these secret messages through encrypted computers and invisible ink.

During its tracking of the spies, the U.S. government had amassed a large amount of evidence against the ten Russians, including recorded conversations, foreign travel, and videotapes of secret meetings with members of the Russian government. There was, however, little reason to act on the information, as the spies never received any information considered to be a threat to the United States. Law enforcement officials instead waited for something significant to catch their attention and force action.

In June, just months after bringing the information to the attention of President Barack Obama, U.S. officials learned that one of the spies was planning to leave the United States permanently for Russia, meaning that if any action was going to be taken, it would need to happen quickly.

It was President Obama who first floated the idea of a swap between Russia and the United States, but his administration holds firm that the swap was not discussed during the June summit in Washington, D.C., between Russia and the United States. The deal was worked out quietly, only raising suspicions of the American media in late June when the ten spies were arrested in New York, Boston, and Virginia. Shortly thereafter, the *New York Times* published the fifty-five-page court document detailing the charges against those who were arrested. Word of a swap first came to light when a man being held in a Russian prison told his family that he was going to be part of a spy trade between the United States and Russia. Russian media outlets celebrated the upcoming exchange, but the U.S. government remained mum. "This is . . . a law enforcement matter," said White House press secretary Robert Gibbs when questioned on the matter.

The United States had been working with the Russian government with the aim of a one-for-one swap. Russia was at the time holding eleven Russians prisoner on suspicion that they were spying for the United States and other Western governments, including the United Kingdom. There were originally eleven Russian agents operating in the United States, but one was released before the swap in Cyprus and immediately disappeared. In the end, the United States and Russia agreed that four of those people being held in Russia would be released to the United States. One of the four released was a Russian scientist named Igor Sutyagin, who had been sentenced to fifteen years in prison for spying for the United States, a charge he consistently denied. Another was a former colonel in Russia's Foreign Intelligence Service, Alexander Zaporozhsky, who received a sentence of eighteen years in prison from the Russian government. The other two accused of spying for Western governments were Sergei Skripal and Gennady Vasilenko, a Russian military intelligence officer and former KGB officer, respectively.

When the ten accused of spying for Russia appeared in a New York courtroom, they all pleaded guilty to the one count against them: acting as an unregistered foreign agent. Prosecutors dropped a charge of conspiracy to money launder and never filed espionage charges. Acting as an unregistered foreign agent carries no minimum sentence, which allowed the United States to quickly release the agents back to Russia with the only caveat that they never again enter the United States. Only one of the spies is not a Russian citizen. Vickey Pelaez, a native of Peru and naturalized citizen of the United States who was working as a journalist in New York, was given the freedom to leave Russia after being transported there and was also promised a visa to anywhere she might live in the future. She was awarded $2,000 per month for the rest of her life to support herself and her children.

In less than two hours after their courtroom appearance, the spies were headed for Russia. The exchange was kept under wraps by the U.S. Department of State, but the exchange culminated in Vienna when a plane from Moscow and one from New York landed within minutes of each other and parked nose-to-tail. The ten Russian spies and four Russians accused of spying for Western organizations were quickly exchanged, and the planes took off. Two of the four prisoners that were being held in Russia were taken to England, while the other two continued on to the United States.

The successful swap was praised by U.S. attorney general Eric Holder. "This was an extraordinary case, developed through years of work by investigators, intelligence lawyers, and prosecutors, and the agreement we reached today provides a successful resolution for the United States and its interests," he said.

The agreement reached by Russia and the United States was not without criticism, however. Some in the intelligence community questioned whether the United States could deter future spy activity when, in this case, it imposed few penalties on the spies that were caught and simply sent them back to their home country. U.S. intelligence officials, however, said that because the spies had been followed for so many years, and the government had as much information on their networks as necessary, there was little reason in continuing to hold or attempting to charge those responsible. "Further incarceration of these individuals wasn't going to bring us any further significant national security benefit, and we did want to take advantage of the opportunity to secure the release of the four Russian individuals who were going to be coming out," said a senior State Department official.

In a briefing with reporters, the State Department celebrated the exchange as another sign of progress in the relationship between the former Cold War foes. "I think in many respects, the handling of this case and its aftermath reflects the progress that we've made in U.S.-Russian relations," remarked an unnamed senior administration official. "After an initial statement by the Russian foreign ministry denying the charges, the Russian government moved very quickly to resolve the spy scandal, including by immediately acknowledging the Russian citizenship of the individuals involved," said the official.

Since the Cold War, a number of American and Russian citizens have been accused or found guilty of spying for one of the two nations. A number of these agents, including Robert Hanssen and Aldrich Ames, caused significant damage to U.S. national security. In contrast, the ten spies sent back to Russia were explicitly told by the Russian government not to collect any data that would be considered classified. Because of that, federal officials are still trying to determine whether the sleeper agents did any significant damage.

RUSSIAN RESPONSE TO THE EXCHANGE

Russian president Dmitry Medvedev and Prime Minister Vladmir Putin welcomed the Russian spies back with open arms. Putin gave the spies a hero's welcome home and was seen with the spies engaging in a patriotic sing-along during their return ceremony in July. Medvedev awarded each of the ten agents with the nation's highest state honor, and Putin, a former spy himself in East Germany where he worked for the KGB, said the spies would enjoy a "bright, interesting life" in Russia and would be assured good jobs.

One Russian spy had little trouble acclimating herself back into Russian society. Anna Chapman, who had received attention in the United States for racy photos posted on the Internet, was hired as the celebrity to represent a Moscow Bank and is also now a spokesperson and model for other companies, including those in the aerospace industry. As for those who exposed the spies, Putin promised to take action against those he called "traitors" and warned that they could end up "in a ditch."

—Heather Kerrigan

Following is a briefing by the U.S. Department of State on July 8, 2010, regarding the exchange of spies between the United States and Russia.

Department of State Briefing on Spy Exchange

July 8, 2010

MR. TONER: Thank you. Good evening, welcome. Thanks for joining us. As you know, there were some significant developments today in the Russian spy case. Ten individuals pleaded guilty today in Manhattan Federal Court to conspiring to act as unlawful agents within the United States on behalf of the Russian Federation.

We're pleased to have with us tonight two Senior Administration Officials who can provide further context to the day's events, both from the legal and from the diplomatic perspective. . . .

SENIOR ADMINISTRATION OFFICIAL ONE: Thank you. Earlier today, in proceedings that ended at approximately 4:45 p.m. in the United States District Court for the Southern District of New York, 10 individuals pleaded guilty to the first count of a two-count indictment or charging instrument. The defendants pleaded guilty in particular, to conspiring to act as agents of the Russian Federation without notifying the attorney general, which is a violation of two federal statutes—Section 951* of Title 18 of the United States Code.

As part of these guilty pleas, the defendants who were here under false names were required to disclose their true Russian identities. And the defendants were also required to forfeit certain money, property, and other assets. At the same hearing, they were also sentenced and ordered removed from the United States. They have agreed as part of their plea agreement never to return to the United States without the prior authorization of the attorney general.

The plea agreements between the United States and each defendant take place against the background of an agreement between the United States Government and that of the Russian Federation, which I or my colleague can describe later in the call.

MR. TONER: Thank you. Senior Administration Official number two, please.

SENIOR ADMINISTRATION OFFICIAL TWO: Sure. Just to add on the diplomatic side—the timing of the arrest of the 10 individuals was driven by our knowledge that one of the individuals intended to depart the United States. The fact that it came on the heels of the President's successful June 24th summit with President Medvedev was coincidental. I think in many respects the handling of this case and its aftermath reflects the progress that we've made in U.S.-Russian relations after an initial statement by the Russian foreign ministry denying the charges, the Russian Government moved very quickly to resolve the spy scandal, including by immediately acknowledging the Russian citizenship of the individuals involved.

As my colleague just said, as part of their plea agreement, the 10 individuals agreed to disclose their Russian identities and be immediately expelled from the United States; in turn, Russia agreed to release four individuals who they had charged with working on behalf of Western governments.

We drove the terms of this arrangement, which was based on national security as well as humanitarian grounds. After many years of monitoring the individuals, we were confident that we'd gain no significant national security benefit from their further incarceration. Instead, we took the opportunity to secure the release of the four Russian individuals, several of whom are in poor health.

Since Monday, we've had contact with the four individuals in Russia who were transferred by the Russian authorities to a prison in Moscow. We explained the opportunity—they had to leave Russia, accompanied by members of their family if they so desired. It was a Russian Government condition that each of the four individuals sign a statement admitting guilt as part of an application for pardon. And I'd leave it to the individuals involved to tell their stories, including their years of imprisonment. But in order to get out of jail, they had no choice but to sign the Russian Government oath.

As the June summit indicated, we have a full agenda to pursue with the Russian Government, and we're confident that the new approach to Russia pursued by President Obama will continue to advance our strategic interests. No one should be surprised that some vestiges of the past remain or that Russia has an active intelligence service. But the rolling up of this network, as my colleague stressed, is a significant success for U.S. law enforcement and intelligence community, and we're pleased that its aftermath has been handled quickly and pragmatically.

MR. TONER: Thank you, very much. Conference moderator, we're ready to open up to questions. . . .

QUESTION: Hi, thanks. And what happens, I guess, to the children of the ten Russian individuals who plead guilty today?

SENIOR ADMINISTRATION OFFICIAL ONE: As far as the government is concerned, we're permitting the children of these defendants to depart the United States at any time as long as the departure complies with the wishes of their parents and with any applicable requirements of U.S. law. . . .

QUESTION: Okay. And also for Vicky—Vicky Pelaez is, I guess, the one U.S. citizen. I mean, what's the—it seems legally like her case may be slightly different from the other nine, and that she's not originally a Russian citizen. Can you speak to that at all?

SENIOR ADMINISTRATION OFFICIAL ONE: It's true she is a citizen, and on the other hand though, as part of her agreement she has also agreed to leave the United States and not to return absent the authorization of the attorney general. . . .

QUESTION: Yes, hi. I was wondering if you could help with a little bit more of the mechanics of the actual exchange. They moved the Russians to Moscow, and then there were reports that one of them was going to Vienna and then on to Britain. Can you explain a little bit of the details of how this—the negotiations for the exchange began and what are the mechanics of the actual swap? There's no (inaudible) bridge this time, I guess.

SENIOR ADMINISTRATION OFFICIAL ONE: Well, we really can't comment on the mechanics of any prisoner exchange and won't get into that kind of operational matter on this call.

QUESTION: Well, how about the actual exchange? Can you actually say where it's going to take place?

SENIOR ADMINISTRATION OFFICIAL ONE: No.

QUESTION: Will it be in Europe?

SENIOR ADMINISTRATION OFFICIAL TWO: Yeah, no, sorry. We just can't get into the operational details as my colleague said. . . .

QUESTION: Hi, and thanks and congratulations on this resolution of the case. My question is, what does "immediate" mean? Have the Russians left? And then to the official number two, is this a result of your recent meeting with the Russian ambassador? And lastly, do you release the names of the people who are to be—who are supposed to be released in Russia? Can you release them? Can you share them?

SENIOR ADMINISTRATION OFFICIAL TWO: Well, just to work backwards through your questions—no, we can't release the names at this stage. Second, this has been an issue that's been handled principally on law enforcement channels which is traditionally the way it's handled. The wider national security team has certainly been involved in this and kept apprised of it. And the meeting that you referred to was focused mainly on other issues. . . .

QUESTION: Hi guys, thanks for doing the call. So, do I take it then you're not going to identify the four at this point?

SENIOR ADMINISTRATION OFFICIAL TWO: No, not at this stage we can't.

QUESTION: Okay. And can you tell us who came up with the idea of trading and how did we pick these four or—

SENIOR ADMINISTRATION OFFICIAL TWO: Well, I mean, the only thing we can say is what I mentioned before is that we drove the terms of this arrangement, but there's been a series of discussions through the channels I mentioned before about how to work out the details of it.

QUESTION: But "we drove the terms"—does that mean we said to Moscow, "Hey, guys, one way to resolve this is if we could effectuate a release of some people there" or did they come to us and say, "Hey, we'd like our people back here—some people we'll offer to you."

SENIOR ADMINISTRATION OFFICIAL TWO: Well, as I said, they took some steps very early on after the individuals in this country were arrested. After an initial statement by the foreign ministry denying the charges, the Russian Government did move quite quickly, including by immediately acknowledging the Russian citizenship of the individuals involved. And after that, we moved relatively quickly to talk about the terms of an arrangement, as I mentioned before. . . .

QUESTION: Okay. And last question is: Is—by exchanging these 10 who we've now convicted—they pleaded guilty—for these other four, are we acknowledging that these four had, in fact, worked for us in some fashion? And if not, isn't that the implication that people are going to get from it?

SENIOR ADMINISTRATION OFFICIAL TWO: No, I mean, the only thing that I'd say again is that these are individuals who had been detained in Russia on charges of working on behalf of Western governments in Russia. Those are the charges on which they were detained, but beyond that can't really offer much. . . .

QUESTION: Yeah, hi. Reading through these documents there—in each case there seems to be reference to if a person wanted to use any type of details of their experience—let's say, in the United States, or I presume during this court case, that they would have to sign over rights and any proceeds to the U.S. Government. It just struck me a little strange that in this type of document you'd be essentially saying, look, if you write—if you get a movie deal, we want the proceeds from that. Am I interpreting that correctly?

And then also, there's a reference to other steps to improve relations between the countries. Is there a further understanding that the countries have that things from now on will be handled differently in this regard?

SENIOR ADMINISTRATION OFFICIAL ONE: I will take the first part of that, and perhaps my colleague can take up the second.

With respect to the provision of the agreements about the profits from any, you know, publication or dissemination of information from the story, that is a not uncommon provision for these kinds of (inaudible) like this, that enjoy a certain notoriety. So it's not something unique to this case, it is something that's been used (inaudible) agreements before.

SENIOR ADMINISTRATION OFFICIAL TWO: Yeah, and I don't have a lot to add on the second part of your question Jill, I mean, except to say that I think it is significant, the way in which the aftermath, the resolution of this case has been handled, quickly and pragmatically. And I think that says something about the progress that we have made, and the relationship.

But there is also no doubt that the rolling up of this network is a significant success for our law enforcement and intelligence community, and I think will have a lasting impact on the capacity of the Russians in the future.

QUESTION: If I could just ask a quick follow-up here—I think we're still questioning that a little bit more. I want to know a few more details of how this was negotiated. I mean, you're saying that it was a success and it shows the relationship. How does it show that? I mean, were they more willing than in previous cases, or—

SENIOR ADMINISTRATION OFFICIAL TWO: No, I think the success that I referred to was the rolling up of the network. I mean, I think that is a significant success for the law enforcement and intelligence community.

Now, I think the only thing I was suggesting about the relative speed, and I think the pragmatic way in which the aftermath has been handled, I think clearly serves the interests of the United States since a further incarceration of these individuals wasn't going to bring us any further significant national security benefit, and we did want to take advantage of the opportunity to secure the release of the four Russian individuals who were going to be coming out. So, in that sense, I think it served our interest.

SENIOR ADMINISTRATION OFFICIAL ONE: Let me just add to that, with respect to the sort of importance of this from a law enforcement/national securities perspective, as my colleague has mentioned, we have—this really is, I think, an important achievement. We have stripped these illegal agents of their ability to operate here, and we have shut down this program here that had been running for many years. And I think, for the future, we have demonstrated our very strong counterintelligence capabilities, and that ought to serve as a warning to any other governments that might try to undertake a similar kind of operation in the future. So, I do think it is an important achievement today. . . .

QUESTION: . . . What's going to happen to the properties and monies that were seized from these 10 individuals?

And what are the kind of circumstances—I think official number one mentioned that, subject to the approval of the attorney general, that there is a—there are circumstances under which they could return to the United States. What are those circumstances?

SENIOR ADMINISTRATION OFFICIAL ONE: Well, on the first part of it, the— each plea agreement specifies certain monies and properties—. . .

SENIOR ADMINISTRATION OFFICIAL ONE: With respect to the forfeiture question, the plea agreements in each case specify certain property that will be forfeited, or that the defendant will not contest the civil or administrative forfeiture of things like, currency, bank accounts, property—real property, houses and so forth.

And so, again, this is not an uncommon term in a plea agreement of this sort. And they will—title will pass to the United States in connection with that forfeiture process.

In terms of the possibility of return, the essential elements of the plea agreement are that they consent and agree to immediate removal or expulsion from the United States, and that they agree never to re-enter the United States after their removal for any purpose, without prior authorization by the attorney general, and recognize that, if they were to re-enter the United States without that approval, it would void the plea agreement and permit prosecution.

I won't comment on the—any situation in which the attorney general might permit a return or re-entry into the United States, but it's obviously solely within the attorney general's discretion under these agreements. . . .

QUESTION: Yes. Were you suggesting—and I may have misunderstood—that your interest in getting four out long predated the arrests? And, secondly, were there discussions, negotiations underway, prior to the arrest in regard to these four?

SENIOR ADMINISTRATION OFFICIAL ONE: No. I mean, I can't really add to what I said before, except to say that we were certainly aware of the health conditions. And once the situation arose, we saw the merits, in terms of our interests, as well as the humanitarian concerns about the individuals involved in moving quickly.

QUESTION: And so you're saying that the discussions post-dated any arrests, in regard to these four?

SENIOR ADMINISTRATION OFFICIAL TWO: Well, I mean, all I would say is that we wanted to move quickly, because we saw it in our interest to see if we could obtain the release of these individuals.

QUESTION: And, again, I'm trying to make sure I understand. The order in which this happened was arrest, discussions, swap—I mean, is that right?

SENIOR ADMINISTRATION OFFICIAL TWO: Yes, it was—. . .

QUESTION: Yes, sorry, it's me again. I guess it's a follow-up to the previous question. Does the fact that you are getting four people in return mean that there are only four people there who you wanted to be returned? In other words, are there any others you are interested in getting released, but maybe who were left behind in this swap?

SENIOR ADMINISTRATION OFFICIAL ONE: Yes, just—that's not one, at least, that I can answer.

SENIOR ADMINISTRATION OFFICIAL TWO: I have no comment on that, either. . . .

QUESTION: Yes, hi. I was just wondering if you can speak to the group that will be leaving New York. Are they all traveling together? And do we have any idea when they are leaving New York, where they are leaving New York from? Anything you can add to that?

SENIOR ADMINISTRATION OFFICIAL ONE: Not really. The—again, the plea agreement provide expressly that they agree to cooperate in immediate removal or expulsion from the United States, but I think that's as far as I would like to go in discussing that. . . .

QUESTION: Yes. Representative Pete Hoekstra questioned whether allowing these illegals to leave early, the U.S. intelligence community might be missing out on some valuable details or secrets about how the Russian intelligence service operates. Can you comment on that?

SENIOR ADMINISTRATION OFFICIAL ONE: Well, I guess as I mentioned earlier, I mean we have reaped a number of significant benefits from these arrests, as well as the very long-term investigation that's detailed and described in the complaints. These people have been under investigation, under surveillance, for quite a long time now.

In addition to depriving these particular illegal agents and others of their ability to operate here, and removing them from the United States and obtaining admission, as we did today, we have effectively shut down the illegal program here, and again demonstrated our capabilities. I think of that as a very important achievement, and a very significant success. . . .

SOURCE: U.S. Department of State. "Background Briefing on U.S.-Russia Relations." July 8, 2010. http://www.state.gov/r/pa/prs/ps/2010/07/144378.htm.

OTHER HISTORIC DOCUMENTS OF INTEREST

DOCUMENT IN CONTEXT

South Africa Assesses the Success of the 2010 FIFA World Cup

JULY 14, 2010

From June 11 to July 11, 2010, South Africa played host to the 2010 Fédération Internationale de Football Association (FIFA) World Cup. As with other major sporting events, the World Cup provided South Africa with a historic opportunity to improve its less-than-favorable public image around the world as well as the potential for long-term social and economic benefits. There is some disagreement about how significant the impact of the World Cup will ultimately be on the country, but government officials declared the event to be an overall success.

SELECTING A HOST

South Africa was selected to host the World Cup through FIFA's competitive bidding process. Shortly before the bidding for the 2010 tournament began, FIFA implemented a new "continental rotation" process, preventing countries from any but the chosen continent from submitting a bid. The organization selected Africa as its continent of choice for the 2010 tournament and accepted bids from South Africa, Morocco, Egypt, and a joint bid by Libya and Tunisia. Both Libya and Tunisia withdrew from the bidding process on May 8, 2004, after the FIFA Executive Committee announced it would not allow joint bids, and it was determined that neither country met the requirements for a host nation on its own. Seven days later, South Africa won the honor of hosting the tournament for the first time, receiving fourteen votes to Morocco's ten.

Despite the high level of excitement surrounding South Africa's win, questions were raised about the country's ability to sufficiently prepare for the tournament, particularly given its lack of accommodations and outdated public transportation system. Some estimates suggested that South Africa would have 120,000 fewer beds than necessary to meet visitor demand, while others predicted that hundreds of fans could miss games for which they had purchased tickets because of transportation problems. In 2006, rumors circulated that FIFA was considering moving the World Cup to Australia due to these and other concerns about crime and HIV rates in the country. However, representatives of the 2010 FIFA World Cup Organizing Committee denied such claims and reaffirmed that FIFA was committed to making the tournament a success in South Africa.

Preparing for the World Stage

Meanwhile, the South African government began its preparations for the World Cup in earnest. As part of the country's hosting agreement with FIFA, officials had promised to make significant investments in improving South Africa's infrastructure, law enforcement, court system, and health and immigration services. Enhancements to the country's public transportation system were sorely needed after decades of under-investment and poor spatial planning during the years of apartheid. The government worked to upgrade roads, airports, and railways, and it introduced Rea Vaya, a rapid bus transit system. Perhaps the most noteworthy transportation project was the completion of the Gautrain, the first high-speed rail line in Africa. The system connected the Sandton neighborhood of the capital city of Johannesburg to the O. R. Tambo International Airport, and it also included a commuter line linking two of the city's suburbs.

To help minimize and punish criminal activity during the tournament, the government recruited and trained forty thousand new police officers and developed the 2010 FIFA World Cup Administration of Justice Operational Plan. The plan called for the creation of a temporary court infrastructure that could fast-track any criminal matters directly related to the tournament. In all, South Africa established fifty-six court rooms throughout the nine host cities, which included thirty-seven district courts and nineteen regional courts.

The government also introduced a unique event visa for foreign visitors travelling to the tournament and promised to issue permits and provide priority treatment for FIFA family members. Airline liaison officers were deployed at airports in Nairobi, Hong Kong, Amsterdam, Dubai, Frankfurt, Lagos, London, and Mumbai to help inspect passengers' travel documents and identify false visas. South Africa also signed an agreement with neighboring countries Lesotho and Mozambique to establish temporary joint border clearance facilities. In addition, the government worked to recruit additional emergency medical services personnel, procured additional ambulances and aero-medical services, renovated hospitals, and provided additional training for existing medical staff. Officials also collaborated with South African Military Health Services to set up the National Health Operations Center, which aimed to ensure an efficient, real-time flow of information between stadiums, fan parks, public viewing areas, and ports of entry about health-related incidents and provide support for the country's provinces in the event of a disease outbreak.

Other preparations included renovations of five existing sports stadiums and the construction of five new venues to accommodate the game schedule. The government spent nearly 12 billion rand ($1.8 billion) on these projects and boasted the creation of sixty-six thousand new construction jobs that generated 7.4 billion rand in wages. However, stadium construction was hampered by a massive labor strike that began on July 8, 2009. Approximately seventy thousand construction workers belonging to the National Union of Mineworkers and the Building Construction and Allied Workers Union refused to continue their work on stadiums, roadways, and the Gautrain rail line until they received a 13 percent wage increase and enhanced benefits from their employers. At the time, the majority of these workers earned approximately 2,500 rand per month, the equivalent of about $375. The workers were also supported by the Congress of South African Trade Unions, part of President Jacob Zuma's governing alliance. After a week of negotiations, the unions reached an agreement with a consortium of employers known as the South African Federation of Civil Engineering Contractors, whereby workers would receive a 12 percent wage increase.

In all, the South African government invested approximately 30 billion rand on improvements to transportation, infrastructure, and event venues. Some questioned whether such a large sum of money would have been better invested in other areas. "We could have used the same money, energy, zeal and enthusiasm to provide water, electricity, houses and free education for millions of poor South Africans," said South African Students Congress president Mbulelo Mandlana. Others questioned the wisdom of building expensive new stadiums that seemed unlikely to be able to sustain themselves as independent businesses once the World Cup had ended.

Another controversy surrounding South Africa's preparations for the World Cup involved the eviction of locals living in slums, hostels, and shantytowns in the nine tournament host cities. In Cape Town, thousands of residents were relocated to an area outside of the city called Blikkiesdorp, or Tin Can Town, which consisted of seventeen hundred metal huts surrounded by high concrete fencing. City officials also planned to evict nearly twenty thousand additional residents to make way for the N2 Gateway housing project that would provide additional accommodations for the World Cup. In other locations, allegations surfaced of police rounding up residents and transporting them to locations miles from where they had been living, while other slum dwellers were relocated to makeshift housing on the outskirts of cities. These actions outraged poverty and housing rights organizations, which claimed that officials were putting South Africa's public image ahead of the needs of its citizens and were violating international human rights standards in the process. "The World Cup is going on at the expense of South Africans who urgently need housing, public services and jobs," said Ruth Tanner, campaigns and policy director for War on Want. City officials countered that many of the individuals being moved were "land-grabbers" and that plans for the clean-up of these urban areas had been in place for some time.

THE GAMES BEGIN

On June 11, the first round of games in the 2010 World Cup began. Thirty-two teams that had been selected through a qualification tournament played a total of sixty-four games in two rounds of play over the course of the thirty-one day event. South Africa's team was eliminated in the first round, and Ghana was the only African nation with a team to make it to round two. The teams from Spain and the Netherlands faced each other in the final match on July 11. Spain scored the winning goal in overtime in the 116th minute of the game, the latest win in a World Cup final, and took home $30 million in prize money.

One constant throughout the tournament that drew considerable attention was fans' use of vuvuzelas, long plastic horns with a sound akin to the buzzing of bees. A number of teams and individual players claimed the noise was a distraction on the field, with French captain Patrice Evra blaming the instruments for the team's poor performance against Uruguay. Some proposed a ban on the vuvuzela for the remainder of the tournament, but FIFA officials said the instruments were "ingrained in the history of South Africa" and would not be prohibited.

Overall, the games took place without any major incidents and, by FIFA's estimates, were attended by approximately 3.18 million fans. Government officials later pointed to the "unanimous opinion by domestic and international observers . . . that the 2010 FIFA World Cup, the first to be hosted in Africa, was a success."

LONG-TERM EFFECTS

A government assessment of the World Cup released on July 14, 2010, stated, "Our preparations for the 2010 tournament have already shown that today is already better than yesterday. Improvements in public transport, security, investment and tourism have already been shown to benefit the people of our country. We only expect to see an increase in this trend." Products of South Africa's World Cup preparations, such as expanded broadband Internet access and a larger police force, were to remain in place after the tournament's completion. Health minister Aaron Motsoaledi said the National Health Operations Center would continue to be used by the Department of Health to help manage disease outbreaks across the country and maintain communications with the various provinces. An expansion of the Gautrain rail line was also planned for 2011. In addition, a study conducted by South African Tourism found that 90 percent of tourists surveyed who attended the World Cup said they would consider visiting South Africa again in the future and would recommend the country to their friends and relatives. The study also noted that roughly 309,000 foreign tourists travelled to South Africa for the World Cup and spent approximately 3.6 billion rand during their stay.

The overall impact on South Africa's economy has been mixed. A study by U.S. tax and audit firm KPMG determined that South Africa only recovered about 10 percent, or 3.5 billion rand, of the money it spent preparing for the games. The growth rate of the country's gross domestic product was also lower in the second quarter of the year, during which the majority of games occurred, than in the first quarter, which some analysts considered evidence that the World Cup did not fulfill economic expectations. Some of the economic benefits generated by the tournament quickly disappeared once the games were completed. Consumer retail spending had grown by 8 percent in July according to Statistics South Africa but only grew by 4.6 percent in August, prompting concerns that the drop in spending may slow longer-term economic growth. However, Finance Minister Pravin Gordhan said that the World Cup did contribute approximately 93 billion rand to the country's economy and that he anticipated additional growth within the next few years.

Government officials also pointed to social benefits of the games. "For the first time ever in the 16 years of freedom and democracy, we see black and white South Africans celebrating together in the stadiums and fan parks," said President Zuma. "This unity and explosion of national pride will go down in our history as one of the most defining moments of the history of our young nation." Yet others expressed concern that anti-immigrant attacks might occur following the tournament, and that labor protests might resurface. As academics and political observers have noted, South Africa must still make important investments in alleviating widespread poverty, unemployment, a housing shortage, and HIV/AIDS infection rates before the country can fully overcome its racial and economic divisions.

—Linda Fecteau

Following is the South African government's assessment of the preparation and carrying out of the 2010 FIFA World Cup, released on July 14, 2010.

South African Government Assesses the World Cup

July 14, 2010

INTRODUCTION

In the last few days, there has been unanimous opinion by domestic and international observers, amongst them international football fans, visiting Heads of State and other dignitaries, and most especially FIFA, that the 2010 FIFA World Cup™, the first to the hosted in Africa, was a success.

Government is hosting this briefing today, three days after the completion of the first FIFA World Cup™ on African soil, to provide an overall assessment on how the event proceeded, particularly as it pertains to government guarantees signed with FIFA. The guarantees included, amongst others, delivery of infrastructure and logistics, policing, justice, finance and tax exemption, as well as immigration services.

According to FIFA, a total of 3.1 million spectators attended the 64 matches of the tournament, the third highest aggregate attendance behind the United States in 1994 and Germany in 2006. This figure excludes the millions of people who watched World Cup games at fan fests, fan parks and public viewing areas.

INFRASTRUCTURE AND LOGISTICS

The South African government identified public transport as the key legacy project for this World Cup. Over the past few years, a major capital injection into transport-related infrastructure and operations has begun to produce some important results.

Given the deep-seated historical legacy of apartheid spatial planning as well decades of under-investment in public transport, it was always appreciated that access and mobility would be a challenge in hosting the 2010 FIFA World Cup™.

However, the investment we've put into the sector has paid off, helping the country to rise to the challenge. Millions of fans travelled around a country three times the size of Germany, primarily through public transport; mainly trains, buses and taxis without any report of a major incidents.

As part of preparations for the World Cup, government upgraded its road and rail infrastructure, airports and introduced new systems such as the Bus Rapid Transit system, known in Johannesburg as Rea Vaya.

The Gautrain on Wednesday, 2 June 2010, finally moved out of testing and into a fully-fledged operation when its safety permit was handed over to the Bombela Operating Company by Transport Deputy Minister Jeremy Cronin. The Gautrain is a catalyst for economic development in South Africa.

It is worth pointing out that the Gautrain was not earmarked as a World Cup project. However, the date of completion for the route between OR Tambo International Airport and Sandton was fast-tracked to be operational just in time to carry World Cup passengers.

The transport milestones developed during the 2010 FIFA World Cup™ form part of the lasting legacy that will be enjoyed by generations of South Africans for many decades, long after the World Cup has come and gone.

All members of the Transport Family, including those spread across the three spheres of government, in particular host cities, and to a range of parastatals in the aviation, rail and road sectors must be credited for their achievements during the World Cup.

We also salute private sector public transport operators, local bus and coach operators and, indeed, the often maligned minibus-taxi industry who have all come to the party and made the country us proud.

POLICING AND JUSTICE

The successful delivery on this guarantee related to a synergistic approach from the criminal-justice cluster, which is made up of departments of Police, Justice and Constitutional Development, the National Prosecuting Authority, State Security, Correctional Services.

Police deployment for the World Cup resulted in 40 000 new, well-trained police officers incorporated into the police force. These recruits will remain on the force, leading to a safer South Africa. Government has financed all of this investment out of current expenditure because of our fiscal prudence, as well as the high levels of tax compliance over the years.

The number of police personnel added to the force, as well as the equipment acquired for their use, is one of the important legacies of the World Cup.

On 9 July 2003, the Department of Justice and Constitutional Development (DoJ&CD) signed a guarantee to FIFA committing to ensure that all justice related requirements for hosting the 2009 FIFA Confederations Cup and the 2010 FIFA World Cup™ events will be provided.

Part of the requirements was the development of a 2010 FIFA World Cup™ Administration of Justice Operational Plan. The plan was developed by all stakeholders of the Integrated Justice System, which includes the Department of Justice and Constitutional Development (DOJ&CD), National Prosecuting Authority (NPA), Legal Aid South Africa and Judiciary.

The primary objective of the Administration of Justice project was to fast track all criminal matters emanating from the 2009/10 events and deal with these cases in a fast and efficient way, especially where foreigners are involved, either as a complainant/witness or an accused.

The Administration of Justice Operational Plan included the following elements that were required to contribute to South Africa hosting a successful world cup tournament: the court infrastructure; personnel; court administration; and court security.

The success of this collaboration between all role-players in the Justice, Crime Preventions and Secu[r]ity (JCPS) cluster was demonstrated by the fact that football fans and visitors have left South Africa largely proclaiming that reports of crime ahead of the World Cup were largely exaggerated.

COURT INFRASTRUCTURE

- 56 Dedicated Court rooms in the 9 host cities. 37 District Courts and 19 Regional Courts
- The breakdown of court allocation per province will be as follows:
- Limpopo province will have four district and three regional courts, totaling seven;
- Mpumalanga province will have three district and one regional court, totaling four;
- Eastern Cape province will have four district and two regional courts, totaling six;

- Kwazulu-Natal province will have four district and one regional court, totaling five;
- Western Cape will have three district and one regional courts; totaling four
- North-West province will have three district and one regional court, totaling four;
- Free State province will have two district and one regional court, totaling three;
- Northern Cape province will have one district and one regional court, totaling two;
- Gauteng province will have 13 district and 8 regional courts, totaling 21

PERSONNEL

- Total number of court officials (all provinces)
- Judiciary—110 magistrates
- National Prosecuting Authority (NPA)—260 prosecutors
- Legal Aid South Africa—110 legal aid attorneys
- DoJ&CD -93 foreign language interpreters, 110 local language interpreters
- Court officials—1140 court officials
- South African Police Service (SAPS)—327 court orderlies
- Through a legacy project of recruiting Volunteers, a pool of about 290 unemployed youths were trained in the accredited Customer Service Management course. SASSETA funded the project with R2.2 million.

COURT ADMINISTRATION

- The operation period for the dedicated courts and dedicated resources will commence two weeks before, during and two weeks after the 2010 FWC tournament, 28 May 2010 until 25 July 2010. These courts will operate from 07:45 in the morning until 23:00 in the evening, seven days a week.

DEFINITION OF THE 2010 FIFA WORLD CUP™ CASE

- A 2010 FIFA World Cup™ case is defined as follows:
  - any offence that is committed by a non-resident supporter of 2010 FIFA World Cup™,
  - committed against a non-resident Supporter of 2010 FIFA World Cup™,
  - to which a non resident is a witness,
  - committed at a tourist attraction or any other place in the country and in the opinion of the Senior Public Prosecutor given time, place, nature and/or publicity of the offence.
- These cases are of various nature and ranges from common theft to serious crimes such as bomb threats and murder.
- These cases will also be subjected to similar due judicial process and dealt with in accordance with the laws of the Republic and the Constitution.

IMMIGRATION

South Africa's guarantees to FIFA in terms of immigration related to the issuance of visas including the unique event visa introduced by the country. It also related to the issuance of permits and priority treatment for FIFA family members and accredited persons.

In support of this objective, the Department of Home Affairs implemented a trio of measures. These comprised the Movement Control System in 34 air and land ports of entry, the Advance Passenger Processing (APP) system and the deployment of Airline Liaison Officers (ALOs) at eight strategic hubs abroad, namely Nairobi, Hong Kong, Amsterdam, Dubai, Frankfurt, Lagos, London and Mumbai to monitor the movement of travellers into South Africa.

The Department of Home Affairs further prioritised 34 air and land ports of entry including OR Tambo, Cape Town and King Shaka International Airports for daily monitoring, provision of early warning signals and the implementation of contingency planning for the FIFA 2010 World Cup.

The department also signed a Memoranda of Understanding (MoU) with its Lesotho and Mozambican counterparts to assist in the establishment of temporary joint border clearance facilities. In addition, government advised several Southern African Development Community (SADC) counterparts to issue their nationals with machine-readable travel documents that will be compatible with our Movement Control System (MCS).

The Movement Control System recorded a total number of foreigners visiting the country for the duration of the tournament as over a million which represented an increase of approximately 25% when compared to the same period in 2009.

During the same period South Africa's Advanced Passenger Processing System witnessed a total of 43 undesirables being prohibited from boarding airlines abroad to enter South Africa.

Meanwhile, the Home Affairs Airline Liaison Officers in various international airports abroad have denied entry into South Africa to 188 persons due to possession of fraudulent (visas, permits, travel documents and stamps) documents and failure to meet immigration requirements.

The Movement Control System has, furthermore enabled the country to facilitate the swift departures of national teams that did not qualify for the next rounds of the FIFA World Cup™ including: Greece, Nigeria, Serbia, Slovenia, New Zealand, Denmark, Italy, Korea Democratic People's Republic (DPR), Korea Republic, Cote d' Ivoire, Australia, Honduras, Mexico, Switzerland, USA, England, Japan, Chile, Cameroon and Algeria.

The Movement Control System has further recorded the following nationalities as among the top visitors into the country for the period coinciding with the FIFA World Cup™: the Southern African Development Community (SADC), (Lesotho, Zimbabwe, Mozambique, Swaziland, Botswana, Malawi and Zambia) followed by the United Kingdom (UK), United States of America (USA), Germany, Australia, Brazil and Mexico.

Media reports have in the last few days quoted fans who said the 2010 World Cup was the best they had ever attended because there was not a single incident of hooliganism for the duration of the tournament. This attests to the efficiency of the systems implemented for the tournament. These systems will be retained following the tournament and will serve as a legacy of the first FIFA World Cup™ hosted by Africa.

FINANCE

South Africa has always viewed the hosting of the World Cup not as an end in itself, but as a catalyst for development whose benefits would be felt long after the tournament. This is why national government has spent R30 billion on transportation (roads, airports, and ports of entry), telecommunications infrastructure, as well as stadiums (building six new ones and upgrading another four).

The R11.7 billion investment in 10 world-class stadiums alone created 66 000 new construction jobs, generating R7.4 billion in wages, with R2.2 billion going to low-income households and therefore contributing to a reduction in poverty.

Though stadiums have been the most visible part of the World Cup-related expenditure, the lion's share of the expenditure has gone into transportation and telecommunications infrastructure, and the renovations of our ports of entry for visitors.

The government spent R13 billion to upgrade train stations near stadiums, improve roads and the massive facelift of our country's airports. Ports of entry received R3.5 billion for renovations, including improved information technology infrastructure equipment at borders.

Some R1.5 billion has been invested in broadcast technology, much of which was used for broadband internet access. This technology will remain an asset to this country for years to come. The fight against crime has also received a fortifying boost, with R1.3 billion being spent on safety and security.

Government always intended that tomorrow should be better than today. Although it is still too early for a precise indication of the economic benefits the 2010 World Cup will have on our economy analysts, scholars and economists are suggesting it could be billions.

During the tournament, a StanLib economist, based on an estimation that half a billion viewers around the world watched the Opening Ceremony in Soweto on 11 June 2010 said, if only 0.5% of these viewers travelled to South Africa to experience the country firsthand, this would have a significant effect on South Africa's economy. He estimated this could treble our tourism figures over the next four years.

HEALTH

The FIFA 2010 Soccer World Cup could not have been successful without an efficient and prepared healthcare system.

To this end, we worked closely with our partners in both the public and private sector to ensure that the country's healthcare system was ready to respond to and cater to the needs of the country and those of FIFA during this period.

It was important to government that the healthcare system continued to function efficiently even beyond the World Cup. We are happy that during this period there was no major health-related incident that compromised the tournament. Most of the incidents that we had to deal with were of a minor nature and we are happy that throughout, the sector displayed its readiness to respond.

Government made massive investments in this regard within the context of its commitment to the country as contained in government programme of action.

The World Cup enabled us to improve on emergency medical services from which our country will benefit from even after the conclusion of the tournament. We have invested massively on ambulance services both ground and aero-medical services as part of our 2010 legacy strategy. Equally, we have been able through this project to recruit more emergency medical services (EMS) personnel who forms an essential element of healthcare delivery in our country.

We worked very closely with the South African Military Health Services to set up the National Health Operations Centre that enabled us to improve our diseases surveillance systems and through this partnership we are confident we will be able to improve on our normal systems as part of providing healthcare services to our people.

Other areas where we have been able to make massive investments include forensic medicine which will now improve the performance of our mortuaries among others which is an area that we always knew needed great improvement.

GENERAL

In light of this short assessment, we are proud to say that everything has gone according to plan and that we hosted a successful tournament. We attribute this to careful planning that began as early as 15 May 2004 when South Africa's name was drawn from the envelope in Geneva declaring us the host country of the 2010 FIFA World Cup.

As South Africans we are proud of what we have achieved in the last few weeks and indeed, in the past 16 years. South Africa will always bear the mark of having hosted the FIFA World Cup™, the first to come to Africa.

Our preparations for the 2010 tournament have already shown that today is already better than yesterday. Improvements in public transport, security, investment and tourism have already been shown to benefit the people of our country. We only expect to see an increase in this trend. . . .

[Annexure A, detailing crime statistics, has been omitted.]

SOURCE: Government of South Africa. "Government Assessment of the 2010 FIFA World Cup™." July 14, 2010. http://www.info.gov.za/speech/DynamicAction?pageid=461&sid=11449&tid=12176.

OTHER HISTORIC DOCUMENTS OF INTEREST

FROM PREVIOUS *HISTORIC DOCUMENTS*

Changes in the Publishing Industry

JULY 19 AND 22, 2010

In January 2010, Apple launched the newest tablet computer, the iPad, and in July, Amazon.com announced that sales of e-books for its electronic reader, the Kindle, which was first released in 2007, had surpassed sales of hardcover books and were expected to surpass soft cover book sales in the coming year. According to the Association of American Publishers, e-book sales in the first half of 2010 were up more than 200 percent. As new, handheld technology became increasingly accessible and more popular, 2010 was a year of significant growth and change for the publishing industry. It also left unanswered questions as to the place for book, magazine, and newspaper publishers in the future.

PRICING THE E-MARKET

The retail book market currently brings in tens of billions of dollars per year across all publishers. The big six trade publishers, Hachette Book Group, HarperCollins, Macmillan, Random House, Penguin Group, and Simon & Schuster, make up 60 percent of the total market. Traditionally, when a book is published, the publishing company sells that book to a wholesaler or a brick-and-mortar store for a wholesale price that is approximately half of the cover price that buyers see. Authors then receive a royalty, or percentage of the sale of each book.

The print book market, however, is slowing and saw annual sales grow only 1.6 percent between 2002 and 2008, leading to decreasing profits. Like newspapers and magazines before them, book publishers have been faced with significantly decreased budgets and layoffs.

With the advent of the iPad, Kindle, and a number of other e-book readers and smartphones with e-book capacity, book publishers have been forced to rely on the sale of e-books without much guidance as to pricing or selling. This opened the door for companies like Amazon.com, which have become the electronic version of the brick-and-mortar book store. Amazon, and its Kindle reader, has become a major player in the e-book marketplace. Amazon takes a 30 percent fee from each e-book that it sells, and most major publishers are giving authors a 25 percent royalty. This leaves 45 percent for the book publisher to pay its bills. E-books present a promising source of revenue for publishers, but pricing became a heated issue that reached a boiling point in 2010.

Since the launch of the Kindle, Amazon set the market standard for the $9.99 e-book, which is a fraction of the cost of new releases and best sellers in hardcover. Most of the big six publishers put up little resistance, but Macmillan said it would not allow Amazon to sell its books in an electronic format unless its best sellers were priced at $15. Amazon, which already had thousands of other titles to offer, called Macmillan's bluff and its titles were pulled from the list of e-book offerings. In the end, backlash from consumers led Amazon to give in to Macmillan's demands. Amazon announced on its website, "We will have to capitulate and accept Macmillan's terms because Macmillan has a monopoly over their own titles, and we will want to offer them to you even at prices we believe are needlessly high for e-books."

Amazon has put itself on a fast track to consume a big portion of the e-book market. In July, the company announced that for the first time, sales of e-books for the Kindle surpassed sales of hardcover books. "Astonishing when you consider that we've been selling hardcover books for 15 years, and Kindle books for 33 months," said Amazon.com founder and chief executive officer Jeff Bezos. Between mid-June and July, the company sold 180 Kindle books for every one hundred hardcover books. Quarterly growth estimates make Amazon poised to consume 50 percent of the overall e-book market share by 2012.

The Opportunity to Self-Publish

The growth in the number of people using e-books and some form of electronic device equipped with e-book capability has led to the growth in the number of books being self-published. Self-publishing was originally done by a number of smaller websites that charged authors a set fee to publish their book and sell it directly through their site. This procedure, however, made it unlikely that authors would reach large audiences. But that is changing as well. Amazon is now going straight to writers and becoming both publisher and seller, offering those who would not have been picked up by agents the opportunity to self-publish through AmazonEncore. Anyone self-publishing with Amazon has the ability to receive 70 percent of book proceeds if they agree to allow their books to be priced anywhere between $2.99 and $9.99. Barnes & Noble has also opened a self-publishing arm.

The likelihood that some authors would leave their agents and publishing houses in favor of direct self-publishing is leaving publishing companies scrambling to rethink their business models. Ted Weinstein, a literary agent, said he's now working with his clients to determine whether self-publishing might be a better option. He called the advent of the self-publishing arms at major companies like Amazon "an enormous transition point." And while he does not believe traditional publishing will go away anytime soon, he said publishers and agents will be facing greater competition and higher demands from writers who can take their books elsewhere.

Waxman Literary Agency, a book agency run by Scott Waxman, is reorganizing the way it does business as well. Waxman has created a new book division separate from his agency that he calls "somewhere in between the big houses and the lonely road of self-publishing." He calls his business different from simple self-publishing because his company offers support to the writers and makes a concerted effort to sell their books, rather than simply putting them on a website.

What Happens to Book Stores?

The brick-and-mortar bookstores also face questions. With companies like Amazon that can sell e-books directly to the consumer in an instant without having the hassle of shipping or warehouse restocking fees, many are now wondering how bookstores will fare in the future. Independent bookstores that cannot rely on high-volume sales are also facing financial challenges. But even the large retailers are feeling the pinch, with Barnes & Noble closing its B. Dalton bookstores. Waldenbooks is also becoming a thing of the past. In February 2011, Borders filed for Chapter 11 bankruptcy protection, hoping to weather its financial storm by closing nearly a third of its stores and focusing on e-book and other online sales.

Sean Feeney, executive vice president of Bookmans Entertainment Exchange, a local bookstore chain in Arizona, is hoping to continue thriving by offering an atmosphere rather than a product. Bookmans has existed in spite of chain bookstores because it acts as a community center and continues to be able to offer old and out-of-print titles that are not currently available to e-book patrons. However, Feeney recognizes that eventually these books will be available to consumers in an e-book format as well. Already, Amazon.com and Google Books are offering a number of titles printed before 1923 for free because their copyright has expired. Amazon has made it a corporate goal to offer "every book, ever published, in any language, in print or out of print, available to be downloaded to one of its Kindle e-readers in less than 60 seconds anywhere in the world."

The decline of hardcopy books does not stop at bookstores, however. Now large retailers like Costco, Walmart, Target, and even Amazon are questioning the future need for warehouses that stock hardcopy books that are shipped to consumers who order them from their websites.

College Texts

The $5 billion U.S. college textbook market is facing similar uncertainties, although not yet to the same extent as the trade market. Due to the uncertainty over future preferences for content delivery and a healthy demand for printed texts, many academic publishers are offering electronic versions of their print titles to satisfy current demand. "Neither the providers nor the consumers of teaching and learning materials have really settled on what the preferred options should be," said Dan Sayre of textbook publisher Wiley Higher Education.

The first electronic college textbooks made available were simply a version of the book that could be read on a computer, without any additional functionality. Today, that is changing. In the simplest form, college textbooks are being presented as e-text, which can be accessed on any computer and many mobile devices. Nearly nine thousand textbook titles are now offered in this format from five of the largest textbook publishers. Models for electronic access and product functionality vary widely between books and platforms. But, says Sayre, "Students want a digital textbook that behaves like a textbook, with the ability to highlight, make notes, dog-ear pages, put Post-it notes on pages, and flip back and forth between pages immediately." In fall 2009, only 9 percent of students purchased an e-textbook.

In 2009, six colleges waded into the e-textbook market and launched a pilot project aimed at reducing the consumption of paper on campus. At Princeton University, one of the six pilot schools, students in three selected courses were given Kindles, paid for by an outside donation, that were loaded with all of the course materials required for the semester. Professor Stanley Katz, whose course on public policy was included in the study, said he hoped to learn "if I can enhance the student learning experience with the e-reader.

The question I start off with is whether, once the novelty wears off, students will find this more attractive to use than its analog counterpart, or whether it will turn out to be more a nuisance than an enhancement."

When study results were announced in February 2010, Katz found that the device had not been useful for his course, because the slow response time of the device made it difficult for students to flip back and forth between pages during class discussions. Princeton reported that the study had been successful in reducing the amount of paper used by approximately 50 percent in each of the three courses. Students reported enjoying the portability of the Kindle over heavy college textbooks, as well as the searchability of the material. But moving forward, participants cited the need for a device that made highlighting and annotating easier; improved navigation; and enhanced PDF readability.

The University of Notre Dame launched a similar study in August 2010, giving iPads to forty students to use as an e-reader in a project management class. The study sought to determine whether the university could become more eco-friendly by going paperless in many of its classes. The first survey of students in the program that was conducted in September found a high rate of satisfaction and a low printing rate. Students reported satisfaction with the devices and cited that they made class more interesting and provided tools not available in traditional textbooks. However, students did have some complaints, including the effect of spending so much time looking at a computer screen, the distraction of easy access to games and the Internet, and difficulty using the highlighting function. The study was expanded to graduate students, where students' perceived usefulness of the iPad declined after two weeks of use.

THE FUTURE OF NEWSPAPERS AND MAGAZINES

Newspapers and magazines are hoping to use the new format offered by the iPad and similar devices to bring tech-savvy readers back—and with them, ad revenue. Agencies looking to advertise in the iPad versions of newspapers and magazines have been reported to pay five times more in an e-reader version of the newspaper than what they would have paid for an ad on a website. One reason advertisers are paying more is because, much like the paper version of a newspaper or magazine, the available ad space is finite. Lou Cona, executive vice president at Condé Nast Media Group, said publishing on the iPad "will redefine publishing and also redefine how advertisers connect with our audience." Publishers still must figure out how to keep readers engaged for long enough to see, or click through, the ads. And with today's ever evolving e-marketplace, there is no telling what advertisers will demand in terms of metrics that prove they are receiving a significant return on their investment.

Questions still need to be answered by publishers interested in joining the electronic device world. Charging for content that is already on the Internet seems to be a non-starter, because with Internet capability, iPad users can simply visit the website of any newspaper or magazine and read the article for free. Some publishers that made content available on the iPad early on offered it for free because no subscription model had been established. Others offered their content for per-issue purchase but sold it at higher-than-newsstand prices. The paid model proved unsuccessful and by December, digital sales had fallen for all iPad-available magazines that release subscriber data to the Audit Bureau of Circulations. The drop renewed the call for Apple to develop a subscription model for iPad users, preferably one that would auto-deliver newspapers and magazines to subscribers rather than forcing users to purchase and download each issue individually. Taking a different approach, News Corporation, the world's third largest media conglomerate, carved out a niche for itself in February 2011, releasing the first iPad-only newspaper, *The Daily*, for $0.99 per week.

That same month, Apple announced its iPad subscription model, offering to sell magazine and newspapers through its iTunes store. In return, Apple asked for 30 percent of the revenue generated through these sales. Publishers continue to be wary of paying such high percentages to Apple to sell its products, and even more so knowing that Apple will keep the subscriber data and not share them with publishers unless the buyer opts to do so.

The instant cry of the death of the publishing industry that rang out when the Kindle and iPad were released seems to have slowed as publishers work to find new niches for themselves in the e-publishing world. Since the Kindle's release in 2007, more than one dozen new e-reader devices have hit the shelves vying for a spot in the market. The flexibility offered by the market gives publishers willing to evolve a number of new ways to explore and develop content that will keep revenues steady, or rising, at least until the next wave of technology comes along.

—Heather Kerrigan

Following are two press releases from Amazon.com, Inc., on July 19 and 22, 2010, announcing that the company is now selling more e-books for its Kindle than hardcover books.

DOCUMENT   *Kindle Sales Surpass Hardcover Sales*

July 19, 2010

Millions of people are already reading on Kindles and Kindle is the #1 bestselling item on Amazon.com for two years running. It's also the most-wished-for, most-gifted, and has the most 5-star reviews of any product on Amazon.com. Today, Amazon.com announced that Kindle device unit sales accelerated each month in the second quarter—both on a sequential month-over-month basis and on a year-over-year basis.

"We've reached a tipping point with the new price of Kindle—the growth rate of Kindle device unit sales has tripled since we lowered the price from $259 to $189," said Jeff Bezos, Founder and CEO of Amazon.com. "In addition, even while our hardcover sales continue to grow, the Kindle format has now overtaken the hardcover format. Amazon.com customers now purchase more Kindle books than hardcover books—astonishing when you consider that we've been selling hardcover books for 15 years, and Kindle books for 33 months."

Kindle offers the largest selection of the most popular books people want to read. The U.S. Kindle Store now has more than 630,000 books, including New Releases and 106 of 110 New York Times Best Sellers. Over 510,000 of these books are $9.99 or less, including 75 New York Times Best Sellers. Over 1.8 million free, out-of-copyright, pre-1923 books are also available to read on Kindle.

Recent milestones for Kindle books include:

- Over the past three months, for every 100 hardcover books Amazon.com has sold, it has sold 143 Kindle books. Over the past month, for every 100 hardcover books Amazon.com has sold, it has sold 180 Kindle books. This is across Amazon.com's entire U.S. book business and includes sales of hardcover books where there is no Kindle edition. Free Kindle books are excluded and if included would make the number even higher.
- Amazon sold more than 3x as many Kindle books in the first half of 2010 as in the first half of 2009.
- The Association of American Publishers' latest data reports that e-book sales grew 163 percent in the month of May and 207 percent year-to-date through May. Kindle book sales in May and year-to-date through May exceeded those growth rates.
- On July 6, Hachette announced that James Patterson had sold 1.14 million e-books to date. Of those, 867,881 were Kindle books.
- Five authors—Charlaine Harris, Stieg Larsson, Stephenie Meyer, James Patterson, and Nora Roberts—have each sold more than 500,000 Kindle books.

Readers are responding to Kindle's uncompromising approach to the reading experience. Weighing 10.2 ounces, Kindle can be held comfortably in one hand for hours, has an e-ink display that is easy on the eyes even in bright daylight, has two weeks of battery life, lets you buy your books once and read them everywhere—on your Kindle, Kindle DX, iPad, iPod touch, iPhone, Mac, PC, BlackBerry, and Android-based devices—and has free 3G wireless with no monthly fees or annual contracts—all at a $189 price.

SOURCE: Amazon.com. Media Room. "Kindle Device Unit Sales Accelerate Each Month in Second Quarter; New $189 Price Results in Tipping Point for Growth." July 19, 2010. http://phx.corporate-ir.net/phoenix.zhtml?c=176060&p=irol-newsArticle&ID=1449176&highlight=.

Amazon.com Announces Second Quarter Sales

DOCUMENT

July 22, 2010

Amazon.com, Inc. (NASDAQ:AMZN) today announced financial results for its second quarter ended June 30, 2010.

Operating cash flow was $2.56 billion for the trailing twelve months, compared with $1.88 billion for the trailing twelve months ended June 30, 2009. Free cash flow increased 29% to $1.99 billion for the trailing twelve months, compared with $1.54 billion for the trailing twelve months ended June 30, 2009.

Common shares outstanding plus shares underlying stock-based awards totaled 465 million on June 30, 2010, compared with 451 million a year ago.

Net sales increased 41% to $6.57 billion in the second quarter, compared with $4.65 billion in second quarter 2009. Excluding the $48 million unfavorable impact from year-over-year changes in foreign exchange rates throughout the quarter, net sales would have grown 42% compared with second quarter 2009.

Operating income increased 71% to $270 million in the second quarter, compared with $159 million in second quarter 2009. The unfavorable impact from year-over-year changes in foreign exchange rates throughout the quarter on operating income was $10 million. Second quarter 2009 operating income was negatively impacted by a $51 million legal settlement.

Net income increased 45% to $207 million in the second quarter, or $0.45 per diluted share, compared with net income of $142 million, or $0.32 per diluted share, in second quarter 2009.

"We're seeing rapid growth in Kindle, Amazon Web Services, third-party sales, and retail. We're also encouraged by what we see in mobile. In the last twelve months, customers around the world have ordered more than $1 billion of products from Amazon using a mobile device," said Jeff Bezos, founder and CEO of Amazon.com. "The leading mobile commerce device today is the smartphone, but we're excited by the potential of the new category of wireless tablet computers. Over time, tablet computers could become a meaningful additional driver for our business."

Highlights

- Readers are responding to Kindle's uncompromising approach to the reading experience. Weighing 10.2 ounces, Kindle can be held comfortably in one hand for hours, has an e-ink display that is easy on the eyes even in bright daylight, has two weeks of battery life, and has free 3G wireless with no monthly fees or annual contracts—all at a $189 price.
- Amazon.com is now selling more Kindle books than hardcover books. Over the past three months, for every 100 hardcover books Amazon.com has sold, the Company has sold 143 Kindle books. Over the past month, for every 100 hardcover books Amazon.com has sold, the Company has sold 180 Kindle books. This is across Amazon.com's entire U.S. book business and includes sales of hardcover books where there is no Kindle edition. Free Kindle books are excluded and if included would make the number even higher.
- Amazon sold more than 3x as many Kindle books in the first half of 2010 as in the first half of 2009.
- The Association of American Publishers' latest data reports that e-book sales grew 163 percent in the month of May and 207 percent year-to-date through May. Kindle book sales in May and year-to-date through May exceeded those growth rates.
- On July 6, Hachette announced that James Patterson had sold 1.14 million e-books to date. Of those, 867,881 were Kindle books.
- Five authors—Charlaine Harris, Stieg Larsson, Stephenie Meyer, James Patterson, and Nora Roberts—have each sold more than 500,000 Kindle books.
- Amazon.com continues to expand Kindle's "Buy once, read everywhere" strategy with this quarter's launch of Kindle for Android. Like all Kindle apps, Kindle for Android includes Whispersync technology, which automatically synchronizes your last page read, bookmarks, notes and highlights across your Kindle, Kindle DX, iPad, iPod touch, iPhone, Mac, PC, BlackBerry, and Android-based devices.
- Kindle offers the largest selection of the most popular books people want to read. The U.S. Kindle Store now has more than 630,000 books, including New Releases and 106 of 110 New York Times Best Sellers. Over 510,000 of these books are $9.99 or less, including 75 New York Times Best Sellers. Over 1.8 million free, out-of-copyright, pre-1923 books are also available to read on Kindle.

- North America segment sales, representing the Company's U.S. and Canadian sites, were $3.59 billion, up 46% from second quarter 2009.
- International segment sales, representing the Company's U.K., German, Japanese, French and Chinese sites, were $2.98 billion, up 35% from second quarter 2009. Excluding the unfavorable impact from year-over-year changes in foreign exchange rates throughout the quarter, sales grew 38%.
- Worldwide Media sales grew 18% to $2.87 billion.
- Worldwide Electronics & Other General Merchandise sales grew 69% to $3.49 billion. Excluding the unfavorable impact from year-over-year changes in foreign exchange rates throughout the quarter, sales grew 70%.
- The Company introduced Textbook Buyback, an easy-to-use program that helps students lower their textbook costs, giving them great value for their used textbooks.
- The Amazon.co.uk and Amazon.de websites each launched Grocery stores offering customers free delivery on thousands of new items from brands such as Kraft, Nestlé, Mars, PepsiCo, Proctor & Gamble, and Unilever.
- Businesses and developers in over 190 countries are taking advantage of Amazon Web Services (AWS). In the first half of 2010, AWS continued significant geographic expansion, launching the first Asia Pacific Region in Singapore as well as extending additional services including Amazon Virtual Private Cloud and Amazon Relational Database Service into the EU.
- AWS announced a new storage option within the Amazon Simple Storage Service (S3), Amazon S3 Reduced Redundancy Storage (RRS), which enables customers to reduce their costs by storing non-critical, reproducible data at lower levels of redundancy than Amazon S3's standard storage.
- AWS introduced Cluster Compute Instances, an Amazon Elastic Compute Cloud (EC2) instance type specifically tailored for high-performance computing.

Financial Guidance

The following forward-looking statements reflect Amazon.com's expectations as of July 22, 2010. Our results are inherently unpredictable and may be materially affected by many factors, such as fluctuations in foreign exchange rates, changes in global economic conditions and consumer spending, world events, the rate of growth of the Internet and online commerce and the various factors detailed below.

Third Quarter 2010 Guidance

- Net sales are expected to be between $6.900 billion and $7.625 billion, or to grow between 27% and 40% compared with third quarter 2009.
- Operating income is expected to be between $210 million and $310 million, or between 16% decline and 24% growth compared with third quarter 2009.
- This guidance includes approximately $130 million for stock-based compensation and amortization of intangible assets, and it assumes, among other things, that no additional business acquisitions or investments are concluded and that there are no further revisions to stock-based compensation estimates. . . .

[Tables containing Amazon.com's finances have been omitted.]

SOURCE: Amazon.com. Media Room. "Amazon.com Announces Second Quarter Sales up 41% to $6.57 Billion." July 22, 2010. http://phx.corporate-ir.net/phoenix.zhtml?c=176060&p=irol-newsArticle&ID= 1451043&highlight=.

Wildfires Impact Russia

JULY 30 AND AUGUST 2, 2010

The worst drought seen in more than one hundred years, coupled with the hottest summer on record, sparked hundreds of wildfires across Russia. The fires destroyed homes and croplands and led to a ban on grain exports that drove up global food prices. With nearly three hundred fires starting each day, Russia's local governments scrambled to deploy fire brigades, while the central government called for increased focus on the protection of military bases and nuclear plants from fire. A 2006 law regarding control of Russia's forest land added to the confusion as local governments questioned who was in charge of the site of each fire. Russian prime minister Vladimir Putin remained highly visible throughout the summer and into the recovery efforts, sparking speculation that he would run for president in 2012 instead of his protégé, Dmitry Medvedev, the nation's current president, who remained deskbound in Moscow.

WILDFIRES RAGE ACROSS RUSSIA

Throughout late July and early August 2010, wildfires sparked by the hottest summer on record broke out across Russia, with most of the fires situated in the western portion of the country. The first fire started in a peat bog on July 29, causing acrid smog to sicken and kill many local residents. As the fires spread, entire villages were burned to the ground. The fires spread quickly because of the lack of warning passed from one government agency to another and a lack of available firefighting equipment. Local law enforcement and firefighters worked around the clock with members of Russia's own law enforcement brigade and military to evacuate Russians from their homes—a peak of seven thousand evacuated in one day was reached at the height of the fires—and secure or save what they could.

Between the wildfires and extreme heat during the summer of 2010, it is estimated by Munich Re, the world's largest reinsurer, that fifty-six thousand were killed. One hundred thousand Russians were forced to evacuate their homes, as two thousand were destroyed by fire.

In addition to the destruction of personal property, of major concern to the central government was the protection of Sarov, the closed city where Russia develops its nuclear bombs. To help protect Sarov, along with other nuclear plants and military bases across the country, the government called on soldiers and firefighters to focus on digging trenches and felling trees. The central government reported that all hazardous nuclear materials had been moved to safe facilities far from the fire.

Russia's daily business newspaper, *Kommersant*, reported that the damage from the fire would reach $15 billion once all of the damage was accounted for, or nearly 1 percent of Russia's gross domestic product (GDP). Russia's emergency minister, Sergei Shoigu, estimated the damage to be closer to 12 billion rubles, or $394 million in damage. "The costs of extinguishing existing fires, plus funding for housing construction and additional resources, including fuel, are currently estimated at 12 billion rubles," he said. The cost could have been much higher, according to Shoigu, had firefighters, law enforcement, and military officials not been able to save four thousand residential areas from the fires.

Putin was the face of the central government throughout the summer, while Medvedev remained in the Kremlin, only appearing on television to advise Russian citizens how to stay safe in the heat or seek help if affected by the fires. "With the cities sweltering in this stifling heat, of course, we want to get out and escape into nature. But here, we have to be extremely attentive, extremely careful, because even a single match left burning could spark an irreparable tragedy," Medvedev said during one of his televised appearances. Behind the scenes, Medvedev was holding a number of meetings with Russia's emergency management officials to determine best steps for managing this and future crises. It was in these meetings that he expressed his concern for the victims of the fire and called for funding to be freed up for rebuilding. "We need to get working," Medvedev told his ministers in one meeting, "so that we can allocate the appropriate amount of money and quickly build at least temporary housing, or begin building permanent housing straight away."

Although he seldom appeared in public, Medvedev was the first to lay blame on those he thought were responsible for not protecting the people and infrastructure in Russia. After a naval base caught fire, Medvedev accused the head of the Russian Navy, Admiral Vladimir Vysotsky, of "incomplete professional responsibility." The damage to more than twenty buildings, supply stockpiles, and vehicles led to the firing of a number of navy officials. "I order the ministry of defense to fire a whole number of officers for the disciplinary infringements that were allowed to take place," said Medvedev. He further ordered an investigation into the local organizations in charge of containing the fires and said he would open criminal investigations into anyone who was found to have skirted his or her duties.

Putin, on the other hand, undertook a shirtsleeves tour of the nation, visiting the areas damaged by fire and drought. Putin met with grieving citizens and lectured local officials who were in charge of aiding those left homeless. During his tour, Putin quickly pledged $200 million to rebuild the fire-damaged homes of Russian citizens. Furthermore, he promised to complete the rebuilding process before Russia's harsh winter set in.

Despite Putin's visibility during the disaster, opinion polls conducted around the country in early August showed his approval rating dropping, as well as that of Medvedev. Putin's popularity only decreased by two percentage points while Medvedev's popularity, which was already lower than Putin's, dropped five percentage points. Some of those surveyed by the Public Opinion Foundation cited Medvedev's vacation on the Black Sea, which was not shortened or postponed during the blazes. His low visibility also contributed to his declining popularity.

Putin's Law

With the spreading fires, members of the Duma, Russia's parliament, and environmentalists criticized Putin's 2006 forestry legislation as a driver behind diminished efforts to stop the raging wildfires. Before this new Forest Code was developed, the Kremlin oversaw a centralized forestry system that was in charge of protecting all forest land in the country, which is nearly twice the size of the entire landmass of the European Union nations combined. Putin's Forest Code disbanded the central forest body, comprised of seventy thousand guards in charge of calling out firefighters when necessary, and moved all protection responsibilities to local authorities. These local authorities rely on firefighting companies and volunteers to fight any fires arising in the forest land, but there exists some confusion related to the boundaries of each local authority.

Opponents of Putin's Forest Code said it was an act aimed at generating a quick profit for timber companies because it made it easier to reclassify the land for development. "This law is good for large companies with [close connections to the authorities], enabling them to quickly cut trees, make money and leave," said Alexei Yaroshenko of Greenpeace Russia. Timber companies were not shy in agreeing. "On the whole, the code is good for us," said Dmitry Chuiko, who acts as adviser to the board of Ilim Group, one of the country's largest timber companies. "It protected the interest of large forest users."

The Federal Forestry Agency, which still exists in a limited role, admits that the former centralized system of forest protection, in the case of the 2010 wildfires, would have made it easier to place blame on those not properly performing their responsibilities and could have eliminated confusion regarding who was in charge of different sections of the forest land. "Maybe [the new system] has some faults," said spokesperson Viktoria Mironova. But it is unlikely, as long as the government remains in the hands of Putin and Medvedev, that responsibility for forest land will be handed back to the Forest Agency. "This is a well-functioning system which only needs some minor adjustments," said Putin's spokesperson Dmitry Peskov.

Export Ban

With thousands of square miles scorched, Russia's grain crop took a serious hit. The Eurasian nation is the world's third largest exporter of wheat, and the threat of a decreased supply sent prices soaring to a twenty-three-month high in early August. Since June 2010, wheat prices had increased 50 percent.

Russia's deputy agriculture minister, Alexander Belyayev, speculated that the extensive drought and wildfires could decrease the year's grain harvest by 25 percent. The Russian Grain Union, which operates under the Ministry of Agriculture, estimated that exports could fall by as much as half the level achieved in 2009. Four percent of the nation's GDP is comprised of agriculture.

After declaring a state of emergency in twenty-eight farming regions, the agriculture ministry's focus shifted to a potential ban on grain exports to stabilize domestic food prices. On August 5, Putin declared that a ban would be placed on exports of all grain and grain products beginning August 15 because of the continuing drought and wildfires. "I think it is expedient to temporarily ban exports of grain and grain products from Russia," Putin said. To serve those in the country in need of grain, the government would distribute what it had from a stock of 9.5 million tons of grain it keeps on hand. Rather than auctioning the grain, as had previously been done, the government doled out the resource based on hierarchy criteria developed by the agriculture ministry, which would determine which regions were most in need of grain.

In late 2010, Russia announced that the ban would be expanded into 2011, driving global prices of grain higher and raising concerns about a repeat of the 2008 worldwide food price crisis. Regardless of its impact on global food prices and demand, Putin insisted that there was nothing Russia could do. "We can only review lifting the ban on grain exports after the next year's crop is harvested and we have clarity on the balances," Putin said in September.

Climate scientists hoped that the drought and wildfires in Europe that led to the export ban would alert other countries to the impact that climate change will have in the coming years. "We are seeing more and more really big fires," cautioned forestry officer Pieter van Lierop of the United Nations' Food and Agriculture Organization. "The control of these fires has become an issue of high importance, not only because of the increasing number of casualties and amounts of area burned, but also because of its link with other global issues, like climate change." The extreme temperatures around the world, scientists said, would make crop shortages more frequent. "With increases in temperature and increasing changes in the global climate, we are experiencing more disasters," said Sherri Goodman, senior vice president at the Center for Naval Analyses.

—Heather Kerrigan

Following is the transcript of a disaster relief meeting held by Russian president Dmitry Medvedev on July 30, 2010, and the transcript of a statement by Medvedev on August 2, 2010, on the effect of the wildfires.

President Medvedev Holds Fire Disaster Meeting

July 30, 2010

PRESIDENT OF RUSSIA DMITRY MEDVEDEV: Good afternoon,

Today is turning out to be a difficult day: there have been many fires and some of them have had a truly catastrophic impact. Right now, the Government is working on my instruction in various Russian regions; Prime Minister is in the Nizhny Novgorod Region; I will be communicating with him later and he will tell me about the situation.

First, I would like to talk with the Regional Development Minister, because in addition to disaster relief (right now, the Ministry of Emergency Situations is working on it, and I hope that everything's on the right course), the events in the Nizhny Novgorod Region will clearly bring on problems.

These problems have to do with the need to provide housing to a very large number of people. Once, a long time ago, I myself participated in disaster relief following an earthquake, so I know how slow this process can be.

And in spite of the fact that summer this year is very hot (abnormally hot, and this is the reason behind the fires), it will end sooner or later. And gradually, it will turn into winter—a very cold winter.

We need to get working, so that we can allocate the appropriate amount of money and quickly build at least temporary housing, or begin building permanent housing straight away. The Government of the Russian Federation and the regional governments must earmark funds in their budgets for these purposes. I would like to know how you plan to organise this process.

MINISTER OF REGIONAL DEVELOPMENT VIKTOR BASARGIN: Mr President,

At this time, experts from the Regional Development Ministry have been sent to all the affected regions. Today, together with the Ministry of Emergency Situations and the regions, we are looking into he [sic] situation, studying it, and analysing everything that has happened.

On the Prime Minister's instruction, we already had a discussion with the Finance Ministry and roughly determined the amount of financing we will need. I can say that according to our data, the average floor space of a house affected by fire ranges between 80 and 100 square metres; in other words, overall, our citizens have lost about 150 thousand square metres of housing.

DMITRY MEDVEDEV: In all the territories?

VIKTOR BASARGIN: Yes. We will continue our monitoring of the situation, for I think these are not the final data.

Our goal now is to look into the possibility of restoring infrastructure in every town; I am referring to public utility infrastructure, including water and gas supply, and the possibility of reconstructing housing on the same sites.

And the challenge before us is a complicate[d] one. We are looking into how we can mobilise the construction sector. We have already analysed our construction capacity for rapidly-constructed housing: we currently have some 36 such facilities in these regions.

We have analysed six regions, and they have between three and eight companies engaged in manufacturing of elements for rapidly constructed housing. But we can look farther out as well, so that we may be able to get additional building materials.

We will be reconstructing metre by metre. A few multiple-apartment buildings were destroyed, in two regions so far. They are small four- and eight-apartment buildings, and we will be reconstructing those as well. Perhaps some other technologies can be used in this case.

This will basically be typical, rapidly constructed housing; the new apartments and houses might be a few square metres bigger than the ones people had before. And even in cases when the previous housing lacked certain amenities, we will try to connect the new housing to utility services, if possible, improving it in parallel.

DMITRY MEDVEDEV: I see. What standards do you use to determine the amount of money needed for construction?

VIKTOR BASARGIN: A standard that is in line with the one established by the Regional Development Ministry; no more than thirty thousand rubles per square metre at most.

Mr President, our data show that the rapidly-constructed housing manufacturers we have identified are currently offering to build just the "box," without any infrastructure, at a price between sixteen and a half thousand to nineteen and a half thousand [rubles] at most.

DMITRY MEDVEDEV: I see. In other words, you feel that this money will be enough—the money allotted based on the construction standards?

VIKTOR BASARGIN: Yes.

DMITRY MEDVEDEV: And how much time will it take?

VIKTOR BASARGIN: It looks like we can get all this reconstruction done—perhaps not before winter starts, but by the end of the year.

DMITRY MEDVEDEV: By the end of this—current—year?

VIKTOR BASARGIN: Yes, this year.

DMITRY MEDVEDEV: If that's how it will be carried out, we do not have much time—just five months—so we will need to think about temporary housing.

Naturally, this is the responsibility of the regions, of regional governors, but we need to analyse the federal capabilities as well—federal reserves related to housing.

VIKTOR BASARGIN: We will certainly make provisions, Mr President.

DMITRY MEDVEDEV: Then let's do just that. We will need to draw up a separate programme for every region affected by the fires, to provide temporary housing for people who have lost their houses and to quickly build housing using modern, high-quality materials, but based on rapid-construction technologies, just as you said, within the financing limits we have set. If there is a need for any additional financing, I am ready to give the appropriate instructions to the Government. It's agreed.

VIKTOR BASARGIN: Very well.

DMITRY MEDVEDEV: Now, Ms Golikova, please, give us a brief report on the situation as regards your work. Unfortunately, the fires claimed several lives, so it is imperative to provide adequate compensation to the families of the victims. There are also individuals who were injured; we do not currently have an exact number. Although the fire-fighters are working very actively and bravely, unfortunately, there are some casualties among them too. There are also those who were injured, and we must take all the necessary steps, make all the decisions concerning those who fell ill and those who have carbon monoxide poisoning, or have simply sustained burns, because we have a number of these individuals in various areas.

And as far as I understand, another problem may have to do with the fact that a significant number of people have lost their housing, and we must at least provide them with temporary housing and ensure normal sanitary and epidemiologic conditions. People need to have access to doctors, because these people have suffered a tremendous psychological stress and are lacking the comforts they used to have, so we must not lose control over medical and sanitary and epidemiologic situation.

MINISTER OF HEALTHCARE AND SOCIAL DEVELOPMENT TATYANA GOLIKOVA: Mr President, Our ministry is a part of the Ministry of Emergency Situations' team, and together with them we monitor the situation as it unfolds in all the regions. Naturally, at this time, we feel that the most alarming situation, based in part on the parameters you spoke about, is in the Voronezh Region. In this regard, I would like to say that in general, we have established a smooth-running interaction plan with the Ministry of Emergency Situations and the regions as regards medical assistance. Nevertheless, if necessary, we are ready to evacuate the injured to central cities if it becomes necessary; the reserve hospital beds that are used in emergency situations are always ready. But just to give you the figures, I will say that according to our data, the Voronezh Region has had 439 individuals admitted to medical facilities; as of today, 377 people have been discharged and 43 people are at hospitals in serious condition. If it becomes necessary to either send specialists there in order to improve medical treatment, or to transfer these patients to other facilities, our Ministry and the Ministry of Emergency Situations are ready—we traditionally work jointly in these cases. As for accommodations, naturally, as a responsible federal agency, we are taking our own measures, but I have a request to our regions: in places where people are being temporarily lodged after having left their homes because of this situation, I request that they are provided with the necessary food products, water, and medicine, and that the infection control is in place, although I understand that it is fairly difficult to do this quickly. Nevertheless, we will make the appropriate recommendations on this matter to the regions.

DMITRY MEDVEDEV: Thank you, Ms Golikova. Please do that, because the situation is very difficult. Today, I spoke with everyone engaged in disaster-relief efforts—the Emergency Situations Minister, the Governors, and the Prime Minister. Overall, I must admit that this kind of disaster can happen in other regions as well. Naturally, We need to take all the necessary preventive measures, but overall, this does not always depend entirely on us or on our capabilities. Thus, we need to be ready to hold all the necessary meetings and videoconferences with regional governors and to give them the appropriate instructions.

SOURCE: Office of the President of Russia. "Transcript of Meeting on Fire-Fighting and Disaster Relief Efforts in Central Russia." July 30, 2010. http://eng.kremlin.ru/transcripts/697.

President Medvedev's Response to the Russian Wildfires

August 2, 2010

PRESIDENT OF RUSSIA DMITRY MEDVEDEV: The heat wave we are experiencing has brought tragedy to several of our country's regions. They are battling with fire. This natural disaster of immense proportions has hit Ryazan, Moscow, Nizhny Novgorod, Vladimir and Voronezh regions, the Republic of Mordovia, and other parts of Russia. Fires are blazing today in 14 of our country's regions, with vast areas engulfed by flames.

The Emergency Situations Ministry and other state institutions are taking all possible measures to bring the fires under control and, most important of all, save people. I have instructed the Defence Ministry and other law enforcement, security and defence agencies to join in this work. We need to use every means available to fight this disaster. This is a very difficult task. The situation remains very serious. The heat is not lessening at all, and the forecasts are not promising. This means the risk of new fires starting remains very high.

I signed an executive order today declaring a state of emergency in several regions that have been hardest hit by the fires. But a lot depends on us, on how we respond and behave. With the cities sweltering in this stifling heat of course we want to get out and escape into nature. But here, we have to be extremely attentive, extremely careful, because even a single match left burning could spark an irreparable tragedy. This is not an oft-repeated word of warning, but is a very real and serious fact.

Our greatest task now is to help those affected by the fires to return to normal life as soon as possible. The fires have left more than two thousand of our fellow citizens homeless. Among them are many children, many old and sick people. Many families have lost everything they owned in the flames. This is a huge tragedy.

The state authorities are acutely aware of their responsibilities in this situation. I have instructed the Government and the regional authorities to make compensation payments to all who have been affected. These payments have already begun. I spoke yesterday with the heads of the affected regions, and they briefed me on what they are doing and that the money is coming in.

Rebuilding homes is another issue we need to address. This is perhaps the most complicated issue we face, but we must build new homes for everyone who has been left without a roof over their head, and we need to do this before the cold weather sets in. Decisions have already been taken and money has already been allocated for this work. But we need to act fast, and so I am going to reduce the normal amount of time it takes to organise this kind of work. I will choose specific sub-contractors, who will begin their work immediately, without going through the normal tender process. In this particular situation this is a justified decision.

The authorities will fulfil their responsibilities. But all of us, all citizens of this country, must do their part to help in this common tragedy. People are already joining forces to help those who have been left with nothing overnight. This is the way people throughout the world respond. People are coming to each other's aid, uniting their efforts to fight the fires together and help those who have lost homes and possessions.

Let's all help those caught up in this misfortune.

SOURCE: Office of the President of Russia. "New Recording on Dmitry Medvedev's Blog in Response to the Serious Situation in the Russian Regions Hit by Fire." August 2, 2010. http://eng.kremlin.ru/tran scripts/709.

OTHER HISTORIC DOCUMENTS OF INTEREST

FROM THIS VOLUME

FROM PREVIOUS HISTORIC DOCUMENTS

China Surpasses Japan to Become the World's Second Largest Economy

JULY 30, 2010

Economic statistics from the first half of 2010 made official a transformation that had long been considered inevitable: the People's Republic of China overtook Japan to become the world's second largest economy. The shift, recorded in nominal gross domestic product figures for the second quarter, reflected the long-term trends of China's powerful export-driven growth and Japan's relative economic inertia. Analysts took the occasion to note China's increasingly outsized influence on the global economy as a leading manufacturer and exporter, a consumer of raw materials, and an investor in infrastructure and natural resources abroad, with trillions of dollars in foreign reserves. China's growing standing in global economic forums, linked with its increasingly assertive position in regional security matters, reinforced the notion that the world's most populous nation sought to raise its geostrategic profile as its economy continued to surge. Chinese officials, however, were quick to note that China remained a developing country with much work ahead of it to convert its economic gains into higher living standards across the population. For their part, Japanese leaders spoke with a tone of resignation about the change in their nation's status.

Nosing Ahead by the Numbers

The Chinese economy, badly shaken in the decades following the communist revolution of 1949, began to grow after the market reforms instituted once Deng Xiaoping came to power in December 1978. Between 1978 and 2010, the nation achieved the remarkable average annual growth rate of 9.5 percent. China tripled its gross domestic product (GDP) in the five-year span between 2004 and 2009, roaring past France, the United Kingdom, and Germany. At the close of 2009, using figures compiled by the World Bank and measured in U.S. dollars, China's GDP was $4.985 trillion, just shy of Japan's $5.069 trillion. The corresponding figure for the United States, the world's leading economy, was $14.119 trillion.

Despite the major financial crisis affecting the global economy in 2009, China posted a robust GDP gain of 8.7 percent, aided by a sizable government stimulus package. Observers concurred that the statistics would show China's output overtaking Japan's imminently, probably sometime in 2010. The actual moment was delayed because the Japanese economy recorded better than expected results—an annualized gain of 4.6 percent—for the fourth quarter of 2009. But by mid-August 2010, when both governments released data for the second quarter, the balance had officially tipped: Japan's nominal GDP for that period totaled $1.286 trillion, bested by China's $1.335 trillion. Given the difference between the two nations' growth rates, it appeared certain that the trend would continue. Using an alternate metric known as purchasing power parity, with adjustments factored in for the different exchange rates between national currencies, the International Monetary Fund (IMF) found that China had vaulted into the number-two position in 2001.

One Runs in Place, One Roars Ahead

In an earlier era, Japan had the world's fastest-growing economy. The Japanese economic "miracle" began with its reconstruction following World War II and lasted through the 1980s. A powerful export sector led by automobiles and electronics, assiduous government direction of the economy, and a firm social contract between corporations and their employees were hallmarks of the Japanese economy at its peak. In the late 1980s, however, the stock market and real estate prices rose to inflated levels, and both bubbles eventually deflated, sapping the economy of its lift.

The 1990s are sometimes called Japan's "lost decade," but the economic malaise persisted throughout the first decade of the twenty-first century. Japan's nominal GDP registered zero growth between 2000 and 2007 and fell a whopping 6 percent in 2009 before regaining 3.9 percent in 2010. Weak corporate investment and consumer demand contributed to a deflationary economy, with interest rates at or near 0 percent. During these years, the yen was strong, curbing the growth of Japanese exports and reducing profits from foreign trade. Japan's public debt was the highest among the world's developed nations, nearly double the level of GDP in 2010, largely due to high social expenditures distributed to an aging population. Despite the stagnant growth, though, Japan remained one of the world's most affluent societies.

Meanwhile, China's economic juggernaut drove it past its Asian rival into an increasingly dominant position in the world market. By 2009, China had become the world's largest exporter; the top steel producer; the number-one consumer of iron ore, copper, and other key raw materials of industry; and the largest market for automobile sales. It also, not coincidentally, had surpassed the United States as the world leader in greenhouse gas emissions, which were rising much faster than previously predicted. In mid-2010, four state-owned Chinese companies were among the world's ten largest corporations by market capitalization, according to the *Financial Times*—the oil company PetroChina, the Industrial and Commercial Bank of China, the China Construction Bank, and the Hong Kong–based telecommunications provider China Mobile.

China's remarkable growth also provided a needed boost to its trading partners. Not the least among these were the Japanese, who used China as an inexpensive manufacturing base and a market for its finished products. Many poorer nations benefited from China's voracious consumption of raw materials. According to Angel Gurría, secretary-general of the Organisation for Economic Co-operation and Development (OECD), one third of the world's economic growth in 2010 could be traced back to China. Without a doubt, the People's Republic contributed immensely to the global economy's recovery during 2009 and 2010.

DISSECTING CHINA'S MARKET POWER

China's rise had much to do with its success at attracting foreign investment. The nation's manufacturing centers offered not only a surfeit of cheap labor but access to every link on the business value chain, from capital to manufacturing and assembly, research and development, and vast and rapidly growing business and consumer markets. Aided by its notoriously undervalued currency, the yuan, China had amassed huge bilateral trade surpluses with the United States and the European Union.

Matching the potency of China's industrial base was its looming financial power. The government's cache of more than $2.4 trillion in foreign exchange reserves gave its investment decisions significant weight on the global market. China had long since emerged as a major holder of U.S. public debt. In the short run, this arrangement contributed to stability in the American and Chinese economies, but its long-term consequences gave American policymakers pause. Beijing also made waves when it proposed eliminating the dollar's status as the world's principal reserve currency.

As a dominant consumer of energy supplies and raw materials for industry, China had gained leverage over the price of many commodities—and thus over the economies of many less powerful nations. During the 2000s, China deepened its trade relationships with African and Latin American states, supplying credit and investing in infrastructure in exchange for assets. These efforts to shore up long-term access to hydrocarbons and other natural resources appeared to be aimed at resolving the problem of China's insufficient domestic supply of these resources. For example, in Sudan, a country that exports half its oil output to China, Chinese capital helped build a pipeline and modern oil refining complex. The Chinese have funded hundreds of projects, such as roads, power plants, and telecommunications systems in Africa. Unlike Western donors and multilateral institutions such as the IMF and the World Bank, China did not impose conditions on these deals, such as restrictions on public spending or improvements in governance. The China Development Bank has also opened multibillion-dollar credit lines for the Venezuelan and Brazilian national oil companies.

A DEVELOPING POWER

Having emerged as the world's number-two economy, China appeared destined to eclipse the United States eventually and ascend to number one, although commentators differed in their estimates of when that was likely to occur. The Japanese Cabinet Office predicted that China would overtake the United States in 2025.

Perhaps the key variable influencing China's future growth would be the level of consumer demand from its massive population of 1.3 billion people. For several years the Chinese leadership has emphasized boosting domestic consumption; it began to see significant results from around 2009. The government's efforts to build future growth around the domestic market rather than relying primarily on exports underscored a critical dimension of current conditions in China: despite the prodigious power it has accumulated, its economic and social development have not matured to the level of the most advanced nations. In the words of Yi Gang, head of the State Administration of Foreign Exchange (SAFE) and deputy governor of the People's Bank of China: "China is still a developing country, and we should be wise enough to know ourselves."

Despite surpassing Japan in nominal GDP—at $5.88 trillion against Japan's $5.47 trillion, according to full-year figures for 2010—China's wealth lagged far behind that of

Japan, and the rest of the industrialized world, when viewed on a per capita basis. China's gross national income per capita of $3,650 for 2009 placed it 125th among nations, according to the World Bank's World Development Indicators database. For purposes of comparison, Japan recorded $38,080 per capita, and the United States $43,360, using the same methodology. The Bank reported that nearly one in ten Chinese—more than 100 million people—live beneath the poverty level of $2 per day. Within China's land mass, roughly comparable to that of the United States, many of its regions lagged behind other industrialized nations in modern infrastructure and living conditions.

With China's rapidly shifting economic status, its position in international affairs was evolving in potentially volatile ways. It possessed enormous clout in its trade patterns and investment decisions. Its growing role in African and Latin American economic development and its investment in the U.S. sovereign debt further strengthened its strategic hand. In bilateral talks with U.S. leaders and in economic forums such as the Group of 8 (G-8), Beijing firmly rebuffed Western criticism of its monetary policy, denying that it was manipulating its currency to favor its exports. President Hu Jintao said in May 2010 that his administration was committed to reforming the regulation of exchange rates, but by year's end, the yuan remained well under its potential market value.

China's military was growing, too, particularly its naval forces. Chinese leaders, for their part, were showing some assertiveness on some foreign policy issues. In the South China Sea, for example, China was pressing its disputed claim to a vast portion of territory, conducting larger naval exercises and, in several instances, harassing foreign vessels. In May, a Chinese policy document referred to the sea as a "core national interest," connoting that it could be treated similarly to China's sovereign policies regarding Taiwan and Tibet. Two months later, at a meeting of the Association of Southeast Asian Nations (ASEAN), U.S. secretary of state Hillary Rodham Clinton claimed that keeping disputes peaceful in the South China Sea was a "national interest" of Washington's.

A contrast to these bold diplomatic stances could be found in the global negotiations on addressing climate change. On this issue, China backed away from a leadership role, advocating to maintain its status as a developing nation under the framework of the Kyoto Protocol and rejecting calls that it assume greater responsibility for emissions reductions.

—Roger K. Smith

Following is an edited interview given by Yi Gang, deputy governor of the People's Bank of China, on July 30, 2010, discussing China's economic plans and its new status as the world's second largest economy.

DOCUMENT *China Discusses Economic Plans*

July 30, 2010

Hu Shuli (hereinafter referred to as Hu): On June 19, 2010, the People's Bank of China announced the decision to further the reform of the RMB exchange rate formation mechanism on the basis of the 2005 reform. Why now? What do you think of the achievements that the exchange rate reform has made so far?

Yi Gang (hereinafter referred to as Yi): China's exchange rate regime is a floating one, which is based on market supply and demand and subject to adjustment and management against a basket of currencies. In fact, this is the best choice at present for the Chinese socialist market economy. How have we arrived at this conclusion? The reform of the exchange rate regime began in 1994, when exchange rates were unified on January 1 and the foreign exchange market was established soon thereafter. From 1994 to 1996, the RMB fluctuated in both directions and appreciated by about 5 percent, from 1: 8.71 to 1: 8.28 against the USD. Then, after the outbreak of the Asian financial crisis, as the Thai Baht and the Korean Won experienced huge depreciations, China refused to devalue the RMB, resulting in a stable 1: 8.28 from 1997 to 2005. We still believed in the benefits of the exchange rate reform and that a managed floating currency is the right exchange rate mechanism for China, but the existence of inertia or path dependence made reform very difficult. Then, on July 21, 2005, the reform started again and we had three years of fluctuations up until 2008.

During this period, the RMB was in fact subject to two-way fluctuations and followed the direction of the currency basket. But in 2008, a series of events occurred, including the outbreak of the sub-prime mortgage crisis. Soon thereafter Bear Stearns went under, and Lehman Brothers declared bankruptcy on September 15, 2008, pushing the financial crisis to a climax. From then on, the RMB remained near the level of RMB 6.83 against the USD, with minor fluctuations, until June 19 of this year, when we again launched the RMB exchange rate reform.

Looking back on history, it is clear that we have never lost sight of this mechanism; we were just interrupted by the outbreak of the crisis and other factors. Nevertheless, this is the best choice for China, a choice that we should uphold.

Hu: What is the ultimate goal?

Yi: Our ultimate goal is to make the RMB a convertible currency. This is the goal that was made in the fall of 1993, at the Third Plenary Session of the 14th CPC Central Committee. . . .

Hu: When can the RMB become convertible? Is there a timetable?

Yi: We don't have an official timetable for RMB convertibility in China. But according to an IMF study, for an average country, it takes about 7 to 10 years to transition to capital account convertibility from current account convertibility, which China achieved in 1996.

Now, 15 years later, China still hasn't achieved capital account convertibility, and we do not have a timetable. People can make their own judgments based on international practices. The main reason is China is too big and our development is too uneven, which makes the problem very complicated and it is difficult to achieve a consensus.

Hu: In terms of currency appreciation, we all know that there are both external pressures and domestic needs. Comprehensively, what are the reasons that the RMB still cannot have a floating exchange rate?

Yi: What really makes a currency's exchange rate float is the real effective exchange rate, which can be altered in two ways. The first is to adjust the nominal exchange rate, and the other is to increase domestic prices. In face of appreciation pressures, we do not have to adjust the nominal exchange rate because inflation can change the real effective exchange rate.

Both methods have been used by China in the past decade, with adjustments in both the nominal exchange rates and prices. The surge in the housing prices is a good example.

Hu: Now after several rounds of exchange rate reform, people's expectations of a RMB appreciation should be pretty low now. Do we still need to continue the adjustment via inflation?

Yi: It is safe to say that the pressure has weakened. In the recent decade, housing prices have gone through the roof in Beijing and Shanghai. In fact, commodity prices as a whole have greatly increased. These price hikes are actually adjustments against imbalances. Ten years ago, if you converted USD into RMB and bought property in China, you could make a lot of money, but now it is no longer a very lucrative deal. The same is true for other assets. All these indicate that, compared with ten years ago, the RMB exchange rate is now much closer to an equilibrium level.

Now, the exchange rate is not likely to fluctuate sharply and we are in a position to maintain a flexible exchange rate regime and to keep the exchange rate stable at a reasonable level of equilibrium.

Every coin has two sides. The constant increase in labor productivity in China has determined the overall trend in currency value. Under such a trend, appreciation can curb inflation; a bit more appreciation would mean a bit less inflation. So if the nominal exchange rate remains the same, the result will be more inflation. Some might argue that the Chinese people do not need imported goods, so a RMB appreciation will result in no benefits. This is wrong. Take soya beans as an example. Over half of the soya beans consumed in China are imported, and bean products are in high demand. Even soya bean pulp is needed to breed pigs, which means soya beans are somehow related to pork prices. If the RMB does not appreciate, then the prices of soya beans, bean oil, and bean pulp will be at least 20 percent higher than they are now. At present, these soya products are becoming very expensive on the international market, but the price increase is not that apparent in China. Why? Because the RMB has gone up and soya prices are mostly calculated in USD. It is the same for crude oil and iron ore, which, believe it or not, are also closely related to every household. So a currency appreciation can control imported inflation. . . .

So we should view this question dynamically. The government is trying all methods to formulate sound policies and to create an enabling environment. For example, instruments for hedging and forward settlement and sales of foreign exchange are offered to help import and export enterprises to hedge against risks.

Another misconception is that a RMB appreciation means losses in our foreign exchange reserves. In 2007, when the RMB was appreciating very rapidly, some observers said that the loss of foreign exchange reserves in one quarter would be worth one aircraft carrier. Now, we have 2.45 trillion USD in foreign exchange reserves (equivalent to more than RMB 16 trillion). With the RMB going up, the foreign exchange reserves, in RMB terms, would appear to be less in number, but that does not mean the money is gone. We would suffer some losses if we were to convert the foreign exchange reserves from USD to RMB, but we haven't converted yet, so there is no such loss. Such a calculation is conversion on book value only.

If such a calculation has to be done, we might as well do the math by calculating how much we will have earned if all RMB assets are put into USD. Take the financial and housing assets in China as an example; the total value of those assets would be RMB 200 trillion (over ten times that of the foreign exchange reserves). If the RMB appreciates and these assets are marked in USD, we can gain at least ten aircraft carriers. But of course, the truth is we neither gain nor lose. . . .

Hu: The foreign exchange reform has been interrupted repeatedly. Is the progress a bit too slow?

Yi: China is a big developing country. In the past three decades, China has created an economic miracle in the history of mankind. In this sense, China's macroeconomic policies have changed track. There might be some criticism concerning the degree of marketization [sic] or the delay of reform, but from 1994 to the present, China has maintained a high growth rate. In addition, since the 1994 inflation, so far we have not experienced another big inflation.

On the whole, China's macro-economic policies are almost optimal. Indeed, we have been interrupted many times, and some might even think that the foreign exchange reform is not occurring fast enough. This question is open to discussion and reflection, but it is fair to say that our macro policies are generally successful.

Hu: Why did the government choose the present time to recover the elasticity of the foreign exchange rate? Is it because it is less risky now, or because there are greater external pressures?

Yi: China has made this decision mainly based on domestic considerations. It is an independent decision. Like I said, during the global financial crisis, the exchange rate was stable for a while. In fact, the crisis is not yet completely over, as is evidenced by the European sovereign debt crisis this year, but the overall picture is much better than before. As the crisis is receding, our growth rate increased last year from 8.7 percent to 9.1 percent. For the U.S., Europe, and Japan, 2010 is also widely predicted to be a year of recovery. Given the domestic and international background, I think now is the ripe time to recover the elasticity. . . .

Hu: Can China become a rule maker?

Yi: This is a huge question. We have always stressed the importance of taking part in the making of international rules. Who makes the rules for the so-called international monetary system? Apparently, major developed countries, especially the U.S. Then how did the U.S. become a rule maker? It was because the US dollar market is open, and it is the main theater for the global financial market. Naturally, whether for stocks or bonds, the rules shall be made by the authorities in charge of those markets, i.e., the U.S. and Europe. We are not yet a rule-maker, but as long as we open up the market and allow foreign players access to our turf, the Chinese monetary and regulatory authorities will then have every right to make our own rules. That is for sure.

Hu: I recently interviewed Russia's first Deputy Prime Minister Igor Shuvalov. He said that sooner or later the RMB will become a reserve currency, whereas the Russian ruble will at most be a regional currency. What do you think?

Yi: We cannot be too complacent. It will do us harm. China is still a developing country. We should bear in mind our limits.

Hu: Then is it possible for the RMB to become a reserve currency? Does the world need it?

Yi: This compliment is half flattery, half prediction. We should be modest and prudent, and keep a low profile. If the RMB is chosen by other countries to be a reserve currency, we will let it happen, because it is market demand. But we are not going to push it. I think the best way is to let things run their own course. We must not take the flattery too seriously; in fact, the RMB is still far from being a reserve currency.

Hu: Are reserve currencies chosen naturally by the market? Or do we need governments to decide which should become a reserve currency? Or is it a bit of both?

Yi: For a currency to become a reserve currency, the first most important factor is the economic strength of that country or confederation; the second is its cultural cohesion and influence; and the third is political and military power.

Economic strength is the deciding factor. As to culture, it is important to have an influential culture, whose core values will be widely accepted by other countries and regions. A reserve currency must be backed by a powerful culture and influential value system.

Do not underestimate the resilience of the US and Europe . . .

Hu: After the financial crisis, both Europe and the U.S. made some adjustments and changes. What do you think of their ability to recover?

Yi: I think they have strong resilience and should not be underestimated. The U.S. financial regulatory reform bill, recently signed into law, marks another milestone after the Glass-Steagall Act of 1933, and the Financial Services Modernization Act of 1999 signed by former President Clinton represents a reflection of the past several decades, especially the recent round of the financial crisis. Aside from the U.S. bill, there is also a new roadmap for a financial regulatory framework drawn up by Britain, and a series of financial regulatory standards formulated by the Financial Stability Board under the G20, the IMF, the Basel Committee, and the Bank for International Settlements. All these have formed global financial regulatory standards and a framework for the coming decade or even longer. Under such a regulatory framework, their capacity to recover is relatively strong and the speed is relatively fast.

Europe has made many contributions to the establishment of an international financial regulatory framework, but, of course, the U.S. is leading the way as it passed the regulatory reform bill.

Hu: Recently, I interviewed Michael Evans, vice chairman of Goldman Sachs. He said that Goldman Sachs is prepared to adjust its strategy. In fact, Wall Street is still resistant to the U.S. financial regulatory reform bill, but Goldman Sachs will adjust its position and embrace the reform. It has set up the Business Standards Committee, which, after investigation and research, has come up with concrete measures to change its business behavior. When talking about the lawsuit against the U.S. Securities and Exchange Commission, he said that although the case has a political bias, we must admit that we made mistakes too. Judging from his attitude, there is a possibility of mediation, but he emphasized that mediation does not mean the end, and Goldman Sachs still needs to adjust its business behavior. But from another perspective, since the financial reform bill has been spoken so highly of, why is it so difficult to implement? Why is the Republican Party so vigorously opposed to the bill?

Yi: The difficulties stem from conflicts of interests. The bill used to contain clauses that harm the interests of investment banks and commercial banks, but they have been watered down now and compromises have been made. On the whole, I think this bill is positive, and the prompt adoption of this bill is so much better than no action at all. Uncertainty would accumulate if no measure were taken. Now the launch of the bill ends the suspense, stabilizes market expectations, and can restore the market to normalcy.

Be Realistic about China's Economic Growth

Hu: I have a question about the macro economy. Do you think there is a big chance of a Double Dip in the world economy?

Yi: The short answer to this question, as far as I see it, is no. But a precise explanation depends on the definition of Double Dip. This year, the U.S. economic growth rate hopefully will be 2.5 percent to 3.5 percent. In Japan, the growth rate will be above zero, probably even above 2 percent; as to Europe, possibly 0.5 percent to 1.5 percent. No one would call this a Double Dip, but there are still many uncertainties, considering the worrying situation in the U.S. housing and job markets.

Hu: China's economic growth rate was 11.1 percent for the first half of 2010. Will it drop in the future?

Yi: For the whole year, the growth rate could reach 9 percent, which is fairly high already. Perhaps we are a bit too obsessed about high growth rates. I hope to see a more moderate approach, which can help extend the long-term growth of the Chinese economy. China has now become the second largest economy in the world. As our economic base expands, growth rates will definitely slow down. In addition, the environmental constraints have reached a bottleneck, with a host of problems concerning underground water, air, and carbon emissions. There are also resource restrictions, including the import of energy. Based on the above reasons and the general rules of economic development, there is no doubt that there will be a slowdown in our economic growth.

In the three decades after the launch of the reform and opening up, China's average GDP growth rate exceeded 9.5 percent. In the first decade of the new century, the rate was over 10 percent. For the second decade, I would say an average growth rate of 7 percent to 8 percent is good enough. The question is whether we can sustain such a growth rate. If in the third decade, we manage to grow at 5 percent to 6 percent, then we would have had 50 years of rapid growth, an unprecedented feat in human history.

In fact, the problem of China's economy lies in the quality of its growth. That is why we have been restructuring and transforming patterns of growth; we are trying to improve the quality and effects of economic growth. We should adjust our mind-set; being too impatient doesn't help.

SOURCE: China State Administration of Foreign Exchange. "Yi Gang, Deputy Governor of the People's Bank of China (PBOC) and Administrator of the State Administration of Foreign Exchange (SAFE), is Interviewed by the Executive Editor-in-Chief of China Reform." July 30, 2010. http://www.safe.gov.cn/model_safe_en/news_en/new_detail_en.jsp?ID=30100000000000000,261&type=&id=2.

OTHER HISTORIC DOCUMENTS OF INTEREST

FROM PREVIOUS HISTORIC DOCUMENTS

August

Proposed Islamic Cultural Center Sparks Controversy

AUGUST 3 AND 13, 2010

On May 25, 2010, Manhattan Community Board 1 gave its approval to a plan to construct an Islamic community center in lower Manhattan, near City Hall and the former World Trade Center site. After a raucous debate between supporters and opponents of the project, the board voted 29 to 1 in favor, with ten abstentions. Developers of the proposed center, originally called Cordoba House and later renamed Park51, envisioned a thirteen-story structure that would house athletic facilities, a library and auditorium, a child care center, a restaurant and culinary school, and a prayer space that could accommodate up to two thousand people. By August, opposition to the project had intensified, with prominent Republican politicians and conservative commentators condemning what they called the "Ground Zero mosque" as an affront to the victims of the September 11, 2001, terrorist attacks and their families. New York City mayor Michael Bloomberg and President Barack Obama were among those who defended the proposal from the standpoint of religious freedom. The situation received substantial media attention during the 2010 midterm election campaigns.

PRAYER AT THE BURLINGTON COAT FACTORY

When the two airplanes struck the World Trade Center on 9/11, felling the twin towers and killing nearly three thousand people, the landing gear from one of the aircraft crashed through the roof of 45 Park Place two blocks to the north. This five-story building, dating back to the 1850s, had once housed the offices of the Merck pharmaceutical company and was being used at the time as a Burlington Coat Factory retail outlet. The store closed and the building stood vacant until it was sold in July 2009 to the real estate developer Soho Properties for just under $5 million. The Cordoba Initiative, an interfaith spiritual organization founded by Imam Feisal Abdul Rauf, was an investor in the property.

Rauf, a Sufi Muslim cleric and prayer leader at the Masjid al-Farah mosque in lower Manhattan's Tribeca district, began holding Friday services at the Park Place location. Rauf and his colleagues conceived a vision of a larger Muslim cultural center at the site. The 92nd Street Y, a successful Jewish community center on the Upper East Side, provided a model for what Rauf and his partners hoped to create. Rauf was well known and widely respected for his efforts to promote interfaith dialogue and bridge the divide between Islam and mainstream America. Establishing a Muslim facility in proximity to the World Trade Center location meshed with the group's vision to help "weave the

Muslim-American identity into the pluralistic fabric of the United States." Rauf's wife, Daisy Khan, was on the advisory board helping to design the proposed September 11 memorial at the site dubbed Ground Zero after the 9/11 attacks.

The couple and their partners attracted the support of local Jewish and Christian leaders and politicians, including Manhattan borough president Scott Stringer and U.S. representative Jerrold Nadler, a Democrat from lower Manhattan. In December 2009, the *New York Times* reported that the project had "drawn early encouragement from city officials and the surrounding neighborhood." That community support was reflected in the lopsided Community Board vote in favor of the proposal five months later.

Sensitivities over "Hallowed Ground"

By the time of the board vote, opposition to the idea had begun to gather. Internet blogger Pamela Geller, cofounder of Stop Islamization of America, warned that a "monster mosque" would make an inappropriate addition to the neighborhood surrounding Ground Zero. Articles in the *New York Post* and *New York Daily News* from May contained quotations from relatives of 9/11 victims who took offense to the proposal, such as Rosemary Cain of Massapequa, Long Island, who said, "I think it's despicable. That's sacred ground." *Post* columnist Andrea Peyser incorrectly reported on May 13 that the house of worship was scheduled to open on September 11, 2011.

The issue spread quickly to the national press, talk radio, and cable television, drawing considerable attention from Fox News. Some commentators attacked Rauf, Khan, and their partners, voicing fears that they intended to build a shrine to terrorism. Others questioned where the $100 million for the community center would come from, implying that the sources could include Muslim extremist groups or adherents of terrorist *jihad*. A larger number objected not to the construction of an Islamic place of worship but to building it so near to where Muslim terrorists had killed thousands. Project foes called this decision insensitive and insulting.

Before the Cordoba House project could go forward, however, the developers needed to surmount another bureaucratic hurdle. The building at 45–47 Park Place was the subject of a pending application for landmark status, filed by a previous owner. Buildings declared landmarks cannot be demolished or undergo major exterior renovation without city approval. Community Board 1 had issued its finding that the existing structure's architectural significance did not merit such a designation, but a ruling by the Landmarks Preservation Commission was nevertheless required. A public hearing of the commission on July 13 turned heated with the presence of many opponents of the center, including former U.S. representative Rick Lazio, a candidate in New York's 2010 gubernatorial race. Real estate developer Carl Paladino, Lazio's rival for the Republican nomination, declared that if elected he would use eminent domain laws to prevent the Cordoba House from being built, adding, "It just doesn't make sense to build a needlessly bold and insulting statement on hallowed ground where radical Islamists declared war on America."

By this time, national political figures from the Republican Party were wading into the conflict. On July 19, former Alaska governor and 2008 vice presidential candidate Sarah Palin used the social media site Twitter to deliver a terse message against the proposal: "Ground Zero Mosque supporters: doesn't it stab you in the heart, as it does ours throughout the heartland? Peaceful Muslims, pls refudiate." Political commentators puzzled over Palin's apparent neologism. Two days later, former House Speaker Newt Gingrich, another prospective GOP presidential hopeful, wrote on his website, "There should be no mosque near Ground Zero in New York so long as there are no churches or synagogues in Saudi Arabia." Gingrich, who characterized Cordoba House proponents as radical Islamists, later said on Fox News that "Nazis don't have the right to put up a sign next to the Holocaust museum in Washington," and a mosque near the World Trade Center was similarly unacceptable. The rhetoric appeared to herald the beginning of the election season, in a midterm year when Republicans hoped to make major gains in congressional races.

President Obama Enters the Debate

On August 3, the Landmarks Commission unanimously denied landmark status to the Park Place property, ruling solely from an architectural standpoint. The judgment cleared the way for the Cordoba House developers to complete their planning for an expansive new building on the site, which would likely take years to erect. That day, Mayor Bloomberg hailed the decision and offered an impassioned defense of religious freedom. He spoke from Governors Island in the East River, where in 1624 Dutch settlers founded the New Amsterdam colony on principles of religious tolerance. Bloomberg acknowledged the special importance of the World Trade Center and its legacy but insisted that the freedoms Americans cherish must prevail in practice. "We would betray our values— and play into our enemies' hands—if we were to treat Muslims differently than anyone else," said the mayor. "In fact, to cave to popular sentiment would be to hand a victory to the terrorists—and we should not stand for that."

On August 13 at the White House, President Obama, while hosting an *iftar* dinner, the evening meal for Muslims observing Ramadan, made his first remarks on the controversy in New York. Conceding that "Ground Zero is, indeed, hallowed ground," he said, "As a citizen and as President, I believe that Muslims have the right to practice their religion as everyone else in this country. And that includes the right to build a place of worship and a community center on private property in lower Manhattan, in accordance with local laws and ordinances. This is America. And our commitment to religious freedom must be unshakeable." The following day, the president explained that he had spoken only of the proponents' right to construct the mosque and that he would have no comment on the wisdom of doing so.

The debate percolated through the media into the fall, touching election contests such as the Nevada senatorial race between Majority Leader Harry Reid and his Tea Party–endorsed Republican challenger, Sharron Angle. On August 22, demonstrators for and against the mosque squared off in lower Manhattan. Imam Rauf was out of the country at the time, on a two-week tour of the Middle East sponsored by the State Department. It was his fourth goodwill visit to the region since 2007 as part of the federal government's diplomatic effort to combat religious extremism.

Koran Burning Scrapped

As the ninth anniversary of the attacks on New York and Washington approached, a Protestant minister in Gainesville, Florida, garnered worldwide headlines by announcing he would burn dozens of copies of the Koran on September 11. Earlier in the year, a pipe bomb had exploded at an Islamic center in Jacksonville, sixty miles northeast of Gainesville. Pastor Terry Jones of the non-denominational Dove World Outreach Center, author of the book *Islam Is of the Devil*, vowed to "stand up and confront terrorism" with his bonfire.

Religious leaders from the Vatican to the Archbishop of Canterbury and political leaders from around the world condemned the gesture. The commander of the North Atlantic Treaty Organization (NATO) forces in Afghanistan, Gen. David Petraeus, warned that televised images of the Islamic scripture ablaze would incite further extremist violence by Muslims worldwide. President Obama said the spectacle would prove a "recruitment bonanza for al-Qaeda." Jones appeared undaunted until September 9, when he abruptly cancelled the event. It appeared that the pastor had been enticed to stand down, in part, by the prospect of a meeting with Imam Rauf in New York. Jones said he wanted to persuade the imam to seek a new location for the Cordoba House. Rauf, however, said he was not willing to meet with Jones and would not entertain the idea of moving the community center as a result of threats.

—Roger K. Smith

Following is New York City mayor Michael Bloomberg's remarks on August 3, 2010, after the vote by the City's Landmark Preservation Commission denying landmark status to 45–47 Park Place; and a statement on August 13, 2010, by President Barack Obama on the construction of the cultural center near Ground Zero.

DOCUMENT

Mayor Bloomberg on Landmark Status Vote

August 3, 2010

[The list of those in attendance during Mayor Bloomberg's remarks has been omitted.]

"We have come here to Governors Island to stand where the earliest settlers first set foot in New Amsterdam, and where the seeds of religious tolerance were first planted. We've come here to see the inspiring symbol of liberty that, more than 250 years later, would greet millions of immigrants in the harbor, and we come here to state as strongly as ever—this is the freest City in the world. That's what makes New York special and different and strong.

"Our doors are open to everyone—everyone with a dream and a willingness to work hard and play by the rules. New York City was built by immigrants, and it is sustained by immigrants—by people from more than a hundred different countries speaking more than two hundred different languages and professing every faith. And whether your parents were born here, or you came yesterday, you are a New Yorker.

"We may not always agree with every one of our neighbors. That's life and it's part of living in such a diverse and dense city. But we also recognize that part of being a New Yorker is living with your neighbors in mutual respect and tolerance. It was exactly that spirit of openness and acceptance that was attacked on 9/11.

"On that day, 3,000 people were killed because some murderous fanatics didn't want us to enjoy the freedom to profess our own faiths, to speak our own minds, to follow our own dreams and to live our own lives.

"Of all our precious freedoms, the most important may be the freedom to worship as we wish. And it is a freedom that, even here in a City that is rooted in Dutch tolerance, was hard-won over many years. In the mid-1650s, the small Jewish community living in Lower Manhattan petitioned Dutch Governor Peter Stuyvesant for the right to build a synagogue—and they were turned down.

"In 1657, when Stuyvesant also prohibited Quakers from holding meetings, a group of non-Quakers in Queens signed the Flushing Remonstrance, a petition in defense of the right of Quakers and others to freely practice their religion. It was perhaps the first formal, political petition for religious freedom in the American colonies—and the organizer was thrown in jail and then banished from New Amsterdam.

"In the 1700s, even as religious freedom took hold in America, Catholics in New York were effectively prohibited from practicing their religion—and priests could be arrested. Largely as a result, the first Catholic parish in New York City was not established until the 1780's—St. Peter's on Barclay Street, which still stands just one block north of the World Trade Center site and one block south of the proposed mosque and community center.

"This morning, the City's Landmark Preservation Commission unanimously voted not to extend landmark status to the building on Park Place where the mosque and community center are planned. The decision was based solely on the fact that there was little architectural significance to the building. But with or without landmark designation, there is nothing in the law that would prevent the owners from opening a mosque within the existing building. The simple fact is this building is private property, and the owners have a right to use the building as a house of worship.

"The government has no right whatsoever to deny that right—and if it were tried, the courts would almost certainly strike it down as a violation of the U.S. Constitution. Whatever you may think of the proposed mosque and community center, lost in the heat of the debate has been a basic question—should government attempt to deny private citizens the right to build a house of worship on private property based on their particular religion? That may happen in other countries, but we should never allow it to happen here. This nation was founded on the principle that the government must never choose between religions, or favor one over another.

"The World Trade Center Site will forever hold a special place in our City, in our hearts. But we would be untrue to the best part of ourselves—and who we are as New Yorkers and Americans—if we said 'no' to a mosque in Lower Manhattan.

"Let us not forget that Muslims were among those murdered on 9/11 and that our Muslim neighbors grieved with us as New Yorkers and as Americans. We would betray our values—and play into our enemies' hands—if we were to treat Muslims differently than anyone else. In fact, to cave to popular sentiment would be to hand a victory to the terrorists—and we should not stand for that.

"For that reason, I believe that this is an important test of the separation of church and state as we may see in our lifetime—as important a test—and it is critically important that we get it right.

"On September 11, 2001, thousands of first responders heroically rushed to the scene and saved tens of thousands of lives. More than 400 of those first responders did not make it out alive. In rushing into those burning buildings, not one of them asked 'What God do you pray to?' 'What beliefs do you hold?'

"The attack was an act of war—and our first responders defended not only our City but also our country and our Constitution. We do not honor their lives by denying the very Constitutional rights they died protecting. We honor their lives by defending those rights—and the freedoms that the terrorists attacked.

"Of course, it is fair to ask the organizers of the mosque to show some special sensitivity to the situation—and in fact, their plan envisions reaching beyond their walls and building an interfaith community. By doing so, it is my hope that the mosque will help to bring our City even closer together and help repudiate the false and repugnant idea that the attacks of 9/11 were in any way consistent with Islam. Muslims are as much a part of our City and our country as the people of any faith and they are as welcome to worship in Lower Manhattan as any other group. In fact, they have been worshipping at the site for the better part of a year, as is their right.

"The local community board in Lower Manhattan voted overwhelming to support the proposal and if it moves forward, I expect the community center and mosque will add to the life and vitality of the neighborhood and the entire City.

"Political controversies come and go, but our values and our traditions endure—and there is no neighborhood in this City that is off limits to God's love and mercy, as the religious leaders here with us today can attest."

SOURCE: Office of Mayor Michael Bloomberg. "Mayor Bloomberg Discusses the Landmarks Preservation Commission Vote on 45–47 Park Place." August 3, 2010. http://www.nyc.gov:80/portal/site/nycgov/menuitem.c0935b9a57bb4ef3daf2f1c701c789a0/index.jsp?pageID=mayor_press_release&catID=1194&doc_name=http%3A%2F%2Fwww.nyc.gov%3A80%2Fhtml%2Fom%2Fhtml%2F2010b%2Fpr337-10.html&cc=unused1978&rc=1194&ndi=1

President Obama on the Muslim Cultural Center

August 13, 2010

Good evening, everybody. Welcome. Please, have a seat. Well, welcome to the White House. To you, to Muslim Americans across our country, and to more than 1 billion Muslims around the world, I extend my best wishes on this holy month. *Ramadan Kareem.*

I want to welcome members of the diplomatic corps, members of my administration, and Members of Congress, including Rush Holt, John Conyers, and Andre Carson, who is one of the two Muslim American Members of Congress, along with Keith Ellison. So welcome, all of you.

Here at the White House, we have a tradition of hosting iftars that goes back several years, just as we host Christmas parties and Seders and Diwali celebrations. And these events celebrate the role of faith in the lives of the American people. They remind us of the basic truth that we are all children of God and we all draw strength and a sense of purpose from our beliefs.

Now, these events are also an affirmation of who we are as Americans. Our Founders understood that the best way to honor the place of faith in the lives of our people was to protect their freedom to practice religion. In the Virginia Act of Establishing Religious Freedom, Thomas Jefferson wrote that "all men shall be free to profess, and by argument to maintain, their opinions in matters of religion." The First Amendment of our Constitution established the freedom of religion as the law of the land, and that right has been upheld ever since.

Indeed, over the course of our history, religion has flourished within our borders precisely because Americans have had the right to worship as they choose, including the right to believe in no religion at all. And it is a testament to the wisdom of our Founders that America remains deeply religious, a nation where the ability of peoples of different faiths to coexist peacefully and with mutual respect for one another stands in stark contrast to the religious conflict that persists elsewhere around the globe.

Now, that's not to say that religion is without controversy. Recently attention's been focused on the construction of mosques in certain communities, particularly New York. Now, we must all recognize and respect the sensitivities surrounding the development of lower Manhattan. The 9/11 attacks were a deeply traumatic event for our country. And the pain and the experience of suffering by those who lost loved ones is just unimaginable. So I understand the emotions that this issue engenders. And Ground Zero is, indeed, hallowed ground.

But let me be clear. As a citizen and as President, I believe that Muslims have the right to practice their religion as everyone else in this country. And that includes the right to build a place of worship and a community center on private property in lower Manhattan, in accordance with local laws and ordinances. This is America. And our commitment to religious freedom must be unshakeable. The principle that people of all faiths are welcome in this country and that they will not be treated differently by their government is essential to who we are. The writ of the Founders must endure.

We must never forget those who we lost so tragically on 9/11, and we must always honor those who led the response to that attack, from the firefighters who charged up smoke-filled staircases to our troops who are serving in Afghanistan today. But let us also remember who we're fighting against and what we're fighting for. Our enemies respect no religious freedom. Al Qaida's cause is not Islam; it's a gross distortion of Islam. These are not religious leaders; they're terrorists who murder innocent men and women and children. In fact, Al Qaida has killed more Muslims than people of any other religion, and that list of victims includes innocent Muslims who were killed on 9/11.

So that's who we're fighting against. And the reason that we will win this fight is not simply the strength of our arms; it is the strength of our values, the democracy that we uphold, the freedoms that we cherish, the laws that we apply without regard to race or religion or wealth or status. Our capacity to show not merely tolerance, but respect towards those who are different from us, and that way of life, that quintessentially American creed, stands in stark contrast to the nihilism of those who attacked us on that September morning and who continue to plot against us today.

In my Inaugural Address, I said that our patchwork heritage is a strength, not a weakness. We are a nation of Christians and Muslims, Jews and Hindus, and nonbelievers. We are shaped by every language and every culture, drawn from every end of this Earth. And that diversity can bring difficult debates. Our—this is not unique to our time. Past eras have seen controversies about the construction of synagogues or Catholic churches. But time and again, the American people have demonstrated that we can work through these issues and stay true to our core values and emerge stronger for it. So it must be—and will be—today.

And tonight we are reminded that Ramadan is a celebration of a faith known for great diversity. And Ramadan is a reminder that Islam has always been a part of America. The first Muslim Ambassador to the United States, from Tunisia, was hosted by President Jefferson, who arranged a sunset dinner for his guest because it was Ramadan, making it the first known iftar at the White House, more than 200 years ago.

Like so many other immigrants, generations of Muslims came to forge their future here. They became farmers and merchants, worked in mills and factories. They helped lay the railroads. They helped to build America. They founded the first Islamic center in New York City in the 19—in the 1890s. They built America's first mosque on the prairie of North Dakota. And perhaps the oldest surviving mosque in America, still in use today, is in Cedar Rapids, Iowa.

Today, our Nation is strengthened by millions of Muslim Americans. They excel in every walk of life. Muslim American communities, including mosques in all 50 States, also serve their neighbors. Muslim Americans protect our communities as police officers and firefighters and first-responders. Muslim American clerics have spoken out against terror and extremism, reaffirming that Islam teaches that one must save human life, not take it.

And Muslim Americans serve with honor in our military. At next week's iftar at the Pentagon, tribute will be paid to three soldiers who gave their lives in Iraq and now rest among the heroes of Arlington National Cemetery. These Muslim Americans died for the security that we depend on and the freedoms that we cherish. They're part of an unbroken line of Americans that stretches back to our founding, Americans of all faiths who have served and sacrificed to extend the promise of America to new generations and to ensure that what is exceptional about America is protected: our commitment to stay true to our core values and our ability, slowly but surely, to perfect our Union.

For in the end, we remain "one nation, under God, indivisible." And we can only achieve "liberty and justice for all" if we live by that one rule at the heart of every great religion, including Islam, that we do unto others as we would have them do unto us.

So thank you all for being here. I wish you a blessed Ramadan. And with that, let us eat.

SOURCE: U.S. Executive Office of the President. "Remarks at the Iftar Dinner." *Daily Compilation of Presidential Documents* 2010, no. 00680 (August 13, 2010). http://origin.www.gpo.gov/fdsys/pkg/DCPD-201000680/pdf/DCPD-201000680.pdf.

OTHER HISTORIC DOCUMENTS OF INTEREST

FROM PREVIOUS *HISTORIC DOCUMENTS*

U.S. District Judge Overturns California Ban on Gay Marriage

AUGUST 4, 2010

The legal status of same-sex marriage in California has followed an emotionally charged course of hairpin turns and sudden reversals, with supporters and opponents alike alternating between cheers and protests. Those in favor of same-sex marriage have focused their arguments on equal rights, while those opposed see the need to safeguard the traditional understanding of marriage. On August 4, 2010, two years after a voter referendum in California amended the state Constitution to prohibit gay marriage, a federal district court judge overturned the marriage ban.

In a forceful opinion, then–U.S. district court judge Vaughn R. Walker ruled in *Perry v. Schwarzenegger* that the marriage ban violated the Due Process and Equal Protection clauses of the U.S. Constitution. This closely watched case marked the first time a federal court had addressed the constitutionality of state prohibitions of gay marriage. The ruling, however, was far from any kind of final adjudication of the issue; that may not come for years. It was immediately appealed to the Ninth Circuit Court of Appeals, which stayed its enforcement pending its determination of the issues. Many expect the case to ultimately be decided by the U.S. Supreme Court.

THE HISTORY OF GAY MARRIAGE IN CALIFORNIA

California voters first faced the issue of same-sex marriages directly in March 2000, when 61 percent of the voters approved Proposition 22, a voter referendum that changed California's Family Code to formally define a valid marriage as one between a man and a woman. In February 2004, Gavin Newsom, then the newly elected mayor of San Francisco, directed city officials to ignore Proposition 22 and to begin granting marriage licenses to same sex couples. Numerous law suits were filed as a result and a month later, the California Supreme Court ordered a stop to same-sex marriage licenses pending resolution of the legal issues.

During that one month before the court order, San Francisco granted marriage licenses to 4,037 same-sex couples. Finding no need to address the substantive legal question of the constitutionality of banning same-sex marriage, the California Supreme Court concluded that public officials of the City and County of San Francisco acted unlawfully by issuing marriage licenses to same-sex couples in the absence of a judicial determination that Proposition 22 was unconstitutional. The court ordered city officials to stop issuing marriage licenses to same-sex couples and nullified all outstanding licenses. But it was not long before the opportunity to address the substantive issue of same-sex marriage did come before the court. The lawsuits filed in the wake of the court's ruling invalidating the San Francisco marriages were consolidated into a single case, *In re Marriage Cases*. On May 15, 2008, the California Supreme Court declared that the right to marry is a fundamental right under the California Constitution that could not constitutionally be granted to opposite-sex couples while being denied to same-sex couples. As a result of the ruling, all California counties were required to issue marriage licenses to same-sex couples.

The celebration of gay marriage supporters was short-lived. While same-sex couples across the state started lining up ballrooms and wedding planners, organized groups opposed to gay marriage started working to pass a voter-initiated referendum banning same-sex marriage. Known as Proposition 8, this referendum would change the California Constitution to overturn the California Supreme Court's finding of a right to gay marriage. It says in its entirety, "Only marriage between a man and a woman is valid or recognized in California." Placing this language into the Constitution itself would invalidate *In re Marriage Cases*. On the ballot, arguments in favor were summarized as follows: "Proposition 8 restores what 61% of voters already approved: marriage is only between a man and a woman. Four judges in San Francisco should not have overturned the people's vote. Proposition 8 fixes that mistake by reaffirming traditional marriage, but doesn't take away rights or benefits from gay domestic partnerships." The ballot also summarized the opponents' arguments: "Equality under the law is a fundamental freedom. Regardless of how we feel about marriage, singling people out to be treated differently is wrong. Proposition 8 won't affect our schools, but it will mean loving couples are treated differently under our Constitution and denied equal protection under the law." In California, voters can amend the state Constitution with a simple majority vote.

After one of the most expensive ballot measure campaigns in U.S. history, with proponents of Proposition 8 raising $39.9 million and those opposed raising $43.3 million, Proposition 8 passed with 52.3 percent of the vote during the general November 2008 elections. Same-sex couples could no longer marry in California. In the almost five months during which it was legal for same-sex couples to marry in California, between the California Supreme Court ruling in *In re Marriage Cases* and the passage of Proposition 8, approximately eighteen thousand same-sex couples had married. On May 26, 2009, the California Supreme Court upheld the validity of Proposition 8 but left undisturbed the then-legal marriages that had taken place.

In May 2009, a federal court challenge to Proposition 8 was filed by an odd pairing of attorneys—David Boies and former U.S. solicitor general Theodore B. Olson—best known for facing off in *Bush v. Gore*, the ballot-recount case that determined the outcome of the 2000 presidential election. The case, *Perry v. Schwarzenegger*, was brought on behalf of two gay couples, one male and one female, who wanted to marry and who challenged the constitutionality of the ballot initiative. The case was filed against then–California governor Arnold Schwarzenegger and then–Attorney General Jerry Brown. (Brown has since succeeded Schwarzenegger as governor.) They refused, however, to support Proposition 8 in court and left the defense to Protect Marriage, the group that had successfully sponsored the voter initiative. During the thirteen-day trial, the plaintiffs challenging the law presented nine experts, including historians, psychologists, economists, political scientists, and a social epidemiologist. Experts testified on issues ranging from the history of marriage laws to the definition of sexual orientation. They also offered emotional testimony from the plaintiffs and four other witnesses. The defense relied primarily on legal conclusions and the cross-examination of just two of the plaintiff's witnesses, including David Blankenhorn, the founder and president of the think tank Institute for American Values.

THE RULING IN *PERRY V. SCHWARZENEGGER*

On August 4, 2010, Judge Walker struck down Proposition 8 after the first trial in federal court to examine if states can legally prohibit same-sex couples from marrying. In a major victory for gay rights supporters, the judge ruled that the voter initiative banning same-sex marriage violated both the Due Process and Equal Protection provisions of the Fourteenth Amendment to the U.S. Constitution. Sidestepping the issue of which level of scrutiny to apply to legal distinctions based on sexual orientation, Judge Walker found that Proposition 8 would fail to pass even the most lenient level of scrutiny. "Excluding same-sex couples from marriage," he writes, "is simply not rationally related to a legitimate state interest." Tradition or moral disapproval of homosexuality, without any other asserted state interest cannot, he concluded, support legislation and satisfy California's obligation to treat its citizens equally.

Judge Walker's lengthy opinion contained fifty-five pages of Findings of Fact, supported by citations to trial testimony and proffered evidence. These findings are traditionally given great deference on appeal, where appellate courts are supposed to take district court findings of fact as true unless they are "clearly erroneous." Among the opinion's eighty factual findings are:

- Marriage in the United States has always been a civil matter. Civil authorities may permit religious leaders to solemnize marriages but not to determine who may enter or leave a civil marriage. Religious leaders may determine independently whether to recognize a civil marriage or divorce but that recognition or lack thereof has no effect on the relationship under state law.
- California, like every other state, has never required that individuals entering a marriage be willing or able to procreate.
- Eliminating marital obligations based on gender and race restrictions in marriage has not deprived the institution of marriage of its vitality.
- Same-sex couples are identical to opposite-sex couples in the characteristics relevant to the ability to form successful marital union.
- Marrying a person of the opposite sex is an unrealistic option for gay and lesbian individuals.
- The availability of domestic partnerships does not provide gays and lesbians with a status equivalent to marriage because the cultural meaning of marriage and its associated benefits are intentionally withheld from same-sex couples in domestic partnerships.
- Permitting same-sex couples to marry will not affect the number of opposite-sex couples who marry, divorce, cohabit, have children outside of marriage, or otherwise affect the stability of opposite-sex marriage.
- The children of same-sex couples benefit when their parents can marry.
- The sexual orientation of an individual does not determine whether that individual can be a good parent. Children raised by gay or lesbian parents are as likely as children raised by heterosexual parents to be healthy, successful, and well-adjusted. The research supporting this conclusion is accepted beyond serious debate in the field of developmental psychology.

Effect of the Ruling on Status of Gay Marriage in California

Same-sex marriages did not resume immediately after the ruling, however, as the judge issued a temporary stay, keeping Proposition 8 in effect until he could rule on the stay issue. Shortly afterward, he issued his final order that would lift the stay on August 18, 2010, allowing same-sex marriages to resume. In an interesting turn, the order lifting the stay suggested that there may be no one with standing to appeal his decision striking down Proposition 8. The courts have taken this technicality very seriously. Article III of the Constitution requires that only those who have been harmed by a case in a way that would be remedied if they won the appeal have standing to bring an appeal. Here, the state of California, which would have standing, chose not to appeal the ruling that banning same-sex marriages violated the Constitution. Instead, Protect Marriage filed the appeal. Regarding Protect Marriage's standing to appeal, Judge Walker wrote that "it appears at least doubtful that proponents will be able to proceed with their appeal without a state defendant."

Same-sex marriage supporters were quickly disappointed. On August 16, 2010, days before Judge Walker's stay could be lifted, the U.S. Court of Appeals for the Ninth Circuit indefinitely extended the stay pending resolution of the case on appeal. No new same-sex couples have married in California since the passage of Proposition 8.

Recent Developments in the Case Lead to Further Delays

As of the spring of 2011, the status of gay marriage in California is in the hands of the federal appellate court, the Ninth Circuit Court of Appeals. But before it can decide the central question—whether gay couples have the constitutionally protected right to marry—it must first decide the issue raised by Judge Walker's order: Who, if anyone, has the right to bring the appeal? The State of California has declined to appeal the lower court's opinion invalidating Proposition 8, so the appeal is being brought by Protect Marriage. Lawyers for the couples challenging Proposition 8 cite a Supreme Court precedent holding that proponents of a ballot initiative in Arizona did not have standing to defend it in federal court. Protect Marriage's attorneys argue that California's laws differ from Arizona's in relevant respects and that someone should be able to speak for the voters.

The Ninth Circuit Court of Appeals decided that the question of who can speak for California is an issue of California state law that should be resolved by California's highest state court. If the California Supreme Court decides that Protect Marriage does not have standing, Judge Walker's opinion will stand, the stay will be lifted, and gay marriages will resume in California. If, on the other hand, Protect Marriage is found to have standing, the Ninth Circuit will rule on the central issue, setting the stage to present the issue to the U.S. Supreme Court.

—Melissa Feinberg

The following is the text of the decision by then–U.S. district court judge Vaughn Walker in Perry v. Schwarzenegger, *issued on August 4, 2010, in which Judge Walker struck down California's Proposition 8, which prohibited same-sex couples from marrying.*

U.S. District Court Rules on
Perry v. Schwarzenegger

August 4, 2010

No C 09–2292 VRW

IN THE UNITED STATES DISTRICT COURT FOR THE NORTHERN DISTRICT OF CALIFORNIA

KRISTIN M PERRY, SANDRA B STIER, PAUL T
KATAMI and JEFFREY J ZARRILLO, Plaintiffs,

CITY AND COUNTY OF SAN FRANCISCO,
Plaintiff-Intervenor,

v

ARNOLD SCHWARZENEGGER, in his official
capacity as Governor of California; EDMUND G
BROWN JR, in his official capacity as Attorney
General of California; MARK B HORTON, in
his official capacity as Director of the California
Department of Public Health and State Registrar
of Vital Statistics; LINETTE SCOTT, in her official
capacity as Deputy Director of Health Information
& Strategic Planning for the California Department
of Public Health; PATRICK O'CONNELL, in his
official capacity as Clerk- Recorder of the County
of Alameda; and DEAN C LOGAN, in his official
capacity as Registrar- Recorder/County Clerk for
the County of Los Angeles,

Defendants,

DENNIS HOLLINGSWORTH,
GAIL J KNIGHT, MARTIN F
GUTIERREZ, HAKSHING

WILLIAM TAM, MARK
A JANSSON and
PROTECTMARRIAGE.
COM—YES ON 8, A
PROJECT OF CALIFORNIA
RENEWAL, as official
proponents of Proposition 8,

Defendant-Intervenors.

Defendant-intervenors Dennis Hollingsworth, Gail Knight, Martin Gutierrez, Mark Jansson and ProtectMarriage.com ("proponents") move to stay the court's judgment to ensure that Proposition 8 remains in effect as they pursue their appeal in the Ninth Circuit. In the alternative, proponents seek a brief stay to allow the court of appeals to consider the matter.

Plaintiffs and plaintiff-intervenor City and County of San Francisco ask the court to deny the stay and order the injunction against Proposition 8 to take effect immediately. California's Governor and Attorney General (collectively the "state defendants") also oppose any stay. Other than proponents, no party seeks to stay the effect of a permanent injunction against Proposition 8. Because proponents fail to satisfy any of the factors necessary to warrant a stay, the court denies a stay except for a limited time solely in order to permit the court of appeals to consider the issue in an orderly manner.

I

"A stay is not a matter of right, even if irreparable injury might otherwise result." Rather, the decision to grant or deny a stay is committed to the trial court's sound discretion. To trigger exercise of that discretion, the moving party must demonstrate that the circumstances justify a stay.

In deciding whether a stay is appropriate, the court looks to four factors:

(1) whether proponents have made a strong showing that they are likely to succeed on the merits;

(2) whether proponents will be irreparably injured absent a stay;

(3) whether the stay will substantially injure other interested parties; and

(4) whether the stay is in the public interest.

The first two factors "are the most critical." The court addresses each factor in turn.

A

The court first considers whether proponents have shown a likelihood of success on the merits of their appeal. The mere possibility of success will not suffice; proponents must show that success is likely. Proponents assert they are likely to succeed "[f]or all the reasons explained throughout this litigation." Because proponents filed their motion to stay before the court issued its findings of fact and conclusions of law, proponents do not in their memorandum discuss the likelihood of their success with reference to the court's conclusions. Neither do proponents discuss whether the court of appeals would have jurisdiction to reach the merits of their appeal absent an appeal by a state defendant.

To establish that they have standing to appeal the court's decision under Article III, Section 2 of the Constitution, proponents must show that they have "suffered an injury in fact, which is fairly traceable to the challenged action and is likely to be redressed by the relief requested." Standing requires a showing of a concrete and particularized injury that is actual or imminent. If the state defendants choose not to appeal, proponents may have difficulty demonstrating Article III standing.

As official proponents under California law, proponents organized the successful campaign for Proposition 8. Nevertheless, California does not grant proponents the authority or the responsibility to enforce Proposition 8. In *Lockyer v City & County of San Francisco*, the California Supreme Court explained that the regulation of marriage in California is committed to state officials, so that the mayor of San Francisco had no authority to "take any action with regard to the process of issuing marriage licenses or registering marriage certificates." Still less, it would appear, do private citizens possess authority regarding the issuance of marriage licenses or registration of marriages. While the court has ordered entry of a permanent injunction against proponents, that permanent injunction does not require proponents to refrain from anything, as they are not (and cannot be) responsible for the application or regulation of California marriage law. The court provided proponents with an opportunity to identify a harm they would face "if an injunction against Proposition 8 is issued." Proponents replied that they have an interest in defending Proposition 8 but failed to articulate even one specific harm they may suffer as a consequence of the injunction. When proponents moved to intervene in this action, the court did not address their standing independent of the existing parties. While the court determined that proponents had a significant protectible interest under FRCP 24(a)(2) in defending Proposition 8, that interest may well be "plainly insufficient to confer standing." This court has jurisdiction over plaintiffs' claims against the state defendants pursuant to 28 USC § 1331. If, however, no state defendant appeals, proponents will need to show standing in the court of appeals.

Proponents' intervention in the district court does not provide them with standing to appeal. The Supreme Court has expressed "grave doubts" whether initiative proponents have independent Article III standing to defend the constitutionality of the initiative. Proponents chose not to brief the standing issue in connection with their motion to stay, and nothing in the record shows proponents face the kind of injury required for Article III standing. As it appears at least doubtful that proponents will be able to proceed with their appeal without a state defendant, it remains unclear whether the court of appeals will be able to reach the merits of proponents' appeal. In light of those concerns, proponents may have little choice but to attempt to convince either the Governor or the Attorney General to file an appeal to ensure appellate jurisdiction. As regards the stay, however, the uncertainty surrounding proponents' standing weighs heavily against the likelihood of their success.

Even if proponents were to have standing to pursue their appeal, as the court recently explained at length the minimal evidence proponents presented at trial does not support their defense of Proposition 8. Proponents had a full opportunity to provide evidence in support of their position and nevertheless failed to present even one credible witness on the government interest in Proposition 8. Based on the trial record, which establishes that Proposition 8 violates plaintiffs' equal protection and due process rights, the court cannot conclude that proponents have shown a likelihood of success on appeal. The first factor does not favor a stay.

B

The second factor asks whether proponents will be harmed if enforcement of Proposition 8 were enjoined. Proponents argue that irreparable harm will result if a stay is not issued because "a state suffers irreparable injury whenever an enactment of its people * * * is enjoined." Proponents, of course, are not the state. Proponents also point to harm resulting from "a cloud of uncertainty" surrounding the validity of marriages performed after judgment is entered but before proponents' appeal is resolved. Proponents have not, however, alleged that any of them seek to wed a same-sex spouse. Proponents admit that the harms they identify would be inflicted on "affected couples and * * * the State." Under the second factor the court considers only whether the party seeking a stay faces harm, yet proponents do not identify a harm to them that would result from denial of their motion to stay.

Both plaintiffs and the state defendants have disavowed the harms identified by proponents. Plaintiffs assert that "gay men and lesbians are more than capable of determining whether they, as individuals who now enjoy the freedom to marry, wish to do so immediately or wait until all appeals have run their course."

Proponents do not adequately explain the basis for their belief that marriages performed absent a stay would suffer from a "cloud of uncertainty." The court has the authority to enjoin defendants from enforcing Proposition 8. It appears, then, that marriages performed pursuant to a valid injunction would be lawful, much like the 18,000 marriages performed before the passage of Proposition 8 in November 2008.

If proponents had identified a harm they would face if the stay were not granted, the court would be able consider how much weight to give to the second factor. Because proponents make no argument that they—as opposed to the state defendants or plaintiffs—will be irreparably injured absent a stay, proponents have not given the court any basis to exercise its discretion to grant a stay.

The first two factors are the "most critical," and proponents have shown neither a likelihood of success nor the possibility of any harm. That alone suffices for the court to conclude that a stay is inappropriate here. Nevertheless, the court turns to the remaining two factors.

C

The third factor considers whether any other interested party would be injured if the court were to enter a stay. Plaintiffs argue a stay would cause them harm. Proposition 8 violates plaintiffs' equal protection and due process rights, and the court presumes harm where plaintiffs have shown a violation of a constitutional right. But no presumption is necessary here, as the trial record left no doubt that Proposition 8 inflicts harm on plaintiffs and other gays and lesbians in California. Any stay would serve only to delay plaintiffs access to the remedy to which they have shown they are entitled.

Proponents point to the availability of domestic partnerships under California law as sufficient to minimize any harm from allowing Proposition 8 to remain in effect. The evidence presented at trial does not support proponents' position on domestic partnerships; instead, the evidence showed that domestic partnership is an inadequate and discriminatory substitute for marriage.

Proponents claim that plaintiffs' desire to marry is not "urgent," because they chose not to marry in 2008. Whether plaintiffs choose to exercise their right to marry now is a matter that plaintiffs, and plaintiffs alone, have the right to decide. Because a stay would force California to continue to violate plaintiffs' constitutional rights and would demonstrably harm plaintiffs and other gays and lesbians in California, the third factor weighs heavily against proponents' motion.

D

Finally, the court looks to whether the public interest favors a stay. Proponents argue that the public interest tips in favor of a stay because of the "uncertainty" surrounding marriages performed before a final judicial determination of the constitutionality of Proposition 8. Proponents also point to the public interest as reflected in the votes of "the people of California" who do not want same-sex couples to marry, explaining that "[t]here is no basis for this Court to second-guess the people of California's considered judgment of the public interest."

The evidence at trial showed, however, that Proposition 8 harms the State of California. Representatives of the state agree. The Governor states that "[a]llowing the Court's judgment to take effect serves the public interest" in "[u]pholding the rights and liberties guaranteed by the federal Constitution" and in "eradicating unlawful discrimination." Moreover, the Governor explains that no administrative burdens flow to the state when same-sex couples are permitted to marry. The Attorney General agrees that the public interest would not be served by a stay.

The evidence presented at trial and the position of the representatives of the State of California show that an injunction against enforcement of Proposition 8 is in the public's interest. Accordingly, the court concludes that the public interest counsels against entry of the stay proponents seek.

II

None of the factors the court weighs in considering a motion to stay favors granting a stay. Accordingly, proponents' motion for a stay is DENIED. The clerk is DIRECTED to enter judgment forthwith. That judgment shall be STAYED until August 18, 2010 at 5 PM PDT at which time defendants and all persons under their control or supervision shall cease to apply or enforce Proposition 8.

IT IS SO ORDERED.

VAUGHN R WALKER
United States District Chief Judge

Source: U.S. District Court for the Northern District of California. No C 09–2292 VRW. *Perry v. Schwarzenegger*. August 4, 2010. https://ecf.cand.uscourts.gov/cand/09cv2292/files/Final_stay_order.pdf.

OTHER HISTORIC DOCUMENTS OF INTEREST

FROM PREVIOUS *HISTORIC DOCUMENTS*

Last U.S. Combat Troops Leave Iraq

AUGUST 19 AND 31, 2010

On August 19, 2010, the last U.S. combat brigade drove three hundred miles to the Kuwait border, signaling the end of Operation Iraqi Freedom, which had begun seven-and-a-half years earlier and had cost some $1 trillion. The end of the combat mission ushered in a new role for the U.S. government in Iraq, that of security force trainer and adviser, operating under the new mission name of Operation New Dawn. The withdrawal of American combat forces was in line with a promise made by President Barack Obama during his first months in office, but it came at a time when instability was increasing in the Middle Eastern nation. In March, Iraqis went to the polls to elect a new government, three months behind schedule, and by the time of troop withdrawal, the leading Iraqi parties had still not reached a consensus on who was in charge. Although some Iraqi leaders said the U.S. departure from Iraq was ill-timed, Washington told the world that it was not abandoning Iraq, but rather working toward a new partnership that would give greater autonomy to the fledgling democracy.

Obama's Promise Kept

During the 2008 presidential campaign and his first months in office, President Obama promised to withdraw all combat troops from Iraq within sixteen months of taking office. After holding discussions on a troop drawdown plan, Obama and his senior military advisors reached an agreement to extend the timeframe to nineteen months to allow for additional security improvements. Speaking before Marines at Camp Lejeune, North Carolina, in February 2009, Obama made it clear that the United States could no longer remain in Iraq. "We cannot rid Iraq of all who oppose America or sympathize with our adversaries. We cannot police Iraq's streets until they are completely safe, nor stay until Iraq's union is perfected. We cannot sustain indefinitely a commitment that has put a strain on our military, and will cost the American people nearly a trillion dollars," he said. With the nineteen-month timetable set, military officials began planning the logistics of withdrawing combat forces and ramped up efforts to train Iraqi security forces to combat the insurgents once the United States switched to an advisory role.

After the 4th Stryker Brigade, 2nd Infantry Division, pulled across the Iraq-Kuwait border on August 19 and signaled the end of combat missions in Iraq, the president told Americans that this was just the beginning of what he had promised when he was elected. "Shortly after taking office," Obama said, "I put forward a plan to end the war in Iraq responsibly. Today, I'm pleased to report that—thanks to the extraordinary service of our troops and civilians in Iraq—our combat mission will end this month, and we will complete a substantial drawdown of our troops."

Further, the president said, the United States will continue its commitment to remove all U.S. troops from Iraq by the end of 2011. In the meantime, the U.S. government would "continue to build a strong partnership with the Iraqi people with an increased civilian commitment and diplomatic effort," he said. "This new approach reflects our long-term partnership with Iraq, one based on mutual interest and mutual respect. Of course, violence will not end with our combat mission. Extremists will continue to set off bombs, attack Iraqi civilians, and try to spark sectarian strife. But ultimately, these terrorists will fail to achieve their goals," President Obama remarked on August 31.

It was the goal of the Obama administration to have no more than 50,000 U.S. troops left on the ground in Iraq by September 1, 2010. The August 19 withdrawal left 52,000 troops in the country, down from the highest point of 165,000 troops. By the end of August, the administration met its 50,000-troop goal. These remaining forces were transitioned to the position of "advise and assist" brigades.

NEW U.S. ROLE IN IRAQ

The shifting focus of U.S. involvement in the region first began in June 2009 when U.S. combat troops left Iraq's major cities. The ongoing role of the United States in Iraq would now be led by the U.S. Department of State, which would oversee the strengthening of the Iraqi government and training of security forces. The task will not be an easy undertaking as the nation's political instability had fueled an increasing number of assassinations and suicide bombings, attacks on civilians and military outposts, and overall unrest. Added to this was the decreased funding available to the State Department to complete the U.S. mission in Iraq. When the Pentagon was in control of the effort, it spent approximately $16 billion per year. The State Department would have $1 billion annually.

As the United States slowly began withdrawing troops from Iraq, the State Department had been preparing for its new role. State Department officials planned to continue manning security checkpoints in Iraq's most dangerous areas, assist with counterinsurgency activities, and advise Iraq's military forces. To do this, the State Department planned to build consulates in Basra and Arbil, along with embassy branches in Kirkuk and Mosul, two areas with the greatest ethnic unrest. Private contractors would also be on hand to assist the continuing U.S. mission.

Some Iraqi leaders were critical of the U.S. decision, even though the Iraqi government had given support to the Obama withdrawal plan. "The Americans are leaving, and they didn't solve the problems," said Falah al-Naqib, a member of parliament from the Iraqiya Party. "So far they've failed and left Iraq to other countries."

The U.S. government disputed these remarks. "There is a misconception that the president's priority is to leave," said Colin Kahl, Pentagon deputy assistant secretary of defense for the Middle East. "It's really laying the foundation for a long-term partnership." P. J. Crowley, then the assistant secretary of state for public affairs, said that the United States continues to have a long-term investment and commitment to the nation and the region as a whole. "We're not ending our involvement in Iraq," Crowley said. "We will have important work to do. This is a transition. This is not the end of something. It's a transition to something different." The continuation of U.S. involvement in Iraq remains necessary, according to Crowley, and the slow withdrawal plan will continue to give stability to the nation. Without this, the United States risks a situation in which American combat troops would need to be sent back into the nation, Crowley warned.

President Obama acknowledged, however, that the Iraqi people and Iraqi government would eventually need to stand on their own. "In the end, only Iraqis can resolve their differences and police their streets, only Iraqis can build a democracy within their borders," the president said.

Still, Iraqi security forces expressed concern about the loss of combat support. "If I were asked about the withdrawal, I would say to politicians: the U.S. army must stay until the Iraqi army is fully ready in 2020," said Iraqi lieutenant general Babakir Zebari. Iraqi foreign affairs minister Hoshyar Zebari called for support from Americans to help the Iraqi government reach an agreement on its governing coalition but recognized that "willingness to compromise is in short supply here, as patience is in short supply in Washington."

The United States and Iraq are still working to determine what will happen when all U.S. forces leave Iraq at the end of 2011. Both governments have expressed an interest in maintaining an ongoing relationship that could include additional training or security patrols in some regions. In August, an unnamed administration official told the *New York Times* that the Obama administration would consider sending seven thousand private security forces to Iraq at the end of 2011.

IRAQ's POLITICAL CRISIS

Part of the purpose behind the U.S. withdrawal in August was the expectation that a new Iraqi government would be in power. Elections were set to take place in January 2010 for new members of parliament and a new president, but because of security concerns, American and Iraqi officials agreed that they needed to be postponed until March 7.

The election marked the first held since 2005 and Iraqis went to the polls in large numbers, undeterred by the threats from Islamic extremists. When the results were released, Prime Minister Nuri Kamal al-Maliki's State of Law coalition had lost by a small margin to the Iraqiya Party. Maliki challenged the outcome, citing voter fraud, and a period of greater political instability was ushered in. Maliki demanded a recount, but election observers, including those from the United Nations, said they saw no indication of election fraud.

The leader of the Iraqiya Party, former prime minister Ayad Allawi, was given thirty days from the election to form a governing coalition as the prime minister caretaker, a sort of interim prime minister. Without Maliki's support, the coalition looked unlikely. Maliki worked to stall Allawi's work, and with support from the United States and Iran, Maliki was able to get Allawi to agree to a governing coalition in which Maliki would continue as prime minister.

In November 2010, a loose agreement was formed under which the nation would build its government. When the parliament chose Maliki to continue as prime minister, Allawi's party walked out of the negotiation session. Regardless, Maliki was given until December 2010 to form his new government and name a cabinet, which he did with support from the nation's parliament on December 21.

—Heather Kerrigan

Following is an edited transcript of the briefing on August 19, 2010, by then–U.S. Department of State spokesman P.J. Crowley on the withdrawal of U.S. combat forces from Iraq; and a statement by President Barack Obama on August 31, 2010, on the end of combat operations in Iraq.

State Department Briefing on
Withdrawal of Combat Forces from Iraq

August 19, 2010

MR. CROWLEY: Good afternoon and welcome to the Department of State. As you know, Secretary Clinton has landed in New York where shortly she will have meetings with Pakistani Foreign Minister Qureshi and United Nations Secretary General Ban Ki-moon, ahead of this afternoon's UN General Assembly meeting where she will discuss the humanitarian situation resulting from the floods in Pakistan. She will announce increased U.S. aid to Pakistan, as well as encouraging other nations to step up and help reach the UN goal of $460 million for emergency flood relief for Pakistan.

And as you heard this morning from Ambassador Richard Holbrooke, USAID Administrator Shah, and Under Secretary McHale, we believe our efforts to date have been very aggressive, as I think Ambassador Holbrooke said, we were first and most. And the Secretary's announcement this afternoon will continue to reflect the partnership that the United States and Pakistan have together, and that this partnership will endure long after the flood waters recede.

We are looking—in the meantime, obviously, we have a great deal of assistance, up to $7.5 billion identified for Pakistan over the next five years under the Kerry-Lugar-Berman legislation. We will be reviewing, in light of the devastation in Pakistan, what the country's most critical infrastructure needs are, work together with Pakistan to address basic needs, but also we'll be reprogramming resources to deal with both the immediate and the intermediate needs that Pakistan has in light of this disaster.

The Secretary, in her remarks, will also announce the establishment of the Pakistan Relief Fund that the United States Government will organize through the Department of State for all Americans to join in this tremendous relief, recovery, and reconstruction effort. And through the relief fund that we will be putting together in the coming days, we will be able to encourage Americans to provide contributions, both small through a texting program, and large through more significant donations, to help show our commitment to the people of Pakistan.

Turning to Iraq, Assistant Secretary Jeff Feltman is on his way back from Iraq. He's been there for the past week. He welcomed the new U.S. Ambassador to Iraq Jim Jeffrey, yesterday. Ambassador Jeffrey has presented his credentials today—I'm sorry, yesterday, to President Talabani and Foreign Minister Zebari, but they have met today with President Talabani and Prime Minister Nuri al-Maliki. Following Ambassador— following Assistant Secretary Feltman's departure, Ambassador Jeffrey today has also met with Dr. Ayad Allawi to discuss the ongoing efforts to form an inclusive government in Iraq.

Also, we are saddened to learn about the attack on UN peacekeepers in the Congo. This attack resulted in the loss of three Indian soldiers with seven wounded. We obviously convey our sympathies to the families and friends of those killed as well as to the Government of India. We are continuing to be—we are grateful for the ongoing support that India is showing to this UN peacekeeping operation. We condemn in the strongest terms these attacks and call on the Government of the Congo to conduct a full investigation and to ensure the perpetrators are swiftly brought to justice.

And finally, the Secretary before heading for New York, did have calls today with Foreign Minister Judeh of Jordan, also, Quartet representative Blair, as part of her ongoing consultations on moving the parties towards direct negotiations.

Last evening she also had a call with Prime Minister Fayyad as part of our ongoing efforts to demonstrate support for the Palestinian Authority and to help with—ensure the resources are there so the Palestinian Authority can continue its efforts to build up its institutions and prepare for the prospect of a Palestinian state at some point and self-government.

Today, we remain in touch with the parties and our international partners. We believe we are getting very close to an agreement to enter into direct negotiations. We think we're well-positioned to get there, but we continue to work on the details of this process. I don't have anything at this point to announce. . . .

[The question and answer section has been omitted.]

Source: U.S. Department of State. "Daily Press Briefing." August 19, 2010. http://www.state.gov/r/pa/prs/dpb/2010/08/146103.htm.

President Obama on the End of Combat Missions in Iraq

August 31, 2010

Good evening. Tonight I'd like to talk to you about the end of our combat mission in Iraq, the ongoing security challenges we face, and the need to rebuild our Nation here at home.

I know this historic moment comes at a time of great uncertainty for many Americans. We've now been through nearly a decade of war. We've endured a long and painful recession. And sometimes in the midst of these storms, the future that we're trying to build for our Nation, a future of lasting peace and long-term prosperity, may seem beyond our reach.

But this milestone should serve as a reminder to all Americans that the future is ours to shape if we move forward with confidence and commitment. It should also serve as a message to the world that the United States of America intends to sustain and strengthen our leadership in this young century.

From this desk 7 1/2 years ago, President Bush announced the beginning of military operations in Iraq. Much has changed since that night. A war to disarm a state became a fight against an insurgency. Terrorism and sectarian warfare threatened to tear Iraq apart. Thousands of Americans gave their lives; tens of thousands have been wounded. Our relations abroad were strained. Our unity at home was tested.

These are the rough waters encountered during the course of one of America's longest wars. Yet there has been one constant amidst these shifting tides. At every turn, America's men and women in uniform have served with courage and resolve. As Commander in Chief, I am incredibly proud of their service. And like all Americans, I'm awed by their sacrifice and by the sacrifices of their families.

The Americans who have served in Iraq completed every mission they were given. They defeated a regime that had terrorized its people. Together with Iraqis and coalition partners, who made huge sacrifices of their own, our troops fought block by block to help Iraq seize the chance for a better future. They shifted tactics to protect the Iraqi people, trained Iraqi security forces, and took out terrorist leaders. Because of our troops and civilians and because of the resilience of the Iraqi people, Iraq has the opportunity to embrace a new destiny, even though many challenges remain.

So tonight I am announcing that the American combat mission in Iraq has ended. Operation Iraqi Freedom is over, and the Iraqi people now have lead responsibility for the security of their country.

This was my pledge to the American people as a candidate for this office. Last February, I announced a plan that would bring our combat brigades out of Iraq, while redoubling our efforts to strengthen Iraq's security forces and support its Government and people.

That's what we've done. We've removed nearly 100,000 U.S. troops from Iraq. We've closed or transferred to the Iraqis hundreds of bases. And we have moved millions of pieces of equipment out of Iraq.

This completes a transition to Iraqi responsibility for their own security. U.S. troops pulled out of Iraq's cities last summer, and Iraqi forces have moved into the lead with considerable skill and commitment to their fellow citizens. Even as Iraq continues to suffer terrorist attacks, security incidents have been near the lowest on record since the war began. And Iraqi forces have taken the fight to Al Qaida, removing much of its leadership in Iraqi-led operations.

This year also saw Iraq hold credible elections that drew a strong turnout. A caretaker administration is in place as Iraqis form a Government based on the results of that election. Tonight I encourage Iraq's leaders to move forward with a sense of urgency to form an inclusive Government that is just, representative, and accountable to the Iraqi people. And when that Government is in place, there should be no doubt: The Iraqi people will have a strong partner in the United States. Our combat mission is ending, but our commitment to Iraq's future is not.

Going forward, a transitional force of U.S. troops will remain in Iraq with a different mission: advising and assisting Iraq's security forces, supporting Iraqi troops in targeted counterterrorism missions, and protecting our civilians. Consistent with our agreement with the Iraqi Government, all U.S. troops will leave by the end of next year. As our military draws down, our dedicated civilians—diplomats, aid workers, and advisers—are moving into the lead to support Iraq as it strengthens its Government, resolves political disputes, resettles those displaced by war, and builds ties with the region and the world. That's a message that Vice President Biden is delivering to the Iraqi people through his visit there today.

This new approach reflects our long-term partnership with Iraq, one based upon mutual interest and mutual respect. Of course, violence will not end with our combat mission. Extremists will continue to set off bombs, attack Iraqi civilians, and try to spark sectarian strife. But ultimately, these terrorists will fail to achieve their goals. Iraqis are a proud people. They have rejected sectarian war, and they have no interest in endless destruction. They understand that in the end, only Iraqis can resolve their differences and police their streets, only Iraqis can build a democracy within their borders. What America can do, and will do, is provide support for the Iraqi people as both a friend and a partner.

Ending this war is not only in Iraq's interest, it's in our own. The United States has paid a huge price to put the future of Iraq in the hands of its people. We have sent our young men and women to make enormous sacrifices in Iraq and spent vast resources abroad at a time of tight budgets at home. We've persevered because of a belief we share with the Iraqi people, a belief that out of the ashes of war, a new beginning could be born in this cradle of civilization.

Through this remarkable chapter in the history of the United States and Iraq, we have met our responsibilities. Now it's time to turn the page. As we do, I'm mindful that the Iraq war has been a contentious issue at home. Here too it's time to turn the page. This afternoon I spoke to former President George W. Bush. It's well known that he and I disagreed about the war from its outset. Yet no one can doubt President Bush's support for our troops or his love of country and commitment to our security. As I've said, there were patriots who supported this war and patriots who opposed it. And all of us are united in appreciation for our service men and women and our hopes for Iraqis' future.

The greatness of our democracy is grounded in our ability to move beyond our differences and to learn from our experience as we confront the many challenges ahead. And no challenge is more essential to our security than our fight against Al Qaida.

Americans across the political spectrum supported the use of force against those who attacked us on 9/11. Now, as we approach our 10th year of combat in Afghanistan, there are those who are understandably asking tough questions about our mission there. But we must never lose sight of what's at stake. As we speak, Al Qaida continues to plot against us, and its leadership remains anchored in the border regions of Afghanistan and Pakistan. We will disrupt, dismantle, and defeat Al Qaida, while preventing Afghanistan from again serving as a base for terrorists. And because of our drawdown in Iraq, we are now able to apply the resources necessary to go on offense. In fact, over the last 19 months, nearly a dozen Al Qaida leaders and hundreds of Al Qaida's extremist allies have been killed or captured around the world.

Within Afghanistan, I've ordered the deployment of additional troops, who, under the command of General David Petraeus, are fighting to break the Taliban's momentum. As with the surge in Iraq, these forces will be in place for a limited time to provide space for the Afghans to build their capacity and secure their own future. But as was the case in Iraq, we can't do for Afghans what they must ultimately do for themselves. That's why we're training Afghan security forces and supporting a political resolution to Afghanistan's problems. And next August, we will begin a transition to Afghan responsibility. The pace of our troop reductions will be determined by conditions on the ground, and our support for Afghanistan will endure. But make no mistake: This transition will begin because open-ended war serves neither our interests nor the Afghan people's.

Indeed, one of the lessons of our effort in Iraq is that American influence around the world is not a function of military force alone. We must use all elements of our power, including our diplomacy, our economic strength, and the power of America's example, to secure our interests and stand by our allies. And we must project a vision of the future that's based not just on our fears, but also on our hopes, a vision that recognizes the real dangers that exist around the world, but also the limitless possibilities of our time.

Today, old adversaries are at peace and emerging democracies are potential partners. New markets for our goods stretch from Asia to the Americas. A new push for peace in the Middle East will begin here tomorrow. Billions of young people want to move beyond the shackles of poverty and conflict. As the leader of the free world, America will do more than just defeat on the battlefield those who offer hatred and destruction. We will also lead among those who are willing to work together to expand freedom and opportunity for all people.

Now, that effort must begin within our own borders. Throughout our history, America has been willing to bear the burden of promoting liberty and human dignity overseas, understanding its links to our own liberty and security. But we have also understood that our Nation's strength and influence abroad must be firmly anchored in our prosperity at home. And the bedrock of that prosperity must be a growing middle class.

Unfortunately, over the last decade, we've not done what's necessary to shore up the foundations of our own prosperity. We spent a trillion dollars at war, often financed by borrowing from overseas. This in turn has shortchanged investments in our own people and contributed to record deficits. For too long, we have put off tough decisions on everything from our manufacturing base to our energy policy to education reform. As a result, too many middle class families find themselves working harder for less, while our Nation's long-term competitiveness is put at risk.

And so at this moment, as we wind down the war in Iraq, we must tackle those challenges at home with as much energy and grit and sense of common purpose as our men and women in uniform who have served abroad. They have met every test that they faced. Now it's our turn. Now it's our responsibility to honor them by coming together, all of us, and working to secure the dream that so many generations have fought for, the dream that a better life awaits anyone who is willing to work for it and reach for it.

Our most urgent task is to restore our economy and put the millions of Americans who have lost their jobs back to work. To strengthen our middle class, we must give all our children the education they deserve and all our workers the skills that they need to compete in a global economy. We must jump-start industries that create jobs and end our dependence on foreign oil. We must unleash the innovation that allows new products to roll off our assembly lines and nurture the ideas that spring from our entrepreneurs. This will be difficult, but in the days to come, it must be our central mission as a people and my central responsibility as President.

Part of that responsibility is making sure that we honor our commitments to those who have served our country with such valor. As long as I am President, we will maintain the finest fighting force that the world has ever known and we will do whatever it takes to serve our veterans as well as they have served us. This is a sacred trust. That's why we've already made one of the largest increases in funding for veterans in decades. We're treating the signature wounds of today's wars, Posttraumatic Stress Disorder and traumatic brain injury, while providing the health care and benefits that all of our veterans have earned. And we're funding a post-9/11 GI bill that helps our veterans and their families pursue the dream of a college education. Just as the GI bill helped those who fought World War II, including my grandfather, become the backbone of our middle class, so today's service men and women must have the chance to apply their gifts to expand the American economy, because part of ending a war responsibly is standing by those who have fought it.

Two weeks ago, America's final combat brigade in Iraq, the Army's 4th Stryker Brigade, journeyed home in the predawn darkness. Thousands of soldiers and hundreds of vehicles made the trip from Baghdad, the last of them passing into Kuwait in the early morning hours. Over 7 years before, American troops and coalition partners had fought their way across similar highways, but this time no shots were fired. It was just a convoy of brave Americans making their way home.

Of course, the soldiers left much behind. Some were teenagers when the war began. Many have served multiple tours of duty, far from families who bore a heroic burden of their own, enduring the absence of a husband's embrace or a mother's kiss. Most painfully, since the war began, 55 members of the 4th Stryker Brigade made the ultimate sacrifice, part of over 4,400 Americans who have given their lives in Iraq. As one staff sergeant said, "I know that to my brothers in arms who fought and died, this day would probably mean a lot."

Those Americans gave their lives for the values that have lived in the hearts of our people for over two centuries. Along with nearly 1.5 million Americans who have served in Iraq, they fought in a faraway place for people they never knew. They stared into the darkest of human creations—war—and helped the Iraqi people seek the light of peace.

In an age without surrender ceremonies, we must earn victory through the success of our partners and the strength of our own Nation. Every American who serves joins an unbroken line of heroes that stretches from Lexington to Gettysburg, from Iwo Jima to Inchon, from Khe Sanh to Kandahar, Americans who have fought to see that the lives of our children are better than our own. Our troops are the steel in our ship of state. And though our Nation may be traveling through rough waters, they give us confidence that our course is true and that beyond the predawn darkness, better days lie ahead.

Thank you. May God bless you, and may God bless the United States of America and all who serve her.

Source: U.S. Executive Office of the President. "Address to the Nation on the End of Combat Operations in Iraq." *Daily Compilation of Presidential Documents* 2010, no. 00716 (August 31, 2010). http://origin .www.gpo.gov/fdsys/pkg/DCPD-201000716/pdf/DCPD-201000716.pdf.

OTHER HISTORIC DOCUMENTS OF INTEREST

FROM THIS VOLUME

- Iraq Parliamentary Elections, p. 75

FROM PREVIOUS *HISTORIC DOCUMENTS*

Violence in Somalia Increases

AUGUST 24 AND DECEMBER 22, 2010

Increasing violence in Somalia rocked the region during the summer and fall of 2010, leading to a number of deaths and thousands of displaced citizens. International security forces seemed unable to control the violence that was centered in the nation's capital city of Mogadishu, and it spilled over into 2011, even as a new, though weak, government was installed. The government in the failed state continued to struggle to maintain control over the capital as antigovernment forces attacked civilians and government officials. The increasing violence brought into question whether the nation would meet the goal of holding its first official election in 2011, as was expected by the international forces that had installed the Somali government in the mid-2000s.

CONTINUED UNCERTAINTY

Somalia has been in a state of near anarchy since 1991 when the central government collapsed. Since that time, it has been unable to install a government in Mogadishu that is strong enough to address the violence caused by militant clans or the pirates operating off its coast. For the most part, a weak central government backed by the United Nations has existed, but its authority in the country is nearly nonexistent. The Supreme Islamic Courts Union (ICU) was formed in 2000 by eleven Islamic militant clans. It was the first successful attempt at creating a coalition government since 1991. The goal of the ICU was to turn Somalia into an Islamic state.

In 2006, the ICU took nearly complete control of the country and was able to provide some basic necessities and government services to Somalia's residents, but the warlords in charge of various constituencies were unable to control ongoing violence and the growing humanitarian crisis. However, the ICU faced significant opposition from the Transitional Federal Government (TFG), which was formed in 2004. The TFG had been created by international mediators and was being run from Kenya until 2005. It overtook the ICU in 2007 and since that time has been the de facto governing body—ruling by a charter rather than a constitution—which set up a parliament and the positions of president and prime minister. Seats in parliament are gained through negotiation among the clans represented in the body. Parliament elects the nation's president, and power is vested in the president to choose the prime minister. The Islamic militant movement, however, continues to threaten the power of the TFG, and Somalis have little faith in the TFG to be able to effectively provide for them.

Military support for the TFG was provided by Ethiopian forces, but they withdrew from the nation in January 2009; since that time, Somalia has existed in a state of lawlessness and increasing violence between militia groups around the country. Citizens are often caught up in the violence and many have fled their homes. The only thing keeping the TFG in power is support from African Union troops, which number nearly seven thousand and fight on the side of the government when violence arises. The United Nations reports that millions of Somalis are in need of basic humanitarian aid.

Without a stable government in power, Somalia has relied on help from international aid organizations and other foreign bodies to quell violence and provide for its citizens. In this state of unrest and poverty, piracy took root as an income generator.

VIOLENCE PEAKS

On August 23, 2010, fighting between the TFG and armed opposition groups broke out in the Somali capital of Mogadishu. At least forty people were killed and hundreds were wounded in what became known as the Ramadan Offensive. The militant groups fighting against TFG forces were attempting to overthrow the government in an effort to install the Islamic state that the ICU had fought for years earlier. The fighting continued throughout the month and targeted civilians and peacekeepers sent to the region from the African nations of Burundi and Uganda. Four Ugandan peacekeepers from the African Union were killed in August. Additional attacks in August resulted in the deaths of members of Somalia's parliament and a number of citizens. In one attack on August 24, a suicide bomber destroyed a Mogadishu hotel, killing 150.

The United Nations Security Council issued a quick condemnation of the new attacks and called on its member nations to provide resources to the international peacekeeping force helping to secure the government and the people. The condemnation was released as a statement to the press, which does not hold any of the binding action that a resolution would. In its condemnation, Security Council members "stressed the need to continue strengthening Somali security institutions and the importance of an inclusive dialogue in the peace process," and it also expressed support for the TFG.

As violence continued into September, the Office of the United Nations High Commissioner for Refugees (UNHCR) reported that at least thirty-two thousand Somalis had been displaced and at least three hundred had been killed. Two radio stations broadcast where residents could travel to for safety or where to turn for help. On September 18, antigovernment forces attacked the two radio stations and shut them down, cutting off all information for Somalis.

In late September, the focus of militant attacks shifted to the African Union peacekeeping forces and government buildings. A suicide bomber detonated herself in front of the presidential palace, while mortar attacks were carried out on the parliament building where lawmakers were meeting. African Union peacekeeping forces were largely successful in repelling attacks targeted toward the government, but civilian deaths continued to pile up. In October, the strength of the African Union peacekeeping forces became clear as they announced that they had taken control of and secured nearly half of Mogadishu. Wafula Wamunyinyi, speaking on behalf of the African Union peacekeepers, said, "Our forces now have a presence across more than forty percent [of Mogadishu]. We anticipate it should be more than fifty percent this month if we continue to make this progress." He said that while the forces were making significant progress, it would take greater numbers to more quickly progress and regain complete control of the capital.

In November, violence continued as a new prime minister was sworn into office. Mohamed Abdullahi Mohamed ("Farmajo") took the position, saying, "I will uphold and protect the laws of the country and I will pursue the common interest of the people and the nation." In his new position of leadership, Farmajo will be expected to increase security around the nation before the TFG's mandate expires in August 2011. Farmajo is the fourth prime minister to be appointed to office since the TFG officially took control of Somalia's government.

The progress being made by the African Union peacekeeping forces faced a significant setback late in the year. Two of the Islamic militant groups fighting against the government—Hizbul Islam and al-Shabaab—agreed to join forces in their pursuit to overthrow the TFG and turn Somalia into an Islamic state. In December, the United Nations called on the African Union to add an additional four thousand peacekeeping troops to its Somali ranks and asked its members "to contribute funds and equipment 'generously and promptly' to enable the force to fulfill a mandate that ranges from restoring peace to helping the Transitional Federal Government (TFG) develop national security and police forces." The United Nations agreed to provide equipment, services, and logistical support to the African Union's mission.

INTERNATIONAL SUPPORT AND NEED

The humanitarian situation in Somalia was off to a rough start in 2010 with no aid money pledged for food, water, medical treatments, sanitation or other vital needs. Donors who commonly supply humanitarian aid to Somalia cited concerns about the effectiveness of continuing aid in the war-torn country and fears that supplies might wind up in the hands of Islamic militants. The worldwide downturn in humanitarian aid, spurred by the global economic crisis, also hampered relief in Somalia. In December 2009, the United Nations made a plea to its members to provide support to the nation or risk violence spilling over into surrounding regions. "The consequences of not addressing the situation in Somalia is that we could expect more displacement into other parts of the region putting a great deal more stress on Djibouti, Ethiopia and Kenya at a time when they can't afford to support them either," said UN resident and humanitarian coordinator Mark Bowden. The United Nations estimated that nearly $700 million in humanitarian assistance would be required for Somalia in 2010.

Some of that money would be directed toward those displaced by the ongoing violence. Even before the August surge in violence, Somalis were already fleeing their homes from the constant danger posed by antigovernment militias. The International Red Cross, one of the organizations working in Somalia, called the situation "extremely critical." The displaced Somalis "are coping through petty trade or by growing crops on small patches of land, and also thanks to the help of resident communities," said Pascal Mauchle, head of the delegation representing the Red Cross in Somalia. "But they cannot hope to cover more than their most urgent needs. They are extremely vulnerable to malnutrition and disease."

When fighting broke out in August and September, six humanitarian groups were barred from entering Somalia to deliver necessary supplies to the nation's citizens. The United States Agency for International Development (USAID) reported that this would stop nearly one-and-a-half million people from receiving basic essentials. A few humanitarian groups were still able to provide support, but they could not provide all that was needed on their own.

Further hampering the relief efforts was the little rain that fell, which reduced the number of locally grown crops available to feed the people of Somalia. Without enough food, prices quickly rose, coupled with a rise in inflation. Those who could not afford to feed their families suffered significant malnutrition and widespread disease. The World Health Organization (WHO) reported that malnutrition has exceeded the emergency threshold of 15 percent of the population, and that nearly thirty-five thousand Somali children were facing severe malnutrition.

International aid organizations were undeterred by the increasing violence. "Our assistance goes to the people affected by the fighting, not to the government," said Benjamin Wahren, the International Red Cross's deputy aid chief for the Horn of Africa. "The government doesn't control much physical territory and we work all over the country." He indicated that no matter who ended up in charge of the country, the Red Cross would continue to support the civilians trapped by the violence.

—Heather Kerrigan

Following is a statement to the press by the UN Security Council on August 24, 2010, condemning the violence in Somalia; and a news release from the United Nations on December 22, 2010, calling on the African Union to add four thousand more troops to its peacekeeping mission in Somalia.

DOCUMENT

UN Security Council Condemns Somali Violence

August 24, 2010

The members of the Security Council condemned in the strongest terms the attack in Mogadishu today, which resulted in the death and injury of innocent civilians, including Members of the Somali Parliament.

The members of the Security Council expressed their condolences to the families of those killed in the attack, as well as to the Transitional Federal Government. They called for the perpetrators to be brought swiftly to justice.

The members of the Security Council reiterated their full support to the Transitional Federal Government and African Union Mission in Somalia (AMISOM), and expressed their continued appreciation for the commitment of troops by the Governments of Uganda and Burundi.

The members of the Security Council stressed the need to continue strengthening Somali security institutions and the importance of an inclusive dialogue in the peace process.

Source: United Nations Political Office for Somalia. "UN Security Council Press Statement on Somalia." August 24, 2010. http://unpos.unmissions.org/Default.aspx?tabid=1931&ctl=Details&mid=2201&ItemID=10129.

United Nations Calls for Increase in Security Forces in Somalia

December 22, 2010

The Security Council today called for a 50 per cent increase to 12,000 troops in the United Nations-backed African Union (AU) peacekeeping force in Somalia, which has been trying to bring stability to a country torn apart by 20 years of factional fighting.

In a unanimous resolution authorizing deployment of the AU mission in Somalia (AMISOM) until 30 September 2011, the 15-member body called on Member States and international organizations to contribute funds and equipment "generously and promptly" to enable the force to fulfil a mandate that ranges from restoring peace to helping the Transitional Federal Government (TFG) develop national security and police forces.

It asks Secretary-General Ban Ki-moon to provide UN logistical support to the enlarged force with equipment and services, while continuing his good offices for reconciliation in a country where Al Shabaab, other Islamist militias, factional groups and foreign fighters control vast tracts of territory in a fight to oust the internationally recognized TFG, based in Mogadishu, the capital.

Somalia has not had a functioning central government since the overthrow of the Muhammad Siad Barre in 1991, and the Council reiterated its serious concern at the impact of the continued fighting on the civilian population, stressing the terrorist threat that the armed opposition, particularly Al Shabaab, constitutes not only for Somalia but for the international community.

Citing human rights violations against civilians, including women and children, and humanitarian personnel, it voiced concern at "the worsening humanitarian situation" and "the significant decline" in humanitarian funding for Somalia and called on all Member States to contribute to current and future appeals.

The Council also reiterated its intent, mentioned in past resolutions, to set up a UN peacekeeping operation when conditions permit. At present the UN maintains a political office for Somalia (UNPOS) in Nairobi, capital of neighbouring Kenya, because of the poor security situation inside Somalia.

As in the past, the resolution called on all parties to support the Djibouti Agreement, a UN-facilitated peace process that began in 2008 and has been joined by one of the rebel groups.

On piracy, which has plagued shipping off the Somali coast, including vital supplies from the UN World Food Programme (WPF) to scores of thousands of hungry civilians, the Council called for a comprehensive international response to tackle both the scourge and its underlying causes.

SOURCE: United Nations News Centre. "Somalia: UN Calls for 4,000 More African Union Peacekeepers." December 22, 2010. http://www.un.org/apps//news/story.asp?NewsID=37141&Cr=somali&Cr1=.

OTHER HISTORIC DOCUMENTS OF INTEREST

FROM PREVIOUS *HISTORIC DOCUMENTS*

Housing Market Hits 15-Year Low

AUGUST 24, SEPTEMBER 23, OCTOBER 25,
NOVEMBER 23, AND DECEMBER 22, 2010

The $8,000 homebuyer's tax credit first offered by the federal government in 2009 bolstered the slowly growing housing market, helping it reach a peak in April 2010 as buyers scrambled to meet the tax credit deadline of April 30. Economists expected that housing sales would decline after the credit's expiration, but no one expected home sales to decrease as much as they did, falling 27 percent in July 2010. With housing sales closely linked to the nation's overall economy, immediate speculation began that one of the major drivers behind the current recession could cause another economic tumble. But by the end of the year, optimism in the real estate market was growing cautiously as existing-home sales began climbing again, even after banks halted foreclosures amid questions regarding the legality of closing paperwork and the actions of bank agents.

RISE AND FALL OF THE U.S. HOUSING MARKET

The long-running crisis of the U.S. housing market has its roots in the economic trends of the 1990s. The little-regulated market, coupled with its volatility, hit a crossroads in the late 1990s when rising housing prices and increasing buyer demand led banks to offer "subprime" mortgages, which allowed people to purchase homes with little or no money down. The catch, however, was that their mortgage rates would end up rising substantially in the years after the home was purchased. This housing bubble, as economists termed it, burst in 2006 when home prices began declining rapidly and many Americans were sitting on property that was worth less than what they still owed on it. The situation quickly spiraled out of control and drove up the number of home foreclosures.

Because the U.S. economy had closely tied itself to the mortgage market during the period of financial deregulation in the mid-1990s when banks bought and sold mortgage debts, the financial industry took a hit as well when the housing bubble burst. As each player in the nation's economy began to crumble, a recession ensued. It was not until December 2008 that the National Bureau of Economic Research, a nonpartisan organization that dates the beginning and ending of economic crises, formally declared that the United States had entered a recession in late 2007.

The collapse of the housing market was hurting banks because they did not have money rolling in from mortgages and, therefore, could not continue lending, meaning that there was less money exchanging hands. With bank-lending stalled, home sales continued to fall and housing prices were subsequently pushed downward. In an attempt to shore up the economy, the federal government undertook a number of steps to infuse money back into financial institutions and, in turn, the pockets of American citizens.

One idea supported by the Barack Obama administration and members of Congress to get money flowing again was to offer a tax credit for first-time and repeat home buyers. The idea behind the program was that it would incentivize those who were thinking about purchasing a home but had been scared off by the housing crisis. The legislation signed by President Obama offered an $8,000 tax credit to first-time buyers and a $6,500 tax credit to repeat buyers who purchased a home after January 1, 2009. The original program was so popular that in November 2009 Congress extended it through April 30, 2010. The extension, which began on November 6, 2009 put an income limit on those who were able to qualify for the credit.

The $30 billion price tag on the tax credit program, coupled with government intervention into the market that allowed less money down on purchases and lender guarantees against default, artificially improved the housing market, economists said. It was long expected that the end of the credit would mean the end of the influx of buyers into the housing market, which would drive housing sales downward.

Housing Market Falls Again

The general consensus of economists was that the April 30 deadline for the homebuyer tax credit would cause a 13 percent decrease in the home sales. When the actual July figures more than doubled that estimate, economists and real estate analysts responded with shock.

Home sales hit a peak in April 2010 as buyers rushed to meet the deadline at the end of the month. July's 27.2 percent decline in homes sales marked a 34 percent decline from peak home sales in April. This was the lowest level of home sales since the National Association of Realtors® (NAR), a trade association representing those involved in residential and commercial real estate, began collecting data on home sales in 1999.

No area of the country and no area of the residential real estate market could escape July's sales fall. Single-family homes, which make up the largest percentage of residential units sold in the United States, hit its lowest level since 1995. Sales of condominiums and co-ops fell more than 28 percent. The Midwest took the hardest hit where home sales fell 35 percent. In the Northwest, sales were down nearly 30 percent, while the sales decline in the South and West hovered in the low- to mid-20 percent range. The bright side was that, with sales down across the country, prices were still edging slightly upward.

Upon news of the decrease in home sales, the financial industry took another hit with the Dow Jones closing down 134 points, marking a six-month low. Two-year Treasury note yields also fell to a record low. "It is becoming abundantly clear that the housing market is undermining the already faltering wider economic recovery," said Paul Dales of Capital Economics, a macroeconomics research consultant. "With an increasingly inevitable double-dip in housing prices yet to come, things could get a lot worse."

However, there was little expectation that the U.S. housing market would drive the country into another recession before it got out of the current one. Instead, it would impede growth and recovery. "It won't be a double dip recession," said economist Joel Naroff, "but it might feel like it." The White House stuck to its position that the economy was still on track to recover, even with the fluctuating housing market. But, said then–White House deputy press secretary Bill Burton, the home sales figures show "that there's a lot more work yet to do."

The real estate market looked slightly better when the August home sale data were released. Overall, existing-home sales were down 19 percent since August 2009 but had increased by 7.6 percent from July to August 2010. The sales climbed again in September, this time by 10 percent, wiping out some expectation of the double-dip in the housing market. After two months of growth, economists became more optimistic about a market recovery, but were still cautious.

One reason for the caution was the foreclosure stoppage announced in October by three of the largest mortgage servicers, Bank of America, JPMorgan Chase, and GMAC. By stopping foreclosure proceedings, the servicers said they would have more time to verify paperwork required for each foreclosed property. The problem that came to light was the large number of foreclosure affidavits and promissory notes that were signed without being authenticated, causing problems for both original owners of a foreclosed property and the current bank owner. This confusion caused some homes to be improperly foreclosed. "If the wrong person is filing a foreclosure action, that means the note has not been properly transferred to them," said Tamara Parker, an attorney from Columbus, Ohio. "They have no right to foreclose on that home. Someone else who actually is the rightful person to collect on that note and mortgage could come back and sue the person for the money." Bank of America took the most wide-reaching approach, halting foreclosure proceedings under its control in all fifty states.

Still, optimism remained. "A housing recovery is taking place but will be choppy at times depending on the duration and impact of a foreclosure moratorium," said NAR chief economist Lawrence Yun. "But the overall direction should be a gradual rising trend in home sales, with buyers responding to historically low mortgage interest rates and very favorable affordability conditions." Unfortunately, this optimism was not enough to buoy the market for a third straight month, and in October, existing-home sales declined 2.2 percent. The expectation of economists and realtors was that the foreclosure stoppage had affected October sales and would affect home sales in the months to come. In addition, said NAR president Ron Phipps, "overly tight credit is making it difficult for some creditworthy borrowers to qualify for a mortgage, and we are continuing to deal with a notable share of appraisals coming in below a price negotiated between a buyer and seller."

Existing-home sales were back up in November and December, rising 5.6 percent and 12.3 percent, respectively. "December was a good finish to 2010, when sales fluctuate more than normal. The pattern over the past six months is clearly showing a recovery," said Yun. "The December pace is near the volume we're expecting for 2011, so the market is getting much closer to an adequate, sustainable level. The recovery will likely continue as job growth gains momentum and rising rents encourage more renters into ownership while exceptional affordability conditions remain."

FUTURE GROWTH OR FUTURE DECLINE?

Steady unemployment that remained above 9 percent for all of 2010 and the slow-growing economy left real estate analysts skeptical that sales or prices would significantly rise before the end of the year. Although December's home sales outpaced expectations, there was no indication that it would remain constant into and throughout 2011, but it would probably look better than originally anticipated. "Nationally, we'll see a bumpy ride instead of a double-dip," said University of Pennsylvania real estate professor Susan Wachter.

The slight rise in home prices was expected to remain stagnant as well. "Given that home values are back in line relative to income, and from very low new-home construction, there is not likely to be any measurable change in home prices going forward," said Yun.

The recovery of home sales now depends greatly on buyers with favorable credit and good jobs, said then–NAR president Vicki Cox Golder. "Mortgage interest rates are at record lows, home prices have firmed, and there is good selection of property in most areas," she said. This sets up a market that, while detrimental to sellers who may be forced to come to a home closing with money and take a loss, is extremely favorable to buyers. Yun echoed Golder's opinion. "Given the rock-bottom mortgage interest rates and historically high housing affordability conditions, the pace of a sales recovery could pick up quickly, provided the economy consistently adds jobs."

—Heather Kerrigan

Following are five press releases issued by the National Association of Realtors® on August 24, 2010, September 23, 2010, October 25, 2010, November 23, 2010, and December 22, 2010, regarding existing-home sales in the United States.

National Association of Realtors® Announces Decline in July Existing-Home Sales

August 24, 2010

Existing-home sales were sharply lower in July following expiration of the home buyer tax credit but home prices continued to gain, according to the National Association of Realtors®.

Existing-home sales, which are completed transactions that include single-family, townhomes, condominiums and co-ops, dropped 27.2 percent to a seasonally adjusted annual rate of 3.83 million units in July from a downwardly revised 5.26 million in June, and are 25.5 percent below the 5.14 million-unit level in July 2009.

Sales are at the lowest level since the total existing-home sales series launched in 1999, and single family sales—accounting for the bulk of transactions—are at the lowest level since May of 1995.

Lawrence Yun, NAR chief economist, said a soft sales pace likely will continue for a few additional months. "Consumers rationally jumped into the market before the deadline for the home buyer tax credit expired. Since May, after the deadline, contract signings have been notably lower and a pause period for home sales is likely to last through September," he said. "However, given the rock-bottom mortgage interest rates and historically high housing affordability conditions, the pace of a sales recovery could pick up quickly, provided the economy consistently adds jobs.

"Even with sales pausing for a few months, annual sales are expected to reach 5 million in 2010 because of healthy activity in the first half of the year. To place in perspective, annual sales averaged 4.9 million in the past 20 years, and 4.4 million over the past 30 years," Yun said.

According to Freddie Mac, the national average commitment rate for a 30-year, conventional, fixed-rate mortgage fell to a record low 4.56 percent in July from 4.74 percent in June; the rate was 5.22 percent in July 2009. Last week, Freddie Mac reported the 30-year fixed was down to 4.42 percent.

The national median existing-home price for all housing types was $182,600 in July, up 0.7 percent from a year ago. Distressed home sales are unchanged from June, accounting for 32 percent of transactions in July; they were 31 percent in July 2009.

"Thanks to the home buyer tax credit, home values have been stable for the past 18 months despite heavy job losses," Yun said. "Over the short term, high supply in relation to demand clearly favors buyers. However, given that home values are back in line relative to income, and from very low new-home construction, there is not likely to be any measurable change in home prices going forward."

Total housing inventory at the end of July increased 2.5 percent to 3.98 million existing homes available for sale, which represents a 12.5-month supply at the current sales pace, up from an 8.9-month supply in June. Raw unsold inventory is still 12.9 percent below the record of 4.58 million in July 2008.

NAR President Vicki Cox Golder, owner of Vicki L. Cox & Associates in Tucson, Ariz., said there are great opportunities now for buyers who weren't able to take advantage of the tax credit. "Mortgage interest rates are at record lows, home prices have firmed and there is good selection of property in most areas, so buyers with good jobs and favorable credit ratings find themselves in a fortunate position," she said. . . .

[Sales data by region and housing type and footnotes have been omitted.]

SOURCE: National Association of Realtors®. "July Existing-Home Sales Fall as Expected but Prices Rise." August 24, 2010. http://www.realtor.org/press_room/news_releases/2010/08/ehs_fall.

National Association of Realtors® Announces August Existing-Home Sales Rise

DOCUMENT

September 23, 2010

Existing-home sales rose in August following a big correction in July, according to the National Association of Realtors®.

Existing-home sales, which are completed transactions that include single-family, townhomes, condominiums and co-ops, increased 7.6 percent to a seasonally adjusted annual rate of 4.13 million in August from an upwardly revised 3.84 million in July, but remain 19.0 percent below the 5.10 million-unit pace in August 2009.

Lawrence Yun, NAR chief economist, said home sales still remain subpar. "The housing market is trying to recover on its own power without the home buyer tax credit. Despite very attractive affordability conditions, a housing market recovery will likely be slow and gradual because of lingering economic uncertainty," Yun said.

According to Freddie Mac, the national average commitment rate for a 30-year, conventional, fixed-rate mortgage fell to a record low 4.43 percent in August from 4.56 percent in July; the rate was 5.19 percent in August 2009.

Yun added, "Home values have shown stabilizing trends over the past year, even as the economy shed millions of jobs, because of the home buyer tax credit stimulus. Now that the economy is adding some jobs, the housing market needs to steadily improve and eventually stand on its own."

The national median existing-home price for all housing types was $178,600 in August, up 0.8 percent from a year ago. Distressed homes rose to 34 percent of sales in August from 32 percent in July; they were 31 percent in August 2009.

NAR President Vicki Cox Golder, owner of Vicki L. Cox & Associates in Tucson, Ariz., said consumers have been getting mixed signals about the housing market. "People understand the good affordability conditions with stable home prices in most areas, but they're concerned about the economy and speculation on Wall Street," she said. "We need to stick with the facts about the long-term value of homeownership and avoid unrealistic assessments. Tight credit and slow short sales are ongoing problems—expediting short sales will help the market to recover more quickly."

Total housing inventory at the end of August slipped 0.6 percent to 3.98 million existing homes available for sale, which represents an 11.6-month supply at the current sales pace, down from a 12.5-month supply in July....

[Sales data by region and housing type and footnotes have been omitted.]

Source: National Association of Realtors®. "Existing-Home Sales Move Up in August." September 23, 2010. http://www.realtor.org/press_room/news_releases/2010/09/ehs_move.

National Association of Realtors® Announces September Existing-Home Sales Rise

October 25, 2010

Existing-home sales rose again in September, affirming that a sales recovery has begun, according to the National Association of Realtors®.

Existing-home sales, which are completed transactions that include single-family, townhomes, condominiums and co-ops, jumped 10.0 percent to a seasonally adjusted annual rate of 4.53 million in September from a downwardly revised 4.12 million in August, but remain 19.1 percent below the 5.60 million-unit pace in September 2009 when first-time buyers were ramping up in advance of the initial deadline for the tax credit last November.

Lawrence Yun, NAR chief economist, said the housing market is in the early stages of recovery. "A housing recovery is taking place but will be choppy at times depending on the duration and impact of a foreclosure moratorium. But the overall direction should be a gradual rising trend in home sales with buyers responding to historically low mortgage interest rates and very favorable affordability conditions," he said.

According to Freddie Mac, the national average commitment rate for a 30-year, conventional, fixed-rate mortgage fell to a record low 4.35 percent in September from 4.43 percent in August; the rate was 5.06 percent in September 2009.

The national median existing-home price for all housing types was $171,700 in September, which is 2.4 percent below a year ago. Distressed homes accounted for 35 percent of sales in September compared with 34 percent in August; they were 29 percent in September 2009.

NAR President Vicki Cox Golder, owner of Vicki L. Cox & Associates in Tucson, Ariz., said opportunities abound in the current market. "A decade ago, mortgage rates were almost double what they are today, and they're about one-and-a-half percentage points lower than the peak of the housing boom in 2005," she said. "In addition, home prices are running about 22 percent less than five years ago when they were bid up by the biggest housing rush on record."

To illustrate the jump in housing affordability, the median monthly mortgage payment for a recently purchased home is several hundred dollars less than it was five years ago. "In fact, the median monthly mortgage payment in many areas is less than people are paying for rent," Golder said.

Housing affordability conditions today are 60 percentage points higher than during the housing boom, so it has become a very strong buyers' market, especially for families with long-term plans. "The savings today's buyers are receiving are not a one-time benefit. Buyers with fixed-rate mortgages will save money every year they are living in their home—this is truly an example of how homeownership builds wealth over the long term," Golder added.

Total housing inventory at the end of September fell 1.9 percent to 4.04 million existing homes available for sale, which represents a 10.7-month supply at the current sales pace, down from a 12.0-month supply in August. Raw unsold inventory is 11.7 percent below the record of 4.58 million in July 2008.

"Vacant homes and homes where mortgages have not been paid for an extended number of months need to be cleared from the market as quickly as possible, with a new set of buyers helping the recovery along a healthy path," Yun said. "Inventory remains elevated and continues to favor buyers over sellers. A normal seasonal decline in inventory is expected through the upcoming months." . . .

[Sales data by region and housing type and footnotes have been omitted.]

Source: National Association of Realtors®. "September Existing-Home Sales Show Another Strong Gain." October 25, 2010. http://www.realtor.org/press_room/news_releases/2010/10/sept_strong.

National Association of Realtors®
Announces October Existing-Home
Sales Decline

November 23, 2010

Existing-home sales retreated in October on the heels of two strong monthly gains, according to the National Association of REALTORS®.

Existing-home sales, which are completed transactions that include single-family, townhomes, condominiums and co-ops, declined 2.2 percent to a seasonally adjusted annual rate of 4.43 million in October from 4.53 million in September, and are 25.9 percent below the 5.98 million-unit level in October 2009 when sales were surging prior to the initial deadline for the first-time buyer tax credit.

Year-to-date there were 4.149 million existing-home sales, down 2.9 percent from 4.272 million at this time in 2009.

Lawrence Yun, NAR chief economist, said the recent sales pattern can be expected to continue. "The housing market is experiencing an uneven recovery, and a temporary foreclosure stoppage in some states is likely to have held back a number of completed sales. Still, sales activity is clearly off the bottom and is attempting to settle into normal sustainable levels," he said. "Based on current and improving job market conditions, and from attractive affordability conditions, sales should steadily improve to healthier levels of above 5 million by spring of next year."

According to Freddie Mac, the national average commitment rate for a 30-year, conventional, fixed-rate mortgage fell to a record low 4.23 percent in October from 4.35 percent in September; the rate was 4.95 percent in October 2009.

The national median existing-home price for all housing types was $170,500 in October, down 0.9 percent from October 2009. Distressed homes accounted for 34 percent of sales in October, compared with 35 percent in September and 30 percent of sales in October 2009.

NAR President Ron Phipps, broker-president of Phipps Realty in Warwick, R.I., clarified that several factors are restraining a housing recovery, even with great affordability conditions. "We'll likely see some impact from the foreclosure moratorium in the months ahead, but overly tight credit is making it difficult for some creditworthy borrowers to qualify for a mortgage, and we are continuing to deal with a notable share of appraisals coming in below a price negotiated between a buyer and seller," he said.

"A return to common sense loan underwriting standards would go a long way toward achieving responsible, sustainable homeownership. In addition, all home valuations should be made by competent professionals with local expertise and full access to market data—there remains an elevated level of appraisals that fail to provide accurate valuation, which is causing a steady level of sales to be cancelled or postponed," Phipps said. . . .

According to FHFA, Fannie- and Freddie-backed mortgages that were recently originated show an outstanding performance, even better than during the pre-housing bubble years.

"A review of recently originated loans suggests that they have overly stringent underwriting standards, with only the highest creditworthy borrowers able to tap into historically low mortgage interest rates. There could be an upside surprise to sales activity if credit availability is opened to more qualified home buyers who are willing to stay well within budget," Yun added.

Total housing inventory at the end of October fell 3.4 percent to 3.86 million existing homes available for sale, which represents a 10.5-month supply at the current sales pace, down from a 10.6-month supply in September.

First-time buyers purchased 32 percent of homes in October, unchanged from September, but down from 50 percent a year ago during the initial surge for the first-time buyer tax credit. Investors accounted for 19 percent of transactions in October; they were 18 percent in September and 14 percent in October 2009; the balance of sales were to repeat buyers. All-cash sales were at 29 percent in October, unchanged from September but up from 20 percent a year ago. . . .

[Sales data by region and housing type and footnotes have been omitted.]

SOURCE: National Association of Realtors®. "Existing-Home Sales Decline in October Following Two Monthly Gains." November 23, 2010. http://www.realtor.org/press_room/news_releases/2010/11/october_retreat.

National Association of Realtors® Announces Existing-Home Sales Climb in November

DOCUMENT

December 22, 2010

Existing-home sales got back on an upward path in November, resuming a growth trend since bottoming in July, according to the National Association of Realtors®.

Existing-home sales, which are completed transactions that include single-family, townhomes, condominiums and co-ops, rose 5.6 percent to a seasonally adjusted annual rate of 4.68 million in November from 4.43 million in October, but are 27.9 percent below the cyclical peak of 6.49 million in November 2009, which was the initial deadline for the first-time buyer tax credit.

Lawrence Yun, NAR chief economist, is hopeful for 2011. "Continuing gains in home sales are encouraging, and the positive impact of steady job creation will more than trump some negative impact from a modest rise in mortgage interest rates, which remain historically favorable," he said.

Yun added that home buyers are responding to improved affordability conditions. "The relationship recently between mortgage interest rates, home prices and family income has been the most favorable on record for buying a home since we started measuring in 1970," he said. "Therefore, the market is recovering and we should trend up to a healthy, sustainable level in 2011."

The national median existing-home price for all housing types was $170,600 in November, up 0.4 percent from November 2009. Distressed homes have been a fairly stable market share, accounting for 33 percent of sales in November; they were 34 percent in October and 33 percent in November 2009.

Foreclosures, which accounted for two-thirds of the distressed sales share, sold at a median discount of 15 percent in November, while short sales were discounted 10 percent in comparison with traditional home sales.

Total housing inventory at the end of November fell 4.0 percent to 3.71 million existing homes available for sale, which represents a 9.5-month supply at the current sales pace, down from a 10.5-month supply in October.

NAR President Ron Phipps, broker-president of Phipps Realty in Warwick, R.I., said good buying opportunities will continue. "Traditionally there are far fewer buyers competing for properties at this time of the year, so serious buyers have a lot of opportunities during the winter months," he said. "Buyers will enjoy favorable afford-ability conditions into the new year, although mortgage rates are expected to gradually rise as 2011 progresses."

According to Freddie Mac, the national average commitment rate for a 30-year, conventional, fixed-rate mortgage rose to 4.30 percent in November from a record low 4.23 percent in October; the rate was 4.88 percent in November 2009.

"In the short term, mortgage interest rates should hover just above recent record lows, while home prices have generally stabilized following declines from 2007 through 2009," Yun said. "Although mortgage interest rates have ticked up in recent weeks, over-all conditions remain extremely favorable for buyers who can obtain credit." ...

Investors accounted for 19 percent of transactions in November, also unchanged from October, but are up from 12 percent in November 2009; the balance of sales were to repeat buyers. All-cash sales were at 31 percent in November, up from 29 percent in October and 19 percent a year ago. "The elevated level of all-cash transactions continues to reflect tight credit market conditions," Yun said. ...

[Sales data by region and housing type and footnotes have been omitted.]

SOURCE: National Association of Realtors®. "Existing-Home Sales Resume Uptrend with Stable Prices." December 22, 2010. http://www.realtor.org/press_room/news_releases/2010/12/existing_prices.

OTHER HISTORIC DOCUMENTS OF INTEREST

FROM PREVIOUS *HISTORIC DOCUMENTS*

Floods Devastate Pakistan

AUGUST 26 AND 27, 2010

During the summer of 2010, provinces across Pakistan were devastated by the worst flooding seen in the country in eighty years. A nation that had already been hampered in its infrastructure development by political instability faced another setback as flood waters rose and destroyed roads, bridges, homes, schools, and government buildings. The government blamed the effects of the flooding partially on the "timber mafia" that had been a driver behind deforestation. Relief flooded in slowly from around the world—even from some organizations deemed "militant" by the United Nations. The large price tag placed on Pakistan's recovery left in question how quickly the government could recover and whether other countries would continue to rely on Pakistan to fight Taliban insurgents.

WORST FLOODS IN EIGHTY YEARS

Water crested the banks of the Indus River, which flows the length of the country, for the first time on July 22, 2010, in the province of Baluchistan. Slowly, the flooding continued into the northwestern province of Khyber Pakhtunkhwa and then into the southern provinces of Punjab and Sindh. In its path, the river destroyed towns and villages, displaced millions of Pakistani citizens, and killed more than fifteen hundred. Floods continued through August, and by the time the flood waters subsided, nearly sixty-two thousand square miles, or approximately one-fifth of the country, had been affected.

In addition to destroying much of the nation's infrastructure, crop damage was also widespread. Many Pakistani families depend on farming for income. The United Nations estimated that nearly 80 percent of all food stocks had been destroyed during the flooding, and seventeen million acres of farmland were left flooded. In addition, the seeds that had been prepared for the following season's harvest were lost as well, signaling that the pain felt by Pakistanis would not be limited to 2010. Pakistan's government provided financial support through the Benazir Income Support Programme (BISP), which had been established in 2008–09 when inflation rose significantly and put increasing financial strain on Pakistani families.

The flooding brought to light the divide between the rich and poor citizens of Pakistan. As water levels continued to rise up and down the Indus River and its tributaries, government officials called for citizens to leave their homes and head for higher grounds, or areas left unaffected by the floods. Wealthier Pakistanis were able to hire transportation to flee their villages before roads and bridges were washed out. Poor Pakistanis, however, were left to flee on foot or fend for themselves at home. The local and central governments called the plight of these Pakistanis exaggerated, indicating that local camps had been set up in government buildings through many provinces.

Trust in Government Hits Another Low

Before the floods, many Pakistanis were still trying to rebuild their homes after a government offensive against Islamic militants that took place in 2009. Millions were displaced during the fighting that followed. The central government sent the military into the northwestern portion of the country to help citizens rebuild and to attempt to restore some of the citizens' trust in the government. Recovery had been slow, however, and many residents reported an increased level of dissatisfaction with Pakistani president Asif Ali Zardari's government.

Adding to the distrust was the August WikiLeaks scandal, during which classified U.S. military documents were made public, some of which suggested that Pakistan's government was secretly supporting the Taliban in Afghanistan (which the government denied), while it told the public that it would use any means necessary to remove these insurgents. Not long after the military documents were leaked, a local politician was assassinated in Karachi, and sectarian violence broke out in the nation's commercial capital leading to murders, arsons, and protests.

For some Pakistanis, trust in the government hit a new low when Zardari toured Europe in the midst of the flooding before he ever visited the areas affected in his own country. During his August trip, the Pakistani president visited France and the United Kingdom, where he attended a political rally for his son. It was not until August 12 that Zardari finally toured the most devastated areas. During the flooding crisis, it was Prime Minister Syed Yousuf Raza Gilani who led the government's efforts to aid citizens affected by the flooding, but most of his work was overshadowed by media focus on Zardari's apparent lack of concern.

Even though Zardari seemed to express little interest in the suffering felt by those affected by the flood after continuing his trip to Europe, those inside Pakistan said that in the long run, it will mean little. "It was a bad decision," said Badar Alam, editor of Pakistan's weekly *Herald* magazine. "But he's been hated for 15 years, and will continue to be hated."

Blame Placed on Timber Mafia

Pakistani government officials placed blame on the so-called timber mafia for significantly increasing the impact of the flooding. The deforestation across the country, which between 2007 and 2009 saw 70 percent of forests illegally cut down, left little ground cover to lessen the impact of flooding. Riaz Ahmad Khan, president of the Sarhad Awami Forestry Ittehad, a group that works to protect Pakistan's forests, said the deforestation was all for militant profit. "Forests were cut ruthlessly by the timber mafia under the protection of the militants," said Khan. The deforestation and logging activities sent large amounts of money directly to the Taliban. Today, Pakistan has only slightly more than five percent forest cover. Officials said the usual 20 to 25 percent expected for a region of its size would have abated the floods.

Furthermore, the felled timber stocked in the country's rivers caused additional problems as waters rose. Some of these stocks were knocked loose and sent downriver, knocking out any bridges in its path and filling dams, preventing water from flowing into them as intended. Without bridges, a number of regions in Pakistan were cut off from neighboring villages, making food and medical aid nearly impossible to deliver.

RELIEF EFFORTS

Pakistani citizens' distrust of the government means that the nation often relies on outside aid, or aid provided by civil society groups set up in major cities around the country. This opened the door for donations from Jamaat-ud-Dawa, a group the United Nations claims has ties to a militant organization believed to have caused the Mumbai, India, bombings of 2008. Jamaat-ud-Dawa immediately took it upon itself to send out thousands of volunteers to aid those in the hardest hit villages, and it also set up medical camps. The group welcomed additional participation in relief efforts and indicated that it was not attempting to gain power through its philanthropy, a charge other organizations had levied. "Everyone should be digging in for humanity's sake, and we shouldn't be politicizing the matter," said the group's deputy spokesman, Yahya Mujahid. "We aren't reaching out with an agenda in mind. The whole world should be putting in aid, America or whoever else, and we want everyone to contribute."

Aid poured in from around the world after the flooding began with $1.7 billion pledged. Leading the aid effort was the United States, which made up nearly 33 percent of the total amount. The World Bank promised an additional $900 million to aid in the recovery efforts, which it would redirect from other projects. The United Nations launched an appeal for $459 million from international groups for immediate flood relief.

Of greatest urgency were the food and medical shortages faced by those who found themselves homeless. Unclean water caused by the flooding put six million people at risk of disease, but with funding for relief moving slowly, water purifiers were hard to come by. The dirty water led to outbreaks of cholera in a number of provinces. Containing the spread of disease was dependent on the ability to reach citizens and provide proper medical care. This effort was hampered by destroyed roads and bridges that prevented aid workers from easily getting to citizens. Those seeking medical attention often travelled through the mountains, their only means of passage to other villages. Because of the damage to food stocks and cropland, even areas in Pakistan that were not affected by the floods would face a food shortage. This resulted in the price of basic food necessities skyrocketing, quadrupling in some areas.

FUTURE IMPACT

International analysts said the flooding damaged such a large swath of infrastructure that Pakistan could be set back decades. The nation had hoped to see 4.5 percent economic growth in 2010, but flooding reduced these targets back significantly, potentially to a deficit of 6 or 7 percent, according to the World Bank.

In October, a financial assessment conducted by the Asian Development Bank and World Bank estimated that $9.5 billion in damage to property, crops, and infrastructure had been caused by the floods. In addition, total recovery costs on the part of the Pakistani government were estimated at $30 billion. Pakistan had originally estimated $43 billion in damage, and although it recognized that its rebuilding effort would be slightly easier, the lower amount of damage also meant less aid from foreign sources.

The public-facing response from Pakistan's government was more positive. "We will prioritize our total budget. We will not wait for the world to give us or not give us [aid]," said Prime Minister Gilani. "We will provide whatever funds are needed to give homes to the homeless people."

This called into question how the United States might respond and what it might be willing to put toward Pakistan's redevelopment efforts. The United States had worked for years to stabilize this part of the world by gaining allies to help remove the Taliban from power. Pakistan has been a key player in this effort. With disaster assistance coming from Islamic militant groups, the Barack Obama administration's plans faced further uncertainty. However, Pakistan and the United States recognized that without quick action on redevelopment, the government risked the Pakistani Taliban becoming increasingly powerful and influential over the people of the nation. Richard Holbrooke, the U.S. special representative for Afghanistan and Pakistan before his death on December 13, 2010, said that the United States would only be able to offer so much, leaving Pakistan to come up with tens of billions of dollars on its own. But with a government that has its focus shifted from one day to the next as it combats attacks from Taliban insurgents, differing political agendas, and growing tension across the country, questions remain as to how or when Pakistan will fully recover.

—Heather Kerrigan

Following are press releases from August 26 and 27, 2010, from the office of President Asif Ali Zardari on the aid for flood victims and reconstruction of damaged provinces.

President Zardari on Aid to Flood Victims

August 26, 2010

President Asif Ali Zardari has said that Benazir Income Support Programme (BISP) has done a commendable job of providing the flood victim much need emergency relief across the country. He said this during a meeting with Federal Minister and BISP, Ms. Farzana Raja here on Thursday. The president also expressed his hope that BISP would continue its relentless efforts of helping poor and downtrodden segments of the society.

Earlier, MS. Farzana Raja briefed away the president regarding BISP's emergency relief plan for the most vulnerable flood-affectees. She said that so far Rs.3.9 billion has already been dispatched and disbursement of it would start from 30th August. She said that this cash grant was imperative and crucial to enable these hapless victims to sustain till returning to normal rehabilitation.

MS. Farzana Raja informed the president Zardari further that more than six million flood affected individuals are already registered by virtue of being part of BISP's beneficiaries' family and identifying them to provide immediate relief is relatively an easy task. She informed the delegation that that BISP has announced Rs. 12000 per family livelihood cash grant for flood affected beneficiaries, which will be distributed in three monthly grant of Rs 4000/ month.

Despite these hectic relief efforts being provided by BISP to most vulnerable flood affectees, she said, the poverty census/survey would be continued as usual to achieve more reliable data of the downtrodden families in Pakistan to maintain an effective mechanism as a selection criteria to avail assistance under any social safety initiative in the future.

President Asif Ali Zardari lauded the timely initiatives of the BISP and said that these efforts would be highly instrumental in rehabilitation of the flood devastating flood victims across the country.

SOURCE: Office of the President of the Islamic Republic of Pakistan. "President Zardari Says BISP's Timely Initiatives Would Be Instrumental for Quick Rehabilitation of the Flood Victims." August 26, 2010. http://www.pid.gov.pk/press26-08-2010.htm.

President Zardari Holds Meeting on Flood Reconstruction

August 27, 2010

President Asif Ali Zardari today called upon the housing sector of the country to adopt innovative approaches in term of technology, design and material while rebuilding houses devastated by floods so as to withstand natural disasters if, God forbid, such disasters struck the nation again. This he said while addressing a meeting on flood reconstruction and rehabilitation by the Housing sector at the Aiwan-e-Sadr today.

Those who were present during the meeting included among others Environment Minister Mr. Hameed ullah Jan Afridi, Housing Minister Mr. Rehmatullah Kakar, Chairman Pakistan Engineering Council Ms. Rukhsana Zubairi, Deputy Chairman ERRA, Chairman NDMA, Deputy Governor State Bank of Pakistan, MD National Construction, Chairpersons Institutes of Architects & Engineers, MD National Housing Authority, federal and provincial secretaries of concerned departments and representatives of private construction companies.

Briefing the journalists Spokesperson to the President Mr. Farhatullah Babar said that the President also called upon the engineers and technologists to consider the possibility of channelling flood waters away from population clusters and diverting it to the desert regions for productive use. A thought should also be given to employing mobile brick and block making machines, steel cutting and bonding machines and machines for prefabricating different structural elements to speed up the reconstruction activity, he said.

In this context, the President advised the Government to consider appointing NESPAK as the lead consultant for undertaking the rehabilitation and reconstruction of the devastated infrastructure and housing in the country, Mr. Babar informed.

The President said that the rehabilitation and reconstruction efforts for the colossal damage to the existing infrastructure requires concerted and coordinated efforts by all the stakeholders and active public private partnership. He said that the Government would accord priority to rehabilitate the flood affected people in their previous localities however new projects would also be undertaken in those localities to equip those areas with modern facilities and safeguards.

The President also directed Communication Ministry to prepare comprehensive estimates of the losses due to washing away of the roads and the amount needed to rebuild them.

The President said that satellite technology should be used in future to map the direction in which columns of flood waters gushed.

The President also said that the environmental degradation and depletion of natural resources was the major factor for erratic climatic changes and freak weather systems and we hope that such situation would not arise in future however, we must equip ourselves for protection against these havocs on one hand and take measures for improvement of the environment through afforestation and reforestation, on the other, he said.

SOURCE: Office of the President of the Islamic Republic of Pakistan. "President Chairs a Meeting on Flood Reconstruction and Rehabilitation by the Housing Sector." August 27, 2010. http://www.pid.gov.pk/press27-08-2010.htm.

OTHER HISTORIC DOCUMENTS OF INTEREST

FROM THIS VOLUME

September

FBI Report on Crime in the United States

SEPTEMBER 13, 2010

The Federal Bureau of Investigation (FBI) released an annual statistical report, *Crime in the United States, 2009*, on September 13, 2010; the document lays out the number of crimes committed in the United States from January 1 through December 31, 2009. The report shows that the number of violent crimes declined for the third consecutive year. In 2007, the decline was 0.7 percent over the previous year; in 2008, the volume of violent crimes declined by 1.9 percent; and in 2009, it declined by 5.3 percent. The volume of property crimes also decreased in 2009, by 4.6 percent, making 2009 the seventh straight year in which the volume of property crime had fallen. The volumes of the four types of violent crime—murder and nonnegligent manslaughter, aggravated assault, robbery, and forcible rape, a category that includes assaults, attempt to commit rape, and forcing a female to have sex against her will, but does not include nonforcible rape (i.e., statutory)—all declined from 2008 to 2009. Murder and nonnegligent manslaughter declined by 7.3 percent; aggravated assault decreased by 4.2 percent; robbery declined by 8 percent; and forcible rape dropped by 2.6 percent.

This year's report was accompanied by a warning against using the crime statistics presented by the FBI to rank cities, counties, and states. "These rough rankings provide no insight into the numerous variables that mold crime in a particular town, city, county, state, tribal area, or region. Consequently, they lead to simplistic and/or incomplete analyses that often create misleading perceptions adversely affecting communities and their residents," according to the report. The FBI writes that a clear analysis of any area is only possible after looking at a number of factors that impact law enforcement in each locality.

The FBI also cautions that its report only includes crimes that are reported to law enforcement. In addition, if multiple crimes are committed during one incident, only the most serious offense is reported in the FBI report; this practice obviously has an effect on the overall numbers associated with certain crimes. The U.S. Department of Justice conducts the National Crime Victimization Survey, which estimates unreported crimes. When the two studies are looked at together, they give the most accurate representation of the actual crime rate in the United States. The version of the National Crime Victimization Survey released on October 13, 2010, showed a decline in both violent crime and property crime, with violent crime falling to its lowest levels since 1973, the first year the U.S. Bureau of Justice Statistics collected data on victims of crime.

CRIME RATES

The FBI does not indicate reasons for the rise and fall of crime rates in its annual reports, and the September 2010 version came as a surprise to some observers who expected to see a rise in crime because of the continuing economic crisis and increasing number of gun purchases. Criminologists, however, said that they have never found a link between either gun ownership or recession and a rise in crime.

The decline in crime was widespread in 2009 according to crime expert Alfred Blumstein at Carnegie Mellon University. "I studied murder and robbery in 23 large high-crime cities, and homicides were down in 19 of them, and robberies were down in 21 of them. That shows this drop was large in magnitude across most big cities in the country," said Blumstein.

The rate of property crime, including burglary, larceny-theft, motor vehicle theft, and arson, fell 4.6 percent from 2008 to 2009 to a rate of 3,036.1 crimes committed per 100,000 people. The property crime rate in 2009 was 11.5 percent lower than in 2005 and 16.1 percent lower than in 2000. The FBI estimates that $15.2 billion in losses were caused by property crime, of which larceny-theft accounted for 67.9 percent, burglary 23.6, and motor vehicle theft 8.5 percent.

Nationwide, 58,871 arsons were reported in 2009, of which 44.5 percent involved structures including houses, storage units, and office buildings; 28.4 percent involved mobile property; and 27.1 percent involved other forms of property, such as crops and fences. Per event, the average dollar amount lost per arson was estimated at $17,411. Arsons decreased 10.8 percent from 2008 to 2009.

In each violent crime category—murder and nonnegligent manslaughter, forcible rape, robbery, and aggravated assault—the number of offenses declined from 2008 to 2009. The violent crime rate in 2009 was 429.4 offenses per 100,000 people, a decrease of 5.3 percent since 2008. When looking at the five- and ten-year trends in violent crime, the 2009 estimate of violent crime showed a decrease of 5.2 percent from 2005 and 7.5 percent from 2000. Aggravated assaults made up the greatest portion of all violent crimes, at 61.2 percent, while robbery accounted for 31 percent, forcible rape for 6.7 percent, and murder for 1.2 percent. The FBI annual crime report also offers information on the type of weapon used during a murder. According to the report, firearms were used during 67.1 percent of murders in the United States in 2009, 42.6 percent of robberies, and 20.9 percent of the aggravated assaults.

In 2009, the FBI reported 13,687,241 arrests for all offenses, excluding traffic violations. Of those, more than 580,000 were for violent crime, while more than 1.7 million were for property crime. Most of the arrests were for drug abuse, driving under the influence, and larceny-theft. From 2008 to 2009, the number of violent-crime arrests declined 2.3 percent; arrests for property crime increased 1.6 percent; arrests of juveniles decreased 8.9 percent; and arrests of adults decreased 1.2 percent. Males were more likely to be arrested than females, accounting for nearly three-quarters of those arrested in 2009. In addition, white Americans were more likely to be arrested than those who are black. Arrests of white citizens accounted for 69.1 percent of all arrests, while the arrest of black citizens was 28.3 percent.

Although the national trend showed crime rates decreasing across the board, not all areas of the country were impacted in a similar fashion. A number of large cities saw an increase in their murder rates in 2009, including Detroit, Michigan; Baltimore, Maryland; and Newark, New Jersey. "Although homicides were down sharply in more affluent areas and among those 25 and over, the sound of gunfire was all too common in some poor neighborhoods. It's not rosy everywhere," said James Alan Fox, a criminologist from Northeastern University.

NATIONAL ATMOSPHERE

While criminologists have never found a clear link between a bad economy and rising crime—specifically violent crime—there is a link between extended poverty and rising crime, a situation residents in some parts of the United States were beginning to find themselves in during 2009, two years into the recession. This is evidenced in cities like Detroit, where the collapse of much of its industry decades earlier caused a rise in violent crime that has yet to subside. As the murder rose in Detroit again in 2009, it was a signal that its own long-term recession could be having an impact.

When President Barack Obama took office in 2009, gun rights advocates purchased new guns in large numbers, fearful of a potential Second Amendment battle. Since his election, gun sales have risen at least 12 percent across the country. With this knowledge, there was expectation that the FBI report would reflect a rise in violent crime in 2010. However, as gun ownership rises, the numbers make it clear that violent crime is continuing to fall. This reflects the correlation researchers have found in the long-running debate on the effects of gun ownership. "There are very consistent findings that the acquisition and obtaining of carrying permits by ordinary law-abiding people has either no or very little impact on the crime rate," said David Kennedy, director of the Center for Crime Prevention and Control in New York. This knowledge has spurred the pro–gun-rights movement, which has been increasingly victorious in 2008 and 2009 in the federal courts. "Anti-gunners have lost another one of their baseless arguments," said Alan Gottlieb, founder of the Second Amendment Foundation, a pro–gun-rights organization.

The Obama administration tied the large decreases in crime rates to its investment in local law enforcement through the American Recovery and Reinvestment Act of 2009 (ARRA). "In 2009, the Obama administration provided over $4 billion in support to law enforcement and criminal justice initiatives through the American Recovery and Reinvestment Act, including $1 billion in COPS [Community Oriented Policing Services] funding to keep police officers on the street," said U.S. attorney general Eric Holder. "Investments in law enforcement play a significant role in reducing violent and property crime."

Criminologists were not as quick to jump on board with Holder's assertions, especially given the short-term nature of funds offered by the ARRA. "What's needed is sustained funding, not just for law enforcement but for prevention programs," said Fox. Fox's concern is that if the crime rate continues to fall, the government may not put as many resources toward crime prevention and crime fighting. One theory for the decrease in crime rates offered by Blumstein was the effect of the election of an African American president. He points to the 2 percent decrease in the arrests of blacks, while arrests of whites increased 2 percent. "Perhaps some youths said, 'This country isn't so bad after all,'" said Blumstein.

HATE CRIMES

In November, the FBI released its annual publication on hate crimes in the United States, which also looked at data collected in 2009. Much like most other forms of crime, the number of hate crimes fell as well, hitting its lowest point in fifteen years. The FBI reports that "while the number of law enforcement agencies submitting data to us increased—topping off at 14,222—the number of hate crime incidents reported for 2009 (6,604) was down from 2008. The number of reported victims (8,336) has also gone down."

As defined by the FBI, victims of hate crimes can be individuals, businesses, institutions, or even society as a whole. In 2009, more than 61 percent of hate crimes were carried out against people, while more than 38 percent were committed against property. More than four thousand were victim to racially motivated crimes, with 71.5 percent of these being victims of offenders prejudiced against African Americans. Antireligious hate crimes accounted for 1,575 victims, nearly three-quarters of which were committed because of an offender's anti-Jewish sentiment. More than 18 percent of hate crimes committed against individuals were motivated by sexual orientation, 13.5 percent dealt with ethnicity or national origin, and 1.2 percent were because of a person's disability.

Approximately one-third of hate crimes took place in or near the victim's home, while another 17.2 percent took place on highways, roads, alleys, or streets. More than 11 percent happened at a school, 6.1 percent in a parking lot or garage, and 4.3 percent in a place of worship.

A majority of the 6,225 known hate crime offenders were white, 18.5 percent were black, and 7.3 percent were multirace groups. More than 10 percent of offenders were of unknown race. More than five thousand of these offenders carried out crimes against individuals, with 40.3 percent committing simple assaults, 34.6 percent intimidating their victims, 23.5 percent committing aggravated assault, and 1.2 percent of offenders committing rape or murder.

After the 2009 passage of the Matthew Shepard and James Byrd, Jr., Hate Crimes Prevention Act, the FBI is now tracking crimes related to actual or perceived gender and gender identity. In addition, law enforcement officials are continuing to expand their civil rights enforcement into areas deemed most in need. "During 2010, the FBI devoted additional resources to combat hate crime in those cities most at risk for bias-motivated violence," said Special Agent Cynthia Deitle, who is in charge of the FBI's civil rights program in Washington, D.C. "Working in collaboration with state and local law enforcement agencies, as well as our non-governmental partners, we are confident we can mitigate the risks and impact hate crimes have on individuals and communities."

—Heather Kerrigan

Following are excerpts from the FBI's annual report, Crime in the United States, 2009, *released on September 13, 2010.*

 # FBI Statistics on Crime in the United States

September 13, 2010

VIOLENT CRIME

Definition

In the FBI's Uniform Crime Reporting (UCR) Program, violent crime is composed of four offenses: murder and nonnegligent manslaughter, forcible rape, robbery, and aggravated assault. Violent crimes are defined in the UCR Program as those offenses which involve force or threat of force. . . .

Overview

- In 2009, an estimated 1,318,398 violent crimes occurred nationwide, a decrease of 5.3 percent from the 2008 estimate.
- When considering 5- and 10-year trends, the 2009 estimated violent crime total was 5.2 percent below the 2005 level and 7.5 percent below the 2000 level.
- There were an estimated 429.4 violent crimes per 100,000 inhabitants in 2009.
- Aggravated assaults accounted for the highest number of violent crimes reported to law enforcement at 61.2 percent. Robbery comprised 31.0 percent of violent crimes, forcible rape accounted for 6.7 percent, and murder accounted for 1.2 percent of estimated violent crimes in 2009.
- Information collected regarding type of weapon showed that firearms were used in 67.1 percent of the Nation's murders, 42.6 percent of robberies, and 20.9 percent of aggravated assaults. (Weapons data are not collected for forcible rape.)...

MURDER

Definitions

The FBI's Uniform Crime Reporting (UCR) Program defines murder and nonnegligent manslaughter as the willful (nonnegligent) killing of one human being by another.

The classification of this offense is based solely on police investigation as opposed to the determination of a court, medical examiner, coroner, jury, or other judicial body. The UCR Program does not include the following situations in this offense classification: deaths caused by negligence, suicide, or accident; justifiable homicides; and attempts to murder or assaults to murder, which are scored as aggravated assaults....

Overview

- An estimated 15,241 persons were murdered nationwide in 2009, which is a 7.3 percent decrease from the 2008 estimate, a 9.0 percent decrease from the 2005 figure, and a 2.2 percent decrease from the 2000 estimate.
- There were 5.0 murders per 100,000 inhabitants in 2009, an 8.1 percent decrease from the 2008 rate. Compared with the 2005 rate, there was a 12.1 percent decrease in the murder rate; compared with the 2000 rate, a 10.4 percent decrease was recorded.
- More than 44 percent (44.8) of murders were reported in the South, the most populous region, with 21.3 percent reported in the West, 20.0 percent reported in the Midwest, and 13.9 percent reported in the Northeast....

FORCIBLE RAPE

Definition

Forcible rape, as defined in the FBI's Uniform Crime Reporting (UCR) Program, is the carnal knowledge of a female forcibly and against her will. Attempts or assaults to commit rape by force or threat of force are also included; however, statutory rape (without force) and other sex offenses are excluded....

Overview

- In 2009, the number of forcible rapes was estimated at 88,097. By comparison, the estimated volume of rapes for 2009 was 2.6 percent lower than the 2008 estimate, 6.6 percent lower than the 2005 number, and 2.3 percent below the 2000 level.

- The rate of forcible rapes in 2009 was estimated at 56.6 per 100,000 female inhabitants, a 3.4 percent decrease when compared with the 2008 estimated rate of 58.6.
- Rapes by force comprised 93.0 percent of reported rape offenses in 2009, and attempts or assaults to commit rape accounted for 7.0 percent of reported rapes. . . .

ROBBERY

Definition

The FBI's Uniform Crime Reporting (UCR) Program defines robbery as the taking or attempting to take anything of value from the care, custody, or control of a person or persons by force or threat of force or violence and/or by putting the victim in fear.

Overview

- Nationwide in 2009, there were an estimated 408,217 robberies.
- The estimated number of robberies decreased from the 2008 and the 2005 estimates—8.0 percent and 2.2 percent, respectively. However, the 2009 robbery estimate increased slightly from the 2000 number.
- The 2009 estimated robbery rate of 133.0 per 100,000 inhabitants reflected a decrease of 8.8 percent when compared with the 2008 rate.
- An estimated $508 million in losses were attributed to robberies in 2009.
- The average dollar value of property stolen per reported robbery was $1,244. The highest average dollar loss was for banks, which lost $4,029 per offense.
- Firearms were used in 42.6 percent of the robberies for which the UCR Program received additional information in 2009. Strong-arm tactics were used in 41.1 percent of the total number of robberies, knives and cutting instruments were used in 7.7 percent, and other dangerous weapons were used in 8.7 percent of robberies in 2009. . . .

AGGRAVATED ASSAULT

Definition

The FBI's Uniform Crime Reporting (UCR) Program defines aggravated assault as an unlawful attack by one person upon another for the purpose of inflicting severe or aggravated bodily injury. The UCR Program further specifies that this type of assault is usually accompanied by the use of a weapon or by other means likely to produce death or great bodily harm. Attempted aggravated assault that involves the display of—or threat to use—a gun, knife, or other weapon is included in this crime category because serious personal injury would likely result if the assault were completed. When aggravated assault and larceny-theft occur together, the offense falls under the category of robbery.

Overview

- There were an estimated 806,843 aggravated assaults in the Nation in 2009.
- According to 2- and 10-year trend data, the estimated number of aggravated assaults in 2009 declined 4.2 percent from 2008 and 11.5 percent when compared with the estimate for 2000.
- In 2009, the estimated rate of aggravated assaults was 262.8 offenses per 100,000 inhabitants.
- A 10-year comparison of data from 2000 and 2009 showed that the rate of aggravated assaults in 2009 dropped 18.9 percent.

- Of the aggravated assault offenses in 2009 for which law enforcement agencies provided expanded data, 26.9 percent were committed with hands, fists, and feet; 20.9 percent were committed with firearms; and 18.7 percent were committed with knives or cutting instruments. The remaining 33.5 percent of aggravated assaults were committed with other weapons. . . .

PROPERTY CRIME

Definition

In the FBI's Uniform Crime Reporting (UCR) Program, property crime includes the offenses of burglary, larceny-theft, motor vehicle theft, and arson. The object of the theft-type offenses is the taking of money or property, but there is no force or threat of force against the victims. The property crime category includes arson because the offense involves the destruction of property; however, arson victims may be subjected to force. Because of limited participation and varying collection procedures by local law enforcement agencies, only limited data are available for arson. Arson statistics are included in trend, clearance, and arrest tables throughout *Crime in the United States*, but they are not included in any estimated volume data. The arson section in this report provides more information on that offense. . . .

Overview

- There were an estimated 9,320,971 property crime offenses in the Nation in 2009.
- The 2-year trend showed that property crime decreased 4.6 percent in 2009 compared with the 2008 estimate. The 5-year trend, comparing 2009 data with that of 2005, showed an 8.4 percent drop in property crime.
- In 2009, the rate of property crime was estimated at 3,036.1 per 100,000 inhabitants, a 5.5 percent decrease when compared with the rate in 2008. The 2009 property crime rate was 11.5 percent lower than the 2005 rate and 16.1 percent under the 2000 rate.
- Larceny-theft accounted for 67.9 percent of all property crimes in 2009. Burglary accounted for 23.6 percent and motor vehicle theft for 8.5 percent.
- Property crimes in 2009 resulted in losses estimated at 15.2 billion dollars. . . .

BURGLARY

Definition

The FBI's Uniform Crime Reporting (UCR) Program defines burglary as the unlawful entry of a structure to commit a felony or theft. To classify an offense as a burglary, the use of force to gain entry need not have occurred. The UCR Program has three subclassifications for burglary: forcible entry, unlawful entry where no force is used, and attempted forcible entry. The UCR definition of "structure" includes apartment, barn, house trailer or houseboat when used as a permanent dwelling, office, railroad car (but not automobile), stable, and vessel (i.e., ship).

Overview

- In 2009, there were an estimated 2,199,125 burglaries—a decrease of 1.3 percent when compared with 2008 data.
- There was an increase of 2.0 percent in the number of burglaries in 2009 when compared with the 2005 estimate and an increase of 7.2 percent when compared with the 2000 estimate.

- Burglary accounted for 23.6 percent of the estimated number of property crimes committed in 2009.
- Of all burglaries, 61.0 percent involved forcible entry, 32.6 percent were unlawful entries (without force), and the remainder (6.5 percent) were forcible entry attempts.
- Victims of burglary offenses suffered an estimated $4.6 billion in lost property in 2009; overall, the average dollar loss per burglary offense was $2,096.
- Burglaries of residential properties accounted for 72.6 percent of all burglary offenses. . . .

LARCENY-THEFT

Definition

The FBI's Uniform Crime Reporting (UCR) Program defines larceny-theft as the unlawful taking, carrying, leading, or riding away of property from the possession or constructive possession of another. Examples are thefts of bicycles, motor vehicle parts and accessories, shoplifting, pocket-picking, or the stealing of any property or article that is not taken by force and violence or by fraud. Attempted larcenies are included. Embezzlement, confidence games, forgery, check fraud, etc., are excluded.

Overview

- In 2009, there were an estimated 6,327,230 larceny-thefts nationwide.
- The estimated number of larceny-thefts dropped 4.0 percent in 2009 when compared with the 2008 estimate. The 2009 figure was a 9.2 percent decline from the 2000 estimate.
- The rate of estimated larceny-thefts in 2009 was 2,060.9 per 100,000 inhabitants.
- From 2008 to 2009, the rate of larceny-thefts declined 4.8 percent, and from 2000 to 2009, the rate decreased 16.8 percent.
- Larceny-thefts accounted for an estimated 67.9 percent of property crimes in 2009.
- The average value of property taken during larceny-thefts was $864 per offense. When the average value was applied to the estimated number of larceny-thefts, the loss to victims nationally was nearly $5.5 billion.
- The largest portion of reported larcenies (36.3 percent) were thefts of motor vehicle parts, accessories, and contents. . . .

MOTOR VEHICLE THEFT

Definition

In the FBI's Uniform Crime Reporting (UCR) Program, motor vehicle theft is defined as the theft or attempted theft of a motor vehicle. In the UCR Program, a motor vehicle is a self-propelled vehicle that runs on land surfaces and not on rails. Examples of motor vehicles include sport utility vehicles, automobiles, trucks, buses, motorcycles, motor scooters, all-terrain vehicles, and snowmobiles. Motor vehicle theft does not include farm equipment, bulldozers, airplanes, construction equipment, or water craft such as motorboats, sailboats, houseboats, or jet skis. The taking of a motor vehicle for temporary use by persons having lawful access is excluded from this definition.

Overview

- There were an estimated 794,616 thefts of motor vehicles nationwide in 2009. The estimated rate of motor vehicle thefts was 258.8 per 100,000 inhabitants.

- The estimated number of motor vehicle thefts declined 17.1 percent when compared with data from 2008, 35.7 percent when compared with 2005 figures, and 31.5 percent when compared with 2000 figures.
- Nationwide, nearly $5.2 billion were lost to motor vehicle thefts in 2009. The average dollar loss per stolen vehicle was $6,505.
- More than 72 percent (72.1) of all motor vehicles reported stolen in 2009 were automobiles. . . .

ARSON

Definition
The FBI's Uniform Crime Reporting (UCR) Program defines arson as any willful or malicious burning or attempting to burn, with or without intent to defraud, a dwelling house, public building, motor vehicle or aircraft, personal property of another, etc. . . .

Data collection
Only the fires that investigation determined to have been willfully set—not fires labeled as suspicious or of unknown origin—are included in this arson data collection. . . .

Overview
- In 2009, 14,957 law enforcement agencies (providing 1-12 months of arson data) reported 58,871 arsons. Of those agencies, 14,693 provided expanded offense data regarding 51,389 arsons.
- Arsons involving structures (e.g., residential, storage, public, etc.) accounted for 44.5 percent of the total number of arson offenses. Mobile property was involved in 28.4 percent of arsons, and other types of property (such as crops, timber, fences, etc.) accounted for 27.1 percent of reported arsons.
- The average dollar loss due to arson was $17,411.
- Arsons of industrial/manufacturing structures resulted in the highest average dollar losses (an average of $93,287 per arson).
- In 2009, arson offenses decreased 10.8 percent when compared with arson data reported in 2008.
- Nationwide, the rate of arson was 21.3 offenses for every 100,000 inhabitants.

OFFENSES CLEARED

In the FBI's Uniform Crime Reporting (UCR) Program, law enforcement agencies can clear, or "close," offenses in one of two ways: by arrest or by exceptional means. Although agencies may administratively close a case, that does not necessarily mean that the agency can clear the offense for UCR purposes. To clear an offense within the UCR Program's guidelines, the reporting agency must adhere to certain criteria, which are outlined in the following text. *(Note: The UCR Program does not distinguish between offenses cleared by arrest and those cleared by exceptional means in collecting or publishing data via the traditional Summary Reporting System.)* . . .

CLEARANCES INVOLVING ONLY PERSONS UNDER 18 YEARS OF AGE

When an offender under the age of 18 is cited to appear in juvenile court or before other juvenile authorities, the UCR Program considers the incident for which the juvenile is being held responsible to be cleared by arrest, even though a physical arrest may not have occurred. When clearances involve both juvenile and adult offenders, those incidents are classified as clearances for crimes committed by adults. Because the clearance percentages for crimes committed by juveniles include only those clearances in which no adults were involved, the figures in this publication should not be used to present a definitive picture of juvenile involvement in crime.

Overview

- In the Nation in 2009, 47.1 percent of violent crimes and 18.6 percent of property crimes were cleared by arrest or exceptional means.
- Of the violent crimes of murder and nonnegligent manslaughter, forcible rape, robbery, and aggravated assault, murder had the highest percentage— 66.6 percent—of offenses cleared.
- When examining the property crimes of burglary, larceny-theft, and motor vehicle theft, larceny-theft was the offense most often cleared with 21.5 percent cleared by arrest or exceptional means.
- In 2009, 34.7 percent of arson offenses cleared by arrest or exceptional means involved juveniles (persons under age 18), the highest percentage of all offense clearances involving only juveniles. . . .

Arrests

Definition

The FBI's Uniform Crime Reporting (UCR) Program counts one arrest for each separate instance in which a person is arrested, cited, or summoned for an offense. The UCR Program collects arrest data on 29 offenses, as described in Offense Definitions. Because a person may be arrested multiple times during a year, the UCR arrest figures do not reflect the number of individuals who have been arrested. Rather, the arrest data show the number of times that persons are arrested, as reported by law enforcement agencies to the UCR Program.

Data collection—juveniles

The UCR Program considers a juvenile to be an individual under 18 years of age regardless of state definition. The program does not collect data regarding police contact with a juvenile who has not committed an offense, nor does it collect data on situations in which police take a juvenile into custody for his or her protection, e.g., neglect cases.

Overview

- Nationwide, law enforcement made an estimated 13,687,241 arrests (except traffic violations) in 2009. Of these arrests, 581,765 were for violent crimes and 1,728,285 were for property crimes.
- The highest arrest counts among the Part I and Part II offenses were for drug abuse violations (estimated at 1,663,582 arrests), driving under the influence (estimated at 1,440,409), and larceny-theft (estimated at 1,334,933).
- The arrest rate was 4,478.0 arrests per 100,000 inhabitants of the total estimated United States population. The arrest rate for violent crime (including murder and nonnegligent manslaughter, forcible rape, robbery, and aggravated assault)

was 191.2 per 100,000 inhabitants, and the arrest rate for property crime (including burglary, larceny-theft, motor vehicle theft, and arson) was 571.1 per 100,000 inhabitants.

- Two-year arrest trends showed violent crime arrests declined 2.3 percent when compared with 2008 arrests, while property crime arrests increased 1.6 percent when compared with the 2008 arrests.
- Arrests of juveniles for all offenses decreased 8.9 percent in 2009 when compared with the 2008 number; arrests of adults declined 1.2 percent.
- Nearly 75 percent (74.7) of the persons arrested in the Nation during 2009 were males. They accounted for 81.2 percent of persons arrested for violent crime and 62.6 percent of persons arrested for property crime.
- In 2009, 69.1 percent of all persons arrested were white, 28.3 percent were black, and the remaining 2.6 percent were of other races. . . .

SOURCE: U.S. Department of Justice. Federal Bureau of Investigation. "Crime in the United States, 2009." September 13, 2010. http://www2.fbi.gov/ucr/cius2009/index.html.

OTHER HISTORIC DOCUMENTS OF INTEREST

FROM PREVIOUS *HISTORIC DOCUMENTS*

Parliamentary Elections Held in Afghanistan

Amid threats of violence from the Taliban, on September 18, 2010, Afghanistan's residents went to the polls to elect members of the Wolesi Jirga, the nation's parliament. Elections had originally been scheduled for May 22 but were postponed by the Independent Election Commission of Afghanistan to allow more time for election reform and fraud monitoring. During initial vote counts, allegations of fraud were widespread, and a number of recounts took place. It was not until December 1 that the results were officially certified and announced, with ethnic Pashtuns claiming a majority of the body's seats.

SYSTEM REFORM

The Afghan constitution indicates that elections should take place on May 22 of the year in which a new parliament is to be elected. However, in January 2010, under pressure from the United Nations and the United States, the Independent Election Commission of Afghanistan announced that it would postpone the election until September. "The Independent Election Commission, due to lack of budget, security and uncertainty and logistical challenges . . . has decided to conduct the [*parliamentary*] election on September 18, 2010," election commission chairman Fazil Ahmad Manawi announced on January 24.

The four-month delay was expected to give the international forces currently fighting in the country a chance to improve the security situation for voters in the southernmost parts of Afghanistan where the Taliban was strongest. There was also the necessity of raising enough money to fund the election, which was estimated to cost $120 million. The Afghan government had $70 million available to put toward the election and needed to raise $50 million from international sources. The United Nations pledged available funds but said that it would not release them until the election system had been reformed in such a way as to prevent corruption and fraud.

The need to reform the election system in Afghanistan became apparent during the August 2009 presidential election. Hamid Karzai was reelected to the presidency, but widespread fraud put the legitimacy of his government in question. After Karzai was declared the winner after an initial vote count, an investigation was launched and overseen by the United Nations, which threw out nearly one-third of the ballots cast for Karzai, determining that they had been cast fraudulently. Without these votes, Karzai did not reach the 50-percent threshold required to win the election, and a runoff was scheduled. It was only after Karzai's opponent, Abdullah Abdullah, a former Afghan foreign minister, withdrew his name from consideration, over complaints that election commission officials refused to resign, that Karzai was declared victorious.

Although the international community congratulated the election commission on its determination to avoid fraud, the United States called on Karzai to reform the election system to eliminate this type of corruption from government. "This has to be a point in time in which we begin to write a new chapter based on improved governance, a much more serious effort to eradicate corruption," said U.S. president Barack Obama. In his inaugural address, Karzai promised to take the necessary steps to control corruption in his government. To assist in this effort, the United States backed two corruption investigation units that have arrested a number of senior Afghan government officials on charges of bribery. After the arrest of one of his closest advisers in July on bribery charges, Karzai fought back against these units and ordered his own investigation into their work. Representatives of Karzai's investigation announced that the corruption investigation units violated the human rights of those being arrested and that the work of the units might be unconstitutional if viewed as a U.S. encroachment on Afghan sovereignty. Karzai announced a plan to issue new rules that would regulate what the investigation units could and could not do. In December 2010, Afghani police began refusing to issue warrants related to the work carried out by the investigation units until an agreement could be reached.

Women Run for Office, Face Threats

The 2010 parliamentary election saw a record number of women campaign for seats in the Jirga. When international officials aided the Afghanis in setting up their government, they created 64 seats in the 249-seat body to be specifically held by women. The male-dominated population of Afghanistan criticized this decision, calling it an example of foreign countries misunderstanding the gender roles in the Middle Eastern nation.

In 2005, only 328 women in Afghanistan ran for seats in the Jirga, but in 2010, at least 406 women offered their names forward as contenders, some campaigning against men for the seats traditionally reserved for male representation. Women running for office faced a number of obstacles, including threatening phone calls from members of the Taliban, which forced some female candidates to withdraw their names and flee their cities. Because urban Kabul is more liberal than the remote parts of Afghanistan, women from areas around the country were more likely to leave their hometowns and campaign for seats in or near Kabul, feeling a greater sense of security. But even these candidates had their posters defaced or torn down.

Female candidates were not the only ones to receive direct threats. All of those participating in the elections—whether running for office or simply voting—faced threats from the Taliban. "We urge people not to participate in the election," said Taliban spokesperson Zabiullah Mujahid. "Everything and everyone affiliated with the election is our target—candidates, security forces, campaigners, election workers, voters are all our targets." The Taliban's threats were more than just vocal. Four of the more than two thousand candidates running for seats in the Jirga were killed during the election campaign, while many others faced serious threats on their lives. A number of campaign workers and those affiliated with the Election Commission were also killed.

Although the lead up to election day was marked by threats of violence, during the vote, only an estimated fourteen Afghanis were killed, far lower than what had been anticipated according to the North Atlantic Treaty Organization (NATO). The violence was also far lower than what was seen during the August 2009 presidential election, during which

479 violent incidents occurred. Only 303 were reported on September 18. These attacks included rocket attacks, gun battles, and a number of explosions in provinces across the country.

WIDESPREAD FRAUD

As was feared by international election observers, the extra time devoted to reforming the Afghan elections system was not enough, even though the United Nations had expressed optimism before the vote. "The electoral authorities have learned many lessons from the experience of last year, in particular in improving their systems to prevent massive fraud. These elections will not be perfect, but I am hopeful that they will be better than last year's election," said Staffan de Mistura, the UN special representative for Afghanistan. Throughout September 18, there were reports across the country of voters being turned away from polling locations or not turning out to vote because of treats from the Taliban and other antigovernment insurgents in the country.

In one polling location in Wardak, where the population is largely Pashtun, few Pashtuns showed up to vote. When vote fraud is suspected, it is up to campaign aides to call the progovernment militia to investigate. When these election guards arrived at the Wardak polling location, they found the doors locked and cardboard over the windows of the polling center. Inside, the election workers were filling out voter identification cards and stuffing the ballot boxes. While only about twenty people had voted at that location on election day, the election guards found hundreds of ballots cast for one of the local candidates, Hajji Wahedullah Kalimzai. The local officials from these areas turned a blind eye to the fraud. "Many people have voted, and almost all of the polling centers are open," Wardak governor Muhammad Haleem Fedayee announced on election day. "It looks as if about 90 percent of the people will vote today."

The candidates who thought their race had been marred by voter fraud called on the Electoral Complaints Commission, the group tasked with investigating cases of alleged fraud, to throw out the votes that could not be verified as authentic. "These elections are a shame. They are an embarrassment," said Roshanak Wardak, one of those running against Kalimzai in Wardak.

When the polls closed, it was the Independent Election Commission of Afghanistan that was set to work with the Electoral Complaints Commission to determine which votes would be counted. Approximately 23 percent of the 5.6 million votes cast were thrown out because of suspected fraud, according to election commission chairman Manawi.

ELECTION RESULTS AND PARLIAMENTARY LIMBO

When the final votes were tallied and election results announced in late November and early December, the biggest surprise was the number of those elected to parliament who were considered President Karzai's political opponents. Nearly 90 percent of those elected fit this description, according to the Kabul Center for Strategic Studies. In fact, a portion of those elected belong to the Change and Hope Party, run by Karzai's 2009 challenger Abdullah.

Only 121 of those elected to parliament in September are affiliated with a political party in Afghanistan, while the remaining 128 are considered independent. Ethnic Pashtuns, who make up the largest portion of Afghanis, took the greatest number of seats, at ninety-six; however, this was a decrease from the number of seats they won during the last parliamentary election in 2005. The group that saw the greatest increase in the number of seats gained was the ethnic Hazara group, whose members voted in higher numbers than any other ethnic group in the country; it took sixty-one seats in the Jirga, eighteen more seats than in 2005. In addition to the Pashtuns, the Tajiks won fifty-three seats. During the 2005 elections, the Pashtuns and Tajiks held 159 seats in the Jirga. The remaining seats are now held by the Uzbeks at fifteen, eight seats each for the Aimaqs and Arabs, three seats for Turkmen, two seats for the Nuristanis, and one seat each for the Balochs, Pashayees, and Turks. Female candidates won 69 of the 249 seats.

The initial results released in late November omitted one province, Ghazni, due to technical problems that prevented the certification of election results. According to election observers, however, the delay was more about the question of fraud. In Ghazni, it was believed that the Taliban had stopped most Pashtuns from voting, leading to the election of eleven candidates from the minority ethnic group in the region, the Hazaras. At the time of the November announcement, the Independent Election Commission of Afghanistan had not yet decided whether to certify the results, which could result in a stronger Taliban in the region, or announce another election, without any guarantees that the outcome would be different.

By December, the body had decided to officially certify the results from the Ghazni province as they were. New accusations of fraud surfaced, and Afghanistan's attorney general, Mohammad Ishaq Alako, called on the nation's Supreme Court to negate the results. However, according to Afghan law, no institution other than the election commission and its fraud arm can certify or overturn the election results.

Afghanistan's constitution does not indicate a specific date upon which the country's parliament must begin work. Only the president can order the start of parliament. Because of the uncertainty surrounding the election results, Karzai waited until January 26, 2011, to officially install the new parliament and begin a new session.

—Heather Kerrigan

The following is a press release from the United Nations on September 16, 2010, expressing support for the Afghan parliamentary elections; and a statement by the Independent Election Commission of Afghanistan on December 12, 2010, regarding the responsibility of election result certification.

United Nations Expresses Support for Afghan Parliamentary Elections

September 16, 2010

Staffan de Mistura, the Special Representative of the United Nations Secretary-General for Afghanistan, today visited the southern city of Kandahar with Abdullah Ahmadzai, Chief Electoral Officer of Afghanistan Independent Election Commission (IEC) to meet with local leaders and electoral officials and express UN support for Saturday's parliamentary polls.

"I visited Kandahar in order to listen to the concerns of those involved in supporting and conducting the elections, as well as to those of tribal elders who are leaders in their communities," said de Mistura.

"The purpose of my visit was to demonstrate the support of the United Nations for the independent electoral authorities and the people of Afghanistan as they prepare to vote."

De Mistura met with Tooryalai Wesa, Provincial Governor of Kandahar, Ghulam Haidar Hamedi, Mayor of Kandahar city, as well as a group of tribal elders, who updated on the final preparations for the ballot. He expressed his hope that the people of Kandahar would come out to vote on 18 September.

"Kandahar is a major centre of Afghanistan, and the people of Kandahar have a vital role to play in strengthening democracy in their country," he said.

Discussions also focused on the importance of the measures being taken by the IEC to improve the electoral process.

"The electoral authorities have learned many lessons from the experience of last year, in particular in improving their systems to prevent massive fraud. These elections will not be perfect, but I am hopeful that they will be better than last year's election."

"I am however concerned about the still low number of female searchers and female polling staff in the city and in particular in the outskirts. A substantial act of participation of women in these important elections is crucial," he concluded.

De Mistura also met with Major General Nick Carter (UK), the International Security Assistance Force (ISAF) Regional Commander, and was briefed on security preparations for the elections.

SOURCE: United Nations Assistance Mission in Afghanistan. "UN Representative Visit Kandahar to Express Support for the Elections." September 16, 2010. http://unama.unmissions.org/Default.aspx?tabid=1760&ctl=Details&mid=2002&ItemID=10434.

Independent Election Commission on Certification of Results

DOCUMENT

December 12, 2010

The Independent Election Commission in accordance to the article 156 of the Constitution of the Islamic Republic of Afghanistan: (The Independent Election Commission, for the purpose of administering and supervising any kind of elections and referring to referendum in the country in accordance with the Law, is established), Is the only legal authority, established for administering, implementing and supervising elections in the country. The IEC has always acted in line with the Law and in the light of ordinances of the operative laws in the country independently.

It is worth mentioning that the Electoral Law specifies the decision-making organizations of electoral issues (i.e. they are the IEC and the ECC.) The ECC is responsible for adjudication of all electoral complaints, decisions of which are final, while certification and announcement of the final results are only under authorities of the IEC.

Unfortunately, two weeks following announcement of the final results for 2010 WJ elections, the Attorney General's Office (AGO) of the Islamic Republic of Afghanistan, expressed various irresponsible statements with reference to the final results of 2010 WJ elections. Moreover, the AGO has tried to interfere in the electoral process by questioning the election results with excuses such as violations of the electoral law, offences and election fraud.

The IEC emphasizes that it is the only legally mandated institution that certifies and announces results of Elections and such authority does not fall under any other organization's jurisdiction. The results of 34 electoral constituencies of 2010 WJ elections were announced by IEC on 24th Nov, 2010 and of the one other constituency, taking note of the technical problems was announced on 01st, Dec, 2010 with one week delay.

Following announcement of the final results, considering article No. 83 and 86 of the constitution, the Lower House (Wolesi Jirga) has been established and the final results cannot be challenged by any institution.

Once again, the IEC insists implicitly that the IEC and the ECC are the only two institutions responsible for organizing elections (IEC) and complaint adjudication (ECC) of elections in Afghanistan. No other organization possesses the authority of expressing a statement and making a decision pertaining to electoral matters. The IEC believes that irresponsible statements of other organizations related to electoral issues issues would lead Afghanistan towards a political crisis and such organization will be responsible for such a crisis.

SOURCE: Independent Election Commission. "Independent Election Commission Press Release with Respect to the Statements of Attorney General's Office about Final Results of 2010 WJ Elections." December 12, 2010. http://www.iec.org.af/pdf/wolesi-pressr/ago_on_2010_wj_elections_results_20101212.pdf.

OTHER HISTORIC DOCUMENTS OF INTEREST

FROM PREVIOUS *HISTORIC DOCUMENTS*

U.S. Poverty Level Hits Fifteen-Year High

SEPTEMBER 16, 2010

In 2009, the poverty rate in the United States rose to its highest level in fifteen years, according to the U.S. Census Bureau's *Income, Poverty, and Health Insurance Coverage in the United States: 2009*, a report that is considered the most complete picture of the effect of the recession on Americans since it began in 2007. As expected, poverty had risen across most sectors of the American population, with the biggest rise in poverty seen in children. The report and accompanying commentary also indicated that investments made in expanding the unemployment insurance, food stamp, and other welfare benefits programs had a significant impact on a number of Americans.

POVERTY RISES ACROSS THE COUNTRY

It seemed that no one, other than senior citizens, was safe from the rising percentage of those considered to be below the poverty level in 2009, which was set at $10,956 for individuals and $21,954 for a family of four. The Census Bureau data labeled 43.6 million Americans as impoverished, or one in every seven. Children were the hardest hit. While the adult poverty rate rose from 11.7 to 12.9 percent, the percentage of children in poverty rose from 19 percent to 20.7 percent. Seniors were the only group that saw a decrease in the percentage of those in poverty with a decline from 9.7 percent to 8.9 percent. The Census Bureau data do not offer an explanation for the level of increase in childhood poverty. However, Kenneth Land, a professor of sociology at Duke University, who coordinates the annual Child and Youth Well-Being Index Project, says that data he has collected, which reflect those of the Census Bureau, can be explained by economics. "Eight million jobs have been lost," says Land. "Even if there are two earners in a family and one earns 40 to 50 percent of income, that's a huge hit on family income if one loses [*his or her*] job."

The state hardest hit by the rise in poverty was Mississippi, with 23.1 percent of its population considered below the poverty line. Arizona, Arkansas, Georgia, and New Mexico were close behind with the greatest percentages of those deemed poor. New Hampshire, on the other hand, had the lowest level of poverty at 7.8 percent of its population. By region, the Midwest saw a growth in those the Census Bureau deemed in poverty from 8.1 million to 8.8 million. In the South, the numbers climbed from 15.9 million to 17.6 million. The increase in the West was from 9.6 million to 10.5 million, and in the Northeast, the number increased from 6.3 million to 6.7 million, though as a percentage the increase was not statistically significant.

The 2009 data also reflected the long-running disparities in income between whites, blacks, and Hispanics in the United States. White, non-Hispanic citizens had a poverty rate of 9.4 percent, while the rates for African Americans and Hispanics were more than 23 percent.

The 14.3 percent overall poverty rate reached in 2009 was the third consecutive increase in the number of those classified as poor. In 2008, slightly less than forty million Americans were living in poverty, and in 2007 that number was 37.2 million. Median household income remained constant at $49,777. "This is the first time in memory that an entire decade has produced essentially no economy growth for the typical American household," said Harvard economist Lawrence Katz.

Poverty experts agree that it is likely that when the Census Bureau calculates the poverty level for 2010, it will result in another increase. Indications of this continuing rise come from food banks that are seeing a significant increase in those requiring services, as well as the rise in food stamp recipients, which is now at one in seven Americans. The likely 2010 increase is also fueled by the increasing number of young adults without a college education who the Census Bureau considers to be in poverty. Because of their lower skill sets, they are not as likely to find employment as those with a college education or more during a recession, making it more difficult to climb out of poverty. Even as the number of unemployed Americans begins to decrease, the percentage of those considered poor will not instantly improve. "Historically," says LaDonna Pavetti, a welfare expert at the Center on Budget and Policy Priorities (CBPP), a Washington, D.C., research group, "it takes time for poverty to recover after unemployment starts to go down."

There is some disagreement over how accurate the Census Bureau's current measures of poverty are. According to the Census Bureau report, "The poverty estimates in this report are based on money income before taxes, do not include the value of noncash benefits, and use the official poverty thresholds." This means that noncash benefits received by individuals and families, including tax breaks, subsidies for food and housing, and government benefits other than those offered for employment, are left out of Census Bureau poverty estimates. In addition, expenses for child care, work, and medical costs are not taken into account. The Census Bureau admits that without these figures being considered in the official poverty threshold, a complete picture is not necessarily created. In September 2011, the Census Bureau expects to release a report based on a supplemental poverty measure that will take these factors into account. This new report will be aimed at determining the success of antipoverty measures offered by federal and state governments. Currently, the Census Bureau releases two annual reports that compile other alternative measures of poverty.

OBAMA'S APPROACH

In his response to the Census Bureau's report, President Barack Obama said the data "illustrates just how tough 2009 was." He continued: "Today's numbers make it clear that our work is just beginning. Our task now is to continue working together to improve our schools, build the skills of our workers, and invest in our Nation's critical infrastructure."

During his speech, Obama gave credit to the American Recovery and Reinvestment Act of 2009 (ARRA), signed during the first months of his presidency, which injected billions of dollars into the economy in an effort to spur growth. "Because of the Recovery Act and many other programs providing tax relief and income support to a majority of working families, and especially those most in need, millions of Americans were kept out of poverty last year," Obama said.

The Census data echoed his remarks. Because of the investment in tax credits and welfare benefits such as food stamps, nearly eight million of those labeled as poor in the report would have been at or above the poverty line if government benefits were taken into account in the calculations. Further, the extensions of unemployment benefits, which are calculated in the report, kept three million families above the poverty level. Jared Bernstein, chief economist and economic policy adviser to Vice President Joe Biden, wrote in a White House blog that the stimulus package and additional economic benefits "made a real difference." He also wrote that the increase in poverty was less than had been expected by many analysts.

The Census Bureau also found that, in addition to government programs, those hoping to avoid falling below the poverty line are often sharing homes with parents, siblings, or friends. This helps to stop the percentage of those in poverty rising higher than it already has. According to the 2009 data, the number of multifamily households has increased more than 11.5 percent during the past two years.

The Brookings Institution, a policy research organization, called for an increase in programs supported by the Obama administration. "We really should be strengthening the safety net programs, not just because people need help but also it will maintain purchasing power among a large group of people," said Isabel Sawhill, a senior fellow with Brookings. Robert Greenstein, executive director of the CBPP, concurred that the focus on unemployment and other welfare benefits will help to slow the anticipated rise of the number of Americans at or below the poverty line. "We are certainly going to see significant mitigation effect again in 2010," he said.

Placing Blame

While Obama and congressional Democrats touted the success of the ARRA and investments made in welfare benefits, Republicans saw things differently. "What poor Americans—like all other Americans—need are jobs, not more government benefits," said then-representative John Linder, R-Ga., a ranking member of the House subcommittee on welfare benefits. Instead of "providing more government stimulus," Linder said, the government needs to "remove impediments to private-sector job creation."

Other conservative organizations placed blame for rising poverty on a number of social factors, including the breakdown of marriage. Robert Rector, a senior research fellow for the conservative think tank Heritage Foundation, said, "Single-mother families are almost five times more likely to be poor than married couples with children." Unwed fathers, he said, are more often employed and earn enough to lift the mother and child out of poverty. However, "few unwed parents marry," he said. Instead of focusing on job creation or additional welfare benefits, the Heritage Foundation believes the country would benefit from additional education about the benefits of marriage. This education, the Heritage Foundation said, should be targeted toward low-income communities.

—Heather Kerrigan

Following is the edited report released by the U.S. Census Bureau on September 16, 2010, on the state of poverty in the United States; and a statement by President Barack Obama on September 16, 2010, responding to the Census Bureau report.

Census Bureau Report on Poverty in the United States

September 16, 2010

[All portions of the report not corresponding to poverty have been omitted.]

[Tables, graphs and footnotes and references to them have been omitted.]

POVERTY IN THE UNITED STATES

Highlights

- The official poverty rate in 2009 was 14.3 percent—up from 13.2 percent in 2008. This was the second statistically significant annual increase in the poverty rate since 2004.
- In 2009, 43.6 million people were in poverty, up from 39.8 million in 2008—the third consecutive annual increase in the number of people in poverty.
- Between 2008 and 2009, the poverty rate increased for non- Hispanic Whites (from 8.6 percent to 9.4 percent), for Blacks (from 24.7 percent to 25.8 percent), and for Hispanics (from 23.2 percent to 25.3 percent). For Asians, the 2009 poverty rate (12.5 percent) was not statistically different from the 2008 poverty rate.
- The poverty rate in 2009 (14.3 percent) was the highest poverty rate since 1994 but was 8.1 percentage points lower than the poverty rate in 1959, the first year for which poverty estimates are available.
- The number of people in poverty in 2009 (43.6 million) is the largest number in the 51 years for which poverty estimates have been published.
- Between 2008 and 2009, the poverty rate increased for children under the age of 18 (from 19.0 percent to 20.7 percent) and people aged 18 to 64 (from 11.7 percent to 12.9 percent), but decreased for people aged 65 and older (from 9.7 percent to 8.9 percent).

IMPACT OF THE 2007 ECONOMIC DOWNTURN

The poverty rate and the number in poverty increased by 1.9 percentage points and 6.3 million between 2007 and 2009. The increase in the overall poverty rate was:

- Larger than the increase in the poverty rate during the November 1973 to March 1975 recession.
- Smaller than the increase in the poverty rates associated with the January 1980 to July 1980 and July 1981 to November 1982 combined recessions.

Between 2007 and 2009, the child poverty rate and the number in poverty increased by 2.7 percentage points and 2.1 million.

RACE AND HISPANIC ORIGIN

Both the poverty rate and the number in poverty increased for non-Hispanic Whites from 2008 to 2009 (9.4 percent and 18.5 million in 2009—up from 8.6 percent and

17.0 million in 2008). The poverty rate for non-Hispanic Whites was lower than the poverty rates for other race groups. Non-Hispanic Whites accounted for 42.5 percent of the people in poverty, compared with 64.9 percent of the total population.

For Blacks, the poverty rate and the number in poverty increased to 25.8 percent and 9.9 million in 2009, higher than 24.7 percent and 9.4 million in 2008. For Asians, the 2009 poverty rate (12.5 percent) was not statistically different from the 2008 rate, while the number of Asians in poverty increased from 1.6 million in 2008 to 1.7 million in 2009. Both the number in poverty and the poverty rate increased for Hispanics—12.4 million or 25.3 percent were in poverty in 2009, up from 11.0 million or 23.2 percent in 2008.

AGE

Between 2008 and 2009, both the poverty rate and the number in poverty increased for people aged 18 to 64 (from 11.7 percent and 22.1 million to 12.9 percent and 24.7 million). Both the poverty rate and the number in poverty decreased for people aged 65 and older (from 9.7 percent and 3.7 million to 8.9 percent and 3.4 million).

Both the poverty rate and the number in poverty increased for children under the age of 18 (from 19.0 percent and 14.1 million in 2008 to 20.7 percent and 15.5 million in 2009). The poverty rate for children was higher than the rates for people aged 18 to 64 and those aged 65 and older. Children comprised 35.5 percent of people in poverty but only 24.5 percent of the total population.

Related children are related to the householder by birth, marriage, or adoption and are not themselves householders or spouses of householders. Both the poverty rate and the number in poverty increased for related children under the age of 18 (from 18.5 percent and 13.5 million in 2008 to 20.1 percent and 14.8 million in 2009). For related children under the age of 18 in families with a female householder, 44.4 percent were in poverty compared with 11.0 percent of related children in married-couple families.

Both the poverty rate and the number in poverty increased for related children under the age of 6 (from 21.3 percent and 5.3 million in 2008 to 23.8 percent and 6.0 million in 2009). Of related children under the age of 6 in families with a female householder, 54.3 percent were in poverty—four times the rate of related children in married-couple families (13.4 percent).

NATIVITY

Of all people, 87.6 percent were native born and 12.4 percent were foreign born. The poverty rate and the number in poverty for the native-born population increased from 12.6 percent and 33.3 million in 2008 to 13.7 percent and 36.4 million in 2009. Among the foreign-born population, 19.0 percent or 7.2 million people lived in poverty in 2009—up from 17.8 percent or 6.5 million people in 2008.

Of the foreign-born population, 42.6 percent were naturalized U.S. citizens; the remaining were not U.S. citizens. The poverty rate and the number in poverty in 2009 for naturalized U.S. citizens were 10.8 percent and 1.7 million, estimates not statistically different from 2008. The poverty rate and the number in poverty for those who were not U.S. citizens rose to 25.1 percent and 5.4 million in 2009—up from 23.3 percent and 5.0 million in 2008.

REGION

The poverty rate increased from 2008 to 2009 in three of the four regions, while all four regions had increases in the number of people in poverty. The Midwest poverty rate increased from 12.4 percent to 13.3 percent, and the number in poverty increased from 8.1 million to 8.8 million; the South increased from 14.3 percent to 15.7 percent and from 15.9 million to 17.6 million; and the West increased from 13.5 percent to 14.8 percent and from 9.6 million to 10.5 million. The 2009 poverty rate for the Northeast was 12.2 percent (not statistically different from the 2008 rate), while the number in poverty increased from 6.3 million in 2008 to 6.7 million in 2009.

RESIDENCE

Inside metropolitan statistical areas, the poverty rate and the number of people in poverty were 13.9 percent and 35.7 million in 2009—up from 12.9 percent and 32.6 million in 2008. Among those living outside metropolitan areas, the poverty rate and the number in poverty were 16.6 percent and 7.9 million in 2009—up from 15.1 percent and 7.3 million in 2008.

Between 2008 and 2009, the poverty rate for people in principal cities increased from 17.7 percent to 18.7 percent, while the number in poverty increased from 17.2 million to 18.3 million. Within metropolitan areas, people in poverty were more likely to live in principal cities. While 38.2 percent of all people living in metropolitan areas in 2009 lived in principal cities, 51.2 percent of poor people in metropolitan areas lived in principal cities. For those inside metropolitan areas but not in principal cities, the poverty rate and the number in poverty rose from 9.8 percent and 15.3 million to 11.0 percent and 17.4 million.

WORK EXPERIENCE

Among all workers aged 16 and older, both the poverty rate and the number in poverty increased to 6.9 percent and 10.7 million from 6.4 percent and 10.1 million.

Between 2008 and 2009, the increase in poverty among workers was driven almost entirely by those who worked less than full-time, year-round. Both the percentage and number in poverty increased among less than full-time, year-round workers from 13.5 percent and 7.3 million to 14.5 percent and 8.0 million. For full-time, year-round workers, the percentage and number in poverty in 2009 were not statistically different from 2008—2.7 percent and 2.6 million.

Among those who did not work at least one week last year, the poverty rate and the number in poverty increased to 22.7 percent and 18.9 million in 2009 from 22.0 percent and 17.1 million in 2008.

FAMILIES

The poverty rate and the number of families in poverty were 11.1 percent and 8.8 million in 2009 compared with 10.3 percent and 8.1 million in 2008.

The poverty rate and the number of families in poverty increased across all types of families: married-couple families (5.8 percent and 3.4 million in 2009 from 5.5 percent and 3.3 million in 2008); families with a female householder (29.9 percent and 4.4 million in 2009 from 28.7 percent and 4.2 million in 2008); and families with a male householder (16.9 percent and 942,000 in 2009 from 13.8 percent and 723,000 in 2008).

Depth of Poverty

Categorizing a person as "in poverty" or "not in poverty" is one way to describe his or her economic situation. The income-to-poverty ratio and the income deficit or surplus describe additional aspects of economic well-being. While the poverty rate shows the proportion of people with income below the appropriate poverty threshold, the income-to-poverty ratio gauges the depth of poverty. It shows how close a family's income is to their poverty threshold. The income-to-poverty ratio is reported as a percentage that compares a family's or an unrelated person's income with the appropriate poverty threshold.

For example, a family with an income-to-poverty ratio of 110 percent has income that is 10 percent above their poverty threshold.

The income deficit or surplus shows how many dollars a family's or an unrelated person's income is below (or above) their poverty threshold. For those with an income deficit, the measure is an estimate of the dollar amount necessary to raise a family's or a person's income to their poverty threshold.

Ratio of Income to Poverty

In 2009, 6.3 percent of all people, or 19.0 million people, had income below one-half of their poverty threshold, up from 5.7 percent and 17.1 million in 2008. This group represented 43.7 percent of the poverty population in 2009. The percentage and number of people with income below 125 percent of their threshold was 18.7 percent and 56.8 million, up from 17.9 percent and 53.8 million in 2008. For children under the age of 18 in 2009, 9.3 percent and 6.9 million lived in families with income below 50 percent of their poverty threshold, up from 8.5 percent and 6.3 million in 2008. The percentage and number of children living in families with income below 125 percent of their poverty threshold in 2009 was 26.3 percent and 19.6 million, up from 25.0 percent and 18.6 million in 2008.

The demographic makeup of the population differs at varying degrees of poverty. Children represented 24.5 percent of the overall population, 35.5 percent of the people in poverty, and 36.3 percent of the people with income below 50 percent of their poverty threshold. On the other hand, the elderly represented 12.7 percent of the overall population, 7.9 percent of the people in poverty, and 5.2 percent of those with income below 50 percent of their poverty threshold. For people with income below 125 percent of their poverty threshold, 34.5 percent were children while 9.7 percent were elderly.

Income Deficit

The income deficit for families in poverty (the difference in dollars between a family's income and its poverty threshold) averaged $9,042 in 2009, which was not statistically different from the 2008 estimate. The average income deficit was larger for families with a female householder ($9,218) than for married-couple families ($8,820).

The average income deficit per capita for families with a female householder ($2,776) was higher than for married-couple families ($2,211). The income deficit per capita is computed by dividing the average deficit by the average number of people in that type of family. Since families with a female householder were smaller, on average, than married-couple families, the larger per capita deficit for female house-holder families reflects their smaller average family size as well as their lower average family income.

For unrelated individuals in poverty, the average income deficit was $6,158 in 2009. The $5,926 deficit for women was lower than the $6,443 deficit for men.

ALTERNATIVE/EXPERIMENTAL POVERTY MEASURES

The poverty estimates in this report are based on money income before taxes, do not include the value of noncash benefits, and use the official poverty thresholds. The money income measure does not completely capture the economic well-being of individuals and families; and there are many questions about the adequacy of the official poverty thresh-olds. Families and individuals also derive economic well-being from noncash benefits, such as food and housing subsidies, and their disposable income is determined by both taxes paid and tax credits received. The official poverty thresholds developed more than 40 years ago do not take into account rising standards of living or such things as child care expenses, other work-related expenses, variations in medical costs across population groups, or geographic differences in the cost of living. Poverty estimates using the new Supplemental Poverty Measure, which the Census Bureau expects to publish for the first time in September 2011, will address these concerns.

National Academy of Sciences (NAS) - Based Measures and Estimates of the Effect of Benefits and Taxes

The Census Bureau currently computes several alternative measures of income and pov-erty which fall into two categories: 1) poverty measures based on the 1995 recommenda-tions of the National Academy of Sciences Panel on Poverty and Family Assistance called NAS-based measures and 2) other income and poverty estimates in the Effect of Benefits and Taxes on Income and Poverty series (R&D). The NAS-based measures use both alter-native poverty thresholds and an expanded income definition. The R&D estimates use the official thresholds but examine the impact of adding or subtracting specific components from an enhanced definition of income.

The Census Bureau will release estimates for these alternative measures for 2009 at a later date. Estimates for 2008 for the R&D series can be found at www.census.gov/hhes/www /cpstables/032009/rdcall/toc.htm and 2008 estimates for the NAS-based measures can be found at <www.census.gov/hhes/www/povmeas/tables.html>.

The Census Bureau also makes available a research file that provides microdata with variables used to construct the NAS-based alternative measures, available at <www.census.gov/hhes/www/povmeas/datafiles.html>, and an expanded version of the CPS ASEC public-use file that includes estimates of the value of taxes and noncash benefits, avail-able at <www.bls.census.gov/cps_ftp.html#cpsmarch>. Both microdata files are currently available for 2008. Data for 2009 will be released before the end of the year.

CPS Table Creator II

CPS Table Creator II is a Web-based tool designed to help researchers explore alternative income and poverty measures. The tool is available from a link on the Census Bureau's poverty Web site <www.census.gov/hhes/www/cpstc/apm/cpstc_altpov.html>. Table Creator II allows researchers to produce poverty and income estimates using their own combinations of threshold and resource definitions and to see the incremental impact of the addition or subtraction of a single resource element. For example:

- If the cash value of Supplemental Nutrition Assistance Program (SNAP) benefits were added to the money income of families, this would move the family resources of 2.2 million people above the official poverty line in 2008.
- Taking into account the value of the federal Earned Income Tax Credit would reduce the number of children classified as poor in 2008 by 2 million.
- In 2008, the number of elderly people in poverty would be higher by 13 million people if Social Security payments were excluded from money income, more than quadrupling the number of elderly people in poverty.

Researchers can also estimate poverty rates using alternative poverty thresholds. Many other countries use relative poverty measures with thresholds that are based on a percentage of median or mean income. Table Creator II allows researchers to estimate poverty rates using a relative poverty threshold calculated as any percentage of mean or median equivalence-adjusted income. For example, using poverty thresholds based on 50 percent of median income rather than the official poverty thresholds would increase the overall poverty rate in 2008 from 13.2 percent to 21.9 percent.

SOURCE: U.S. Census Bureau. "Income, Poverty, and Health Insurance Coverage in the United States: 2009." September 16, 2010. http://www.census.gov/prod/2010pubs/p60-238.pdf.

President Obama on the Census Bureau Poverty Report

DOCUMENT

September 16, 2010

Our economy plunged into recession almost 3 years ago on the heels of a financial meltdown and a rapid decline in housing prices. Last year, we saw the depths of the recession, including historic losses in employment not witnessed since the Great Depression. Today the Census Bureau released data that illustrates just how tough 2009 was: Along with rising unemployment, incomes failed to rise for the typical household, the percentage of Americans without health insurance rose to 16.7 percent, and the percentage of Americans living in poverty increased to 14.3 percent.

But the data released today also remind us that a historic recession does not have to translate into historic increases in family economic insecurity. Because of the Recovery Act and many other programs providing tax relief and income support to a majority of working families, and especially those most in need, millions of Americans were kept out of poverty last year.

The substantial expansion of the Children's Health Insurance Program (CHIP) helped inoculate our children from the economic distress experienced by their parents, as there was little change in the percentage of children without health insurance. The

Affordable Care Act will build on that success by expanding health insurance coverage to more families.

Even before the recession hit, middle class incomes had been stagnant and the number of people living in poverty in America was unacceptably high, and today's numbers make it clear that our work is just beginning. Our task now is to continue working together to improve our schools, build the skills of our workers, and invest in our Nation's critical infrastructure.

For all of our challenges, I continue to be inspired by the dedication and optimism of America's workers, and I am confident that we will emerge from this storm with a stronger economy.

SOURCE: U.S. Executive Office of the President. "Statement on the Release of Census Bureau Data on Income, Poverty, and Health Insurance Coverage." *Daily Compilation of Presidential Documents* 2010, no. 00758 (September 16, 2010). http://www.gpo.gov/fdsys/pkg/DCPD-201000758/pdf/DCPD-201000758.pdf.

OTHER HISTORIC DOCUMENTS OF INTEREST

FROM PREVIOUS *HISTORIC DOCUMENTS*

France Imposes Ban on Face Veils and Deports Roma Gypsies

SEPTEMBER 29 AND OCTOBER 7 AND 19, 2010

In September 2010, the French parliament approved a ban on wearing face veils in public places after months of contentious public debate over the necessity and true motive of the proposal. The new law passed several years after France instituted a similar ban on wearing headscarves and other religious symbols in schools. Coupled with an aggressive program of repatriating Roma Gypsies living in France to Romania and Bulgaria, the ban drew allegations of racism and xenophobia from international observers.

Roots of a Controversy

Tensions between the French government and the country's immigrant populations, particularly the estimated five million Muslims living primarily in the suburbs of Paris and other metropolitan areas, had been brewing for several years. As a country, France had long believed in the importance of assimilating diverse communities into the broader society, to the point of forbidding the collection of any demographic statistics that are based on ethnicity or religion. Some viewed France's large Muslim population and its failure to thoroughly assimilate as a threat to national unity and a challenge to the country's secular identity. Others pointed to the recent rise of Islamic militancy since the beginning of the global War on Terror as sufficient reason to be distrustful of these immigrants. This suspicion ultimately led to feelings of alienation among Muslim communities and accusations of discrimination in schools and in the workplace.

The government's move under President Jacques Chirac and his party, the Union pour un Mouvement Populaire (UMP), to ban the wearing of headscarves and other "conspicuous signs of religious affiliation" in public schools in 2004 further fed these tensions. While the ban also applied to items such as large Christian crosses and Jewish skullcaps, many suspected the law was targeted primarily at the Muslim headscarf. Then, in 2005, a series of youth protests broke out in Clichy-sous-Bois, an eastern suburb of Paris, and spread to cities across the country. A police pursuit of several Muslim teenagers, two of whom were killed when they climbed the wall of a power substation, spurred the riots. While the police claimed to be pursuing a different group of alleged burglars and had not harmed the teens, those living in similar suburban communities described the incident as yet another example of police harassment of Muslims and part of a broader pattern of social and racial prejudice.

Veils Are "Not Welcome"

In June 2009, President Nicolas Sarkozy ignited a new round of controversy during his first state of the nation speech when he said full veils and face coverings were "not welcome" in France. "The problem of the burqa is not a religious problem, it's a problem of liberty and women's dignity. It's not a religious symbol, but a sign of subservience and debasement," he said. Sarkozy echoed his statement in his New Year's address in January 2010 and took one step further, calling for an "unambiguous" parliamentary resolution against such veils, including the burqa and the niqab.

On January 26, a parliamentary committee released a report recommending that parliament adopt a ban on wearing full face veils on public transportation and in hospitals, schools, and government offices, despite the interior ministry's estimates that a relatively small number of women, approximately nineteen hundred, wear such veils. The committee further suggested that any woman who defied the ban should be denied the services offered in those locations, including state benefits, and that foreign women who insist on wearing the veils in public should be prevented from obtaining asylum or French citizenship. "It is the symbol of the repression of women, and ... of extremist fundamentalism," said National Assembly president Bernard Accoyer. "This divisive approach is a denial of the equality between men and women and a rejection of co-existence side-by-side, without which our republic is nothing."

In April 2010, the Pew Global Attitudes Project conducted a survey that found that 82 percent of French citizens polled supported the proposal, while only 17 percent opposed a ban. Then–justice minister Michèle Alliot-Marie defended the ban against claims that the law was intended to target a specific religion, arguing that it simply reinforced French values of integration and dignity of all individuals. Some French Muslim leaders also seemed accepting of a ban on face veils. "Islam, in the West, must adapt its faithful," said Dalil Boubakeur, rector of the Great Mosque of Paris. The Socialist Party denounced the proposed ban, claiming it would be too difficult to enforce and expressing concerns that such a law would stigmatize Muslim women, rather than grant them greater equality. Other critics claimed such a ban would violate basic human rights to freedom of speech and expression. In a rare display of concurring opinions, U.S. president Barack Obama and al-Qaida leader Ayman al-Zawahiri criticized the proposal as an insult to Muslims. Muslim women also argued that the ban would force them to stay home, as they would not be able to hide their faces in public.

Yet the UMP pushed forward with a formal bill that closely mirrored the key recommendations of the committee's report and declared, "No one shall, in any public space, wear clothing designed to conceal the face." The proposed bill did include several exceptions, stating that the ban would not apply "if such clothing is prescribed by law or regulations, is justified on medical or professional grounds or is worn in the context of sporting practices, festivities, or artistic or traditional events." If a woman defied the law, she would be charged a $190 fine, while anyone who forced a woman to wear a full veil would face a fine of up to $38,000 and one year in jail. If approved, the law would not take effect until six months following its passage, in order to provide the government with sufficient time to educate Muslim women about the change of policy and enforcement measures.

On July 13, the National Assembly voted overwhelmingly in favor of the ban's passage, 335 to 1, with most members of the Socialist Party abstaining. The Senate followed suit on September 14, approving the measure 246 to 1, again with most Socialist Party representatives abstaining. Following the vote, the bill was referred to the Constitutional Council to ensure it was in line with the French constitution. On October 7, the Council ruled that "the law forbidding concealing the face in public conforms to the Constitution" but noted that the law should not be applied to places of worship that are open to the public lest it "restrict the exercise of religious freedom."

SENDING THE ROMA HOME

While the French parliament pursued the ban on wearing face veils, government officials began executing a plan to repatriate thousands of Roma, a nomadic people whose ancestors are believed to have originated in northern India, to their home countries. In 2010, an estimated four hundred thousand Roma were living in long-term communities in France, while another twelve thousand Roma who had immigrated to France from Romania and Bulgaria were living in illegal camps.

A 2004 European Union (EU) directive guarantees freedom of movement and residency for citizens of the European Economic Area as long as they can prove that they are working as an employee, are working as a self-employed person, are studying, or have enough income to avoid relying on the public funds available in whichever European state they choose to settle in. If they are unable to provide such evidence, their right of free movement is limited to three months. Many of the Roma living in France were in violation of this directive, as they did not have work permits or other documentation to prove they were self-sufficient.

In addition, police in the town of Saint-Aignan clashed with dozens of Roma in July after an officer shot and killed a twenty-two-year-old Roma who drove through a security checkpoint without stopping. Roma attacked the local police station with hatchets and iron bars, burned cars, and cut down trees in protest, prompting President Sarkozy to call an emergency ministerial meeting. Officials ultimately decided to begin dismantling three hundred illegal camps, which Sarkozy described as "sources of illegal trafficking, of profoundly shocking living standards, of exploitation of children for begging, of prostitution and crime."

Police began taking down Roma camps in August 2010, and the government made arrangements for the Roma to be flown back to their countries of origin. Those who agreed to leave received 300 Euros each and an additional 100 Euros per child. Those who did not were relocated to temporary shelters or other accommodations.

The program generated immediate criticism from human rights organizations, who claimed the campaign deliberately stigmatized a peaceful and law-abiding community in order to strengthen Sarkozy's support among right-wing voters. The European Roma Rights Centre said the plan "reinforces discriminatory perceptions about Roma and travelers and inflames public opinion against them." Former prime minister Dominique de Villepin described the deportations as "a stain of shame on our flag," and Vatican officials called on France to halt the program. Romanian officials also warned against "xenophobic reactions" and questioned the legality of the program under EU law. "We understand the position of the French government," said Romanian president Traian Basescu. "At the same time, we support unconditionally the right of every Romanian citizen to travel without restrictions within the EU." The policy also caused divisions within the UMP, with then–French foreign and European affairs minister Bernard Kouchner claiming he was "shocked" by the government's singular focus on the Roma.

On August 31, then–French secretary of state for European affairs Pierre Lellouche and then–immigration and integration minister Eric Besson met with EU commissioners in Brussels to defend the program. Lellouche claimed Romania was to blame, because the country had not taken sufficient steps to integrate its Roma minority into society. Besson denied that authorities were carrying out systematic deportations, insisting that each Roma's case was considered individually on the same merits as any European migrant.

Nearly two weeks later, an internal government memo was leaked to the press that seemed to refute Besson's argument and suggested that officials were in fact deliberately targeting the Roma. The memo sought to remind police chiefs of a "specific objective" set by Sarkozy and ordered that "three hundred camps or illegal settlements must be evacuated within three months; Roma camps are a priority." The document reignited the anger of human rights groups and political opponents. Viviane Reding, vice president for justice of the European Commission, decried the program as "a disgrace," saying, "This is a situation I had thought Europe would not have to witness again after the Second World War." Her comments brought a sharp reaction from Lellouche, who noted, "A plane ticket back to the European Union country of origin is not the same thing as death trains and the gas chambers" and said the government would continue with its program.

On September 29, the European Commission informed French officials that they had two weeks to prove that they were not violating the EU's free movement directive and were not deliberately targeting the Roma, or else the country could face litigation proceedings. By October 19, the commission reported that it was satisfied with the French response to its request, and that it would not pursue further disciplinary action.

POLITICAL MOTIVES

Throughout both controversies, Sarkozy's opponents claimed he was pandering to far-right voters in an attempt to distract from France's economic issues and bolster his sagging poll numbers. Others within the UMP insisted the face-veil ban and deportation of Roma were merely part of a broader effort to fight crime. While the UN Committee on the Elimination of Racial Discrimination has argued that racism and xenophobia are undergoing a "significant resurgence" in France, it remains to be seen whether Sarkozy will continue to pursue similar policies and maintain his hard-line stance as the 2012 election approaches.

—Linda Fecteau

Following is a press release from the European Union on September 29, 2010, assessing France's Roma deportation policy; the October 7, 2010, French Constitutional Council decision regarding the country's full-face veil ban; and an October 19, 2010, press release from the European Union following up on its request to France for additional information on its Roma policy.

European Commission on France's
Roma Deportation

September 29, 2010

EUROPEAN COMMISSION ASSESSES RECENT DEVELOPMENTS IN FRANCE, DISCUSSES OVERALL SITUATION OF THE ROMA AND EU LAW ON FREE MOVEMENT OF EU CITIZENS

As announced earlier this month, the European Commission today assessed recent developments in France and discussed the overall situation of the Roma and EU law on free movement of EU citizens.

The Commission heard presentations by Vice-President Viviane Reding, responsible for Justice, Fundamental Rights and Citizenship, Commissioner László Andor, responsible for Social Affairs, Employment and Inclusion, and Commissioner Cecilia Malmström, responsible for Home Affairs.

The Commission concluded the following:

1. The right of every EU citizen to free movement within the Union is one of the fundamental principles of the EU. As the guardian of the Treaties, it is the Commission's duty to ensure its full and effective implementation by all Member States.

2. The Member States are responsible for and entitled to take the measures to protect public safety and public order on their territory. In doing so, they must respect the rules laid down in the 2004 Directive on Free Movement, the fundamental rights of EU citizens and avoid discrimination, notably on grounds of nationality or the belonging to an ethnic minority.

3. Recent developments in France have led to a detailed exchange between the Commission and the French authorities on the application of EU law on free movement of people. The Commission took note today of the assurances given by France at the highest political level on 22 September 2010 that

- Measures taken by the French authorities since this summer did not have the objective or the effect of targeting a specific ethnic minority, but treated all EU citizens in the same manner;
- The administrative instruction ("circulaire") of 5 August 2010 that was not in conformity with this orientation was annulled and replaced by a different instruction on 13 September 2010;
- The French authorities fully ensure an effective and non-discriminatory application of EU law in line with the Treaties and the EU Charter of Fundamental Rights.

4. The Commission noted equally that France reaffirms its commitment to a close and loyal cooperation on these matters. The Commission will pursue the exchange with the French authorities and is sending a letter to the French authorities with detailed questions regarding the practical application of the political assurances provided.

5. In order to provide legal certainty to Member States and EU citizens, in particular in controversial situations, it is of utmost importance that the procedural and

substantive safeguards included in the 2004 Directive on Free Movement are fully and correctly transposed by and in the Member States. At this stage, the Commission considers that France has not yet transposed the Directive on Free Movement into national legislation that makes these rights fully effective and transparent. Therefore, the Commission decided today that it will issue a letter of formal notice to France requesting the full transposition of the directive, unless draft transposition measures and a detailed transposition schedule are provided by 15 October 2010. The letter of formal notice would be sent in the context of the October 2010 package of infringement procedures.

6. At the same time, the Commission is analysing the situation of all other EU Member States under the Directive on Free Movement to assess whether it will be necessary to initiate infringement proceedings also in other cases. Consequently, it will send a letter of formal notice in similar cases also in the context of the next packages of infringement procedures.

7. The Commission reiterated today that the social and economic integration of the Roma represents a common challenge and a common responsibility for all EU Member States. The Commission's Communication on this issue adopted on 7 April 2010 lists a series of important measures that need to be taken at national and EU level to improve the situation of the Roma as quickly as possible.

8. To this effect, and on the basis of the work of the Roma platform and of the Roma Task Force set up by the Commission on 7 September 2010 to analyse the use and effectiveness of EU and national funds by all Member States for Roma inclusion, the Commission will present an EU Framework for National Roma Integration Strategies in April next year. This EU Framework, based on the report of the Roma Task Force, will notably assess the use of national and European funding and make proposals for a more effective implementation of EU funds in tackling Roma exclusion for the current and forthcoming programming periods. The multidimensional problems of Roma minority will be dealt with in the context of the ten basic principles of the Communication for Roma inclusion and within the frame of enhanced cooperation among all stakeholders. In addition, the EU Framework will seek to ensure a more efficient monitoring of and support to national and European efforts with regard to Roma integration. To that end, and in the frame of the Europe 2020 Strategy, the Commission will invite Member States to present their own national strategies for the inclusion of Roma which could feature in their national reform programmes. The forthcoming flagship initiative on a "Platform against poverty" will constitute an integrated framework of actions to support horizontal priorities such as the integration of Roma citizens. The European Commission also expects Member States to be explicit and ambitious about Roma when setting their national Europe 2020 targets in the fields of poverty reduction, employment and education.

9. The Commission will closely work together with all EU Member States in the preparation of the EU Framework for National Roma Integration Strategies. The EU's Fundamental Rights Agency will be associated to this work.

10. The Commission will report on progress made to the European Parliament and the European Council before summer 2011.

SOURCE: European Union. Press Releases. "European Commission Assesses Recent Developments in France, Discusses Overall Situation of the Roma and EU Law of Free Movement of EU Citizens." September 29, 2010. http://europa.eu/rapid/pressReleasesAction.do?reference=IP/10/1207.

France Prohibits Wearing of Full Face Veil in Public

October 7, 2010

Decision n° 2010 - 613 DC of October 7th 2010

Act prohibiting the concealing of the face in public.

On September 14th 2010 the Constitution Council received a referral, pursuant to paragraph 2 of Article 61 of the Constitution, from the President of the National Assembly and the President of the Senate, pertaining to the Act prohibiting the concealing of the face in public

THE CONSTITUTIONAL COUNCIL

Having regard to Ordinance n° 58-1067 of November 7th 1958 as amended (Institutional Act on the Constitutional Council);
Having heard the Rapporteur;
ON THE FOLLOWING GROUNDS:

1. The President of the National Assembly and the President of the Senate have referred for review by the Constitutional Council the Act prohibiting the concealing of the face in public. They have not raised any particular contention regarding this statute.

2. Section 1 of the statute referred for review provides: "No one shall, in any public space, wear clothing designed to conceal the face". Section 2 of the same statute provides: "I. For the purposes of the application of the foregoing section, the public space shall be composed of the public highway and all premises open to the public or used for the provision of a public service. – II The prohibition set forth in section 1 hereinabove shall not apply if such clothing is prescribed by law or regulations, is justified on medical or professional grounds or is worn in the context of sporting practices, festivities, or artistic or traditional events." Section 3 of the same statute provides that failure to comply with the prohibition set forth in section 1 of the statute shall be punishable by a fine imposed for offences of the second category.

3. Article 4 of the Declaration of the Rights of Man and the Citizen of 1789 proclaims: "Liberty consists in being able to do anything which does not harm others: thus the exercise of the natural rights of every man has no bounds other than those which ensure to other members of society the enjoyment of these same rights. These bounds shall be determined solely by the law". Article 5 of the same Declaration proclaims: "The Law shall prohibit solely those actions which are harmful to society. Nothing which is not prohibited by law shall be impeded and no-one shall be compelled to do that which the law does not prescribe". Article 10 proclaims: "No one shall be harassed on account of his opinions and beliefs, even religious, on condition that the same do not disturb public order as determined by law". Lastly, paragraph 3 of the Preamble to the Constitution of 1946 provides: The law shall guarantee women equal rights to those of men in all spheres".

4. Sections 1 and 2 of the statute referred for review are intended to respond to practices, which until recently were of an exceptional nature, consisting in concealing the face in the public space. Parliament has felt that such practices are dangerous for public safety and security and fail to comply with the minimum requirements of life in society. It also

felt that those women who conceal their face, voluntarily or otherwise, are placed in a situation of exclusion and inferiority patently incompatible with constitutional principles of liberty and equality. When enacting the provisions referred for review Parliament has completed and generalized rules which previously were reserved for ad hoc situations for the purpose of protecting public order.

5. In view of the purposes which it is sought to achieve and taking into account the penalty introduced for non-compliance with the rule laid down by law, Parliament has enacted provisions which ensure a conciliation which is not disproportionate between safeguarding public order and guaranteeing constitutionally protected rights. However, prohibiting the concealing of the face in public cannot, without adversely affecting Article 10 of the Declaration, result in restricting the exercising of religious freedom in places of worship open to the public. With this qualification, sections 1 to 3 of the statute referred for review are not unconstitutional.

6. Section 4 of the statute referred for review, which punishes by a term of one year's imprisonment and a fine of € 30 000 any person forcing another person to conceal the face, and sections 5 to 7 thereof concerning the coming into effect of said statute and the application thereof, are not unconstitutional.

HELD

<u>Article 1</u>: With the qualification set forth in paragraph 5 hereinabove, the Act prohibiting the concealing of the face in public is constitutional.

<u>Article 2</u>: This decision shall be published in the Journal officiel of the French Republic. Deliberated by the Constitutional Council sitting on October 7th 2010 and composed of Mr Jean-Louis DEBRE, President, Mr Jacques BARROT, Mrs Claire BAZY MALAU-RIE, Messrs Guy CANIVET, Michel CHARASSE, Jacques CHIRAC, Renaud DENOIX de SAINT MARC, Valéry GISCARD d'ESTAING, Mrs Jacqueline de GUILLENCHMIDT and Mr Pierre STEINMETZ

SOURCE: Constitutional Council of France. "Act Prohibiting the Concealing of the Face in Public." October 7, 2010. http://www.conseil-constitutionnel.fr/conseil-constitutionnel/root/bank_mm/anglais/en2010_613dc.pdf.

European Union Reassesses French Deportation of Roma

October 19, 2010

STATEMENT BY VIVIANE REDING, VICE-PRESIDENT OF THE EUROPEAN COMMISSION, EU COMMISSIONER FOR JUSTICE, FUNDAMENTAL RIGHTS AND CITIZENSHIP, ON THE RECENT DEVELOPMENTS CONCERNING THE RESPECT FOR EU LAW AS REGARDS THE SITUATION OF ROMA IN FRANCE

"The situation of Roma in France over this summer has raised substantial concerns. Therefore, the Commission, and I personally, have been following developments very closely during the past months.

On 29 September, the Commission emphasised that procedural safeguards must be respected whenever the right of EU citizens to free movement is restricted by public authorities. The Commission believes that procedural safeguards, as they are included in the EU's Free Movement Directive of 2004, serve to protect EU citizens against arbitrary, discriminatory or disproportionate decisions.

The Commission therefore asked the French government to ensure that these procedural safeguards are included in French legislation. And that this legislation is put into place swiftly.

We formally requested France to reply to our concerns by 15 October. In parallel, we prepared a letter of formal notice to be sent to France in case of a non-satisfactory response.

I'm glad to say today that France has responded positively, constructively and in time to the Commission's request.

Last Friday, the French authorities submitted detailed documentation to the Commission. This documentation includes draft legislative measures and a credible calendar for putting the procedural safeguards required under the EU's Free Movement Directive into French legislation by early 2011. France has thus done what the Commission had asked for.

This is proof of the good functioning of the European Union as a Community governed by the rule of law.

Following the official commitments made by France last Friday, the European Commission will now, for the time being, not pursue the infringement procedure against France decided by the College of Commissioners on 29 September.

The European Commission will closely watch over the full implementation of the commitments made by France, in the interest of EU law and EU citizens. The Commission also stands ready to assist the French authorities in ensuring that the new legislation is put in place swiftly and in full compliance with EU law.

In addition, the Commission will continue its work on promoting the economic and social integration of Roma in all EU Member States, whether country of origin or host country. We need to go to the root of the problem and encourage stronger national efforts in providing access to housing, education, health and the labour market and in eradicating poverty. In the context of the work of the Roma Task Force established by the Commission in September, we will examine how EU funds can help to further strengthen national measures for Roma integration. On this basis, the Commission will present an EU Framework for national Roma strategies next April.

It is now for all policy-makers, national as well as European, to show that the commitment to this largest European minority is not just a one-off matter. But that we now move on to action and results, on the basis of our European values and the fundamental right of non-discrimination".

SOURCE: European Union. Press Releases. "Statement by Viviane Reding, Vice-President of the European Commission, EU Commissioner for Justice, Fundamental Rights and Citizenship, on the Recent Developments Concerning the Respect for EU Law as Regards the Situation of Roma in France." October 19, 2010. http://europa.eu/rapid/pressReleasesAction.do?reference=MEMO/10/502&type=HTML.

OTHER HISTORIC DOCUMENTS OF INTEREST

FROM PREVIOUS *HISTORIC DOCUMENTS*

Ecuador in Crisis

SEPTEMBER 30, 2010

On September 30, 2010, a protest by Ecuadorian police and military forces escalated into a crisis. A state of emergency was put in place after protestors erected road blocks, shut down the country's main airports, and attacked Ecuadorian president Rafael Correa with tear gas. The president sought treatment in a hospital, which was then surrounded by protestors. After a thirty-five-minute gun battle with protestors, which left two police officers dead, Correa left the hospital unharmed. The rebellion has renewed concerns over political stability in the country and put Correa's hard-line approach to implementing his policies in the spotlight.

Political Tensions Mount as Controversial Laws Are Passed

In the months leading up to the crisis, Ecuador's National Assembly faced paralysis. Political tensions, which had been high since late 2009, peaked as the left-wing president and his ruling party, Alianza País (AP), put forward a number of pieces of controversial legislation. Upon entering office in 2007, Correa pledged to fulfill his promise of a "Citizens' Revolution," which would increase the role of the state in the economy by building new infrastructure and passing new laws. But given financial constraints and opposition from rival political parties, by mid-2010, the reform process had stalled. Correa largely laid the blame for the delays on a conspiracy by the opposition. To add to his woes, there were signs that the fragmented opposition could unite in its opposition to the bills, which included reforms of the media, hydrocarbons sector, education, and water management.

With widespread opposition to the legislation and holding only 53 out of 124 seats in the legislature, in mid-2010 the AP postponed debate over the important bills in order to avoid defeat by the opposition. The postponement of the debate was in itself controversial, as the president of the National Assembly, Fernando Cordero (AP), moved to unilaterally block the debate. Ecuador's constitution requires that two-thirds of assembly members approve a postponement. Cordero's action was largely seen as undermining the rule of law in Ecuador.

Nevertheless, in the month leading up to the legislative holiday beginning in mid-August, the controversial bills came up for debate. In late July, a bill that would have reformed Ecuador's central bank, allowing it to channel private deposits into public investment schemes, was defeated in the National Assembly. The defeat—the first for President Correa since he assumed office—came as a blow to his administration, which saw the bill as a centerpiece of its reform agenda. In late July, however, controversial political maneuvers by the president ensured the passage of the hydrocarbon legislation without legislative debate. Then again in early August the AP was successful in pushing through its reforms to higher education, although the party was forced to make concessions to some of the smaller political parties to ensure its passage. After the legislation was passed, Correa threatened to veto any changes made to original legislation. On September 3, the president acted on his warning, issuing partial vetoes on aspects of legislation regarding the civil service, land use, and higher education.

The alienation of the radical left-wing Maoist and indigenous parties, which were initially loyal to the AP, combined with opposition to parts of President Correa's legislative agenda from large interest groups, including public employees, indigenous groups, student unions, and teachers, led to increased political squabbling in the National Assembly and accusations from both the AP and the vote-buying opposition. Correa's combative political style and belligerent rhetoric compounded the infighting, creating an atmosphere ripe for political unrest in a country that has seen seven presidents since 1996—and three ousted prematurely.

With political tensions running high, on September 29, a public austerity bill passed the National Assembly. Again, Correa had used his veto power to change legislation after it passed in early September. Critics claimed that the legislation would cut benefits and eliminate promotions, but government officials countered that the bill would only slow the rate of salary increases, in part by ending the practice of awarding bonuses after each promotion. Despite the government's attempt to reassure those who would be affected, protests erupted the following day.

Protests Erupt

The unrest began when members of the military and police, angered by the austerity measures, set up road blocks around the country and occupied several barracks. Local media broadcast images of police burning tires in the streets of Ecuador's major cities, including the largest city, Guayaquil, and the capital, Quito. Protestors occupied the building housing the National Assembly. Correa responded to the unrest by issuing a statement from a military barrack in Quito: "If you want to kill the president, here he is. Kill him, if you want to. Kill him if you are brave enough." The president went on to say, "If you want to seize the barracks, if you want to leave citizens undefended, if you want to betray the mission of the police force, go ahead. But this government will do what has to be done. This president will not take a step back." After attempting to negotiate with the protestors, Correa was attacked with tear gas, physically assaulted, and doused with hot water, forcing him to flee.

Correa claimed that one of the tear gas canisters exploded near his head, causing minor injuries and forcing him to seek treatment at a hospital. From the hospital, the president claimed that the violence was "a coup attempt led by the opposition and certain sections of the armed forces and the police." In particular, Correa placed the blame on Lucio Gutiérrez, a former president and head of the opposition Patriotic Society Party. Meanwhile, the protestors had followed Correa to the hospital, where they allegedly fired tear gas at his civilian supporters, who had amassed at the hospital in a show of solidarity. Further unrest flared up when it was reported that Correa was being held against his will inside the hospital as protestors laid siege.

Elsewhere, around three hundred military personnel took control of the runways at the Mariscal Sucre International Airport in Quito, causing the cancellation of all flights. The airport closure was, however, short-lived, as the runways reopened approximately nine hours later. The country's second largest airport at Guayaquil was also closed for a time. Many Ecadorian businesses and schools closed due to the civil unrest. The governor of the central bank, Diego Borja, warned Ecuadorians not to withdraw money from banks after reports surfaced of looting.

Support for the President

The head of the country's Armed Forces Joint Command, General Luis Ernesto Gonzalez, expressed the support of his troops for President Correa: "We live in a state which is governed by laws, and we are subordinate to the highest authority which is the president of the republic. We will take whatever appropriate action the government decides on." The military leadership's support for the president suggested that the military was not directly involved in the unrest. Nevertheless, General Gonzalez did "emphatically request" that the president revise the controversial civil service legislation in a bid to soothe tensions and calm the uprising.

Meanwhile, Ecuador's neighbors and close allies also vocalized their support for President Correa. Both Colombia and Peru closed their borders with Ecuador, while Venezuelan president Hugo Chavez posted a message on Twitter, a social networking website, encouraging neighboring countries to "wake up" to the situation that the protestors "are trying to oust President Correa." The U.S. government also backed Correa's presidency and was "closely monitoring" events there.

A Dramatic Rescue Attempt

After nightfall, soldiers stormed the hospital in which Correa was holed up. The troops reportedly used automatic weapons and stun grenades in order to end the siege and free the president. The operation, in which two police officers were killed, was successful and Correa emerged unharmed. In a speech from the balcony at the presidential palace, the president stated that the events of September 30 were an attempt to topple his government and not, as many observers agreed, a protest that got wildly out of control. The president said that "those people made the institution look so bad that they attacked their co-citizens, that they abused the weapons given to them by the society to which they belong, that they dishonoured the police uniform. Of course, all the people who can be identified will have the corresponding sanction. There will be no forgiving nor forgetting."

The President's Coup Claims Are Disputed

Correa's claims that the drama of September 30 was a coup attempt appear to be ill-founded. Neither the protestors or members of the opposition called for the president to step down, nor was there a clear leader of the uprising. Indeed, Guayaquil mayor Jaime Nebot, a fierce opponent of Correa, denounced the protests and any attempt to bring down the administration of the president. Some viewed the uprising as a culmination of the dissatisfaction of many groups in Ecuadorian society over Correa's policies. A member of the opposition Pachakutik indigenous party, Lourdes Tibán, blamed the president for the uprising, claiming that various sectors of society had been "trampled on by the government." Correa's apparent unwillingness to negotiate on many issues has spurred growing opposition, raising the risk of further political instability in Ecuador.

—Hilary Ewing

Following is a September 30, 2010, press release from the Ecuadorian president Rafael Correa on the violence in his country; a statement from September 30, 2010, by the spokesperson for UN secretary-general Ban Ki-moon expressing concern over the events in Ecuador; and a letter from Rep. Dennis Kucinich, D-Ohio, on September 30, 2010, urging the United States to take action in Ecuador.

DOCUMENT

Ecuador's President's Remarks on *Recent Violence in His Country*

September 30, 2010

FROM THE GOVERNMENT OF ECUADOR TO THE WORLD:

In light of the current attempt to destabilize democracy in Ecuador through the illegal actions of elements of the police force, the international community should know that:

Today, a group of police officers decided to violate the constitution and the law through an act of mutiny with the excuse of rejecting the approval by the National Assembly of a new law regulating the public sector. This illegal action, pushed by groups seeking the rupture of democratic order, has as its end goal the disruption of a historical process of political, economic and social change supported by the vast majority of Ecuadorian citizens.

The struggle of the Ecuadorian Government to create a revolutionary citizens movement transcends the national arena and is based on universal principles of democracy and the dedication to the equality and sovereignty of all people. The government's commitment to these principles has been made manifest through social policies representing unprecedented milestones in the history of this country:

1. More than US$6 billion invested to ensure free, high-quality public health care.
2. The defense of labor rights, including the elimination of all forms of worker exploitation and an increase in salaries to provide a fair, living wage for all Ecuadorians (including the police force, whose salaries doubled under this administration).
3. More than US$5.6 billion in credit for private enterprise development, with an emphasis on small and medium-sized businesses.
4. More than 200,000 families benefiting from housing subsidies.

National sovereignty lies with the people, whose will is the basis for any governmental authority and which is exercised through the legitimate institutions of public power. Therefore, it is the irrefutable right of the people to vigilantly defend, as they have, democracy and the continuation of the Government that they have entrusted to oversee the Ecuadorian state.

We reaffirm the public commitment expressed by President Rafael Correa to defend democracy and the process of change embodied by the Citizens Revolution to the end. We will never give in to pressure from economic and political sectors that have conspired with certain members of the national police to attempt a coup d'etat.

The Citizens Revolution belongs to the people and against the people no conspiracy can triumph.

SOURCE: Embassy of Ecuador in the United States. "Press Release from the Presidency of Ecuador on the Current Situation." September 30, 2010. http://www.ecuador.org/blog/?p=887.

UN Secretary General Expresses Support for Ecuadorian Democracy

September 30, 2010

Secretary-General Ban Ki-moon has voiced deep concern at today's developments in Ecuador, where the President has been hurt during protests and some members of the police and military forces have reportedly been insubordinate.

Mr. Ban "expresses his strong support for the country's democratic institutions and elected government," his spokesperson said in a statement.

"The Secretary-General is also concerned about the physical condition and personal welfare of President Rafael Correa."

Media reports say Mr. Correa was taken to hospital after being hit by tear gas during a demonstration in the capital, Quito. The protests relate to Government measures that will cut some benefits for public servants such as police officers.

"The Secretary-General calls on all actors to intensify efforts to resolve the current crisis peacefully, within the rule of law," today's statement added. "He welcomes the endeavours of the Organization of American States and other regional actors to contribute to an early, constructive resolution."

SOURCE: United Nations. News Centre. "Ecuador: UN Chief Expresses Deep Concern at Civil Unrest." September 30, 2010. http://www.un.org/apps/news/story.asp?NewsID=36304&&Cr=ecuador&&Cr1=.

Rep. Kucinich Calls on United States to Support Ecuador

September 30, 2010

After the President of Ecuador was injured in what he called an attempted Coup D'état, Congressman Dennis Kucinich (D-OH) today wrote to President Obama, urging him to make it clear that the United States will only recognize the democratically elected government of Ecuador led by President Rafael Correa.

The full text of the letter follows:

September 30, 2010
The Honorable Barack Obama
President of the United States
The White House
Washington, D.C.

Dear Mr. President:
I write to express my deep concern over reports of violence and a possible attempted coup in Ecuador.

Reports indicate that violence in the country is at such a level that Ecuadorian President Rafael Correa has been hospitalized and that police seem to have also shut down the main airport. It appears as though the government is attempting to stabilize the country without resorting to violence.

It is of utmost importance at this time that the United States makes its support for democracy unequivocal and well-known. The United States needs to clearly state that we will only recognize democratically elected President Correa and that we will work together with regional partners and the Organization of American States to ensure the continuity of Correa's democratically elected government in Ecuador.

Unfortunately, such a statement was not made last year at the onset of the coup in Honduras. Our silence contributed to an atmosphere in the country characterized by widespread reports of brutal oppression, killing, torture and disappearances that continue today. We cannot allow such a dangerous precedent to be set in Ecuador.

I urge you to immediately announce unequivocal support by the US for democracy in Ecuador.

Sincerely,

/s/

Dennis J. Kucinich

Member of Congress

SOURCE: U.S. Congress. Office of Rep. Dennis Kucinich. "Kucinich Requests Support for Ecuadorian Democracy." September 30, 2010. http://kucinich.house.gov/News/DocumentSingle.aspx?Document ID=209615.

OTHER HISTORIC DOCUMENTS OF INTEREST

FROM PREVIOUS *HISTORIC DOCUMENTS*

October

UN Releases Report on War Crimes in the Congo

OCTOBER 1, 2010

After two years of field research and hundreds of interviews, on October 1, 2010, the United Nations released a mapping report on the human rights and humanitarian law violations committed in the Democratic Republic of the Congo (DRC) between 1993 and 2003. The report reviewed hundreds of murders, detentions, and acts of torture that were committed during this time and implicated eight foreign actors, including the African nations of Rwanda, Burundi, and Uganda, and twenty-one armed Congolese groups as responsible for the crimes. Rwanda, Burundi, and Uganda attacked the United Nations for releasing the report and demanded that it be retracted. The United Nations stood by the report and called for an investigation to determine whether those responsible for the atrocities—the names of whom the United Nations kept out of the report—could be tried for their crimes.

DRAFT REPORT RELEASED

In 1997, the United Nations began formulating a plan to investigate human rights violations in the DRC but did not revisit the plan until 2005 when the UN peacekeeping mission in the country found three mass graves, believed to contain the bodies of Hutu civilians. At that point, the United Nations announced that it would undertake "a mapping exercise of the most serious violations of human rights and international humanitarian law." It hoped that the report would lead to justice for the people and government of the DRC for atrocities suffered inside the nation, formerly known as Zaire.

Work on the mapping report began in mid-2008. The authors were tasked with reporting violations of human rights in the DRC between March 1993 and June 2003; determining whether the DRC's justice system could effectively try and prosecute anyone found responsible of such violations; and making recommendations to the government of the DRC on how to deal with any uncovered human rights violations and what role the international community could play in bringing those responsible to justice. The human rights specialists who acted as authors of the report interviewed more than one thousand people and compiled fifteen hundred documents of evidence. For each instance of human rights violations, the United Nations required two independent sources to ensure that all data were accurate and verifiable.

During the ongoing investigation, the United Nations made clear that it was not seeking to find and hold anyone personally responsible for the violence, but instead wanted to expose what had happened during the decade between 1993 and 2003. For that reason, no one involved was named in the report, but the UN high commissioner for human rights, Navi Pillay, kept a confidential database of the names of those alleged to have committed war crimes. These names would only be used if a trial was held in the DRC or the International Criminal Court (ICC).

Before its official release in October 2010, a copy of the report was leaked. The draft report concluded that what took place in the DRC severely violated human rights. "The vast majority of incidents listed in this report point to the commission of prohibited acts such as murder, willfully causing great suffering, or serious injury to body and health, rape, intentional attacks on the civilian population, and unlawful and arbitrary pillage and destruction of civilian goods, which are sometimes essential to survival of a civilian population, primarily against protected persons." The report focused most of its attention on attacks carried out by the Rwandan army and the Congolese rebel movement, which was led by Laurent Kabila, father of the DRC's current president, Joseph Kabila.

The attacks carried out by these groups were targeted toward the thousands of ethnic Hutus from Rwanda who fled across the border into the DRC. In 1994, the Hutu-backed government undertook a genocidal campaign that killed more than eight hundred thousand people based in Rwanda, most of whom were ethnic Tutsis. Hutus—both those responsible for the Tutsi genocide and those escaping to save their lives—fled to the DRC. Rwanda claims that it entered the Congo in an effort to find those responsible for the 1994 Tutsi genocide, but findings in the UN report said the murder of Hutus in the DRC between 1996 and 1997 suggest "circumstances and facts from which a court could infer the intention to destroy the Hutu ethnic group in the DRC in part," the mapping report states. It continues: "The extensive use of edged weapons . . . and the apparently systematic nature of the massacres of survivors after the camps had been taken suggest that the numerous deaths cannot be attributed to the hazards of war or seen as equating to collateral damage." The draft report did not specifically call the Hutu murders genocide, but it did determine that an international court could make such an inference based on the UN's evidence. "The apparent systematic and widespread attacks described in this report reveal a number of inculpatory elements that, if proven before a competent court, could be characterized as crimes of genocide," the report states.

Rwanda struck back. "The desire to validate the double genocide theory is consistently present throughout the draft Mapping Report by mirror-imaging the actors, ideology, and methods employed during the 1994 Rwandan genocide," the Rwandan government said in a statement. Rwanda called the UN mapping report a tactic meant to diminish the magnitude of the 1994 Tutsi genocide. In response, the nation threatened to withdraw its peacekeeping troops from Darfur, but later backed down under the condition that it would be allowed to submit comments to the United Nations before the final report was released.

Uganda and Burundi, two other nations named in the report, came out strongly against the draft's findings. The report stated that Ugandan troops entered the DRC in 1997 in support of Congolese rebel troops that were trying to overthrow the DRC government. The rebel troops are said to have been responsible for mass murders of Hutu refugees from Rwanda, as well as members of the former Hutu-backed Rwandan government.

The Ugandan troops remained until 2003, and during that time the United Nations alleges that the troops committed multiple war crimes, including executions of civilians, unlawful detentions, and torture. In a letter sent to the United Nations, which was released in conjunction with the final report, Uganda called the findings a "compendium of rumors deeply flawed in methodology, sourcing and standard of proof" and called on the United Nations not to publish the final version of the report. If the United Nations did choose to publish the report, Uganda threatened to remove its international peacekeeping forces from Somalia. "Such sinister tactics undermine Uganda's resolve to continue contributing to, and participating in, various regional and international peacekeeping operations," said Uganda's foreign affairs minister, Sam Kutesa.

The United Nations claims in its mapping report that at the same time Hutus fled Rwanda, they also left Burundi in search of refuge in the DRC to escape Hutu-Tutsi ethnic violence. Tutsi-backed Burundian troops entered the DRC in search of Hutu refugees, killing those they found. Following the release of the draft report, Burundi's statement to the United Nations demanded that any and all allegations about its army be removed and called it a report aimed at destabilizing the region.

The DRC called the UN report credible. "The victims deserve justice and they deserve that their voices are heard by my government and by the international community," said the Congolese representative to the United Nations, Atoki Ileka. While the nation said the crimes committed came as no surprise to a government that had for years dealt with the fallout, Ileka said the government was "appalled at the horrific nature and scope" of the crimes detailed. The DRC did criticize the United Nations for not responding to the nation's earlier calls for a panel to investigate possible war crimes committed by Burundi, Rwanda, and Uganda in the DRC.

FINAL REPORT RELEASED

After the leak of the draft report, the United Nations decided to delay publication of the final version until comments could be received from all nations implicated. On October 1, 2010, the final five-hundred-fifty-page report was issued and was accompanied by responses from Angola, Burundi, the DRC, Rwanda, and Uganda. In all, 617 serious human rights violations that occurred between 1993 and 2003 were detailed in the report. "The period covered by this report is probably one of the most tragic chapters in the recent history of the DRC," the report states. "Indeed, this decade was marked by a string of major political crises, wars and multiple ethnic and regional conflicts that brought about the deaths of hundreds of thousands, if not millions, of people."

Much of the media coverage after the August leak of the draft report was focused on the violence in DRC on the part of Rwanda, Burundi, and Uganda. But upon final release, Pillay wanted to shift the focus back to the DRC, which had suffered the most. "First and foremost, the Mapping Report is a report about the DRC. Yes, it does refer to the presence of foreign forces which were involved in the conflict in the DRC, and it does point to the responsibility of those forces for human rights violations," Pillay said.

The purpose of the mapping report was not only to make an official record of the crimes that occurred in the DRC, but also to help the government seek justice for those who were harmed. As part of its exercise, the mapping report team made recommendations to the DRC as to how to seek criminal prosecution against those allegedly responsible for the 617 violations. The report suggests that the DRC rely on its international partners and the United Nations to bring those responsible to justice. "The millions of Congolese victims of violations committed by an extraordinarily wide range of actors deserve nothing less," said Pillay. The necessity of bringing closure to the issue is especially essential for the thirty thousand children who were recruited to fight during the violence and the thousands more who suffered rape, torture, displacement, and other tragedies. "If this situation is allowed to continue, there is a risk that a new generation will be created that has known nothing but violence, and violence as a means of conflict resolution, thus compromising the country's chances of achieving lasting peace," the report states.

UNITED NATIONS FOLLOW-UP

After the final report was released, the United Nations called for a full investigation to determine whether the incidents discussed in the report could be considered genocide. For years, human rights activists have claimed that the crimes committed against Hutus in the DRC should be tried in the ICC as genocide. The UN mapping report instead chose not to label the reported crimes as genocide, stressing the importance of further criminal investigations and trials to reach this decision. "The report stresses that this question can only be addressed by a competent court," said Pillay.

As to those responsible for the human rights violations detailed in the report, it will be up to the DRC to decide whether it wants to seek action in the ICC and rely on international assistance or if it will bring those responsible to its own judicial system, which the United Nations recognizes as weak and lacking in any punishment structure. In her introduction to the report, Pillay stressed the importance of using the data collected by the United Nations to seek justice. "It is inherently difficult to render justice in a situation where the violence and suffering is so widespread. Yet, grievances and allegations of abuses which are not investigated and resolved all too often serve as grounds for groups seeking to mobilize constituencies for armed conflict. The culture of impunity in the DRC—which continues today—has encouraged the creation and evolution of armed groups and the use of violence to resolve disputes and gain control over natural resources," she said.

The Rwandan government of President Paul Kagame had the most to lose from the release of the report and any possible investigation. Prior to his term in office, in 1994, the Hutu-backed government killed more than eight hundred thousand Rwandan citizens, most of whom were ethnic Tutsis. Kagame's rebel movement took control of the government and has been credited with ending the Tutsi genocide. However, in the years since he first took office, the tactics of his administration have been called into question regarding the Rwandan government's entry into the Congo to seek out the Hutus who fled across the border into the DRC after Kagame's Rwandan Patriotic Front toppled the Hutu-backed government. But whether a charge of genocide against Kagame's government could hold up in court is questionable because his government did invite the Hutu refugees back into the country, and he extended other gestures of goodwill toward the Hutu citizens even after conducting a military-like campaign in the DRC. It is anticipated that members of Kagame's government could be first to go to trial.

—Heather Kerrigan

Following are excerpts from the United Nations report on war crimes in the Congo, released on October 1, 2010.

DOCUMENT

United Nations Report on War Crimes in the Congo

October 1, 2010

[The table of contents and footnotes have been omitted.]

FOREWORD

This report is the result of interviews with several hundred interlocutors, both Congolese and foreign, who witnessed atrocities in the country: it substantiates their accounts and reflects their aspirations for justice. No report however, can adequately describe the horrors experienced by the civilian population in Zaire, now the Democratic Republic of the Congo (DRC), where almost every single individual has an experience to narrate of suffering and loss. In some cases, victims became perpetrators, while perpetrators were themselves sometimes subjected to serious violations of human rights and international humanitarian law, in a cycle of violence that has not yet abated. The report is intended to be representative of the grave acts of violence that affected—directly or indirectly—a vast number of people living in the DRC. While it neither aims to establish individual responsibility, nor lay blame, the report—in full candour—reproduces the often shocking accounts by victims and witnesses of the tragedies they experienced. The report is intended as a first step towards the sometimes painful but nonetheless essential process of truth-telling after violent conflict.

This report makes an assessment of the justice system in the DRC, based on insights from various stakeholders in the justice sector, including those who were victims of its shortcomings. It presents a number of options to be considered by both Congolese and international actors in the difficult task of reforming the justice system, which faces multiple challenges. It calls for renewed Government commitment to ensure that justice becomes one of the fundamental pillars of Congolese democracy. Lastly, it looks to the future by identifying a number of paths that could be pursued by Congolese society to come to terms with its past, to fight impunity, and to face its contemporary challenges in a manner that prevents the re-occurrence of such atrocities.

Through their testimonies in this report, the Congolese people have demonstrated their commitment to truth and to justice. The ultimate impact of this project will depend on follow-up actions by the Government and the people of the DRC. While the primary responsibility to define and implement an approach to transitional justice lies with the Government and the people of the DRC, they deserve the support of the international community in this endeavour. The Office of the United Nations High Commissioner for Human Rights will remain a committed partner of the Democratic Republic of the Congo in the important quest for truly sustainable peace.

Navanethem Pillay
United Nations High Commissioner for Human Rights

EXECUTIVE SUMMARY

[The sections detailing mandate, background, and implementation of the mapping exercise have been omitted.]

I. Inventory of the most serious violations of human rights and international humanitarian law committed on the territory of the DRC between March 1993 and June 2003

15. The period covered by this report is probably one of the most tragic chapters in the recent history of the DRC. Indeed, this decade was marked by a string of major political crises, wars and multiple ethnic and regional conflicts that brought about the deaths of hundreds of thousands, if not millions, of people. Very few Congolese and foreign civilians living on the territory of the DRC managed to escape the violence, and were victims of murder, mutilation, rape, forced displacement, pillage, destruction of property or economic and social rights violations. Aside from its historical contribution to documenting these serious violations and fact-finding during this period, the ultimate purpose of this inventory is to provide the Congolese authorities with the elements they need to help them decide on the best approach to adopt to achieve justice for the many victims and fight widespread impunity for these crimes.

16. The Mapping Exercise report is presented chronologically, reflecting four key periods in the recent history of the DRC, each preceded by an introduction explaining the political and historical background in which the violations were committed. Each period is organised by provinces and sometimes subdivided into groups of victims and presents a description of the violations committed, the groups allegedly involved and the approximate number of victims.

A. March 1993–June 1996: Failure of the democratisation processes and regional crisis

17. The first period covers violations committed in the final years of the regime of President Mobutu and is marked by the failure of the democratisation process and the devastating consequences of the Rwandan genocide on the declining Zairian state, in particular in the provinces of North Kivu and South Kivu. During this period, 40 incidents were listed. The most serious violations of human rights and international humanitarian law documented, were concentrated for the most part in Katanga, North Kivu and in the city-province of Kinshasa.

B. July 1996–July 1998: First Congo War and the Alliance des forces démocratiques pour la libération du Congo-Zaire (AFDL) regime

18. The second period concerns violations allegedly committed during the First Congo War and the first year of the regime established by President Laurent-Désiré Kabila. With 238 listed incidents, this period has the greatest number of incidents in the whole of the decade under examination. The information available today points to the significant role of other countries in the First Congo War and their direct implication in the war, which led to the overthrow of the Mobutu regime. At the start of the period, serious violations were committed against Tutsi and Banyamulenge civilians, principally in South Kivu. This period was then characterised by the apparently relentless pursuit and mass killing (104 reported incidents) of Hutu refugees, members of the former Armed Forces of Rwanda (later "ex-FAR") and militias implicated in the genocide of 1994 (Interahamwe), allegedly by the Alliance des forces démocratiques pour la libération du Congo-Zaïre (AFDL). A proportion of the AFDL's troops, arms and logistics were apparently supplied by the

Armée patriotique rwandaise (APR), the Uganda People's Defence Force (UPDF) and by the Forces armées burundaises (FAB) throughout the Congolese territory. Hutu refugees, who it appears were often rounded up and used by the ex-FAR/Interahamwe as human shields during their flight, began a long trek across the country from east to west towards Angola, the Central African Republic or the Republic of the Congo. This period was also marked by serious attacks on other civilian populations in all provinces without exception, in particular allegedly by the Forces armées zaïroises (FAZ) retreating towards Kinshasa, the ex-FAR/Interahamwe driven back by the AFDL/APR and the Mayi-Mayi.

C. AUGUST 1998–JANUARY 2000: SECOND CONGO WAR

19. The third period concerns the inventory of violations committed between the start of the Second Congo War in August 1998, and the death of President Laurent-Désiré Kabila. This period includes 200 incidents and is characterised by the intervention on the territory of the DRC of the government armed forces of several countries, fighting alongside the Forces armées congolaises (FAC) (Zimbabwe, Angola and Namibia) or against them, and also the involvement of multiple militia groups and the creation of a coalition under the banner of a new political and military movement, the Rassemblement congolais pour la démocratie (RCD), which would later split on several occasions. During this period the DRC was racked by numerous armed conflicts: "Some [...] international, others internal and [...] national conflicts that became internationalised. Participants in these conflicts include at least eight national armies and irregular armed groups". In spite of the signing of the Lusaka Ceasefire Agreement on 10 July 1999 by all the parties, which called for the respect of international humanitarian law by all parties and the definitive withdrawal of all foreign forces from the national territory of the DRC, the fighting continued, as did the serious violations of human rights and international humanitarian law allegedly by all parties to the conflict. On 16 June 2000, the UN Security Council, in its Resolution 1304 (2000), called for all parties to cease hostilities and demanded that Rwanda and Uganda withdraw from the territory of the DRC. It was not until the signing of two new agreements with Rwanda (Pretoria Agreement) and Uganda (Luanda Agreement) in 2002, that these foreign forces began to withdraw from the country.

20. This period was marked by attacks on civilians believed to be Tutsi, in particular in Kinshasa, Katanga, Orientale Province, East and Kasai Occidental, Maniema and North Kivu. Within the context of the war and the conflicts across the whole of the territory, civilian populations were broadly speaking the victims of serious violations of human rights and international humanitarian law allegedly by all parties in the conflicts and throughout the territory, but especially in North Kivu and South Kivu, Orientale Province (in particular in Ituri), Katanga, Équateur and also Bas-Congo.

D. JANUARY 2001–JUNE 2003: TOWARDS TRANSITION

21. Lastly, the final period lists 139 incidents describing the violations committed in spite of the gradual establishment of a ceasefire along the front line and the speeding up of peace negotiations in preparation for the start of the transition period on 30 June 2003. During this period, fighting that had shaken the province of Ituri, in particular the ethnic conflicts between the Lendu and the Hema, reached an unprecedented peak. The period was marked by clashes between the Forces armées congolaises (FAC) and the

Mayi-Mayi forces in Katanga province. As in previous periods, the main victims of the parties involved in the conflict were civilian populations throughout the territory, particularly in Orientale Province, North Kivu, South Kivu, Maniema and Kasai Oriental provinces.

E. LEGAL CLASSIFICATION OF ACTS OF VIOLENCE COMMITTED IN THE DRC BETWEEN MARCH 1993 AND JUNE 2003

22. It must be stated that the vast majority of the 617 most serious incidents described in this report could, if investigated and proven in a judicial process, point to the commission of multiple violations of human rights but above all of international humanitarian law. It did not appear either appropriate or essential to classify in law each of the hundreds of violent incidents listed. It was therefore decided instead to identify the legal framework applicable to the main waves of violence and to point to the possible general legal classification of the incidents or groups of incidents reported.

WAR CRIMES

23. This term is generally used to refer to any serious breaches of international humanitarian law committed against civilians or enemy combatants during an international or domestic armed conflict, for which the perpetrators may be held criminally liable on an individual basis. Such crimes are derived primarily from the Geneva Conventions of 12 August 1949 and their Additional Protocols I and II of 1977, and the Hague Conventions of 1899 and 1907. Their most recent codification can be found in article 8 of the Rome Statute of the International Criminal Court (ICC) of 1998.

24. The vast majority of incidents listed in this report could, if investigated and proven in a judicial process, point to the commission of prohibited acts such as murder, willfully causing great suffering, or serious injury to body or health, rape, intentional attacks on the civilian population, pillage, and unlawful and arbitrary destruction of civilian goods, including some which were essential to the survival of the civilian population. The vast majority of these acts were committed against protected persons, as defined in the Geneva Conventions, primarily people who did not take part in the hostilities, particularly civilian populations and those put out of combat. This applies in particular to people living in refugee camps, who constitute a civilian population that is not participating in the hostilities, in spite of the presence of military personnel among them in some cases. Finally, there is no doubt that the violent incidents listed in this report almost all fall within the scope of armed conflict, whether international in nature or not. The duration and intensity of the violent incidents described, and the apparent level of organisation of the groups involved, could lead to the conclusion that, with few exceptions, that this was an internal conflict and not simply domestic disturbances or tensions or criminal acts. In conclusion, the vast majority of violent incidents listed in this report are the result of armed conflict and if proven in a judicial process, point to the commission of war crimes as serious breaches of international humanitarian law.

CRIMES AGAINST HUMANITY

25. The definition of this term was codified in paragraph 1 of article 7 of the Rome Statute of the ICC. The notion encompasses crimes such as murder, extermination, rape,

persecution and all other inhumane acts of a similar character (wilfully causing great suffering, or serious injury to body or to mental or physical health), committed "as part of a widespread or systematic attack directed against any civilian population, with knowledge of the attack", they constitute crimes against humanity.

26. This report shows that the vast majority of incidents listed, if investigated and proven in a judicial process, fall within the scope of widespread or systematic attacks, depicting multiple acts of large-scale violence, apparently carried out in an organized fashion and resulting in numerous victims. Most of these attacks were directed against non-combatant civilian populations consisting primarily of women and children. As a consequence, the vast majority of acts of violence perpetrated during these years, which formed part of various waves of reprisals and campaigns of persecution and pursuit of refugees, became collectively, a series of widespread and systematic attacks against civilian populations and could be found by a competent court to constitute crimes against humanity.

CRIME OF GENOCIDE

27. Since it was initially formulated in 1948, in article 2 of the Convention on the Prevention and Punishment of the Crime of Genocide, the definition of the crime has remained substantially the same. It can be found in article 6 of the Rome Statute, which defines the crime of genocide as "any of the following acts committed with intent to destroy, in whole or in part, a national, ethnical, racial or religious group, as such". The definition is followed by a series of acts representing serious violations of the right to life and the physical or mental integrity of the members of the group. The Convention also provides that not only the acts themselves are punishable, but also conspiracy to commit genocide, direct and public incitement to commit genocide, the attempt to commit genocide and complicity in genocide. It is the specific intention to destroy an identified group either in whole or in part that distinguishes the crime of genocide from a crime against humanity.

28. The question of whether the numerous serious acts of violence committed against the Hutus (refugees and others) constitute crimes of genocide has attracted a significant degree of comment and to date remains unresolved. In practice, this question can only be decided by a court decision on the basis of evidence beyond all reasonable doubt. Two separate reports by the United Nations, in 1997 and 1998, examined whether or not crimes of genocide had been committed against Hutu and other refugees in Zaire, subsequently the DRC. In both cases, the reports concluded that there were elements that might indicate that genocide had been committed but, in light of the shortage of information, the investigative Teams were not in a position to answer the question and requested that a more detailed investigation be carried out. The Mapping Exercise also addressed this question in accordance with its ToR and made the following observations.

29. At the time of the incidents covered by this report, the Hutu population in Zaire including refugees from Rwanda, constituted an ethnic group as defined in the aforementioned Convention. Several of the incidents listed suggest that multiple attacks targeted members of the Hutu ethnic group as such, and not only the persons responsible for the genocide committed in 1994 against the Tutsis in Rwanda and that no effort was allegedly made by the AFDL/APR to distinguish between Hutu members of the ex- FAR/Interahamwe and Hutu civilians, whether or not they were refugees.

30. The intention to destroy a group in part is sufficient to constitute a crime of genocide and the international courts have confirmed that the destruction of a group can be limited to a particular geographical area. According to relevant jurisprudence, even if only a part of the Hutu population in Zaire was targeted and destroyed, it could nonetheless constitute a crime of genocide if this was the intention of the perpetrators.

31. Several incidents listed in this report, if investigated and judicially proven, point to circumstances and facts from which a court could infer the intention to destroy the Hutu ethnic group in the DRC in part, if these were established beyond all reasonable doubt. The scale of the crimes and the large number of victims, probably several tens of thousands, all nationalities combined, are illustrated by the numerous incidents listed in the report (104 in all). The extensive use of edged weapons (primarily hammers) and the apparently systematic nature of the massacres of survivors after the camps had been taken suggests that the numerous deaths cannot be attributed to the hazards of war or seen as equating to collateral damage. The majority of the victims were children, women, elderly people and the sick, who were often undernourished and posed no threat to the attacking forces. Numerous serious attacks on the physical or mental integrity of members of the group were also committed, with a very high number of Hutus shot, raped, burnt or beaten. If proven, the incidents' revelation of what appears to be the systematic, methodological and premeditated nature of the attacks listed against the Hutus is also marked: these attacks took place in each location where refugees had allegedly been screened by the AFDL/APR over a vast area of the country. The pursuit lasted for months, and on occasion, the humanitarian assistance intended for them was allegedly deliberately blocked, particularly in the Orientale province, thus depriving them of resources essential to their survival. Thus the apparent systematic and widespread attacks described in this report reveal a number of inculpatory elements that, if proven before a competent court, could be characterized as crimes of genocide.

32. There are however a number of countervailaing factors that could lead a court to find that the requisite intent was lacking, and hence that the crime of genocide was not committed. . . .

33. In light of the competing considerations reviewed above, a full judicial investigation into the events that occurred in Zaire in 1996 to 1997 will be necessary, in order to permit a competent court to decide on the matter. . . .

[The inventory of the violations described in the report, and a discussion as to the effectiveness of the various judicial systems to handle the report's allegations, have been omitted.]

CONCLUSION

85. Drawing up an inventory of the most serious violations of human rights and international humanitarian law that were committed on DRC territory between March 1993 and June 2003, the report concludes that the vast majority of the 617 listed incidents could constitute crimes under international law, given full judicial investigation and prosecution. These include war crimes committed during armed conflict, either internal or international, or crimes against humanity committed in the context of a generalised or systematic attack against a civilian population, or in many cases both. The issue of whether the many serious acts of violence committed against Hutus in 1996 and 1997 constitute crimes of genocide can only be decided by a competent court.

86. In terms of justice, the response of the Congolese authorities in the face of the overwhelming number of serious crimes committed within the territory of the DRC has been very limited or even non-existent. The lack of political will on the part of the Congolese authorities to prosecute those who are allegedly responsible for serious violations of human rights and of international humanitarian law committed in the DRC has only encouraged further serious violations, which continue to this day. The report notes that, because of the multiple dimensions of seeking justice for the possible crimes committed in the DRC, it is crucial that a holistic policy of transitional justice be implemented, which will involve the creation of diverse and complementary mechanisms, both judicial and non-judicial. While the report is careful not to give any recommendations or directives as such, it does, however, examine the advantages and drawbacks of various transitional justice options in terms of truth, justice, reparation for and rehabilitation of victims, and reform of judicial and security institutions (including vetting measures), in the current Congolese context. These options, which must be examined by the Government of the DRC and civil society, include: a) the creation of a hybrid judicial mechanism; b) creation of a new Truth and Reconciliation Commission; c) reparation programmes; and d) reforms of both the legal sector and the security forces. In order to ensure that the Congolese people are fully involved in assessing needs, establishing priorities and finding solutions—in short, to ensure that they assume ownership of these new mechanisms and understand their function and scope—it is essential that the authorities carry out national consultations on transitional justice. Such prior consultations will be important to ensure the credibility and legitimacy of any undertakings in this area. . . .

[The remainder of the report, which provides details on the human rights violations summarized above, has been omitted.]

SOURCE: United Nations. Office of the High Commissioner for Human Rights. "Report of the Mapping Exercise Documenting the Most Serious Violations of Human Rights and International Humanitarian Law Committed Within the Territory of the Democratic Republic of the Congo Between March 1993 and June 2003." October 1, 2010. http://www.ohchr.org/Documents/Countries/ZR/DRC_MAPPING_REPORT_FINAL_EN.pdf.

OTHER HISTORIC DOCUMENTS OF INTEREST

FROM PREVIOUS *HISTORIC DOCUMENTS*

Brazilians Elect
First Female President

OCTOBER 4 AND NOVEMBER 1, 2010

On October 31, 2010, Dilma Rousseff, the governing party candidate for president, secured the top office in Brazil, defeating her opponent by a double-digit margin in the second round of voting, thereby becoming the first woman president in Brazil. Rousseff was a relative unknown before the campaign, but her position as the heir apparent to the incumbent, Luiz Inácio Lula da Silva, combined with the current positive economic climate in Brazil, boosted her popularity. Despite two significant pre-election scandals—one involving corruption allegations against her former executive secretary—Rousseff managed to maintain a solid lead in the polls in the run-up to the first vote on October 31. Nevertheless, her showing at the polls suffered, and she failed to garner enough votes to avoid a run-off later in the month.

CLOSE POLLING

Brazil's presidential race heated up in May 2010 as Rousseff, the candidate of the ruling left-wing Partido dos Trabalhadores (PT), closed the gap in the opinion polls with her main rival, José Serra, of the main opposition Partido da Social Democracia Brasileira (PSDB). Rousseff had been campaigning unofficially for a year, while Serra had only begun his bid for the top office in April 2010. Serra was the minister of health in the 1990s before becoming governor of São Paulo state in 2007, giving him the upper hand in terms of political experience. Meanwhile, Rousseff held the unelected position of civil chief-of-staff for the outgoing president, Lula.

Official campaigning began on July 7, by which point the two main candidates were still tied in the opinion polls. However, just a few weeks later, Rousseff opened up a double-digit lead over Serra. Meanwhile, the candidate for the left-leaning Partido Verde (PV), Marina Silva, was polling at just 8 to 9 percent. The turnaround in Rousseff's campaign—Serra had enjoyed a significant lead in the polls for nearly a year despite not announcing his candidacy until April—was largely a reflection of three factors. The first was the support of her former boss—Lula was a hugely popular president, who enjoyed an unprecedented level of popular support from the Brazilian public. With his approval ratings steady at around 80 percent, Lula energetically campaigned for his hand-picked successor. Lula's campaigning at times fell afoul of Brazilian election laws, and as a result the president was fined around $27,000 for seven offenses. Lula even publicly promised to continue to provide support for Rousseff after she took office, which provided the public with peace of mind after eight years under the Lula administration. Moreover, Lula's popularity prevented Serra from attacking Rousseff, as doing so would likely have led to a backlash among voters.

Secondly, the popularity of the president's socioeconomic policies, which have helped to provide many poor Brazilians with higher wages and greater access to credit and social benefits, served to boost the PT candidate's ratings. More broadly, with the Brazilian economy faring well and with a general feeling of contentment among the population, Rousseff benefited from the country's economic upturn. Finally, despite initially coming across to voters as stiff and technocratic, Rousseff was able to improve her public image and her campaigning skills with the help of her public relations team. Indeed, her popularity among women improved after she appeared on television to discuss her bout with cancer and becoming a grandmother.

Nevertheless, Rousseff's campaign faced significant challenges. Foremost was her ability to assert her authority over a coalition of nine parties that supported her candidacy, as well as over leftist factions within the PT. Secondly, Rousseff needed to establish political legitimacy given that she was selected by the incumbent president as his successor and owed much of her support to his public popularity.

By September Serra's campaign was flagging, as even some of his political allies distanced themselves from his campaign. Serra was unable to expose any major weaknesses in his opponent. He was also blighted by a number of mistakes relating to his choice for vice presidential nominee.

Corruption Scandals Damaged Rousseff

The presidential campaign's outcome appeared less certain after a series of high-profile corruption scandals came to light in August and September. While Rousseff was not directly implicated in the scandals, her popularity at the polls nevertheless suffered. The first scandal related to improper access to the tax returns of Serra's daughter and son-in-law, as well as of a few PSDB party officials, by inland tax revenue officials linked to the PT. Serra claimed that the alleged "crime" may have been intended to boost his opponent's campaign.

More worrisome for Rousseff was the second scandal, which involved her successor as Lula's chief of staff. Erenice Guerra, who was Rousseff's executive secretary when Rousseff was chief of staff, was forced to resign following allegations that several of her family members had attempted to charge fees to various parties in return for facilitating loans and public contracts through the Banco Nacional do Desenvolvimento Economico e Social, the state development bank.

As a result of the scandals, Rousseff's standing in the polls was damaged. According to a Datafolha poll of voting intentions taken on September 27, 49 to 53 percent of those polled supported her, down five points from a week earlier. However, Serra failed to make major gains in the polls, despite Rousseff's setbacks. The PSDB's candidate trailed Rousseff by around 20 percentage points in the poll, with just 28 percent indicating that they would vote for him. Surprisingly, Silva made a significant gain, garnering 14 percent of votes according to the Datafolha poll, up from around 8 to 9 percent in previous polls.

Runoff Declared

A week later, on October 3, Brazilians headed to the polls. Voting is compulsory in Brazil, although the repercussions for those abstaining are generally minimal. Despite leading her opponents by a significant margin in the run-up to the election, Rousseff was unable to secure an outright victory. She secured 46.9 percent of the total votes, a full 14 percentage points ahead of Serra, but just short of the 50 percent plus one vote required to secure an outright victory. The outcome was viewed in part as a reflection of her lack of personal charm and a repercussion of the corruption scandals. In addition, Rousseff may have lost some votes due to her previous support of liberalizing Brazil's abortion laws.

Rousseff performed particularly well in the northeast and southeast parts of the country. The northeast is a relatively poor region that benefited from Lula's social benefit programs. One notable exception to her wins in the southeast was in the state of São Paulo, which is the country's largest electoral district. Serra served as governor of the state from 2007 until April 2010, making his win there almost inevitable. Serra also garnered more votes than his opponent in the southern states.

The big surprise of the first round of voting was the strong performance of Silva, who attracted 19.3 percent of the total vote. This was the highest percentage attained by a third-party candidate since direct presidential elections resumed in Brazil in 1989. Silva had both personal appeal as well as an attractive agenda. Her party espouses environmental issues, which attracted particular support from young, urban, middle-class Brazilians. She performed strongly in the capital, Brasília, as well as another major city, Belo Horizonte. In the state of Rio de Janeiro, Silva attracted more than 30 percent of the vote. In addition, she benefited from the support of evangelical Christians, who are thought to represent around 24 percent of voters in the country. In the aftermath of the first round of the presidential election, both Serra and Rousseff attempted to gain Silva's explicit support. On October 17 the PV voted instead to not support either candidate, stating that neither had adequate environmental policies.

Rousseff Victory

Silva's neutral stance worked in Rousseff's favor. Without the former's support, it was nearly impossible for Serra to drum up enough votes to overcome Rousseff's lead. Indeed, Serra needed to attract the votes of around 90 percent of the Brazilians who voted for Silva in the first round of voting in order to win, and without her explicit support, that would not be possible. His only other chance was to gain the support of most of the 18 percent of Brazilians who abstained from voting in the first round, or to convince Rousseff's supporters to instead vote for him. Neither scenario was likely.

On October 31 the second round of presidential elections was held. As expected, Rousseff beat her opponent by a comfortable margin, gaining more than 55 percent of votes, compared with Serra's 44 percent. The margin of victory was large enough to give Rousseff a mandate for office, despite not securing the victory in the first round of voting. She became the first woman to be elected president in Brazil.

—Hilary Ewing

Following are two news releases from the government of Brazil. The first, issued on October 4, 2010, details the presidential election results that set up a runoff election; the second, issued on November 1, 2010, announces the election of Brazil's first female president.

Brazil Presidential Election Results in Runoff

October 4, 2010

Brazil's presidential election will go to a second round with Ms Rousseff of the Workers Party (PT) who finished with 46,90% and José Serra of Party of Brazilian Social Democracy (PSDB) trailing on 32,61%, according to figures from the Superior Electoral Court (TSE). Thirdly, the candidate Marina Silva of the Green Party (PV) polled 19.33%.

Position	Candidate Name	Votes Qty	Party
1	Dilma Rousseff	47.649.079 (46,91%)	PT
2	José Serra	33.130.514 (32,61%)	PSDB
3	Marina Silva	19.636.000 (19,33%)	PV
4	Plínio	886.800 (0,87%)	PSOL
5	Eymael	89.346 (0, 09%)	PSDC
6	Zé Maria	84.609 (0, 08%)	PSTU
7	Levy Fidelix	57.958 (0, 06%)	PRTB
8	Ivan Pinheiro	39.134 (0, 04%)	PCB
9	Rui Costa Pimenta	12.206 (0, 01%)	PCO

Candidate backed by President Luiz Inacio Lula da Silva's and former chief of staff Dilma, 62, and Jose Sierra, 68, the opposition candidate, former governor of São Paulo, Minister of Health and Planning, senator and congressman.

The first round of general elections in Brazil was held on Sunday (3), to elect seats to president, state governors, senators (two per state), congressmen along with federal and state deputies.

Brazil's presidential election is to continue at an October 31 runoff, when Brazilian will decide between Dilma Rousseff and José Serra. There will also be a run-off voting for governor in states where the first round ruling party candidate fails to win 50 percent plus one vote.

SOURCE: Government of Brazil. Portal Brasil. "Rousseff and Serra Face Off for Brazil's Presidency." October 4, 2010. http://www.brasil.gov.br/news/history/2010/10/04/rousseff-will-face-serra-for-brazil2019s-presidency.

Brazil Elects First Female President

November 1, 2010

Dilma Vana Rousseff, has been elected president of Brazil. With over 90% of the votes counted, Dilma has more than 55% of the valid votes and her opponent, Jose Serra, over 44%. The inauguration ceremony is on January 1, 2011.

Without ever running for office she has won the highest office in the land. Dilma is an economist who became the minister of Mines and Energy in the Luiz Inacio Lula da Silva administration when Lula was elected back in 2003. In 2007 she took over as the president's Chief of Staff ("ministra chefe da Casa Civil").

Dilma's campaign focused on the progress made during the eight years that Lula was president and promised continuity.

She was Lula's handpicked candidate to succeed him and got a big boost by the president's 80% approval ratings. Her campaign emphasized the need for the country to continue growing economically while providing assistance to the needy ("inclusão social"). She pointed out that over the last eight years some 28 million Brazilians had risen above the poverty line and promised to eradicate extreme poverty in Brazil.

Dilma Rousseff had a reputation as a demanding taskmaster in the Casa Civil where she coordinated the government's main development project, the Accelerated Growth Program ("PAC"). Dilma was also behind a huge housing program ("Minha Casa, Minha Vida") that had strong social appeal.

Dilma was born in Minas Gerais in 1947, in an upper middle class family. Her mother, Dilma Jane Rousseff, was a teacher, and her father, a Bulgarian who became Brazilian, was a successful lawyer. She says her father taught her to read and like him she has devoured books all her life.

Dilma studied at an elite school in Belo Horizonte but later moved to a public school and got involved in politics. She was soon actively opposing the military dictatorship (1964–85). She was arrested (1970) and tortured. Released from prison (1973), she married Carlos Araujo, a politician, and they lived in Porto Alegre. They had a daughter, but later divorced.

In Porto Alegre, Dilma was a member of the PDT, founded by Leonel Brizola, and was an official in the city and state government (secretariat of Mines and Energy, among other posts) in the 1980s and 90s. In 2000 she left the PDT and joined the PT.

SOURCE: Government of Brazil. Portal Brasil. "Dilma Rousseff is First Woman to be President of Brazil." November 1, 2010. http://www.brasil.gov.br/news/history/2010/11/01/dilma-rousseff-is-first-woman-to-be-president-of-brazil.

OTHER HISTORIC DOCUMENTS OF INTEREST

FROM PREVIOUS *HISTORIC DOCUMENTS*

Toxic Sludge Blankets Hungarian Villages

OCTOBER 5, 6, 7, AND 9, 2010

On October 4, 2010, a reservoir in Hungary storing the byproduct of aluminum oxide production burst, sending toxic red sludge into neighboring villages in waves reaching more than six feet high. Nearly two hundred million gallons covered three Hungarian villages. The spill killed at least 9 people and injured more than 150. As it flowed through the villages, destroying homes, roads, and bridges, it moved toward Danube river tributaries, killing all life in one and putting downstream nations on high alert for possible contamination.

DEVASTATION

On October 4, at approximately noon local time, the corner of a dam at the Ajkai Timfoldgyar alumina plant, located one hundred miles from the Hungarian capital city of Budapest, collapsed, sending millions of gallons of toxic red sludge into surrounding villages. The spill covered more than fifteen square miles, wiping out cars, bridges, roads, homes, and everything else in its path. Sándor Pintér, Hungary's interior minister, called the spill the "greatest ecological disaster" to hit Hungary.

The sludge that poured into the streets is created when bauxite is turned into aluminum oxide, a form of alumina that is used to manufacture products made from the metal. It is highly alkaline and contains a number of heavy metals. However, according to the company that owns the plant, Magyar Alumínium Zrt (MAL Zrt.), the level of heavy metal was allowed under European Union (EU) environmental standards and posed no serious health threats.

Even so, the government suggested that residents who remained in the three hardest hit villages—Kolontár, Devecser, and Somlóvásárhely—not eat any fruits or vegetables produced in the soil that was now covered in the thick sludge. Additionally, the government encouraged residents to wear face masks, as the heat during the early fall months was causing the sludge to dry into an airborne toxin. The Hungarian Academy of Sciences announced that while precaution is necessary in any disaster, the level of heavy metal in the toxic sludge would not pose severe health hazards to those who came into contact with it. Residents near the spill, however, disagreed. "The academy can say whatever it wants," said Barbara Szalai Szita, a resident of a village hard hit by the sludge. "All I know is that if I spend 30 minutes outside I get a foul taste in my mouth and my tongue feels strange."

Those who came into contact with the toxic sludge suffered severe burns and eye damage because of its corrosive properties. Ten people were reported to have been killed by the dam breach, mostly those who were swept away by the waves of sludge, which in some instances reached more than six feet high.

Most of the damage done by the dam breach affected infrastructure. Shortly after the dam burst, Hungarian prime minister Viktor Orbán declared a state of emergency to allow for government funds to be easily released to the hardest hit villages. During a visit to Kolontár, which was located closest to the dam, Orbán said, "It is difficult to find the words. Had this happened at night everybody would be dead." Because of the extensive damage caused in the village of Kolontár, Orban said it was unlikely that anyone would be able to rebuild or live in the village ever again. Residents agreed, also expressing distrust of living near the company.

The Hungarian government estimated that it would cost tens of millions of dollars and take at least one year to complete cleanup of the affected area. "The area is very big, very heavy contamination, lots of human resources are needed, definitely machinery is needed," said Hungarian environmental minister Zoltán Illés, who said financial assistance from the EU would likely be necessary. The cleanup process included the removal of one inch of topsoil from any area that had been contaminated by the sludge to prevent further soil contamination.

Although the damage was severe, initial fears that the sludge would contaminate drinking water and kill all life in the Danube River were alleviated by continued testing of drinking water, which showed that the metal in the water was at a level allowed by government standards. Greenpeace reported differently. Its officials announced that high levels of arsenic had been found in the drinking water of one waterway near the spill. In addition, they claimed that farmland located near the breached dam had been affected by arsenic, chrome, and mercury, which it said would affect the safety of crops and livestock.

In response to the spill, the Hungarian government ordered the shutdown of the alumina plant until it could determine that the plant could continue safe operations. On October 15, the plant reopened, but it had been nationalized and was brought under the control of a state commissioner whose primary responsibility was to focus on disaster containment and avoidance. The government estimated that it would retain control of the plant for at least two years.

CLEANUP AND RESPONSIBILITY

On October 7, the Hungarian government called on the EU Civil Protection Mechanism for pollution cleanup and assessment assistance. Hungary asked the EU to send three to five experts who could help develop a plan for decontamination of the affected area. This team would also assist with water- and air-quality monitoring. The Civil Protection Mechanism responded with experts from its member states. "Hungary has been affected by an environmental catastrophe," said Kristalina Georgieva, commissioner of the mechanism responsible for crisis response. "Disasters like this do not stop at national borders and a combined European response can help deliver the most effective assistance possible. In this moment of need, I call all EU Member States to respond with generosity to the request of Hungary."

Beyond his focus on cleanup, Prime Minister Orbán vowed to take action against those responsible for the dam breach. "This is so irresponsible that it is impossible to find words," he said of the disaster. An investigation was launched to determine whether the breach was caused by human error or the heavy rains that had fallen in Hungary during the spring and summer of 2010, but the government made it clear that evidence pointed toward human error.

"We all are astonished because we are not aware of any information that could reduce human responsibility," Orbán said. "My point is that behind this tragedy, there must have been some human errors and mistakes." He promised to seek "the toughest possible" consequences against anyone found responsible for the spill. MAL Zrt. denied responsibility, saying that safety checks on the day of the breach had shown no irregularities. "The last physical review, on the same day, and the most recent laboratory evaluation of a water sample from within the reservoir didn't show any sign of the disaster that occurred," MAL Zrt. said in a statement.

On October 11, Zoltan Bakonyi, chief executive of MAL Zrt., was arrested. Orbán assured the Hungarian people that Bakonyi and others responsible would be forced to pay for the damage claims estimated at $102 million. "Since this is not a natural catastrophe but the damage was brought about by people, the damages must be paid first and foremost not by taxpayers but by those who caused the damage," he said. He further stated that Bakonyi knew that the dam walls had been weakened by the spring and summer weather, but chose to take no action for repair.

Protecting the Danube and Threat of a New Spill

As the toxic sludge crept toward the Danube River, emergency crews worked to dilute the pollutant. The spill had first reached the river's tributaries, including the Raba, Mosoni-Danube and Marcal rivers. The Raba and Mosoni-Danube rivers escaped extensive damage, but the toxic sludge killed all life in the Marcal River. "Life in the Marcal River has been extinguished," said Tibor Dobson, a spokesman for the Hungarian national disaster unit. "The main effort is now being concentrated on the Raba and the Danube. That's what has to be saved." A decade before the October 2010 alumina dam spill, the Danube had been contaminated after an accident in Romania. Following the cleanup efforts, Danube River nations installed warning systems that can alert shore cities to contaminants that enter the water, leading to an earlier intervention. This system proved critically important after the Hungary spill.

A major concern for the Raba and Mosoni-Danube rivers was the rising alkalinity of the water. In an effort to bring the pH level in the water under control, plaster and vinegar were dumped in. Countries downriver from Hungary were also put on high alert, including Croatia, Serbia, and Bulgaria. The World Wildlife Fund reported that it did not expect the sludge to cause river problems downstream because any toxic material would be diluted by the volume of water in the river by the time it reached another country. But downstream countries took all precautions and tested the water in the Danube several times each day. "It is clear that the consequences of this are greatest in the local area and that the implications on a trans-boundary level, we understand, will not be significant which doesn't mean they don't exist," said Philip Weller, the executive secretary of the United Nation's International Commission for the Protection of the Danube River.

As nations rushed to protect the Danube, fears of a second toxic sludge spill began to take root. The second reservoir at the alumina plant, containing more than 132 million gallons of the red toxic sludge began cracking. "Last night, the interior minister informed us that cracks have appeared in the northern wall of the reservoir, whose corner collapsed," Orbán reported. "The detached parts of the dam are growing apart. The distance between them widened by 7 cm from late last night until this morning so it is very likely that we have to reckon on this wall collapsing."

As a precaution, with assistance from EU crews, the government began construction on a sixteen-foot-high barrier to protect towns in the anticipated path of the sludge. It also began evacuation of nearby towns and readied trains and vehicles for a quick removal of citizens and soldiers in the event of another breach. Luckily, the second containment dam did not rupture.

REGULATING ALUMINA

The collapse of the dam in Hungary, a center of aluminum oxide production in Europe, brought the regulation of toxic material in Europe into question. The EU does not classify the sludge byproduct as a hazardous material, and the Hungarian government began a fight to ensure that it would be added, which would guarantee tighter control of its production and storage. The EU told government regulators that it was open to reviewing its policy but would wait until the Hungarian investigation was complete.

Determining who was responsible for inspections at the dam was central to this investigation. MAL Zrt. said its inspections had shown nothing out of the ordinary, and a September 23 inspection by Hungary's National Inspectorate for Environment, Nature and Water also showed no irregularities. After the dam burst, however, István Csepregi, director of the Inspectorate, said that his organization was not responsible for any safety inspections. "It did not fall within the remit of the environmental inspectorate to ascertain the technical condition of the structure," he said. The Inspectorate believes MAL Zrt. must accept responsibility for the spill.

Environmental groups hope that the lessons from Hungary's spill will be carried throughout the world to encourage better safety standards for alumina plants. "The safety of such plants may be worse here than in Western Europe," said Greenpeace Hungary spokesperson Márton Vay. "But they are far better than those in parts of Asia or Africa. . . . If we continue to demand cheap aluminum for everything from chocolate bar wrappers to drink cans, these catastrophes will happen again."

—Heather Kerrigan

Following are four statements issued by the government of Hungary. The first, from October 5, 2010, declares a state of emergency in some Hungarian counties due to the toxic sludge; the second, from October 6, 2010, encourages visitors to continue travel plans to Hungary even after a dam burst; the third, issued October 7, 2010, outlines the activities undertaken by the Hungarian government to alleviate the toxic sludge problem; and the fourth, issued on October 9, 2010, details remarks made by Prime Minister Viktor Orbán upon visiting the hardest hit areas.

DOCUMENT *Hungary Declares State of Emergency*

October 5, 2010

The Government has issued an order to declare a state of emergency in Veszprém, Győr-Moson-Sopron and Vas counties due to the burst of a red sludge reservoir in Kolontár.

The Minister of Internal Affairs convened the Government Coordination Committee this afternoon in order to decide upon further measures to be taken. The catastrophe has caused a severe situation but the Government and its relevant agencies keep it under control and rescue and recovery operations have been underway since the dam burst took place.

Coordination is at an unprecedented high level between the Police, the Army, the National Emergency Response Directorate and the National Ambulance Service, as a result of their close ties forged in their collaboration in previous rescue operations.

SOURCE: "Redsludge" Tragedy. Government of Hungary. Ministry of Internal Affairs. "Statement of the Minister of Internal Affairs." October 5, 2010. http://redsludge.bm.hu/?p=1.

DOCUMENT *Toxic Sludge Does Not Impede Travel*

October 6, 2010

Staying in Hungary is completely safe, experts reassure travellers to Budapest. The rupture of the red sludge reservoir in Hungary has caused a localised emergency situation afflicting three villages 160 km from the capital, Budapest. The dam burst poses no threat at all to anyone planning to travel to Budapest or stay elsewhere in Hungary.

The disaster triggered by a ruptured sludge reservoir near Ajka, a town situated 160 km from the capital, is localised in nature and has no damaging impact on areas located farther away. The most favoured tourist destinations, such as Budapest and Pécs, the Cultural Capital of Europe, are not affected by the dam burst in any manner. Visitors arriving in Hungary continue to have unlimited access to the entire tourism infrastructure, including airports, places of accommodation and other tourism service providers and attractions.

On 4 October, red sludge escaped from a containment pond of a privately owned alumina production company 160 km from Budapest. The ruptured dam caused severe damage in two settlements, killing 4 people and seriously injuring 12. The Hungarian Government took immediate measures to ensure the safety of the local population, and today clean-up and decontamination operations are underway along with efforts to reinforce the banks of the reservoir. The sludge poses a direct health hazard to the local population only; consumption of locally grown food-products is not allowed. Outside the afflicted areas the disaster has no adverse health effects whatsoever. The Government launched an immediate investigation to detect the cause of the calamity; human error cannot be ruled out.

Source: "Redsludge" Tragedy. Government of Hungary. Ministry of Internal Affairs. "Hungary Is a Totally Safe Place to Stay." October 6, 2010. http://redsludge.bm.hu/?p=6.

Hungarian Government Details Action on Toxic Sludge

DOCUMENT

October 7, 2010

The Hungarian government and the national bodies under its leadership have immediately started and are continuously managing all defence and reconstruction activities following the red sludge disaster. The catastrophe occurred 160 kilometres from Budapest, flooding 3 villages, but clean-up operations are already on the way. Prime Minister Viktor Orbán visited the affected villages today and told the people that they would not be abandoned by the government.

State of the rivers, including the Danube: the alkaline contamination is being reduced continuously.

The red sludge contamination reached nearby rivers, increasing the alkalinity of the water. Disaster management experts started working on avoiding the contamination of the rivers immediately after the catastrophe: in order to reduce alkalinity and protect the water quality, they pour plaster and organic acetic acid into the River Marcal and construct underwater weirs to slow the speed of the water flow and help to deposit the sludge and its heavy metal content.

However, in spite of immediate intensive efforts, they were unable to prevent the contamination of the River Marcal. Although the river's pH-level was reduced to around 10 by the early hours of Thursday, all the fish in the River Marcal have been destroyed and the vegetation could not be saved either.

The contamination advanced from the Marcal and reached the River Rába around 3 a.m., by which time the pH-level of the water was under 10. The red sludge has reached the Moson branch of the Danube by Thursday morning with pH 9.3.

The toxic sludge contamination advanced from the Marcal, the Rába and the Moson branch to the main branch of the Danube with a pH-level of 8–9. We must stress that on reaching the Danube, the alkalinity of the river-water has been reduced continuously and considerably. Experts continue to monitor contamination levels in the water.

FOOD SAFETY

Hungarian food products are completely safe.

The only restrictions concern the consumption of consumables, produced in the gardens of the flood-hit areas.

Events on site

Following Monday's disaster, when a large amount of red sludge flooded from the burst dam of a reservoir, the government passed all decrees that are required by disaster recovery efforts. Police and defence forces, disaster management units and ambulance services work in unison in the affected areas.

At the moment, experts focus on the most important tasks: to localise the dam failure, reinforce the reservoirs, provide for the villagers, neutralise contaminated surfaces and reduce freshwater contamination.

Reservoir dams have been reinforced and are guarded 24 hours a day in order to avoid any subsequent bursts and sludge floods.

NO radiation danger

There is no danger of radiation anywhere, because radiation levels in the red sludge are well under levels that would be harmful to health. Experts from the Hungarian Academy of Sciences had studied samples from the site and concluded that the proportion of heavy metal particles in the red sludge did not reach the threshold limit that would be dangerous to health and it contained less lead than normal soil.

Drinking water

Initial tests show that the drinking water supply of the flooded villages has not been contaminated, nevertheless experts continue to monitor the quality of the drinking water.

Housing

Prime Minister Viktor Orbán visited the site of the disaster today and said that the government would not abandon people in times of need and everyone would have a roof over their head, but they need all the help they can get. In the prime minister's view that is no point in rebuilding part of the disaster-hit area. He reassured villagers that after the recovery efforts it would be their decision to choose whether they wanted to move back to their original homes. If not, appropriate solutions must be found for them. This means that a new area should be opened for them in another part of the village to build their houses and carry on with their lives.

Responsibility

According to the government, the tragedy was not caused by natural disaster, but presumably by human negligence, therefore all those responsible must be found. The National office of Investigation under the Ministry of the Interior launched a probe into the spill, using a special investigation unit, due to the priority status and complexity of the case. A criminal inquiry has been opened on suspicion of occupational negligence causing death. The inquiry shall also examine whether the company, operating the reservoir with hazardous materials, followed all regulations and conducted all necessary inspections.

INTERNATIONAL AID

Hungary wishes to thank the international organisations and states that offered their support. Hungary has received help, among others, from Austria, India, Japan, France, the Czech Republic, Slovakia, Serbia, Germany, Canada, Switzerland, Romania, Poland, Luxembourg, Belgium, Spain, the USA and the United Kingdom for the recovery efforts of the red sludge disaster. We were offered assistance in the form of sending mineral water supplies, iodine tablets, soldiers, rescue teams and toxicology experts.

Tourism

The reservoir, affected by the red sludge spill, is situated 160 kilometres from Budapest, near the town of Ajka. It is a local disaster, with no detrimental effects to any further areas. Favourite tourist destinations, such as Budapest or Pécs, the current cultural capital of Europe, are in no way affected by the disaster. Our entire tourism infrastructure is ready to welcome all foreign visitors.

The disaster

Hungary's largest ecological disaster occurred on 4 October, when around one million cubic metres of red sludge inundated the Veszprém County villages of Devecser, Kolontár and Somlóvásárhely. The red sludge reservoir is owned and operated by a private company: Hungarian Aluminium Producing and Trading Company (MAL).

The sludge flooded 800 hectares (8 square kilometres) of surrounding areas. It was caused by the rupture of a sludge reservoir at the nearby alumina plant. The red sludge, which is a highly alkaline material, escaped from the ruptured reservoir and flooded 500 houses. The disaster claimed four lives, with three people still missing and over 150 people injured, currently 11 of them in serious or critical condition. Many lost their houses and all their belongings in this tragic event.

SOURCE: "Redsludge" Tragedy. Government of Hungary. Ministry of Internal Affairs. "The Hungarian Government Uses Coordinated Efforts in Red Sludge Disaster Recovery." October 7, 2010. http://red sludge.bm.hu/?p=6.

DOCUMENT   *Prime Minister Responds to Disaster*

October 9, 2010

The Hungarian Premier held a special press conference for the Hungarian and international media in Ajka on Saturday morning.

The Premier stated that late last night cracks appeared in the northern wall of the reservoir; it is assumed that there is the danger of another failure. Experts have analysed the condition of the wall and have determined that there is a real risk that the wall will collapse and that the red sludge behind it will spill out. "At present we do not have exact information about the composition of the material in the reservoir," said the Premier, and therefore helicopters were being used to obtain samples.

The evacuation of Kolontár has become necessary in order to protect inhabited areas. During the night the army was put on standby, and is ready to relocate as many as 3000 people. Thus far 750 people have been evacuated from Kolontár. Public safety and the protection of property in the settlements have been assured.

"After Kolontár the next issue is nearby Devecser," the Premier explained, stating that Devecser has 6000 residents. So far there has been no evacuation, but law enforcement personnel are standing by for this purpose: 319 soldiers, 127 transport vehicles, and even trains are available. There is no panic in the settlements, and the residents are also prepared for a potential evacuation.

The sections of dam wall are moving apart from each other, and they have moved 7 cm between yesterday evening and this morning. There is a high probability that the wall will collapse. "We have prepared for such a crisis, and are ready to protect residents and the rivers," emphasised Viktor Orbán.

The construction of new dams has begun between the reservoir and the village to capture or slow the flow of sludge in the event of another collapse. The fourth and final dam is being built in the village of Kolontár itself. If the reservoir dam wall suffers a second collapse there is the danger of a spillage of around 500 000 cubic metres of toxic waste: equivalent to half of Monday's volume.

Multiple cracks in the wall have been observed, and a zone of moisture has formed around resulting leaks; this confirms that there is the realistic chance of a rupture, and the collapse of the entire wall. If the material escapes, it will take the same course as before.

The Premier once again stressed that the river water's pH level has been successfully reduced from a value of 13 to about 9—a level which does not endanger the Danube's ecosystem. The pH level of the river water is decreasing continuously.

When asked whether other reservoirs might fail, the Premier responded that this possibility is also under investigation: "We have an appropriate response for the worst possible scenario," he said.

"The inspection of every Hungarian red sludge reservoir is already taking place," confirmed the Premier.

The facility may only restart operations with government permission, and this decision will most certainly not be made on Monday. This matter will not be handled in the "way that has been customary up to now," said Orbán, referring to the investigation into responsibility for the disaster, adding that "A few months ago a new era began in Hungary." The Premier will give a speech in Parliament on Monday—he also said that he will supply Parliament with comprehensive information. In response to questions from the media, he stated that at present there is no information enabling the precise determination of responsibility for the incident, but he unequivocally stated that the allocation of personal responsibility must be looked into.

SOURCE: "Redsludge" Tragedy. Government of Hungary. "Victor Orbán's Special On-Site Press Conference." October 9, 2010. http://redsludge.bm.hu/?p=117#more-117.

Guinea Election
Sparks Delays and Violence

OCTOBER 8 AND 25, NOVEMBER 9
AND 19, AND DECEMBER 3, 2010

The first democratic election in one of Africa's poorest nations, Guinea, stretched on from June into December 2010. Violent clashes between ethnic groups after allegations of fraud surfaced after the June 27 vote led to two postponements of a runoff election. But calls for peace by the two presidential candidates, former prime minister Cellou Dalein Diallo and opposition leader Alpha Condé, paid off on November 7 as Guinea residents peacefully went to the polls in overwhelming numbers. That peace rapidly devolved into violence, as Condé's declaration as the winner of the runoff election was disputed by Diallo, who accused Condé's party, Rally of the Guinean People (RPG), of suppressing votes from Diallo's ethnic Peuhl supporters.

GUINEA GOES TO THE POLLS

Since gaining its independence from France in 1958, mineral-rich Guinea has been ruled by dictators and a military junta that has suppressed personal freedom and wealth across the country, hoarding mineral profits for its own gain. In 2008, a military coup overthrew the government, assassinating President Lansana Conté, who had held dictatorial power for twenty-four years. The coup, led by a group called the National Council for Democracy and Development, took control and suspended the nation's constitution. This new military junta said it would hold a democratic election in December 2010, but regional pressure, led by the Economic Community of West African States (ECOWAS), called for an election to be held in 2009. The National Council for Democracy and Development rejected the call and brutally cracked down on political opponents.

In September 2009, the nation descended into chaos when government troops killed more than 150 pro-democracy demonstrators. Shortly thereafter, the junta leader who had been acting as president, Moussa Dadis Camara, was shot and injured by an aide, giving way for a new military leader to take power. Regional organizations helped bring General Sékouba Konaté to power as the interim leader of the government in January 2010, and he promised to seek an election for civilian rule of Guinea.

The promised civilian election came on June 27 and resulted in no clear winner out of a field of twenty-four candidates. Former prime minister Diallo received 44 percent of the vote, while opposition leader Condé received 18 percent. No candidate could be declared the winner without at least 50 percent of the vote. A runoff was scheduled for July 18 but was soon postponed because of allegations of fraud during the June 27 vote. These charges resulted in the dismissal of Louceny Camara as head of Guinea's National Independent Electoral Commission (CENI). Camara's position in the CENI was contested by Diallo, who believed Camara's support of Condé's candidacy would render him unable to make a sound judgment of the election results. Camara's predecessor had been sentenced for election fraud just weeks earlier. Camara was replaced by Siaka Toumani Sangaré. In this position, it would be Sangaré's duty to organize and certify the final results of the presidential election.

In mid-July, Guinea's prime minister, Jean-Marie Doré, announced that the government and military leaders had uncovered a violent plot to disrupt the runoff election. This was not the first threat to the security of elections. Before the first round of voting occurred in June, supporters of former president Camara said they would undertake any means necessary to stop the vote unless Moussa Dadis Camara was returned to the position of president. In both cases, violence never materialized.

A second runoff date was scheduled for October 24 but was again postponed to allow time to calm the ethnic violence between Guinea's two largest ethnic groups, the Peuhl and Malinke, that had remained steady since the the June 27 vote. The United States and France carefully watched the situation in Guinea and expressed concern about the continued election delays. In a statement, the two nations encouraged Guinea to hold its presidential election "with no further delay that could provide opportunities for antidemocratic forces to thwart this historic transition."

Guinea Votes Again

The runoff was rescheduled for November 7, with a promise from election commission leader Sangaré that there would be no further delay. "It is a date that has been agreed upon, cannot be changed, and, dare I say it, I think will be the last one set for this election that the Guinean people are waiting for so much," he said. Because Diallo won a significant portion of the June 27 vote, he was heavily favored to win the runoff because Guinea's Supreme Court had thrown out nearly one-third of the votes cast for Condé in the first election because of allegations of ballot rigging and vote stuffing.

Seeking a swift and peaceful end to the election process, the presidential candidates appeared together, calling for an end to violence before the November 7 vote. "We urgently appeal to all citizens of our country to carry out their civic duty in peace, tranquility and serenity . . . and that they make election day on 7 November and the post-election period, a historic moment of rediscovered brotherhood," said Diallo. Their request appeared to work. International election observers reported few irregularities during runoff voting, other than late-arriving ballots and ink. "There were no major irregularities or incidents likely to taint the freedom, credibility and transparency of the 7 November 2010 presidential election in Guinea," said ECOWAS observation mission leader Theodore Holo.

The high turnout and small number of incidents reported gave ECOWAS hope that the political transition could be carried out peacefully, installing Guinea's first civilian government. "ECOWAS is pleased with the efforts made by the Guinean authorities and all the stakeholders to ensure a good conduct of the poll in a peaceful environment. It also lauded the commitment and the sense of civic responsibility the voters showed during this historic electoral process. It urged all the stakeholders to continue the rest of the electoral process in the same state of mind and respect for order and discipline until the declaration of provisional then final results," the organization said in a statement.

Results Spark Violence

The Election Day calm was short lived. On November 15, the Guinea election commission announced Condé as the winner of the presidential election, gaining more than 52 percent of the vote to Diallo's 47 percent. Almost immediately, violence broke out in Guinea's capital city, Conakry. According to the United Nations' Office of the High Commissioner for Human Rights, a number of human rights violations followed the election outcome, including hundreds of injuries and deaths. The office expressed deep concern regarding the use of force and weapons by Guinea officials to stop demonstrations, saying that UN staff had witnessed security forces "brutally beating, arresting and shooting" unarmed civilians. Konaté's government declared a state of emergency in an effort to restore order. The nation's borders were closed and the head of the army was fired to avoid any uprising as Condé's government attempted to take office.

Shortly before the election commission's announcement of Condé's victory, Diallo declared himself the winner. He refused to participate in the certification of the election results until all allegations of voter fraud had been investigated. These allegations came from Diallo's Peuhl party, the Union of Democratic Forces of Guinea (UFDG), and claimed that vote totals were higher in some areas than the number of registered voters. But the biggest complaint from Diallo was the inclusion of election results from the Siguiri region of Guinea. Prior to the election, a number of ethnic Peuhls had been driven from Siguiri because of violence in the region, but they were granted the right to vote on a provisional ballot. Diallo, however, claimed that his party was not able to independently verify whether the displaced Peuhls' votes had been counted.

The results were sent to Guinea's Supreme Court for verification. In December, the election results were certified, and the United Nations led the call for a peaceful transition of the government from military rule to civilian rule. The international body further promised that "all reported acts of violence will be closely scrutinized by the Office in order to determine whether crimes falling under the [International Criminal Court's] jurisdiction are committed and should warrant an investigation."

It was not until December 22 that Condé was able to officially take control of Guinea's government. In his speech upon becoming the first democratically elected president of Guinea, Condé said, "Today Guinea is cited as an example . . . in the sub-region." The United Nations concurred, encouraging other African countries to look to Guinea as an example of a relatively successful election. "As the dust settles on a most demanding electoral process in Guinea and a new legitimate president is about to assume office, it is appropriate to commend the Guinean people and leaders for this historic achievement," according to Said Djinnit, special representative of the UN secretary-general for West Africa.

In his first official speech as president and leader of Guinea's army, Condé promised to help the nation overcome its challenges, including poverty and ethnic violence. "We shall get Guinea out of great poverty and end impunity across the entire national territory," he said. He promised that his government would not retain funds from the nation's mineral wealth for his own personal gain and would end the corruption that had been commonplace under the military rule. "I will try to be the Mandela of the republic of Guinea," Conte said. "Guinea is back."

—Heather Kerrigan

Following is a statement by the embassies of France and the United States in Guinea on October 9, 2010, expressing concern over election delays; a statement by the Economic Community of West African States (ECOWAS) on October 25, 2010, calling on the transitional government to conduct a peaceful election; a November 9, 2010, statement by ECOWAS regarding the outcome of the Guinea presidential election; a November 19, 2010, press release from the United Nations expressing concern about post-election violence in Guinea; and a December 3, 2010, statement by the United Nations welcoming the conclusion of the Guinea presidential election.

United States and France Address Guinea Election Delay Concern

October 9, 2010

The United States and France, echoing the strong views expressed by the AU and ECOWAS, are deeply concerned with the continued delay in completing the second round of presidential elections in Guinea. Elections must take place on October 24 with no further delay that could provide opportunities for anti-democratic forces to thwart this historic transition. The entire world is watching this historic event in Guinea.

All of Guinea's political class, especially the candidates and members of the interim government, must place the national interests of Guinea above any other consideration. We urge presidential candidates Cellou Dalein Diallo and Apha Condé to act responsibly, control their supporters and prevent provocations or acts of harassment that could incite violence, in accordance with the principles of the Ouagadougou Accord.

Meantime, Guinea's interim leaders and electoral officials must for their part remain neutral and advance the electoral process as non-partisan actors. We salute Sekouba Konate's continued efforts towards finalizing this electoral process and promoting democratization of the country. Guineans want and deserve this pivotal moment in their history. It is time for Guinea's dream of democracy, a dream that has been deferred for more than 50 years, to become a reality.

SOURCE: Embassy of the United States in Conakry, Guinea. "Press Release by American and French Embassies in Guinea." October 8, 2010. http://conakry.usembassy.gov/pr_08102010d.html.

ECOWAS Calls on Transitional Government to Conduct Peaceful Election

October 25, 2010

The Economic Community of West African States (ECOWAS) expresses its satisfaction with the consultations that were recently held and which opportunely resulted in a consensus in the choice and appointment of Brigadier General Siaka Toumany Sangaré as President of the CENI in Guinea. CENI or the National Independent Electoral Commission is in charge of organizing the Second Round of the Presidential Elections.

It is the hope of ECOWAS that this appointment and that of the two Vice-Presidents will provide a lasting solution to the leadership crisis within that body. ECOWAS has also taken note of the useful consultations that resulted in the postponement of the Second Round of the Presidential Elections previously scheduled for 24th October 2010.

To ensure the best conditions for calm and peaceful elections in Guinea, ECOWAS urges all members of the CENI to strengthen unity and inclusivity around the new leadership and to collaborate with all stakeholders involved in the preparations for the elections in order to overcome all challenges identified and thus decide, as soon as possible, on a new date for the effective holding of the Second Round of the Presidential Elections.

Concerned with the sporadic and repeated acts of violence that have characterized the electoral campaign and in conformity with the spirit of the Protocol on peaceful elections in Guinea signed in Ouagadougou on 3rd September 2010 by the two candidates in contention in the Second Round, ECOWAS reiterates its appeal for calm and also urges all stakeholders in the process as well as the entire Guinean population to put the national interest above any militant or ethnic factor.

ECOWAS congratulates General Sékouba Konaté, the Transitional President, for his commitment and leadership in the search for a peaceful solution to the political stalemate that had bedeviled the electoral process during the past few weeks. It encourages him to continue his invaluable efforts for the successful conduct of the democratic and electoral process in Guinea.

ECOWAS reaffirms its commitment to support Guinea in this critical process to ensure a return to political integrity, cohesion, unity and constitutional order in the country.

SOURCE: Economic Community of West African States. Press Releases. "Postponement of the Second Round of Presidential Elections in Guinea." October 25, 2010. http://news.ecowas.int/presseshow .php?nb=168&lang=en&annee=2010.

ECOWAS Announces Satisfaction with Second Round of Guinea Voting

DOCUMENT

November 9, 2010

«There were no major irregularities or incidents likely to taint the freedom, credibility and transparency of the 7 November 2010 presidential election in Guinea». This is how the Leader of the ECOWAS Observer Mission for this election, Professor Theodore HOLO, President of the High Court of Justice of Benin summarized his preliminary statement at a press conference this day in the presence of the President of ECOWAS Commission, Ambassador James Victor Gbeho.

This statement indicated that during preparations for the poll and the handling of pending issues that could jeopardize the success of the process, concrete steps were taken by various stakeholders involved in the electoral process to ensure optimum conditions for the effective holding of the poll. Among these arrangements, Professor HOLO mentioned the technical competence of the Independent National Electoral Commission (INEC) to organize the poll, the commitment of the authority of the transition to make every effort to ensure security before, during and after the vote and until the declaration of results as well as the joint declaration signed by the two candidates in contention on 5 November 2010 in which they reiterated their commitment to work for a peaceful, free and democratic poll all over the country.

Regarding the conduct of the poll, the Mission noted, inter alia, the huge voter mobilization and turnout at the various polling stations, the availability of polling materials and polling officials as well as the presence of the Special Force for Securing the Electoral Process (FOSSEPEL).

The Mission also found out that the voting process was smooth and in accordance with current standards, particularly in terms of collation and vote counting as well as the presence of representatives of both candidates in contention for this second round of presidential election in almost all the polling stations.

However, the Mission noted some shortcomings in some polling stations relating among others to inadequate polling materials, inconsistency between the attendance sheets and the displayed voters' register. These various shortcomings to which a progressive and agreed settlement were found during the vote, did not in any way affect the good conduct of the poll. The ECOWAS Observer Mission concluded therefore that there were no major irregularities or incidents likely to taint the freedom, credibility and transparency of the 7 November 2010 presidential election in Guinea, stated Professor Theodore Holo.

To this end, ECOWAS is pleased with the efforts made by the Guinean authorities and all the stakeholders to ensure a good conduct of the poll in a peaceful environment. It also lauded the commitment and the sense of civic responsibility the voters showed during this historic electoral process. It urged all the stakeholders to continue the rest of the electoral process in the same state of mind and respect for order and discipline until the declaration of provisional then final results.

ECOWAS reiterated its appeal to both candidates, their supporters and sympathizers to respect the results of the poll and urged them to resort to legal channels in case of any dispute in conformity with the Memorandum of Understanding for a peaceful election signed in Ouagadougou, Burkina Faso on 3 September 2010. It reminded both candidates that victory is not an end in itself. «This presidential election rather opens new ways for future elections that will ensure the participation of all the political parties in the exercise of power in the interest of Guinea», stressed Professor Theodore Holo.

ECOWAS seized the opportunity to thank the Chairman of the Transition, General Sekouba Konate for his commitment and leadership in the successful completion of the transition and expressed its gratitude to the Burkinabe President Blaise Compaore, Mediator in the Guinean crisis, for his remarkable efforts in this completion. It reiterated its commitment to support Guinea in the next stages for a successful transition and to consolidate democracy and good governance in this country[.]

SOURCE: Economic Community of West African States. Press Releases. "ECOWAS Welcomes the Proper Conduct of the Second Round of the Presidential Election in Guinea." November 9, 2010. http://news .ecowas.int/presseshow.php?nb=177&lang=en&annee=2010.

UN Concerned About Post-Election Violence in Guinea

November 19, 2010

The United Nations human rights office today voiced deep concern at reported abuses committed during the violence that erupted in Guinea following the presidential election, including excessive force, use of live fire and incitement to ethnic hatred.

The violence began on Monday after Guinea's Independent Electoral Commission declared Alpha Condé the winner of the run-off poll held on 7 November.

Four people have been confirmed to have been killed and over 300 other reported injured in the violence that took place in the capital, Conakry, according to the Office for the High Commissioner for Human Rights (OHCHR).

"OHCHR staff in Guinea have documented numerous allegations of human rights violations and continue to carry out investigations," spokesperson Rupert Colville told a news conference in Geneva.

The Office is deeply concerned by the manner in which Guinea's security forces, while reacting to a series of demonstrations linked to the election, have used excessive force and resorted to live fire, he stated, adding that a number of members of the security forces have also been injured.

Mr. Colville said agents of the Force Spéciale de Securisation du Processus Electoral (FOSSEPEL) and red beret troops have fired on crowds with live ammunition in several parts of Conakry. OHCHR staff witnessed heavily armed red beret soldiers and FOSSE-PEL police and gendarmes "brutally beating, arresting and shooting" at unarmed civilians in various locations.

In addition, human rights staff have received several reports that ethnically-motivated violence between Peuhl and Malinké youths was taking place in several neighborhoods, Mr. Colville noted.

According to victims interviewed by OHCHR, red beret troops have been collaborating with groups of ethnic Malinké youth to target property and homes owned by members of the Peuhl ethnic group.

"OHCHR urges the authorities and security forces, political leaders and their activists to refrain from violence and from inciting ethnic hatred," said the spokesperson.

The Office also called on the transitional Government, which proclaimed a state of emergency, to scrupulously adhere to international norms regarding states of emergency, and to ensure that the security forces adhere to international standards governing the use of force and firearms.

Meanwhile, the Office of the Prosecutor of the International Criminal Court (ICC) said today it is keeping a close eye on the situation in Guinea.

Deputy Prosecutor Fatou Bensouda issued a statement in which she urged the security forces to refrain from any excessive use of force against civilians, and encouraged the political leaders to call on their supporters and fellow citizens to maintain calm and avoid unrest.

"All reported acts of violence will be closely scrutinized by the Office in order to determine whether crimes falling under the Court's jurisdiction are committed and should warrant an investigation," she stated.

Members of the Security Council yesterday deplored the violence in Guinea and urged political leaders in the West African country to refrain from actions likely to incite tensions.

They appealed to all parties to follow the existing legal procedure to "resolve their differences peacefully," Philip John Parham, Deputy Permanent Representative of the United Kingdom, which holds the Council's rotating presidency this month, told reporters after a closed-door meeting with the Secretary-General's Special Representative for West Africa, Said Djinnit, who briefed them on the latest developments.

SOURCE: United Nations. News Centre. "UN Rights Office Concerned at Reported Abuses in Post-Electoral Guinea." November 19, 2010. http://www.un.org/apps/news/story.asp?NewsID=36804&Cr=+Guinea+&Cr1.

UN Secretary General Welcomes
Conclusion of Guinea Election

December 3, 2010

Secretary-General Ban Ki-moon today welcomed the certification of the results of the presidential poll in Guinea and urged the people of the West African country to accept the outcome and to move towards peace and national reconciliation.

Mr. Ban congratulated the president-elect, Alpha Conde, and encouraged him to work to consolidate and promote national unity.

Guinea's Supreme Court certified the results of the run-off presidential election held on 7 November in which Mr. Conde was pitted against the country's former Prime Minister Cellou Dalein Diallo.

The run-off poll followed the first round of the election in June. It was the final stage of the interim Government's efforts to restore democracy after Captain Moussa Dadis Camara seized power in a coup in 2008 following the death of long-time president Lansana Conté.

Mr. Ban deplored the incidents of violence and violations of human rights that followed the release of the provisional results on 15 November.

"He emphasizes the need to respect international human rights standards and calls on the security forces to ensure the protection of all Guineans. He warns those who may incite or perpetrate violence that they will be held accountable," said a statement issued by the Secretary-General's spokesperson.

Mr. Ban commended all those who facilitated the transition process in Guinea, including the country's leaders, President Blaise Compaoré of Burkina Faso—in his capacity as the mediator mandated by the Economic Community of West African States (ECOWAS), the African Union and Guinea's other international partners.

"The United Nations will continue to support national reconciliation, peace building and development efforts in Guinea," the statement added.

Source: United Nations. News Centre. "Ban Welcomes Conclusion of Presidential Election in Guinea, Urges Reconciliation." December 3, 2010. http://www.un.org/apps/news/story.asp?NewsID=36944&Cr=+guinea+&Cr1=.

OTHER HISTORIC DOCUMENTS OF INTEREST

FROM THIS VOLUME

Chinese Dissident
Awarded Nobel Peace Prize

OCTOBER 9 AND DECEMBER 7, 10, AND 11, 2010

On October 8, the Norwegian Nobel committee announced that imprisoned Chinese dissident Liu Xiaobo would be awarded the 2010 Nobel Peace Prize. In announcing the award, Nobel chair Thorbjørn Jagland said that Liu was chosen for his "long and non-violent struggle for fundamental human rights in China." Jagland explained that it was the belief of the Nobel committee that human rights and peace are closely linked. Jagland called on the world to keep close watch on China as it continues its rise to global dominance. "We have to speak when others cannot speak. As China is rising, we should have the right to criticize. . . . We want to advance those forces that want China to become more democratic," he said.

Immediately after the announcement, the Chinese government struck back, furious that the prize was going to someone who had been convicted of violating Chinese law. "Liu Xiaobo is a criminal who has been sentenced by Chinese judicial departments for violating Chinese law," the Chinese foreign ministry said. According to the ministry, awarding the Nobel Peace Prize to Liu "runs completely counter to the principle of the prize." China called on nations around the world to boycott the ceremony and warned that relations with Norway and countries supporting the award could be tarnished.

LIU XIAOBO

A former teacher, Liu first gained notoriety for his writings and lectures, in which he called for justice for those who had suffered under the reign of the former Chinese communist leader Mao Zedong. In 1989, while teaching at Columbia University in New York, violence broke out in China's Tiananmen Square, and Liu returned to his home to support the demonstrators. Liu and three other intellectuals staged a hunger strike to protest the military crackdown on pro-democracy demonstrators in the square. On June 4, the military closed in and the group, headed by Liu, negotiated with the military to allow protestors to peacefully leave the square. Liu was arrested and labeled a traitor who had worked to assemble the Tiananmen Square rebellion.

When Liu was released in 1991, he began petitioning for democracy and human rights in China. His work was closely watched by the Chinese government, who arrested him again in 1995 and held him for eight months, and again in 1996, when he was sentenced to three years in a labor camp for his writings that called on the Chinese government to end its corruption and hold democratic elections.

Upon his release in 1999, Liu used the Internet to reach a new overseas audience to spread his message about human rights violations in China. The dawn of Internet communication and research in China also enabled Liu to complete further research on the U.S. Constitution, the French Declaration of the Rights of Man and of the Citizen, and other democratic documents. His research led to the creation of a group of intellectuals that spent three years writing and finding signatories for the document known as Charter 08, a call for the end of communism and the installation of a democratic government in China. Charter 08 was first released on the Internet in 2008; since then, more than ten thousand people have signed onto the document.

The charter, along with other writings by Chinese dissidents, led to a Chinese government crackdown on electronic communication. Liu and the original three hundred signatories of Charter 08 were questioned, and Liu was held under house arrest until a trial in December 2008. The verdict after the trial: Liu was "openly slandering and inciting others to overthrow our country's state power." When he was sentenced to eleven years in prison, Liu stated, "I firmly believe that China's political progress will never stop, and I'm full of optimistic expectations of freedom coming to China in the future, because no force can block the human desire for freedom."

Liu's arrest and detention did not signal the end of the human rights and democratic movements in China. To gain momentum for their cause, a number of Chinese dissidents sent a nomination to the Nobel committee to express their support for Liu for the 2010 Nobel Peace Prize. Xu Youyu, a philosopher who joined the dissidents, wrote to the committee that Liu and his writings were "characterized by an unwavering bravery and refusal to back down in the face of danger and suppression, by the pursuit and defense of human rights, humanism, peace and other universal values and, finally, adherence to the practice of rational dialogue, compromise and non-violence." The letters aided the Nobel committee's decision to honor Liu as the 2010 Nobel Peace Prize laureate.

CHINA PROTESTS THE AWARD

Statements from the Chinese government came quickly following the Nobel announcement, criticizing the committee for violating the traditions of the prize. "The Nobel Peace Prize should be awarded to those who work to promote ethnic harmony, international friendship, disarmament and who hold peace meetings. These were Nobel's wishes," a spokesperson for the foreign ministry said. "Liu Xiaobo was found guilty of violating Chinese law and sentenced to prison by Chinese judicial organs. His actions run contrary to the purpose of the Nobel Peace Prize. By awarding the prize to this person, the Nobel committee has violated and blasphemed the award."

After learning that Liu was being awarded the Nobel Peace Prize, China immediately cracked down on activists across the country. Liu's friends and family were kept under close surveillance and were barred from leaving the country to attend the December 10 Nobel ceremony. In some instances, cell phone service was cut off to stop communication among political activists, some of whom were reported to have gone missing. The Chinese government refused to release Liu from his prison in Northeast China to receive the award, marking the first time the award would not be accepted since 1935.

As the government tried to control the flow of information, BBC and CNN news feeds were cut off from Chinese television. State media reports throughout China featured polls meant to reflect the attitude of Chinese citizens, which the government said were unhappy with the Nobel committee's decision to award Liu. In state-run newspapers, articles appeared in defense of the nation's human rights records and attacked the United States and other nations that had congratulated Liu for his award or had called for his release.

In November, China issued a diplomatic note to nations with embassies in Oslo, Norway, requesting that they boycott the Nobel Peace Prize ceremony. The note further pressed the governments not to issue the customary congratulatory statements regarding Liu or the award. While few heeded China's warning, some diplomats, particularly those of European nations, chose to proceed with caution because China is a large, and ever more increasing, investor in Europe. "European nations are facing these choices now—do they want to be part of the political game? Or do they want to act responsibly and develop friendly ties with the Chinese government and people?" Chinese vice minister of foreign affairs Cui Tiankai said of the relationship as it related to the Nobel Peace Prize.

The Chinese government warned that nations attending the ceremony could face "consequences" from China. The sixteen nations that chose not to attend were Chinese allies and trade partners, including Cuba, Afghanistan, Russia, Iran, Pakistan, and Egypt. Although the number was small, the Chinese government claimed it received widespread support of its cause. "As far as I know, at present, more than 100 countries and organizations have expressed explicit support for China opposing the Nobel peace prize, which fully shows that the international community does not accept the decision of the Nobel committee," said foreign ministry spokesperson Jiang Yu. Jiang noted that support for China would be clear in the number of countries that would not attend the ceremony. "Facts have fully shown that the decision of the Norwegian Nobel Committee does not represent the wish of the majority of the people in the world, particularly that of the developing countries," she said. Although only sixty-five nations were invited to the ceremony, the Nobel committee would only acknowledge that China was one element in each nation's decision of whether to attend. "Some have obviously been influenced by China, for others this has nothing to do with China," said the Nobel committee's secretary, Geir Lundestad.

In the United States, where the relationship with China is often tenuous, President Barack Obama, the 2009 Nobel Peace Prize laureate, and his administration continued to press for Liu's release. "Over the last thirty years, China has made dramatic progress in economic reform and improving the lives of its people," Obama said. "But this award reminds us that political reform has not kept pace, and that the basic human rights of every man, woman and child must be respected."

Nobel Peace Prize Ceremony

Liu is not the first to be awarded the Nobel Peace Prize while serving a prison sentence. German Carl von Ossietzky, who had been convicted of high treason for publishing information on Germany's violation of the Treaty of Versailles, won the award in 1935 while imprisoned in a German concentration camp. And Aung San Suu Kyi, a Burmese political opposition leader kept under house arrest until her release in 2010, received the award in 1991. She was not allowed to travel to receive her award, but her husband and son accepted it on her behalf.

Because Liu was unable to attend, the Nobel committee set an empty chair with his picture on the stage. Committee chair Jagland spoke during the ceremony about Liu's contribution to world peace and called for his release. "Liu has exercised his civil rights. He has done nothing wrong. He must therefore be released," Jagland said. Jagland's speech was also highly critical of the human rights record of the Chinese government, noting that the nation is a signatory of many human rights declarations, which the Nobel committee believes the government is in clear violation of. "More or less authoritarian states may have long periods of rapid economic growth, but it is no coincidence that nearly all the richest countries in the world are democratic. Democracy mobilizes new human and technological resource. China's new status entails increased responsibility. China must be prepared for criticism and regard it as positive—as an opportunity for improvement," Jagland said of China's position in the world.

Jagland called on China to look differently at those labeled as political dissidents. "The human rights activists in China are defenders of the international order and the main trends in the global community," he said. "Viewed in that light, they are thus not dissidents, but representatives of the main lines of development in today's world."

After the ceremony, China took another opportunity to attack the Nobel committee's decision and the nations that supported the award. "Mutual respect for sovereignty and non-interference in internal affairs are the basic norms governing international relations," Jiang said.

—Heather Kerrigan

Following are four statements issued by the Chinese government in response to the awarding of the Nobel Peace Prize to Liu Xiaobo. The first, from October 9, 2010, is a statement by foreign ministry spokesperson Ma Zhaoxu on the announcement by the Nobel committee of Liu's award; the second, from December 7, 2010, announces support given to China by one hundred nations and organizations in opposition to the award; in the third, from December 10, 2010, foreign ministry spokesperson Jiang Yu expresses opposition to the award; and the fourth, from December 11, 2010, questions Western support for the award. In addition, the speech given by Nobel committee chair Thorbjørn Jagland on December 10, 2010, upon awarding the Nobel Peace Prize to Liu has been included.

Chinese Government Responds to Nobel Peace Prize

DOCUMENT

October 9, 2010

Q: On Oct. 8, the Norwegian Nobel committee awarded the Nobel Peace Prize for 2010 to Chinese "dissident" Liu Xiaobo. How do you comment?
A: As described in Nobel's will, the Nobel Peace Prize should be awarded to the person who "shall have done the most or the best work for fraternity between nations, the abolition or reduction of standing armies and for the holding and promotion of peace congresses". Liu Xiaobo is a criminal who broke China's laws and was convicted by Chinese judicial authorities. What he did runs in opposite directions to the purposes of the Prize. It completely violates the principles of the prize and discredits the peace prize itself for the Nobel committee to award the prize to such a person.

Q: Will the award undermine China-Norway relations?

A: Over the past years, China-Norway relations have maintained sound development, which is in the fundamental interests of both countries and peoples. The award of the Nobel Peace Prize to Liu Xiaobo by the Nobel committee not only contravenes the principles of the Nobel Peace Prize but also will damage China-Norway relations.

SOURCE: Ministry of Foreign Affairs of the People's Republic of China. "Foreign Ministry Spokesperson Ma Zhaoxu's Remarks." October 9, 2010. http://www.fmprc.gov.cn/eng/xwfw/s2510/2535/t759708.htm.

Chinese Government Claims Support of One Hundred Nations and Organizations for Its Opposition

December 7, 2010

More than 100 countries and international organizations have expressed support for China's stance on this year's Nobel Peace Prize, which will be awarded to convicted Chinese criminal Liu Xiaobo, Chinese Foreign Ministry spokesperson Jiang Yu said Tuesday.

"This shows that the majority of international community members do not accept the Nobel Committee's wrong decision," said Jiang at a news briefing.

Liu was sentenced to 11 years in jail on Dec. 25, 2009, after a Beijing court convicted him of violating Chinese law and engaging in activities aimed at overthrowing the government.

Jiang said the Nobel Committee's decision to grant the Peace Prize to a convicted criminal was tantamount to overt support for criminal activities in China, and a gross interference in China's judicial sovereignty.

"This wrong decision will incur firm opposition from the Chinese people, and it is unacceptable to the vast majority of countries that uphold justice," said Jiang.

In China, human rights experts and legal experts aired their opposition to the award.

A spokesperson of Beijing Municipal Higher People's Court pointed out that the court's decision on Liu's case was based on an adequate factual and legal foundation.

Liu had incited others to subvert state power and overthrow the socialist system through writing incendiary articles and releasing them on the Internet and organizing and inducing others to sign in support of his articles, said the spokesperson.

His actions violated Article 105 of the Criminal Law of the People's Republic of China and he had committed the crime of inciting others to subvert state power, said the spokesperson.

Professor Zhang Xiaoling, director of the human rights research center of the Party School of the Communist Party of China Central Committee, said China respected the rule of law, and the Chinese courts handled Liu Xiaobo's case according to the law, which was a judicial act of a sovereign country that should be respected.

The Nobel Committee had awarded the prize to an imprisoned Chinese criminal, which challenged China's judicial authority, and interfered in China's internal affairs, said Zhang.

Zhu Wenqi, a professor of international law at Renmin University of China, said China was a vast and populous country, and its stability had direct bearing on the world order. Responsible international organizations and institutions should weigh their actions against the interests of a peaceful world order.

Zhu said different countries had different legal provisions, but many Western countries had also criminalized the incitement of hatred. China's law was appropriate to its own social and cultural circumstances, which should be respected and understood by other countries.

SOURCE: Government of the People's Republic of China. "China Has Backing of More than 100 Countries, Organizations on Nobel Peace Prize." December 7, 2010. http://www.gov.cn/misc/2010-12/07/content_1761034.htm.

DOCUMENT

China Says Nobel Peace Prize Interferes with Internal Affairs

December 10, 2010

China voiced strong opposition to this year's Nobel Peace Prize Friday, saying the country is firmly against attempts to use the prize to interfere in its internal affairs.

"We are firmly against attempts by any country or individual to use the Nobel Peace Prize to interfere in China's internal affairs and infringe on China's judicial sovereignty," said Foreign Ministry spokeswoman Jiang Yu.

She made the remarks when commenting on the Nobel Peace Prize Award Ceremony in Oslo that gave this year's prize to convicted Chinese criminal Liu Xiaobo, who was sentenced to 11 years in prison for engaging in activities aimed at overthrowing the government.

Jiang said that China's position "has won the understanding and support over 100 countries and major international organizations."

"Facts have fully shown that the decision of the Norwegian Nobel Committee does not represent the wish of the majority of the people in the world, particularly that of the developing countries," Jiang added.

The spokeswoman noted that prejudice and lies are untenable and the Cold War mentality has no popular support, saying that "this political farce will in no way shake the resolve and confidence of the Chinese people to follow the path of socialism with Chinese characteristics."

"The scheme by some people will get nowhere," Jiang said.

SOURCE: Embassy of the People's Republic of China in the United States of America. "China Voices Strong Opposition of Nobel Peace Prize to Interfere in Its Internal Affairs." December 10, 2010. http://us.chineseembassy.org/eng/gdxw/t777298.htm.

Nobel Prize Presentation Speech

December 10, 2010

Your Majesties, Excellencies, Ladies and Gentlemen,

"The Norwegian Nobel Committee has decided to award the Nobel Peace Prize for 2010 to Liu Xiaobo for his long and non-violent struggle for fundamental human rights in China. The Norwegian Nobel Committee has long believed that there is a close connection between human rights and peace. Such rights are a prerequisite for the "fraternity between nations" of which Alfred Nobel wrote in his will."

This was the first paragraph of the Norwegian Nobel Committee's announcement on the 8th of October of the award of this year's Peace Prize.

We regret that the Laureate is not present here today. He is in isolation in a prison in north-east China. Nor can the Laureate's wife Liu Xia or his closest relatives be here with us. No medal or diploma will therefore be presented here today.

This fact alone shows that the award was necessary and appropriate. We congratulate Liu Xiaobo on this year's Peace Prize.

There have been a number of previous occasions when the Laureate has been prevented from attending. This has in fact been the case with several awards which have proved in the light of history to have been most significant and honourable. Even when the Laureate has come, he or she has several times been severely condemned by the authorities of his or her own country.

There was a great deal of trouble in 1935, when the Committee gave the award to Carl von Ossietzky. Hitler was furious, and prohibited all Germans from accepting any Nobel Prize. King Haakon did not attend the ceremony. Ossietzky did not come to Oslo, and died a little over a year later.

There was considerable outrage in Moscow when Andrej Sakharov received his Prize in 1975. He, too, was prevented from receiving the award in person. He sent his wife. The same thing happened to Lech Walesa in 1983. The Burmese authorities were furious when Aung San Suu Kyi received the Peace Prize in 1991. Once again, the Laureate could not come to Oslo.

In 2003, Shirin Ebadi received the Nobel Peace Prize. She came. Much could be said of the reaction of the Iranian authorities, but the Iranian Ambassador did in fact attend the ceremony.

The Norwegian Nobel Committee has given four Prizes to South Africa. All the Laureates came to Oslo, but the awards to Albert Lutuli in 1960 and to Desmond Tutu in 1984 provoked great outrage in the apartheid regime in South Africa, before the applause broke out thanks to the awards to Nelson Mandela and F.W. de Klerk in 1993.

The point of these awards has of course never been to offend anyone. The Nobel Committee's intention has been to say something about the relationship between human rights, democracy and peace. And it has been important to remind the world that the rights so widely enjoyed today were fought for and won by persons who took great risks.

They did so for others. That is why Liu Xiaobo deserves our support.

Although none of the Committee's members have ever met Liu, we feel that we know him. We have studied him closely over a long period of time.

Liu was born on the 28th of December 1955 in Changchun in China's Jilin province. He took a Bachelor's degree in literature at Jilin University, and a Master's degree and a PhD at Beijing Normal University, where he also taught. Stays abroad included visits to Oslo, Hawaii, and Columbia University, New York.

In 1989 he returned home to take part in the dawning democracy movement. On the 2nd of June he and some friends started a hunger strike on Tiananmen Square to protest against the state of emergency that had been declared. They issued a six-point democratic manifesto, written by Liu, opposing dictatorship and in favour of democracy. Liu was opposed to any physical struggle against the authorities on the part of the students; he tried to find a peaceful solution to the tension between the students and the government. Non-violence was already figuring prominently in his message. On the 4th of June he and his friends tried to prevent a clash between the army and the students. He was only partially successful. Many lives were lost, most of them outside Tiananmen Square.

Liu has told his wife that he would like this year's Peace Prize to be dedicated to "the lost souls from the 4th of June." It is a pleasure for us to fulfil his wish.

Liu has said that "The greatness of non-violent resistance is that even as man is faced with forceful tyranny and the resulting suffering, the victim responds to hate with love, to prejudice with tolerance, to arrogance with humility, to humiliation with dignity, and to violence with reason."

Tiananmen became a turning-point in Liu's life.

In 1996, Liu was sentenced to three years in a labour camp for "rumour-mongering and slander." He was president of the independent Chinese PEN-centre from 2003 to 2007. Liu has written nearly 800 essays, 499 of them since 2005. He was one of the chief architects behind Charter 08, which was made known on the 10th of December 2008, which was, in the words of the document's Preamble, on the occasion of "the one hundredth anniversary of China's first Constitution, the 60th anniversary of the promulgation of the Universal Declaration of Human Rights, the 30th anniversary of the birth of the Democracy Wall, and the 10th anniversary of the Chinese government's signature of the International Covenant on Civil and Political Rights." Charter 08 defends fundamental human rights and has in due course been signed by several thousand persons both in China itself and abroad.

On the 25th of December 2009, Liu was sentenced to 11 years' imprisonment and two years' loss of political rights for, in the words of the sentence, "incitement to the overthrow of the state power and socialist system and the people's democratic dictatorship." Liu has consistently claimed that the sentence violates both China's own constitution and fundamental human rights.

There are many dissidents in China, and their opinions differ on many points. The severe punishment imposed on Liu made him more than a central spokesman for human rights. Practically overnight, he became the very symbol, both in China and internationally, of the struggle for such rights in China.

Your Majesties, ladies and gentlemen,

During the cold war, the connections between peace and human rights were disputed. Since the end of the cold war, however, peace researchers and political scientists have almost without exception underlined how close those connections are. This is, allegedly, one of the most "robust" findings they have arrived at. Democracies may go to war against dictatorships, and have certainly waged colonial wars, but there is, apparently, not a single example of a democracy having gone to war against another democracy.

The deeper "fraternity between nations" which Alfred Nobel mentions in his will, and which is a prerequisite for real peace, can hardly be created without human rights and democracy.

There are scarcely any examples in world history of a great power achieving such rapid growth over such a long period of time as China. Since 1978, year by year, decade after decade, the country's growth rate has stood at 10 percent or more. A few years ago the country's output was greater than Germany's; this year it exceeded Japan's. China has thus achieved the world's second largest gross national product. The USA's national product is still three times greater than China's, but while China is continuing its advance, the USA is in serious difficulties.

Economic success has lifted several hundred million Chinese out of poverty. For the reduction in the number of poor people in the world, China must be given the main credit.

We can to a certain degree say that China with its 1.3 billion people is carrying mankind's fate on its shoulders. If the country proves capable of developing a social market economy with full civil rights, this will have a huge favourable impact on the world. If not, there is a danger of social and economic crises arising in the country, with negative consequences for us all.

Historical experience gives us reason to believe that continuing rapid economic growth presupposes opportunities for free research, thinking and debate. And moreover: without freedom of expression, corruption, the abuse of power, and misrule will develop. Every power system must be counterbalanced by popularly elected control, free media, and the right of individual citizens to criticise.

More or less authoritarian states may have long periods of rapid economic growth, but it is no coincidence that nearly all the richest countries in the world are democratic. Democracy mobilises new human and technological resources.

China's new status entails increased responsibility. China must be prepared for criticism and regard it as positive—as an opportunity for improvement. This must be the case wherever there is great power. We have all formed opinions on the role of the USA through the years. Friends and allies criticised the country both for the Vietnam War and for the lack of civil rights for the coloured people. Many Americans were opposed to the award of the Nobel Peace Prize to Martin Luther King in 1964. Looking back, we can see that the USA grew stronger when the African-American people obtained their rights.

Many will ask whether China's weakness—for all the strength the country is currently showing—is not manifested in the need to imprison a man for eleven years merely for expressing his opinions on how his country should be governed.

This weakness finds clear expression in the sentence on Liu, where it is underlined as especially serious that he spread his opinions on the Internet. But those who fear technological advances have every reason to fear the future. Information technology can not be abolished. It will continue to open societies. As Russia's President Dmitrij Medvedev put it in an address to the Duma: "The new information technology gives us an opportunity to become connected with the world. The world and society are growing more open even if the ruling class does not like it."

No doubt Medvedev had the fate of the Soviet Union in mind. Compulsory uniformity and control of thought prevented the country from participating in the technological revolution which took place in the 1970s and 80s. The system broke down. The country would have stood to gain a great deal more from entering into a dialogue at an early stage with people like Andrej Sakharov.

Your Majesties, ladies and gentlemen,

Today neither the nation-state nor a majority within the nation-state has unlimited authority. Human rights limit what the nation-state and the majority in a nation-state can do. This must apply to all states that are members of the United Nations and who have acceded to the Universal Declaration of Human Rights. China has signed and even ratified several of the UN's and the ILO's major international conventions on human rights. It is interesting that China has accepted the supranational conflict-resolving mechanism of the WTO.

China's own constitution upholds fundamental human rights. Article 35 of the country's constitution thus lays down that "Citizens of the People's Republic of China enjoy freedom of speech, of the press, of assembly, of association, of procession and of demonstration." Article 41 begins by stating that citizens " . . . have the right to criticise and make suggestions regarding any state organ or functionary."

Liu has exercised his civil rights. He has done nothing wrong. He must therefore be released!

In the past 100 to 150 years, human rights and democracy have gained an ever-stronger position in the world. And with them, peace. This can be clearly seen in Europe, where so many wars were fought, and whose colonial powers started so many wars around the world. Europe today is on the whole a continent of "peace." Decolonization after the Second World War gave a number of countries, first in Asia and then in Africa, the chance to govern themselves with respect for basic human rights. With India in the lead, many of them seized the opportunity. Over the latest decades, we have seen how democracy has consolidated its position in Latin America and in Central and Eastern Europe. Many countries in the Muslim part of the world are treading the same path: Turkey, Indonesia, Malaysia. Several other countries are in the process of opening up their political systems.

The human rights activists in China are defenders of the international order and the main trends in the global community. Viewed in that light, they are thus not dissidents, but representatives of the main lines of development in today's world.

Liu denies that criticism of the Communist Party is the same as offending China and the Chinese people. He argues that "Even if the Communist Party is the ruling party, it cannot be equated with the country, let alone with the nation and its culture." Changes in China can take time, a very long time: political reforms should, as Liu says, " be gradual, peaceful, orderly and controlled." China has had enough of attempts at revolutionary change. They only lead to chaos. But as Liu also writes, "An enormous transformation towards pluralism in society has already taken place, and official authority is no longer able to fully control the whole society." However strong the power of the regime may appear to be, every single individual must do his best to live, in his words, "an honest life with dignity."

The answer from the Chinese authorities is to claim that this year's Peace Prize humiliates China, and to give very derogatory descriptions of Liu.

History shows many examples of political leaders playing on nationalist feelings and attempting to demonize holders of contrary opinions. They soon become foreign agents. This has sometimes happened in the name of democracy and freedom, but almost always with a tragic outcome.

We recognise this in the rhetoric of the struggle against terrorism: "You are either for me or against me." Such undemocratic methods as torture and imprisonment without sentence have been used in the name of freedom. This has led to more polarisation of the world and harmed the fight against terrorism.

Liu Xiaobo is an optimist, despite his many years in prison. In his closing appeal to the court on the 23rd of December 2009, he said: "I, filled with optimism, look forward to the advent of a future free China. For there is no force that can put an end to the human quest for freedom, and China will in the end become a nation ruled by law, where human rights reign supreme."

Isaac Newton once said, "If I have seen further, it is by standing on the shoulders of giants." When we are able to look ahead today, it is because we are standing on the shoulders of the many men and women who over the years—often at great risk—have stood up for what they believed in and thus made our freedom possible.

Therefore: while others at this time are counting their money, focussing exclusively on their short-term national interests, or remaining indifferent, the Norwegian Nobel Committee has once again chosen to support those who fight—for us all.

We congratulate Liu Xiaobo on the Nobel Peace Prize for 2010. His views will in the long run strengthen China. We extend to him and to China our very best wishes for the years ahead.

SOURCE: Nobel Foundation. "Presentation Speech by Thorbjørn Jagland, Chairman of the Norwegian Nobel Committee." December 10, 2010. http://nobelprize.org/nobel_prizes/peace/laureates/2010/presentation-speech.html.

China Criticizes Western Nation
Support of Nobel Peace Prize

DOCUMENT

December 11, 2010

China on Friday night hit back at some western politicians' support for this year's Nobel Peace Prize that was awarded to a convicted Chinese criminal, reiterating its opposition to interference in its internal affairs.

"We oppose anyone to make an issue of this matter, and oppose anyone to interfere in China's internal affairs in any way," said Foreign Ministry spokeswoman Jiang Yu.

Jiang made the remarks while answering a question on reports that some leaders from western countries have voiced support for the award.

The Nobel Committee awarded the Nobel Peace Prize at a ceremony in Oslo to Liu Xiaobo, who was sentenced to 11 years in prison for engaging in activities aimed at overthrowing the government.

"China has repeatedly expressed its principle and position," Jiang said.

"Mutual respect for sovereignty and non-interference in internal affairs are the basic norms governing international relations," said Jiang.

She hoped that "relevant countries could abide by the norms and do more things conducive to mutual trust and cooperation, and not the opposite."

SOURCE: Government of the People's Republic of China. "China Hits Back at Some Western Politicians' Support for Nobel Peace Prize." December 11, 2010. http://english.gov.cn/2010–12/11/content_1763575.htm.

OTHER HISTORIC DOCUMENTS OF INTEREST

FROM THIS VOLUME

FROM PREVIOUS *HISTORIC DOCUMENTS*

Thirty-three Chilean Miners Rescued

OCTOBER 13, 14, AND 18, 2010

In August 2010, Chile vaulted into the spotlight following a potentially tragic mining accident. Defying all odds, a group of thirty-three missing miners, feared dead, were found alive deep in the mine. The lengthy and heroic efforts to rescue the men captured the world's attention and united Chileans as never before.

SEARCHING FOR SURVIVORS IN A TROUBLED MINE

On August 5, a group of miners reported to work at the San José copper and gold mine, located in the arid Atacama Desert near Copiapó, Chile. The mine was one of several owned by the San Esteban Mining Company, which had a history of safety problems at a number of its properties. Between 2004 and 2010, three people died in mines owned by San Esteban, including one man who was killed in an explosion at the San José mine in 2007. During that same period, the Chilean government fined the company forty-two times for failing to take sufficient action to protect its workers.

At 2:00 p.m., the roof of the San José mine caved in, trapping thirty-three of the men who were working approximately 2,300 feet below the surface. Rescuers immediately began drilling exploratory boreholes into the mine to try to make contact with the missing men. On August 22, seventeen days after the mine collapse, the rescuers' drill bit came back to the surface with a note attached that read, "Estamos bien en el refugio los 33," or, "All 33 of us are well inside the shelter."

The men were eating lunch in a shelter located near their work area when the cave-in occurred. The impact of the collapse and falling rock created a dust storm that reached the men and temporarily blinded them for six hours. Once the dust cleared, shift leader Luis Urzua organized several men to search the tunnels for a way out. The men later reported that rocks blocked the main tunnel and that none of the escape tunnels had safety ladders, leaving them trapped in a mine shaft measuring 540 square feet. The shelter had emergency air and food stores the miners could use, but those supplies were only intended to last for forty-eight hours. The men survived by drinking water drained from the work vehicles in the mine, and Urzua imposed a strict system of food rations. He limited each man to eating two spoonfuls of tuna, a sip of milk, a piece of cracker, and a sliver of peach every 48 hours. While waiting on a hoped-for rescue, Urzua divided the shaft into three separate areas for sleeping, working, and for waste, and he devised a twelve-hour work shift schedule for the men to keep busy.

Rescuers quickly began working to stabilize the physical condition of the miners once they made contact. With little food, and living in an average temperature of 85 degrees

Fahrenheit with 90 percent humidity, the men had lost a tremendous amount of weight. Rescuers began to send metal cylinders down a series of air shafts with deliveries of water, hydration gels, and a calorie- and protein-enriched milk drink that supplied the miners with vital calories without overwhelming their deprived digestive systems. Rescuers also sent letters from family members, moisture-wicking clothes, and special socks intended to prevent athlete's foot, as well as flu and tetanus vaccinations. Doctors on hand as part of the rescue team were also concerned about the miners' lack of sunlight, fearing that without sunlight to dictate their normal routines and sleep patterns, the men could develop irregular metabolisms, vitamin deficiencies, and even heart disease, or that their motor skills would be impaired. The men received Vitamin D supplements to help combat these problems, and the rescue team later installed electric wires down one of the supply holes, enabling the miners to connect and turn on custom-made LED lights to help simulate night and day.

The rescue team also worked to establish a daily routine for the men to help combat the negative psychological effects of being trapped in isolation. The miners woke each day at 7:30 a.m., and following breakfast at 8:30, they worked to clean their living area before a morning bath. Each man also had morning chores, such as checking the oxygen and carbon dioxide levels in the air, working to reinforce the mine walls, or clearing rocks that fell due to the rescuers' drilling effort. Each day the miners ate lunch at noon and held an afternoon meeting. They sometimes held video conferences or made phone calls. The men would later be able to watch a live soccer match between Chile and the Ukraine, projected onto the wall of the mine, and enjoy music from an iPod with speakers.

Several of the men took on specialized roles while in the mine. Yonni Barrios, a miner trained in first aid, served as the group medic. With guidance from medical personnel at the surface, Barrios conducted daily medical rounds, watching particularly for the development of fungal infections or bad teeth. He also vaccinated the men against diphtheria, tetanus, and pneumonia, and participated in a daily phone call with the Chilean government's medical team.

PLANNING THE RESCUE

Meanwhile, a team assembled by the Chilean government began to drill a rescue shaft. Given the distance the drill would need to penetrate, officials estimated the shaft would not be completed for three to four months. At first, the rescue team did not tell the miners of this timeline, fearing their reactions. Yet when the men were informed several days later, officials said they reacted fairly calmly to the news.

On August 28, mine engineers announced a second rescue plan, to be executed at the same time as Plan A. Plan B would use a special "downhole hammer" drill that featured several air-powered bits that pounded the rock as the drill rotated; this feature made the drill particularly well-suited to cutting through hard volcanic rock and minerals. The team would drill at an 80 degree angle into a part of the mine shaft that was just over 2,000 feet from the surface. They would also use one of the boreholes through which supplies were transported and work to widen the hole from 3.19 inches to 28 inches. Officials estimated Plan B would take approximately two months to complete. Then, on September 5, officials announced they would set up a third drill as part of Plan C. However, because the drill had to be transported from the northern region of Iquique, officials predicted the drill would not be operational until mid-September. The benefit of Plan C was that the drill would only need to penetrate approximately 1,900 feet of rock.

In the meantime, Chilean Navy engineers began constructing a rescue capsule. Dubbed Phoenix, after the mythical bird that rose from its own ashes, the capsule was approximately twenty-one inches wide. It featured a reinforced roof to help protect the men against falling rocks or debris, as well as its own oxygen supply. The capsule had wheels along its side to ease its ascent and descent, as well as an escape hatch and safety device that would enable a miner to lower himself back to the shelter if the capsule got stuck. A video link would allow the rescue team to communicate with each miner as he rose to the surface.

Leaving the Mine

Ultimately, Plan B proved to be the most efficient and successful. Despite several technical difficulties that caused minor delays, the drill reached its target destination within six weeks. Extraction began on October 12, once the shaft and capsule had been tested. Two nurses were sent down into the mine to help prepare the men. Each man wore a chest strap that monitored his heart rate and blood pressure, as well as a special pair of sunglasses donated by Oakley to help protect his eyes against the light.

The rescue team chose Florencio Ávalos as the first man to leave the mine, as he was relatively healthy and was believed to be the best prepared to deal with any problems that might arise during transport. Ávalos reached the surface shortly after 12:00 a.m. on October 13, greeting the gathered crowd, Ávalos's family, and President Sebastián Piñera triumphantly. The exuberant crowd greeted each man with cheers of "Chi-chi-chi / Le-le-le / Los mineros de Chile!" and President Piñera remained on hand throughout the entire rescue.

At 8:50 p.m. on October 13, shift leader Urzua became the last man to reach the surface. After embracing President Piñera, Urzua said, "I've delivered to you this shift of workers, as we agreed I would." Piñera replied, "I gladly receive your shift, because you completed your duty, leaving last like a good captain. You are not the same after this, and Chile won't be the same either."

Life after the Mine

After leaving the mine, each man was taken on a stretcher to a field hospital for triage before traveling to Copiapó Hospital. One miner had acute pneumonia, and two needed dental surgery. Some had skin problems caused by the moisture of the mine, while others had lesions in their eyes. Yet overall the men appeared to be in surprisingly good health. "Things are extraordinarily well, better than expected," said Chilean health minister Jaime Mañalich. "They really are in good . . . emotional condition and physical condition." Doctors watched carefully for nightmares, panic attacks, or claustrophobia, as they could be symptoms of longer-term disorders such as post-traumatic stress disorder (PTSD). The medical team also warned that the miners' reintegration into society should occur slowly and that their sudden global fame would be a shock. President Piñera visited the miners in the hospital on October 14, vowing that never again would Chileans be permitted to work in conditions as unsafe and inhumane as the San José mine.

All of the miners were allowed to leave the hospital by October 19. Immediately, they found themselves at the center of global attention. Offers for book contracts, movie deals, paid interviews, and all-expense-paid trips to Greece, Israel, and the Dominican Republic poured in. One Chilean mining executive wrote a $10,000 check to each miner, while

Chilean philanthropist Leonardo Farkas created funds for the miners and their families to collect donations. On October 25, the men attended a formal ceremony at the presidential palace in Santiago, where President Piñera presented them with medals of commendation. Later that afternoon, the men played a soccer match at National Stadium against the president and members of the rescue team.

As the country celebrated the miners' return, the political and legal impact of the incident continued to play out. Public polling data showed a jump in approval ratings for both President Piñera and mining minister Laurence Golborne. The successful rescue operation also provided a boost to Chile's image around the world. Many analysts speculated that Chile's decision to keep the entire rescue operation open to the media helped establish it as an advanced, well-organized country in a way that might draw increased foreign investment.

Meanwhile, twenty-seven of the miners filed a $10 million negligence lawsuit against the San Esteban Mining Company, while miner Raul Bustos filed a lawsuit that also blamed Chile's National Geology and Mine Service, also known as Sernageomin, for its failure to enforce safety regulations at the San José Mine. President Piñera called for the resignation of three top Sernageomin officials while promising to triple the budget of the notoriously under-staffed agency. Piñera also closed eighteen mines and said officials would examine the potential closure of some three hundred additional mines where major safety issues had been cited. In addition, Piñera established the Commission on Work Safety to investigate the San José Mine accident and provide recommendations for preventing similar incidents in the future. The commission's preliminary report, presented on October 25, presented thirty proposals ranging from improvements in hygiene to better coordination among local regulators. However, Piñera rejected these proposals, and the Chilean Congress will not consider the commission's full recommendations until the spring of 2011.

—Linda Fecteau

Following are two press releases from the Chilean government, issued on October 13 and 14, 2010, detailing the rescue of the thirty-three trapped miners; and a statement by Chilean president Sebastián Piñera on October 18, 2010, upon the safe rescue of all thirty-three miners.

DOCUMENT   *Mine Rescue Operation Begins*

October 13, 2010

The first 12 hours of the rescue of 33 miners, trapped for 70 days in the depths of a gold and copper mine, have passed without delay in the Atacama Desert in the northern tip of Chile.

By noon local time on Wednesday October 13th, a total of 15 workers had surfaced after a journey of just over 15 minutes in the Phoenix II capsule, a cage of 54 cm in diameter, 3.9 meters in length and weighing 450 kilos.

The first worker to appear on the surface was foreman Florencio Ávalos (31) at 00:12 local time (03:12 GMT), and, like his colleagues who followed, he was in good spirits and walking unaided.

However, all the workers spent two hours in a stabilization zone, and were then taken in Chilean Air Force (FACH) Bell 412 helicopters to the hospital in the city of Copiapó for a precautionary medical examination.

It is estimated that the 33 workers will remain hospitalized for at least 48 hours in what is the leading medical center of the Atacama Region, located 800 kilometers north of Santiago.

The president of Bolivia, Evo Morales, arrived in Camp Hope at the San José mine and spoke with his counterpart President Sebastian Piñera about the rescue of fellow Bolivian Carlos Mamani (23).

The foreign leader declared he was "surprised and impressed" by the "great humanitarian action" taking place in the area. "Bolivia will never forget this historic and unprecedented moment," promised Morales.

Subsequently, the leaders received a call from the Brazilian president Luiz Inacio Lula da Silva, who called the work of the Chilean people and authorities "extraordinary." "The world is proud" of Chile, he said, according to sources cited by EFE.

The speed with which the process has developed prompted President Piñera to announce that everything could end today: "The deadlines have been shortened because the rescue operation for each miner took one hour, but now we are rescuing three miners every two hours. We have seven or eight hours of work left.

"The great wealth of our country is not the copper, but the miners; it is not the natural resources, but the Chileans," said the Head of State, while confirming he will remain in the area until "we rescue the last miner."

SOURCE: ThisisChile.cl. "15 Miners Recovered in the First 12 Hours of the Rescue in Chile." October 13, 2010. http://www.thisischile.cl/Articles.aspx?id=5478&sec=193&eje=&t=15-miners-recovered-in-the-first-12-hours-of-the-rescue-in-chile&idioma=2.

DOCUMENT *Final Miner Rescued*

October 14, 2010

After a full day of uninterrupted work, the 33 miners trapped since August 5th more than 600 meters deep at a mine in northern Chile, were rescued unharmed on Wednesday night.

With the rescue of the group leader, Luis Urzúa (54), recorded at 21:55 local time (00:55 GMT) after 70 days of isolation, authorities declared the end of the salvage operation. The six brigades had yet to return to the surface.

"I hand over my shift and I hope this never happens again. Thanks to all of Chile and to those who have cooperated. I feel proud of being a Chilean," the miner said to President Sebastián Piñera when he stepped out of the capsule of only 54 centimeters in diameter that had hauled him up the 622 meter duct.

The surfacing of Urzúa caused an explosion of joy at Camp Hope, the village set up by relatives of the workers in the mine near San Jose, where around 2,000 media professionals from all over the world arrived.

The joy was also expressed in the streets and squares across the country, with motorists honking their horns, citizens waving flags and fire stations making their alarms sound in unison.

"We had the strength, grit and spirit to fight for ourselves and for our families," the miner said in his brief conversation with the head authority, while the official television signal showed the six brigades who remained in the depths of the shelter displaying a canvas which read: "Chile: Mission Accomplished."

"I receive your shift and I congratulate you for doing your duty and coming out last," President Piñera answered Urzúa, before he shook his hand, gave him a warm hug and sang the Chilean national anthem with all those who participated.

Emerging at 00:21 local time (03:21 GMT), Manuel González, from the brigade of state-owned Codelco who spent 24 hours in the mine having been the first one to go down in the Phoenix 2 cage, said: "Officially, we declare this over. I am returning happy thanks to God and all my team-mates." 12 minutes later, the San Lorenzo operation ended with full success.

SOURCE: ThisisChile.cl. "Successful Rescue of 33 Miners in Chile." October 14, 2010. http://www.thisis chile.cl/Articles.aspx?id=5493&sec=193&eje=&t=successful-rescue-of-33-miners-in-chile&idioma=2.

Chilean President on the Rescue of Thirty-three Miners

DOCUMENT

October 18, 2010

"This story, that started as a possible tragedy, I hope it will end as a real blessing", President Sebastián Piñera stated moments before he left to the San José mine to witness the rescue of the 33 miners, on October 12th.

The final stage of this operation lasted over 30 hours and all of the workers were brought safely to the surface, after 69 days trapped 700 meters below. Their relatives, the technical group in charge of the rescue and the Chief of State himself waited for them as they came out of the mine. The last miner ascending was Luis Urzúa, who was the leader of the group. He symbolically handed the shift over to President Piñera.

After receiving proper medical attention, all of the miners are healthy and back home with their families.

SOURCE: Government of Chile. "Rescue of the 33 Chilean Miners." October 18, 2010. http://www.gob.cl/ rescate-mineros-san-jose/rescue-of-the-33-chilean-miners/.

OTHER HISTORIC DOCUMENTS OF INTEREST

FROM THIS VOLUME

- Earthquakes Devastate Haiti and Chile, p. 13

United Nations Announces Rinderpest Virus Eradication

OCTOBER 14, 2010

On October 14, 2010, the Food and Agriculture Organization (FAO) of the United Nations declared the end of its Global Rinderpest Eradication Programme (GREP), signaling that the virus, which kills 80 percent of the cattle it infects, had been wiped out. Rinderpest is only the second virus considered to be eradicated—the first was smallpox more than three decades earlier—and the first virus eradicated that affects only animals. The disease has been largely overlooked by those in Western nations, but in Africa and Asia, it has done extensive damage to cattle herds and caused widespread famine. The eradication efforts that had begun sixteen years earlier culminated in the FAO's announcement of what it called "a powerful example of what can be achieved when the international community and individual country's veterinary services and farming communities cooperate."

History of Rinderpest

It is believed that rinderpest originated in Asia and moved to Egypt more than five thousand years ago through cattle herding and trading. In the late 1800s, the virus spread across Africa and wrought widespread havoc. Ninety percent of cattle herds in sub-Saharan Africa were wiped out, leading to famine. In Ethiopia, one-third of the human population was killed by rinderpest-induced famine in the late nineteenth century, according to the FAO. Two-thirds of the Maasai people in Tanzania died as well.

The virus was rarely seen in Western nations or Australia and New Zealand because any shipments containing diseased cattle that reached ports in these parts of the world were slaughtered. A small outbreak occurred in Great Britain in the mid-1800s, however. In response, the government set up the National Veterinary Service in 1865 and wiped out any trace of the disease there by 1867.

Asia and Africa continued to be afflicted by the virus into the twentieth century because of porous borders. A number of localized eradication campaigns were started, and then quickly ended, after it was falsely determined that the virus was gone. In the 1950s, the African Union established the Inter-African Bureau of Epizootic Diseases (now known as the African Union–Interafrican Bureau for Animal Resources) to eradicate the disease from the African continent without success. During the 1960s and 1970s, a localized vaccination project called JP15 was reported to have eliminated rinderpest from every African nation except Sudan. In 1987, after another outbreak of rinderpest in Africa, the Organization of African Unity launched the Pan-African Rinderpest Campaign, which declared all regions except Sudan and Somalia free of the disease by the 1990s. A similar program took root in Asia after an outbreak of rinderpest in Afghanistan in 1969, but after it had been removed from nearly every part of the continent, the program ended and the virus materialized again.

United Nations Takes Action

The Global Rinderpest Eradication Programme (GREP), which began in 1994, set out to eradicate the virus by 2010, and along the way gain additional information about the disease strain, the way it spreads, and the best techniques for surveillance. When the GREP was initiated, organizers initially faced difficulty deciding which areas to target with eradication efforts. Affected nations, skeptical of the program, were slow to release data on the extent of their rinderpest problem. But as success slowly spread, cooperation increased as well.

To treat affected animals, the FAO used the vaccine first developed in the 1950s by British veterinary pathologist Walter Plowright. Before the availability of the vaccine, local eradication efforts consisted of slaughter and quarantine, coupled with unsuccessful attempts at inoculation, which actually spread the virus further. Although it was no easy task eradicating smallpox, rinderpest proved more difficult because it occurs only in animals—most commonly in cattle—that can be easily moved across borders, spreading the virus to new herds. But scientists working on the rinderpest eradication program had one thing working on their side—a single virus strain. Most often, as a virus spreads, it mutates into multiple strains, which requires creation of more than one vaccine. Since it was first introduced thousands of years ago, the rinderpest virus strain has been detected in three different lineages, each affecting a specific part of the world—Lineages I and II affect cattle and other animals in Africa, while Lineage III targets animals in Asia and the Middle East.

Eradicating the virus was a global effort that encompassed a number of partnerships, including those with the African Union, South Asian Association for Regional Cooperation, European Union, U.S. Agency for International Development, United Kingdom Department for International Development, the government of the Republic of Ireland, the Italian Development Cooperation, and other partners and individual countries. These groups worked together to raise funds and offer laboratories, scientists, and data to help complete the eradication process. "Together we have defeated rinderpest. Together we are stronger. Together we will defeat hunger," said FAO director-general Jacques Diouf.

Through their efforts, nations in Asia, Africa, and the Middle East have slowly been declared free of the virus. India was declared free of the virus in 2004, and Pakistan followed three years later. China was declared free of the disease in 2008. A number of other Asian nations will receive a declaration of eradication in 2011. Central Asia has not seen the disease for decades. In the Middle East, no clinical cases of the virus have been reported in more than a decade. A number of Middle Eastern nations received their eradication declaration beginning in 2005, while others are due to receive theirs in 2011.

In Africa, rinderpest eradication has varied from country to country. In West and Central Africa, the virus has not been seen since 1988. Northern and southern Africa have been mostly free of the disease, except for an outbreak in Egypt in 1987. The Somali ecosystem, which comprises southern Somalia, Ethiopia, and Kenya, is a different story. This is the area in which the last rinderpest outbreak was reported in 2001. The porous borders in this area of Africa made it increasingly difficult for FAO scientists to contain the disease, and scientists at one point thought they would not be able to stop the spread in the region. It was not until 2008 that Ethiopia was declared free of the virus, followed by Kenya in 2009 and Somalia in 2010.

The last-known case of rinderpest occurred in Kenya in 2001. Scientists are typically slow to declare successful eradication for fear that the virus could crop up again, as was the case in the earliest attempts at rinderpest eradication, before FAO involvement. But the announcement was readily welcomed by animal health and food supply experts around the world. "There has never been such an important and devastating disease as rinderpest in livestock," said Michael Baron of the Institute for Animal Health. "We've known about it and its problems for a thousand years and we've got rid of it."

Final Steps Toward Eradication

Official declaration of the eradication of rinderpest is a three-phase process. First, the director-general of the FAO declared the end of GREP operations. This was done on October 14, 2010. Next, when the chief veterinary officers meet at the World Organisation for Animal Health (OIE) World Assembly in May 2011, they will adopt a resolution, after having received all necessary information from participating countries, that declares the virus eradicated. And finally, the resolution will be endorsed by the FAO at its June 2011 conference. OIE director general Bernard Vallat is confident the process will be successful. "We are confident that the World Assembly of Delegates of the OIE will officially recognize all remaining countries as free from the disease in May 2011 and thus close on that day OIE Pathway activities for rinderpest eradication. The OIE programme was launched back in 1989 and has been extremely reliable in assessing the presence or absence of the virus in all countries worldwide. It should serve future ventures in eradicating other animal diseases," he said.

As the FAO works through each of these steps, it is also planning post-eradication activities that will help countries continue to monitor rinderpest and will build a network for quickly alerting veterinary services to any conditions arising in animals that resemble the disease. Future studies are being planned that will look at the history of the ecosystems where the virus thrived to identify the likelihood of reemergence. Decisions will also need to be made to determine how many vaccines and how much of the live virus should be kept. Virologists argue for keeping a large stock on hand for testing purposes, but public health experts prefer that most of the virus be destroyed out of concern of biological warfare if the virus falls into the wrong hands. When the laboratories that will house the virus have been chosen, an official declaration will be made by all GREP nations and organizations that the virus has been destroyed in all other locations. Scientists at FAO have also announced plans to use what they have learned from rinderpest eradication to target a similar virus that kills sheep and goats—peste des petits ruminants.

Other Eradication Efforts

More than thirty years ago, United Nations scientists announced the successful eradication of smallpox, a contagious and sometimes fatal disease that affected humans, killing nearly 30 percent of those infected. It took more than ten years of work from the time the World Health Organization launched the campaign to eradicate smallpox before scientists were convinced that the virus was no longer affecting humans in any part of the world.

Seven other viruses are currently targeted for eradication efforts—the most public of which is polio. Guinea worm, elephantiasis, measles, mumps, rubella, and cysticercosis are the remaining six. Billions of dollars have been put toward polio eradication, and scientists have thought multiple times that eradication had been achieved, only for another case to be identified. Scientists say they will be able to use knowledge gained during both smallpox and rinderpest eradication to target these seven viruses.

—Heather Kerrigan

Following is a document released by the Food and Agriculture Organization of the United Nations on October 14, 2010, announcing the end of rinderpest eradication efforts.

UN Declares End of Rinderpest Eradication Activities

October 14, 2010

An ambitious global effort that has brought rinderpest, a deadly cattle plague, to the brink of extinction is ending all field activities, paving the way for official eradication of the disease.

It would be the first time in history that humankind has succeeded in wiping out an animal disease in the wild, and only the second time, after smallpox in 1980, that a disease has been eliminated thanks to human efforts.

Rinderpest does not affect humans directly, but its ability to cause swift, massive losses of cattle and other hoofed animals has led to devastating effects on agriculture for millennia, leaving famine and economic devastation in its wake.

"The control and elimination of rinderpest has always been a priority for the Organization since its early days in its mission to defeat hunger and strengthen global food security," FAO Director-General Jacques Diouf said as ministers, animal health experts and partners gathered in Rome (13–14 October) for a Global Rinderpest Eradication Symposium.

The meeting got underway as representatives from many of FAO's member countries prepared to take part in the 15 October World Food Day 2010 observance, whose theme is "United Against Hunger."

"The disease has affected Europe, Asia and Africa for centuries and has caused widespread famine and decimated millions of animals, both domestic and wild. In the 1880s, rinderpest caused losses of up to one million head of cattle in Russia and central Europe," said Diouf.

When it entered Africa in the nineteenth century, it decimated millions of heads of livestock and wildlife and triggered widespread famine. It is estimated that in that pandemic alone, up to one-third of the human population of Ethiopia died of starvation as a result. The last known outbreak of rinderpest occurred in 2001 in Kenya.

A joint FAO/OIE announcement of global rinderpest eradication is expected in mid-2011, pending a review of final official disease status reports from a handful of countries to the World Organisation for Animal Health (OIE).

"We are confident that the World Assembly of Delegates of the OIE will officially recognize all remaining countries as free from the disease in May 2011 and thus close on that day OIE Pathway activities for rinderpest eradication. The OIE programme was launched back in 1989 and has been extremely reliable in assessing the presence or absence of the virus in all countries worldwide. It should serve future ventures in eradicating other animal diseases," Dr Bernard Vallat, OIE Director General declared.

Participants of the symposium discussed lessons learned from international efforts to stamp out the disease, how to apply lessons learned to eradicate other diseases, and reviewed what remains to be done before and after a final declaration of eradication.

A GLOBAL EFFORT

FAO has spearheaded a coordinated, global effort to study the pattern and nature of rinderpest, help farmers and veterinary services recognize and control the disease, develop and implement vaccination campaigns and, ultimately eradicate the disease within the framework of the OIE pathway.

That effort has involved a broad alliance of international partners such as the OIE, IAEA and donors, most recently under the Global Rinderpest Eradication Programme (GREP).

GREP was launched in 1994 as a global coordination mechanism that would allow the international community to jointly undertake rinderpest control in a systematic and comprehensive way. It was the decisive, final push in a decades-long campaign of scientific research, field surveillance and vaccination of animals in the field.

"The extraordinary success of this programme would not have been possible without the united efforts and determined commitment of the governments of all affected and exposed countries, without the African Union's Inter-African Bureau on Animal Resources and the responsible regional organizations in Asia and Europe, without the donor agencies committed to this endeavor," said FAO Director-General Jacques Diouf.

Special gratitude was expressed to the European Union and other major donors as well as dedicated professionals in research institutions and bilateral and multilateral development agencies.

"Together we have defeated rinderpest. Together we are stronger. Together we will defeat hunger," concluded Jacques Diouf.

DEVASTATING HISTORY

Caused by a virus and spread by contact and contaminated materials, rinderpest has destroyed countless millions of cattle, buffalo, yaks and their wild relatives, with mortality rates in extreme cases reaching close to 100 percent.

Many centuries after it was first seen in Asia and Europe, rinderpest reached its height in the 1920s. At one time, the disease's footprint extended from Scandinavia to the Cape of Good Hope and from the Atlantic shore of Africa to the Philippine archipelago, with one outbreak reported in Brazil and another in Australia.

In the early 1980s, rinderpest was still ravaging livestock herds around the world, with devastating epidemics hitting South Asia, the Middle East and Africa. Losses in Nigeria in the 1980s totalled $2 billion. A 1994 outbreak in northern Pakistan wiped out more than 50 000 cattle and buffalo before being brought under control with help from FAO and its partners.

SOURCE: Food and Agriculture Organization of the United Nations. "Campaign Against Deadly Cattle Plague Ending." October 14, 2010. http://www.fao.org/news/story/en/item/46383/icode/.

OTHER HISTORIC DOCUMENTS OF INTEREST

FROM PREVIOUS *HISTORIC DOCUMENTS*

- General Accounting Office on Bioterrorism Preparation, *2001*, p. 672
- World Health Organization on Infectious Diseases, *1996*, p. 302

Europeans Protest Austerity Measures and EU Monetary Policy

OCTOBER 21, 26, AND 29, 2010

Throughout 2010, European citizens took to the streets, protesting austerity measures passed by a number of European Union (EU) member governments to reduce government spending. The global economic crisis hit public coffers hard, prompting a public debt crisis and the loss of millions of jobs. In an effort to stabilize banking and financial systems, Greece, Spain, Portugal, Slovenia, Poland, Italy, Serbia, and Ireland introduced measures that would reduce public spending and the availability of government services. The protests across the continent were led by public employee unions facing layoffs and pension reductions.

In November, the EU approved the recommendations of a financial task force that would institute new economic governance policies for all EU member states. The policies would limit public debt and were intended to avoid future bank bailouts, such as those in Greece and Ireland in 2010. The recommendations were not as stringent as those proposed by the European Council's president, who wanted to fine nations billions of dollars for noncompliance with debt-reduction strategies, which sparked anger from member states.

DEMONSTRATORS PROTEST AUSTERITY MEASURES

Protests took root in Greece in the spring of 2010 when the nation appealed to the EU for financial assistance to shore up its crumbling financial system and received $100 billion in rescue loans. But it was not until late September that massive protests, led by labor unions, broke out in European capitals. The first nation to experience such protests was Spain, where labor unions organized the first strike in eight years. This strike stopped trucks from making deliveries in the capital city of Madrid, slowed public transportation, and led to the cancellation of two-thirds of all flights entering and leaving the country. The protest organizers said they were walking off the job to express discontent with decreases in public employee wages and what they saw as a lack of government intervention into continuing high unemployment, which reached 20 percent in May. The public cuts were aimed at bringing Spain's budget deficit from 11 percent of its gross domestic product (GDP) down to 3 percent by 2013 to comply with EU regulations and avoid a possible sanction.

Greek transportation and hospital workers joined the September protests, as did Slovenia's public unions, whose members protested a two-year freeze on public employee wages. The concern voiced by these and other workers was not only the wage cuts but also the massive government spending on bailing out banks. Jean-Claude Mailly, who leads the French Force Ouvrière (FO) union, said, "Those responsible for the crisis, the banks, the financial markets and the ratings agencies are all too quick in asking for help from states and public budgets and today want the workers to pay for their debts."

In London, students and professors protested university tuition and fee hikes, passed as one part of a larger austerity program. British universities are public institutions, and tuition has been kept low to allow all citizens to take advantage of higher education. In cutting government spending, Prime Minister David Cameron's Conservative Party proposed raising tuition to $14,000 per year, which protestors said would create a university system primarily used by the wealthy. "This is about turning colleges and universities from learning institutions into finishing schools for the rich," said Frances O'Grady, deputy general secretary of the Trades Union Congress, the United Kingdom's national trade union.

The European protests of 2010 made their way to EU headquarters in Brussels, Belgium. Estimates of the number of protestors ranged from sixty thousand to one hundred thousand. "We're here to say 'no' to the multiplying number of austerity plans, whether adopted by governments or by European institutions," said Bernard Thibault, secretary of French trade union Confédération Générale du Travail (CGT). In response, police barricaded the building where members of the European Parliament were meeting to discuss a new monetary policy for member states.

Calls for a New Monetary Policy

When the eurozone was established, it left most debt and budget considerations and tracking up to member states, which international economic observers at the time said would cause either greater political unification or failure of the euro. While neither has occurred, the recognition by the EU that greater financial controls of member states housed in the EU's central government were necessary was evidence of the fragile state of the joint financial system.

In June 2010, the EU's monetary arm, the European Central Bank, called for tighter regulations to control member state compliance with the bank's budget rules, including a prohibition on deficits above 3 percent of an individual nation's GDP. "The benefits and protection that are derived from membership of monetary union bring with them responsibilities and obligations," said Jean-Claude Trichet, president of the Central Bank. Current policy allowed states to borrow funds from the bank at low cost as long as they complied with the deficit rule. Some of these nations were in clear violation of the debt and deficit thresholds set by the body, but there were few controls in place to ensure compliance. When a violation was discovered, a nation only received a report with recommendations on how to reduce its deficit. EU law allowed the Central Bank to hand out fines to nations found in noncompliance, but it had never done so.

When Trichet spoke before a meeting of the European Parliament in June, borrowing costs had skyrocketed as the number of bailouts rose, and member nations began seeking bailout funds from the International Monetary Fund (IMF), which offered lower borrowing rates and fewer regulations. To better enforce monetary rules, Trichet called on a task force, currently working under the direction of European Council president Herman Van Rompuy, to make recommendations on how the EU could best monitor the economic activities of its member states. He further called for the development of more severe sanctions, which could include hefty fines or a loss of voting rights.

The European Commission responded first, proposing a new financial model based on Trichet's recommendations. The commission's proposal called for multibillion-dollar fines to be charged to any country that did not hold firm to stringent budget cuts aimed at avoiding a euro financial meltdown. "Governments are not always right," commission president José Manuel Barroso said. "If governments were always right we would not have the situation that we have today. Decisions taken by the most democratic institutions in the world are very often, or can be, wrong." As demonstrated in Greece and Ireland, Barroso said, individual governments could not be trusted to control their spending and debt plans.

Barroso's proposal would require all sixteen euro members to deposit billions of dollars into Brussels bank accounts controlled by the European Central Bank. The total required deposit of each country would be equal to 0.2 percent of its GDP. If any nation failed to follow through on implementation of austerity measures, the deposit would be forfeited. Each government would also be required to keep its deficit under 3 percent of its GDP and to cut one-twentieth of its debt every year, to help each nation reach a debt threshold of no more than 60 percent of its GDP. In some countries, this would be an extremely large undertaking that could result in quick forfeiture of their deposits. In Italy, for example, in 2009, debt was at 116 percent of its GDP.

The forfeiture of the deposit would be automatic, as called for by Trichet. This raised the ire of France, which, defying European recommendations, proposed to reduce its deficit by increasing growth rather than decreasing spending. Under the commission's proposal, France would have faced a loss of its deposit. Discontent from other euro nations was apparent. "There is a complete absence of democratic sensitivity. People want an approach that promotes job creation not imposed sanctions from on-high," said former Danish prime minister Poul Nyrup Rasmussen. Germany was one of the few countries to agree with Barroso's proposal. The recommendations of the commission would not be implemented until 2012.

TASK FORCE RELEASES REPORT

On October 21, 2010, the European Council's Task Force on Economic Governance released its final report on recommendations to strengthen the financial stability of all twenty-seven EU member states. Upon conclusion of the last meeting of the task force, Van Rompuy said, "Today, the European Union made a great step forward in the European Union's economic governance. The package agreed by the Task force . . . will be the biggest reform of the Economic and Monetary Union since the Euro was created." The report contained five recommendations: creation of a system to track macro-economics in each member nation; enforcement of greater fiscal discipline on all members; greater financial coordination among nations; better crisis management aimed at earlier financial intervention when a problem is recognized; and the creation of independent institutions that can analyze the fiscal environment in each member state.

Trichet responded, noting that he did not agree with all of the suggestions, specifically because he did not think the measures would effectively prevent financial distress in the sixteen eurozone states. For those states, he said, he thought the proposal "could be more ambitious." Trichet had hoped the task force would adopt the commission's recommendations on automatic sanctions against nations with higher-than-allowed debt levels, but Van Rompuy's commission only recommended sanctions to be applied after six months of warnings. It also allowed EU member states to vote to block any financial sanctions.

The agreed-upon monetary policies were met by resistance from some EU member states, who saw it as another encroachment on their sovereignty. In the United Kingdom, former cabinet minister John Redwood called the measures "a massive extension of European economic governance." But supporters accepted the move as a necessity to avoid a future financial crisis. UK Treasury financial secretary Mark Hoban admitted that additional reporting would be required but that it was nothing more than what the nation currently compiles. "Will we have to give Europe access to information for budgetary surveillance that is not similarly shared with organizations such as the IMF that is publicly available on the internet? . . . No," said Hoban.

All member states agreed to the task force report, which Van Rompuy acknowledged was only a first step in avoiding another financial crisis. The work of the central government, he said, can only be effective if both member states and the central government strengthen their financial institutions and carefully track the effectiveness of new debt reduction strategies. "Heads of State or Government stressed that, at the same time as fiscal discipline is reinforced in the European Union, it is essential that the European Union budget and the forthcoming Multiannual Financial Framework reflect the consolidation efforts being made by Member States to bring deficit and debt onto a more sustainable path. Respecting the role of the different institutions and the need to meet Europe's objectives, the European Council will discuss at its next meeting how to ensure spending at the European level can make an appropriate contribution to this work," he said.

—Heather Kerrigan

Following are excerpts from the European Council task force report on monetary policies issued on October 21, 2010; an October 26, 2010, statement by European Council president Herman Van Rompuy calling for European nations to come together on economic policy; and an October 29, 2010, statement by Rompuy announcing the endorsement of the task force report.

Task Force Report to the European Council on Monetary Policy

October 21, 2010

[Footnotes have been omitted.]

EXECUTIVE SUMMARY

The financial crisis and the more recent turmoil in sovereign debt markets have clearly highlighted challenges in the European Union's economic governance.

To address these challenges, a fundamental shift in European economic governance is needed, commensurate to the degree of economic and financial integration already achieved through the monetary union and the internal market. The recommendations in the Task Force Report address the high degree of economic inter-dependence, particularly in the euro area, while preserving national responsibilities on fiscal and economic policies. The recommendations should be implemented in five main directions:

1. Towards greater fiscal discipline

The budgetary surveillance framework currently in place, defined in the Stability and Growth Pact (SGP), remains broadly valid. However, it needs to be applied in a better and more consistent way. In particular, there is a need for a greater focus on debt and fiscal sustainability, to reinforce compliance and to ensure that national fiscal frameworks reflect the EU's fiscal rules.

The criterion of public debt needs to be better reflected in the budgetary surveillance mechanism by paying greater attention to the interplay between deficit and debt. Therefore, the Task Force recommends to operationalise the debt criterion in the Treaty by defining an appropriate quantitative reference, and to apply it effectively—due account taken of all relevant factors—notably as a trigger in the excessive deficit procedure.

To increase their effectiveness in the future, a wider range of sanctions and measures, of both financial and reputational/political nature, should be applied progressively in both the preventive and the corrective arms of the SGP, starting at an earlier stage in the budgetary surveillance process. Fairness, proportionality and equal treatment between Member States must be ensured.

The recommended political and reputational measures range from enhanced reporting requirements to ad-hoc reporting to the European Council, and enhanced surveillance, eventually followed by a public report.

The recommended financial sanctions range from interest-bearing deposits to fines. They will be first applied to euro area Member States only. As soon as possible, and at the latest in the context of the next multi-annual financial framework, the enforcement measures will be extended to all Member States, by making a range of EU expenditures conditional upon compliance with the SGP.

A more effective compliance regime will also be brought about by a higher degree of rule-based decision making. Therefore it is proposed to introduce a reverse majority rule for the adoption of enforcement measures. This means in practice that Commission recommendations would be adopted unless a qualified majority of Member States in the Council votes against within a given deadline.

A set of agreed minimum requirements for national fiscal frameworks needs to be met before the end of 2013, covering the essential areas. Moreover, a set of non-binding standards should be agreed upon. The Commission and the Council will assess the national fiscal frameworks.

The task Force also recommends a number of measures to further strengthen Eurostat and the European statistical system.

2. Broadening economic surveillance: a new surveillance mechanism

The global crisis has demonstrated that compliance with the Stability and Growth Pact is not sufficient to ensure balanced growth in the EU.

The Task Force therefore recommends the introduction of a new mechanism for macroeconomic surveillance underpinned by a new legal framework alongside the budget-focused SGP.

An annual assessment of the risk of macroeconomic imbalances and vulnerabilities will be undertaken, using an alert mechanism based on a limited number of indicators. In case of actual or potential excessive imbalances, the Commission should conduct an in-depth analysis. In particularly serious cases, an "excessive imbalance position" should be launched by the Council, with a deadline to take a set of policy measures to address the problem. Euro area Member States may ultimately face sanctions in case of repeated non-compliance.

3. Deeper and broader coordination: the 'European Semester'

One of the earliest Task Force recommendations to reinforce policy coordination, the so-called "European semester", has already been decided and will be implemented as of 1st January 2011. Each spring, it will allow a simultaneous assessment of both budgetary measures and structural reforms fostering growth and employment. This will contribute to ensure that the EU/euro area dimension is better taken into account when countries prepare budgets and reform programmes.

4. Robust framework for crisis management

Since the creation of the Task Force, the European Financial Stability Facility (EFSF) for the euro area and the European Financial Stability Mechanism (EFSM) have been set up and are now fully operational, offering therefore a good line of defence for the next three years.

The Task Force considers that in the medium term there is a need to establish a credible crisis resolution framework for the euro area capable of addressing financial distress and avoiding contagion. It will need to resolutely address the moral hazard that is implicit in any ex-ante crisis scheme. The precise features and operational means of such a crisis mechanism will require further work.

5. Stronger institutions for more effective economic governance

Stronger institutions both at national and EU level will contribute to improve economic governance. At the national level, the Task Force recommends the use or setting up of public institutions or bodies to provide independent analysis, assessments and forecasts on domestic fiscal policy matters as a way to reinforcing fiscal governance and ensuring long-term sustainability. . . .

[The remainder of the report, which expands upon the suggestions in the executive summary, has been omitted.]

Source: Council of the European Union. "Strengthening Economic Governance in the EU: Report of the Task Force to the European Council." October 21, 2010. http://www.consilium.europa.eu/uedocs/cms_data/docs/pressdata/en/ec/117236.pdf.

European Council President Calls for Shared Responsibility

October 26, 2010

[An outline of the Lisbon Treaty and the powers given to the European Commission, European Council, and individual parliaments has been omitted.]

One reason for the perception of a shift of powers to the European Council is simply because, in recent months, the main preoccupation of the European Union has been to do with macro economic governance. Macroeconomic policy is inevitably a matter of coordinating national policies, given that 98% of public spending in the EU is national or sub-national, while only 2% is carried out through the European budget. It is therefore natural that the European Council plays a significant role.

Indeed, the work of the Task Force that I have had the honour to chair illustrates the need to respect this reality.

We sought to get the right balance between laying down an overall European framework regarding the need to avoid fiscal deficits and allowing national governments freely to choose what they want to tax, and on what they want to spend, in accordance with their national political procedures (and the prerogatives of their national parliaments!). All the steps we take will leave the basic unique situation of the Euro as it is: the responsibility for monetary decisions lies at the European level, and the responsibility for budgetary matters and for economic policy remains essentially for the Member States, albeit in a jointly agreed framework.

Respecting that situation, while also drawing the lessons of the recent crisis, the Task Force report proposes basically actions on two levels: on the one hand, making sure that each Member State fully takes into account the impact of its economic and fiscal decisions on its partners and on the stability of European Union as a whole, and on the other hand, strengthening the capacity of the EU level to react when policies in a Member State present a risk to the rest of the Union.

In particular, we looked at:

- Reviewing and tightening up the Stability and Growth Pact, with more effective sanctions and a greater emphasis on public debt levels, and not just focusing on the current level of deficit
- Broadening the scope of monitoring national economic developments (after all, Spain and Ireland were perfectly within the criteria of the Stability and Growth Pact before the crisis hit) so as to include macroeconomic imbalances, balance of payments developments, asset bubbles and other significant indicators. This surveillance mechanism is in my view the biggest innovation: it will be a macro-economic counterpart to the budget-focused Pact and really make the European economies more crisis-proof.
- Deeper coordination. Already, the so-called "European semester" has been agreed whereby member states will confer at an earlier stage on the assumptions (in terms of growth projections, inflation rates, etc) on which their national budgets based. This will allow you to bring the European consequences of national policy decisions into your national parliamentary debate. This is one of the means by which emphasize how the decisions of each Member State affect all.

I will ask for the political backing of the Heads of State and Government for the final report in the European Council meeting later this week. The European Council will also decide on what form the further work should take, in particular on a future robust crisis resolution mechanism, and whether or not a treaty change is needed in this context.

Before concluding, I would like to underline that the work on the Stability Pact is not simply about being punitive to member states or about rectifying past mistakes. It is important to look at it in a wider context.

After all, we have just been hit by the biggest economic tsunami since the Great Depression. Yet we avoided most of the mistakes that were made in the 1930s:

- We avoided protectionism—in no small part thanks to the single European market.
- We largely avoided competitive currency devaluations—in no small part thanks to the euro.
- We agreed on a fiscal stimulus at the depth of the recession which helped turn the corner.

Problems arose when a number of member states could not maintain their fiscal stimulus because their levels of public debt made that impossible. They had been profligate in the good times, meaning that they no longer had a margin of manoeuvre for the bad types.

One of our objectives is to make sure that this does not happen again. It is neither in the interests of the Union, nor in the interest of the member states concerned, that they remain in the vulnerable situation that arises when excessive deficits are maintained for too long.

At the same time as the fiscal reforms that will flow from the work of Task Force, we must not lose sight of the wider challenge of improving Europe's structural growth rate and its general economic performance. This was the focus of the 2020 strategy agreed by the European Council earlier this year. The answer to those who fear that fiscal retrenchment will cut economic growth rates, is to focus better on the underlying structural factors that hinder our economic performance and to remedy them.

This entails an overall approach, drawing on both Union instruments and national instruments.

Indeed, the bulk of the instruments needed are national, for instance in terms of improving educational attainment, social inclusion and a large part of boosting research and development.

Here too, it is up to you in the national parliaments to play your part in ensuring that all member states join in this effort, which will determine whether we, collectively as Europeans, make a success of a 21st-century or not.

All governments and institutions need to cooperate. We cannot be rivals. We have a common goal: the well-being of our citizens—and not just because they are our voters!

SOURCE: Council of the European Union. "'Sharing the Responsibility for European Decisions': President Herman Van Rompuy Addresses the Representatives of the European Parliament and 27 National Parliaments (COSAC-Meeting)." October 26, 2010. http://www.consilium.europa.eu/uedocs/cms_data/docs/pressdata/en/ec/117412.pdf.

European Council Accepts Task Force Report on Economic Governance

October 29, 2010

Today we took important decisions to strengthen the Euro. We have endorsed the final report of the Task Force. We have also found an agreement about the procedure to decide upon a crisis mechanism for the Euro zone.

This spring, we overcame a deep crisis of the Economic and Monetary Union. Our next political duty was to draw the lessons for the future, to make the European economies more crisis-proof.

That's exactly what the recommendations of the Task Force will do. That's why all Heads of State and Government agreed with the proposals today, as a huge improvement compared to the current situation.

Let me highlight the three main elements, before coming to the follow-up.

Firstly, the creation of a **new macro-economic surveillance framework**. This is the biggest innovation. It will detect imbalances and risks, like housing bubbles. It will observe the competitiveness of Member States. If a country loses too much competitiveness, action will have to be undertaken, in particular within the Eurozone.

I have said before that the Euro has acted as a sleeping pill, especially in good times. We now propose a system of timely awakening. This will enhance confidence.

Second main element: a **stronger Stability and Growth Pact**, improving fiscal responsibility.

- Compared to the current situation, sanctions will kick in earlier and progressively.
- Public debt will be taken more into account, alongside the deficit criterion.
- Sanctions will be possible before the 3 percent annual deficit is reached (if not enough preventive action is taken): that is totally new.
- Moreover, sanctions can be decided more easily.

All this will deter bad budgetary behaviour. These recommendations, as the others of the Task Force, are also extremely close to the Commission proposals.

One clarification: some people claim to be disappointed there is not more "automaticity" in the decision-making. Well, more "automaticity" is exactly what we propose! Ministers of Finance will decide on sanctions on the basis of a so-called reversed majority: this means a Commission proposal for sanctions stands, unless a qualified majority votes against (whereas until now a majority had to approve the sanction). The judgement of the Finance Ministers is foreseen in the Treaty and therefore cannot be eliminated.

Only a few weeks ago, some Member States were very reluctant about the reversed majority. It is really a break-through.

Furthermore, the Task Force proposes a whole series of other measures aimed at strengthening the Stability Pact, such as more policy-coordination (the European Semester), sound statistics, and independent fiscal councils. Member States should feel that their policy decisions affect all their partners and the Union as a whole. It is the big lesson of the crisis.

A general remark. The Task Force was a political framework, aimed at generating rapidly consensus. All the break-throughs we achieved, now need to be translated into legislative texts. The work needs to be done by the Council, the Commission and the Parliament. I trust all the institutions will keep up the momentum. It is our duty.

Now the third and final main element of the Task Force, which also brings me to the follow-up of the Task Force: we recommend a robust and credible permanent crisis mechanism to safeguard the financial stability of the euro area as a whole. Today, all Heads of State and Government agreed on that need.

Why?

Because even if all the right budgetary and economic measures are taken by everybody, one may never exclude surprises. Politics is not a zero-risk business.

This spring, the absence of a crisis mechanism almost brought down the Eurozone as a whole. It made people think.

Under pressure, a temporary crisis mechanism was improvised. It will last for three years, until mid-2013. So we need to think beyond that date, starting now.

The guiding principles are clear: a permanent crisis mechanism should be able to address financial distress and avoid contagion from one country to another. It should also avoid moral hazard.

Now the question is whether such a robust crisis mechanism requires a change of the Treaty. There are legal aspects and political considerations, both for individual Member States and for the Union as a whole.

Tonight, we have had a good exchange of views on this and we decided upon the following:

"Further to the report of the Task Force, and in order to ensure balanced and sustainable growth, Heads of State or Government agree on the need for Member States to establish a permanent crisis mechanism to safeguard the financial stability of the euro area as a whole and invite the President of the European Council to undertake consultations with the members of the European Council on a limited treaty change required to that effect, not modifying article 125 TEU ("no bail-out" clause).

The European Council welcomes the intention of the Commission to undertake, in close consultation with the President of the European Council, preparatory work on the general features of a future new mechanism, i.a. the role of the private sector, the role of the IMF and the very strong conditionality under which such programmes should operate.

The European Council will revert to this matter at its December meeting with a view to taking the final decision both on the outline of a crisis mechanism and on a limited treaty amendment so that any change can be ratified at the latest by mid-2013.

The President of the European Council intends to subsequently examine in consultation with the Member States the issue of the right to participate in decision making in EMU related procedures in case of a permanent threat to the stability of the eurozone as a whole."

We took also a position on the budgetary perspectives:

"Heads of State or Government stressed that, at the same time as fiscal discipline is reinforced in the European Union, it is essential that the European Union budget and the forthcoming Multiannual Financial Framework reflect the consolidation efforts being made by Member States to bring deficit and debt onto a more sustainable path. Respecting the role of the different institutions and the need to meet Europe's objectives, the European Council will discuss at its next meeting how to ensure spending at the European level can make an appropriate contribution to this work."

We will examine how the impact of pension reform can be accounted for in the implementation of the Stability Pact.

So those are the main elements of our discussion today and the most important conclusion is that we endorsed the report of the Task Force.

SOURCE: Council of the European Union. "Press Remarks by Herman Van Rompuy President of the European Council Following the First Session of the European Council." October 29, 2010. http://www .consilium.europa.eu/uedocs/cms_data/docs/pressdata/en/ec/117489.pdf.

OTHER HISTORIC DOCUMENTS OF INTEREST

U.S. Officials on Intercepted Package Bombs

OCTOBER 29, 2010

In late October 2010, two package bombs were seized in the United Kingdom and Dubai, bound for the United States on United Parcel Service (UPS) and FedEx Corporation cargo planes. The bombs were concealed in printer cartridges to escape detection during the package screening process. Neither package, each of which was addressed to synagogues in Chicago, Illinois, made it to U.S. soil, and both were defused before any damage could be done. Global cooperation between Saudi Arabia, the United States, and the United Kingdom helped avoid disaster and also aided investigators in quickly pinpointing the al Qaeda affiliate responsible for making the bombs, a group known as al Qaeda in the Arabian Peninsula.

INTERNATIONAL COOPERATION

On October 28, 2010, senior intelligence officials in Saudi Arabia received a tip about two suspected package bombs. They alerted the United States that packages bound for the country had just left Yemen. Saudi and U.S. officials worked together to determine the route and stops that each package would make. The first package left Yemen on a passenger aircraft and stopped in Dubai, where it was transferred to a UPS cargo plane that continued to Germany, and then on to East Midlands Airport in Great Britain, where it landed during the early morning hours of October 29. It was there that United Kingdom officials intercepted the package before it would have continued on two more flights, scheduled to stop in Philadelphia, Pennsylvania, before reaching its ultimate destination in Chicago.

The second package was found at a Dubai FedEx facility, after traveling on two commercial airliners from Yemen to Qatar on October 28, and then from Qatar to Dubai. Security officials intercepted the package on October 29, before the FedEx plane it had been loaded onto left for Newark, New Jersey, before continuing to Chicago. Both package bombs were similar in nature and featured a printer and ink cartridge containing wires and circuit boards set up to explode with a timed mechanism, not through remote detonation.

According to British home secretary Theresa May, the first package could have exploded in the cargo plane on which it was being carried. The question, however, was how those shipping the bomb could know when or where the bomb would explode.

"We do not believe that the perpetrators of the attack would have known the location of the device when they planned for it to explode," said May.

Although package routes are changed daily depending on the time necessary to get to and from the United States, British officials suspected that the bomb found in Great Britain would have exploded somewhere over a remote area of Canada, although they believed that the intention was to explode the plane somewhere over the East Coast of the United States. Those responsible for shipping the bomb could have tracked its location, and it was likely that they used data available on the Internet to determine typical routes of UPS cargo planes. But, said one U.S. official involved in the case, "when you send something by cargo, you don't control all the variables."

Knowledge of the package bombs set off a number of tense situations around the United States as cargo and passenger planes and package delivery trucks were held and searched in New York, New Jersey, and Pennsylvania. "Based on close cooperation among U.S. government agencies and with our foreign allies and partners, authorities were able to identify and examine two suspicious packages, one in London and one in Dubai," wrote White House press secretary Robert Gibbs in a statement. "As a result of security precautions triggered by this threat, the additional measures were taken regarding the flights at Newark Liberty and Philadelphia International Airports." President Barack Obama's assistant for homeland security and counterterrorism, John Brennan, said that packages following routes similar to those of the two package bombs were also being investigated. "What we are doing is making sure that we take a close look at other packages that might also have some type of materials in them of concern. Both of these packages that we've identified to date originated in Yemen, and so I think it is very prudent for us to make sure that other packages that might be coming in similar routes or from Yemen, as well, are looked at very carefully," Brennan said.

Synagogues and other places of worship in Chicago, the intended destination of the package bombs, went on high alert. "Since two of the suspicious packages that were intercepted were addressed to religious institutions in Chicago, all churches, synagogues and mosques in the Chicago area should be vigilant for any unsolicited or unexpected packages, especially those originating from overseas locations," said Chicago FBI spokesman Ross Rice. Both the United States and United Kingdom, however, believed that the cargo planes, rather than the synagogues, were the intended targets.

President Obama phoned Saudi Arabia's King Abdullah II shortly after the incident to thank his government and intelligence units for acting quickly and playing a "critical role" in bringing the bomb plot to a successful conclusion. The United States also thanked its close ally, the United Kingdom. "We greatly appreciate the highly professional nature of the U.K. investigation and the spirit of partnership with which the U.K. authorities have pursued this matter," said White House spokesperson Nick Shapiro.

WHO'S RESPONSIBLE?

On October 31, investigators involved in the case announced that the materials used in the explosive devices, as well as other evidence that had been collected, pointed to the likelihood that the responsible party was an al Qaeda affiliate based in Yemen, known as al Qaeda in the Arabian Peninsula, which operates largely autonomously of central al Qaeda leadership. The sophistication of the device and the pentaerythritol trinitrate (PETN) used in the bomb led investigators to suspect that Ibrahim Hassan al-Asiri was personally responsible for both the UPS and FedEx bombs.

Al-Asiri, a 28-year-old Saudi national, has most recently been linked to two attempted attacks—one in Saudi Arabia and one in the United States. In 2009, al-Asiri built a sophisticated PETN bomb, which he concealed in his younger brother's body cavity, sending him to the home of Saudi prince Muhammad bin Nayef, head of the Saudi intelligence service, under the pretext that he was turning himself in for another crime. The bomb exploded, killing al-Asiri's brother and wounding a top Saudi counterterrorism official, but the target was left unscathed. In December 2009, it is believed that al-Asiri was responsible for building the bomb used by the Christmas Day "underwear bomber," Umar Farouk Abdulmutallab, who attempted to blow up a flight bound for Detroit, Michigan. The bomb used in the Christmas Day incident differed slightly from those found in the UPS and FedEx packages because it was set up to use chemical reactions to create an explosion, rather than using electronic means to set off the bomb.

Although al Qaeda had never before attempted to ship bombs into the United States through mail or package delivery services, the method of packaging the bomb materials into a printer is similar to what had been seen in other parts of the world. "The targeting manner carries characteristics similar to methods previously carried out by terrorist organizations like al Qaeda," said authorities in Dubai after finding and investigating the FedEx package bomb.

On October 30, a medical student in her twenties and her mother were arrested in San'a, Yemen, on suspicion that they were responsible for dropping the two package bombs off at local UPS and FedEx facilities. Both suspects were subsequently released after it was learned that that the student's identity had been stolen and was used when dropping off the packages. The actual shipper remains unknown.

U.S.-YEMEN RELATIONSHIP

After the attempted Christmas Day bombing in 2009, the United States increased its military and logistical aid to Yemen, where a weak central government allows the al Qaeda affiliate and other radical organizations to operate largely untouched. The Yemeni government has lost control over large portions of its land to Shiite rebels and is facing the threat of civil war. These factors, coupled with the United States' desire to stop Middle Eastern nations from creating safe havens for al Qaeda and its affiliates, led to an increase in U.S. military aid.

The assistance offered by the United States in battling al Qaeda, however, has been met with resistance from the Yemeni government, which has maintained its desire to avoid foreign intervention. "We do not want anyone to interfere in Yemeni affairs by hunting down al Qaeda," Yemen's president, Ali Abdullah Saleh, announced on October 30 after word spread that the United States was considering sending armed drones to areas of the country believed to be al Qaeda strongholds. Still, the United States has pressed on, working to strengthen its relationship with the nation. "I would say that the ... cooperation right now with Yemen is better than it's been ever before. That doesn't mean that it can't improve more," said Brennan, who had visited the region four times in 2009 and 2010 to build the partnership.

Before the package bomb plot was uncovered, the United States and United Kingdom had both increased vigilance in Yemen. In early 2010, the two nations temporarily closed their embassies there under threat of a possible terrorist attack. In the months leading up to the UPS/FedEx package bomb incident, U.S. investigators had been tracking other packages coming from Yemen that it now believes were practice runs for the October bomb shipment.

Following the October plot, the United States, United Kingdom, and France announced that they would ban mail and freight originating in Yemen from entering their countries until the security situation could be fully vetted. The United States also said it would continue to monitor and review its own security measures for incoming airborne mail and packages. Former FBI agent David Williams, an explosives expert who investigated the 1993 World Trade Center bombing, said it was logical that al Qaeda would continue using mail and freight to attack the United States, recognizing that the screening procedures for packages are not as stringent as those undergone by passengers boarding airplanes. President Obama promised to work with the Department of Homeland Security to implement any new security measures deemed necessary. "We will continue to pursue additional protective measures for as long as it takes to ensure the safety and security of our citizens," he said.

—Heather Kerrigan

Following is a statement by U.S. president Barack Obama on October 29, 2010, on the suspicious packages sent from Yemen to the United States; and a press briefing held on October 29, 2010, by John Brennan, assistant to the president for homeland security and counterterrorism, on the Yemen package bombs.

DOCUMENT

President Obama Discusses U.S.-bound Package Bomb

October 29, 2010

Good afternoon, everybody. I want to briefly update the American people on a credible terrorist threat against our country and the actions that we're taking with our friends and our partners to respond to it.

Last night and earlier today, our intelligence and law enforcement professionals, working with our friends and allies, identified two suspicious packages bound for the United States, specifically, two places of Jewish worship in Chicago. Those packages have been located in Dubai and East Midlands Airport in the United Kingdom. An initial examination of those packages has determined that they do apparently contain explosive material.

I was alerted to this threat last night by my top counterterrorism adviser, John Brennan. I directed the Department of Homeland Security and all our law enforcement and intelligence agencies to take whatever steps are necessary to protect our citizens from this type of attack. Those measures led to additional screening of some planes in Newark and Philadelphia.

The Department of Homeland Security's also taking steps to enhance the safety of air travel, including additional cargo screening. We will continue to pursue additional protective measures for as long as it takes to ensure the safety and security of our citizens.

I've also directed that we spare no effort in investigating the origins of these suspicious packages and their connection to any additional terrorist plotting. Although we are still pursuing all the facts, we do know that the packages originated in Yemen. We also know that Al Qaida in the Arabian Peninsula, a terrorist group based in Yemen, continues to plan attacks against our homeland, our citizens, and our friends and allies.

John Brennan, who you will be hearing from, spoke with President Salih of Yemen today about the seriousness of this threat, and President Salih pledged the full cooperation of the Yemeni Government in this investigation.

Going forward, we will continue to strengthen our cooperation with the Yemeni Government to disrupt plotting by Al Qaida in the Arabian Peninsula and to destroy this Al Qaida affiliate. We'll also continue our efforts to strengthen a more stable, secure, and prosperous Yemen so that terrorist groups do not have the time and space they need to plan attacks from within its borders.

The events of the past 24 hours underscores the necessity of remaining vigilant against terrorism. As usual, our intelligence, law enforcement, and homeland security professionals have served with extraordinary skill and resolve and with the commitment that their enormous responsibilities demand. We're also coordinating closely and effectively with our friends and our allies, who are essential to this fight.

As we obtain more information, we will keep the public fully informed. But at this stage, the American people should know that the counterterrorism professionals are taking this threat very seriously and are taking all necessary and prudent steps to ensure our security. And the American people should be confident that we will not waver in our resolve to defeat Al Qaida and its affiliates and to root out violent extremism in all its forms.

Thank you very much.

SOURCE: U.S. Executive Office of the President. "Remarks on Explosive Devices Found Aboard Flights Bound for the United States." *Daily Compilation of Presidential Documents* 2010, no. 00919 (October 29, 2010). http://origin.www.gpo.gov/fdsys/pkg/DCPD-201000919/pdf/DCPD-201000919.pdf.

Senior Presidential Advisor Brennan Addresses Package Bomb Incident

October 29, 2010

MR. GIBBS: Good afternoon. Before I bring John up to answer a few of your questions, I wanted to run you all briefly through a tick-tock of some of the events of the last few hours, starting, as you know from our earlier statement, that at 10:35 p.m. last night, Assistant to the President for Homeland Security and Counterterrorism John Brennan alerted the President of the credible terrorist threat. The President directed U.S. intelligence and law enforcement agencies and the Department of Homeland Security to take steps to ensure the safety and security of the American people and to determine whether these threats are a part of any additional terrorist plot.

John provided the President with additional updates throughout the evening. . . .

[The update timeline has been omitted.]

Q Mr. Brennan, if you could talk about what we know beyond the fact that this was from Yemen, there are people in Yemen with AQAP who want to harm us—if there is more that can be established to create a direct link beyond the country of origin?

MR. BRENNAN: I think, as Robert said, this is an active and ongoing investigation. We are working very closely with our partners in Yemen and United Arab Emirates, as well as in the United Kingdom and other countries, as well.

We know that al Qaeda in the Arabian Peninsula has been trying to carry out attacks against U.S. and Western interests, as well as against Yemenis. So as we continue with this investigation, we are trying to understand who is behind it, the responsibility, and make sure that we understand the scope of the threat that we might face.

We've identified these two packages right now. They have been isolated and they have been made inert. So, therefore, what we're trying to do now is to make sure that we are able to address any other threats that might be out there.

Q Just a quick follow, you said you've identified two. What about reports that there are up to 15 packages out there that you're looking for? Is that possible?

MR. BRENNAN: What we are doing is making sure that we take a close look at other packages that might also have some type of materials in them of concern. Both of these packages that we've identified to date originated in Yemen, and so I think it is very prudent for us to make sure that other packages that might be coming in similar routes or from Yemen, as well, are looked at very carefully. And that's what we're doing right now. But there are only two packages right now that have materials of concern.

Q The President described this is as a credible terrorist threat against the United States. Can you say whether this was actually an attempted terrorist attack, or some sort of practice run for something down the line?

MR. BRENNAN: I think, as the President noted, it is—does appear that there were explosive materials in both of these packages, that they were in a form that was designed to try to carry out some type of attack. The forensic analysis is underway. We are relying heavily and working closely with our partners in this regard. But clearly, from the initial observations, the initial analyses that's done, that the materials that were found and the device that was uncovered was intended to do harm.

MR. GIBBS: Chip.

Q "Do harm." Do you have any sense on the extent of the harm or the extent of the damage that could have been done by this? And secondly, are you looking into the possibility that al-Aulaqi was involved in this?

MR. BRENNAN: I don't want to speculate at this point in terms of what the damage could be from the devices, the explosive material that we have found. That's the analysis that's underway. It's still at the very early stage of that analysis. We're working, as I said, closely with our partners.

Clearly, what we are doing is looking at all individuals that we think might be involved in this. Al Qaeda in the Arabian Peninsula has been rather open in its venom towards the United States, towards Western interests. There are a number of individuals there that we're very concerned about, so we're looking at all possibilities.

When I had my conversation with President Saleh this morning he did pledge the full cooperation of the Yemeni government. We are working closely with them and we are going to get to the bottom of this plot.

Q Did al-Aulaqi's name come up? Is he considered a top suspect?

MR. BRENNAN: Anybody who's associated with al Qaeda in the Arabian Peninsula is a subject of concern.

Q Do you have a sense of the quantity of the explosive, even if your analysis hasn't determined the quality of it yet?

MR. BRENNAN: We have had some preliminary discussions with our partners. I don't want to go into the details about the quantity or the exact types of materials because I think this is still preliminary and I wouldn't want to say something that was going to be then corrected in the future.

Q Are there any suspects in custody?

Q Prior to learning about the plot was the intelligence community aware of this option as a possibility, using cargo planes with packages to attack?

MR. BRENNAN: I think over the years al Qaeda has demonstrated that it has focused intently on the aviation sector. A lot of its plots have focused on trying to carry out attacks against aircraft, using aircraft also as potential missiles, as we well know. So the aviation industry has taken those steps over the years expressly because al Qaeda—and when I'm talking about al Qaeda I'm not just talking about al Qaeda in the FATA area in Afghanistan. I'm talking about the franchises, including in Yemen, which have demonstrated very clearly that not only are they intending to do certain things against this homeland, but that, as we saw last Christmas Day with Umar Farouk Abdulmutallab, that they will, in fact, take steps to carry out those intentions.

Q Were cargo planes, though, were those ever focused on as a possibility?

MR. BRENNAN: We've been concerned about passenger aircraft and cargo planes, commercial airliners, others, for many, many years.

MR. GIBBS: I cut off the questions on the fourth row. You had your hand up.

Q Oh, yes. Were there any suspects—are there any suspects in custody?

MR. BRENNAN: Not to my knowledge, no.

Q Is there any reason to believe that this plot goes beyond cargo flights to regular passenger travel, and is there any consideration being given to putting an embargo on packages from Yemen—originating in Yemen, or even urging people to reconsider travel plans?

MR. BRENNAN: We're looking at all possibilities at this point. We don't want to presume that we know the bounds of this plot, so we are looking at all types of packages, air travel, whatever. We just want to make sure that we are going to whatever length we need to, to ensure the safety and security of air travel at this point.

Q And an embargo on any packages originating in Yemen?

MR. BRENNAN: We are working with the Yemeni government right now. I do believe that it would be prudent and we have taken some steps to ensure that packages that come from Yemen are going to be carefully screened. We're working with the Yemeni government right now.

So at this point, one of the reasons why we looked at some planes that were coming down into Philadelphia and Newark today is because they were, in fact, carrying cargo from Yemen. So we have had these interagency meetings to discuss all these options. I don't want to go into the details of this because this is all part of the security measures that are in place, but several of these measures have already been instituted.

MR. GIBBS: Helene.

Q Can you walk us through the decision to send fighter jets to escort that Emirates flight into JFK today?

MR. BRENNAN: These are decisions that are made by U.S. military/Canadian military air force. If there's a threat—and my understanding—and I've only seen some of the preliminary reports about this—is that there was concern about possible cargo on that flight. And so, again, with an abundance of caution, sometimes air force—our air force, the Canadian air force—will scramble some jets to make sure that everything is okay.

Q There's been a lot of concern about threats against European targets. Is this at all related to any of that chatter that was picked up in recent weeks?

MR. BRENNAN: Well, as you well know, we issued the travel alert because of concerns about al Qaeda carrying out attacks in Europe; that one package was uncovered in East Midlands Airport in the UK. We are looking at all the parts of the puzzle that we have been piecing together over the past several weeks from al Qaeda. But we're not presuming that this is part of that plot. We're not presuming that we've disrupted that plot. We need to maintain our vigilance. And that's the message that we share with our European partners.

MR. GIBBS: Chuck.

Q Considering what the targets were in Chicago, the Jewish places of worship, any extra precautions that you're putting out for synagogues?

MR. BRENNAN: The FBI, Department of Homeland Security and other domestic agencies are looking at that very carefully and have reached out to the appropriate private-sector entities as well as organizations to ensure that any other potential targets of such attacks are alerted. So we're working very closely with state and local officials.

Q And a quick big picture—the Yemeni cooperation—considering this is now multiple attempted terrorist attacks it looks like emanating from Yemen, is it fair to say that we don't have the best cooperation yet with the Yemeni government?

MR. BRENNAN: I would say that over the past 22 months or so, during this administration, and even in the prior administration, there has been a steady improvement in that cooperation. I would say that the CT cooperation right now with Yemen is better than it's been ever before. That doesn't mean that it can't improve more. It needs to improve more. I've been out to Yemen four times during the past two years. We're working very closely with them. And we found that they are courageous partners. Many Yemenis have lost their lives in the battle against al Qaeda.

MR. GIBBS: Wendell.

Q Have U.S. authorities been able to inspect these packages? Have we increased our presence, or do we plan to do so in Yemen?

    And, Robert, Philadelphia and Chicago involved in this—will the President's travel plans this weekend change?

Q Robert, do you expect this issue to come up at all during the campaign events at all in the next few days?

MR. GIBBS: I have not talked to—I'll get some guidance from the speechwriters to see if this gets mentioned. Certainly, I will say, as the President said, we will take the opportunity if need be throughout the weekend to continue to update the public on information as it comes in.

Q Considering what al Qaeda has done in the past in targeting other countries during an election season, are you taking that into account that there's anything—that this is more than just a coincidence of timing?

MR. BRENNAN: There's never a day that we relax our guard against al Qaeda and its potential to carry out attacks or attempt to do that—whether it's Election Day or any other day of the year.

Q I wonder, Mr. Brennan, if you can back that tick-tock up just a little bit. What did you know at the time when you briefed the President last night? And were these packages just discovered through random screenings? Or was there something that tipped you off to these packages?

MR. BRENNAN: Well, I knew enough last night to be able to brief the President, number one. Number two, I think the American people should feel particularly good that since 9/11, the U.S. government has built up a very, very capable and robust intelligence, law enforcement, homeland security system. And as a result of the strength of that system, information became available that we were able to act upon very quickly and that we were able to locate these packages.

So I'm not going to go into the details about how we became aware of it. But the redundant layers of security, the tremendous work of the counterterrorism professionals, law enforcement, homeland security, intelligence, was the reason why we were able to succeed.

Q If I can just follow up on that—you're saying then that you were aware of this plot not because of the packages but because of something else?

MR. BRENNAN: I'm saying that whenever you pull a string, there's a reason why you start to pull that string. And we had a reason to pull it. And as a result of what we were able to uncover in East Midlands Airport, with the very strong cooperation of British authorities, we were able to also then take additional steps. And that's why those prudent measures were taken today to ensure that we were able to identify any other packages that might be out there of concern.

Q Can I just follow up on that? Were you able to—did you direct the authorities in the East Midlands to look for this package?

MR. BRENNAN: We were working very closely with our British partners to identify—locate, identify and isolate that package.

Q To be clear, which of the two packages was found first? Was it Dubai, and that led you to East Midlands? Or was there any connection—

MR. BRENNAN: The first one that was found was East Midlands. . . .

Q Mr. Brennan, can you just clarify—so you found the first package after the President was briefed on this issue last night, is that correct?

MR. BRENNAN: Yes, from a sequencing standpoint, yes.

Q And is it your belief that the institutions in Chicago were the targets of the attack and not, say, the cargo flights? Because you made some reference to the security of cargo flights and so forth. The intent was to injure people at these institutions?

MR. BRENNAN: It is less than 24 hours since we first started to look at this very intensively and so it's still the very early stage of the investigation, and the analysis as far as the intended target, the impact of the explosives, how it could have been used, and I don't want to speculate at this point, at this time. . . .

Q Mr. Brennan, early on there had been a lot of speculation that this might be some kind of a dry run. Given what you do know about these packages now, would you say that this was more than just a dry run?

MR. BRENNAN: I'm concerned that since there were explosive materials in it, a traditional dry run is something that you would not necessarily use with explosive materials.

That said, I don't know yet what exactly the intent was at this point. There are a lot of different scenarios that some people have speculated about, but—and what we're trying to do is wrestle this to the ground by doing a good forensic analysis, as well as taking a look from an intelligence standpoint and trying to piece together what we might have known in the past and that would give us a sense of how this was going to be used. . . .

Q Do you think, Mr. Brennan, in the past when there have been specific attacks, as has been highlighted by the administration, that terrorists have had to modify their ways because of the hurdles that the government has thrown up in front of them—do you think that's the case that we saw here, the use of cargo planes instead of passenger planes reflect the intense scrutiny that passenger aircraft have gotten in the last year or so since they've come under—being used as a vehicle for attacks?

MR. BRENNAN: Absolutely. The al Qaeda organization has tried to adapt to all of the obstacles and hurdles we've put in front of it. And that's why we have to remain very agile. We have to make sure that we stay one step ahead of them.

But clearly, they are looking to identify vulnerabilities in our system and take advantage of those vulnerabilities. But fortunately, because of, again, the good work of the people here, as well as the very important partnership that we have with our allies overseas, we've been able to stay ahead of them.

Q Are you surprised that they keep focusing on airplanes—so long after 9/11, that still remains an attraction for them?

MR. BRENNAN: There's nothing about al Qaeda that surprises me anymore. And that's why we have to be prepared to deal with every eventuality that is out there.

Q How did your response to this in the last 24, 36 hours, to this incident, differ from the response to Abdulmutallab over the holidays last year? And what did you learn from the last year attempted Christmas Day bombing that helped you better prepare for this?

MR. BRENNAN: In some respects, they're very different because you're dealing with two packages as opposed to an individual, but in other respects, there are similarities.

What we—whenever something like this happens, what we want to do is to make sure that we take all appropriate measures to identify additional threats that are out there. Whether it's somebody who arrived in Detroit or whether a package is found in East Midlands, we're trying to find are there other individuals that are trying to blow up a plane? Are there other packages out there?

And so the community kicked into gear right away and took those steps so that we would find out where those packages were and take the appropriate steps with TSA, FAA and others, and the system worked very, very well. . . .

Q Mr. Brennan, how many credible threats have come from Yemen in the last two years?

MR. BRENNAN: There are a number of threat streams that we've been following, a number of individuals that we're very concerned about.

Q What number?

MR. BRENNAN: I wouldn't put a number to it.

Q Dozens? We know of under 10. How many—

MR. BRENNAN: Well, it's a question about whether or not there's reports of a threat that may be separate from other reporting. Is it part of the same threat stream? Sometimes we're concerned that al Qaeda is trying to carry out some type of attack, so we might have dozens upon dozens of reports related to that one attack.

So over the past year, the intelligence community, the counterterrorism community has been kept very busy with reports about al Qaeda in the Arabian Peninsula trying to carry out attacks in Yemen and in that region, as well as against the United States. . . .

SOURCE: The White House. Office of the Press Secretary. "Press Briefing by Press Secretary Robert Gibbs and Assistant to the President for Homeland Security and Counterterrorism John Brennan." October 29, 2010. http://www.whitehouse.gov/the-press-office/2010/10/29/press-briefing-press-secretary-robert-gibbs-and-assistant-president-home.

OTHER HISTORIC DOCUMENTS OF INTEREST

FROM THIS VOLUME

FROM PREVIOUS *HISTORIC DOCUMENTS*

International Collaboration on Settlement of Nagorno-Karabakh Region

OCTOBER 29 AND DECEMBER 1, 2010

Violence between Armenia and Azerbaijan over Nagorno-Karabakh, an autonomous region located within Azerbaijan, reignited in 2010, as both countries violated a ceasefire agreement and promised full-scale military action against one another. Armenia claims that it is the rightful owner of the land, in which a majority of the inhabitants are ethnic Armenians. Azerbaijan claims the land for itself, as it is fully surrounded by the country, and blames Armenia for escalating violence against the people of Azerbaijan. International organizations and countries, including the United Nations, European Union, Organization for Security Co-operation in Europe (OSCE), and the United States, worked together to secure a settlement over the disputed land. Throughout 2010, these groups held a number of meetings and passed resolutions. Few breakthroughs in the stalemate were made, and governments on both sides of the conflict remained unconvinced that peace would soon come to the region.

HISTORY OF THE NAGORNO-KARABAKH CONFLICT

The 2010 increase in violence between Armenia and Azerbaijan was centered on a decades-long conflict over the Nagorno-Karabakh region, located in the South Caucasus. The region was considered autonomous but under Azerbaijani jurisdiction by the then-Soviet government, even though it remained populated by a majority of ethnic Armenians into the late twentieth century. The minority ethnic Azerbaijanis attempted to enforce discriminatory rule against Armenians in the region. In the late 1980s, the Soviet government granted increased authority to Azerbaijan to rule the Nagorno-Karabakh region, resulting in a push by Armenians in the region's national council to secede from Azerbaijan.

Violent protests against Azerbaijani rule led by Armenians broke out, and the Azerbaijani army cracked down on the Armenian rebellion. Moscow initially supported Azerbaijan's troops but backed down in September 1991. Armenian militants took the opportunity to launch renewed attacks on Azerbaijan's army. Independence from Azerbaijan was approved in 1991 through referendum, but the violence showed no sign of slowing.

Between 1992 and 1994, some thirty thousand were killed as a result of Nagorno-Karabakh violence. With Russian troops gone, Armenia's forces were able to advance and take control of the former capital city of Shusha, which had previously been dominated by Azerbaijanis. Azerbaijanis fled the region, leading the United Nations to call for an end to the advance of Armenian troops. It promised to send peacekeeping forces to the region if hostilities ended. The violence stopped in May 1994, at least temporarily, after Russia helped Azerbaijan and Armenia reach a cease-fire, leaving Armenia holding tentative control. The ceasefire created the Line of Contact, which divides troops from Armenia and Azerbaijan. Both nations maintain snipers on the line and often trade fire.

CONFLICT REIGNITED, PEACE STALLED

Azerbaijan had been unhappy with the terms of the 1994 ceasefire and hoped to end Armenia's occupation. After 1994, Armenian troops occupied 20 percent of Azerbaijan, and the Azerbaijan government accused the troops of forcing Azerbaijanis located in Nagorno-Karabakh to flee their homes. Azerbaijan first turned to its international partners for assistance.

The OSCE Minsk Group, consisting of France, the United States, and Russia, was created to lead the mediation efforts since they began in 1992, but failed to produce results amenable to both sides. Azerbaijan took its case to the United Nations General Assembly, with a draft resolution that would allow Azerbaijanis who had been driven from their homes in Nagorno-Karabakh to return home. The resolution further called upon the OSCE to look into allegations that Armenia was violating humanitarian law. Armenia's foreign ministry struck back against the draft resolution, saying that it would derail the negotiations over the Nagorno-Karabakh region, and also asked that the United Nations be excluded from all Nagorno-Karabakh negotiations.

With pleas from Azerbaijan's government, a group of world leaders led by the OSCE came together to work toward a resolution of the Nagorno-Karabakh conflict in November 2009. The summit began with Azerbaijan's president, Ilham Aliyev, threatening to use his nation's military force to gain control over the region if no agreement could be reached. "If this meeting ends without a result, then our hopes in the negotiating process will be exhausted in which case we will not have any other choice," said Aliyev. "We have the full right to liberate our lands by military means." The summit did end without a resolution, and violence was renewed in early 2010 when Armenia violated the ceasefire agreement and killed three Azerbaijani soldiers.

TOWARD A COMPROMISE

Russian president Dmitry Medvedev took the lead on negotiations between Armenia and Azerbaijan in 2010, working both with the Minsk Group and independently. The basis for negotiations was the Basic Principles for the Peaceful Settlement of the Nagorno-Karabakh Conflict, first introduced in 2005 by the Minsk Group. The principles in this agreement call for the regions surrounding Nagorno-Karabakh to be returned to Azerbaijan; the creation of a land corridor linking Armenia to Nagorno-Karabakh; allowing refugees to return to their homes; the establishment of an international peacekeeping force in Nagorno-Karabakh; and a self-governance model to be created in the disputed territory by legal agreement. Up until 2010, the presidents of Armenia and Azerbaijan had agreed to little more than the preamble to this agreement.

In March, President Aliyev stated that the two nations, with the help of their mediators, had made important steps toward reaching a final agreement on the Nagorno-Karabakh settlement. "We have reached the crucial stage in settling the conflict," he announced. "The negotiations can be said to have mainly been completed. Most of the proposals, for a few exceptions, meet Azerbaijan's interests. They ensure territorial integrity and return of all the occupied territories to Azerbaijan," Aliyev stated. Furthermore, Aliyev said that Azerbaijan had held firm on its position that it would not allow Nagorno-Karabakh to become an independent settlement. "Any status of Nagorno-Karabakh outside Azerbaijan is out of the question. It will not happen—neither tomorrow, nor in 100 years, never. We cannot accept it, and it is our position of principle. Nagorno-Karabakh will never be granted independence."

In June, another breakthrough occurred. One month before it was set to meet with the OSCE Minsk group, Armenian foreign affairs minister Edward Nalbandian announced that a meeting held by Russia had brought the nations one step closer to an agreement. "The process is continuing," said Nalbandian. "We can say the negotiations were quite constructive and useful. They played an important part in the regulation of the problem." Russia announced that the meeting helped to settle a number of disagreements over the basic principles framework, which was necessary in ensuring a peaceful resolution to the conflict, but still no agreement had been reached on the major elements, including the independence of Nagorno-Karabakh.

Throughout the summer months of 2010, little progress toward an agreement was made. Violence along the Line of Contact increased, and by late June Azerbaijan was holding full-scale military exercises at the boundary. The increase in violence ramped up international efforts for an agreement. U.S. secretary of state Hillary Rodham Clinton visited both Armenia and Azerbaijan in July 2010, shortly after the visit of U.S. defense secretary Robert Gates in June, calling the region a "high priority" in U.S. foreign affairs. The focus placed on the region by the United States is driven by Azerbaijan's border with Iran, making Azerbaijan a key strategic partner in military and political intervention in the Middle East. In Azerbaijan, Clinton told reporters, "The final steps toward peace often are the most difficult, but we believe peace is possible." Although she had not expected much progress, Secretary Clinton left Azerbaijan without any agreement or concessions on either side of the Nagorno-Karabakh dispute.

UN secretary general Ban Ki-moon intervened in the dispute in September 2010, meeting with Nalbandian and asking that he remove snipers and other troops from their positions on the Line of Contact. Azerbaijan said the simple removal of snipers would do nothing to end the violence. "Let's see whether by withdrawing the snipers the aggressor will give up its unfair claims, or release the Azerbaijani territories. This is the major problem. Suppose that this proposal is realized and snipers are withdrawn from the contact line. Does it mean that shots from other weapons will not be heard?" asked Azerbaijan's defense ministry spokesperson Eldar Sabiroglu. "Within the past month, Armenian servicemen have fired on opposite positions across the contact line from machine and sub-machine guns and grenade throwers. These weapons have even been used against civilians," Sabiroglu claimed. He called on the United Nations to work with the OSCE Minsk Group to ensure that the four resolutions calling for Armenia to end the violence in Nagorno-Karabakh be fully enforced.

Prior to the final OSCE meeting of 2010, leaders from Russia, Armenia, and Azerbaijan met again in Russia with President Medvedev to continue settlement discussions. Little progress was made on the Nagorno-Karabakh region specifically, but Armenia and

Azerbaijan did agree to return the other nation's prisoners of war and bodies of those killed in the conflict. "Any kinds of talks are better than having the conflict become active," said Medvedev of the meeting that produced few concrete results.

Armenia remained skeptical after the October meeting with Russia that the OSCE December summit would produce any results. "I do not think any fundamental agreements may be reached [at the OSCE Summit] in Astana, as the sides are too far from each other now. Azerbaijan is not at all ready for any compromise. If the international community and mediators are expecting the summit to produce any results, it means they hope for concessions by the Armenian side. They are mistaken, however. The Armenian side will not do it," said Armen Rustamyan, chairman of the Armenian parliament's Foreign Relations Committee. Aliyev opened the OSCE December summit calling for increased focus on the humanitarian situation in Azerbaijan, particularly within the Nagorno-Karabakh region. "Armenia continues to occupy not only Nagorno-Karabakh but also seven other regions of Azerbaijan. . . . They committed war crimes, genocide in Khodjaly where hundreds of civilians were killed by Armenian armed forces only because they were Azerbaijanis. Among the innocent victims of Khodjaly, more than 100 were children." Aliyev committed his country to the peace process, and criticized the unwillingness of Armenia to agree to suggested peace provisions. "The way how Armenia behaves during the negotiation process leads us to the conclusion that Armenia does not want peace, doesn't want to liberate occupied territories, but wants to keep the status-quo as long as they can and make negotiation process endless."

—Heather Kerrigan

Following is a statement by the Armenian Socialist Party on October 29, 2010, after a meeting between Russia, Armenia, and Azerbaijan to discuss mediation over the disputed Nagorno-Karabakh region; and a speech given by Azerbaijan's president, Ilham Aliyev, on December 1, 2010, at the Organization for Security and Co-operation in Europe (OSCE) summit on security concerns in Nagorno-Karabakh.

Presidents of Russia, Armenia, and Azerbaijan Meet

October 29, 2010

President of the Russian Federation Dmitry Medvedev, President of Armenia Serzh Sargsyan, and President of Azerbaijan Ilham Aliyev discussed future possibilities for reaching a settlement of the Mountainous (Nagorno) Karabakh conflict.

At the talks, in Astrakhan, the parties approved a joint statement. The document, which is humanitarian in purpose, has great importance for resolving the conflict in view of the various difficulties still apparent today in Azerbaijani-Armenian relations over the Mountainous Karabakh issue, Dmitry Medvedev said and added that the statement aims to bolster the ceasefire regime and strengthen confidence-building measures. The Armenian and Azerbaijani presidents agreed that their first step would be an immediate exchange of prisoners of war and the return of the bodies of those killed. This would be organised with the help of the co-chairs of the OSCE Minsk Group and the International Committee of the Red Cross.

Answering journalists' questions after the meeting, Mr Medvedev noted that the general principles for settling the Nagorno-Karabakh problem could be drafted in time for the OSCE summit that will take place on December 1–2, 2010 in Astana. "Overall, I think that these are very useful meetings even though they are not easy and the talks involve quite intense and sometimes emotional debate, and even though this is not an easy undertaking for the mediators either, for the Minsk Group, and for Russia as one of the Minsk Group's co-chairs. First of all, any kinds of talks are better than having the conflict become active. Second, and perhaps most important, these are not just talks but are steps forward.

"I can inform you now that the two parties have just signed a joint statement. This is a humanitarian agreement, but at the same time it is very important given the various difficulties that we still see in Azerbaijani-Armenian relations over the Nagorno-Karabakh issue. This is a special declaration aimed at bolstering confidence-building measures so as to organise as swiftly as possible the exchange of prisoners of war and return the bodies of those killed. Though at first glance this is a serious but nonetheless private issue, it is very important because the two sides have not been engaged in open and direct confrontation for quite a long time now, but there are still problems, there are still shots being fired and people killed. The point comes when it is essential to look openly at the situation and take steps towards each other, attempting to work out perhaps small but nevertheless very important problems.

"Another subject that we discussed today was of course the issue of a peace treaty and overall settlement. This has been on the agenda at all of our meetings since the meeting in Maiendorf in the Moscow Region, when the joint declaration was adopted. Today we discussed this subject too and agreed on the following points.

"The general settlement principles that will later lay the peace treaty's foundations have still to be agreed on, but we have nonetheless made progress that gives hope that if the two sides work hard over the coming month—and we will give this instruction to our foreign ministers—we could have an approved draft of the general settlement principles in time for the OSCE summit in Kazakhstan on December 1–2.

"I emphasise that there are still many issues to sort out, but both sides seek to reach agreement on the differences over wording that still remain. Russia will continue its efforts. I believe that we can reach results and I think we have grounds for being reasonably optimistic. Of course, the main part of the work is still ahead."

The Astrakhan trilateral meeting was the seventh so far and the third this year.

JOINT DECLARATION ADOPTED AFTER THE TRILATERAL MEETING OF THE PRESIDENTS OF ARMENIA, THE RUSSIAN FEDERATION AND AZERBAIJAN IN ASTRAKHAN

"On October 27, 2010 the Presidents of the Republic of Armenia, the Republic of Azerbaijan and the Russian Federation met in Astrakhan at the invitation of the President of the Russian Federation and discussed thoroughly the process and the prospects of the resolution of the Nagorno Karabakh conflict.

"Reaffirming the provisions of the Joint Declaration signed in Moscow on November 2, 2008, the Presidents underlined that the resolution of the conflict through the political and diplomatic means requires additional efforts aimed at the reinforcement of the cease-fire and enhancement of confidence building in the military sphere. Toward that end, the Presidents of Armenia and Azerbaijan agreed as a first step, assisted by the Minsk Group and the International Committee of Red Cross, to immediately exchange prisoners of war and return remains of the dead, and driven by the utterly humanistic nature of these issues, to act upon this principle hereafter."

ARF-D DISAPPOINTED AN[D] IS NOT OPTIMISTIC

The Armenian Revolutionary Federation-Dashnaktsutyun (ARF-D) is disappointed at the results of the Astrakhan meeting and does not have any special hopes in connection with the OSCE Summit in Astana.

The Armenian-Azerbaijani-Russian presidential meeting has fallen short of ARF-D's expectations. The sides did not discuss the principal aspects of the Mountainous Karabakh conflict, particularly Mountainous Karabakh's status and security guarantees, Armen Rustamyan, the chairman of the Armenian parliament's Foreign Relations Committee and chairman of ARF-D Supreme Council of Armenia, told journalists on October 28.

The statement adopted in Astrakhan will, to a certain extent, contribute to security and atmosphere of confidence in the conflict zone, provided the agreements are put into effect and not violated by Azerbaijan, said Rustamyan. "Baku's position does not inspire any optimism—Azerbaijan organized a provocation just on the threshold of the Astrakhan meeting. Athough the present situation in the Mountainous Karabakh conflict zone is a neither-war-nor-peace situation, but official statements talk about exchange of POWs," Rustamyan said. He is not optimistic about the OSCE Summit in Astana. "I do not think any fundamental agreements may be reached [at the OSCE Summit] in Astana [in early December], as the sides are too far from each other now. Azerbaijan is not at all ready for any compromise. If the international community and mediators are expecting the summit to produce any results, it means they hope for concessions by the Armenian side. They are mistaken, however. The Armenian side will not do it," Rustamyan said.

ASTRAKHAN MEETING EASED TENSED ATMOSPHERE

The main objective of the recent trilateral meeting of Armenian and Azerbaijani presidents initiated by their Russian counterpart Dmitry Medvedev was to some extent "to calm the atmosphere," Giro Manoyan, director of the International Secretariat of the ARF-D Bureau told journalists on October 29. According to him, the atmosphere between the Armenian and Azerbaijani relations had reached a high level of tension due to the statements by Azerbaijani President Ilham Aliyev and some of the statements Armenia's president Serzh Sargsyan made in response, as well as due to the ceasefire violations that frequently take place in the recent months.

"Medvedev succeeded in doing so," said Manoyan, adding that the meeting in Astrakhan gave nothing else. Even more, there are no grounds to have any expectations from the December meeting to be held in Astana, Kazakhstan. According to Mr Manoyan, in a best-case scenario, the Organization for Security and Cooperation in Europe may at its year-end summit come up with a statement over the Mountainous Karabakh conflict, by reaffirming the principles of the settlement of the conflict as already declared by the presidents of the co-chair countries of the OSCE Minsk Group or by the OSCE Ministerial Council, on 2 December 2009, in Athens.

Speaking about the agreement reached between Serzh Sargsyan and Ilham Aliyev to swap prisoners of war and repatriate the remains of all those killed on the line of contact, Giro Manoyan said that Azerbaijan will perhaps be committed to its pledge only to show to its people that there is some progress in the talks process.

Furthermore, Mr Manoyan said that Turkey continues linking the settlement of the Karabakh conflict to the normalization of the Armenia-Turkey relations—something that is "clear to all, including the US." According to him, Turkey's attitude is another reason Armenia to withdraw its signature from the Armenia-Turkey Protocols.

Manoyan considers that opening of Heydar Aliyev's statue in Astrakhan was a gesture made by Moscow to the returning Azerbaijani leader to Russia who was upset at the results of their last trilateral meeting in Saint Petersburg, in June. One should not consider it as Russia's serious change of position, he noted.

OSCE ASTANA SUMMIT NOT TO YIELD RESULTS

No critical breakthroughs in the Moutnainous Karabakh peace process is expected at OSCE Summit in Astana, December 1–2, leader of the Armenian Revolutionary Federation-Dashnaktsutyun parliamentary faction, Vahan Hovhannesyan, stated at a press briefing in the Armenian National Assembly on October 29.

"Did any such meeting achieve significant progress in the Karabakh conflict resolution before? Why should we expect a breakthrough this time?" Hovhannesyan asked.

The ARF-D leader stressed it would be better if Azerbaijan changed its uncompromising stance and it too made concessions, then it would be possible to speak of the light at the end of the tunnel then, but. . . .

SOURCE: Armenian Socialist Party. "Meeting of the Presidents of Armenia, Azerbaijan and the Russian Federation." October 29, 2010. http://www.arfd.info/2010/10/29/meeting-of-the-presidents-of-armenia-azerbaijan-and-the-russian-federation/.

President of Azerbaijan Speaks on Conflict at OSCE Summit

DOCUMENT

December 1, 2010

Mr. Chairman,

Ladies and Gentlemen,

First of all, I would like to express my gratitude to President Nursultan Nazarbayev and all our Kazakh friends for excellent organization of this summit, warm hospitality and for chairing the OSCE throughout the year.

I'd like to draw Your attention to the issues of security in our region. The ongoing armed conflict between Armenia and Azerbaijan continues to represent a major threat to international and regional peace and stability.

As a result of the policy of ethnic cleansing conducted by Armenia against Azerbaijanis 20% of the territory of Azerbaijan is under occupation, 1 mln. Azerbaijanis became refugees and internally displaced persons on their own land.

Armenia continues to occupy not only Nagorno-Karabakh but also 7 other regions of Azerbaijan. Armenia destroyed our cities and villages, our homes and sacred places, graves of our ancestors and our mosques. They committed war crimes, genocide in Khodjaly where hundreds of civilians were killed by Armenian armed forces only because they were Azerbaijanis. Among the innocent victims of Khodjaly more than 100 were children.

Nagorno-Karabakh is a historic part of Azerbaijan. It is internationally recognized part of Azerbaijan. Today Armenia continues to use force to sustain the control over the occupied territories and to hinder the return of the IDPs to their homes. But nevertheless Azerbaijan was always and remains committed to the peaceful negotiations and still hopes that they will bring results. Solution to the conflict must be based only on the respect to the norms and principles of international law, implementation of 4 UN Security Council resolutions, decisions of OSCE, resolutions of European Parliament, the Council of Europe and other international organizations. But Armenia instead of negotiating in good faith with a view to finding a durable solution to the conflict as soon as possible, gives preference to its escalation with unpredictable consequences. Armenia permanently violates the cease-fire regime, conducts military trainings in the occupied territories, tries to rename the historical names of our occupied cities and villages. Armenia illegally settles civilians in the occupied territories, tries to make the situation irreversible and peace process meaningless.

Illegal activity by Armenia in the occupied territories was reflected in the report of the OSCE fact-finding mission to the region in 2005.

The way how Armenia behaves during the negotiation process leads us to the conclusion that Armenia does not want peace, doesn't want to liberate occupied territories, but wants to keep the status-quo as long as they can and make negotiation process endless.

OSCE Minsk Group was created in 1992, negotiations are held for almost 20 years, but without any results.

Azerbaijan values the proposals that the Minsk Group Co-Chairing countries have elaborated over past six years within the Prague Process. We are ready to continue negotiations and to finalize them as soon as possible and to achieve a solution which will be based on the norms and principles of international law within the framework of the territorial integrity of Azerbaijan.

Thank You.

SOURCE: Office of the President of Azerbaijan. "Speech by Ilham Aliyev at the VII OSCE Summit." December 1, 2010. http://president.az/articles/1208?locale=en.

OTHER HISTORIC DOCUMENTS OF INTEREST

FROM PREVIOUS *HISTORIC DOCUMENTS*

■ Armenian President on Shootings in Parliament, *1999*, p. 639
■ Clinton, Yeltsin at European Security Summit, *1994*, p. 583

November

Responses to the 2010 Midterm Elections

NOVEMBER 2 AND 3, 2010

The November 2010 elections returned a historic victory to the Republican Party. At the federal level, the GOP took control of the House of Representatives with a net gain of sixty-three seats, the biggest legislative landslide since 1948. The Democrats lost six Senate seats but maintained control of the upper house by a 53 to 47 margin. The Republicans also swept elections for state legislatures, flipping control of nineteen of the ninety-nine legislative chambers. Although the bleak economic picture made 2010 a year the opposition party could expect to make gains, the margin of the Republican victory exceeded most predictions. Campaign spending reached an all-time high in the 2010 cycle, exceeding $4 billion in expenditures, mostly on advertisements. Many observers pointed to the U.S. Supreme Court's 2010 decision in *Citizens United v. Federal Election Commission*, which removed restrictions on corporate and union electoral contributions, thus markedly changing the political environment of the United States.

THE "ENTHUSIASM GAP"

The congressional results dramatically reversed the Democratic gains of 2006 and 2008. The 2008 election that put Barack Obama in the White House was viewed at the time as a watershed vote, notable for the energetic participation of young voters. However, two years into Obama's presidency, a great deal of energy had been drained away from the Democrats' liberal base. The economic recession that officially began in December 2007 had developed into a severe and lasting recession, and even when the economy began to recover, unemployment remained above 9.5 percent. President Obama spent much of 2009 waging a fierce battle to enact health care reform legislation. By the time the measure finally passed in March 2010, many Democrats found the bill too watered down. Meanwhile, thousands of American troops remained at war in Iraq, although their combat mission officially ended in September 2010, and the war in Afghanistan appeared to be expanding with no end in sight.

All these factors spelled electoral trouble for Democratic legislators and candidates, especially in swing districts. From early in 2010, opinion polling revealed that likely Republican voters were far more eager than their Democratic counterparts to go to the polls in November. Studies showed that in state primary elections, Republican turnout exceeded Democratic for the first time since the 1930s. Republican leaders sensed an opportunity to replicate the success they enjoyed in the 1994 midterm elections during Bill Clinton's presidency. Emulating the 1994 tactics of U.S. representative Newt Gingrich, R-Ga., House Republicans released a policy document called "A Pledge to America" in September, aiming to craft a national campaign message that would help them retake the House. Campaign ads called on the voters to "fire" House Speaker Nancy Pelosi, D-Calif. Minority Leader John Boehner, R-Ohio, vowed that if he became Speaker of a Republican-controlled House, his top priority would be to repeal the new health care law.

For the Republican rank and file, the paramount issues appeared to be taxes, spending, and budget deficits. Fiscal conservatives were outraged by such government outlays as the $700 billion Wall Street bailout, passed in the waning months of President George W. Bush's second term, and Obama's $787 billion economic stimulus package, the American Recovery and Reinvestment Act of 2009.

A new populist movement calling itself the Tea Party arose in 2009 and emerged as a potent and very visible force in the 2010 election cycle. Tea Party activists, galvanized by their opposition to excessive government spending, mounted several successful primary challenges to incumbent Republican office-holders across the nation. Political analysts agreed that the Tea Party phenomenon represented a new energy and momentum on the right. They differed, however, over whether to characterize the Tea Party as an authentic grassroots uprising or a rebranding of libertarian conservatism underwritten by elite organizations such as FreedomWorks, run by former House majority leader Dick Armey, R-Texas, and the foundations of the billionaire brothers Charles G. and David H. Koch.

CITIZENS UNITED AND THE ROLE OF MONEY

The role of corporations and interest groups in campaign spending sparked a major controversy in the 2010 elections. In January, the Supreme Court overturned campaign finance restrictions in its *Citizens United v. Federal Election Commission* decision. By a 5 to 4 majority, the Court ruled that the First Amendment rights of corporations, unions, and other independent organizations permitted them to spend essentially unlimited amounts from their general treasuries on independent political advertisements for candidates and political parties. Although the ruling itself did not eliminate the legal requirement to disclose political donations, in practice the number of donors failing to disclose rose astronomically.

The 2010 election was thus the most expensive congressional race in the nation's history. By many measures, the new regulatory framework worked to the clear advantage of the Republican Party. Organizations such as the U.S. Chamber of Commerce and the Koch Family Foundations and media baron Rupert Murdoch pledged millions to help GOP candidates. The groups American Crossroads and Crossroads GPS, which Republican consultant Karl Rove helped to found, strategically directed anonymous donations toward attack ads in competitive House races. The flood of political advertising by both parties brought well over $2 billion in revenue to the television networks during the election season. The ubiquitous campaign ads, often broadcast with no disclosure of their funding sources, were instrumental in setting the agenda of dozens of close races.

As Election Day neared, President Obama and leading Democratic figures raced around the country urging their supporters to go to the polls. Predictions of a Republican landslide proliferated, with many pundits projecting that the party would likely capture one or both houses of Congress. The nation's attention went to a number of tight Senate races. Senate majority leader Harry Reid, D-Nev., was battling against Sharron Angle, a Tea Party–endorsed conservative. Another Tea Party favorite, Christine O'Donnell, who defeated former governor Michael Castle to win the Republican Senate nomination in Delaware, was in a tight race with former New Castle County executive Chris Coons. Both Democrats hung on to win their races, but the Tea Party notched dozens of other victories on a very Republican night.

WINNERS AND LOSERS

The sixty-three-seat swing in the House was larger than almost all projections before Election Day. The majority of seats that flipped were in competitive or Republican-leaning districts where Democrats had won in 2006 and 2008. The "Blue Dog" caucus of conservative Democrats was especially hard-hit, shrinking from fifty-four members to twenty-six in the new Congress. By contrast, only three out of eighty members of the Congressional Progressive Caucus were defeated. Overall, roughly 85 percent of House incumbents were reelected, the lowest percentage since the 1970 midterm elections. Republicans would hold a sizable 242 to 193 majority in the 112th Congress.

The drama on election night centered on the Senate, with Republicans needing to pick up ten or more seats to gain control. Only two Democratic incumbents fell to challengers: in Wisconsin, Ron Johnson, a political novice, turned back progressive Russ Feingold's quest for a fourth term; and in Arkansas, Rep. John Boozman soundly defeated Blanche Lincoln, a conservative Democrat who had provided a key vote in favor of health care reform. Republican representative Mark Kirk won the Illinois seat formerly held by President Obama, defeating Alexi Giannoulias. In another closely watched Senate contest, Pat Toomey prevailed over representative Joe Sestak, who had defeated incumbent Arlen Specter in Pennsylvania's Democratic primary. Republicans also won open seats in Indiana and North Dakota. In Florida, rising GOP star Marco Rubio won a three-way race over former governor Charlie Crist, a moderate Republican who ran as an independent, and Democrat Kendrick Meek. Perhaps the biggest Tea Party victory came in Kentucky, where libertarian Rand Paul, son of the iconoclastic Texas representative Ron Paul, took the Senate seat vacated by former baseball star and longtime politician Jim Bunning.

Democrats won enough key victories to retain their Senate majority. California's junior senator, Barbara Boxer, won a fourth term by defeating Carly Fiorina, former CEO of the technology firm Hewlett-Packard. Colorado's Michael Bennet squeaked by Weld County, Colorado, district attorney Ken Buck. Washington's Patty Murray hung on to defeat Dino Rossi, who conceded two days after Election Day. Connecticut's attorney general, Richard Blumenthal, kept in Democratic hands the seat that Christopher Dodd occupied for 30 years, besting the CEO of World Wrestling Entertainment, Linda McMahon.

Perhaps the year's most unusual Senate campaign took place in Alaska. Incumbent Republican Lisa Murkowski, who was appointed to the Senate in 2002 by her father, Governor Frank Murkowski, narrowly lost the Republican primary to Joe Miller, who had the endorsement of Alaska's famous former governor, Sarah Palin. After exploring a run as a Libertarian, Murkowski declared she would contest the general election as a write-in candidate. She thus became only the second senator in history elected as a write-in, surpassing Miller by ten thousand votes; Democrat Scott McAdams ran third.

Republicans were equally successful at the state level. In gubernatorial races, the GOP made a net gain of six and did especially well in swing states, taking from Democrats the governorships of Iowa, Kansas, Michigan, New Mexico, Ohio, and Pennsylvania. Conservative Republican Scott Walker won the Wisconsin governor's race over Milwaukee mayor Tom Barrett. In California, however, Democrat Jerry Brown completed his twenty-eight-year pilgrimage back to the governor's office. After serving two terms from 1975 to 1983, Brown returned to power by defeating Meg Whitman, the former head of eBay who spent more than $175 million of her own money on the campaign.

The GOP picked up a total of 680 seats in state legislatures across the nation, the biggest gain for either party since 1966. In 2011 the party would control both legislative houses and the governor's office in sixteen states. Moreover, since states would be redrawing district boundaries in accordance with 2010 census data, the Republicans were in a strong position to consolidate their gains.

Turnout and the demographic makeup of the electorate helped influence the outcome of many close contests in the 2010 elections. Nationwide turnout fell more than a third from 2008. Voters between the ages of eighteen and twenty-nine comprised 11 percent of the total, compared to 18 percent two years prior. Those above sixty-five years of age, on the other hand, rose from 16 percent in 2008 to 23 percent in 2010. Exit polls revealed that voters were upset about the economy and employment and believed both were getting worse.

—Roger K. Smith

Following is a statement by Republican National Committee chair Michael Steele on November 2, 2010, in response to the 2010 midterm election results; a November 3, 2010, statement by DNC chair Tim Kaine on the midterm election results; November 3, 2010, statements by Rep. John Boehner, R-Ohio, and Sen. Harry Reid, D-Nev., in response to the 2010 midterm election results; and an article from the National Conference of State Legislatures on November 3, 2010, on the results of the 2010 state legislative elections.

RNC Chairman Steele on Election Results

November 2, 2010

"Tonight, we learned that our democracy is alive and well and that voters, not politicians, will be the ones who direct the course of our great nation. After two years of arrogance on behalf of Democrats towards their constituents, the American people have taken an important step to reclaim the reins of their country by making the important decision to fire Nancy Pelosi. Tonight, voters rejected the economic policies that have resulted in nearly double-digit unemployment and record-breaking budget deficits. They have rejected the belief that government can run our health care system, automobile companies, and student loan industry better then we can. Most importantly, they have rejected the politics of President Obama where the people's business is conducted behind closed doors.

"Two years ago, the Republican Party was said to be in the wilderness without a cohesive message or a plan of action. So we listened to the American people and remained true to our core principles of limited government and fiscal responsibility. Today, the Republican Party has reemerged stronger and closer to the people who put their faith in us. The new Republican Majority in the House of Representatives was elected on a promise to put a check on the liberal agenda and reckless spending of the Obama Administration. We intend to make good on that promise so that the families of today can once again afford the American dream."

Source: Republican National Committee. "Statement from RNC Chairman Michael Steele on the Republican Party Gaining Control of the U.S. House." November 2, 2010. http://www.gop.com/index .php/news/comments/statement_from_rnc_chairman_michael_steele_on_the_republican_party_ gaining_.

DNC Chairman Kaine on the 2010 Midterm Election Results

November 3, 2010

In November 2008, the American people voted for change—for a President that would stand up for the needs of middle-class families and a government that would work together to address America's biggest challenges. In the two years since then, Democrats have worked hard to rebuild America's economy and renew the American Dream. But tonight, voters sent a message that change has not happened fast enough. The American people are rightly frustrated by the economy, and Democrats are ready to redouble our efforts to create jobs and accelerate growth. With the two houses of Congress now divided between Democrats and Republicans, it is incumbent upon both parties to take responsibility for governing so we can move the nation forward.

In the face of stiff historical and economic headwinds, many of our candidates—with the help of committed volunteers and supporters across the country—outperformed expectations tonight. Democrats will maintain control of the Senate and we are fighting hard in key governors' races across the country. I am extremely proud of our Party and the Democrats across the country who ran strong races based on records of fighting for the middle class, holding Wall Street accountable, ending the worst insurance industry abuses, and repairing the economic damage created by nearly a decade of failed economic policies.

While there are many races still undecided, we must turn our attention back to the business of the American people and in that, we hope that Republicans will join us in looking for common ground from which we can make the progress the American people expect and deserve.

Source: Democratic National Committee. "DNC Chairman Tim Kaine's Statement on the Midterm Election Results." November 3, 2010. http://www.democrats.org/news/blog/dnc_chairman_tim_ kaines_statement_on_the_midterm_election_results.

Rep. Boehner on the 2010 Midterm Election Results

November 3, 2010

"As you heard me say last night, we are humbled by the trust that the American people have placed in us and we recognize this is a time for us to roll up our sleeves and go to work on the people's priorities: creating jobs, cutting spending and reforming the way Congress does its business. It's not just what the American people are demanding—it's what they are expecting from us.

"And the real question now is this: are we going to listen to the American people? Republicans have made a pledge to America, and our pledge is to listen to the American people and to focus on their priorities, and that's exactly what we're going to do.

"Last night, the President was kind enough to call me. We discussed working together on the American people's priorities: creating jobs and cutting spending. We hope that he will continue to be willing to work with us on those priorities.

"But as I said last night, the new majority here in Congress will be the voice of the American people, and I think we clearly expressed that last night. We're going to continue to renew our efforts for a smaller, less costly, and more accountable government here in Washington, DC."

SOURCE: U.S. House of Representatives. Office of Representative John Boehner, R-Ohio. "Boehner Remarks at Press Conference with Sen. McConnell & Gov. Barbour." November 3, 2010. http://john boehner.house.gov/News/DocumentSingle.aspx?DocumentID=213655.

Sen. Reid Responds to 2010 Midterm Election Results

November 3, 2010

"While we await the full results of outstanding races throughout the country, I welcome the newest members of Congress, including those who will be joining our Senate Democratic caucus. I congratulate them for earning the confidence of their constituents and look forward to working with these new members on both sides of the aisle to find shared solutions to our shared problems.

"The message that voters throughout Nevada and all across the nation sent to Washington is that they want Democrats, Republicans and Independents to work together to find the common ground needed for real solutions and real progress. I will keep fighting to make sure that big banks, big oil, those who want to privatize Social Security and other powerful special interests are prevented from taking advantage of middle-class families and small businesses. And I also welcome every opportunity to work with our Republican colleagues as we know the challenges that lie ahead of us know no political affiliation.

"While this could be considered a tough election for some who were on the ballot this year it is nothing compared to the fight that Nevada families are facing to stay in their homes, workers are facing to find good jobs and keep them, and small businesses are facing to keep their doors open and remain competitive.

"The time for politics is now over. And now that Republicans have more members in both houses of Congress, they must take their responsibility to present bipartisan solutions more seriously. Simply saying 'no' will do nothing to create more jobs, support our middle-class and strengthen our economy. We must spare no effort to get back to work immediately in order to restore the American Dream for the millions of Nevadans and all Americans."

SOURCE: U.S. Senate. Office of Senator Harry Reid, D-Nev. "Reid Statement on 2010 Midterm Elections." November 3, 2010. http://reid.senate.gov/newsroom/pr_101103_midtermelection.cfm.

Republican State Legislature Gains in 2010 Midterm Elections

November 3, 2010

THE 2010 ELECTION WILL SHAPE THE NATIONAL POLITICAL LANDSCAPE FOR AT LEAST THE NEXT 10 YEARS

Tuesday night's GOP power sweep exceeded expectations, giving the party its largest number of seats since the Great Depression.

Republicans now hold about 3,890, or 53 percent, of the total state legislative seats in America, the most seats in the GOP column since 1928. The GOP will now control at least 54 of the 99 state legislative chambers, its highest number since 1952. As a result, state legislatures will likely reflect a more conservative political agenda when they convene in 2011.

"2010 will go down as a defining political election that will shape the national political landscape for at least the next 10 years," said Tim Storey, elections specialist with the National Conference of State Legislatures. "The GOP, in dramatic fashion, finds itself now in the best position for both congressional and state legislative line drawing than it has enjoyed in the modern era of redistricting."

With their gains in state legislatures, Republicans now have a decided advantage in shaping congressional and state legislative districts when legislatures start the redistricting process next year. The GOP will have unilateral control of about 190 U.S. House districts. Storey says this is the best position for the GOP in redistricting since the landmark Supreme Court decision, Baker vs. Carr, in 1962, which established the "one-person, one-vote" rule that requires districts to be redrawn every 10 years.

The night marked a 20-year march by Republicans across the South. In 1990, the GOP held no legislative chambers and only 26 percent of legislative seats in the region. With Tuesday's results, the GOP now controls 18 legislative chambers and 54 percent of the seats. The Midwest, traditionally a Democratic stronghold, now has just 38 percent Democrat members, the lowest percentage there since 1956.

Storey said Democrats were overwhelmed by an "enthusiasm gap." Of the roughly 11,000 candidates running for the 6,115 legislative seats up this year, the GOP had 822 more Republicans running for office than in 2008. Democrats actually had 50 fewer candidates than two years ago.

Based on unofficial, preliminary returns, legislative chambers that have switched so far are:

- Alabama House and Senate
- Indiana House
- Iowa House
- Maine House and Senate
- Michigan House
- Minnesota House and Senate
- Montana House
- New Hampshire House and Senate
- North Carolina House and Senate
- Ohio House
- Pennsylvania House
- Wisconsin Assembly and Senate

Undecided chambers that could still switch are the Colorado Senate and House; the New York Senate; the Oregon House; and the Washington Senate.

Other key observations from this year's election include:

- Republicans gained at least 680 seats on Tuesday, the largest gain by either party since 1966, surpassing Democratic gains in the post-Watergate election of 1974.
- The North Carolina Senate is now in Republican control for the first time since 1870.
- The Minnesota Senate, which held nonpartisan elections until 1974, is under Republican control for the first time.
- The Alabama legislature is under Republican control for the first time since Reconstruction.

The leaders of America's state legislatures will change dramatically as a result of Tuesday's elections. Eleven sitting Democratic leaders lost their reelection bids on Tuesday, including one speaker, one lieutenant governor, two Senate President Pro Tems, six majority leaders and one Senate minority leader.

There will be significant turnover in House and Senate leadership when legislatures convene next year. Currently, 32 House Speakers are Democrats and 17 are Republican. Next year, this will change to 30 Republicans and 15 Democrats. Chambers in Colorado, Oregon and Washington remain undecided and Nebraska is nonpartisan. In terms of Senate presidents, in January 30 Senate chambers will be led by Republicans and 17 by Democrats. Currently, there are 26 Democrats and 24 Republicans. Chambers in New York, Oregon and Washington remain undecided.

Source: National Conference of State Legislatures. "Republicans Exceed Expectations in 2010 State Legislative Elections." November 3, 2010. http://www.ncsl.org/default.aspx?tabid=21634.

Other Historic Documents of Interest

National Cancer Institute on the Link between CT Scans and Lung Cancer Deaths

---

NOVEMBER 4 AND 26, 2010

On November 4, 2010, the results of a large, eight-year, $250 million study funded by the National Cancer Institute (NCI) concluded that receiving a preventative CT scan could help reduce the number of deaths caused by lung cancer. Lung cancer is the leading cause of cancer death in the United States, often because the disease is caught too late for treatment to be effective. The NCI study is the first to show a potential link between preventative screening and a reduction in lung cancer death. "This is the first time we have seen clear evidence of a significant reduction in lung cancer mortality with a screening test in a randomized controlled trial," said the NCI's Dr. Christine Berg, who acted as the project officer on the study. But scientists cautioned that additional research and testing must be completed before anyone can conclude whether lung cancer screenings for smokers should become a routine, preventative medical test.

LUNG CANCER IN THE UNITED STATES

Despite government attempts to crack down on tobacco companies and reduce smoking rates, 46.6 million, or 20 percent, of U.S. adults were smokers in 2009. A number of attempts have been made to decrease this number, including raising health insurance premiums for tobacco users who refuse to participate in cessation programs, cracking down on tobacco advertisements and marketing, and making the danger of tobacco use more readily apparent on cigarette packages. Most recently, in 2009, President Barack Obama signed the Family Smoking Prevention and Tobacco Control Act into law, which brought sweeping changes to the ways tobacco products are marketed and regulated. Although these efforts have had some effect, the number of annual deaths due to smoking remains high. According to the American Cancer Society (ACS), in 2010, an estimated 29 percent of cancer deaths in men and 26 percent in women will be linked to lung or bronchus cancers, higher than the percentage of death from any other form of cancer. More than 150,000 Americans were expected to die in 2010 from lung cancer.

The large number of deaths due to lung cancer can be partially linked to a lack of routine strategy for caring for smokers. Studies have been conducted on various forms of treatment starting with preventative screenings, but these studies have not shown that CT scans or x-rays are effective in preventing death. Four studies conducted in the 1970s on the effectiveness of chest x-rays in preventing lung cancer death concluded only that the disease can be caught earlier, not that the test has an effect on mortality. Without this link, medical specialists have been left to treat lung cancer in late stages, when other symptoms of the disease necessitate a CT scan or x-ray.

National Cancer Institute Trial

The National Lung Screening Trial (NLST) followed more than fifty-three thousand current and former heavy smokers between the ages of fifty-five and seventy-four. Smokers involved in the trial smoked a minimum of one pack per day for thirty years, or two packs per day for fifteen years. None of the participants had any lung cancer symptoms at the start of the trial. Beginning in 2002, the participants were randomly assigned to one of two groups: one that would receive helical CT scans, and one that would receive chest x-rays. During the twenty-month trial period, the participants were given three annual screenings. Those participating in the study were then tracked for five years. Participants who received positive screening tests were encouraged to meet with their doctors to discuss possible methods of treatment. The NCI did not provide medical care beyond the screenings, nor did it pay for follow-up medical care.

The eight-year study, which ended earlier than expected when researchers determined that there was a clear CT scan benefit, was intended to produce results on one key objective: the difference between lung cancer mortality rates in those receiving chest x-rays and those receiving helical CT scans. The difference between the two scans is that an x-ray produces a single, flat image that stacks all of the internal structures on top of one another. A helical CT scan, on the other hand, takes multiple pictures of the entire chest to produce a complete picture of the separate pieces, making it easier to identify problem areas. Before the eight-year study, scientists suggested that the CT scan could help detect the disease at an earlier stage than an x-ray because of its more comprehensive picture, but no studies were conducted on the topic.

In October 2010, preliminary results showed that 354 people who received CT scans had died from lung cancer, while 442 in the x-ray group had died from the disease. Scientists involved in the study believe the 20-percent difference in the number of deaths in the CT scan group was caused by an ability to more easily detect lung cancer and, therefore, provide treatment during the earliest stages of the disease. Another preliminary result to come out of the study was a 7-percent reduction in death by all causes. Research has not yet been completed to determine why an overall reduction in death was caused; however, statisticians working on the study said it could be because the CT scans and x-rays help detect other diseases, including various cancers and heart conditions.

Some medical experts said it was possible that the NLST test underestimated the benefits of preventative screening because only three scans were conducted during the eight-year trial. Dr. Claudia Henschke, a professor of radiology at Mount Sinai Medical Center, says that if additional screenings had been added and continued over ten years, 80 percent of lung cancer deaths could have been avoided. Her own work in this field has produced similar results, but her studies are considered largely unreliable because she has earned royalties from CT scan machine manufacturers.

Others are skeptical that the NLST study proves that preventative scans save lives. "If we look at this study carefully, we may suggest that there is some benefit in high-risk individuals, but I'm not there yet," says Dr. Edward Patz Jr., a professor of radiology at Duke University. He helped devise the methods for the NLST study, but believes that the size of a lung cancer tumor cannot help determine whether the disease is advanced or not. Tumor size was a key component of the treatment decisions made in the NLST study.

ADDITIONAL RESEARCH NECESSARY

The study leaves open a number of questions that are now being researched by medical groups including the ACS and U.S. Preventative Services Task Force. The results will need to be analyzed to determine how cost-effective CT scans are for lung cancer screening, how screening itself impacts a person's health, and what additional medical care is needed after a screening is complete. Scientists involved in the study are optimistic that the CT scan link will produce positive benefits for the overall health of tobacco users. "This is a major step in the formulation of appropriate screening strategies for this deadly disease," said Brown University biostatistician Constantine Gatsonis, who participated in the study.

The risks of CT scans are weighing heavily on whether experts will recommend preventative screening. Radiation exposure and false positives are two potential problems that arise when a person receives a scan. The helical CT scans used in the NLST study have approximately 80 percent lower doses of radiation than regular CT scans, but the level is higher than that of an x-ray. Scientists admit that the radiation level is still lower in either case than what an average person is exposed to annually, but the effect of radiation, coupled with the number of screenings a person may need, is being taken into consideration.

A false positive is also a risk of screening. Between 20 and 60 percent of CT scans of current and former smokers show abnormalities. But this abnormality is not always cancerous. It can be inflammation, a scar, or a benign tumor. Often, these false positive patients undergo additional screenings, biopsies, or surgeries, which increase anxiety and risk. Approximately 25 percent of those in the CT scan group in the NLST study had false positives.

The risks of radiation and false positives could be more harmful than the benefits for those who are casual smokers or who have not smoked as heavily as the trial group. "For people who may have smoked a pack a day for 10 years and stopped," said Dr. Len Lichtenfeld of the ACS, "this study has no implication for them, and in fact the harms of the test could outweigh the benefits."

Further analysis will also be conducted to determine what screening recommendations would do to the overall cost of health care in the United States. The NLST study estimates that to save one life, three hundred heavy smokers need to receive a helical CT scan. Few health insurance plans currently cover these screening tests as a preventative measure. The cost of a preventative CT scan can cost upwards of $300, which patients are currently expected to pay out of pocket. The high number of screenings required to save one life will be compared to the high cost of treating advanced lung cancer in future analysis. The Centers for Medicare & Medicaid Services (CMS) announced that it would review the findings to determine whether to add preventative lung cancer screenings to health coverage benefits of those participating in Medicare and Medicaid programs. "CMS looks forward to evaluating the results of the National Lung Screening Trial as soon as the study is published and reviewing low-dose spiral CT as a screening procedure of potential value for Medicare and Medicaid beneficiaries," the organization said in a statement.

The changing face of health care in the United States, led by President Obama's health reform initiatives, will play a leading role in the additional studies and analysis that will be conducted on the NLST study results. The Obama administration has suggested that receiving too many preventative screenings not only increases the cost of health care but also puts a patient's health at risk. The NLST study seems to suggest otherwise.

Legal backlash is another potential effect of the additional analysis of the study results. A number of lawsuits have been brought against tobacco companies by current and former smokers seeking cost coverage of CT scans. Because there has been no proven link between reduction in death from lung cancer and CT scans before the NLST study, those suits have largely been thrown out. The NLST study opens the door for a number of new cases to be filed.

Medical experts and scientists continue to stress that quitting smoking, or never starting to smoke, remains the best way to avoid lung cancer. People who have never smoked account for only 15 percent of lung cancer deaths. "No one should come away from this believing it's now safe to continue to smoke or to start smoking," says NCI director Harold Varmus. "This screening does not protect the large majority of subjects from death from lung cancer." Varmus also stressed the importance of continued efforts to prevent smoking. "These findings should in no way distract us from continued efforts to curtail the use of tobacco, which will remain the major causative factor for lung cancer and several other diseases," he said.

—Heather Kerrigan

Following is a November 4, 2010, press release from the National Cancer Institute on the conclusion of the lung cancer screening study; and a questions-and-answers article about the lung cancer study updated by the National Cancer Institute on November 26, 2010.

National Cancer Institute Concludes Lung Cancer Screening Study

November 4, 2010

[Notes have been removed.]

The National Cancer Institute (NCI) is today releasing initial results from a large-scale test of screening methods to reduce deaths from lung cancer by detecting cancers at relatively early stages.

The National Lung Screening Trial (NLST), a randomized national trial involving more than 53,000 current and former heavy smokers ages 55 to 74, compared the effects of two screening procedures for lung cancer—low-dose helical computed tomography (CT) and standard chest X-ray—on lung cancer mortality and found 20 percent fewer lung cancer deaths among trial participants screened with low-dose helical CT. The NLST was sponsored by NCI, a part of the National Institutes of Health, and conducted by the American College of Radiology Imaging Network (ACRIN) and the Lung Screening

Study group. A paper describing the design and protocol of the NLST, "The National Lung Screening Trial: Overview and Study Design" by the NLST research team, was published yesterday by the journal Radiology and is openly available at http://radiology.rsna.org/cgi/content/abstract/radiol.10091808.

"This large and well-designed study used rigorous scientific methods to test ways to prevent death from lung cancer by screening patients at especially high risk," said Harold Varmus, M.D., NCI Director. "Lung cancer is the leading cause of cancer mortality in the U.S. and throughout the world, so a validated approach that can reduce lung cancer mortality by even 20 percent has the potential to spare very significant numbers of people from the ravages of this disease. But these findings should in no way distract us from continued efforts to curtail the use of tobacco, which will remain the major causative factor for lung cancer and several other diseases."

The NCI's decision to announce the initial findings from the NLST was made after the trial's independent Data and Safety Monitoring Board (DSMB) notified the NCI director that the accumulated data now provide a statistically convincing answer to the study's primary question and that the trial should therefore be stopped. A fuller analysis, with more detailed results, will be prepared for publication in a peer-reviewed journal within the next few months. Participants in the NLST are being notified individually of the findings by the study's investigators. The participant notification letter, as well as the DSMB letter, can be viewed at http://www.cancer.gov/clinicaltrials/noteworthy-trials/nlst.

Starting in August 2002, the NLST enrolled about 53,500 men and women at 33 trial sites nationwide over a 20 month period. Participants were required to have a smoking history of at least 30 pack-years and were either current or former smokers without signs, symptoms, or history of lung cancer. Pack-years are calculated by multiplying the average number of packs of cigarettes smoked per day by the number of years a person has smoked.

Participants were randomly assigned to receive three annual screens with either low-dose helical CT (often referred to as spiral CT) or standard chest X-ray. Helical CT uses X-rays to obtain a multiple-image scan of the entire chest during a 7 to 15 second breath-hold. A standard chest X-ray requires only a sub-second breath-hold but produces a single image of the whole chest in which anatomic structures overlie one another. Previous efforts to demonstrate that standard chest X-ray examinations can reduce lung cancer mortality have been unsuccessful.

The trial participants received their screening tests at enrollment and at the end of their first and second years on the trial. The participants were then followed for up to another five years; all deaths were documented, with special attention given to the verification of lung cancer as a cause of death. At the time the DSMB held its final meeting on October 20, 2010, a total of 354 deaths from lung cancer had occurred among participants in the CT arm of the study, whereas a significantly larger 442 lung cancer deaths had occurred among those in the chest X-ray group. The DSMB concluded that this 20.3 percent reduction in lung cancer mortality met the standard for statistical significance and recommended ending the study.

"This is the first time that we have seen clear evidence of a significant reduction in lung cancer mortality with a screening test in a randomized controlled trial. The fact that low-dose helical CT provides a decided benefit is a result that will have implications for the screening and management of lung cancer for many years to come," said Christine Berg, M.D., NLST project officer for the Lung Screening Study at NCI.

An ancillary finding, which was not the main endpoint of the trial's design, showed that all-cause mortality (deaths due to any factor, including lung cancer) was 7 percent lower in those screened with low-dose helical CT than in those screened with chest X-ray. Approximately 25 percent of deaths in the NLST were due to lung cancer, while other deaths were due to factors such as cardiovascular disease. Further analysis will be required to understand this aspect of the findings more fully.

The NCI and its partners conducted this trial to obtain the most reliable results possible about the potential benefits of lung cancer screening. Others will begin to use the extensive data from this trial to conduct further analyses and to propose clinical guidelines and policy recommendations for lung cancer screening.

"The results of this trial provide objective evidence of the benefits of low-dose helical CT screening in an older, high-risk population and suggest that if low-dose helical CT screening is implemented responsibly, and individuals with abnormalities are judiciously followed, we have the potential to save thousands of lives," said Denise Aberle, M.D., NLST national principal investigator for ACRIN. "However, given the high association between lung cancer and cigarette smoking, the trial investigators re-emphasize that the single best way to prevent lung cancer deaths is to never start smoking, and if already smoking, to quit permanently."

The possible disadvantages of helical CT include the cumulative effects of radiation from multiple CT scans; surgical and medical complications in patients who prove not to have lung cancer but who need additional testing to make that determination; and risks from additional diagnostic work-up for findings unrelated to potential lung cancer, such as liver or kidney disease. In addition, the screening process itself can generate suspicious findings that turn out not to be cancer in the vast majority of cases, producing significant anxiety and expense. These problems must, of course, be weighed against the advantage of a significant reduction in lung cancer mortality.

It should also be noted that the population enrolled in this study, while ethnically representative of the high-risk U.S. population of smokers, was a highly motivated and primarily urban group that was screened at major medical centers. Thus the results may not accurately predict the effects of recommending low-dose helical CT scanning for other populations.

SOURCE: National Cancer Institute. "Lung Cancer Trial Results Show Mortality Benefit with Low-Dose CT." November 4, 2010. http://www.cancer.gov/newscenter/pressreleases/2010/NLSTresultsRelease.

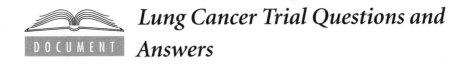

Lung Cancer Trial Questions and Answers

November 26, 2010

[Graphics have been omitted.]

1. What is NLST?

The National Lung Screening Trial (NLST) is a lung cancer screening trial sponsored by the National Cancer Institute (NCI) and conducted by the American College of Radiology Imaging Network (ACRIN) and the Lung Screening Study group.

Launched in 2002, NLST compared two ways of detecting lung cancer: low-dose helical (spiral) computed tomography (CT) and standard chest X-ray, for their effects on lung cancer death rates in a high-risk population. Both chest X-rays and helical CT scans have been used as a means to find lung cancer early, but the effects of these screening techniques on lung cancer mortality rates had not been determined. Over a 20 month period, more than 53,000 current or former heavy smokers ages 55 to 74 joined NLST at 33 study sites across the United States.

This trial is a randomized clinical trial – the gold standard of research studies.

2. Why are the initial NLST results being released now?

The NLST Data and Safety Monitoring Board (DSMB), a group of independent experts, has been meeting twice yearly since 2003, and has reviewed annual interim analyses since 2006, to ensure the safety of participants and determine if the primary scientific objective of the trial had been met.

By October 2010, sufficient data were available for the first time for the DSMB to ascertain that the study could provide a statistically significant answer to the study's primary objective and that the group receiving low-dose helical CT scans had a benefit. The conclusions were conveyed in a letter to the NCI director, in which the DSMB recommended that this information be made public. NCI concurred with the recommendation.

3. What was the primary initial result of the NLST?

NLST researchers found 20 percent fewer lung cancer deaths among trial participants screened with low-dose helical CT relative to chest X-ray. This finding was highly significant from a statistical viewpoint.

4. Were there any other important findings from this study?

An additional finding, which was not the main endpoint of the trial's design, showed that all-cause mortality (deaths due to any factor, including lung cancer) was 7 percent lower in those screened with low-dose helical CT relative to those screened with chest X-ray. This finding should not be interpreted to mean that the general population should now get regular CT. These results apply to a high-risk population. Additionally, the risks of regular CT screens could be considerable, especially for relatively healthy people.

5. When will the full set of results from this study be released?

After a more comprehensive analysis of the findings from the NLST, the investigators will prepare manuscripts for publication in peer-reviewed journals. The NCI will ensure that the analysis and manuscript preparation are performed as swiftly as possible and that the formal presentations are fully and rapidly made available to the public.

IMPLICATIONS OF NLST FINDINGS

6. Is it OK to keep smoking because there is a screening test that has benefit?

No. Tobacco is one of the strongest cancer-causing agents. Tobacco use is associated with a number of different cancers, including lung cancer, as well as with chronic lung diseases and cardiovascular diseases. The damage caused by smoking is cumulative and the longer a person smokes, the higher the risk of disease. Conversely, if a person quits smoking, the damage may be partially reversible. Finally, many participants in the trial died of lung cancer despite receiving CT screening....

7. Should all smokers have low-dose helical CT to screen for lung cancer and/or other diseases?

Not necessarily. The NLST participants were a very specific population of men and women ages 55 to 74 who were heavy smokers. They had a smoking history of at least

30 pack-years but no signs or symptoms of lung cancer at the beginning of the trial. Pack-years are calculated by multiplying the average number of packs of cigarettes smoked per day by the number of years a person has smoked. It should also be noted that the population enrolled in this study, while ethnically representative of the high-risk U.S. population of smokers, was a highly motivated and primarily urban group, and these results may not fully translate to other populations.

Men and women in a similar age group and with a similar smoking history should be aware that not all lung cancers found with screening will be early stage. They should also be aware, that at this time, reimbursement for screening CT scans is not provided by most insurance carriers. The current estimated Medicare reimbursement rate for a non-contrast helical diagnostic CT of the lung is $300, but varies by geographic location. A diagnostic CT is done after a person has a sign or symptom of disease, while a screening CT looks for initial signs of disease in healthy people.

A statement provided by the Centers for Medicare & Medicaid Services (CMS) at the time the initial results of the NLST were announced said, "CMS looks forward to evaluating the results of the National Lung Screening Trial as soon as the study is published and reviewing low-dose spiral CT as a screening procedure of potential value for Medicare and Medicaid beneficiaries."

For physicians and other practitioners, the Fleischner Society (http://www.fleischner.org), an international medical society for thoracic radiology, has established guidelines for diagnosing indeterminate lung nodules. Other organizations have developed guidelines for many other types of lung nodules.

8. Are there radiation exposure risks associated with repeat CT scans?

The radiation exposures from the screening done in the NLST will be modeled to see how exposure to three low-dose CT scans changed a person's risk for cancer over the remainder of his or her life, but that analysis will take a while to conduct.

Previous studies show that there can be an increased lifetime risk of cancer due to ionizing radiation exposure. It is important to recognize that the low-dose CT used for screening in the NLST delivers a much lower dose of radiation than a regular diagnostic CT. Additionally, the benefit of potentially finding a treatable cancer in current or former heavy smokers, ages 55 to 74, using helical CT appear to outweigh the risk from receiving a low dose of radiation.

For comparison purposes, a standard low-dose helical CT scan as used in the NLST delivers a small amount of radiation to several organs in the body, primarily the lung (4 mGy, or milligray, which is a measure of absorbed radiation dose) and the breast (4 mGy) but also the red bone marrow, stomach, liver and pancreas (each about 1 mGy) while a standard screening mammogram results in a similar radiation exposure to both breasts (about 4 mGy) but the doses to all other organs are negligible (less than 0.1 mGy). The total whole body effective dose that is ultimately delivered via a CT scan is calculated as a weighted average of the dose to each organ and is therefore higher for a low-dose lung CT scan, about 1.5 mGy, compared to 0.7 mGy for a mammogram. As a final comparison, a chest X-ray delivers only about 0.02 mGy.

9. Does screening with chest X-rays reduce lung cancer mortality?

No. The NLST consisted of two study groups, one of which included sites also involved in the Prostate, Lung, Colorectal and Ovarian Cancer Screening Trial, or PLCO. The PLCO started in 1992 and looked at chest X-rays for lung cancer screening in half of its 155,000 participants. The other half received usual care, or no screening, from their healthcare providers and served as the control group. A special analysis of about 30,000 PLCO participants who were similar in age and smoking history to the population of NLST participants showed no lung cancer mortality benefit for those who got chest X-rays. Independent of the NLST, investigators from the lung cancer component of the PLCO will report their full set of findings in the near future.

10. What do NLST participants do now?

In the NLST, participants received three screening tests after they were randomized to either the CT or chest X-ray arm: one screen at the time of enrollment and then two more annually. All of the participants finished receiving NLST screening tests by 2007 and have been under the care of their personal health care providers rather than study personnel.

Participants are being sent a letter with the initial study results. It is being recommended that those who received chest X-rays talk to their health care providers about having low-dose helical CT scans. Because it is not known if having more than three low-dose helical CT scans has any benefit, those who received helical CT scans in NLST are advised to talk to their personal health care providers about lung cancer screening, including the possibility of having additional helical CT scans. Reimbursement for screening CT scans is not provided by most insurance carriers.

11. Will screening recommendations for lung cancer change based on these results?

As with all cancer clinical trials, the NLST provided answers to a set of very specific questions related to a specific population. Whether those answers can be used to provide general recommendations for the entire population must be the subject of future analysis and study. The vast amount of data generated by NLST, which is still being collated and studied, will greatly inform the development of clinical guidelines and policy recommendations. Those, however, are decisions that will ultimately be made by other organizations.

12. What additional questions will be answered as a result of the NLST?

The NLST results reported on November 4, 2010, were initial mortality findings. Many more analyses will be done in the coming months to try to answer questions such as:

- What medical resources are utilized when CT screening tests or chest X-ray tests are positive in individuals at high risk of lung cancer?
- What is the overall cost-effectiveness of CT screening in the most commonly accepted health services research metric: dollars per quality-adjusted life year?
- How does lung cancer screening affect an individual's quality of life overall, when the screening test is positive, and when the test determines that there is a lung cancer?
- How does lung cancer screening influence smoking behaviors and beliefs, both short-term and long-term?
- What early biomarkers for lung cancer in a high risk group can be validated in the associated biospecimen archive (blood, sputum, urine)? Other information, such as germline (inherited) mutations that might predict increased risk of lung cancer, or somatic (non-heritable) mutations in the archived lung cancer specimens associated with outcomes from the cancer, may also be determined. . . .

Background about the Trial

13. Why was this study needed?

Lung cancer, which is most frequently caused by cigarette smoking, is the leading cause of cancer-related deaths in the United States. It is expected to claim 157,300 lives in 2010. Lung cancer kills more people than cancers of the breast, prostate, and colon combined. There are more than 94 million current and former smokers in the United States, many of whom are at high risk of lung cancer.

Most lung cancers are detected when they cause symptoms. By the time lung cancer is diagnosed, the disease has already spread outside the lung in 15 percent to 30 percent of cases. Therefore, researchers have sought to develop methods to screen for lung cancer before symptoms become evident. Helical CT, a technology introduced in the 1990s, can pick up tumors well under 1 centimeter (cm) in size, while chest X-rays detect tumors about 1 to 2 cm (0.4 to 0.8 inches) in size. It is sometimes hypothesized that the smaller the tumor, the higher the chance of long-term survival. However, in other randomized trials, chest X-ray screening has not been found to reduce deaths from lung cancer, even though it does increase the detection of small tumors. The NLST, with a large number of participants in a randomized trial, was able to provide the evidence needed to determine whether low-dose helical CT scans are better than chest X-rays in helping to reduce a person's chances of dying from lung cancer.

14. What is the relationship between the NLST and the I-ELCAP trial?

The International Early Lung Cancer Action Program (I-ELCAP) was a non-randomized trial that used CT screening to detect early lung cancer. Its results, which were reported in 2006, suggested that CT screening might be beneficial. However, the combination of I-ELCAP not being a randomized trial and not using the endpoint of lung cancer mortality led many clinical investigators to recommend waiting until the NLST results were available so that they could determine definitively the utility of this screening approach. Another non-randomized study of CT screening, which was published in 2007, failed to demonstrate the benefits inferred from the I-ELCAP trial. These negative results underscored the importance of NLST and its randomized trial design.

15. How do lung screening tests work?

A chest X-ray produces a picture of the organs within a person's chest. Throughout the procedure, the person stands with the chest pressed to a photographic plate, hands on hips and elbows pushed forward. During a single, large sub-second breath-hold, a beam of X-rays passes through the person's chest to the photographic plate, which creates an image. When processed, the image is a two-dimensional picture of the lungs.

Low-dose helical CT uses X-rays to scan the entire chest in about 7 to 15 seconds during a single, large breath-hold. The CT scanner rotates around the person, who is lying still on a table as the table passes through the center of the scanner. A computer creates images from the X-ray information coming from the scanner and then assembles these images into a series of two-dimensional slices of the lung at very small intervals so that increased details within the organs in the chest can be identified.

In the NLST, four different brands of machines were used: GE Healthcare (5 models); Philips Healthcare (3 models); Siemens Healthcare (4 models); and Toshiba (2 models).

16. What happened during the study?

- Participants talked with NLST staff about the study and their eligibility was determined.
- Participants read and signed a consent form that explained NLST in detail, including risks and benefits.

- Participants were assigned by chance (randomly assigned) to have either chest X-rays or CT scans, and were offered the same test each year for three years.
- Expert radiologists reviewed the chest X-ray or CT scan. Test results were mailed to the participants and their doctors, who determined if follow-up tests were needed.
- Participants were asked to update information about their health periodically, for up to seven years.
- Some NLST screening centers collected blood, urine, or sputum (phlegm) specimens from participants for future lung cancer studies. Specimens of lung cancer and normal lung tissue that were removed during surgery have also been collected from some of the participants. These specimens, also known as biospecimens, will be used for future research to look for biomarkers that may someday help doctors better screen for, and diagnose, lung cancer.
- During the trial, if participants were current smokers they were encouraged to quit, and if they wished, they were referred to smoking cessation resources. They did not have to quit smoking in order to take part in the study.

17. What happened if lung cancer was found during the study?

For participants with positive screening tests (a positive test means that it revealed an abnormality that might be cancer), the study centers notified the participants and their primary care doctors and encouraged a consultation with a cancer expert. Names of cancer experts were provided on request, but decisions regarding further evaluation were made by participants and their doctors. Any tests performed to follow up on a positive screening result could have been performed at the study center if the participants and their doctors so chose.

18. Who paid for the testing?

People participating in the trial were screened free of charge with either low-dose helical CT or chest X-ray.

Costs for any diagnostic evaluation or treatment for lung cancer or other medical conditions were charged to the participants in the same way as if they were not part of the trial. A participant's medical insurance plan paid for diagnosis and treatment according to the plan's policies. Participants who had no insurance were referred to local community resources to receive needed evaluations.

In addition to the low-dose helical CT scans and chest X-rays that all of the centers performed, some NLST centers also collected samples of blood, urine, or sputum for future lung cancer studies. These procedures were performed without charge.

ABOUT SCREENING FOR LUNG CANCER

19. What are some of the possible risks of screening for lung cancer?

Recent studies indicate that 20 percent to 60 percent of screening CT scans of current and former smokers will show abnormalities. Most of these abnormalities are not lung cancer. However, these abnormalities – scars from smoking, areas of inflammation, or other noncancerous conditions – can mimic lung cancer on scans and may require additional testing. These tests may cause anxiety for the participant or may lead to unnecessary biopsies or surgery.

Lung biopsy, a potentially risky procedure, involves the removal of a small amount of tissue, either through a scope fed down the windpipe (called bronchoscopy) or with a needle through the chest wall (called percutaneous lung biopsy). Though they happen infrequently, possible complications from biopsies include partial collapse of the lung, bleeding, infection, pain, and discomfort.

Depending on the size and location of the abnormality detected, chest surgery (called thoracotomy or thoracic surgery) to obtain a larger biopsy specimen may be required. Thoracotomy is major surgery that often results in the removal of substantial amounts of lung tissue. The procedure can damage nerves in the chest, and is more dangerous in people with lung or heart conditions, which tend to be common in current or former smokers.

In addition, studies suggest that both CT and X-ray screening for lung cancer may detect small tumors that would never become life threatening. This phenomenon, called overdiagnosis, puts some screening recipients at risk from unnecessary diagnostic biopsies or additional surgeries as well as unnecessary treatments for cancer, such as chemotherapy or radiation therapy.

20. Why is mortality the measure of the effectiveness of a screening test? Why not case survival?

Mortality refers to the number of deaths from the disease within the whole population screened. Case survival refers only to the number of people with the disease remaining alive at a certain point in time after diagnosis.

Changes in lung cancer mortality rates (rates of death from lung cancer) are the accepted measure of screening effectiveness. The major reason that case survival cannot be used when determining the effectiveness of screening is that it does not take into account specific biases that affect its measurement. These biases are lead time, length, and overdiagnosis bias.

Screening tests are performed in ostensibly healthy people who do not have symptoms of cancer. If the screening detects a cancer, the time of diagnosis is advanced (made earlier). The time between a screening diagnosis and death will be longer just because of early diagnosis, even if the screen does not ultimately change the time of death.

Secondly, studies of other types of cancer show that screening tends to detect more slowly growing cancers and may not be helpful with very fast-growing tumors. This is called length bias. Screen-detected cancers may be less aggressive and slower growing cancers than the cancers picked up by symptoms, which would make screening appear to prolong life, when in fact, it is simply picking up the less lethal cancers. An extreme of this tendency is overdiagnosis bias, in which the tumor detected by screening has the pathologic features of malignancy but grows so slowly that it may never cause death.

Case survival measurements cannot adjust for the effects of lead time, length, and overdiagnosis and may overestimate the benefit of screening. Showing a decrease in lung cancer deaths in those who are screened versus those who are not screened (or those receiving a different kind of screening test) through a randomized trial provides definite evidence of screening benefit and circumvents the biases of lead time, length and overdiagnosis.

Definition of Terms

Lead time bias: Lung cancer-specific survival is measured from the time of diagnosis of lung cancer to the time of death. If a lung cancer is screen-detected before symptoms (Sx), then the lead time in diagnosis equals the length of time between screening detection and when the first signs/symptoms would have appeared. Even if early treatment had no benefit, the survival of screened persons is longer simply by the addition of the lead time. To be beneficial, screening tests should detect disease before signs or symptoms occur and must lead to decreased mortality.

Length bias refers to the tendency of the screening test to detect cancers that take longer to become symptomatic; therefore, the more indolent, slower growing cancers. Not all cancers have the same behavior: some are very aggressive, while some grow more slowly. The cancers that grow slowly are easier to detect because they have a longer pre-symptomatic period of time when they are detectable. Thus, the screening test detects more slowly growing cancers. The survival in patients with screen-detected cancers is longer in part because the screened cancers are more indolent, but the improved survival cannot be accurately attributed to the early treatment.

Overdiagnosis bias is an extreme form of length bias in which the screening test detects a lung cancer that is not lethal—it behaves like a benign process and does not result in the death of the individual. This benign process, sometimes called pseudodisease, is a tumor you die with and not from. It looks like cancer both to the naked eye and under the microscope, but it does not have the potential to kill. When a screening test detects such a tumor, it appears to have been treated successfully, making the screening test look effective when in fact, the test detected something non-lethal.

Survival refers to the number of people remaining alive at a certain point in time relative to diagnosis. For example, a 5-year survival rate of 60 percent means that 60 percent of people will be alive five years from diagnosis. Survival is the most important measure used to compare different methods of treatment to one another. People with the same disease and severity of disease are treated with different agents (or in different ways); their survival is measured to determine which treatment is associated with longer survival. . . .

SOURCE: National Cancer Institute. "National Lung Screening Trial: Questions and Answers." Updated: November 26, 2010. http://www.cancer.gov/newscenter/qa/2002/nlstqaQA.

OTHER HISTORIC DOCUMENTS OF INTEREST

FROM THIS VOLUME

FROM PREVIOUS HISTORIC DOCUMENTS

Pro-Democracy Leader
Aung San Suu Kyi Released

NOVEMBER 13, 2010

To cheering crowds, Burma (Myanmar) pro-democracy leader Aung San Suu Kyi was released from house arrest on November 13, 2010. Suu Kyi had spent fifteen of the past twenty-one years under house arrest, only released for brief periods by the ruling junta to be arrested again for participation in opposition-movement events. The long negotiations that led to her most recent release left a number of questions unanswered as to whether Suu Kyi's release would truly be unconditional or whether, as had happened in the past, Suu Kyi would be returned to house arrest.

Aung San Suu Kyi

Suu Kyi is the daughter of General Aung San, who led Burma to independence from British rule in 1943 and founded the Burmese Communist Party. Aung San was assassinated in 1947, just two years after Suu Kyi's birth. After spending years abroad for schooling and eventually to raise a family, Suu Kyi returned to Burma in 1988 to care for her dying mother and became involved in the nation's pro-democracy movement.

A military coup that overthrew the Burmese government in 1988 gave rise to the pro-democracy party, National League for Democracy (NLD), of which Suu Kyi was chosen general secretary. In this position, she gave a number of speeches throughout the country, calling for democracy and personal freedom. In 1990, the dictatorship in power in Burma was forced by international pressure to hold an election. Suu Kyi campaigned on behalf of the NLD but was detained and placed under house arrest by the Burmese government. Although she was unable to run for election herself, her party won more than 80 percent of the seats in parliament. The government at the time, however, refused to certify the results of the election and NLD was barred from coming to power.

In 1991, while under house arrest, Suu Kyi was awarded the Nobel Peace Prize. The Burmese government did not allow her to travel to Oslo, Norway, to receive the award, so her husband and son accepted it on her behalf. In presenting the award, then-Nobel committee chairman Francis Sejersted remarked, "In the good fight for peace and reconciliation, we are dependent on persons who set examples, persons who can symbolize what we are seeking and mobilize the best in us. Aung San Suu Kyi is just such a person. She unites deep commitment and tenacity with a vision in which the end and the means form a single unit. Its most important elements are: democracy, respect for human rights, reconciliation between groups, non-violence, and personal and collective discipline."

Suu Kyi was held under house arrest until 1995, when she was released under the condition of restricted travel. However, she was arrested again in 2000 after attempting to leave the Burmese capital of Rangoon to hold political meetings elsewhere in the nation. In 2002, the Burmese junta again released Suu Kyi from house arrest in what it called a move toward national reconciliation. But in 2003, Suu Kyi was arrested when the government grew wary of the large crowds of support that followed her wherever she spoke on behalf of the NLD.

In 2009, Suu Kyi was sentenced to three years of hard labor for violating the terms of her house arrest when an American named John William Yettaw swam across a lake and entered her home. The Burmese government said she had violated her arrest by not immediately reporting Yettaw's presence to authorities. Suu Kyi reported that she did not want Yettaw to be arrested by the Burmese government because he was complaining of cramps. The three years of hard labor was commuted to an additional eighteen months of house arrest. Yettaw was sentenced to seven years in prison for breaking immigration laws.

UNCONDITIONAL RELEASE AND CAUTION

In August 2010, junta leader Than Shwe and Suu Kyi reached an agreement to end her house arrest. The junta government had originally proposed that Suu Kyi not leave the capital and not give public speeches. After she refused, the government proposed that her freedom from house arrest be based on a delay in her return to public speaking. Again, Suu Kyi refused. In the end, her lawyer was able to reach an agreement that guaranteed her unconditional release and included freedom to travel throughout the country and abroad, as well as the freedom to continue public speaking.

When she stepped out of her home on November 13 to greet the cheering crowds, her first remark was "I'm very happy to see you all again." She called on those at her home to work together to achieve their shared democratic goals. Her release came just six days after a general election took place that put the junta's party, the Union Solidarity and Development Party, squarely in charge of all government posts in what the junta called a civilian government. The United Nations and its member states labeled the election a sham because, after promising to release political prisoners before the election to allow their participation in the vote, election laws announced in early 2010 banned prisoners from participation, and their freedom never materialized. Burma banned election monitors from the nation, and the violence in the run-up to Election Day led to low turnout, especially of opposition supporters.

Because Suu Kyi had previously been granted release from house arrest, only to have that freedom revoked, there was reason for skepticism in November. Jared Gensler, a Washington, D.C.–based lawyer who works with political prisoners in Burma, cautioned, "She has been out three times before and nothing has changed in the country. In fact, in recent years, there has not been any indication from the military regime that it intends to compromise in any way whatsoever by engaging in any sort of dialogue with her."

However, as opposed to previous releases, the November 13 release was marked by a number of conciliatory gestures by the Burmese government, including a positive article regarding her release published in the state-run *New Light of Myanmar* newspaper. The article indicated that Suu Kyi was being released on good behavior and because of the status of her late father in the nation. The article also stated that Burmese state police "stand ready to give her whatever help she needs."

The United Nations and United States celebrated Suu Kyi's release, and encouraged the Burmese government to grant her freedom to travel and participate in discussions with junta leaders to ensure national reconciliation. "We urge Burma's leaders to break from their repressive policies and begin an inclusive dialogue with Aung San Suu Kyi and other democratic and ethnic leaders towards national reconciliation and a more peaceful, prosperous, and democratic future," said U.S. secretary of state Hillary Rodham Clinton. UN secretary general Ban Ki-moon further asked that the Burmese government release all twenty-one hundred political prisoners who are believed to be held in the country. The secretary general urged "the Myanmar authorities to build on today's action by releasing all remaining political prisoners." Ambassador Susan Rice, U.S. permanent representative to the United Nations, spoke of Suu Kyi's involvement in elections. "For more than two decades, Aung San Suu Kyi has stood as an inspiration and provided a voice to those around the world who fight for justice, democracy, and human rights. While Aung San Suu Kyi was not able to participate in recent elections that were neither credible nor legitimate, it is imperative that the Burmese authorities allow her and other Burmese citizens the unrestricted right to freedom of speech, movement and the ability to participate in the political process."

FUTURE PLANS

Suu Kyi's NLD party dissolved on May 7, 2010, in a symbolic gesture after the pro-democracy group denounced the junta's November elections as undemocratic. Burmese law requires the dissolution of any political party that fails to register for an election. After her release, Suu Kyi defended the decision of her party to boycott the election because of its disagreement with the new election laws. "The people have to want it, and they have to be united," she said of the change necessary in the country.

Suu Kyi's release six days after the Burmese elections took place was seen as politically motivated by the ruling junta, who believed they could easily control her opposition movement after receiving nearly 80 percent of the vote. But the incoming leaders, though still a part of the oppressive military regime, offered Suu Kyi the opportunity to work with the junta to change the face of Burma. After her release, Suu Kyi announced that she would work toward a nonviolent revolution. "I think of revolution as significant change," she said. "I say this because we are in need of significant change." Her new movement is operating in opposition to the government, but Suu Kyi makes it clear that she does not want to be confrontational. She has said that she would be willing to meet with any of the junta leadership. "Democracy is when the people keep a government in check," Suu Kyi said the day after her release. "To achieve democracy we need to create a network, not just in our country but around the world. I will try to do that. If you do nothing you get nothing." Suu Kyi announced her willingness to meet with any members of the Burmese regime to discuss the political situation in the nation, but no one readily came forward.

Suu Kyi's ultimate goal, she said, was to change not the regime in Burma but rather the values held by the government and its people. "What we want is value change," she said. "Regime change can be temporary, but value change is a long-term business. We want the values in our country to be changed. We want a sound foundation for change. Even if there's regime change, if these basic values have not changed, then one regime change can lead to another regime change and so on and so on."

In a speech on December 31, Suu Kyi called on the people of Burma to work together to achieve national reconciliation. "We must struggle by establishing people's political and social networks to get national reconciliation as well as a truly united spirit." Suu Kyi had questioned the political will of her followers when she was released in November, telling them that before any change would occur in Burma, they would need to decide what goal they want to achieve.

—Heather Kerrigan

Following is a statement from the United Nations on November 13, 2010, following the release of Aung San Suu Kyi in Burma; a statement by Susan Rice, U.S. permanent representative to the United Nations, on November 13, 2010, welcoming the release of Aung San Suu Kyi; and a statement on November 13, 2010, by U.S. secretary of state Hillary Rodham Clinton upon the release of Aung San Suu Kyi.

UN Statement on Release of Aung San Suu Kyi

DOCUMENT

November 13, 2010

Secretary-General Ban Ki-moon and the United Nations human rights chief welcomed the freeing on Saturday of pro-democracy leader Aung San Suu Kyi and urged the authorities in Myanmar to release all remaining political prisoners.

Ms. Suu Kyi, the head of the National League for Democracy (NLD) and a Nobel Peace Prize laureate, had been under house arrest for much of the past two decades. Her release comes one week after the South-east Asian nation held its first elections in 20 years.

"Her dignity and courage in the face of injustice have been an inspiration to many people around the world, including the Secretary-General, who has long advocated her freedom," Mr. Ban's spokesperson said in a statement.

"The Secretary-General expects that no further restrictions will be placed on her, and he urges the Myanmar authorities to build on today's action by releasing all remaining political prisoners."

The statement also noted that it was "deeply regrettable" that Ms. Suu Kyi was effectively excluded from participating in the recent elections.

"Democracy and national reconciliation require that all citizens of Myanmar are free to participate as they wish in the political life of their country."

UN High Commissioner for Human Rights Navi Pillay called Ms. Suu Kyi's release a "positive signal" that the Myanmar authorities are willing to move forward with the serious challenge of democratic transition.

"Clearly, Aung San Suu Kyi can make a major contribution to this process," Ms. Pillay stated, adding that she remained "extremely disappointed" that the pro-democracy leader was not released before the elections.

The High Commissioner urged the authorities to now release the other 2,200 political prisoners as "a clear sign that the new Government intends to respect human rights and forge a new future for the country."

Source: United Nations. News Centre. "UN Officials Welcome Release of Myanmar's Aung San Suu Kyi." November 13, 2010. http://www.un.org/apps/news/story.asp?NewsID=36752&Cr=myanmar&Cr1.

U.S. Permanent Representative to the UN on Release of Aung San Suu Kyi

November 13, 2010

I welcome the long delayed and overdue release of Nobel laureate Aung San Suu Kyi from house arrest. At the same time we must not forget that the regime's decision to detain her for the peaceful expression of political views can never be justified.

For more than two decades, Aung San Suu Kyi has stood as an inspiration and provided a voice to those around the world who fight for justice, democracy, and human rights. While Aung San Suu Kyi was not able to participate in the recent elections that were neither credible nor legitimate, it is imperative that the Burmese authorities allow her and other Burmese citizens the unrestricted right to freedom of speech, movement and the ability to participate in the political process.

Burma's long struggle for freedom is far from over. The United States continues to call for the release of the more than 2,100 other political prisoners who languish in the Burmese regime's jails. We call on Burma's leaders to enter into a genuine dialogue with the democratic opposition and ethnic minority groups. Only by taking concrete steps toward national reconciliation and democratic reform can the Burmese regime end its international isolation and build a better future for its people.

Source: United States Mission to the United Nations. "Statement by Ambassador Susan E. Rice, U.S. Permanent Representative to the United Nations, on the Release of Aung San Suu Kyi." November 13, 2010. http://usun.state.gov/briefing/statements/2010/150877.htm.

U.S. Secretary of State Clinton on Aung San Suu Kyi's Release

November 13, 2010

Today I join with billions of people around the world to welcome the long-overdue release of Burmese democracy leader and Nobel Peace Prize Laureate Aung San Suu Kyi from house arrest.

Aung San Suu Kyi has endured enormous personal sacrifice in her peaceful struggle to bring democracy and human rights to Burma, including unjustified detention for most of the past twenty years. The Burmese regime has repeatedly rejected her offers to engage in dialogue and work together, trying instead to silence and isolate her. Through it all, Aung San Suu Kyi's commitment to the Burmese people has not wavered.

The United States calls on Burma's leaders to ensure that Aung San Suu Kyi's release is unconditional so that she may travel, associate with her fellow citizens, express her views, and participate in political activities without restriction. They should also immediately and unconditionally release all of Burma's 2,100 political prisoners.

We urge Burma's leaders to break from their repressive policies and begin an inclusive dialogue with Aung San Suu Kyi and other democratic and ethnic leaders towards national reconciliation and a more peaceful, prosperous, and democratic future.

SOURCE: U.S. Department of State. "Release of Aung San Suu Kyi." November 13, 2010. http://www.state.gov/secretary/rm/2010/11/150872.htm.

OTHER HISTORIC DOCUMENTS OF INTEREST

FROM THIS VOLUME

- Chinese Dissident Awarded Nobel Peace Prize, p. 498

FROM PREVIOUS *HISTORIC DOCUMENTS*

- Burma's Military Leaders Bar Relief Workers After Cyclone, *2008*, p. 174
- Reports on Violence and Unrest in Myanmar, *2007*, p. 528

EU and IMF Help Stabilize Ireland's Banking System

NOVEMBER 28 AND 29, 2010

In November 2010, the European Union (EU) and International Monetary Fund (IMF) announced a $118 billion bailout of Ireland to help stabilize its banking system. This illustrates the remarkable changes Ireland has experienced in the past few decades. Following its independence in 1922, Ireland, at the occasional behest of its leaders, maintained a Catholic and largely rural culture, in which living standards were considered secondary to tradition. When the economy opened to globalization in the 1990s, Irish lifestyles and opportunities began to reflect Western European norms. Companies seeking a European base were attracted by low taxes and an educated, comparatively inexpensive English-speaking workforce. Emigration for work, long the bane of Irish parents, was considered part of history.

ADOPTION OF THE EURO

With "catch-up growth" believed by analysts to have been achieved by 2001, Ireland adopted the euro in 2002. Joining the eurozone granted Ireland lower interest rates and greater availability of cross-border credit, creating an economic boom fueled by consumption and property investment. Ireland shed its quiet, provincial image and was christened the Celtic Tiger.

Annual output tripled in the ten years leading up to 2006, with Ireland becoming home to major international technology and health care corporations. Consumers and businesses assumed that the trend of low interest rates, rising living standards, and buoyant property prices would continue indefinitely in Ireland's new economy. Tax deductions were offered to lessen the weight of mortgages in household budgets, and property sales were facilitated by simpler approval procedures. Subsidies encouraged investment in commercial property, the principal driver of construction. Ballooning commercial development was initiated by a small group of investors, within which the majority of the sector's loans were concentrated. Their initiatives were further supported by an inflow of credit from banks in richer European countries.

THE CRISIS

This growth, however, was unsustainable, relying heavily on a textbook property bubble and an oversized banking sector. The Organisation for Economic Co-operation and Development (OECD) reported that Ireland was the most overheated European economy.

The impact of the subsequent crash was deepened by poor risk assessment in the private sector, where incentives encouraged excessive confidence at all levels, from executives to loan officers. More harmful still was the insufficient implementation of regulation and imprudent government spending. In the midst of the boom, policy was staunchly pro-cyclical, increasing spending on public sector pay and social programs: public sector workers earned as much as 25 percent more than their counterparts in the private sector. At the same time, the government enthusiastically cut taxes, relying on revenue from foreign capital, investments, and property transactions, which proved to be unreliable sources of income when the economy soured.

Meanwhile, wages rose dramatically from the late 1990s, diverging from the average increase for the eurozone in 1997 to record average increases that were two or three times the regional average through 2008. Loss of competitiveness combined with a loose regulatory environment to expose a weakened Ireland, slow to respond to the international crisis. Pro-cyclical policy during this time left no flexibility to soften the effects of the coming recession. By autumn 2008, the property market had slowed and Ireland's economy had lost momentum. Nevertheless, when faced with a series of international bank failures in the autumn of 2008, the government pledged to guarantee all Irish banks. This would prove to be its undoing.

THE BAILOUT

Ireland's economy contracted in 2009 and 2010 as consumer demand plummeted in line with rising unemployment and emigration. As the crisis in the private sector abated, the implications of government-guaranteed debt became more apparent. Europe's fiscal outlook was darkened by the 2010 debt crisis, which had compelled Greece to accept a $146 billion bailout from the EU and IMF in May and prompted the creation of the European Financial Stability Facility in June. German chancellor Angela Merkel, whose country was looked to for the majority of the bailout funds, indicated in September that investors would have to share in future losses, further unsettling the market.

International analysts feared that contagion from the crisis would take Ireland hostage as well. The Irish government insisted that its aggressively orthodox economic program was not analogous to the situation in Greece. However, the costly nationalization of private Irish debt was highlighted in September by an additional $48 billion bailout for the disgraced Anglo Irish Bank, which was viewed as one of the main culprits of the crisis. Despite cuts in welfare benefits and services, officials announced a projected annual deficit worth 32 percent of economic output in October, reflecting the heavy burden that bank debt imposed on the country's fundamentals. Investors were unconvinced by the sharp austerity measures being adopted by the Irish government, and the yield difference between Irish and German bonds rose to a punishing 10 percent. Shortly after the November 4 announcement of 2011 budget cuts worth $8.5 billion, then–Irish finance minister Brian Lenihan acknowledged grim circumstances but claimed that Ireland had sufficient funds to operate until at least mid-2011.

However, in late 2010, EU officials, concerned about growing investor unrest over European debt, urged Ireland to seek a bailout in order to settle market sentiment. Ireland reluctantly agreed to a $112.5 billion bailout from the EU and the IMF on November 28, prompting outrage among the Irish electorate. The perceived loss of sovereignty to external advisers was more provocative than the stringent conditions attached to the aid package, with some Irish commentators bemoaning the imposition of a new imperial regime, with bitter allusions to the British occupation of the country. Opposition parties demanded early elections and threatened not to approve the program. Brian Cowen, the beleaguered prime minister at the time, promised early elections, but only after the passage of the package and the 2011 budget, presenting the terms as a non-negotiable alternative to national insolvency.

In response to the passage of the budget and bailout, voters questioned the justice of being made to pay for what they perceived to be the losses of risk takers who had made handsome profits during the boom. Although the outsized role that the financial sector held during the Celtic Tiger years seemingly compelled the government to nationalize its burgeoning debts, the temptation of moral hazard for financial decisionmakers in the future was increased and threatened to delegitimize Ireland's social contract with its government and businesses. The implicit taxpayer backing of private debt and risk undermined political stability, particularly in the face of rising joblessness and emigration. The government's plan to restructure the banking sector also seemed insufficiently punitive toward financiers, despite the criminal investigations initiated against Irish Anglo Bank. Normally stoic Irish voters now viewed themselves as the victims of government appropriation, being forced to finance the poor decisions of others while ceding national honor to foreign powers.

FALLOUT

The impact of the 2010 bailout will continue to reverberate through Irish politics in the coming years. Facing a wave of public anger, Prime Minister Cowen resigned as head of the Fianna Fáil party for the remainder of his term in office and approved early elections held in March 2011. The erstwhile ruling party, which had governed for sixty of the previous eighty years, then suffered its worst defeat since the country's independence, forfeiting fifty-eight of seventy-eight seats. Ultimately, victory in the March 2011 elections may prove costly for the former opposition parties, Fine Gael and Labour. Their policy choices are extremely constrained by those made by their predecessor, and by the terms of the IMF-EU bailout agreement. Although the governing coalition campaigned on a promise to soften these conditions, it is unlikely that international bodies will grant more than the minimum concessions required to preserve political stability, such as a reduction in the nominal interest rate on Ireland's loans.

The economy also remains extremely fragile. Half of Ireland's banks were predicted to close by December 2011. Ahead of a stress test to determine banks' vulnerability to another crisis in March that year, it was believed that the banks would require more than what was allocated for bank support in the bailout package. The Irish government hesitated to acquire more debt and may impose a haircut on investors instead, deepening skepticism among wary bond vigilante investors. These concerns were heightened by the increasingly fragile position of Portugal, which faced a political crisis and was widely seen as the next European candidate for a bailout in the spring of 2011. Spain was also viewed as a potential victim of the crisis. Despite Ireland's unwilling acceptance of a bailout, capital infusions have not resolved the eurozone's debt problems, which will not be addressed without painful restructuring and deleveraging throughout Europe's weaker economies.

The "pace of deleveraging" was highlighted as a key policy concern during this period. European officials debated whether to sell underperforming assets and bankrupt institutions quickly for less profit, or whether to construct a costly "holding instrument" to steward the assets until conditions improved and a higher profit could be made. The European

Central Bank also debated whether to allow the Bank of Ireland to provide emergency funding to underwater banks on an ongoing basis.

These questions have implications for all struggling European economies, as well as the long-term survival of the euro currency. Held variously as a symbol of unity, progress, or independence, the collapse of the euro would seriously undermine the credibility of the European project. Nevertheless, so long as monetary and fiscal policies are not coordinated, the eurozone faces the threat of imbalance between productive, disciplined economies and uncompetitive or extravagant counterparts.

Alternative compromises have included suggestions for a two-tier euro system that recognizes the relative strengths of member economies, or the expulsion of fundamentally insolvent members from the currency union. While the latter option would allow strained states the leverage to devalue debt and boost export competitiveness, it would seem a concession of the failure on the part of the member state and the EU. Ireland, for its part, is reluctant to consider such an option, as the consequences of the market's reaction are unpredictable and could undermine trade with its European partners. Additionally, British suggestions of the reintroduction of the Irish pound, pegged to the British pound, have offended patriotic sensibilities. It is clear, however, that the country will pay heavily for its attachment to the euro, both in the form of the debt it incurred in response to attractive interest rates and in its subjection to a monetary policy it cannot control.

RECOVERY

The path to recovery remains uncertain, and economic growth is not expected to resume in Ireland before 2012. Conditions are more challenging than in the aftermath of the recessions of the late 1990s and early 2000s. Ireland cannot simply export its way out of debt on the back of global demand, though exports are growing. Nevertheless, despite an oversized, debt-ridden banking sector, the wider economy boasts a mobile and skilled workforce, as well as several industries with long-term growth potential, such as pharmaceuticals and biotechnology. It is also a major food exporter, particularly of dairy and beef products.

The business environment is favorable, and the government is unlikely to agree to European demands that it increase the 12.5 percent corporate tax rate. While other EU members claim that it undermines competition, the government holds that its business would simply go to other low-tax regimes, rather than European alternatives with higher government burdens. Ireland views its pro-business tax structure as a chief attraction that will support its eventual economic recovery. Meeting the terms of the bailout in the intervening period will be a social project as well as an economic one, and it will require the cooperation of an ideologically diverse coalition government as well as the support of the Irish people.

—Anastazia Skolnitsky

Following is a statement by International Monetary Fund (IMF) managing director Dominique Strauss-Kahn on November 28, 2010, announcing Ireland's acceptance of the IMF's monetary assistance; a statement from the government of Ireland on November 28, 2010, announcing its plan to restructure its banking system; and a joint statement on November 29, 2010, by Strauss-Kahn and Olli Rehn, the European commissioner for economic and monetary affairs, on Ireland's banking plan.

IMF Statement on Restoration Plan for Irish Banking System

November 29, 2010

Mr. Dominique Strauss-Kahn, Managing Director of the International Monetary Fund (IMF), issued the following statement today on Ireland:

"The Irish authorities have today proposed a clear and realistic package of policies to restore Ireland's banking system to health and put its public finances on a sound footing. Immediate actions to tackle vulnerabilities in the banks and continued strong fiscal adjustment are set in a multi-year policy framework for sustained growth and job creation.

"In recent years, Ireland has resolutely carried out bold policies in a very challenging environment, and I have confidence in its ability to implement this new program. Supported by substantial financing, this program can underpin market confidence and bring Ireland's economy back on track.

"The strategy for the financial system rests on twin pillars: deleveraging and reorganization; and ample capitalization. A fundamental downsizing and reorganization to restore the viability of the system will commence immediately.

"At the end of this process, a smaller, more robust, and better capitalized banking system will emerge to effectively serve the needs of the Irish economy. The transition to this goal will be buttressed by substantial recapitalization based on higher capital standards and stringent stress tests and asset valuation to accurately determine the quality of banks' loan portfolios. In addition, structural measures—a special resolution scheme for deposit-taking institutions and a further strengthening of the supervisory system—will impart greater stability.

"On the fiscal side, the program incorporates a comprehensive National Recovery Plan that covers a period of four years. The plan will form the basis for the 2011 budget and also details fiscal consolidation measures through 2014. The process of budget formation will be reformed to safeguard these gains and bring greater sustainability to public finances.

"The fiscal plan strikes an appropriate balance between revenue and spending measures, and maintains Ireland's due regard to a social safety net.

"To restore strong sustainable growth the program includes a strategy to remove potential structural impediments to enhancing competitiveness and creating new employment opportunities. It also details appropriate sectoral policies to encourage exports and a recovery of domestic demand, thereby supporting growth and reducing long-term unemployment.

"A financing package of €85 billion (about US$113 billion) will support Ireland's effort to get its economy back on track. Of this, the European Union and bilateral European lenders have pledged a total of €45.0 billion (about US$60 billion). The Irish authorities have decided to contribute €17.5 billion to this effort from the nation's cash reserves and other liquid assets. The Fund's contribution would be through a three-year SDR 19.5 billion (about €22.5 billion; or US$30.1 billion) loan, representing about 2,320 percent of quota, under the Extended Fund Facility (EFF). The IMF has activated its fast-track procedures for consideration of Ireland's funding request, and I expect the EFF will go to the IMF Executive Board for approval in December."

The choice of an EFF offers Ireland a facility with a longer repayment period, with repayments to the Fund starting after four and a half years and ending after 10 years. The IMF charges member countries a uniform interest rate on nonconcessional loans, which is a floating rate based on the SDR interest rate, which is updated weekly. (The SDR interest rate is a weighted average of yields on three-month Treasury bills for the United States, Japan, and the United Kingdom, and the three-month Eurepo rate.) For amounts up to 300 percent of quota, the lending interest rate is currently 1.38 percent, while the lending rate on amounts over 300 percent of quota includes a surcharge that is initially 200 basis points and rises to 300 basis points after three years. At the current SDR interest rate, the average lending interest rate at the peak level of access under the arrangement (2,320 percent of quota) would be 3.12 percent during the first three years, and just under 4 percent after three years.

SOURCE: International Monetary Fund. "IMF Reaches Staff-level Agreement with Ireland on 22.5 Billion Extended Fund Facility Arrangement." November 28, 2010. http://www.imf.org/external/np/sec/pr/2010/pr10462.htm.

Ireland Announces EU-IMF Financial Stabilization Plan

November 28, 2010

The Government today agreed in principle to the provision of €85 billion of financial support to Ireland by Member States of the European Union through the European Financial Stability Fund (EFSF) and the European Financial Stability Mechanism; bilateral loans from the UK, Sweden and Denmark; and the International Monetary Fund's (IMF) Extended Fund Facility (EFF) on the basis of specified conditions.

The State's contribution to the €85 billion facility will be €17½ billion, which will come from the National Pension Reserve Fund (NPRF) and other domestic cash resources. This means that the extent of the external assistance will be reduced to €67½ billion.

The purpose of the external financial support is to return our economy to sustainable growth and to ensure that we have a properly functioning healthy banking system.

The external support will be broken down as follows: €22½ billion from the European Financial Stability Mechanism (EFSM); €22½ billion from the International Monetary Fund (IMF); and €22½ billion from the European Financial Stability Fund (EFSF) and bilateral loans. The bilateral loans will be subject to the same conditionality as provided by the programme.

The facility will include up to €35 billion to support the banking system; €10 billion for the immediate recapitalisation and the remaining €25 billion will be provided on a contingency basis. Up to €50 billion to cover the financing of the State. The funds in the facility will be drawn down as necessary, although the amount will depend on the capital requirements of the financial system and NTMA bond issuances during the programme period.

If drawn down in total today, the combined annual average interest rate would be of the order of 5.8% per annum. The rate will vary according to the timing of the drawdown and market conditions.

The assistance of our EU partners and the IMF has been required because of the present high yields on Irish bonds, which have curtailed the State's ability to borrow. Without this external support, the State would not be able to raise the funds required to pay for key public services for our citizens and to provide a functioning banking system to support economic activity. This support is also needed to safeguard financial stability in the euro area and the EU as a whole.

PROGRAMME FOR SUPPORT

The Programme for Support has been agreed with the EU Commission and the International Monetary Fund, in liaison with the European Central Bank. The Programme builds on the bank rescue policies that have been implemented by the Irish Government over the past two and a half years and on the recently announced National Recovery Plan. Details of the measures are set out in the accompanying Notes for Editors.

The Programme lays out a detailed timetable for the implementation of the measures contained in the National Recovery Plan.

The conditions governing the Programme will be set out in the Memorandum of Understanding and the Government will work closely with the various bodies to ensure that these conditions are met. The funding will be provided in quarterly tranches on the achievement of agreed quarterly targets.

The Programme has two parts—the first part deals with bank restructuring and reorganisation and the second part deals with fiscal policy and structural reform. The requirement for quarterly progress reports covers both parts of the programme. When the documentation on the Programme is finalised, it will be laid before the Houses of the Oireachtas.

BANK RESTRUCTURING AND REORGANISATION

The Programme for the Recovery of the Banking System will be an intensification of the measures already adopted by the Government. The programme provides for a fundamental downsizing and reorganisation of the banking sector so it is proportionate to the size of the economy. It will be capitalised to the highest international standards, and in a position to return to normal market sources of funding.

FISCAL POLICY AND STRUCTURAL REFORM

The Ecofin has acknowledged the EU Commission's analysis that a further year may be required to achieve the 3% deficit target. This analysis is based on a more cautious growth outlook in 2011 and 2012 and the need to service the cost of additional bank recapitalisations envisaged under the programme. The Council has today extended the time frame by 1 year to 2015.

The Programme endorses the Irish Government's budgetary adjustment Plan of €15 billion over the next four years, and the commitment for a substantial €6 billion frontloading of this plan in 2011. The details of the Programme closely reflects the key objectives set out in the National Recovery Plan published last week. The adjustment will be made up of €10 billion in expenditure savings and €5 billion in taxes.

The Programme endorses the structural reforms contained in the Plan which will underpin a return to sustainable economic growth over the coming years.

The Government welcomes the support shown to Ireland by our Eurozone partners and in particular by the United Kingdom, Sweden and Denmark who have expressed their willingness to offer bilateral assistance. The Government also welcomes the assistance of the IMF.

As part of the Programme, Ireland will discontinue its financial assistance to the Loan Facility to Greece. This commitment would have amounted to approximately €1 billion up to the period to mid-2013.

Ends

28th November 2010

Notes for Editors—Programme Measures

Fiscal Measures in the Programme

Taxation

Lowering of personal income tax bands and credits or equivalent measures

A reduction in pension tax relief and pension related deductions

A reduction in general tax expenditures

Excise and other tax increases

A reduction in private pension tax reliefs

A reduction in general tax expenditures

Site Valuation Tax to fund local services

A reform of capital gains tax and acquisitions tax

An increase in the carbon tax

Programme Expenditure

Savings in Social Protection expenditure through enhanced control measures, structural reform measures, a fall in the live register and if necessary, further rate reductions.

Increase the state pension age to 66 years in 2014, 67 in 2021 and 68 in 2028.

Nominal value of State pension will not be increased over the period of the plan.

Public Service Costs

Reduction of public service costs through a reduction in numbers and reform of work practices as agreed in the Croke Park Agreement.

A reduction of existing public service pensions on a progressive basis averaging over 4% will be introduced.

New public service entrants will also see a 10% pay reduction.

Reform of Pension entitlements for new entrants to the public service

including a review of accelerated retirement for certain categories of public servants and an indexation of pensions to consumer prices.

Pensions will be based on career average earnings.

New entrants' retirement age will also be linked to the state pension retirement age.

Other

Other programme expenditure and reductions in public capital investment

Structural fiscal reforms

a Fiscal Responsibility Law will be introduced including a medium-term expenditure framework with binding multi-annual ceilings on expenditure in each area

Additional unplanned revenues must be allocated to debt reduction.

The government will establish a budgetary advisory council to provide an independent assessment of the Government's budgetary position and forecasts.

the voluntary 15 day rule for prompt payments is extended to the health service executive, local authorities and state agencies

measures to be put in place to cap the contribution of the local government sector to general government borrowing at an acceptable level.

Structural reforms in the Programme

Labour market adjustment

Minimum wage:

Reduce national minimum wage by €1.00 per hour to foster job creation for categories at higher risk of unemployment and to prevent distortions associated with sectoral minimum wages

Enlarge the scope for the "inability to pay clause"

An independent review of the Registered Employment Agreements and Employment Regulation Orders. Terms of Reference to be agreed with European Commission Services.

Reform of the unemployment benefit system to incentivise early exit from unemployment.

Steps to tackle unemployment and poverty traps including reducing replacement rates for individuals receiving more than one type of benefit (including housing allowance).

Streamline administration of unemployment benefits, social assistance and active labour market policies, to reduce the overlapping of competencies among different departments;

Enhanced conditionality on work and training availability;

Reform of activation policies:

improved job profiling and increased engagement;

a more effective monitoring of jobseekers' activities with regular evidence-based reports;

the application of sanction mechanisms for beneficiaries not complying with job-search conditionality and recommendations for participation in labour market programmes

Review of the personal debt regime:

New legislation to be prepared which will balance the interests of both creditors and debtors.

Competition

Removal of restrictions to competition in sheltered sectors including:

Legal profession:

establish an independent regulator;

implement the recommendations of the Legal Costs Working Group and outstanding Competition Authority recommendations.

Medical Profession:

eliminate restrictions on the number of GPs qualifying, remove restrictions on GPs wishing to treat public patients and restrictions on advertising.

Pharmacy Profession:

ensure the recent elimination of the 50% mark-up paid for medicines under the State's Drugs Payments Scheme is enforced.

Enhanced competition in open markets

empower judges to impose fines and other sanctions in competition cases in order to generate more credible deterrence

require the competition authorities to list restrictions in competition law which exclude certain sectors from its scope and to identify processes to address them.

Examination of the impact of eliminating the cap on the size of retail premises

Bank Recapitalisation and Restructuring Measures

The Programme for the recovery of the banking system will be an intensification of the measures already adopted by the Government. The programme provides for a recapitalisation, fundamental downsizing, restructuring and reorganisation of the banking sector. The outcome will lead to a smaller banking system more proportionate to the size of the economy, capitalised to the highest international standards, with renewed access to normal market sources of funding and focused on strongly supporting the recovery of the economy.

The proposed programme has been developed with the assistance of, and is endorsed by, our international partners.

The main elements of the programme are as follows:-

Building on the results of the Central Bank of Ireland's Prudential Capital Assessment Review (PCAR) carried out earlier this year additional capital requirements have been set.

The domestic banking system will benefit from a substantial and immediate recapitalisation raising Core Tier 1 capital ratios to at least 12%.

This action, along with early measures to support deleveraging set out below will result in an immediate injection of €10bn of fresh capital into the banking system, above and beyond that already committed.

Further recapitalisations will take place in the first half of 2011 as necessary based on the results of a detailed review and updating of the banks' capital needs following a revised PCAR exercise undertaken by the Central Bank of Ireland and involving stringent stress testing.

A Prudential Liquidity Assessment Review (PLAR) will be implemented by the Central Bank of Ireland for the domestic banks to identify deleveraging actions necessary to significantly reduce their reliance on short term funding.

A substantial downsizing of the banking system will be achieved through early and decisive actions including:-

Banks will be required to run down non-core assets, securitize and or sell portfolios or divisions with credit enhancement provided by the State, if needed.

The NAMA Scheme will be extended to remove remaining vulnerable land and development loans from Bank of Ireland and Allied Irish Bank by end-Q1 2011

This process will be carried out in a carefully balanced and controlled manner with the benefit of the substantial resources available to the banks for their funding and capital needs.

Banks will be required to promptly and fully provide for all nonperforming assets.

The restructuring of Anglo Irish Bank and Irish Nationwide Building Society will be swiftly completed and submitted for EU State aid approval.

A significant strengthening of the regulation and stability of the credit union sector will be carried out by end-2011

A special legislative regime to resolve distressed credit institutions will be introduced early in 2011.

Specific legislation to support immediate restructuring actions is in preparation.

The credibility and implementation of the programme is underpinned by the availability of a very substantial capital pool comprised of both national and international resources.

The programme builds on and complements the broad set of actions taken by the Government over the past two years to resolve the difficulties of the banking sector including the provision of guarantees, recapitalisation of the banks and NAMA.

The primary objective of this far-reaching programme is to rebuild international market confidence in the Irish banking system to enable the banks to revert to normal market funding in due course and reduce progressively their reliance on funding from the Eurosystem and guarantees and other financial support from the Exchequer.

The programme provides a strong foundation for a reformed and restructured banking system. The programme is underpinned by the large commitment of financial resources to recovery of the banking system and the support and endorsement of the programme by the IMF and the EU.

This will be crucial to ensuring that the banks play a full and vital role in underpinning economic recovery and the achievement of the Government's objectives detailed in the National Recovery Plan.

SOURCE: Government of Ireland. Department of Finance. "Announcement of Joint EU-IMF Programme for Ireland." http://www.finance.gov.ie/viewdoc.asp?DocID=6600.

EU and IMF Issue Joint Statement on Ireland's Financial Recovery Plan

November 29, 2010

"We strongly support the economic program announced today by Ireland. It is a forceful response to vulnerabilities in the banking system imposing a heavy cost on the budget and, in turn, hurting the prospects for growth that Ireland needs for an enduring solution to the crisis.

This program articulates a clear strategy for tackling today's problems and for harnessing the enormous growth potential of this open and dynamic economy. Swift and sustained implementation of this program will create a smaller banking sector that is robust and well capitalized, and able to serve the needs of Ireland's economy.

It also offers a road map for sound public finances by setting strong, upfront actions in a multi-year framework.

On the financial side, the program shows the authorities' determination to reorganize the banking sector while deleveraging the banks and injecting fresh capital into them. The program will also strengthen regulation and supervision to prevent a repeat of the costly mistakes of the past.

On the fiscal side, the program spells out both spending and revenue efforts over several years to repair the budget position, with due regard for Ireland's system of strong social protection.

Carrying out this plan calls a sustained effort by the Government and the people of Ireland. But it also offers a sound basis for stable, job-creating growth.

Ireland's international partners will support this effort. The European Commission and the bilateral lenders, together with the international community through the IMF, will offer financing that will be complemented by the Irish authorities so as to amount to €85 billion.

By shielding Ireland from the need to go to the markets for a considerable period of time, this support places financing at Ireland's disposal on more favourable terms than it could obtain elsewhere for the foreseeable future. This package also offers assurance that Ireland's banking system will be adequately funded, including through the buffer of €17.5 billion from the nation's cash reserves and other liquid assets."

SOURCE: European Union. "Joint Statement of European Commissioner for Economic and Monetary Affairs Olli Rehn and Managing Director of the International Monetary Fund Dominique Strauss-Kahn on Ireland." November 29, 2010. http://europa.eu/rapid/pressReleasesAction.do?reference=MEMO/10/6 24&format=HTML&aged=1&language=EN&guiLanguage=en.

OTHER HISTORIC DOCUMENTS OF INTEREST

FROM THIS VOLUME

FROM PREVIOUS *HISTORIC DOCUMENTS*

U.S. Department of State Responds to WikiLeaks

NOVEMBER 29 AND DECEMBER 1, 2010

Beginning in April 2010, a website called WikiLeaks began publishing thousands of confidential government documents revealing potentially embarrassing and politically damaging information about key elements of U.S. foreign policy. The most significant leak occurred in late November 2010, prompting a harsh reaction from U.S. officials and igniting a global debate on who or what was protected by the principle of freedom of the press.

LAUNCH OF A MOVEMENT

WikiLeaks, first launched in 2007, describes itself as a "non-profit media organization dedicated to bringing important news and information to the public" that also provides a "universal way for the revealing of suppressed and censored injustices." The website features an encrypted drop box that enables anonymous sources to submit, or leak, information to the organization's volunteer journalists. Perhaps the most unique aspect of the WikiLeaks site is that it publishes the documents it receives in their entirety, a feature that supporters claim enables readers to draw their own conclusions from the documents.

The site was founded by Julian Assange, a thirty-nine-year-old Australian who worked in computer security before launching the WikiLeaks project. Assange is also believed to have been a computer hacker in his youth. His associates describe him as someone who believes that the use of technology to expose hidden information is a key tool to achieving social and political change. A string of emails written by Assange later revealed his hopes that transparency would result in the "total annihilation of the current U.S. regime."

Indeed, the United States had been the subject of several WikiLeaks reports prior to 2010. In 2007, the site posted the operations manual for the U.S. military's Guantánamo Bay detention facility, which revealed several controversial policies, such as instructions on how to use military dogs to intimidate prisoners. The following year, WikiLeaks released the confidential Rules of Engagement for the U.S. War in Iraq.

The flow of secret information from the United States reached a fever pitch in 2010. On April 5, Assange held a press conference in Washington, D.C., to unveil a military video of a group of civilians being shot down in Baghdad by a U.S. Apache helicopter in 2007. In the video, the American soldiers can be heard congratulating themselves on their shooting skills and mocking the dead, making comments such as "look at those dead bastards." One soldier expresses hope that an injured man would try to fire on the helicopter so that they could shoot him again, per the rules of engagement. Military officials claimed the helicopter had been called in to assist coalition forces that were engaged in combat, but the video showed no such thing.

On July 25, WikiLeaks began to release a series of some 92,000 internal records of U.S. military action in Afghanistan between January 2004 and December 2009. The documents included threat reports from intelligence agencies, plans for and accounts of coalition operations, records of meetings with local politicians, and reports on incidents of friendly fire and civilian casualties. Some of the documents also suggested that Pakistan's Inter-Services Intelligence agency was working with the Taliban. U.S. officials immediately expressed outrage over the leak, claiming the publication of such sensitive information was a threat to national security. Then in October, WikiLeaks began posting more than 390,000 reports on the war in Iraq and U.S. military action in that country between January 2004 and December 2009. Each document offered details on the events of the war as told by soldiers on the ground in Iraq.

The most significant leak of confidential U.S. documents began on November 28, as WikiLeaks released an initial set of more than 250,000 diplomatic cables collected from approximately 250 embassies from around the world. None of the documents were top secret, and many had even been unclassified, but some had been labeled as "secret" or "noforn," meaning the material was considered too delicate to be shared with foreign governments. WikiLeaks also claimed that, in accordance with the organization's "harm minimization" policy, names and identifying information had been removed from the documents, though many officials could still be identified by other characteristics noted in the cables. Five major newspapers—*El País, Le Monde, Der Spiegel,* the *Guardian,* and the *New York Times*—published excerpts of the documents, as WikiLeaks provided those outlets with advance copies.

Some of the more notable cables detailed appeals to the United States from Arab governments, including the king of Saudi Arabia, to attack Iran and destroy its nuclear missiles. Other Arab officials described Iran as "evil" or an "existential threat." Another cable noted a promise from Yemeni president Ali Abdullah Saleh to General David Petraeus that his country would pretend a series of American missile strikes against an al-Qaida group had actually come from Yemeni forces. One cable suggested that Italian prime minister Silvio Berlusconi was the "mouthpiece of Putin" in Europe and may have been reaping personal benefit from energy deals with Russia. Still others outlined some of the tactics used by the United States to pressure countries to take detainees released from Guantánamo Bay, such as generous payments made to the Pacific Island nation of Kiribati and an offer made to Slovenian president Danilo Türk of a one-on-one meeting with President Barack Obama. Several of the more controversial leaked documents cited U.S. memos that encouraged diplomats to gather extensive personal information on other diplomats, beyond what was considered standard practice, such as Internet passwords, credit card numbers, and frequent flyer numbers.

THE U.S. REACTS

U.S. officials swiftly condemned WikiLeaks's decision to release the documents. U.S. secretary of state Hillary Rodham Clinton described it as "an attack against the international community," while U.S. assistant secretary of state for public affairs P. J. Crowley said the leak had a "real impact on the national security of the United States." Officials were also quick to defend the diplomatic corps, claiming that what the cables really showed were diplomats going about their jobs, working collaboratively with others and engaging foreign officials in conversations. "Our diplomats are doing what diplomats do around the world every day, which is build relationships, negotiate, advance our interests, and work to find common solutions to complex problems," said Susan Rice, U.S. permanent representative to the United Nations.

U.S. officials had known for several months that such a release was imminent and had worked to warn diplomats of the leak. They also reached out to foreign governments, describing in general terms what might be contained within the documents to help minimize any damage to diplomatic relationships, though the documents themselves were not shared. Officials cut the connection between the State Department's Net-Centric Diplomacy database and the Pentagon's classified Secret Internet Protocol Router Network (SIPRNet), the Department of Defense's largest computer network for exchanging classified information, to tighten communications and prevent any further leaks. The State Department also worked to relocate sources and intelligence officers who may have been compromised by the leaks.

The leak was quickly labeled as a criminal act, and U.S. attorney general Eric Holder announced a "very serious, active, ongoing" criminal investigation to determine how Assange received the cables. Army private first class Bradley Manning was widely suspected to have been Assange's contact. Manning had been arrested in May after confiding in computer hacker Adrian Lamo that "someone he knew" had been downloading and encrypting confidential data and uploading it to Assange. In some instances, Manning admitted to leaking the material himself. Manning was charged in July with improperly downloading and releasing information after it was determined that he had leaked the controversial helicopter video. Following the leak of the diplomatic cables, the FBI began seeking foreign-intelligence warrants to search for additional evidence of contact between Manning and Assange. U.S. officials also began to explore the possibility of filing criminal charges against Assange under the Espionage Act of 1917.

Journalist or Irresponsible Delinquent?

Officials' harsh reaction and pursuit of Assange generated criticism and allegations of U.S. hypocrisy from some foreign officials. Russian prime minister Vladimir Putin questioned, "If it is a full-fledge democracy, then why have they put Mr. Assange away in jail? You call that democracy?" Then–Brazilian president Luiz Inácio Lula da Silva also expressed support for Assange and accused the United States of a "siege on freedom of expression," while Bolivian vice president Álvaro García Linera hosted several of the cables on his official government website. The *Financial Times Deutschland* also alleged U.S. bias in investigating the leak, claiming that "no one can explain what crimes Assange allegedly committed with the publication of the secret documents, or why publication by WikiLeaks was an offense, and in the *New York Times*, it was not."

U.S. officials sought to reassure the media that going after WikiLeaks did not mean they would try to limit freedom of the press, and they emphasized that Assange was not a journalist, but an anarchist. Others supported the U.S. stance. Italian foreign minister Franco Frattini called the leak the "September 11 of world diplomacy," while Pakistan's Ministry of Foreign Affairs condemned the "irresponsible disclosure of sensitive official documents."

Assange Pursued

On December 3, Swedish prosecutors announced that they had reissued international and European arrest warrants against Assange for two alleged sex crimes that occurred in

August. Swedish authorities originally sought Assange for questioning in September after two women accused him of forcing them to have sex. Assange had reportedly gone into hiding in the United Kingdom since leaving Sweden, telling one newspaper that he was afraid of potential assassination attempts if anyone found out where he was. Assange's attorneys questioned the motivation behind the warrants and suggested that Swedish officials may be facing external political pressure from the United States to arrest Assange so that he could be extradited for questioning and possible trial.

Shortly thereafter, Swiss officials closed a bank account at PostFinance held by Assange for the purpose of receiving donations for WikiLeaks. PayPal announced that it would no longer process payments to WikiLeaks, as did Visa and MasterCard. Amazon.com announced it would no longer host WikiLeaks content in the United States. Several governments acted to prevent WikiLeaks from hosting its content on servers in their countries, and hackers attempted to take the site down on several occasions. Yet WikiLeaks supporters had set up roughly thirteen hundred "mirror" sites, or carbon-copy websites, to store the classified cables in case the site was taken down, and the Swiss Pirate Party ultimately offered to host the WikiLeaks site on its servers.

Other supporters fought back against the "censorship" of WikiLeaks more aggressively, using digital tactics to bring down the websites of companies and organizations that sought to disable WikiLeaks. Soon a group called Operation Payback flooded target websites with false requests, preventing them from handling genuine communications. The group claimed credit for shutting down PostFinance's website and threatened to do the same to PayPal. The group also disabled the websites of the Swedish prosecution authority and MasterCard.

On December 7, Assange turned himself in at a London police station and was arrested by the UK Metropolitan Police Service's Extradition Unit. He appeared before a judge at the City of Westminster Magistrates' Court that afternoon. The judge denied him bail, arguing that he had "substantial grounds" to believe Assange would not show up for later court proceedings, and placed Assange into custody until an extradition hearing could be arranged. Assange said he would fight extradition to Sweden, while his lawyers claimed that political overtones had infected the case. The following week, the Magistrates' Court overturned its decision and granted Assange bail after various supporters made monetary assurances that he would not leave the country, and his passport was confiscated. Assange was freed on bail on December 17 and has been living at a supporter's country estate.

A full hearing of Sweden's extradition request took place in January 2011. The UK judge granted the request, but Assange immediately appealed, calling the extradition a breach of his human rights. Assange remains out on bond until his July appeal hearing. U.S. officials have yet to file charges against Assange. Bradley Manning will also face a court-martial in 2011 with the possibility of a significant jail sentence. In late April, Manning was deemed physically and mentally able to stand for the court-martial, which will take place at a later date.

—Linda Fecteau

Following is a November 29, 2010, statement by U.S. permanent representative to the United Nations Susan Rice responding to the release of government documents by the WikiLeaks website; and an edited transcript of a press conference held on December 1, 2010, by U.S. assistant secretary of state for public affairs P. J. Crowley, in response to WikiLeaks.

Ambassador Rice on Release of WikiLeaks Documents

November 29, 2010

Ambassador Rice (Nov. 29): "Let me be very clear. Our diplomats are just that—they're diplomats. That's what they do every day. They get out and they work with other countries, with partners here and in the United Nations and around the world to confront the most pressing global challenges that we face and to advance U.S. national interests. And they do so with enormous skill and integrity. I couldn't be more proud of them as they conduct the work of the U.S. Government and do the work that diplomats do around the world.

"Our diplomats are doing what diplomats do around the world every day, which is build relationships, negotiate, advance our interests, and work to find common solutions to complex problems. That's what they do. And they do it extremely well, with great integrity, with hard work. And I want to just underscore that in the complex world in which we live, the work that U.S. diplomats do here in the United Nations and around the world is indispensible to our national security and substantially advances our shared interests in international peace and security.

"I'm not going to get into commenting on classified material or alleged classified material and its contents. I have said what I'm going to say on that topic.

"I can say with confidence that American diplomats here at the United Nations and around the world will continue to do with—excellently the work they do every day in supporting and advancing the interests of the United States, and I am confident that their ability to do so will endure and indeed strengthen.

"This has been a time when the United States, under President Obama's leadership, has made enormous progress in repairing and rebuilding our relationships with partners and allies around the world. It's a time when we've come together here in the United Nations and many other fora to tackle issues from proliferation, to terrorism, to environmental degradation and climate change, and we've done so in a way that has been helpful to the interests and the wellbeing of the American people and indeed people around the world. We're very proud of that work, and we're going to continue to do it. Thank you very much."

SOURCE: U.S. Department of State. "Remarks on WikiLeaks." November 29, 2010. http://www.state .gov/p/io/rm/2010/152079.htm.

Assistant Secretary of State Crowley on WikiLeaks

December 1, 2010

MODERATOR: Good afternoon, everybody. Welcome to the Foreign Press Center. We are happy to have with us, yet again, Assistant Secretary P.J. Crowley for Public Affairs. Please remember when you ask questions, say your name and media organization. If you have a follow-up, please don't just talk. Wait for the microphone so it can show up on the transcript and everybody can read your very interesting questions. All right. And here's Assistant Secretary Crowley.

MR. CROWLEY: A few of you I just saw a few minutes ago. (Laughter.) So I suggest that there should be no double-dipping here. Good afternoon. You probably have seen, either in person or on the TV screens, the State Department briefing that we just finished. I won't repeat everything I said at the start there, but if there's any topic of conversation, I'll be happy to go back over it.

We promised to talk to you about WikiLeaks, and I should say at the outset we will not engage in any conversation about any specific cable. These are still classified, but by the same token, we will—we would be willing talk about the potential implications here. And I would say clearly first there has been real impact on the national security of the United States. The release of this volume of material in our view does harm our interests, but it's not just our interests; it is the interests of other countries and other people.

But by the same token, what you see in the full context of these documents is United States diplomats fully engaged around the world working cooperatively and collaboratively with other countries, conversations with diplomats and officials of other countries, conversations with members of civil society of other countries, pursuing our interests, but pursuing also our mutual interests consistent with our values and our laws and the laws of other countries. And that is not going to change.

I think what the most significant response to what has happened is exactly what Secretary Clinton is doing in Astana, Kazakhstan as we speak. She is there working constructively together with other leaders of European nations, nations of the Central Asian states, on cooperation and security in a very important part of the world. That is what diplomats led by Secretary Clinton do every single day. It's what we're going to continue to do every single day.

Clearly, the release of—the unauthorized release of these documents represents risk to the United States and to others with whom we collaborate. We are very conscious of the fact that individual cables report on confidential conversations that we have with sources inside governments, inside the civil society, and we are genuinely concerned that the release of these documents without regard to the welfare of individual people does, in fact, put real people and real interests at significant risk.

We have taken aggressive steps anticipating the release of these documents to contact our sources and to warn them of the potential release of these cables and we will do everything in our power to help to protect people who have helped us understand events around the world. And this is why we condemn what WikiLeaks has done, because these cables are being released without regard to the welfare of individual citizens around the world who do help us day in and day out interpret events in various countries, understand developments in various regions, and that information helps us in the conduct of the foreign policy of the United States.

But as Secretary Clinton is demonstrating in Astana, is that we will continue to engage fully with countries. Our interests have not changed; these are mutual interests. And we—those interests have not changed. We will continue to engage. We'll continue to cooperate. We'll continue to work constructively along with other countries, allies, friends around the world to try to solve the global challenges that confront our people and the people of the rest of the world. And with that, I will be happy to take your questions. . . .

[The following three pages have been omitted; they contain media questions related to the impact of the cables on U.S. relations with Latin American countries and Turkey.]

QUESTION: Hello, it's Zdenek Fucik from Czech news agency. Could you please specify the way or the manner in which you notified the foreign partners about the WikiLeaks before these cables were published? Did you make the content concerning them available to them? In other words, does the Czech Government, for example, right now know what is in these cables concerning them, or does it have to wait till they be released on the WikiLeaks sites, just like everybody else?

MR. CROWLEY: Good question. In anticipation of this release, obviously this has been something that we have been investigating for several months, and we did understand, having done significant forensic analysis, roughly speaking, the potential breadth of documents that have been compromised through this—what we believe is a criminal act. In anticipation of this release, our embassies and then senior leaders here within the Department of State have reached out to capitals, including the Czech Republic, and both to warn governments about what we anticipated might be among documents released. We've had conversations and described in general terms what is in these documents.

I'm not aware that we have shared any of these documents. They are classified and they—we obviously want to protect them. But we are doing whatever we can to help nations understand both the general content, but most importantly, to reassure that notwithstanding this unfortunate disclosure, which we are investigating, we will prosecute those responsible and we will take steps to try to protect this information and make sure that this does not happen again.

And then our message to governments is that we will continue to engage. We will—to the extent that the trust between our respective countries has been challenged, we will do everything necessary to rebuild that trust. We believe that we can continue to interact with governments in confidence, and we hope that we will never confront this again. . . .

[The following two pages have been omitted; they contain media questions related to the impact of the cables on U.S. relations with Canada, how the U.S. could allow the leak to happen, and an election in the Ivory Coast.]

QUESTION: Thank you. David Nikuradze, Georgian Broadcasting Company Rustavi 2, Washington Bureau. I have two questions. First, what legal actions are you going to take against WikiLeaks? And second, I was wondering if you could give us an update about OSCE summit. I heard there were some statements on Georgia. Thanks, sir.

MR. CROWLEY: Well, on your latter point, I am here and not there, so I do know that the Secretary had a bilateral with President Saakashvili today. And I believe that she has had some comments that I'm sure we are putting out in the transcripts, so I'll defer on that.

Clearly, her meeting with the Georgian leader underscores our ongoing commitment to Georgia's territorial integrity, and I'm sure that was a major topic of discussion today.

What are we going to do on WikiLeaks? Well, we have an investigation that is ongoing both within the United States Government but also understanding the implications of what has occurred. Under our laws, the transfer of classified information to those who are not authorized to receive it is a crime. And the fact that we still have our classified information in possession of WikiLeaks is a continuation of that crime.

We are going to investigate this fully, and I won't prejudge the results of that investigation. . . .

QUESTION: Yeah. Thank you. Andrei Sitov from TASS. As a journalist, I need to ask this. The responsibilities with the people who released the documents without authorization, it's not only the journalist who published the documents, right? I'm asking you if you can tell us that the American officials who keep talking to journalists, legitimate journalists—

MR. CROWLEY: (Laughter.)

QUESTION:—legitimate journalists, journalistic requests—no, it's a serious question.

MR. CROWLEY: No, it is a serious question and—

QUESTION: P.J., and—

MR. CROWLEY: Andrei, let me—it's a very, very important point. Nothing that's happened here changes our view regarding the vital importance of freedom of the press, even when we believe that the press may or may not be taking actions that we agree with. That doesn't change the fact that a vibrant press is vital to democracy and to the building of a civil society in any country in any part of the world.

What's crucial here is that Mr. Assange is not a journalist. He is an anarchist and he is not worthy of the protections of a journalist. But we understand that the reporting of this is something that is what journalists do, and it won't change our willingness to engage, just as we are here today.

QUESTION: That was the last part of my question. Do you believe that actually capturing Mr. Assange and prosecuting him will send the right kind of signal, especially given that around the world people will be watching and saying, okay, then we will also clamp down on everything?

MR. CROWLEY: Well, I don't want to misconstrue that the release of 250,000 classified cables is something that does damage to our national security and our interest, and we believe puts at risk the interests of others around the world. I have had conversations with a number of media outlets who have been reporting on these documents this week, and I do respect that those outlets I have been personally in contact with have taken care where we have been able to identify for them areas where individuals in particular who are cited in various documents are potentially at risk with these disclosures. And we appreciate the seriousness with which real journalists and real outlets have understood that the disclosure of these materials can, in fact, put real people and real interests at risk. And I respect these conversations that we've had on a case-by-case basis.

But Mr. Assange is in a different category entirely. He has disclosed this material without regard to the risk that it does generate to real people in difficult circumstances around the world. We have taken steps in recent days to have direct conversations with people with whom we have had conversations in confidence and where we believe that the disclosure of their names or their descriptions puts them at risk. As we've said, we are prepared, if necessary, to take steps to help protect these people who we believe are at serious risk, including risk of loss of their freedom or loss of their lives.

WikiLeaks has taken no such—has expressed no such concern for the welfare of these people, and I think that says a great deal about Mr. Assange.

MODERATOR: We're going to take another question from New York. New York, go ahead with your question.

QUESTION: Okay, my name is Renzo Cianfanelli from the Italian media group Corriere della Sera and Il Secolo. Under Secretary, as you probably know, the Italian Foreign Minister Mr. Frattini characterized what happened as the 9/11 of diplomacy. Even people such as myself who do not agree with this characterization still think that there has been a systemic failure, let's call it, once again, after 9/11, of the established procedures which must safeguard confidential and classified communication. So the question is what are you going to do about it? Is the system still valid, the emailing dispatches all over the world which can be intercepted?

MR. CROWLEY: That's a very good question. We do not underestimate the seriousness of this disclosure. It is a huge volume of classified documents and it does, in fact, represent an unfortunate violation of the trust which is inherent in the relationship that we have with many, many countries and many individuals around the world. People should understand that this was not an act of a government, this was a criminal act by at least one individual who violated the trust and confidence that the American people place in those of us who serve the national interest.

We are aggressively investigating this crime and we will punish those who are responsible. And the disclosure of this is in violation of our laws and our values. And we are making that clear in our conversations with leaders around the world, including the conversations that Secretary Clinton has had with her counterparts in Kazakhstan this week. There have been a lot of hyperbole in terms of what this represents. And we do understand that this has impact. It puts real lives and real interests at risk.

By the same token, when you look at the breadth of what has been released—and I'm not going to talk about any particular cable—but what do you see? You see the United States engaged across the world, unique among countries in terms of the breadth of our engagement. You actually see diplomats who are day in and day out having serious conversations, frank conversations, with other governments and people in various countries, and you see diplomats who are actively working to carry out the foreign policy of the United States and work constructively with other countries and other leaders to try to solve local, regional, and global challenges. We are very proud of our diplomacy. We are very proud of our country. We are very proud of the work that we do working constructively and cooperatively with other countries.

And certainly the Secretary's presence at the OSCE Summit in Kazakhstan is a perfect representation of what we are doing and will continue to do. So this doesn't change our policy. This doesn't change our willingness to engage. This doesn't change our interest in solving the world's problems. So from this point, what will we do? The Secretary will be in the region for the rest of this week. She will be at Manama later this week, working constructively with regional leaders to try to bring peace and stability to the Middle East.

We will have Under Secretary Bill Burns in Geneva next week working with the P-5+1 to demonstrate our willingness to sit down with even a country like Iran, with which we have very, very difficult relations to try to find a way to answer the questions that we the United States have, but also the questions that the international community has about the nature of Iran's nuclear program. We will be willing to engage with Iran on the nuclear issue and any other issue with which Iran has questions of us. We will do this in pursuit of peace, stability, and prosperity for our people and the people of the rest of the world. That is what we do as a country, and that is what we're going to continue to do as a country going forward. It doesn't change anything. This revelation doesn't change those fundamentals. . . .

[The following five and a half pages have been omitted. They contain media questions related to a meeting of the OSCE; efforts to close the Guantánamo Bay Detention Center; the impact of the cables on U.S. relations with Brazil, Italy and Turkey; previous documents distributed by WikiLeaks; and possible impact of the leak of diplomatic cables on perceptions of Secretary Clinton's work.]

SOURCE: U.S. Department of State. "WikiLeaks and Other Global Events." December 1, 2010. http://fpc .state.gov/152229.htm.

European Union Begins Google Antitrust Investigation

NOVEMBER 30, 2010

In late November, the European Commission announced that it would open a formal antitrust investigation into California-based Google after allegations that the world's top search engine was using its search algorithm to demote the sites of its competitors. In a statement, the regulatory body of the European Union (EU) said, "The Commission will investigate whether Google has abused a dominant market position in online search by allegedly lowering the ranking of unpaid search results of competing services." The EU investigation was not the first to be taken up against Google. A number of smaller technology companies have filed suit, alleging that Google has priced competitors out of the market through its AdSense platform and demotes search results of any website it views as direct competition. Google continues to defend its algorithm, saying that it was not created to benefit the company, but rather to benefit the user.

ALLEGATIONS

The European Commission announced that it would launch its Google antitrust investigation more than nine months after three websites—Foundem, ejustice.fr, and Ciao!, all rivals of Google—claimed that their sites were being demoted in Google results. Foundem, a shopping comparison site located in the United Kingdom, claimed that Google had imposed penalties on the company for more than three years, leading to its demotion, and in some instances removal, in search results. Foundem told the European Commission that it was being penalized because Google was threatened by its business model. According to Google, the penalty was lifted in December 2009, when it changed its search policies. "What we are asking for is more transparency about the criteria and rationale for penalties and for Google to introduce a more effective, transparent appeals process," said Foundem chief executive Shivaun Raff. Although Foundem argued that Google was using its "universal search" to steer traffic back to Google sites, Google claimed that sites such as Foundem only duplicate information from other websites, making it less useful to a user, which causes its low Google search result ranking.

When the EU received the three complaints in early 2010, it requested information from Google on how it uses its algorithm to rank search results and paid advertisements. In reply, Google posted on its blog, "While we will be providing feedback and additional information on these complaints, we are confident that our business operates in the interests of users and partners, as well as in line with European competition law." It also responded to the complaint by Microsoft-owned Ciao!, a price comparison site, claiming that the independent company had a positive relationship with Google and AdSense before being acquired by Google competitor Microsoft.

Following the November announcement of the EU investigation, Google maintained its claim that it would not be found guilty of any wrongdoing. "Those sites have complained and even sued us over the years, but in all cases there were compelling reasons why their sites were ranked poorly by our algorithms," a Google spokesperson said. In an emailed statement, the company wrote, "Since we started Google we have worked hard to do the right thing by our users and our industry—ensuring that ads are always clearly marked, making it easy for users and advertisers to take their data with them when they switch services, and investing heavily in open source projects. But there's always going to be room for improvement, and so we'll be working with the Commission to address any concerns."

In addition to the algorithm complaints, the European Commission announced that it would look into secondary concerns during its investigation, such as allegations that Google forced advertisers to comply with certain obligations, including a prohibition on the placement of competitors' ads on their websites. In addition, the commission reviewed whether data collected by Google for online campaign advertising could be moved to competing platforms if a company chose to leave Google AdSense. "The Commission's probe will additionally focus on allegations that Google imposes exclusivity obligations on advertising partners, preventing them from placing certain types of competing ads on their web sites, as well as on computer and software vendors, with the aim of shutting out competing search tools. Finally, it will investigate suspected restrictions on the portability of online advertising campaign data to competing online advertising platforms," the commission announced.

POSSIBLE FINES

Under EU rules, the commission has the ability to fine Google up to 10 percent of its annual global revenue if it is found guilty of violating EU antitrust rules, which could total $2.4 billion based on Google's 2009 revenue figures.

In December 2009, the European Commission ended a ten-year battle with Microsoft over software sold by the technology company and installed on Windows-based computers that gave limited access to non-Windows Internet browsers. In the end, Microsoft agreed to increase access, as well as pay $2.4 billion in antitrust fines. Technology giant Intel has also faced fines from the EU, totaling $1.45 billion, for paying computer makers to use Intel chips rather than those of its competitors. To avoid a similar fine, in 2008, Apple stopped its practice of charging more to British iTunes users than those using the store in other European countries.

THE INVESTIGATION BROADENS

After less than one month, the European Commission announced in mid-December that it would expand its investigation into Google to include complaints from a German online mapping company and a group of newspaper and magazine publishers. EU rules allow the regulatory body to take on cases from member nations when the topics in question overlap with current commission investigations.

The German magazine and newspaper publishers, known as BDZV and VDZ, released a statement upon learning of the commission's decision, saying, "We appreciate that the EC is now investigating the case as it could be one of the most important topics for the digital press in the coming years. From our point of view, Google is no longer a mere search engine but filling the result pages with more and more own content." The group called Google a "direct competitor" with its ability to publish news and books, and claimed that Google's refusal to compensate publications for content it reproduces was illegal. The mapping company, Euro-Cities, claimed that because Google Maps could be imbedded onto other websites for free, its business model was being destroyed.

OTHER GOOGLE INVESTIGATIONS

Google has come under scrutiny a number of times in the EU and United States as it rose to be the world's dominant search engine. In Europe, the company makes up 90 percent of the search engine and search advertising market, and in the United States, it holds two-thirds of the market share.

Since the Barack Obama administration began in January 2009, it has taken up a number of cases against Google. But in a change from previous antitrust investigations and rulings against telecom giants like AT&T, the U.S. Justice Department has chosen to investigate what Google might do, rather than what it has done. In September 2009, the Justice Department ruled on what Google had called "a historic settlement," which would have given it the exclusive right to publish digital editions of certain types of books. The case stemmed from a 2005 lawsuit filed after Google digitized a number of copyright-protected books that were out of print. The case was settled out of court in October 2008, and the deal gave Google the right to electronically publish some of these books. Opponents have argued that Google cannot have sweeping power to publish books that are still protected by a U.S. copyright, even if they are out of print. The Justice Department asked for the agreement to be rewritten but recognized the importance of access to digital books. It stated in a filing with the U.S. District Court for the Southern District of New York, "As presently drafted, the Proposed Settlement does not meet the legal standards this Court must apply."

In September 2010, Texas attorney general Greg Abbott announced an investigation into Google's algorithm as well. The investigation will review complaints of Foundem, SourceTool/TradeComment, and myTriggers. Each site has complained that Google forces it to be ranked low in search results. Both SourceTool and myTriggers have filed lawsuits in the past, alleging that Google raised the prices of advertisements by as much as 10,000 percent, thereby pricing them out of the market. A New York court dismissed the suit, saying it did not have jurisdiction to rule on a California company.

As it did in the European case, Google maintained that Foundem, which is closely tied to a Microsoft-financed group in Brussels that lobbies for legislation favorable to their corporate interests, has little legitimacy in its claims because of its ties to one of Google's major competitors. Both myTriggers and SourceTool/TradeComment are being represented in Texas by Microsoft attorneys. "Given that not every website can be at the top of the results, or even appear on the first page of our results, it's unsurprising that some less relevant, lower quality websites will be unhappy with their ranking," said Google deputy general counsel Don Harrison.

The cases taken up around the world against Google's algorithm recognize that placement on a search engine can make or break companies. By being buried near the bottom—or excluded, as Foundem claims—companies can lose a significant amount of business. On the other hand, being the top search result ensures a number of click-throughs, driving up traffic and, in turn, revenue. TripAdvisor, a website offering reviews of hotels and sites in cities around the world, has been an outspoken advocate for claims against Google. According to the company's chief executive, Stephen Kaufer, since mid-October 2010, when Google announced that it would change the way it displays information about local businesses by placing Google-generated results first, traffic to TripAdvisor through Google has fallen by more than 10 percent. Mayo Clinic, on the other hand, has seen traffic from Google improve with the invention of Google Health, which produces top search engine results when a user types in the name of a certain ailment. Mayo Clinic web pages often appear next to the Google Health links.

These cases also call into question a growing demand for "search neutrality." Much like net neutrality prevents Internet service providers (ISPs) from reducing bandwidth access to certain websites and online platforms it sees in direct competition to its own business, there are those who believe that search providers should not be able to determine how results are ranked. For a search neutrality case to stick in the United States, it would need to be proven that search engines can be considered a utility under the Communications Act.

—Heather Kerrigan

Following is a statement by the European Union on November 30, 2010, announcing an investigation into antitrust allegations made against Google.

EU Announces Antitrust Investigation Against Google

DOCUMENT

November 30, 2010

[Footnotes have been omitted.]

The European Commission has decided to open an antitrust investigation into allegations that Google Inc. has abused a dominant position in online search, in violation of European Union rules (Article 102 TFEU). The opening of formal proceedings follows complaints by search service providers about unfavourable treatment of their services in Google's unpaid and sponsored search results coupled with an alleged preferential placement of Google's own services. This initiation of proceedings does not imply that the Commission has proof of any infringements. It only signifies that the Commission will conduct an in-depth investigation of the case as a matter of priority.

Google's internet search engine provides for two types of results when people are searching for information. These are unpaid search results, which are sometimes also referred to as "natural", "organic" or "algorithmic" search results, and third party advertisements shown at the top and at the right hand side of Google's search results page (so-called paid search results or sponsored links).

The Commission will investigate whether Google has abused a dominant market position in online search by allegedly lowering the ranking of unpaid search results of competing services which are specialised in providing users with specific online content such as price comparisons (so-called vertical search services) and by according preferential placement to the results of its own vertical search services in order to shut out competing services. The Commission will also look into allegations that Google lowered the 'Quality Score' for sponsored links of competing vertical search services. The Quality Score is one of the factors that determine the price paid to Google by advertisers.

The Commission's probe will additionally focus on allegations that Google imposes exclusivity obligations on advertising partners, preventing them from placing certain types of competing ads on their web sites, as well as on computer and software vendors, with the aim of shutting out competing search tools. Finally, it will investigate suspected restrictions on the portability of online advertising campaign data to competing online advertising platforms.

What is the legal base for the decision?

The legal base of this procedural step is Article 11(6) of Council Regulation No 1/2003 and article 2(1) of Commission Regulation No 773/2004.

Article 11(6) of Regulation No 1/2003 provides that the initiation of proceedings relieves the competition authorities of the Member States of their authority to apply the competition rules laid down in Articles 101 and 102 of the Treaty.

Article 2 of Regulation No 773/2004 provides that the Commission can initiate proceedings with a view to adopting at a later stage a decision on substance according to Articles 7–10 of Regulation No 1/2003.

The Commission has informed the company about this decision. The Competition Authorities of the Member States have also been informed.

There is no legal deadline to complete inquiries into anticompetitive conduct. Their duration depends on a number of factors, including the complexity of each case and the extent to which the undertakings concerned co-operate with the Commission.

SOURCE: European Union. Press Room. "Antitrust: Commission Probes Allegations of Antitrust Violations by Google." November 30, 2010. http://europa.eu/rapid/pressReleasesAction.do?reference= IP/10/1624&format=HTML&aged=0&language=EN&guiLanguage=en.

OTHER HISTORIC DOCUMENTS OF INTEREST

FROM PREVIOUS *HISTORIC DOCUMENTS*

■ U.S. District Court on Microsoft Settlement, *2002,* p. 797

December

Child Nutrition Bill Signed into Law

DECEMBER 1, 2, AND 13, 2010

After stalling in the U.S. House of Representatives shortly before the midterm elections, on December 13, 2010, the $4.5 billion Healthy, Hunger-Free Kids Act of 2010 was signed by President Barack Obama. The legislation was a key component of first lady Michelle Obama's fight to end childhood obesity through her Let's Move campaign. The Healthy, Hunger-Free Kids Act, referred to as the child nutrition reauthorization bill, is aimed at improving the quality of school lunches, increasing the number of students eligible for free and reduced-fee lunches, and increasing the number of physical activity programs for children. To the dismay of many Democrats in Congress, the act was paid for in part with funds from a temporary increase in the Supplemental Nutrition Assistance Program (SNAP), which provides a monthly stipend for groceries to families in need.

LET'S MOVE

When her husband became president in January 2009, Michelle Obama made it a goal to fight childhood obesity across the country by improving nutrition and increasing physical activity. "This isn't just a policy issue for me," she said. "This is a passion. This is my mission. I am determined to work with folks across this country to change the way a generation of kids thinks about food and nutrition."

Her first public step in this initiative came when Washington, D.C., elementary school students helped the first lady plant a garden at the White House for the kitchen staff to use. This first step grew into the Let's Move campaign, which was launched in February 2010 when President Obama created the Task Force on Childhood Obesity. This group was given the role of reviewing childhood nutrition and activity programs and developing a plan to maximize federal dollars to improve the health of America's children. The five key elements of the task force's plan, which fell in line with the Let's Move campaign, are: creating a healthy start for children, empowering caregivers, providing healthy food at school, improving access to healthy food and making it affordable, and increasing physical activity.

SENATE PASSES, HOUSE STALLS

President Obama put his weight behind passage of the bill, writing an op-ed piece in the *Washington Post* before the Senate vote and calling the bill "groundbreaking legislation that will bring fundamental change to schools and improve the food options available to our children." In August 2010, the Senate easily passed its version of the child nutrition reauthorization bill through unanimous consent, without a voice vote. The bill, written primarily by Sen. Blanche Lincoln, D-Ark., was fully paid for and garnered a large amount of support from national organizations including the American Heart Association and the American Academy of Pediatrics. Upon passage, Michelle Obama remarked, "While childhood obesity cannot be solved overnight, with everyone working together, there's no question that it can be solved—and today's vote moves us one step closer to reaching that goal."

Passage in the House of Representatives was less certain. The Child Nutrition Act of 1966, which provides federal funds to defray the costs of school lunch programs and would be reauthorized by the Healthy, Hunger-Free Kids Act, was set to expire on September 30, 2010. Advocates of the reauthorization said that expiration of the Child Nutrition Act could mean higher lunch costs, a decline in the number of at-risk students receiving free or reduced-fee lunches, and fewer healthy food options for students. But because of a protest by 106 members of the Democratic Party, a final vote was put on hold, and instead a stop-gap spending measure was passed to continue funding the program until Congress returned for its lame-duck session after the midterm elections.

The 106 Democrats opposed the funding method for the reauthorization because it would remove $2 billion from SNAP. Anti-hunger advocates joined these Democrats, saying that the cut would result in a decrease of $59 per month from an average family of four's food budget. "That additional amount of food stamps is absolutely fundamental to children and families' well-being," said James Weill, president of the Food Research and Action Center. "The people who belittle that are ignoring at their peril what is happening to the 41 million poorest people in the country." Democrats also criticized the president for cutting SNAP funds to push through Michelle Obama's legislation while many families were struggling with job loss and other effects of the slow-growing U.S. economy.

Advocates of reauthorization, however, said that the effect of the cut was not necessarily true. The $2 billion was being taken from a temporary SNAP increase, first passed in 2009, because of anticipated inflation of food costs which never materialized. Advocates also criticized the Democrats because all 106 had previously voted in August for $12 billion to be taken from the temporary SNAP increase to protect teachers' jobs.

The delay in the House was also blamed on the impending midterm elections. Voters around the country had made it clear that they wanted to see less government spending and less federal intervention. The Healthy, Hunger-Free Kids Act, some argued, meant bigger government and more spending.

The School Nutrition Association called on the House to act as quickly as possible to ensure passage of the reauthorization when it returned for its lame-duck session. "We can no longer afford to voice our concerns about rising rates of childhood obesity and the need to promote healthier lifestyles at school without investing in the programs that reach children in their school cafeterias each day," said Nancy Rice, president of the organization. Advocates of the bill knew that a delay into the 112th Congress would almost assuredly result in the passage of a reauthorization that would not guarantee any improvement in the school lunch program because Republicans would not make it a top spending priority.

When the House returned after the election, it took up the reauthorization bill. Democratic leadership and President Obama were able to bring most of the Democrats back to the table. A majority of the 106 conceded and agreed to vote for the bill after Obama said that he would try to help find other ways to fund the program and restore SNAP funds.

The most controversial portion of the legislation, other than its funding method, was a provision regulating lunch prices for children in families above 185 percent of the poverty level. The Congressional Budget Office said this stipulation would lead to an increase in lunch prices, and Rep. John Kline, R-Minn., ranking member of the House Education and Labor Committee compared it to little more than a tax increase on working families. The concern voiced by a number of advocacy groups was that schools would need to reallocate subsidies for low-income children to those in higher-income families. During debate on the House floor, Rep. George Miller, D-Calif., chair of the House Education and Labor Committee, appealed to those who thought the bill would raise school lunch prices. "It's very clear in this legislation that it does not require school districts to raise any meal prices," he said. "In fact, in the best sense of local control, it lets school districts decide and determine how they will ensure that there's adequate revenue to support the paid meal program." He rested his speech on the idea that the nation spends billions of dollars per year to treat obesity in children and adults, so helping Americans stay healthy at a young age is a step toward reducing those costs. "Child nutrition is not a political issue. It's not a partisan issue. It's a question of what's a moral thing to do for our children. It's about being on the right side of history and ensuring a healthy and productive future for our country. Our children will make and determine our future, and that is what is at stake," Miller said.

Kline recognized the necessity of extending nutrition programs for children but said expansion and additional spending was unnecessary. "The American people have spoken, and they continue to speak loud and clear. I have been listening, and I know what I have been hearing. . . . Stop growing government." He criticized Democrats for not allowing Republican members of the House to present a similar child nutrition program that would cost taxpayers nothing. "I support extending and improving child nutrition programs. I believe we can do so in a bipartisan way, but that opportunity is lost with this bill, and so I must oppose it," Kline said.

House Republicans made a last-minute attempt to block the bill by introducing an amendment that would bar federal funds from being distributed to child care programs that hire workers who lie about their past or refuse background checks. The Democrats stopped the amendment, and the bill passed 264 to 157 on December 2. Seventeen Republicans joined the Democrats to pass the bill, while four Democrats voted no.

PROGRAM PROVISIONS

Obama signed the Healthy, Hunger-Free Kids Act on December 13, 2010, with his wife by his side. Both spoke during the signing event, with the president pledging his support for the SNAP program and the first lady congratulating the organizations that came together in support of the bill. "These folks come at this issue from all different angles. But they've come together to support this bill because they know it's the right thing to do for our kids. And they know that in the long run, it won't just save money, but it's going to save lives," the first lady said.

As signed by the president, the act funds a number of childhood nutrition programs for ten years and provides reauthorization for these programs for five years. The thirty-one million children who receive school lunches each school day would begin seeing a number of changes as the act takes effect.

To improve childhood nutrition and reduce obesity, the act allows the U.S. Department of Agriculture (USDA) to regulate nutritional standards for all foods served and sold during the school day; improves the nutritional quality of foods served during school breakfasts and lunches; provides funds to give schools access to more locally grown foods by establishing partnerships with local farms and building community gardens; expands breastfeeding support; promotes nutrition in non-school child care programs; sets basic physical activity standards; and increases drinking water access. For the first time in nearly three decades, the act also provides a real increase in the reimbursement rate for federally subsidized school lunches. The increase is set at six cents per meal, as long as the school adheres to the guidelines set forth in the act. The National School Boards Association was highly critical of the rate, claiming that complying with all provisions of the act would cost nearly double the six-cent increase.

Increasing access to healthy meals is another key component of the act. To reach this goal, provisions include: giving the USDA additional authority to support meals offered to low-income children in afterschool programs; eliminating paper applications to instead draw on census data to determine the eligibility of high-poverty community students to receive school-provided meals; helping states improve their free-meal certification process to add an additional 4,500 students per year to the rolls of those receiving school meals; and increasing the number of children in school meal programs by 115,000 students.

Finally, the act seeks to increase the monitoring of school nutrition and food programs. To do this, the act requires audits of school districts every three years to ensure that the district is complying with nutrition standards; requires schools to make nutritional information about school meals available to parents; provides training for school food service staff; and improves the safety of school foods.

—Heather Kerrigan

Following is a floor speech by Rep. George Miller, D-Calif., on December 1, 2010, in support of the Healthy, Hunger-Free Kids Act of 2010; a floor speech by Rep. John Kline, R-Minn., on December 1, 2010, in opposition to the Healthy, Hunger-Free Kids Act of 2010; a statement by agriculture secretary Tom Vilsack on December 2, 2010, applauding the passage of the act; and the signing statement on December 13, 2010, by President Barack Obama and first lady Michelle Obama.

Rep. Miller in Support of the Childhood Nutrition Bill

December 1, 2010

Mr. GEORGE MILLER of California. I yield myself such time as I may consume.

Mr. Speaker, today I rise for our Nation's children, for the poorest children in our country who are hungry and malnourished. I rise because children need our help. Child nutrition is not a political issue. It's not a partisan issue. It's a question of what's a moral thing to do for our children. It's about being on the right side of history and ensuring a healthy and productive future for our country. Our children will make and determine our future, and that is what is at stake.

In a country as great as ours, no child should go hungry, but, in fact, millions of children do go hungry at various times throughout the year and very often throughout the day. And the fact of the matter is we cannot afford to let that continue.

At the same time we are in the middle of this crisis of food insecurity, it's called, better known as hunger. We also face the public problem of obesity. And what we understand and what we know is that our schools, through the school nutrition programs and other programs that serve nutritional meals to children, are an opportunity to educate them about eating better, eating healthier. This legislation addresses those concerns because it provides the resources necessary so that we can improve the meal selection for our children in the various feeding programs.

It's very important for us because it also provides for increased transparency of the program, for increased efficiency of the program, for increased simplicity of the program both for parents who are enrolling their children, for school districts who are enrolling and accountable for those children and for those meals. Those combinations of accountability and transparency for healthier meals should be a goal and is the goal, in fact, of this Congress and of this Nation.

It also provides accountability within the legislation, and it also provides the means by which we can assure that we will have healthy foods during the school day for the children and in other educational settings and care settings for these children so that we can also address the problems of childhood obesity.

We have had hearings in our committee where we have had experts from various scientific organizations and health organizations, that we now have very young children presenting with adult diseases and illnesses. We spend some $140, $150 billion on the excess costs of obesity, much of which starts with children, with their diet.

That's what this legislation is really about, is making sure that we can, in fact, provide for a healthier school-age population, a smarter school-age population about the foods that they choose, a better meal program for them, and increased simplicity and transparency and accountability for those who administer the program. . . .

First of all, it's very clear in this legislation that it does not require school districts to raise any meal prices. In fact, in the best sense of local control, it lets school districts decide and determine how they will ensure that there's adequate revenue to support the paid meal program. We should not have the Federal taxpayers underwriting the support of meals for those who can afford it as is required by the law. This bill passed unanimously from the United States Senate. It passed unanimously because they knew that it is paid for. . . .

SOURCE: Rep. George Miller. "Healthy, Hunger-Free Kids Act of 2010." *Congressional Record* 2010, pt. 156, H7800. http://www.gpo.gov/fdsys/pkg/CREC-2010-12-01/pdf/CREC-2010-12-01-pt1-PgH7778.pdf.

Rep. Kline in Opposition to the Childhood Nutrition Bill

December 1, 2010

Mr. KLINE of Minnesota. Mr. Speaker, I rise in opposition to S. 3307, and I yield myself such time as I may consume.

The American people have spoken, and they continue to speak loud and clear. I have been listening, and I know what I have been hearing in the Second District of Minnesota is being repeated from coast to coast: Stop growing government. The people are telling us, Stop spending money we do not have. It's a simple request and a sensible one, yet it continues to be ignored.

Today's vote will be among our final acts as we move through the few remaining days of the 111th Congress. As we cast those votes, we have a choice to make. Will we continue spending more and increasing the role of government in Americans' lives, or will we listen to the people and begin to step on the brakes?

Each of us must make that choice as we cast our votes on the bill before us. Everyone recognizes the importance of extending child nutrition programs, but extending these programs does not mean expanding them. We could extend these programs and improve them with no added cost to taxpayers. We could listen to our constituents and do right by our children.

In fact, my Republican colleagues and I tried to do precisely that, but the Democrats on the Rules Committee denied us the opportunity to offer such an option on the floor today. Instead, this bill spends another $4.5 billion on various programs and initiatives and creates or expands 17 separate Federal programs. It imposes a tax on the middle class by empowering the U.S. Secretary of Agriculture to require schools to increase—that's right—require schools to increase the price they charge families for school meals.

This is a dangerous foray into Federal price controls, and it's one of many concerns outlined by the National Governors Association and leading school groups. In fact, the school leaders who would be responsible for implementing these new requirements have urged us to vote "no" on S. 3307 because of its higher cost for local districts and its rigid mandates.

Earlier this month, the American Association of School Administrators, the Council of the Great City Schools, and the National School Boards Association told us, "All of the national organizations representing the Nation's public school districts do not support the Senate version of the Child Nutrition reauthorization bill pending before the House." This is a strong statement that should leave every Member questioning the wisdom of imposing these added costs and mandates on our school systems.

In fact, the cost of this proposal has been a sticking point throughout the process. The majority claims this bill is paid for. They want us to believe we can grow government with no cost or consequences. But the American people know that's just not true. More spending is more spending whether or not those dollars are offset elsewhere in the massive Federal budget. But one offset in this bill is particularly questionable.

The truth is, at least some portion of the billions the new program costs is deficit spending. This money was borrowed from our children and grandchildren in 2009 when it was put in the stimulus; that borrowed money is simply being redirected today. It was borrowed then; it is borrowed now.

This bill, with its so so-called pay-for, is merely a stalling tactic. It obscures government expansion in the short term so this bill can become law and its spending can become permanent. So here we stand, playing a shell game with the Federal budget and hoping the American people do not notice that government continues to grow, spending continues to expand, and our children continue to fall deeper and deeper into debt.

Mr. Speaker, I support extending and improving child nutrition programs. I believe we can do so in a bipartisan way, but that opportunity is lost with this bill, and so I must oppose it.

I reserve the balance of my time.

SOURCE: Rep. John Kline. "Healthy, Hunger-Free Kids Act of 2010." *Congressional Record* 2010, pt. 156, H7800. http://www.gpo.gov/fdsys/pkg/CREC-2010-12-01/pdf/CREC-2010-12-01-pt1-PgH7778.pdf.

Secretary Vilsack on Passage of the Childhood Nutrition Bill

December 2, 2010

Agriculture Secretary Tom Vilsack today issued the following statement regarding House passage of S. 3307 "The Healthy Hunger-Free Kids Act."

"This is an historic victory for our nation's youngsters. This legislation will allow USDA, for the first time in over 30 years, the chance to make real reforms to the school lunch and breakfast programs by improving the critical nutrition and hunger safety net for millions of children.

"When President Obama first asked me to be the Secretary of Agriculture, he identified healthier school meals as one my top priorities and together with First Lady Michelle Obama's Lets Move! initiative, this administration has made it a goal to end childhood obesity within in a generation.

"Our national security, economic competitiveness and health and wellness of our children will improve as a result of the action Congress took today."

"I applaud Speaker Pelosi, Leader Hoyer, Chairman Miller, and Chairwoman DeLauro for their leadership on this legislation."

The Healthy Hunger-Free Kids Act includes the following provisions which USDA will begin implementing after President Obama signs the legislation:

1. Upgrading nutritional standards for school meals by increasing the federal reimbursement rate for school lunches by 6 cents for districts who comply with federal nutrition standards. This is the first real reimbursement rate increase in over 30 years.

2. Improving the nutritional quality of all food in schools by providing USDA with the authority to set nutritional standards for all foods sold in schools, including in vending machines, the "a la carte" lunch lines, and school stores.

3. Increases the number of eligible children enrolled in the school meals programs by using Medicaid data to directly certify children who meet income requirements without requiring individual applications connecting approximately 115,000 new students to the school meals program.

4. Enhances universal meal access for eligible children in high poverty communities by eliminating paper applications and using census data to determine school wide income eligibility.

5. Provides more meals for at-risk children nationwide by allowing Child and Adult Care Food Program (CACFP) providers in all 50 states and the District of Columbia to be reimbursed for providing a meal to at-risk children after school paving the way for an additional 21 million meals to children annually.

6. Empowering parents by requiring schools to make information more readily available to parents about the nutritional quality of school meals, as well as the results of any audits.

7. Improving the quality of foods supplied to schools by building on and further advancing the work USDA has been doing to improve the nutritional quality of the commodities that schools get from USDA and use in their lunch and breakfast programs.

8. Improving WIC by making it easier for children to get recertified as eligible for the program, requiring greater use of EBT technology (debit cards), and expanding support for breastfeeding.

SOURCE: United States Department of Agriculture. "Agriculture Secretary Vilsack Statement on Passage of the Healthy, Hunger-Free Kids Act." December 2, 2010. http://www.usda.gov/wps/portal/usda/usdah ome?contentidonly=true&contentid=2010/12/0632.xml.

President and First Lady Remarks upon Signing Healthy, Hunger-Free Kids Act

December 13, 2010

THE PRESIDENT: Well, I want to thank all the students and faculty and staff here at Tubman Elementary for hosting us today at your beautiful school. And we want to thank Principal Harry Hughes for doing outstanding work here. Thank you—give them all a big round of applause. (Applause.)

We are thrilled to be here with all of you as I sign the Healthy, Hungry-Free Kids Act—a bill that's vitally important to the health and welfare of our kids and to our country. But before I do this, I just want to acknowledge a few of the folks who are here, as well as a few who are not here but who played a hugely important role in getting this legislation passed. . . .

It is worth noting that this bill passed with bipartisan support in both houses of Congress. That hasn't happened as often as we'd like over the last couple of years, but I think it says something about our politics. It reminds us that no matter what people may hear about how divided things are in Washington, we can still come together and agree on issues that matter for our children's future and for our future as a nation. And that's really what today is all about.

At a very basic level, this act is about doing what's right for our children. Right now, across the country, too many kids don't have access to school meals. And often, the food that's being offered isn't as healthy or as nutritious as it should be. That's part of the reason why one in three children in America today are either overweight or obese.

And we're seeing this problem in every part of the country in kids from all different backgrounds and all walks of life. As a result, doctors are now starting to see conditions like high blood pressure, high cholesterol and Type II diabetes in children—these are things that they only used to see in adults. And this bill is about reversing that trend and giving our kids the healthy futures that they deserve.

And this bill is also about doing what's right for our country, because we feel the strains that treating obesity-related health conditions puts on our economy. We've seen the connection between what our kids eat and how well they perform in school. And we know that the countries that succeed in the 21st century will be the ones that have the best-prepared, best-educated workforce around.

So we need to make sure our kids have the energy and the capacity to go toe to toe with any of their peers, anywhere in the world. And we need to make sure that they're all reaching their potential. That's precisely what this bill—the Healthy, Hungry-Free Kids Act—will accomplish.

This legislation will help 115,000 children gain access to school meal programs. And wherever we can, we're doing away with bureaucracy and red tape, so that families don't have to fill out mountains of paperwork to get their kids the nutrition they need.

We're improving the quality of those meals by reimbursing schools an additional six cents per lunch to help them provide with healthier options—the first real increase, by the way, in over 30 years. Because when our kids walk into the lunchroom, we want to be sure that they're getting balanced, nutritious meals that they need to succeed in the classroom.

We're empowering parents by making information more available about the quality of school meals—helping families understand what their kids are eating during the day.

And to support our schools' efforts to serve fresh fruits and vegetables, we're connecting them with local farmers.

We're also improving food safety in schools, and boosting the quality of commodities like cheese that schools get from the Department of Agriculture and use in their lunch and breakfast programs.

It's also important to note that while this bill is fully paid for, it won't add a dime to the deficit, some of the funding comes from rolling back a temporary increase in food stamp benefits—or SNAP as it's now called—starting in the fall of 2013. I know a number of members of Congress have expressed concerns about this offset being included in the bill, and I'm committed to working with them to restore these funds in the future.

We know that every day across this country, parents are working as hard as they can to make healthy choices for their kids. Schools are doing everything possible to provide the nutritious food they need to thrive. Communities are coming together to help our young people lead healthier lives right from the beginning. And it's time that we made that work a little bit easier.

So these folks are fulfilling their responsibilities to our kids. This legislation helps ensure that we fulfill our responsibilities as well.

Shortly after signing the first law establishing school lunches, Harry Truman said that "Nothing is more important in our national life than the welfare of our children, and proper nourishment comes first in attaining this welfare."

So today, I'm very proud to sign this bill that continues that legacy. Not only am I very proud of the bill, but had I not been able to get this passed, I would be sleeping on the couch. (Laughter and applause.)

So now I am—now I am very proud to introduce somebody who's done so much to shine a light on these critical issues related to childhood nutrition and obesity and exercise: America's First Lady, my First Lady, Michelle Obama. (Applause.) . . .

MRS. OBAMA: And thank you, Mr. President—(laughter)—for that very kind introduction. And all kidding aside, my husband worked very hard to make sure that this bill was a priority in this session. And I am grateful to you.

THE PRESIDENT: Because I would have been sleeping on the couch. (Laughter.)

MRS. OBAMA: But I am thrilled to be here—we won't go into that. (Laughter.) Let's just say it got done, so we don't have to go down that road. (Laughter.)

But I am thrilled to be here with all of you today as my husband signs the Healthy, Hunger-Free Kids Act into law.

Now, usually, we hold these bill signings in the White House. But we felt it was important to do this one right here at Tubman Elementary because we wanted to share this moment with our partners—with the students, the parents, the teachers, the community leaders, like all of you here, who have been so instrumental.

Our White House chefs have worked closely with educators at this school, and they've seen your commitment to serving high-quality school meals to all of your students. I've worked side by side with kids from this school, as well as from Bancroft Elementary School, to harvest our White House garden. We couldn't have done it without all our students helping us. And I saw how hard they worked, and I also saw how brave they were to try vegetables that many of them never even heard of, so—(laughter)—and I also understand that there are students from Murch Elementary School who are here today as well, and we all had just a great time last spring working up a sweat and exercising and playing on the South Lawn of the White House.

So with everything that all of you are doing to give these children a healthy start in life, you are fulfilling the mission of this legislation every single day. That's why we're here. So I want to thank you all, all of our partners, for what you've done, not just in hosting us here today but in making sure that we're doing the right thing by our kids.

I also want to echo my husband's thanks to leaders and members of Congress, many of whom are on the stage, many of whom are not and are down here, and you all have done just a tremendous thing in making this day possible. As he said, this was truly a bipartisan effort, with passionate supporters from both parties putting in late nights and long weekends, working around the clock to make sure that this bill got passed, because while we may sometimes have our differences, we can all agree that in the United States of America, no child should go to school hungry.

We can all agree—(Applause.)—that in the wealthiest nation on Earth, all children should have the basic nutrition they need to learn and grow and to pursue their dreams, because in the end, nothing is more important than the health and well-being of our children. Nothing. And our hopes for their future should drive every single decision that we make.

These are the basic values that we all share, regardless of race, party, religion. This is what we share. These are the values that this bill embodies. And that's why we've seen such a groundswell of support for these efforts—not just from members of Congress here in Washington, but from folks in every corner of the country. It's been beautiful to see.

From educators working to provide healthier school meals, because they know the connection between proper nutrition and academic performance.

From doctors and nurses who know that unhealthy kids grow into unhealthy adults—at risk for obesity-related diseases like diabetes, heart disease, cancer.

From business and labor leaders who know that we spend nearly $150 billion a year to treat these diseases and who worry about the impact on our economy.

From advocates and faith leaders who know that school meals are vital for combating hunger, feeding more than 31 million children a day.

And from military leaders who tell us that when more than one in four young people are unqualified for military service because of their weight, they tell us that childhood obesity isn't just a public health issue; they tell us that it is not just an economic threat—it is a national security threat as well.

Now, these folks come at this issue from all different angles. But they've come together to support this bill because they know it's the right thing to do for our kids. And they know that in the long run, it won't just save money, but it's going to save lives.

And particularly in these tough economic times, when so many families are struggling, when school meals sometimes are the main source of nourishment for so many kids, we have an obligation to make sure that those meals are as nutritious as possible.

But by improving the quality of school meals—and making sure that more children have access to them—that is precisely what the Healthy, Hunger-Free Kids Act is going to do. Because while it might seem counterintuitive, child hunger and child obesity are really just two sides of the same coin. Both rob our children of the energy, the strength and the stamina they need to succeed in school and in life. And that, in turn, robs our country of so much of their promise.

Both, though, can be solved when we come together to provide our children with the nutritious food that they need and deserve. That's why for well over half a century, we've made child nutrition a national priority.

The bill we're signing into law today actually has its roots in the National School Lunch program signed into law by President Truman after World War II. And it also has roots in the Child Nutrition Act that was passed just two decades after that in 1966. Now, the idea for that act came from a priest named Revered C.B. Woodrich, who worked with children in Denver, Colorado.

Many of these kids were going hungry because they couldn't afford to buy lunch. Reverend Woodrich thought that was unconscionable, and he decided to do something about it. So he somehow managed to talk his way into a meeting with President Johnson. He arrived at the Oval Office without any kind of report or presentation or speech. Instead, he simply brought an enormous album filled with the photos of children in need, which he promptly spread across the President's desk.

The Reverend, he wanted—later explained that the size of the photo album was deliberate, because he wanted to be sure that it would be big enough to cover up everything else on the President's desk. And that's hard to do. It's a big desk. (Laughter.)

It is to this day a moving reminder that the most important job of any President is to ensure the well-being of our nation's children, because we know that the success of our nation tomorrow depends on the choices we make for our kids today. It depends on whether they can fulfill every last bit of their potential, and we, in turn, can benefit from every last bit of their promise.

That is our obligation, not just as parents who love our kids but as citizens who love this country. That's the mission of this legislation—to give all of our children the bright futures that they deserve. And that is why I am so proud to be here. I am so proud to have worked on this bill with all of you, and now I am pleased to stop talking and turn this over to my husband so that he can get to work signing that bill.

THE PRESIDENT: Let's go sign this bill.

MRS. OBAMA: Let's go do it.

SOURCE: The White House. Office of the Press Secretary. "Remarks by the President and First Lady at the Signing of the Healthy, Hunger-Free Kids Act." December 13, 2010. http://www.whitehouse.gov/the-press-office/2010/12/13/remarks-president-and-first-lady-signing-healthy-hunger-free-kids-act.

OTHER HISTORIC DOCUMENTS OF INTEREST

FROM PREVIOUS *HISTORIC DOCUMENTS*

Violence Increases after Election in Côte d'Ivoire

DECEMBER 5 AND 23, 2010

The long-awaited presidential election held in Côte d'Ivoire in October and November 2010 resulted in two candidates claiming victory. With no agreed-upon winner, violence broke out as supporters and security forces controlled by the current president, Laurent Gbagbo, killed, wounded, and kidnapped supporters of opposition leader, former prime minister, and would-be president Alassane Ouattara. United Nations (UN) peacekeeping forces in the country tried to uphold an Ouattara government, being run from the heavily guarded Golf luxury hotel in Abidjan, but by the end of 2010, fears were renewed that another civil war would break out in the West African nation if a power agreement was not soon reached.

CIVIL WAR

Gbagbo first came to power in 2000, after a violent uprising overthrew then-president Robert Guéï. Gbagbo used violence to silence rebels in the northern part of the country, who were led by Ouattara. In 2002, a rebellion broke out and northern Muslims, led by Ouattara, who called for democratic elections to be held to choose a new leader of Côte d'Ivoire, clashed with southern Ivorians who supported Gbagbo. The year-long civil war effectively split the nation in two, leaving the government in control of the southern portion of the country, while rebels, known as the New Forces, controlled the north. Peacekeepers from France and the United Nations have kept a patrol on the dividing line since 2003.

Gbagbo's term as president was set to expire in 2005, the year an election was scheduled, but Gbagbo's government delayed it six times because of the violence in the country and what Gbagbo called difficulty organizing the election. In 2007, Gbagbo's government signed a peace agreement with the leaders of the New Forces, agreeing to schedule the election, which it promised would be free and fair, but it was not until 2009 that the presidential election was finally scheduled. In May 2009, Gbagbo's government announced another delay, until late 2009, and then again delayed the election until spring 2010. Ivorians did not end up going to the polls until October 31, 2010.

PRESIDENTIAL ELECTION

The October 31, 2010, presidential election in Côte d'Ivoire featured fourteen candidates. Gbagbo received 38 percent to Ouattara's 32 percent. Ouattara's opposition party called on the nation's Constitutional Council for a recount, but the body, which is backed by Gbagbo, certified the results as they were. Because neither candidate received a minimum of 50 percent of the vote, a runoff election was scheduled for November 28, 2010.

In the lead-up to the runoff, both candidates went on the offensive. Gbagbo's supporters called Ouattara the instigator of the violence that had plagued Côte d'Ivoire since the civil war. Gbagbo called the runoff "a true battle between the democrats and the coup leaders." Ouattara and his supporters said that Gbagbo would not stop the violence in the nation if he was elected, but would rather rob the people of their wealth and happiness.

The first votes to be counted in the runoff election were those cast by Ivorian expats. Ouattara came out ahead, 56 percent to 40 percent in the count of the initial ten thousand ballots. Before the final results were announced, Gbagbo alleged that Ouattara and his supporters had committed vote fraud and threatened Gbagbo supporters to keep them away from the polls in northern Côte d'Ivoire. On November 30, the Independent Electoral Commission (CEI) called a press conference to announce preliminary results of the election. Before the spokesperson for the body could take the stage, a Gbagbo supporter on the commission stole the results and tore them apart. The spectacle led to fraud and vote-tampering allegations against Gbagbo from Ouattara supporters.

On December 2, 2010, Côte d'Ivoire's election commission declared Ouattara the winner with 54 percent of the vote. Ivorian law requires the Constitutional Council to certify all election results, and immediately after the announcement, the body called the election commission's announcement illegal. "CEI was supposed to declare the results by latest on Wednesday midnight, but due to disagreements over results from some regions, it was not able to do so and therefore the Constitutional Council will take up the issue and make a ruling," said council president Paul Yao N'dre. Gbagbo's army sealed off land and sea borders, and a number of media outlets were closed after the CEI announcement. In an effort to certify himself the winner, Gbagbo called on the Constitutional Council to throw out votes from the northern part of the country, which he claimed were fraudulent.

The United Nations responded to the voting controversy, warning of possible sanctions for falsifying election results. UN secretary general Ban Ki-moon said in a statement that the organization "assures the people of Ivory Coast that the [UN mission] . . . will undertake all possible action, within its mandate, to help keep the electoral process on track, to preserve peace and security in the country and to support their efforts to successfully conclude the peace process."

On December 3, the Constitutional Council defied the United Nations and certified Gbagbo as the winner of Côte d'Ivoire's election after throwing out a half million votes from the northern part of the country. Ouattara, with the support of the United Nations and a number of other foreign countries, refused the Constitutional Council's decision and instead began building his government from inside a luxury hotel, which was heavily guarded by eight hundred UN peacekeeping forces.

North-South Rivalry Reignites

Both Gbagbo and Ouattara took the oath of office for the position of president on December 4. Gbagbo wrapped himself in the nation's flag and denounced the international opinion that he had lost the election. Hours later, Ouattara took his own oath of office in the hotel, saying, "These last days have been difficult, but I can tell you now that Ivory Coast is in good hands."

As the rivals declared their leadership of the government, supporters on both sides took to the streets in protest. The United Nations vowed to keep close watch over the humanitarian situation, which quickly spiraled out of control as Gbagbo supporters targeted Ouattara's supporters. The UN high commissioner for human rights, Navi Pillay, announced that the United Nations had received information that hundreds of citizens had been abducted "from their homes, especially at night, by armed individuals in military uniform." According to Pillay, the reports also stated that the gunmen were joined by government security forces. UN peacekeepers were also at risk. Choi Young-jin, the UN special representative for Côte d'Ivoire, said, "Armed men have been coming to the personal houses of United Nations employees, asking them to leave and searching their houses under the pretext of looking for arms."

The Economic Community of West African States (ECOWAS) issued a statement on the violence in Côte d'Ivoire, urging Gbagbo to respect the will of the people and hand the government over to Ouattara. "In the prevailing circumstances, ECOWAS strongly condemns any attempt to usurp the popular will of the people of Côte d'Ivoire and appeals to all stakeholders to accept the results declared by the electoral commission."

Because of the security situation in the nation, the United Nations agreed to Ouattara's request to keep the ten thousand UN peacekeeping forces in the country for an additional six months. The UN Security Council called on its member states to support Ouattara as the rightful president of Côte d'Ivoire after the United Nations independently verified the election results, determining that Ouattara had received 54 percent of the vote. Some member nations froze Gbagbo's assets, while the United Nations imposed a travel ban on Gbagbo, his family, and a number of his closest advisers.

Gbagbo's government accused the United Nations of supporting rebel forces. "The UN is giving weapons to the rebels in Côte d'Ivoire to attack the government and overthrow Mr. Gbagbo from power," said youth minister Charles Blé Goudé, who has been on a UN sanction list since 2006 for advocating violence. "We are using legal means to show the outside world the majority of the Ivorian people are supporting president Gbagbo. What the western media are saying is not true. Mr. Gbagbo is the winner and we are going to show it in the street," he continued. Gbagbo himself issued a statement on state-run television, speaking against the mission of the United Nations. "The international community and the others are doing it not because the Ivoirians want it, but because they want to install a person they want as president," he said.

Ouattara's supporters struggled to gain complete control of Côte d'Ivoire as 2010 came to a close. Gbagbo maintained his hold on the military, state-run media outlets, and a number of government institutions, and he also held the nation's revenue from oil and cocoa. In late December, the World Bank attempted to put a stop to some of Gbagbo's money flow, cutting off all loans to the African nation. As Ouattara worked via fax from the Golf Hotel to communicate with foreign embassies to cut off Gbagbo's monetary access, Gbagbo forces, which surrounded the UN peacekeeping troops at the hotel, prevented food, water, and medicine from being delivered to Ouattara's government.

On December 23, the United Nations called a special meeting of the human rights commission to discuss the humanitarian crisis ensuing in Côte d'Ivoire. Since the election, hundreds had been killed and countless more arrested, wounded, or tortured by Gbagbo's government. Thousands more fled their homes, seeking refuge in neighboring countries. At the start of the meeting, Kyung-wha Kang, the UN deputy high commissioner for human rights, said: "Following the proclamation of the results of the elections, the political stalemate has been characterized by the use of excessive force by the supporters of

Mr. Laurent Gbagbo to repress public gatherings and marches; harassment and intimidation; arbitrary arrest and detention; torture; disappearances; and extrajudicial killings. . . . I must stress that international law requires that the right to life be respected at all times, all persons deprived of their liberty be treated humanely and according to due process." The United Nations and its member states called on Gbagbo to give them access to the people and institutions of the nation to help peacefully transition the government and bring to justice those responsible for human rights violations.

Gbagbo's government continued to reject calls for his resignation and instead began work assembling an international commission that would oversee a vote recount. His anticipation that he would find sympathy in the Zimbabwean government of Robert Mugabe was met by silence from the dictator, who said he would respect the will of the African Union, which supported Ouattara as Côte d'Ivoire's rightful leader.

As violence intensified, and UN peacekeepers found mass graves they believed to be filled with Ouattara supporters. In January 2011, Ouattara vowed to take the oath of office before month's end. "I'm confident I will take power this month in January, not in three months," he said. "I am not a dictator. I am a democrat and I shall still be." It was not until May 6, 2011, that Ouattara was sworn in following the April arrest of Gbagbo by UN peacekeepers, bringing an end to the armed conflict the nation had endured since November 2010.

—Heather Kerrigan

Following is a statement by the Economic Community of West African States (ECOWAS) on December 5, 2010, following elections in Côte d'Ivoire, expressing concern about the violence and difficulties in leadership transition; a statement by Kyung-wha Kang, the UN deputy high commissioner for human rights, on December 23, 2010, on the violence against the citizens of Côte d'Ivoire; and edited proceedings of a meeting on December 23, 2010, of the UN Human Rights Commission.

ECOWAS on the Situation in Côte d'Ivoire

December 5, 2010

Following the unexpected turn of events in Côte d'Ivoire after the run-off of the presidential elections recently held there, the ECOWAS Commission wishes to express its deep disappointment and concern at the anomalies that have attended the leadership transition in that Member State, especially the reported inauguration today of the incumbent President.

This is more so, in view of the part played recently by the ECOWAS Observer Team in ascertaining the true wish of the electorate and the concerted efforts made by ECOWAS and the international Community to ensure peaceful and democratic election in line with the ECOWAS Declaration on Political Principles and the ECOWAS Protocol on Democracy and Good Governance.

In the prevailing circumstances, ECOWAS strongly condemns any attempt to usurp the popular will of the people of Côte d'Ivoire and appeals to all stakeholders to accept the results declared by the electoral commission.

The ECOWAS Authority of Heads of State and Government will consequently meet in an Extraordinary Summit in Abuja, Nigeria on Tuesday, 7th December, 2010 with the sole objective of examining the situation and deciding on subsequent action on the crisis in Côte d'Ivoire in accordance with the ECOWAS relevant texts.

The ECOWAS Commission hereby appeals to the Ivorian political leaders and the people of Côte d'Ivoire to refrain from any further acts that would lead to violence and deterioration in the fragile situation.

SOURCE: Economic Community of West African States. "ECOWAS Commission's Statement on the Political Situation in Côte d'Ivoire." December 5, 2010. http://news.ecowas.int/presseshow.php?nb=187&lang=en&annee=2010.

UN Deputy High Commissioner for Human Rights on the Situation in Côte d'Ivoire

December 23, 2010

Mr. Vice President,
    Distinguished Members of the Human Rights Council,
    Excellencies,
    Ladies and Gentlemen,
    I am very honoured and delighted to address this assembly on behalf of the High Commissioner who is abroad. We commend the Human Rights Council for convening this Special Session on the situation in Côte d'Ivoire. I reiterate her deep concerns regarding violations of human rights in Côte d'Ivoire and the alarm of the Secretary-General that the current spate of violence triggered by the October-November 2010 presidential polls may escalate further.

Following the proclamation of the results of the elections, the political stalemate has been characterized by the use of excessive force by the supporters of Mr. Laurent Gbagbo to repress public gatherings and marches; harassment and intimidation; arbitrary arrest and detention; torture; disappearances; and extrajudicial killings. These acts are ominously reminiscent of the violence that blighted the country in 2004, and are blatant violations of obligations under international human rights law. I must stress that international law requires that the right to life be respected at all times, all persons deprived of their liberty be treated humanely and according to due process. Further, there should be no unacknowledged detention, abduction, or enforced disappearances. Deportation or transfer of population, or forced displacement by expulsion or other coercive means are forbidden.

Despite the extremely difficult circumstances on the ground, the Special Representative of the Secretary-General Mr. Choi Young-jin and all United Nations staff continue to seek a peaceful and fair outcome to the crisis and valiantly endeavor to provide assistance to the population. UN human rights officers are deployed across the country, particularly in areas most affected by the violence. They are doing their utmost to monitor the situation and provide protection where they can. The Human Rights Council should lend its support to these brave colleagues on the ground.

The UN Operation in Côte d'Ivoire (UNOCI) has established a 24-hour "green line" through which allegations of human rights violations can be reported. On average, 300 calls per day are received on this line.

Between 16 and 21 December, human rights officers have substantiated allegations of 173 killings, 90 instances of torture and ill treatment, 471 arrests and detentions and 24 cases of enforced or involuntary disappearances.

Unfortunately, it has been impossible to investigate all the allegations of serious human rights violations, including reports of mass graves, due to restrictions on movement by UN personnel. Indeed, the Special Representative of the Secretary-General was stopped at gunpoint, as he sought to verify such allegations.

Yet, it is precisely at times of strife that human rights monitoring and reporting are essential. On 20 December, the Security Council unanimously renewed the mandate of the UNOCI for six months and emphasized the need for protection of civilians.

The current restrictions imposed by security forces and youth groups loyal to Mr. Gbagbo, must be lifted immediately. Such infringements on freedom of movement have also hindered the capacity of the United Nations to deliver much-needed services and humanitarian assistance.

The deteriorating conditions and general insecurity have severely hampered economic and social activities for many Ivoirians, especially the poorest, resulting in the serious infringement of economic and social rights.

Some 6,000 Ivoirians have fled to Liberia and over 200 to Guinea since 3 December. Hundreds of persons are internally displaced.

I remain very concerned about the monopolization of many means of communication, including state television and radio, by those loyal to Mr. Gbagbo. Foreign TV and radio broadcasters considered favorable to President-elect Alassane Ouattara have been banned for several weeks and their radio broadcasts are constantly scrambled.

I repeat the United Nations' call upon Ivoirian leaders to prevent violations of all human rights and to refrain from any incitement to violence and hatred. Perpetrators of this and other abuses must be held accountable.

Excellencies,

The Security Council urged all Ivorian parties and stakeholders to respect the will of the people and the outcome of the election in view of ECOWAS and African Union's recognition of Alassane Ouattara as President-elect of Cote D'Ivoire and representative of the freely expressed voice of the Ivorian people.

This position is fully grounded in human rights norms, particularly the Universal Declaration of Human Rights (UDHR) which establishes that the authority of a government flows from the will of the people. Article 25 of the International Covenant on Civil and Political Rights, to which Côte 'd'Ivoire is a party, echoes such principle and recognizes and protects the right of every citizen to take part in the conduct of public affairs, the right to vote and to be elected. Moreover, the Human Rights Committee, the body that monitors the implementation of the Covenant, in its General Comment 25 confirmed the importance of independent scrutiny of the voting and counting processes.

I remind the Human Rights Council of the strong condemnation by the Economic Community of Western Africa States and the African Union of human rights violations in Côte d'Ivoire. Such violations must cease, the United Nations must be granted unfettered access to the population and perpetrators must be held accountable. I exhort all Ivoirians to exercise their rights peacefully and respect the rights of others. I convey again the High Commissioner's call on the country's leadership to ensure that abuses are stopped and further abuses prevented and those responsible for violations held to account.

Let me conclude by assuring you that OHCHR stands by all efforts to promote justice, peace, security and respect for human rights in Côte d'Ivoire.

SOURCE: Office of the United Nations High Commissioner for Human Rights. "Statement by Ms. Kyung-wha Kang, Deputy High Commissioner for Human Rights, Human Rights Council 14th Special Session on 'The Situation of Human Rights in Côte d'Ivoire Since the Elections on 28 November 2010.'" December 23, 2010. http://www.ohchr.org/EN/NewsEvents/Pages/DisplayNews.aspx?NewsID=10616 &LangID=E.

UN Human Rights Commission Holds Special Session on Côte d'Ivoire

December 23, 2010

The Human Rights Council this morning opened a Special Session on "The situation of human rights in Côte d'Ivoire since the elections on 28 November 2010".

Kyung-wha Kang, Deputy High Commissioner for Human Rights, speaking on behalf of High Commissioner for Human Rights Navi Pillay, reiterated the deep concerns of the High Commissioner, regarding the violations of human rights in Côte d'Ivoire. . . .

Member States of the Council and Observer States then took the floor. . . .

[The list of speakers has been omitted.]

STATEMENTS BY MEMBER STATES

OSITADINMA ANAEDU (Nigeria), on behalf of the African Group, said that the African Union was deeply concerned about the human rights situation in Côte d'Ivoire in relation to the results of the 2010 presidential elections in the country and the violence which had led to loss of lives and property. The African Group welcomed a number of initiatives undertaken by various international, regional and sub-regional bodies and said that it became imperative for the Human Rights Council to pronounce itself on the situation in Côte d'Ivoire and address the issues within the limits of its mandate. The African Groupe condemned the violence, loss of lives and property and called for restoration of democracy and rule of law. The African Union also urged all media outlets to guard against inciting violence and propaganda of hate speech in the publications and broadcasts as this had a potential of setting the country unto internal conflict. The African Group believed that the success of today's endeavour would be judged by the collective resolve to assist Côte d'Ivoire to return to normalcy and enhance the capacity of its institutions for the promotion and protection of human rights for all.

ALEX VAN MEEUWEN (Belgium), speaking on behalf of the European Union, said the European Union had joined the call for this session because it believed that the Human Rights Council could not remain silent when there was growing evidence of massive violations of human rights. The European Union condemned in the strongest terms the persistence of violations against civilians. It did not forget the thousands of refugees who fled the violence and was prepared to launch a humanitarian action in support of those refugees. Also, the European Union had adopted yesterday an emergency humanitarian aid decision of 5 million Euros as contingency planning to ensure that humanitarian aid was available for the victims of the crisis and for those who had sought refuge in neighbouring countries. The European Union underscored that all those who used violence to oppose the democratic choice of the Ivorian people would be held responsible for their actions and be brought to justice. The European Union reiterated its full support for the action of the United Nations and the efforts of the African Union and the Economic Community of West African States in Côte d'Ivoire, and it underlined the importance for the United Nations Operation in Côte d'Ivoire to implement its protection mandate. . . .

BETTY KING (United States) said the United States was pleased that the Human Rights Council was holding this Special Session. The membership of the Council had a strong interest in speaking up, and by convening this session it was sending a strong, unified and clear message that the human rights violations occurring in Côte d'Ivoire would not be tolerated. The United States deplored the ongoing violence and recent human rights violations and abuses occurring in Côte d'Ivoire and the deterioration of the security situation. It deeply regretted the loss of life and called on all Ivorians to remain calm and peaceful. Hundreds of people had been arrested or detained and according to credible reports more than 200 people had already been killed, with many more tortured. Others had been snatched in the middle of the night. The United States was disturbed by reports that the Laurent Gbagbo-controlled media were encouraging conflict, among other things by propagating hate speech against members of ethnic groups and those who opposed Laurent Gbagbo. The United Nations was doing critical work, but their movement was being severely restricted, and United Nations staff had already been attacked. Attacks on the vital work of the United Nations must be universally condemned and rejected. Today the United States stood united with the United Nations and the international community in support of the people of Côte d'Ivoire, condemning all human rights violations and abuses in Côte d'Ivoire. The United States called for an immediate end of human rights violations and to ensure that all perpetrators would be held responsible. . . .

SHINICHI KITAJIMA (Japan) said Japan shared the international concern over the present political and human rights situation in Côte d'Ivoire. They believed that the views expressed at this Special Session added an important voice to the discussions on this matter that had already taken place at various international and regional fora. The violence, which had escalated over the past week amid the stand-off between the supporters of Laurent Gbagbo and those of Alassane Ouattara, must be halted as soon as possible. Japan joined others in condemning the killings of many civilians and other serious human rights violations, as well as the attacks on United Nations Operation in Côte d'Ivoire personnel. All those responsible for such actions must be held accountable. All Ivorian parties and stakeholders must respect the human rights of all Ivorians without discrimination and play a constructive role in consolidating peace and democracy in the country. If they did so, the international community, including Japan, was ready to help in that process. As a first step, all Ivorian parties must respect the result of the recent election which had shown Alassane Ouattara to be the rightful president-elect.

VALERY LOSHCHININ (Russian Federation) said that the Russian Federation was concerned by the upsurge in violence in Côte d'Ivoire. Any irresponsible acts and calls could lead to further violence. The Russian Federation appealed to the parties to stop violence and demonstrate restraint. The existing problems needed to be resolved on the basis of the Ivorian Constitution and the existing laws of the country and it was not a responsibility of the United Nations or Human Rights Council to enforce the results of the elections. The key role must be played by the African community and the Russian Federation continued to support the efforts of the African Union and the Economic Community of West African States in establishing stability in Côte d'Ivoire. The Russian Federation was convinced that regional bodies and institutions would be able to find a solution this crisis. . . .

PROSPER VOKOUMA (Burkina Faso) said Burkina Faso welcomed the holding of this Special Session on the human rights situation in Côte d'Ivoire since the presidential elections. After over three years of efforts that had led to considerable progress in terms of peace, the Ivorian people had been able to hold presidential elections at the end of 2010. The elections were supposed to bring the people peace and stability. In contrast, the crisis following the announcement of the election results was dangerously undermining efforts made by the Economic Community of West African States and the international community, among other actors. In fact, the current situation could lead to a new crisis which, if not managed in time, could in turn lead to a new conflict. In the view of Burkina Faso it was thus urgent to uphold the choice of the Ivorian people, protect the population and foreigners in the country and put an end to the human rights violations. . . .

DARLINGTON MWAPE (Zambia) said Zambia supported the initiative of the African Union to convene this Special Session on the situation in Côte d'Ivoire and that Zambia was deeply concerned with the situation in the aftermath of the 2010 Presidential elections. Zambia joined others in strongly condemning human rights violations, including loss of life and property, abductions and use of mercenaries which were aimed at terrorising the people into submission. The way out of the crisis through dialogue must be supported, but such efforts would bear fruit only if parties refrained from violence. Zambia reiterated the position of the African Union for Mr. Gbagbo to respect the result of the election and facilitate, without delay, the transfer of power to the elected president in the best interest of Côte d'Ivoire, the Region and Africa as a whole. . . .

WU HAITAO . . . (China) said China followed closely the developments in Côte d'Ivoire after the elections and was concerned about the human rights and humanitarian situation there. China took note of the constructive assistance provided by the UN High Commissioner for Refugees and hoped the Human Rights Council would play a similar role. China called for the respect of Côte d'Ivoire's sovereignty and called on all parties to resolve their internal disputes through dialogue. China would work together with the parties concerned to promote peace in Côte d'Ivoire to achieve stability and development in the country. . . .

ELLEN S. NEE-WHANG (Ghana) said that, as a member of the Economic Community of West African States, Ghana considered this African initiative important and timely. Since the beginning of the crisis, Ghana had been closely involved in efforts at fostering peace and ensuring a return to normalcy. Ghana was deeply concerned about the situation and condemned the ongoing human rights violations. In this regard, Ghana urged all factions to exercise the utmost restraint and to refrain from further incitement towards violence. It was Ghana's hope that the Council would be part of the international effort to restore normalcy to Côte d'Ivoire and further assist it to deepen its democratic institutions. In this connection, Ghana looked forward to the Council's engagement and to an appropriate mechanism to facilitate its contribution . . .

[Statements by Observer States have been omitted.]

STATEMENTS BY NON-GOVERNMENTAL ORGANISATIONS

JULIE DE RIVERO, of Human Rights Watch, said high-level officials connected to Gbagbo were using threatening rhetoric, apparently aimed at inciting violence against the United Nations and French Forces. Human Rights Watch thus called on the Council to remind to those who incited to and carried out unlawful attacks against United Nations peacekeepers that they might be prosecuted by the International Criminal Court for such actions. Human Rights Watch was likewise concerned that those attempting to report on these mounting abuses had come under attack and said the Council must thus take immediate action to prevent further deterioration of the human rights situation in Côte d'Ivoire. . . .

PATRIZIA SCANELLA, of Amnesty International, said they were alarmed by the situation in Côte d'Ivoire and the human rights violations that had came to their attention, included extrajudicial killings, violence against women, denial of medical treatment, amongst others. They urged the Council to demand that the armed forces of Laurent Gbagbo immediately stopped the human rights violations; demand an immediate end to hostility and violence; recall the declaration made by Côte d'Ivoire accepting the International Criminal Court's jurisdiction with respect to crimes committed on Ivorian territory since 2002; and call on United Nations Operation in Côte d'Ivoire to act robustly in the implementation of its mandate. Also, Amnesty International requested the Human Rights Council to urge the international community to ensure the United Nations Operation was being provided with the resources it needed and to make arrangements for the Council to be kept informed about the developments in Côte d'Ivoire. . . .

SOURCE: Office of the United Nations High Commissioner for Human Rights. "Human Rights Council Debates Situation of Human Rights in Côte d'Ivoire." December 23, 2010. http://www.ohchr.org/EN/ NewsEvents/Pages/DisplayNews.aspx?NewsID=10614&LangID=E.

OTHER HISTORIC DOCUMENTS OF INTEREST

FROM THIS VOLUME

■ Guinea Election Sparks Delays and Violence, p. 490

FROM PREVIOUS *HISTORIC DOCUMENTS*

■ UN Security Council Resolution on Civil War in Ivory Coast, *2004*, p. 818
■ UN Security Council on Peace Agreement for Ivory Coast, *2003*, p. 237

U.S. Census Bureau Releases 2010 American Community Survey and Census Data

DECEMBER 14 AND 21, 2010

Once each decade, the U.S. Census Bureau is mandated by the Constitution to count every person in the United States. These numbers are used to determine representation in the U.S. House of Representatives. When the bureau released the preliminary data on December 21, 2010, from its 2010 count, it was clear that the population was shifting heavily toward western states. The population growth in that part of the country, at least in the short term, would place additional power in the hands of the Republican Party. But it would also place increasing power in the hands of immigrants, both legal and illegal, who made up a majority of the population growth in the United States during the past decade. States will use data from the 2010 census to redraw congressional district lines and reapportion House seats.

Prior to the release of the decennial census data, the bureau released five-year data from the American Community Survey (ACS), which provides demographic and population characteristics of the American public. With more than eleven billion individual pieces of data used to create the report, the ACS is considered to give a far more detailed look at the United States and is relied on by government officials to make informed policy decisions.

AMERICAN COMMUNITY SURVEY

Since 2005, the ACS has provided annual data on sixty-six hundred areas of the United States that have a population of sixty-five thousand or more. While the data were useful to big-city mayors, small towns, cities, and counties were forced to wait for decennial census data to be released to determine basic demographic data about their citizens, which were often outdated by the time they were tabulated. The 2010 ACS data release provided the first five-year look at localities large and small across the United States, compiling in-depth demographic data for 670,000 geographies. The Census Bureau plans to make the release of five-year ACS data an annual occurrence.

Upon releasing the 2010 five-year data, Robert Groves, director of the Census Bureau, remarked, "The ACS represents the first time such a massive compilation of data estimates for small geographic areas is available. These estimates deliver on our commitment to Congress to provide timely statistics on our communities and our economy, allowing for a more efficient government."

The decennial census provides a complete picture of the number of people living in the United States, and it also gives very basic demographic characteristics. The ACS digs deeper, covering seventy-two topics, including data on poverty, housing values, education, household income, and language spoken at home. The 2010 data release reported that poverty remained concentrated on American Indian reservations. Five U.S. counties had poverty rates higher than 39 percent, and four contain or are contained on Indian reservations located in South Dakota. At the county level around the rest of the nation, individual poverty rates ranged from 4 percent to more than 40 percent of the population. This number can be directly related to household income. Owsley County, Kentucky, had one of the lowest median household incomes at $18,869. Only three counties/independent cities in the United States had median household incomes above $100,000, and all three were located in Northern Virginia—Falls Church independent city, Fairfax, and Loudoun counties. Conversely, eighteen counties—mainly in the South—had a median household income of less than $25,000.

Educational attainment was wide-ranging, according to ACS data. At its lowest, the percentage of those aged twenty-five and older who had completed high school was at 46.5 percent in Starr County, Texas. The highest percentage of high school attainment for those twenty-five and older was 98.7 percent, in Hinsdale County, Colorado, and Los Alamos County, New Mexico. The percentage of those twenty-five and older who had attained a bachelor's degree ranged from 4.6 percent in Owsley County to 69.5 percent in Falls Church. These statistics fall directly in line with median household income, with Owsley County at the bottom and Falls Church at the top.

The influx of immigrants into the United States has been a topic of debate for many years. According to the ACS, nine U.S. counties had more than one-third of their population foreign-born between 2005 and 2009. Three of these counties are located in California, two in Alaska, two in New York, and one each in New Jersey and Florida. Nearly three hundred counties had a population that was less than 1 percent foreign-born. The ACS also collected data on the number of Spanish speakers in the United States. In Maine, no county had more than 2 percent of its population made up of Spanish speakers, while Starr County, Texas, had 95.9 percent of its population speaking Spanish at home.

Go West

With preliminary census data tallied on December 21, the Census Bureau announced that the U.S. population surpassed the 300 million mark, coming in at 308,745,538 people as of April 1. Over the past decade, this population represents a growth of twenty-seven million new residents. Only two other times in history has a decade seen such large numerical growth. As a percentage, however, the U.S. population is growing slowly. Since 2000, it had grown only 9.7 percent. The only decade with slower growth was the Great Depression years of 1930–1940, when the U.S. population grew by only 7.3 percent. "Over the last 100 years, the rate of growth of the U.S. population has gradually slowed," said Groves. "But there is a lot of variation across decades."

The slow growth percentage can be linked to two causes. First is simple mathematics. The bigger the U.S. population gets, the larger the number of people that need to be added to achieve a high percentage gain. Second is the economy. As with the decade during the Great Depression, a bad economy can cause families to put off having children; it can also mean that potential immigrants stay in their own countries, or return to their home countries, instead of seeking work in the United States.

The geographical results of the 2010 Census were largely unsurprising—the U.S. population has been shifting westward over time, away from traditional population centers in the Northeast and Midwest, and the 2010 Census illustrated this shift. But the 2010 data made the West officially larger than the Midwest, a position of dominance it had never before held. The Northeast and Midwest have been experiencing gradual population decline as unemployment remains high and companies continue relocating to western and southern states that have more lenient business tax policies and fewer unions.

THE IMMIGRANT QUESTION

The growth in the U.S. population between 2000 and 2010 was largely driven by immigrants, both legal and illegal. In fact, three-quarters of the twenty-seven million new citizens in the United States were immigrants in the past decade, according to a review of census data by the Center for Immigration Studies. Census data showed more than thirteen million new immigrants after 2000. These immigrants gave birth to more than eight million children.

By law, the Census Bureau is required to include a count of illegal immigrants in each census. Because the total number of U.S. citizens is used to determine congressional representation, it is likely that some areas of the country will gain congressional seats but have a high number of citizens who are unable to vote. "Literally we'll have districts like we have right now where half the adult population can't vote," said Steven Camarota, research director with the Center for Immigration Studies.

Even so, both legal and illegal immigration will have a significant impact on the upcoming redistricting of congressional seats. States with large increases in their immigrant populations, including Arizona, Florida, Georgia, Nevada, South Carolina, Texas, and Washington, all saw a population increase that will lead to a gain of at least one congressional seat.

REPUBLICANS GAIN POWER?

Twelve congressional seats will shift once redistricting is completed, with eleven moving away from states in the Northeast and Midwest. "The trend is a growth in seats for Western and Southern states and a tendency to lose seats from the Midwest and Northeastern states," said Groves. But that trend is not new. New York and Pennsylvania will each lose seats, just as they have every ten years since World War II. Illinois, Iowa, and Massachusetts will also suffer losses, but these three states have not gained a seat since World War II. The additional five states that will experience a loss—Louisiana, Michigan, Missouri, New Jersey, and Ohio—have all lost seats since 1980. For the first time in history, the Midwest and Northeast will hold less than 40 percent of seats in the U.S. House of Representatives. The first Congress to convene under this new reapportionment will meet in January 2013.

The rise in the immigrant population, led by Hispanics, raises the question of what will happen to the power struggle between Democrats and Republicans. The western states that saw population increases and will gain congressional seats are typically Republican strongholds, led by Texas, which will gain four seats. Some Republicans expressed delight at this, as Texas has remained firmly in Republican hands for years. All statewide offices are held by Republicans, and the state has not voted for a Democratic president since 1976.

During the 2010 midterm elections, Republicans made gains in a number of state-houses, putting them in control of redistricting in some states. Having the power to draw congressional lines is expected to give them a boost in the 2012 congressional and presidential elections. "More seats equals more votes," says Bruce Buchanan, a government professor at the University of Texas at Austin. "And since most of these are going to be Republican seats, that translates into more difficulty for Democrats recapturing the House." These early gains, however, might not be sustained. Hispanics typically support Democratic candidates, and the influx of Hispanics into western states could work against Republicans in the future. "The fact that [Republican-leaning states] are gaining seats does not automatically mean an extra seat for the GOP," says Eric Ostermeier, a research associate at the University of Minnesota's Center for the Study of Politics.

—Heather Kerrigan

Following is a press release issued on December 14, 2010, by the U.S. Census Bureau detailing data collected for the 2010 American Community Survey; and a second press release, issued on December 21, 2010, by the U.S. Census Bureau, announcing the first results of the 2010 decennial census.

Census Bureau Releases American Community Survey Data

December 14, 2010

[Website links have been omitted.]

The U.S. Census Bureau today released 5-year American Community Survey (ACS) estimates for the first time, making available social, economic, housing and demographic statistics for every community in the nation.

Up until now, small geographic areas had to rely on outdated 2000 Census figures for detailed information about the characteristics of their communities. Consisting of about 11.1 billion individual estimates and covering more than 670,000 distinct geographies, the 5-year ACS estimates give even the smallest communities more timely information on topics ranging from commute times to languages spoken at home to housing values.

"The ACS represents the first time such a massive compilation of data estimates for small geographic areas is available," said Census Bureau Director Robert Groves. "These estimates deliver on our commitment to Congress to provide timely statistics on our communities and our economy, allowing for a more efficient government."

The data released today are based on a rolling annual sample survey mailed to about 3 million addresses between Jan. 1, 2005, and Dec. 31, 2009. By pooling several years of survey responses, the ACS can generate detailed statistical portraits of smaller geographies. The Census Bureau will release a new set of 5-year estimates every year, giving these communities a powerful tool to track local trends over time.

Public officials, including mayors and governors, and private organizations such as chambers of commerce, rely on ACS estimates on education, housing, jobs, veteran status and commuting patterns to help them make informed decisions that will affect their community, such as where to build new schools, hospitals and emergency services.

"The data provided through the ACS provide a statistical foundation to evaluate our nation's needs, and we now share them with communities across the country as a powerful resource for decision making," Groves said.

The new 2005–2009 ACS estimates are not related to the 2010 Census population counts that will be released Dec. 21. The ACS complements the decennial count and provides estimates of population characteristics that are far more detailed than the basic demographic information that will be released from the 2010 Census, which will be available starting in February.

As a complete count of the population, the 2010 Census data are critical for knowing how many people live in the United States, where they live and their basic demographic information such as race, sex and Hispanic origin. The ACS estimates, on the other hand, are based on a sample survey of the nation and are intended to describe the characteristics of the U.S. population, not to provide population counts.

Before the ACS, estimates about characteristics were only produced once every 10 years through tabulations of responses to the decennial census "long form" sent to a subset of the nation's addresses. Those estimates required two years to tabulate and provided an increasingly outdated picture of the country. By the end of any given decade, decision and policy makers often had to rely on 10-year-old data.

Given the critical role that these long form estimates played in national and local decision making, the Census Bureau responded by developing a continuous measurement concept that would provide more timely data. Approval by Congress helped turn the Census Bureau's innovation into the American Community Survey. . . .

Because it is a survey based on a sample of the population rather than the entire population, the ACS (like the census long form it replaces) produces estimates, not actual counts. To aid data users, the Census Bureau calculates and publishes a margin of error for every ACS estimate it produces, a step not taken for estimates from the 2000 Census long form. However, the technical documentation provided with Census 2000 Summary File 3 does contain the information needed to calculate a margin of error for those published estimates.

ACS 5-year estimates on 72 topics can be downloaded for more than 670,000 geographic areas, including states, counties, cities, tribal areas and more. . . .

As an illustration of the kinds of information provided in these new ACS 5-year estimates, below are some examples of available statistics derived from the tables at the county level.

POVERTY . . .

The county-level poverty rate for individuals ranged from less than 4 percent to more than 40 percent.

In 19 counties or county equivalents, the poverty rate was below 5 percent. These included five counties or independent cities in Virginia, three counties in New Jersey, two in Colorado and Wisconsin, and one in Illinois, Maryland, Minnesota, Missouri, New Mexico, Ohio and South Dakota.

- Douglas County, Colo.
- Hinsdale County, Colo.

- Kendall County, Ill.
- Howard County, Md.
- Scott County, Minn.
- St. Charles County, Mo.
- Hunterdon County, N.J.
- Morris County, N.J.
- Somerset County, N.J.
- Los Alamos County, N.M.
- Delaware County, Ohio
- Lincoln County, S.D.
- Fairfax, Va.
- Falls Church, Va.
- Loudoun County, Va.
- Stafford County, Va.
- York County, Va.
- Ozaukee County, Wis.
- Waukesha County, Wis.

In 21 counties, more than one-in-three individuals were living in poverty. Of the five counties with poverty rates greater than 39 percent, four contain or are contained within American Indian reservations: Sioux County, N.D., which is contained within the Standing Rock Indian Reservation; Buffalo County, S.D., which contains the Crow Creek Indian Reservation; Shannon County, S.D., which is contained within the Pine Ridge Indian Reservation; and Todd County, S.D., which is contained within the Rosebud Indian Reservation. The fifth, Willacy County, Texas, is on the Gulf Coast.

The poverty rate for individuals 65 and over ranged from 0 percent to more than 30 percent for Owsley County, Ky.; Holmes County, Miss.; Shannon County, S.D.; and Kenedy, Maverick, Starr and Willacy counties in Texas.

Housing Value . . .

The counties with the lowest median home values for owner-occupied housing units included Reeves, Texas, at $29,400. Counties with the highest median home values included Nantucket, Mass., at about $1 million.

Thirty-two counties had median home values of greater than $500,000, the majority of which were in California.

Thirty-three counties had median home values of less than $50,000, 19 of which were in Texas.

Mean Travel Time . . .

The counties with the lowest mean travel time to work included King, Texas, at 3.4 minutes, while counties with the highest mean travel time to work included Richmond, N.Y., at 42.5 minutes.

Four counties, all in New York, had mean travel times to work in excess of 40 minutes: Richmond, Queens, Kings and Bronx.

Fourteen counties or county equivalents, all but two in Alaska, had mean travel times to work of less than 10 minutes.

- Aleutians East Borough, Alaska
- Aleutians West Census Area, Alaska
- Bethel Census Area, Alaska
- Dillingham Census Area, Alaska
- Lake and Peninsula Borough, Alaska
- Nome Census Area, Alaska
- North Slope Borough, Alaska
- Northwest Arctic Borough, Alaska
- Skagway Municipality, Alaska
- Wade Hampton Census Area, Alaska
- Yakutat City and Borough, Alaska
- Yukon-Koyukuk Census Area, Alaska
- Kalawao County, Hawaii
- King County, Texas

MARRIED COUPLE FAMILIES WITH CHILDREN UNDER 18 . . .

In 24 counties, more than one-third of all households were married couple families with children under 18, including about one-quarter of the counties in Utah. Of the remaining 17 counties, most were relatively wealthy suburban counties (e.g. Douglas, Colo.; and Loudon, Va.).

By contrast, there were 10 counties or county equivalents where less than one-in-10 households were married couple families with children. These included the cities of Richmond, Petersburg and Williamsburg in Virginia; Baltimore, Md.; and the District of Columbia.

- Washington, D.C.
- Taliaferro County, Ga.
- Baltimore, Md.
- Claiborne County, Miss.
- Mineral County, Nev.
- Catron County, N.M.
- Mason County, Texas
- Petersburg, Va.
- Richmond, Va.
- Williamsburg, Va.

EDUCATIONAL ATTAINMENT . . .

The percent of those 25 and over who had completed high school ranged from 46.5 percent in Starr County, Texas, to 98.7 percent in Hinsdale County, Colo., and Los Alamos County, N.M.

In 10 counties, more than 95 percent of the population 25 and over had completed high school. Of the 10 counties with high school completion rates over 95 percent, three were in Colorado (Hinsdale, Douglas and Routt) and three were in Nebraska (Wheeler, Logan and Grant).

- Douglas County, Colo.
- Hinsdale County, Colo.

- Routt County, Colo.
- Hamilton County, Ind.
- Washington County, Minn.
- Gallatin County, Mont.
- Grant County, Neb.
- Logan County, Neb.
- Wheeler County, Neb.
- Los Alamos County, N.M.

Five counties had less than 60 percent of the population 25 and over that had completed high school. Among these five counties, four were in Texas (Maverick, Presidio, Starr and Willacy) and the fifth was Holmes County, Ohio.

The percent of those 25 and over who had completed a bachelor's degree ranged from 4.6 percent in Owsley County, Ky., to 69.5 percent in Falls Church, Va.

Seventeen counties or county equivalents had populations where more than 50 percent of those 25 and over had a bachelor's degree. Seven of these counties were in the suburbs of the District of Columbia, three in Colorado (Boulder, Douglas and Pitkin) and two in California (Marin and San Francisco). Pitkin County, Colo., with an estimated population of just over 15,000, is the smallest of these counties.

- San Francisco County, Calif.
- Marin County, Calif.
- Boulder County, Colo.
- Douglas County, Colo.
- Pitkin County, Colo.
- Hamilton County, Ind.
- Howard County, Md.
- Montgomery County, Md.
- Los Alamos County, N.M.
- New York County, N.Y.
- Orange County, N.C.
- Albemarle County, Va.
- Alexandria, Va.
- Arlington, Va.
- Fairfax County, Va.
- Falls Church, Va.
- Loudoun County, Va.

There were 62 counties where less than 10 percent of the population 25 and over had a bachelor's degree. Fourteen of these counties were in Georgia, nine in Tennessee, eight in Kentucky and five each in Florida and West Virginia.

LANGUAGE, SPANISH SPEAKERS . . .

The county with the highest percentage of the population 5 and over that spoke Spanish at home was Starr, Texas, at 95.9 percent. Starr was one of 28 counties, and one of 22 counties in Texas, where more than half the population 5 and over spoke Spanish at home. More than 200 counties had less than 1 percent of the population 5 and over that spoke Spanish at home, including 25 counties in West Virginia and 22 in Kentucky. In Maine, there were no counties where the percent of Spanish speakers exceeded 2 percent.

Household Income . . .

Counties with the lowest median household income included Owsley County, Ky., at $18,869, while counties or county equivalents with the highest median household income included Falls Church, Va., at $113,313. In addition to Falls Church, only two other counties had median household incomes greater than $100,000 — Fairfax and Loudoun counties, both in Virginia.

Eighteen counties had a median household income of less than $25,000. These included six counties in Kentucky, three counties in Mississippi and Texas, two counties in Alabama, and one county in Arkansas, Georgia, South Carolina and West Virginia.

- Sumter County, Ala.
- Wilcox County, Ala.
- Chicot County, Ark.
- Taliaferro County, Ga.
- Bell County, Ky.
- Breathitt County, Ky.
- Knox County, Ky.
- Lee County, Ky.
- Magoffin County, Ky.
- McCreary County, Ky.
- Holmes County, Miss.
- Issaquena County, Miss.
- Leflore County, Miss.
- Allendale County, S.C.
- Brooks County, Texas
- Starr County, Texas
- Zapata County, Texas
- McDowell County, W.Va.

Foreign-Born . . .

Nine counties in the United States had populations that were greater than one-third foreign-born. These included three counties in California (Los Angeles, Santa Clara and San Francisco), two county equivalents in Alaska (Aleutian East Borough and Aleutians West Census Area), and two counties in New York (Kings and Queens), along with Miami-Dade, Fla., and Hudson, N.J. Two of these—Aleutians East Borough and Aleutians West Census Area—were in counties with total populations of less than 20,000 people.

There were 292 counties with populations that were less than 1 percent foreign-born, including 34 counties in Kentucky, 27 in West Virginia, 26 in Missouri and 21 in Mississippi. Of those 292 counties, 222 had total populations less than 20,000 people. . . .

SOURCE: U.S. Census Bureau. "U.S. Census Bureau Releases First Set of 5-Year American Community Survey Estimates." December 14, 2010. http://www.census.gov/newsroom/releases/archives/american_community_survey_acs/cb10-cn90.html.

DOCUMENT *Preliminary Census Data Released*

December 21, 2010

The U.S. Census Bureau announced today that the 2010 Census showed the resident population of the United States on April 1, 2010, was 308,745,538.

The resident population represented an increase of 9.7 percent over the 2000 U.S. resident population of 281,421,906. Commerce Secretary Gary Locke, Acting Commerce Deputy Secretary Rebecca Blank and Census Bureau Director Robert Groves unveiled the official counts at the National Press Club in Washington, D.C.

"A big thanks to the American public for its overwhelming response to the 2010 Census," U.S. Commerce Secretary Gary Locke said. "The result was a successful count that came in on time and well under budget, with a final 2010 Census savings of $1.87 billion."

Rebecca Blank, now Acting Deputy Secretary of Commerce who has overseen the 2010 Census as Under Secretary for Economic Affairs, echoed Locke. "The 2010 Census was a massive undertaking, and in reporting these first results, we renew our commitment to our great American democracy peacefully, fairly and openly for the 23rd time in our nation's history."

The U.S. resident population represents the total number of people in the 50 states and the District of Columbia.

The most populous state was California (37,253,956); the least populous, Wyoming (563,626). The state that gained the most numerically since the 2000 Census was Texas (up 4,293,741 to 25,145,561) and the state that gained the most as a percentage of its 2000 Census count was Nevada (up 35.1% to 2,700,551).

Regionally, the South and the West picked up the bulk of the population increase, 14,318,924 and 8,747,621, respectively. But the Northeast and the Midwest also grew: 1,722,862 and 2,534,225.

Additionally, Puerto Rico's resident population was 3,725,789, a 2.2 percent decrease over the number counted a decade earlier.

Just before today's announcement, Locke delivered the apportionment counts to President Obama, 10 days before the statutory deadline of Dec. 31. The apportionment totals were calculated by a congressionally defined formula, in accordance with Title 2 of the U.S. Code, to divide among the states the 435 seats in the U.S. House of Representatives. The apportionment population consists of the resident population of the 50 states, plus the overseas military and federal civilian employees and their dependents living with them who could be allocated to a state. Each member of the House represents, on average, about 710,767 people. The populations of the District of Columbia and Puerto Rico are excluded from the apportionment population, as they do not have voting seats in Congress.

"The decennial count has been the basis for our representative form of government since 1790," Groves said. "At that time, each member of the House represented about 34,000 residents. Since then, the House has more than quadrupled in size, with each member now representing about 21 times as many constituents."

President Obama will transmit the apportionment counts to the 112th Congress during the first week of its first regular session in January. The reapportioned Congress will be the 113th, which convenes in January 2013.

Beginning in February and wrapping up by March 31, 2011, the Census Bureau will release demographic data to the states on a rolling basis so state governments can start the redistricting process.

Article I, Section 2 of the U.S. Constitution calls for a census of the nation's population every 10 years to apportion the House seats among the states. The 2010 Census is the 23rd census in our nation's history.

SOURCE: U.S. Census Bureau. "U.S. Census Bureau Announces 2010 Census Population Counts—Apportionment Counts Delivered to President." December 21, 2010. http://2010.census.gov/news/releases/operations/cb10-cn93.html.

OTHER HISTORIC DOCUMENTS OF INTEREST

FROM THIS VOLUME

FROM PREVIOUS *HISTORIC DOCUMENTS*

9/11 First Responder
Health Bill Signed into Law

DECEMBER 20 AND 22, 2010

In its final act of the 111th Congress, on December 22, 2010, the U.S. Senate and House of Representatives passed the James Zadroga 9/11 Health and Compensation Act, guaranteeing coverage of medical care for the rescue and cleanup crews that worked at Ground Zero after the September 11, 2001, terrorist attacks. Passage of the bill, introduced unsuccessfully in each Congress since 2004, was hard-fought on both sides of the aisle. In an eleventh-hour deal to secure the bill's passage, Senate Democrats agreed to Republican concessions that reduced the cost of the bill and increased oversight and transparency. President Barack Obama signed the bill on January 2, 2011.

LONG WAITING PERIOD

A health care bill specifically for those involved in the September 11, 2001, rescue and cleanup efforts was first introduced in 2004. The bill was intended to pay for the medical expenses of those who needed to be treated for illnesses thought to be related to the dust, glass, and metal debris they had breathed in at Ground Zero. Medical experts made it clear that it can take decades for a link to be established between cancers or other diseases and a specific event, but New York Democrats pushed for a bill sooner rather than later, arguing that by waiting for the link to become clear, it would be too late to provide the necessary care to save the lives of some responders. Democrats outside of New York never put the bill at the forefront of each congressional calendar, and Republicans, who were largely opposed to the total cost of the program, kept it from coming to a floor vote.

While waiting for federal legislation, New York took up the issue in its own assembly and senate. Then-governor George Pataki, a Republican, signed three pieces of legislation in 2006 to aid first responders in medical and monetary claims. One bill extended the period of time given to those wanting to file workers compensation claims for their work at Ground Zero. A second law gave New York City fire and rescue workers who had spent time at Ground Zero additional time to file for accidental disability pensions. And a third bill, which was opposed by New York City mayor Michael Bloomberg, gave more generous death benefits to the relatives of Ground Zero workers from New York City who died from a number of cancers and respiratory illnesses. The law ordered New York City to pay half the cost of the benefits, which Bloomberg said would cost the city between $5 million and $10 million per year. "I have no objections to the purpose of the bill, but I want them to fund it if that's what they want to do," Bloomberg said of Pataki's law.

When the bill was reintroduced in the 111th Congress, it was titled the James Zadroga 9/11 Health and Compensation Act, named after a New York police detective who participated in cleanup and rescue efforts after the terrorist attack. Zadroga developed breathing difficulties that were thought to be related to the conditions at Ground Zero because a number of first responders had developed symptoms similar to those of Zadroga. Zadroga died in 2006, but the New York City medical examiner's report found that the cause of death was not linked to the attack.

FINDING THE VOTES

The House of Representatives passed the Zadroga bill in late September, by a party-line vote of 268 to 160. Its version of the bill, costing a total of $7.4 billion, called for $3.2 billion to be used over the next eight years to monitor and treat injuries caused by the dust and debris at Ground Zero. An additional $4.2 billion would be allocated to reopen the September 11th Victim Compensation Fund, which provides benefits to compensate for job and economic loss stemming from rescue and cleanup work. The $4.2 million in this fund would be paid to those receiving payment from New York City under the settlement of ten thousand lawsuits filed against the city by cleanup and rescue crews.

Senate passage was expected to be difficult. In September, Senate Republicans promised not to pass any other legislation until a tax cut package was agreed to. Even with this threat, Senate Democrats scheduled a test vote on the bill for December 9, 2010. The test vote, a procedural move to end debate on the bill, came up short. Democrats needed sixty votes to move the bill to a final floor vote, but garnered only fifty-seven, with forty-two voting in opposition. Republicans voting no along party lines said their concern still rested with the cost and how the $7.4 billion bill would be paid for.

Democratic supporters of the bill were determined to pass it before the 111th Congress adjourned. With Republicans set to take control of the House of Representatives in January 2011, House and Senate Democratic leaders knew they had little chance to pass the bill if they waited for the next Congress. The first proposal by Democrats, introduced by Rep. Carolyn Maloney, D-N.Y., was to add the legislation to the tax cut package that had strong Republican support. The Senate rejected the plan.

As negotiations continued, a number of supporters of the bill, including Bloomberg, spoke out against Senate Republicans. "The attacks of 9/11 were attacks on America," Bloomberg said. "And we have a collective responsibility to care for the heroes, from all 50 states, who answered the call of duty, saved lives and helped our nation recover."

DEMOCRATS CONCEDE

In mid-December, political analysts began suggesting that Republicans would concede to a vote because they had come under heavy fire by both Democrats and Republicans across the country. Comedian Jon Stewart used his cable television show, *The Daily Show*, to attack Republicans who were not supporting the bill. In his last show of the season, Stewart invited September 11 first responders to share their thoughts on the bill. During the debate, Stewart called the Republican failure to agree to the bill "an outrageous abdication of our responsibility to those who were most heroic on 9/11." He continued, "The party that turned 9/11 into a catchphrase [is] now moving suspiciously into a convenient pre-9/11 mentality when it comes to this bill." Even high-profile Republican supporters lashed out. Speaking on Fox News, former New York City mayor Rudolph Giuliani, who was in office at the time of the attacks, criticized Republicans for not allowing the bill to come to a vote. "I think this is a very big mistake. Anytime you treat September 11 as a political issue, which is what they are doing . . . I think is just wrong. That's the wrong thing to do," he said.

On December 18, Democrats announced that they had the votes needed to pass the bill. Negotiations that had dragged on for two weeks finally resulted in a breakthrough. "We have the votes we need," said bill sponsor Sen. Kirsten Gillibrand, D-N.Y. "We have indications from several Republicans that they very much want to vote for this bill." Behind closed doors, senators had been working to convince Republican holdout Tom Coburn, R-Okla., to cast a vote in favor of the bill. Coburn refused because of the cost and demanded that it be reduced before he would agree to cast a yes vote. Democrats did not want to bend to Coburn's demands, fearing that it would reduce the benefits available to 9/11 workers.

In the end, Democrats conceded in order to gain Coburn's vote to pass the measure using unanimous consent rather than a standard cloture vote, which they feared would delay the bill until after the Christmas recess. The total cost of the bill was reduced to $4.2 billion, with $1.5 billion set to cover health benefits and $2.7 billion going to the Victim Compensation Fund, which would be closed after five years, another concession to Republicans who wanted to avoid fraud and abuse of the system. Other details of the deal included additional reporting of claims data to ensure that victims were not taking advantage of the system and assurances that the most cost-effective route of care was being pursued. This, Democrats said, could include handing over care of 9/11 cleanup and rescue workers to the Department of Veterans Affairs. In addition, the deal changed the way in which the program would be paid for. Initially, Democrats had proposed paying for the bill by taxing foreign companies. The deal removed that provision and instead placed a fee on certain foreign companies that sell goods and services to the U.S. government's overseas operations.

Before debate on the bill closed, Republicans applauded their colleagues for sticking with their desire to cut the cost of the bill, while Democrats gave impassioned speeches. "I beg, I plead, I implore two brave colleagues from the other side to join us," said Sen. Charles Schumer, D-N.Y. "[First responders] are not asking for welfare. They are not asking for a huge handout. They are simply asking that they be able to meet the high health care costs that occur when you develop cancers and other illnesses because particles of glass and cement and other materials get lodged in your lungs or your gastrointestinal tract," he continued.

Speaking to widespread criticism before the vote, Sen. Mitch McConnell, R-Ky., said, "Some have tried to portray this debate as a debate between those who support 9/11 workers and those who don't. This is a gross distortion of the facts. There was never any doubt about supporting the first responders. It was about doing it right." But he said the delay was necessary. "Thanks to the hard work of a number of Senators . . . we have come a long way in improving this bill."

Both Democrats and Republicans applauded the deal and the bill's ultimate passage. Coburn called it "a good deal that takes care of the people we need to take care of." To the cheers of emergency workers and the families of 9/11 victims, Gillibrand said, "To the firefighters here, the police officers here, everyone involved in the recovery, all the volunteers, the family members: Thank you! It was your work, it was your heroism, it was your dedication that made the difference. It was your effort, coming here week after week to tell senators and Congress members about your stories and what you went through."

The House quickly voted and passed the bill 206 to 60. President Barack Obama signed the legislation on January 2, 2011, while on vacation in Hawaii.

—Heather Kerrigan

Following is a statement by New York City mayor Michael Bloomberg on December 20, 2010, urging the U.S. Senate to pass the James Zadroga 9/11 Health Care and Compensation Act; a floor statement in support of the 9/11 health care act by Sen. Charles Schumer, D-N.Y., on December 22, 2010; a statement by Sen. Mitch McConnell, R-Ky., on December 22, 2010, in support of the 9/11 health care act; and a statement by Reps. Carolyn Maloney, D-N.Y., Jerrold Nadler, D-N.Y., and Peter King, R-N.Y., on December 22, 2010, announcing U.S. House of Representatives passage of the 9/11 health care bill.

DOCUMENT

Mayor Bloomberg Urges Passage of 9/11 Health Bill

December 20, 2010

"Good morning. I want to thank the distinguished members of Congress, our police and fire commissioners, Mr. Joseph Zadroga, some of our first responders, and labor leaders who have joined us today. For years now, all of us have been working very hard to pass a bill through the United States Congress guaranteeing that the first responders and survivors of the attacks of 9/11 receive the health care they need.

"These attacks were attacks on America by a foreign enemy. They were acts of war, and they led us to war in Afghanistan. Caring for the men and women who rushed to our defense on that dark day, and in the days that followed, is nothing less than a national duty. America is too great a country to shirk this duty. We are too strong. Too proud. Too patriotic. And this is the week that we have to show it.

"Getting anything done in Washington is never easy, but thanks to years of hard work by so many people—and thanks to the strong leadership of Pete King, Carolyn Maloney, Jerry Nadler, and many others, the bill did pass the House earlier this year. Earlier this month, the Senate fell several votes short of the 60 required to end debate and take a vote. At the time, Republicans said that they voted against ending debate because they did not believe that any bill should move until a deal on tax cuts had been completed.

"That deal, as you know, is now done. And the time for excuses is over. Very simply: it's time to end the debate and let the bill be voted on.

"It's encouraging that the bill has been gaining more Republican support—and I believe that if the Senate ends the debate and takes a vote, other Republicans will join in passing it. I understand the concerns that have been raised about increasing federal spending but this bill will be paid for with other revenue generators—unlike the tax cuts that just won overwhelming support in the Senate. So this is not a vote on whether we should increase the deficit.

"It's a vote on whether we should stand by those who stood by America in its hour of greatest need. It's a vote on whether we should fulfill our obligation to the men and women in uniform, and in hard hats, whom we rightly call heroes. And it's a vote on whether the thousands of Americans who are suffering from 9/11-related illness will at least have the peace of mind that their government has not abandoned them.

"Two weeks ago, many thought that the 9/11 bill was dead. But we didn't give up. And thanks to the determined leadership of Senators Schumer and Gillibrand—not to mention the tireless support of many first responders—the bill now has a very real chance of passing. Our two senators deserve a great deal of credit for brokering changes to the bill over the weekend, which ought to bring more Republicans on board.

"The Senate has a full week ahead of it, and it should not adjourn until it passes this bill. I've talked to many Senators on behalf of this bill, and I will do whatever I can to help get it passed this week. I know that's also true of Pete King, Carolyn Maloney and Jerry Nadler—who have been fighting like crazy on this issue for years. Along with the rest of New York's Congressional delegation, they've been great champions for 9/11 victims and responders.

"I'd like to ask each of them to say a few words, starting with Congresswoman Maloney who has been nothing but relentless when it's come to moving this bill forward. Congressman King? Congressman Nadler? Congressman Rangel? Congressman Weiner? Congressman Engel? Congressman McMahon? Congressman Crowley?

"Before introducing some of the other speakers, I'd also like to thank the members of the World Trade Center Medical Work Group. For years, they've documented the ongoing health effects of exposure to the dust cloud in rescue and recovery work and made passage of this bill its primary recommendation.

"Now, many of the people who have fought hardest for this bill have been members of the FDNY and the NYPD, and I'd like to ask Commissioners Sal Cassano and Ray Kelly to say a few words. Commissioner Kelly? Commissioner Cassano?

"We are joined this morning by the father of James Zadroga, Joseph.

"Joseph, thank you, and we all understand that you endured a terrible tragedy with the death of your son, and nothing short of a tremendous champion for this bill you have been, and we are proud to have you stand with us today.

"We are happy to welcome some of the construction workers and first responders who bravely and selflessly took part in the cleanup efforts. That includes John Feal, a construction worker who lost part of his foot during the recovery operation and has since started his own organization, The Feal Good Foundation, to lobby for help for first responders. John, if you could speak briefly about the importance of this bill?

"Kenny Specht is a former lieutenant in the FDNY, and has worked in the recovery efforts. Kenny, you want to say a few words?

"We're also joined by some of our city's labor leaders—and I'd like to ask each of them to speak, starting with the president of the Uniformed Firefighters Association, Steve Cassidy. Pat Lynch, is the president of the Patrolmen's Benevolent Association. Pat? Also here is Uniformed Fire Officers Association president Al Hagan. Al?

"Finally, let me introduce Richard Wood, president of Plaza Construction, one of the major construction contractors that responded after 9/11."

SOURCE: Office of New York City Mayor Michael Bloomberg. "Mayor Michael R. Bloomberg Urges Senate Passage of Revised James Zadroga 9/11 Health and Compensation Act." December 20, 2010. http://www.nyc.gov/portal/site/nycgov/menuitem.c0935b9a57bb4ef3daf2f1c701c789a0/index.jsp?pageID=mayor_press_release&catID=1194&doc_name=http%3A%2F%2Fwww.nyc.gov%2Fhtml%2Fom%2Fhtml%2F2010b%2Fpr515-10.html&cc=unused1978&rc=1194&ndi=1.

Sen. Schumer in Support of the 9/11 Health Care Bill

December 22, 2010

Madam President, I rise to speak on a bill that the Chair has spearheaded the charge for—and done it with such hard work and determination and commitment and vigor—and that is the bill to provide health care for our 9/11 heroes, those men and women who at a time of war rushed to danger to save lives and protect our freedom.

We have met with these brave men and women repeatedly. Some of them are suffering already with cancers they acquired for their acts of bravery. Others know it is an almost certainty that they will come down with similar diseases and illnesses that are extremely costly to fight.

Madam President, we have had a grand tradition in America: Those who risk their lives to protect us and volunteer to do it under no compunction, we remember them when they get hurt in that brave endeavors. We do it for our veterans and we should be doing it for our 9/11 heroes—the first responders, the police, the firefighters, the EMT workers, the construction workers, and the ordinary citizens who rushed into danger at a time when no one knew how many people might be living and entrapped in those collapsed towers.

I plead with my colleagues on the other side of the aisle, this should not be a moment of politics. One can come up with reason after reason why not to vote for this bill, and we have heard many and the reasons keep changing. But one fact doesn't change: There are those who need help and who deserve our help—from New York, New Jersey, Connecticut, and from every other State of the Union. To them, a parliamentary decision that we can't vote on this because there is another bill we want to vote on first, because we would change this or that, is going to ring very hollow.

This should not be a partisan issue. This should be an issue where America unites. When it comes to helping our veterans, we are united. That is not a Democratic or Republican issue. That is not a northeast or southwest issue. It is an issue of being an American. This vote is about being an American because from the days at Bunker Hill, when the patriots put down their plows and took up muskets to defend and create our freedom, we have always tried to take care of them, and we have done it better and better for our veterans. The heroes of 9/11 are no different.

So I beg, I plead, I implore two brave colleagues from the other side to join us. Put aside the political considerations. Remember what these people did for us. You have seen them when they have visited your offices, the suffering, all for an act of voluntary heroism. They are not asking for welfare. They are not asking for a huge handout. They are simply asking that they be able to meet the high health care costs that occur when you develop cancers and other illnesses because particles of glass and cement and other materials get lodged in your lungs or your gastrointestinal tract.

So this is our last call. It is a plea. We will keep at this, but today is the day to step to the plate. I urge my colleagues to please support those brave men and women who were there for us—for America. Do not come up with an excuse as to why you cannot do it. We have marched and marched and marched, and this is the finish line. Help us get over it, please.

SOURCE: Sen. Charles Schumer. "Development, Relief, and Education for Alien Minors Act of 2010—Motion to Proceed." *Congressional Record* 2010, pt. 156, S8663–8664. http://www.gpo.gov/fdsys/pkg/CREC-2010-12-09/pdf/CREC-2010-12-09-pt1-PgS8662.pdf.

Sen. McConnell on the 9/11 Health Care Bill

December 22, 2010

Mr. President, I am delighted the Senate was able to reach an agreement to provide health care for the men and women who helped in the rescue, recovery, and cleanup efforts after the 9/11 attacks.

In the years since then, as we all know, a number of these brave Americans have become ill. Today represents an important step in making sure they receive the care they need as a result of their extraordinary service. No one has ever questioned whether to provide the care they need. The only question was how to do so.

Like many of my colleagues, I have been concerned that attempts to rush this legislation at the end of the session would prevent us from ensuring the bill was written in a responsible fashion. I still believe this cause and this legislation would have benefited from a bipartisan committee process. But thanks to the hard work of a number of Senators—most notably Senators COBURN and ENZI and their staffs—we have come a long way in improving this bill.

We have made sure that more compensation will go to victims than trial lawyers. It has got improved oversight, so money isn't siphoned away from the people who need it. We put time limits on the legislation so Congress can come back and review what has worked and where improvements can be made. So this is a much better product.

Some have tried to portray this debate as a debate between those who support 9/11 workers and those who don't. This is a gross distortion of the facts. There was never any doubt about supporting the first responders. It was about doing it right.

SOURCE: Sen. Mitch McConnell. "First Responders Bill." *Congressional Record* 2010, pt. 156, S10990. http://www.gpo.gov/fdsys/pkg/CREC-2010-12-22/pdf/CREC-2010-12-22-pt1-PgS10990-4.pdf.

Reps. Maloney, Nadler, and King on Passage of 9/11 Health Care Bill

December 22, 2010

Today, the House of Representatives passed, for the second time, legislation to address the health crisis caused by the terrorist attacks of September 11, 2001. H.R. 847, the James Zadroga 9/11 Health and Compensation Act, will provide health care for those exposed to toxins released by the collapse of the World Trade Center towers. The bill will also reopen the federal Victim Compensation Fund to provide economic relief to those harmed by the attacks. Earlier today, the Senate passed an amended version of the bill that reduces the bill's cost to $4.3 billion over five years. A summary of the Senate's changes can be found below.

The bill, sponsored by New York Reps. Carolyn Maloney (D-NY), Jerrold Nadler (D-NY), and Peter King (R-NY), with the support of the entire New York Congressional delegation, will now be sent to President Obama's desk. The President has said that he supports and will sign the legislation.

The passage of H.R. 847 represents a victory for ailing 9/11 first responders and survivors who have waited more than nine years for the federal government to approve a comprehensive plan to deal with the public health disaster caused by the attacks.

"To 9/11 responders and survivors who have suffered for so long: help is finally here. With this vote, Congress repaid a long-overdue debt and answered the emergency calls of thousands of ailing 9/11 first responders and survivors. This bipartisan compromise is a strong program that will save lives," said Maloney. "I thank Speaker Pelosi and Leader Hoyer for their dedication to those who are sick or injured because of 9/11, I applaud Senators Gillibrand and Schumer for brokering the compromise reached today, and I remain eternally grateful to my friends and co-authors, Jerry Nadler and Peter King, and all our colleagues in the New York delegation."

"Today's victory is without a doubt the proudest moment of my 34-year career in government," said Nadler. "Along with Carolyn Maloney, my staff and I have worked on this legislation for literally nine years. We have stood with first responders and community survivors through the numerous lows and battles over the course of years. We have grieved at the many losses—losses due to 9/11-related illnesses and due to cold political odds and seemingly insurmountable hurdles. But, today, thanks to the work and patience of so many responders, survivors, elected officials, and our allies in disparate corners, we have achieved the sweetest of victories. And it comes not a moment too soon. The plight of 9/11 responders and survivors is very serious and immediate. Thousands are sick and, until now, justice has seemed so far away. I am so proud that our government has done precisely what it is here for—to take responsibility for its citizens after the ugliest of attacks against our nation. Thanks goes out in particular to Congresswoman Maloney, Congressman King, Senators Gillibrand and Schumer, John Feal, Manhattan's Community Board 1, my entire staff, and so many others who have done so much."

"This is a great victory for the heroes of September 11th, the firefighters, police officers and construction workers. Justice is finally being served. A great day for America," said King.

The Zadroga Act is historic, but not unprecedented, legislation. In the aftermath of the Pearl Harbor attacks, Congress passed the War Hazards Compensation Act of 1942, which provided health care and financial relief to civilians who helped recover the dead and salvage what remained of our Pacific fleet. In passing the Zadroga Act, Congress has once again demonstrated that our nation will not abandon those harmed by an attack on our shores.

Fact Sheet on Bipartisan Agreement on 9/11 Health and Compensation Act:
The terms of the Senate agreement adopt H.R. 847 with the following changes:

- Provide a total of $4.3 billion in funding for the health and compensation titles of the bill.
- Cap federal funding for the health program over five years at $1.5 billion (New York City will contribute 10% of the cost). Any funds not spent in the first five years may be carried over and expended in the sixth year of the program.
- Reopen the Victim Compensation Fund (VCF) for five years to file claims, with payments to be made over six years. Fund the VCF at $2.8 billion for six years, with $.8 billion available for payments in the first five years and $2.0 billion available for payment in year six. Claims will be paid in 2 installments—one payment in the first five years, and a second payment in the sixth year of the program.

- The payfor in the House-passed version of the bill has been replaced by a 2 percent fee on government procurement from foreign companies located in non-GPA countries and a one-year extension of H-B1 and L-1 Visa fees for outsourcing companies. These are estimated by CBO to collect $4.59 billion over the 10-year scoring period for the bill.
- The bill is not only fully paid for, but will reduce the deficit by $450 million over the 10-year scoring period.

Others changes made in the bill to address Republican concerns:

- Requiring that the Centers of Excellence report claims data to HHS so that costs and utilization of services can be fully monitored.
- Specifying the non-treatment services furnished by Centers of Excellence to be funded under the health program (e.g. outreach, social services, data collection, development of treatment protocols).
- Authorizing the World Trade Center Program Administrator to designate the Veteran's Administration as a provider for WTC health services.
- Directing the Special Master to develop rules to implement the VCF within 180 days of passage of the legislation.

SOURCE: Rep. Carolyn B. Maloney. "9/11 Health Bill Passes U.S. House, Will Be Signed by President." December 22, 2010. http://maloney.house.gov/index.php?option=com_content&task=view&id=2247&Itemid=61.

OTHER HISTORIC DOCUMENTS OF INTEREST

FROM PREVIOUS *HISTORIC DOCUMENTS*

- Bush on Terrorist Attacks Against the United States, *2001*, p. 614

Credits

"American Red Cross Releases $10 Million to Help Haiti," January 15, 2010; "Red Cross Aid Reaches Haitian Earthquake Survivors," January 17, 2010. Used with permission. American Red Cross, www.redcross.org.

"Announcement of Joint EU-IMF Programme for Ireland," November 28, 2010. © The Department of Finance.

"Award Ceremony Speech," December 10, 2010. © The Nobel Foundation 2010.

"July Existing-Home Sales Fall as Expected by Prices Rise," August 24, 2010; "Existing-Home Sales Move Up in August," September 23, 2010; "September Existing-Home Sales Show Another Strong Gain," October 25, 2010; "Existing-Home Sales Decline in October Following Two Monthly Gains," November 23, 2010; "Existing-Home Sales Resume Uptrend with Stable Prices," December 22, 2010. Copyright © NATIONAL ASSOCIATION OF REALTORS®. Used with permission.

"Kindle Device Unit Sales Accelerate Each Month in Second Quarter; New $189 Price Results in Tipping Point for Growth." July 19, 2010; "Amazon.com Announces Second Quarter Sales up 41% to $6.57 billion." July 22, 2010. © Amazon.com, Inc.

"Republicans Exceed Expectations in State Legislative Elections," November 3, 2010. © National Conference of State Legislatures.

"Volcanic Ash Crisis: Frequently Asked Questions," April 20, 2010; "Joint Statement on Greece by EU Commissioner Olli Rehn and IMF Managing Director Dominique Strauss-Kahn," May 2, 2010; "European Commission Assesses Recent Developments in France, Discusses Overall Situation of the Roma and EU Law on Free Movement of EU Citizens," September 29, 2010; "Statement by Viviane Reding, Vice-President of the European Commission, EU Commissioner for Justice, Fundamental Rights and Citizenship, on the Recent Developments Concerning the Respect for EU Law as Regards the Situation of Roma in France," October 19, 2010; Antitrust: Commission Probes Allegations of Antitrust Violations by Google," November 30, 2010. © European Union, 1995-2011.

"Government Assessment of the FIFA 2010 World Cup," July 14, 2010. © GCIS2004: ALL RIGHTS RESERVED

Cumulative Index, 2006–2010

*The years in **boldface type** in the entries indicate which volume is being cited. Names starting with al- are alphabetized by the subsequent part of the name.*

A

Aaron, Hank (major league baseball player), **2007**: 716

AARP (*formerly* American Association of Retired Persons)
  health care reforms, **2009**: 401
  National Commission on Fiscal Responsibility and Reform, **2010**: 55

ABA. *See* American Bar Association

Abbas, Mahmoud (*aka* Abu Mazen; chairman, PLO)
  Annapolis Conference and, **2007**: 683
  Gaza Strip violence response, **2010**: 284
  Hamas government and Fatah party response, **2006**: 16–17, 19–20; **2010**: 282
  Palestinian leader, successor to Arafat, **2007**: 39, 681
  Palestinian president, **2006**: 195
  peace negotiations and cease-fire agreement, **2007**: 40, 41
  peace talks with Olmert, **2007**: 680–682
  presidential election, **2006**: 13
  speeches, **2007**: 41, 47–49
  U.S. government support of, **2006**: 13, 20

Abbott, Greg (attorney general, Texas), **2010**: 607

Abdel-Rahman, Arouf (judge, Saddam Hussein war crimes trial), **2006**: 638–640

Abdullah, Abdullah (foreign minister, Afghanistan), **2009**: 579; **2010**: 432, 434

Abdullah bin Abdul Aziz (crown prince, Saudi Arabia), **2006**: 228

Abdullah II (king, Jordan)
  package bombs, information on, **2010**: 534
  summit meeting with Bush and Maliki, **2006**: 176–177

Abdulmutallab, Umar Farouk ("Christmas Day bomber"), **2009**: 663–670; **2010**: 296, 535

Abe, Shintaro (foreign minister, Japan), **2006**: 583

Abe, Shinzo (prime minister, Japan)
  "policy speech," **2006**: 585–591
  resignation of, **2007**: 504–506, 508–509; **2008**: 373

Abhisit Vejjajiva (politician, Thailand), **2008**: 551; **2010**: 213, 215

Abizaid, John (general, U.S.), **2006**: 119–120

Abkhazia, rebel region of Georgia, **2008**: 346, 347

Abortion. *See also* Birth control
  health care reform and, **2009**: 535, 536; **2010**: 84–85
  "morning-after pill" (Plan B) controversy, **2006**: 466–471
  parental notification or consent for, **2006**: 469–470
  partial-birth abortion
    federal ban on, **2007**: 176–179
    Supreme Court rulings, **2006**: 468–469; **2007**: 180–189
  state restrictions on, South Dakota ban rejected, **2006**: 466, 468
  Supreme Court rulings on, **2007**: 180–189
  teenagers and, **2009**: 338

Abramoff, Jack (lobbyist), **2006**: 103, 264–266; **2007**: 466, 469

Abramov, Sergei (prime minister, Chechnya), **2006**: 207

Abrams, Donald (professor), **2009**: 496

al-Abssi, Shakir (Palestinian leader), **2007**: 628

Abstinence Education Program, **2009**: 332

Abubakar, Atiku (vice president, Nigeria), **2007**: 267–268, 269

Abu Dhabi (capital, UAE), **2009**: 612

Abu Ghraib prison abuse scandal
  abuses as isolated incidents, **2006**: 512
  anti-American sentiments, **2006**: 286–287
  Gonzales, Alberto, and, **2007**: 458

Abu Mazen. *See* Abbas, Mahmoud

Abu Nidal (Sabry al-Banna), Libyan connections with, **2006**: 225

AbuZayd, Karen (UN aid official), **2008**: 647, 648, 649

Accelerate Florida, **2008**: 453, 455, 456

Accoyer, Bernard (president, French National Assembly), **2010**: 449

Acheson, David W. K., foodborne illness and fresh produce safety, **2006**: 538–546

ACIP. *See* Advisory Committee on Immunization Practices

Acker, Tanya, **2010**: 248

ACLU. *See* American Civil Liberties Union

ACLU v. National Security Agency, **2006**: 64

ACORN (Association of Community Organizations for Reform Now), **2008**: 521

Acquired immunodeficiency syndrome. *See* HIV/AIDS

ACS. *See* American Cancer Society

ACT (testing organization), **2009**: 485

Action contre le Faim (Action against Hunger), **2006**: 251

Acute myelogenous leukemia (AML). *See* Cancer—specific types

ADA. *See* Americans with Disabilities Act of 1990

Adada, Rodolphe (representative for Darfur, UN), **2007**: 393

Adair, Rod (state senator, New Mexico), **2009**: 138

Adams, Bill (spokesperson, DOT), **2009**: 358

Adams, Gerry (leader, Sinn Féin), **2007**: 214, 215

Adan, Sharif Hassan Sheikh (leader, Somalia), **2006**: 717, 718

Adelphia Communications Corp., corporate scandal, **2006**: 239, 243

Administrative Procedure Act (1946), **2008**: 7

Adolescents. *See* Teenagers; Youth

ADP. *See* Automatic Data Processing, Inc.

Advanced Energy Initiative, **2006**: 32, 147–148

Advani, L. K. (politician, India), U.S.-India nuclear agreement, **2006**: 97

Advertising. *See also* Elections
  Massachusetts regulation of, **2009**: 211–212